Design Annual 2004 Graphis Mission Statement: *Graphis* is committed to presenting exceptional work in international design, advertising, illustration and photography. Since 1944, we have presented individuals and companies in the visual communications industry who have consistently demonstrated excellence and determination in overcoming economic, cultural and creative hurdles to produce true brilliance.

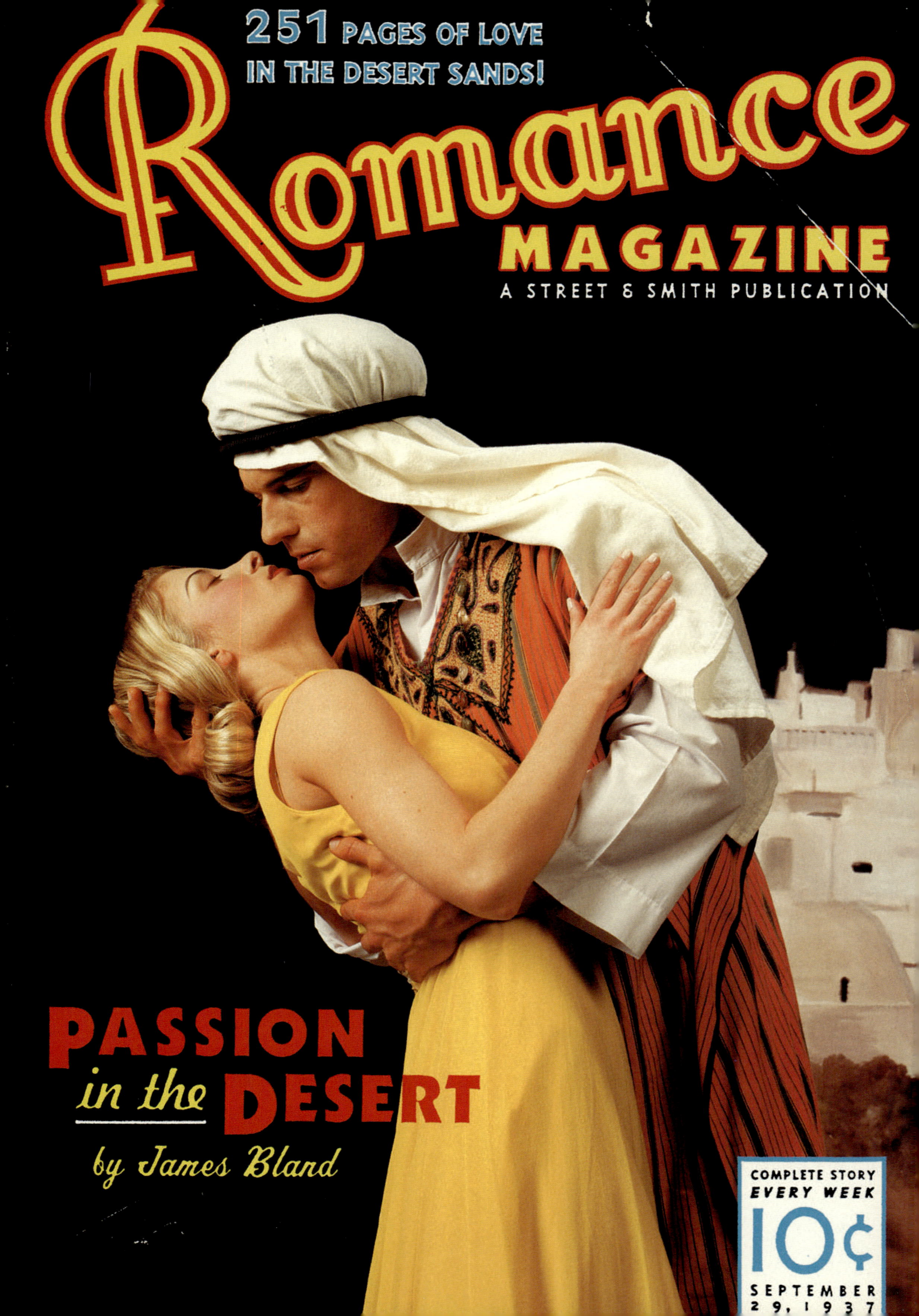
251 PAGES OF LOVE IN THE DESERT SANDS!
Romance MAGAZINE
A STREET & SMITH PUBLICATION
PASSION in the DESERT
by James Bland
COMPLETE STORY EVERY WEEK
10¢
SEPTEMBER 29, 1937

DesignAnnual2004

CEO & Creative Director: B. Martin Pedersen

Editor: Michael Porciello

Art Director: Lauren Prigozen
Design & Production: Luis Diaz, Jennifer Kinon and Andrea Vélez
Design Interns: Sanaâ Akkach and Julian Jaramillo

Photographer: Alfredo Parraga

Published by Graphis Inc.

This book is dedicated to
Fred Troller

(opposite) Promo piece for the photographer James Bland by Squires and Company and (next page) "Letting the Germ Out of the Bottle" by Mirko Ilić

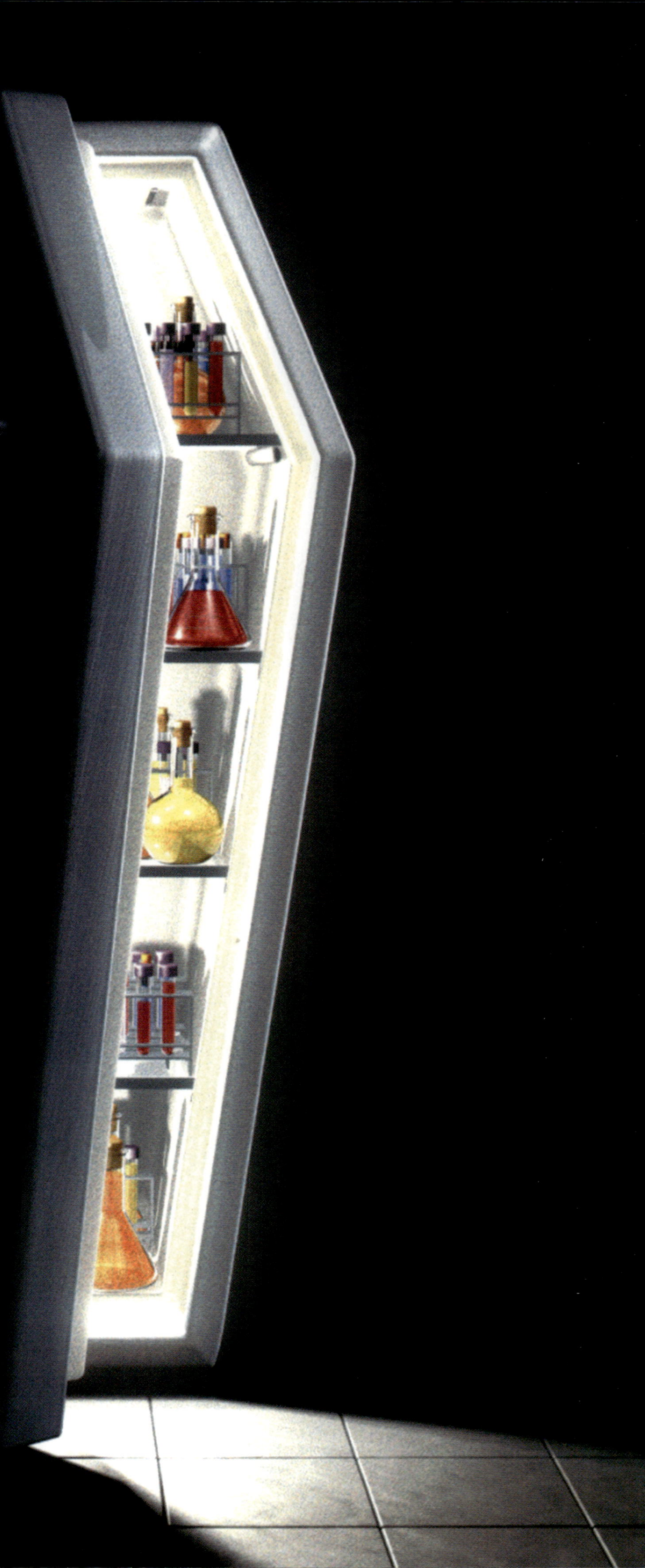

ContentsInhaltSommaire

Remarks: We extend our heartfelt thanks to contributors throughout the world who have made it possible to publish a wide and international spectrum of the best work in this field. Entry instructions for all Graphis Books may be requested from: **Graphis Inc.**, 307 Fifth Avenue, Tenth Floor, New York, New York 10016, or visit our Web site at www.graphis.com.

Anmerkungen: Unser Dank gilt den Einsendern aus aller Welt, die es uns ermöglicht haben, ein breites, internationales Spektrum der besten Arbeiten zu veröffentlichen. Teilnahmebedingungen für die Graphis-Bücher sind erhältlich bei: **Graphis Inc.**, 307 Fifth Avenue, Tenth Floor, New York, New York 10016. Besuchen Sie uns im World Wide Web, www.graphis.com.

Remerciements: Nous remercions les participants du monde entier qui ont rendu possible la publication de cet ouvrage offrant un panorama complet des meilleurs travaux. Les modalités d'inscription peuvent être obtenues auprès de: **Graphis Inc.**, 307 Fifth Avenue, Tenth Floor, New York, New York 10016. Rendez-nous visite sur notre site web: www.graphis.com.

ISBN: 1-931241-32-5 Printed in Korea.

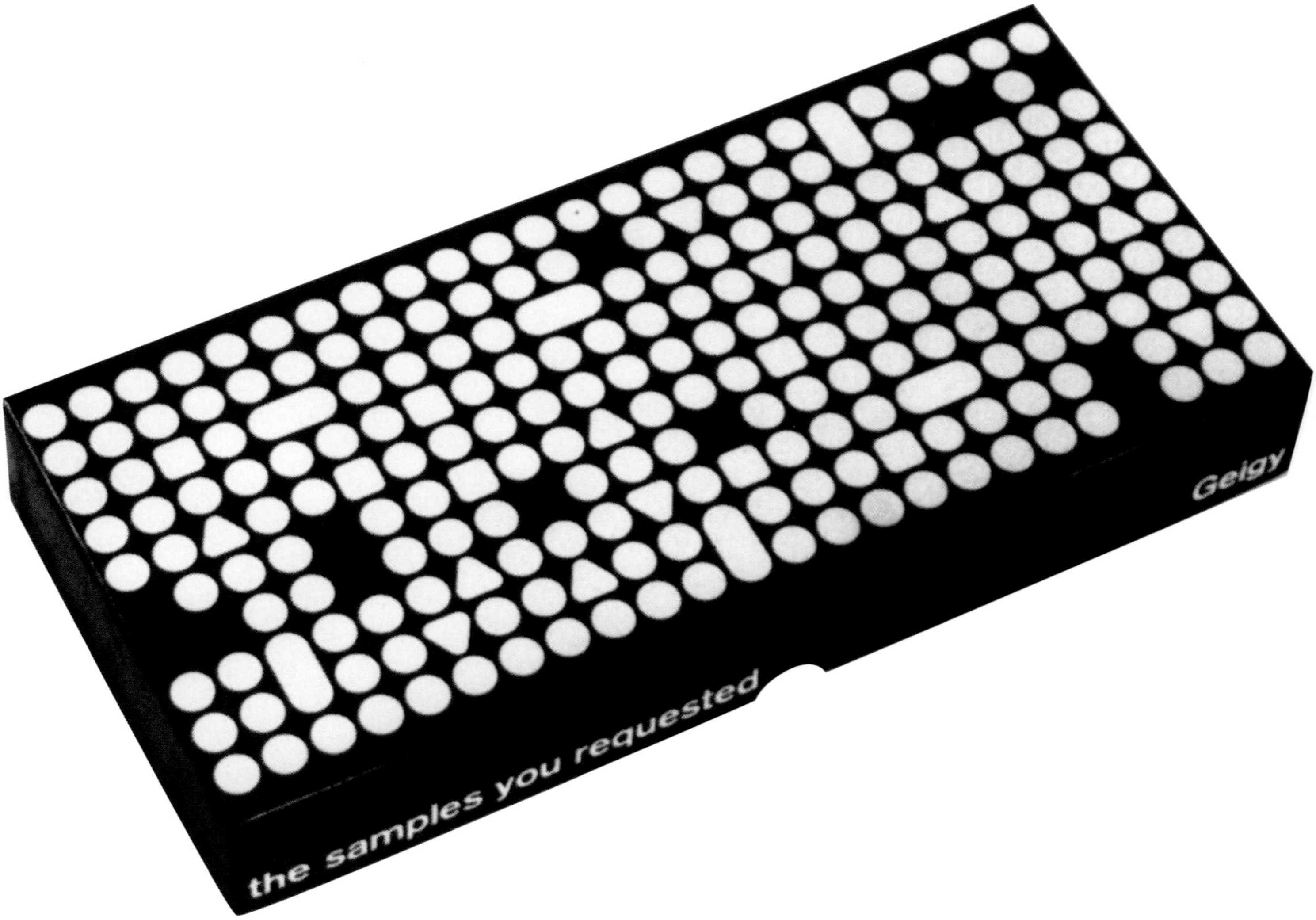
Geigy
the samples you requested

Fred Troller

(December 12, 1930 - October 11, 2002)

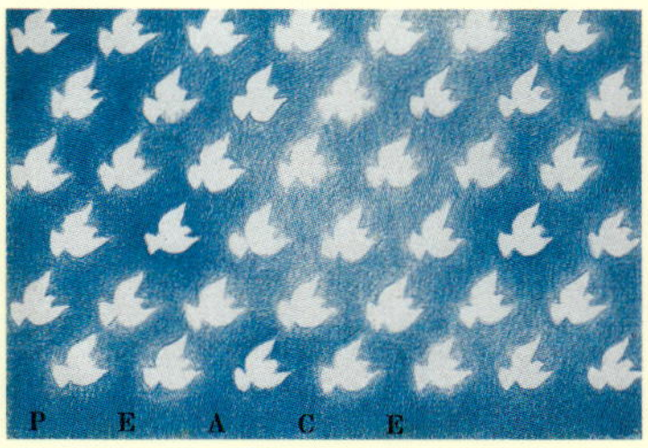

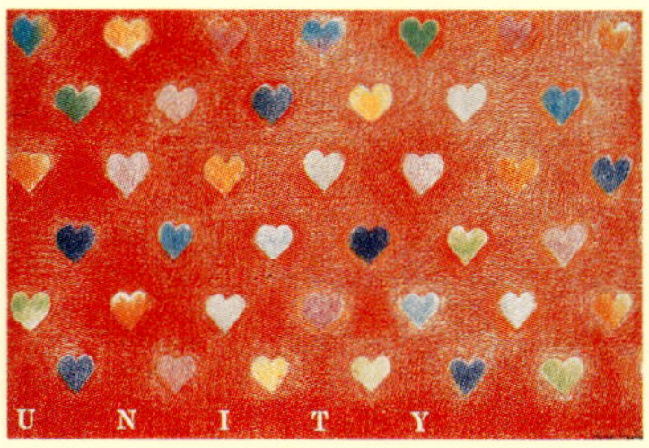

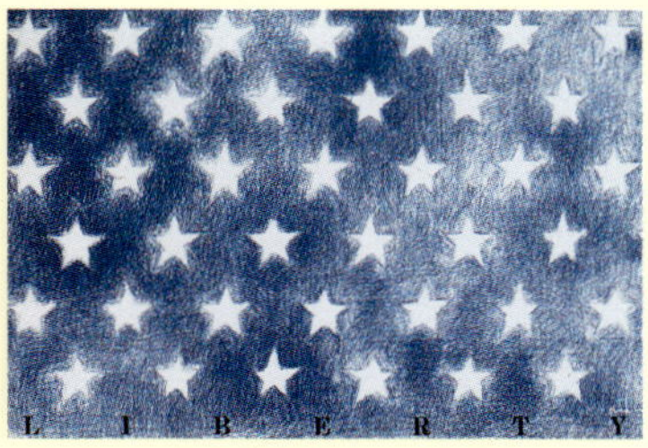

Fred Troller, died of cancer at his home in Rye, New York, on October 11. He was 71. ■ A graphic designer who helped popularize Swiss New Typography in the United States in the 1960s. Troller was part of a movement that embraced the clean photography and sans-serif typefaces of the Bauhaus over the more ornamental graphic-design styles popular at the time. ■ Corporations were drawn to this straightforward style for its ability to communicate clearly and logically—qualities that simplified the broad application of graphic identity systems. Troller's work for clients including American Airlines, Exxon, IBM and General Electric are marked by their use of geometric forms and disproportionate typography. "Symbolism, geometry and typography play an important part in my graphic work," he once wrote. "By the imaginative use of these elements it is possible to create strong recognition and communication values, which stand out in contrast to the man-made visual pollution surrounding us everywhere." ■ He had recently retired after a twelve-year tenure at the College of Ceramics at Alfred University, in western New York, where he was chair of the design department. ■ Troller was born in Zurich. He attended the Kunstgewerbeschule in Zurich and began teaching there after graduating in 1950. ■ In 1954 Troller was invited to work for the film producer Louis de Rochemont—one of the creators of the "March of Time" newsreels. Working with Rochemont, Troller was able to travel throughout the Americas. In 1955, Troller and his wife Beatrice starred in Rochemont's "Cinerama Holiday," a documentary style film about two young couples one from the Midwest the other from Switzerland—each traveling in the other's country. Shot with three cameras running simultaneously to create a panoramic effect, "Cinerama Holiday" was the highest grossing film of 1955. ■ Back in Zurich, Troller ran his own design firm until 1960, then spent six years as art direcctor for the Geigy Chemical Corporation. In 1968 he opened Troller Associates in Rye, where he worked on advertising and corporate identity for a wide range of corporate clients. ■ He was assigned to create an identity program for the Federal Energy Administration in June 1974. The symbol he created, the Federal Energy Star, won him a certificate of excellence from the Federal Design Council. Unfortunately, Congress quickly disbanded the agency. Tony Speath, who worked with Troller on the F.E.A. project, remembers these words from Paul Rand: "If it's really important and I can't do it, I want Fred to do it." ■ In addition to Alfred University, Troller taught at the School of Visual Arts, Purdue Univer-sity, The Philadelphia College of Art, SUNY Purchase, Ohio State University, Southeastern Massachusetts University, Rhode Island School of Design and the Cooper Union. ■ In 1995, Georgia State University mounted an retrospective exhibition on Troller's design. He was also a painter and sculptor, and exhibited at Grace Borgenicht Gallery in New York. ■ In addition to his wife, Troller is survived by a son, Simon, of Portchester, New York, a daughter, Meret Piderman of Treviso, Italy; and three grandchildren.

(opposite page) Samples box designed for Geigy Chemical Corporation and (above) Public service poster series

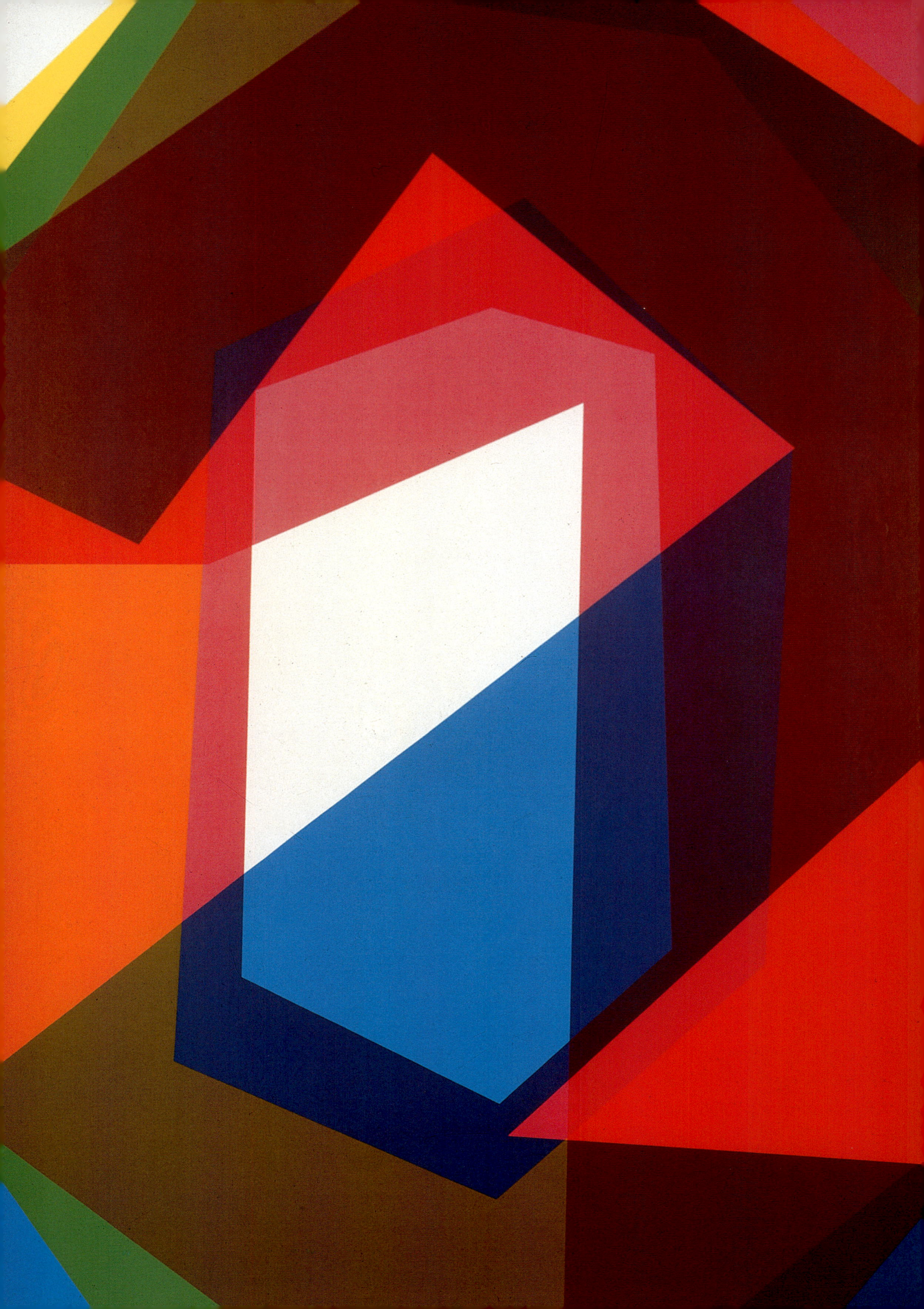

Commentary Kommentar Commentaire

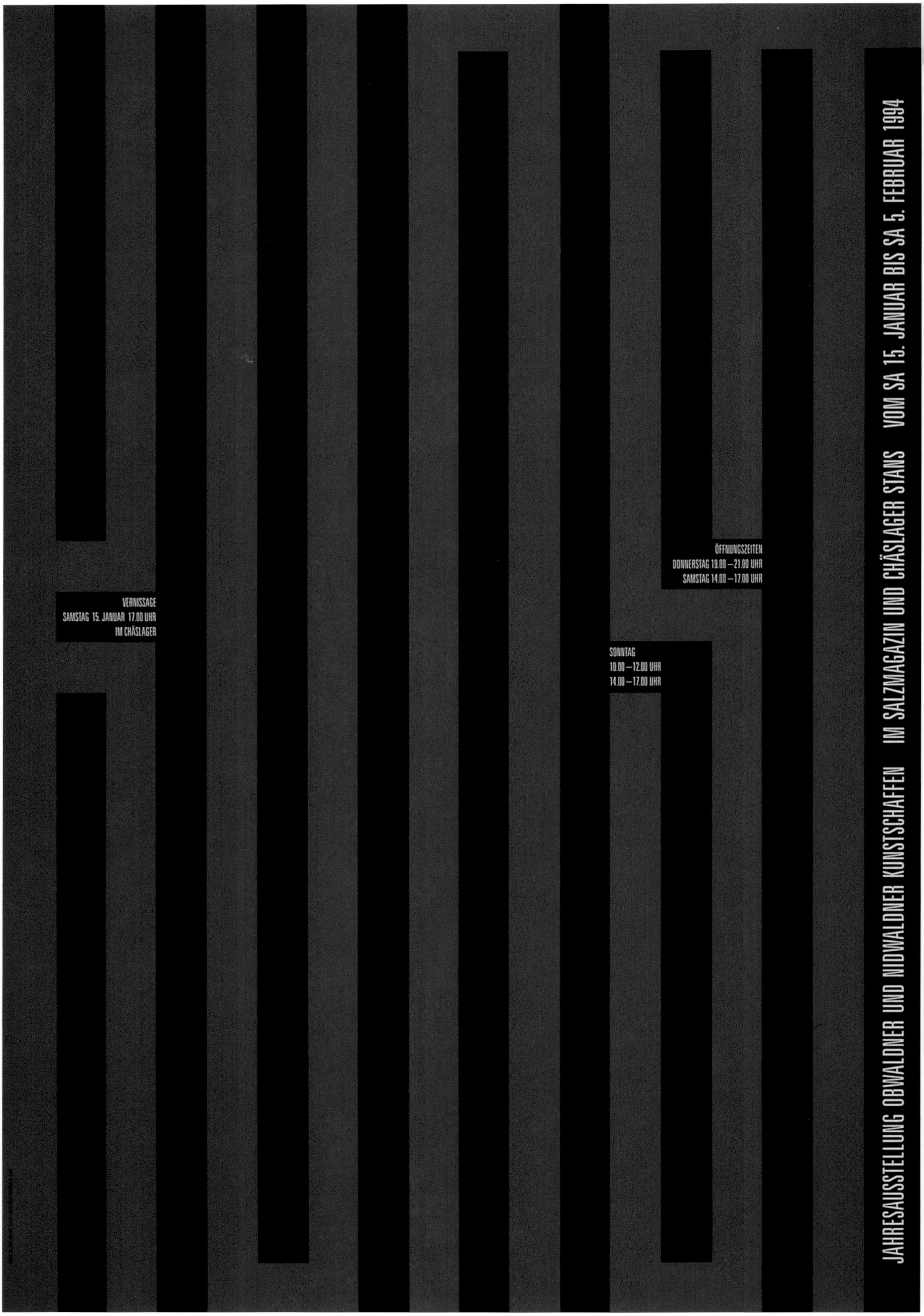
JAHRESAUSSTELLUNG OBWALDNER UND NIDWALDNER KUNSTSCHAFFEN IM SALZMAGAZIN UND CHÄSLAGER STANS VOM SA 15. JANUAR BIS SA 5. FEBRUAR 1994
VERNISSAGE
SAMSTAG 15. JANUAR 17.00 UHR
IM CHÄSLAGER
ÖFFNUNGSZEITEN
DONNERSTAG 19.00 –21.00 UHR
SAMSTAG 14.00 –17.00 UHR
SONNTAG
10.00 –12.00 UHR
14.00 –17.00 UHR

Q&A with Melchior Imboden, Buochs, Switzerland

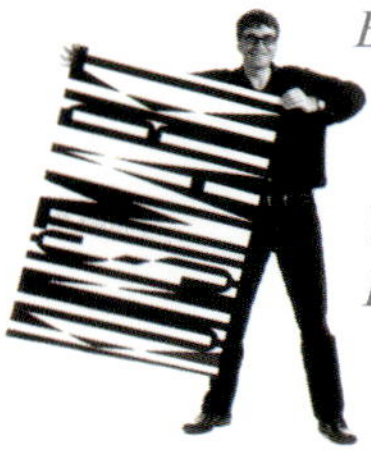

Born in Stans, Switzerland in 1956, Imboden studied Graphic Design at the Art School of Lucerne and started his own Graphic Studio in '92. His main activities are in the field of poster design, book design and catalogue design for art and photo exhibitions and cultural institutions. He has participated of many international exhibitions, including Essen, Chaumont, Brno, Lahti, Warsaw, Toyama, Ogaki, Trnava, Colorado, Helsinki and Moscow and his works are included in many different collections. His Art-Exhibition posters have been awarded several prizes, including '94 Gold Medal at the 16th International Poster Biennial in Brno, '95 Special Prize at the 11th International Poster Biennial in Helsinki, '96 Silver Medal at the 15th International Poster Biennial in Warsaw, '96 First Prize IBCC Award at the World poster-winners competition at the Golden Bee 3 in Moscow.

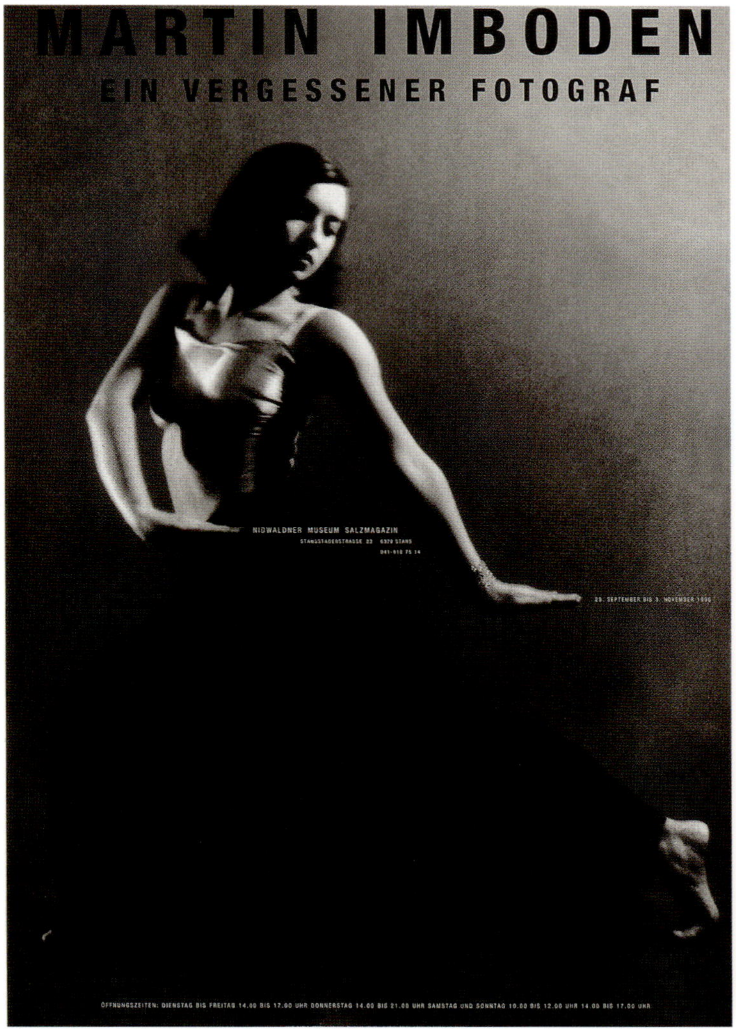

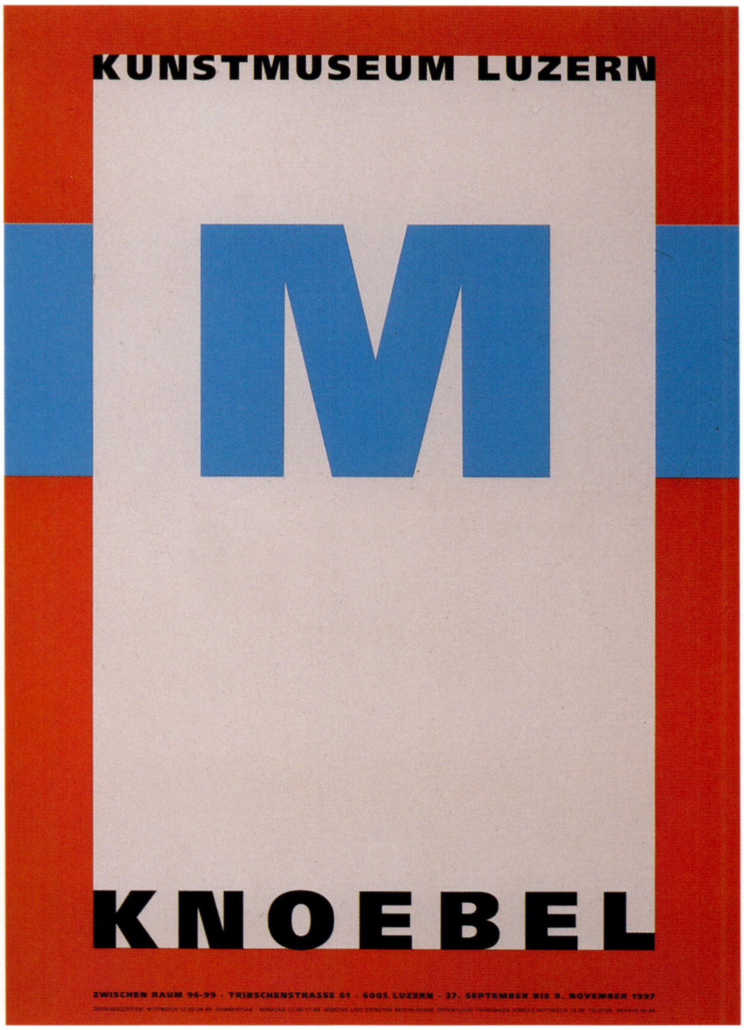

What is your proudest achievement in design so far?

It is not easy to limit my answer to just one achievement. I would have to begin with my international recognition as a poster designer. This started with exhibitions all over the world, which resulted in various awards and then led to the possibility of giving speeches at international design exhibitions and conferences as well as at universities. In addition, I am also very proud of the various art and photography books that I have designed and published. My current book project is on the work of a Swiss photographer who took 7,000 portraits of daily life from 1911 till 1938, all in the same location. My interest in these projects stems from the fact that I am also a photographer. My artistic activity in this field has also led to international exhibitions and recognition.

How important is it to win awards?

Winning awards is an important recognition and provides motivation to pursue my work. During my own studies, I won an award in a competition for poster design, which had a great influence on me and reflected an interest in that field which has continued until the present.

How much does technology influence your work?

My work could not be completed without the help of computers. However, I always begin by hand: sketches, collages, experiments with materials and colors. I belong to the last generation which did not grow up with computers, and am therefore accustomed to taking pen in hand when starting a project. In my activities as a university guest Professor, I always make a point of encouraging my students to sketch their inspirations first by hand before turning to the computer.

How do you keep up with current trends in design?

It would be unthinkable not to keep oneself up-to-date with the latest trends in this profession, for they are an important source of inspiration. I buy and read books and magazines on design, art and photography, go to exhibitions and have regular contact with foreign designers. Because a critical analysis of a design is extremely important, this enables me to compare and evaluate the latest works.

What part of your work do you find most demanding?

Book design is the most demanding part of my work because of the many facets involved. When I am the publisher of a book, I am responsible for the concept, the design, the text and authors, the financing, the deadlines, and often—as is the case with my latest book on photography—the poster design, invitations and creation of the exhibition itself.

What interests do you have outside work?

Travel, hiking, skiing, music, and visiting exhibitions are among my most important interests outside work.

Have you ever turned down a client—and why?
It has happened that I have had to turn down a project, usually either for lack of time or for lack of interest in the project. For a project which interests me, however, I can always find the time.

What questions do your clients most often ask?
Today, most clients ask how much time will be involved and what the costs will be. As a result of not having planned far enough in advance, they often ask for last-minute changes, which they assume must be possible with the computer.

How involved are you with the design community?
For the very reason that I work alone, I value contact—both personally and professionally—with other designers in the world.

Do you teach a course on design?
I am currently teaching as a guest professor in communication design at the Staatliche Hochschule für Gestaltung in Karlsruhe, Germany.

Do you enjoy speaking at design conferences?
It is always a challenge to speak at various design congresses and exhibitions. I especially enjoy the opportunity to exchange ideas and having contact with other designers, teachers and students.

What creative philosophy do you communicate to a student audience? a professional audience? a client?
At the university, I tell my students that they should feel very free to explore and collect information on the assigned theme in order to discover their own creative identities. Once they are working in their profession, they will soon find themselves limited by their employer, a client, given specifications, and so on. With a professional audience—when giving a speech at an international design conference, for example—I have often said that it is important for the designers to maintain and respect their own cultural identity. I try to encourage my clients to be open to fresh, new design solutions; to have the courage to overcome their preconceived ideas.

Which of your skills would you most like to perfect?
It would be helpful to my work if I were more adept with the computer.

Who are the three to five designers you most admire?
A design must be seen within the context of a particular field. Often it is only after a designer has been active in his field for years that his work can truly be evaluated. In the history of design, there are names that can still hold their own when compared to contemporary design. Given these observations, it is difficult for me to name those I admire most.

Where would you like to be five or ten years from now?
I would particularly like to increase my activities in the field of photography by exhibiting my photographic work internationally. However, because my activities in design take up so much of my time, there is not enough space for that at the moment.

(commentary intro) Silkscreen poster rendered in twenty different vesions for an art exhibition at Galery Sust, Stansstad, 2001, and also a millenium poster for 2000/2001 (previous spread-left page) 'Kunst 1994' silkscreen poster for an exhibition of artists from central Switzerland for the Museum of Modern Art, Stans, Switzerland, 1994 (previous spread-right page, left side) Silkscreen poster for a Martin Imboden Photo exhibition, City of Lucerne, 1996 (previous spread-right page, right side) Silkscreen poster for an Imi Knoebel Art Exhibition, Museum of Modern Art, Lucerne, 1997 (this spread-left page, left side) 'Plakat Kultur' silkscreen poster for an exhibition of poster artists from central Switzerland, Art Galerie Sust, Stansstad, 1999 (this spread-left page, right side) Silkscreen poster for the IMF Classic Music Festival, City of Lucerne, 1996 (this spread-right page) 'Kunst 1999' silkscreen poster for an exhibition of artists from central Switzerland for the Museum of Modern Art, Stans Switzerland, 1999

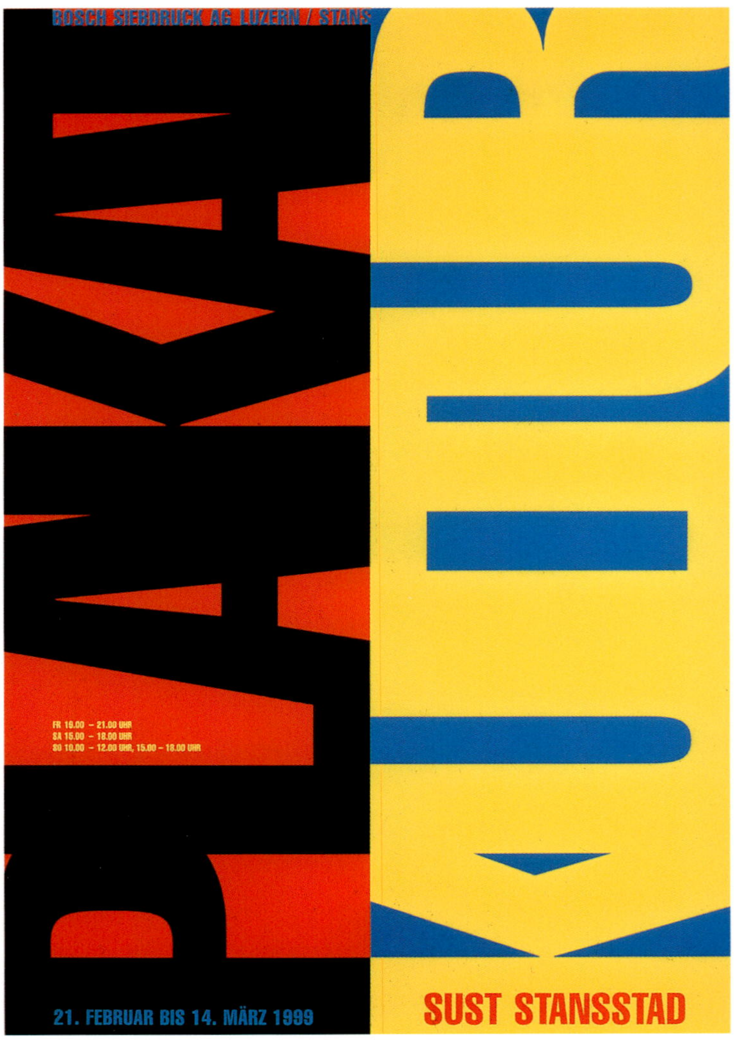

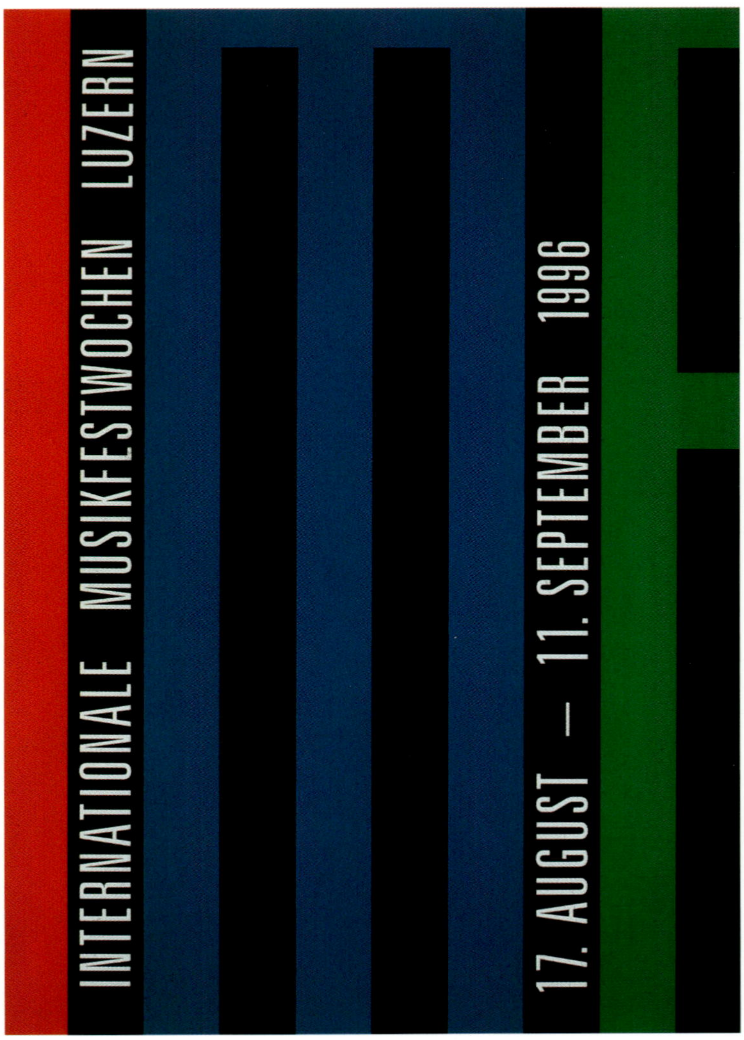

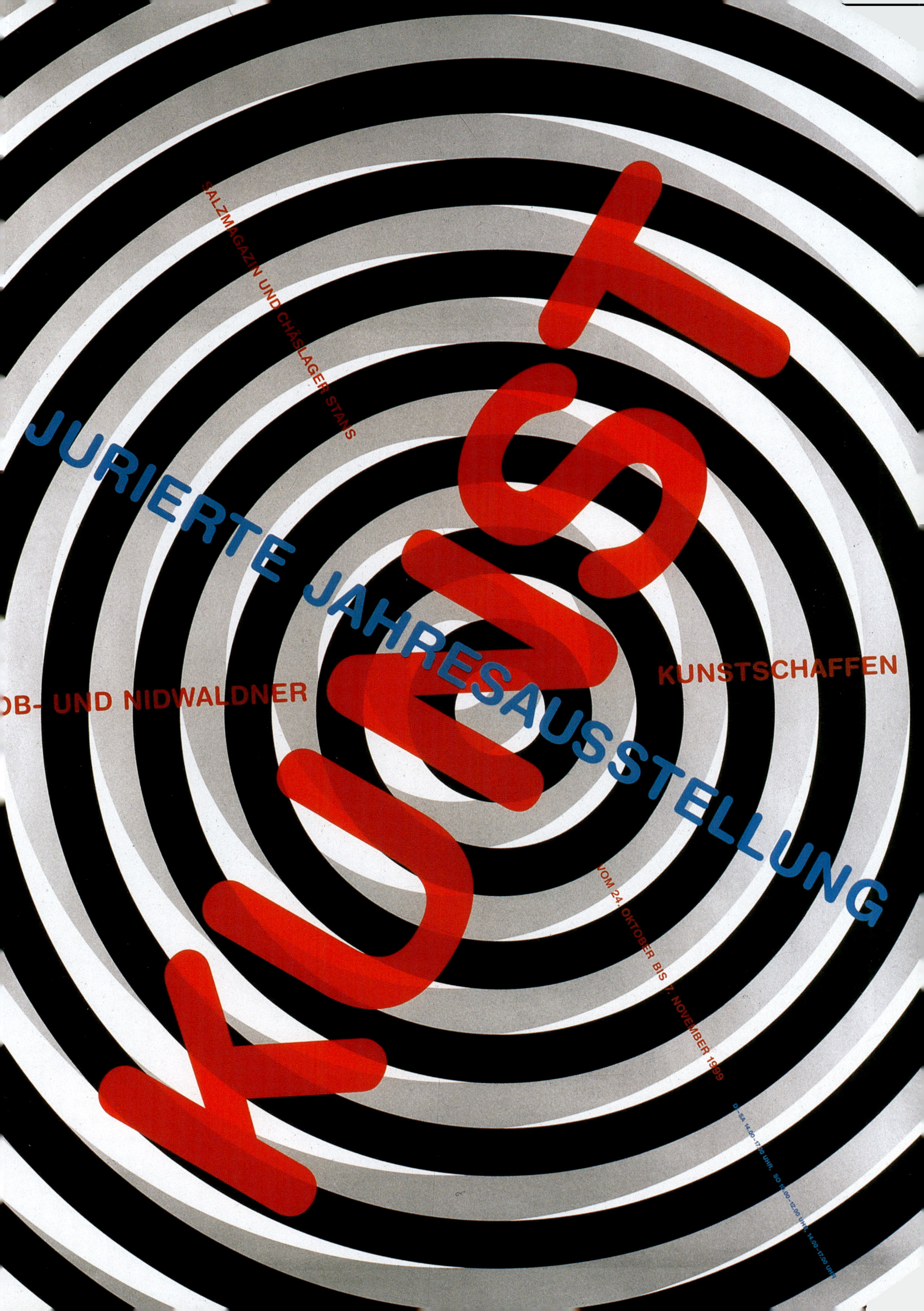
SALZMAGAZIN UND CHÄSLAGER STANS
JURIERTE JAHRESAUSSTELLUNG
KUNST
OB- UND NIDWALDNER
KUNSTSCHAFFEN
VOM 24. OKTOBER BIS 7. NOVEMBER 1999
DI–SA 14.00–17.00 UHR, SO 10.00–12.00 UHR, 14.00–17.00 UHR

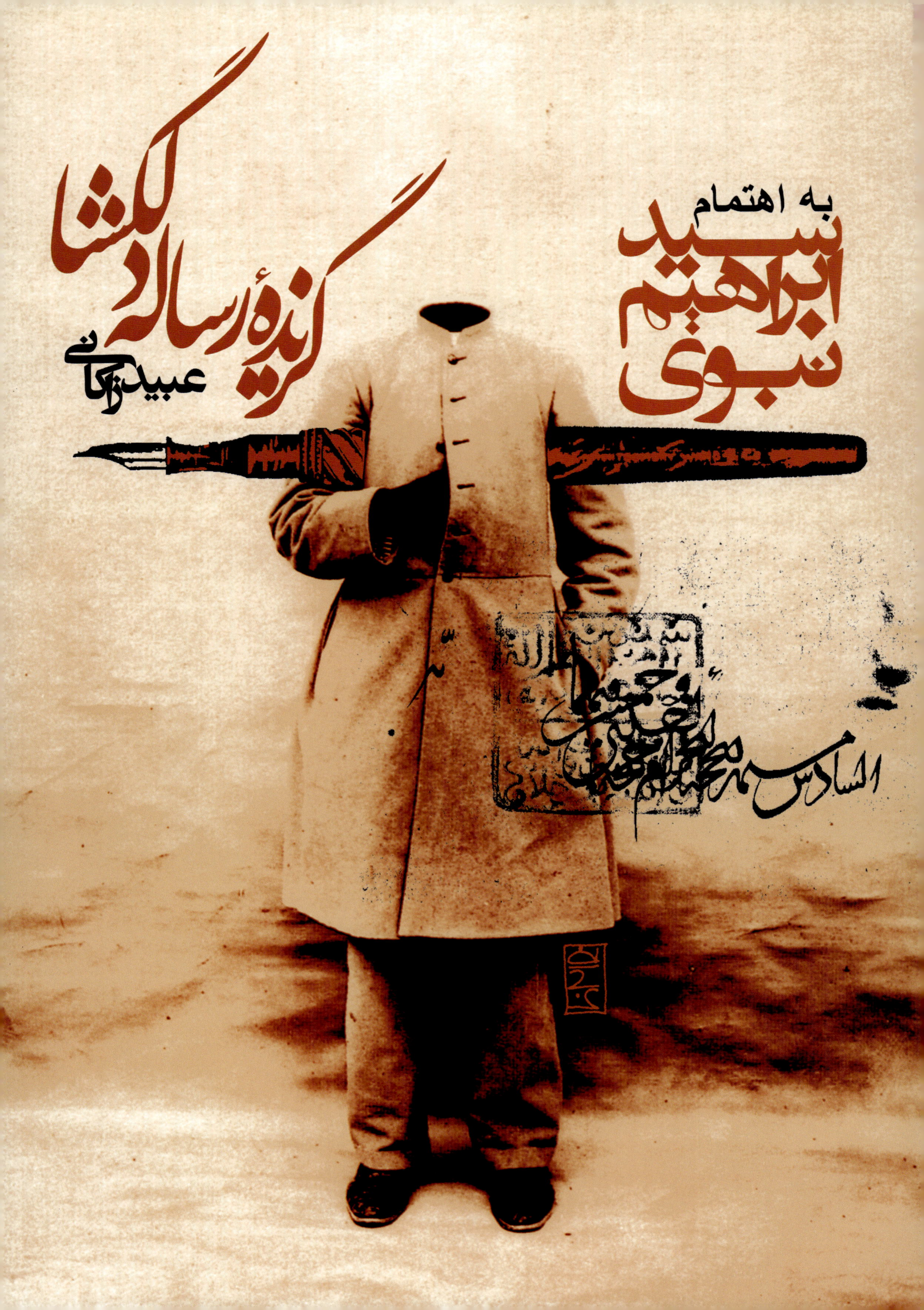
گزیدهٔ رساله دلگشا
عبید زاکانی
به اهتمام
سید ابراهیم نبوی

Q&A with Reza Abedini, Tehran, Iran

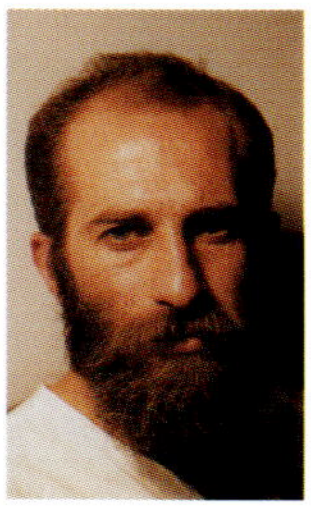

Born in 1967 Tehran, Iran, Reza Abedini graduated in Graphic Design from the School of Fine Arts, 1985 and earned a B.A. in Painting from Tehran Art University, 1992. He's had a professional career as a graphic designer since 1989. His work has been exhibited in numerous shows, including "An Exhibition of Film Posters," Tehran 1993, '94 and '96, "The Biennial of Iranian Graphic Designers," Tehran 1991 and '99 and "Self-promotional Posters," Tehran 2001, as well as the solo exhibitions "In The Opposite Direction (Visual Experiment)" 2001, "In The Beginning (Poster Exhibition)" 2001, "Return (Visual Experiment)" 2002 and "Answer? (Poster Exhibition)" 2002. Internationally, his work has appeared at exhibitions in Essen, Brno, Taiwan, Paris, Warsaw and Chaumont. Additionally, Abedini has received numerous awards for his work, including "Best Film Poster," International Film Festival, Tehran 1993, '94 and '96, the Film Critics Special Award for the best film poster, Tehran 1994, Poster Award from the 6th Biennial of Iranian Graphic Designers, Tehran 1999, and the "Special Award for Creativity" from Iranian Graphic Designers Society, Tehran 1999. He has been a member of Iranian Graphic Designers Society since 1997 (Supervisor of the Cultural Committee since 1999), and a member of Alliance Graphique International (AGI) since 2001. Reza Abedini is also very active in the literary field: since 1990 he's been a writer and critic in the field of visual arts. From 1992-93 he served as editor of the visual section of the monthly magazine Sureh *and is managing director and editor-in-chief of* Manzar, *a pictorial magazine. His book covers include* Qeseye Kutuleha va Deraza (A Tale of Dwarfs and Lankier), *2000,* Manzar Pictorial Book 1999, *Khalil Jibran's* The Prophet, *1997,* The Art of Print—The Textbook of Iran Art Schools *(Iran Educational Ministry), 2000 and* Autobiographic, A Selection of Works, *2002. Since 1996 he's taught classes in Graphic and Visual Design, Printmaking, Poster and Editorials, as member of The Faculty of Art and Architecture, Fine Arts School and Tehran University.*

What is your proudest achievement in design so far?
To design and to review Persian fonts and type as my main focus. In a general sense, to update, to revive and to give a new identity to Persian typography and to strive towards creating a graphic atmosphere based on our visual culture and heritage.

Who are the three to five designers you most admire?
Aleksander Rodchenko, Morteza Momayez, Roman Cieslewicz, and Ikko Tanaka.

How much does technology influence your work?
Graphic design is basically a technological form of art and the two cannot be separated. But if what you mean by "technology" is modern devices and equipment—which are mainly digital—it doesn't affect my work very much and I am really careful about using it. I hate the competition of using technology in design work and the pressure being technologically up-to-date. I always try to keep technology under my esthetic control.

How do you keep up with current trends in design?
By studying and understanding the trends and getting to know their roots, origins and the real reason behind them. I never ignore what is going on with trends! We need to be careful because they have a great power for a short period of time. However these trends sometimes change the way that graphic design is defined and this worries me a lot.

What part of your work do you find most demanding?
I think the part of the design which comes after the creative part and only takes time and energy doing non-creative, redundant and precise operations and the preparation of work for printing!

What interests do you have outside work?
Watching movies and television documentaries, driving, writing, smoking, drinking tea and discussion.

Have you ever turned down a client—and why?
Yes, it has happened a lot because they have gone the wrong way! Or they gave me a short time to do an important and big job, or because of redundant and typical requests and sometimes because of design order, which were not my field of expertise.

What questions do your clients most often ask?
The questions usually are: "Is this the best design work you have ever done or have you put all your talent and energy into this job?" And yes, sometimes: "Can I pay less?" or "What did you mean by this design?" And I say, "DESIGN is all that I meant, that is all."

What creative philosophy do you communicate to a student audience? a professional audience? a client?
To my students: To always present novel and unpredictable subjects rather than what's on the curriculum or the usual design basics. To my clients: I try to make an image in the client's mind on the progress of the job and its impact. To the professional audience: To demonstrate my ideas unexpectedly, to constantly study the current and routine design works around me and to do the opposite and also to wear "ear plugs" and "bulletproof vest!"

How involved are you with the design community?
A lot. I am involved in all the local and IGDS (Iranian Graphic Designers Society) events and exhibitions. I am also informed about the most graphic design events and exhibitions around the world and I try to take part in them, if it is possible.

Do you enjoy speaking at design conferences?
Yes, because I come across many new subjects, ideas and points of view in design. At the same time what surprises me is that my colleagues around the world and I have the same problems, issues and worries to take care of despite all the cultural, political, social and even economical conditions and differences.

Do you teach a course on design?
I have been teaching in public design schools and centers for six years and at the same time I have my own private design courses at my own studio. I select a group of my students each year and work with them in different field of design.

How important is it to win awards?
It will be a lie if I say it's not that important. But when I see the way awards are given out and the relationship between winners and judges and what goes in between, I lose a bit of my enthusiasm.

Which of your skills would you most like to perfect?
Discovering the infinite relations and combinations between type and image. Especially Persian type as a visually rich and pure phenomenon.

Where would you like to be five or ten years from now?
In five years: known as an Iranian graphic designer! In ten years: known as a more Iranian graphic designer!! At the same time being actively present, along with all other graphic designers around the world and creating a new dialect in graphic design language.

(opposite page) 'A Selection of Resale Delgosha' book cover for Rozaneh Publication, Iran, 2000 and (next spread - left) A Page of Karname Literature Magazine, 1999 and (next spread - right) 'Imagination Thought Drawing' poster for the Iranian Artists House Gallery, 2002

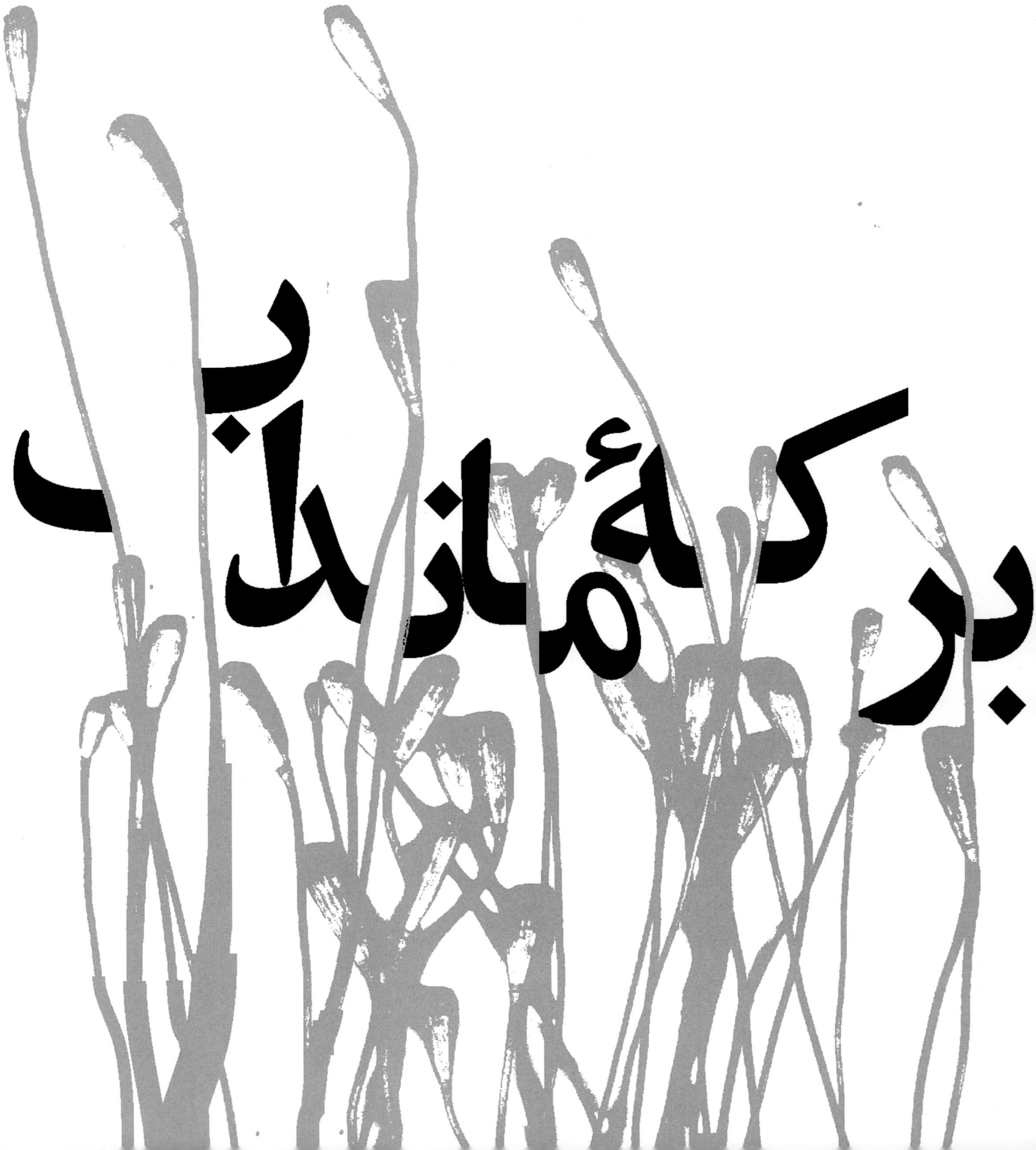

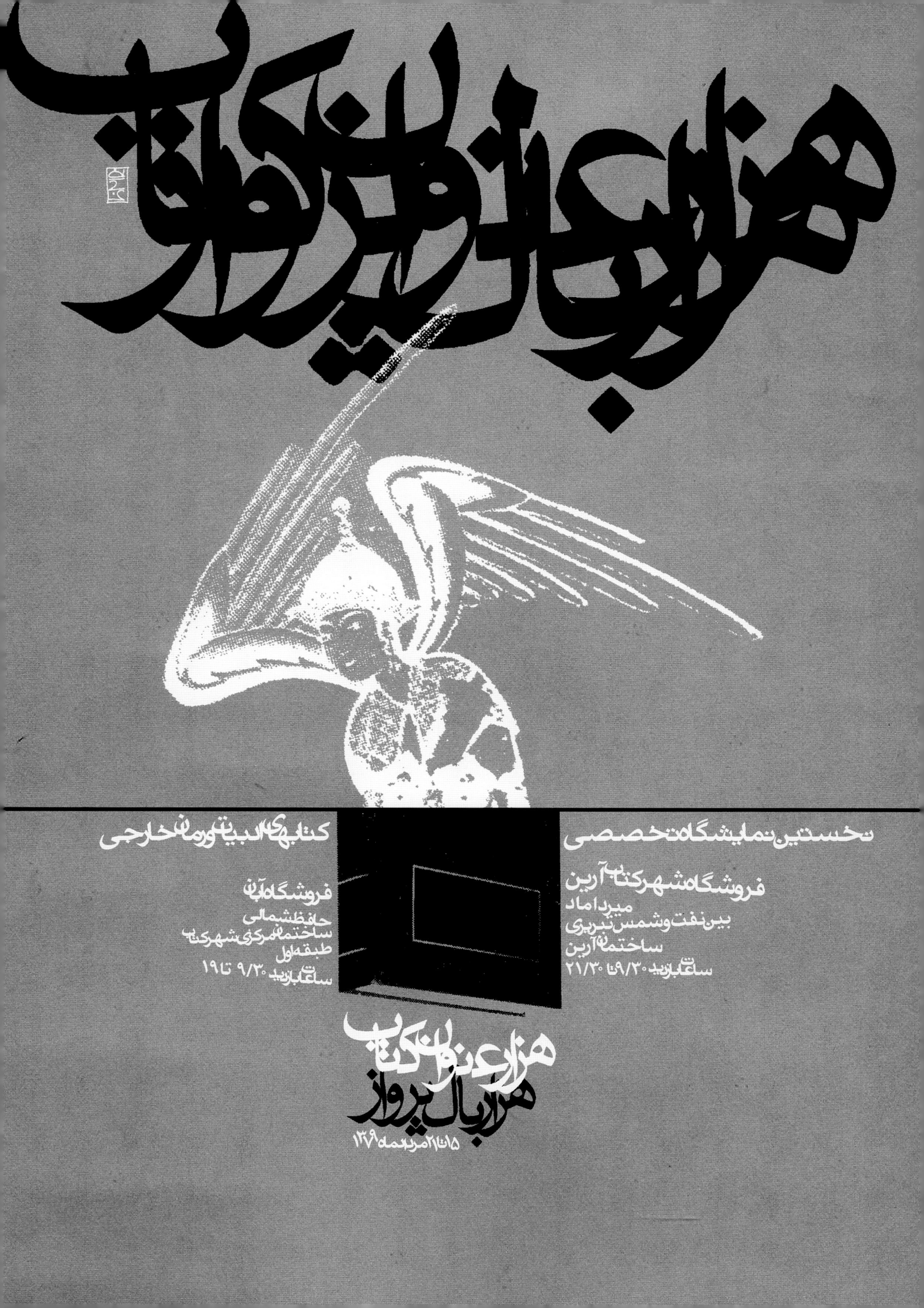
هزار عنوان کتاب هزار بال پرواز
نخستین نمایشگاه تخصصی
کتابهای ادبیات و رمان خارجی
فروشگاه شهر کتاب آرین
میرداماد
بین نفت و شمس تبریزی
ساختمان آرین
ساعت بازدید ۹/۳۰ تا ۲۱/۳۰
فروشگاه آبان
حافظ شمالی
ساختمان مرکزی شهر کتاب
طبقه اول
ساعت بازدید ۹/۳۰ تا ۱۹
هزار عنوان کتاب
هزار بال پرواز
۱۵ تا ۲۱ امردادماه ۱۳۷۹

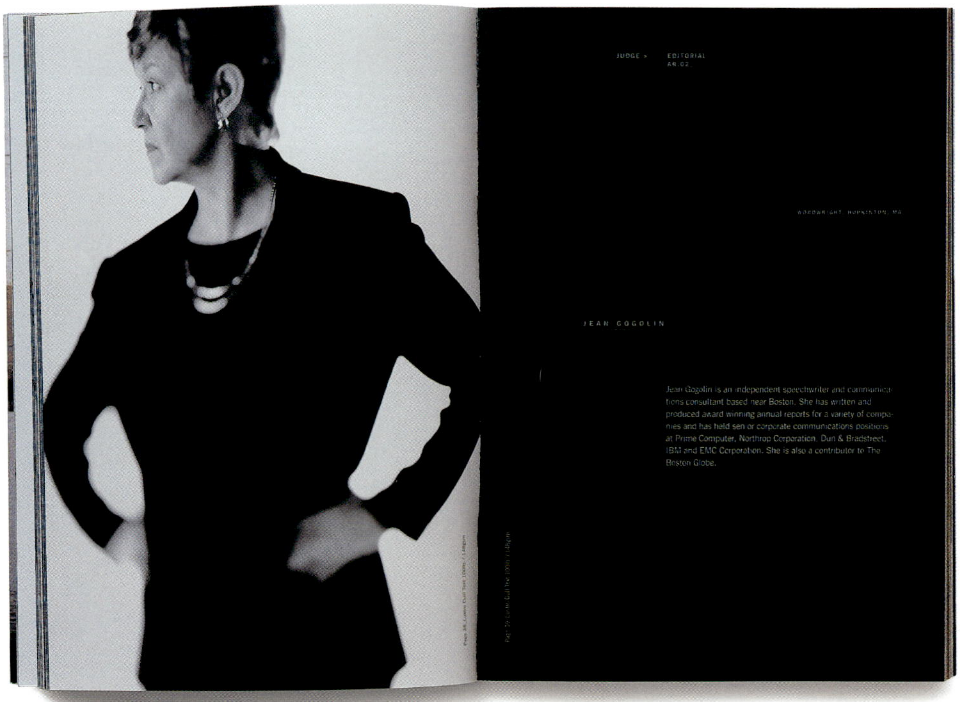

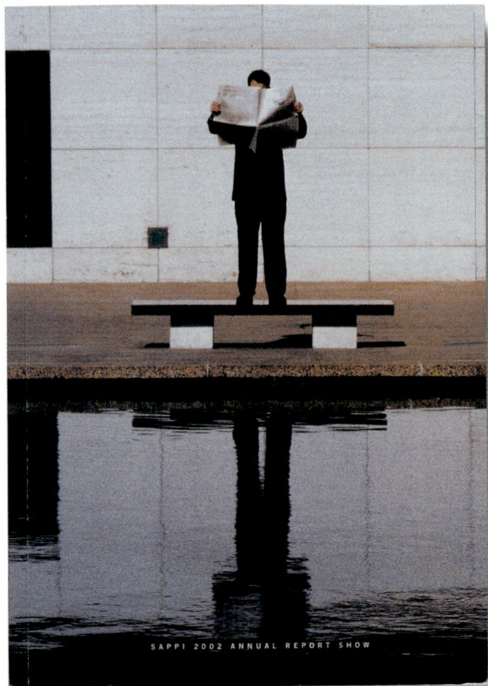

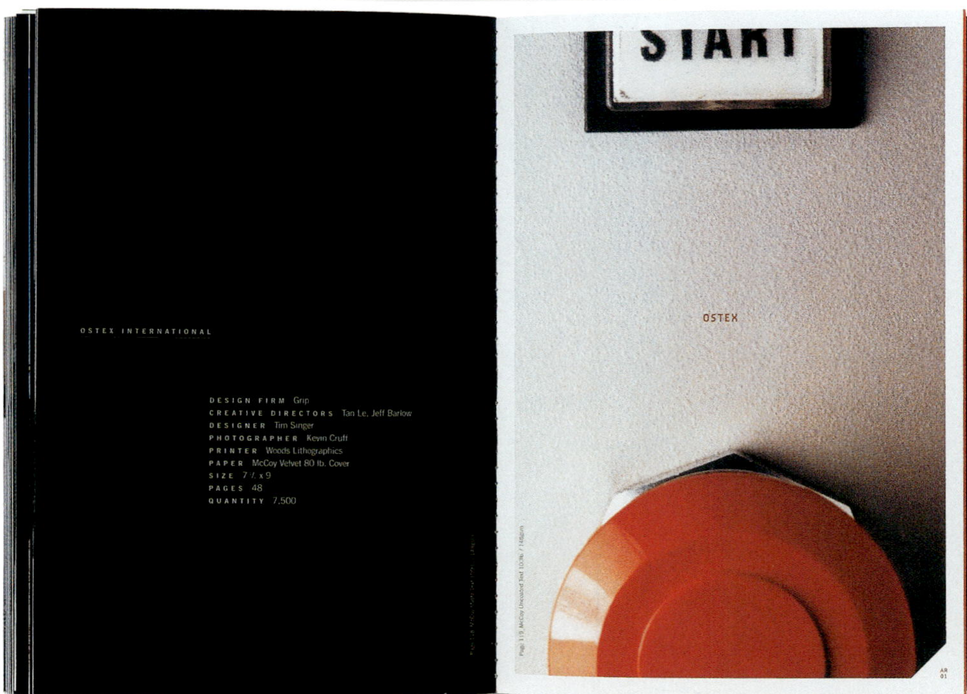

(this spread) 'Sappi 2002 Annual Report Show' Design Firm: Weymouth Design Art Director: Tom Laidlaw Designers: Robert Krivich and Brad Lewthwaite Photographers: Michael Weymouth, Jonathan Torgovnik, Francois Robert and Steven Crowley Copywriter: Jean Gogolin Client: Sappi Fine Paper

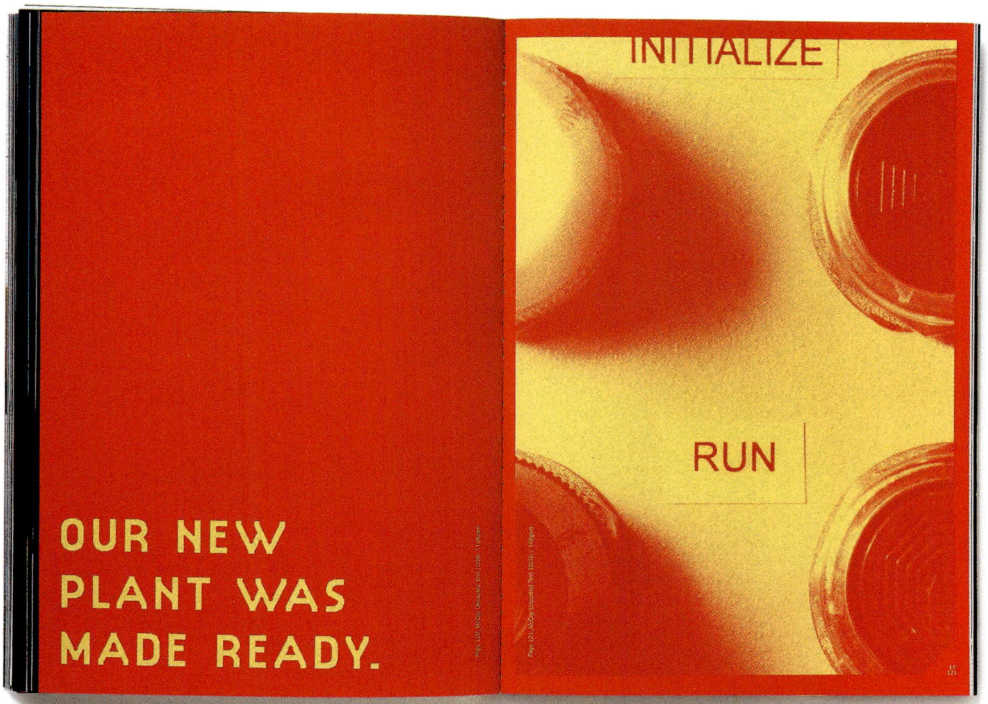
INITIALIZE
RUN
OUR NEW
PLANT WAS
MADE READY.

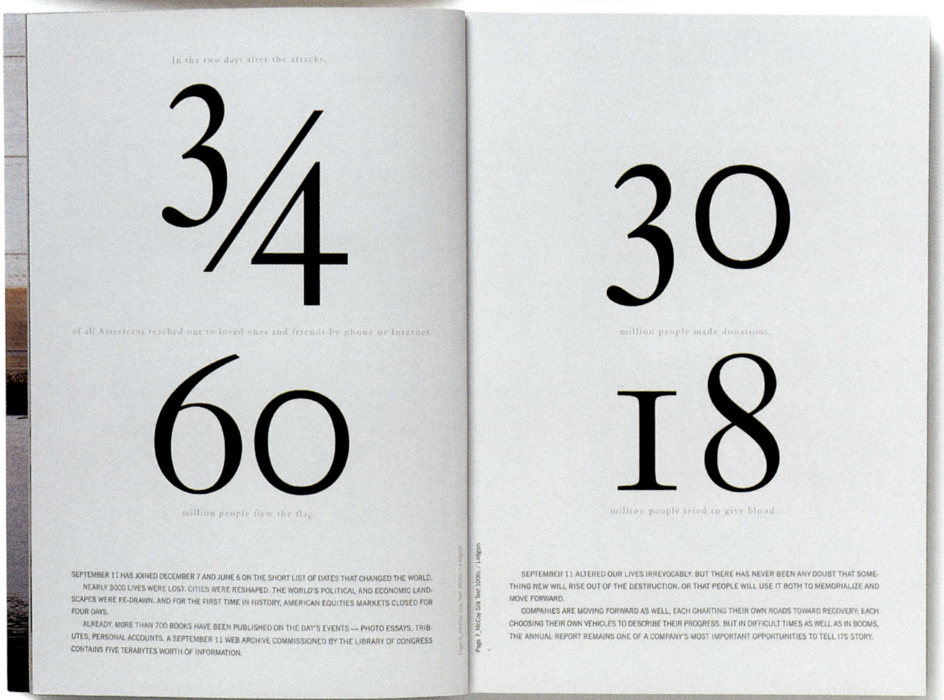
In the two days after the attacks,
3/4
of all Americans reached out to loved ones and friends by phone or Internet.
60
million people flew the flag.
SEPTEMBER 11 HAS JOINED DECEMBER 7 AND JUNE 6 ON THE SHORT LIST OF DATES THAT CHANGED THE WORLD.
NEARLY 3000 LIVES WERE LOST. CITIES WERE RESHAPED. THE WORLD'S POLITICAL AND ECONOMIC LANDSCAPES WERE RE-DRAWN. AND FOR THE FIRST TIME IN HISTORY, AMERICAN EQUITIES MARKETS CLOSED FOR FOUR DAYS.
ALREADY, MORE THAN 700 BOOKS HAVE BEEN PUBLISHED ON THE DAY'S EVENTS — PHOTO ESSAYS, TRIBUTES, PERSONAL ACCOUNTS. A SEPTEMBER 11 WEB ARCHIVE COMMISSIONED BY THE LIBRARY OF CONGRESS CONTAINS FIVE TERABYTES WORTH OF INFORMATION.
30
million people made donations.
18
million people tried to give blood.
SEPTEMBER 11 ALTERED OUR LIVES IRREVOCABLY. BUT THERE HAS NEVER BEEN ANY DOUBT THAT SOMETHING NEW WILL RISE OUT OF THE DESTRUCTION, OR THAT PEOPLE WILL USE IT BOTH TO MEMORIALIZE AND MOVE FORWARD.
COMPANIES ARE MOVING FORWARD AS WELL, EACH CHARTING THEIR OWN ROADS TOWARD RECOVERY; EACH CHOOSING THEIR OWN VEHICLES TO DESCRIBE THEIR PROGRESS. BUT IN DIFFICULT TIMES AS WELL AS IN BOOMS, THE ANNUAL REPORT REMAINS ONE OF A COMPANY'S MOST IMPORTANT OPPORTUNITIES TO TELL ITS STORY.
Page 7_McCoy Silk Text 100lb. / 148gsm

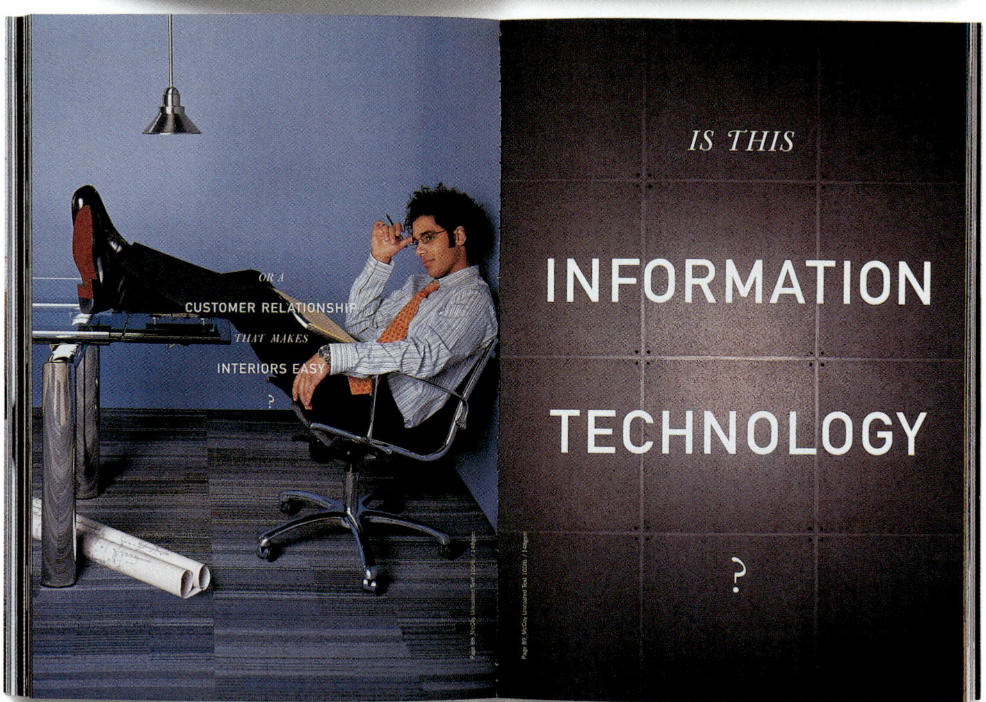
OR A
CUSTOMER RELATIONSHIP
THAT MAKES
INTERIORS EASY
?
IS THIS
INFORMATION
TECHNOLOGY
?

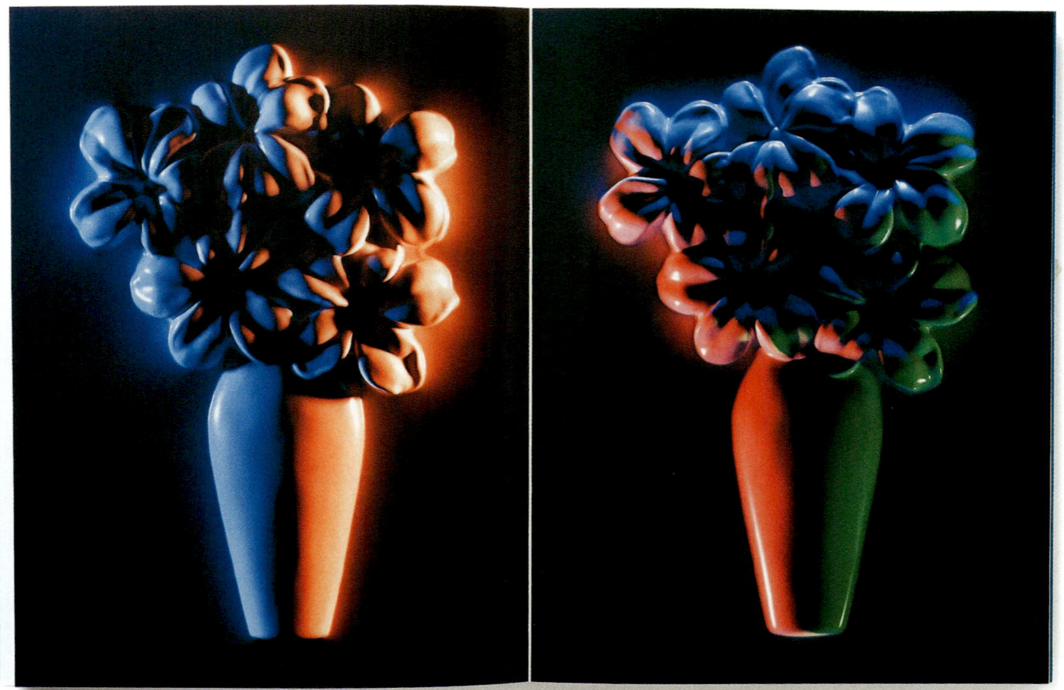

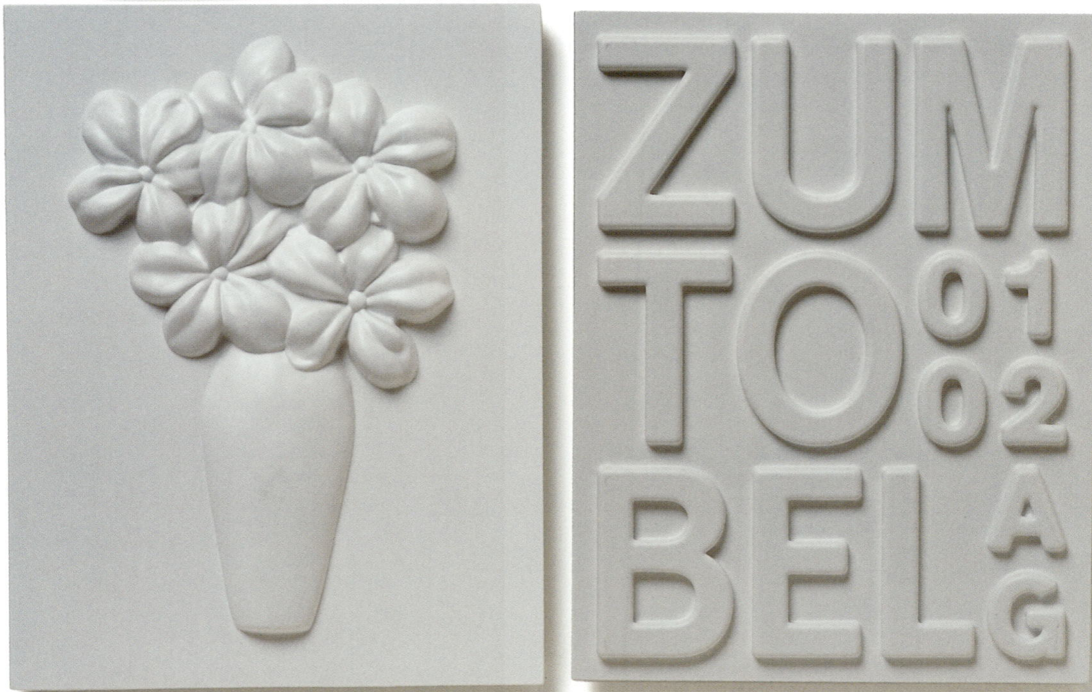

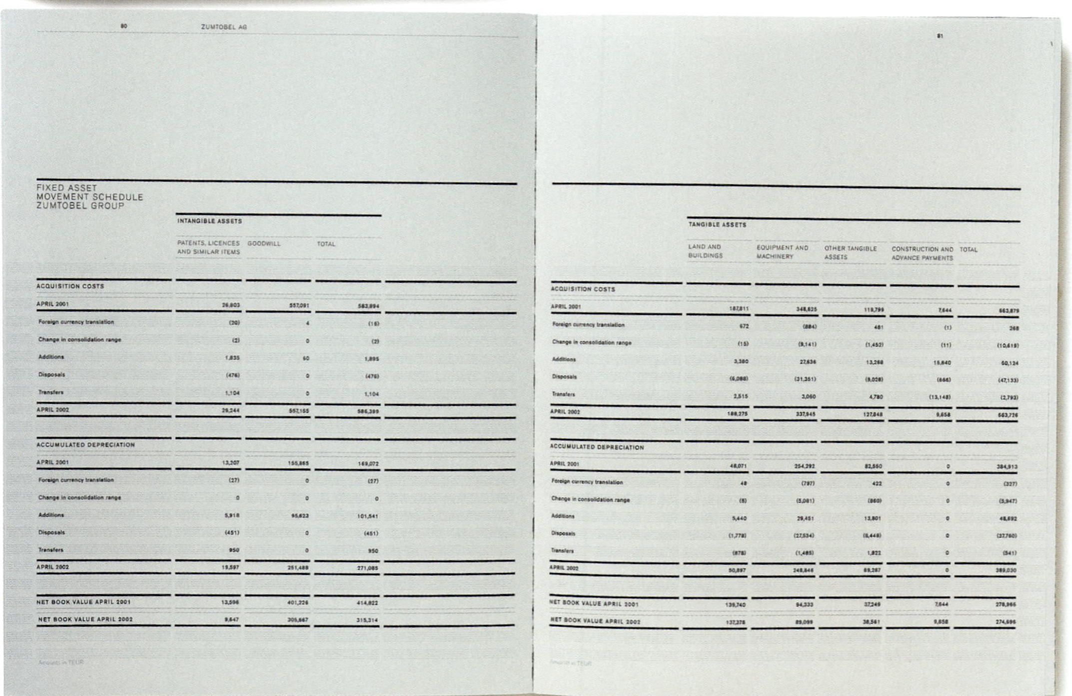

'Zumtobel Annual Report' Design Firm: Sagmeister Inc. Art Director: Stefan Sagmeister Designer: Matthias Ernstberger Photographer: Belov Borsodi Illustrator: Matthias Ernstberger Copywriter: Otto Riewoldt Client: Zumtobel AG

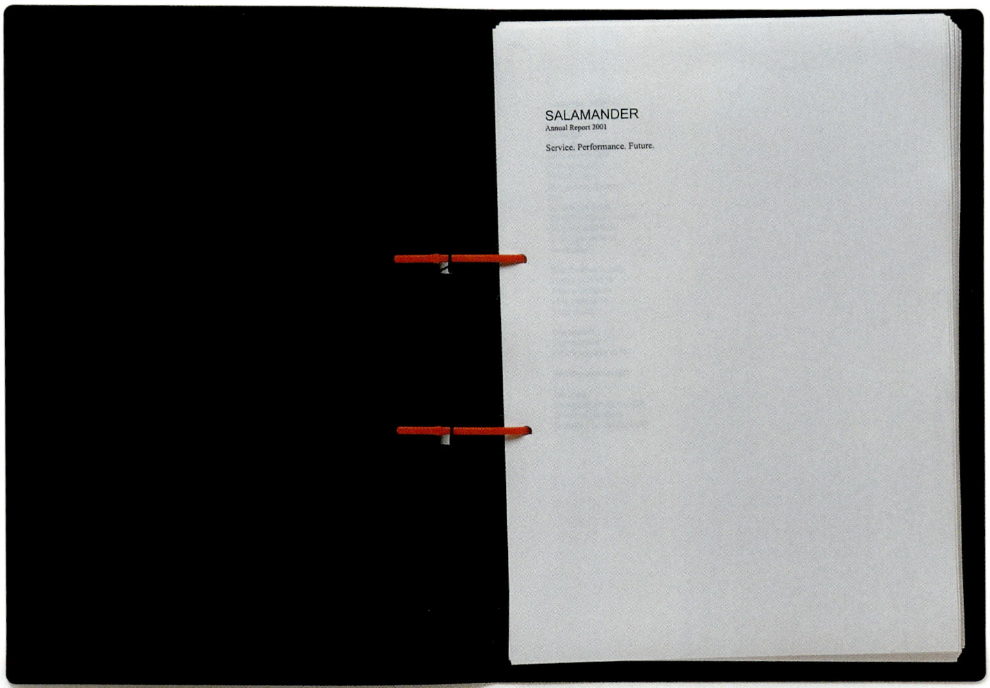

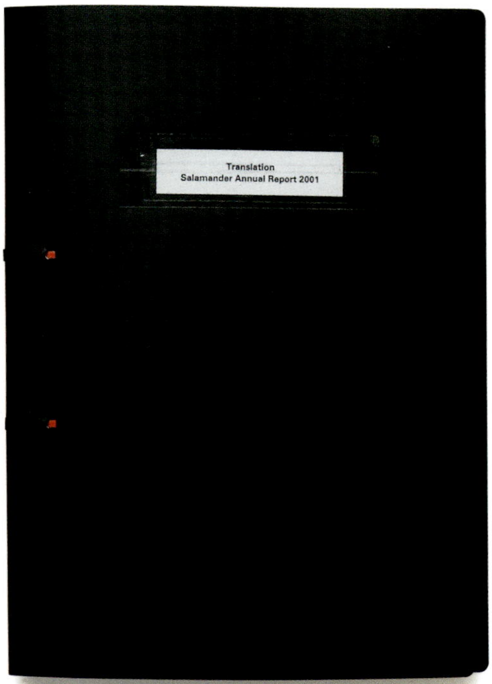

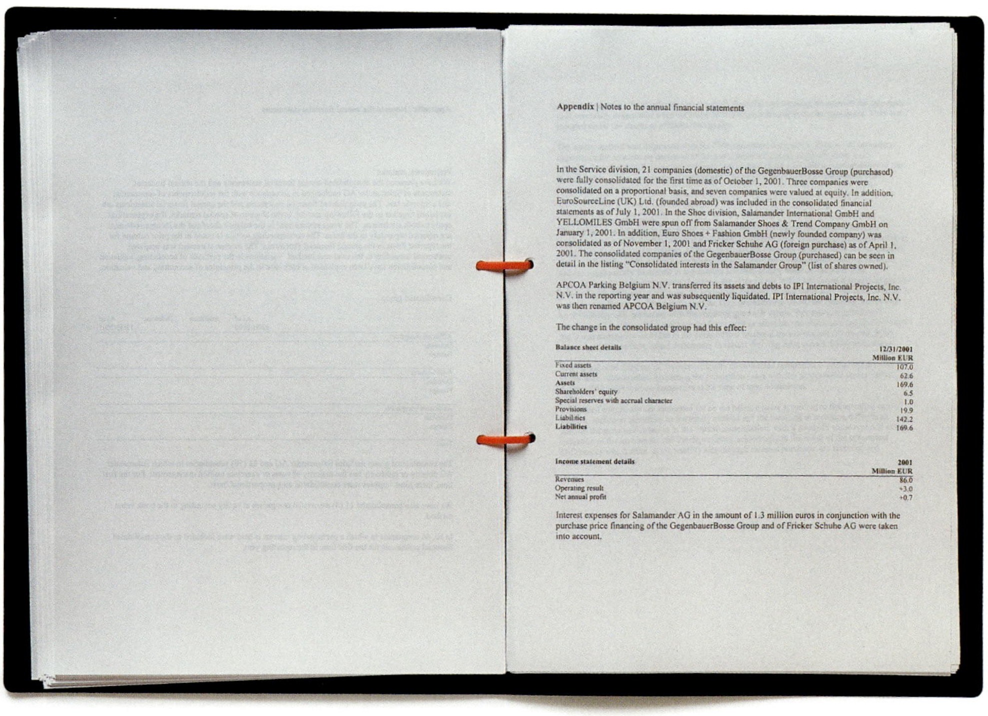

'Salamander Annual Report 2001: Service, Performance, Future' Design Firm: TC Gruppe GmbH, Target Communications Creative Director: Maike Heyn-SeGares Art Director: Daniela Rota Photographer: Thomas Weecard Consulting: Angela Tybussek Client: Dr. Albrecht Bamler, Salamander AG

'The McKnight Foundation Annual Report' Design Firm: Gage Creative Director: David Whitman Designer: Dawn Selg Copywriter: McKnight Foundation Client: McKnight Foundation

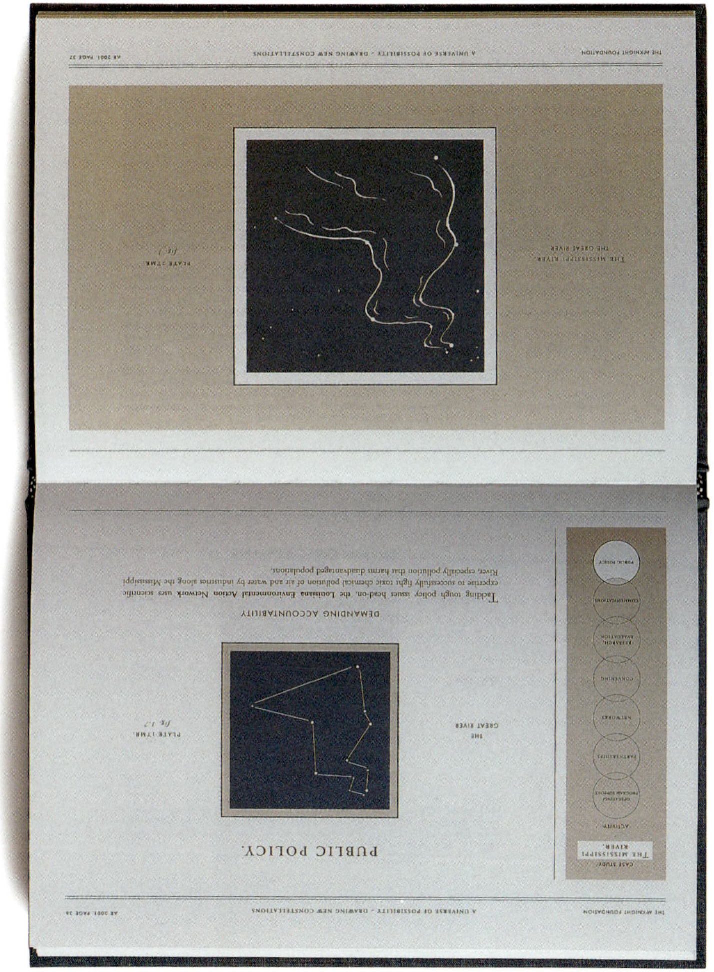

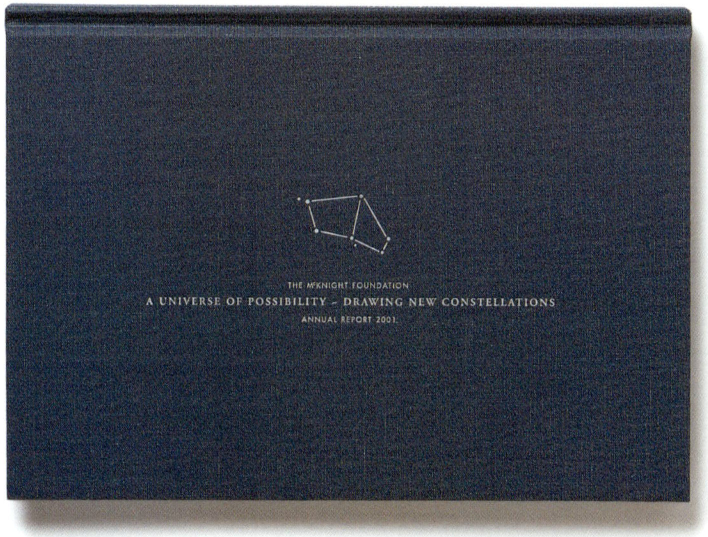

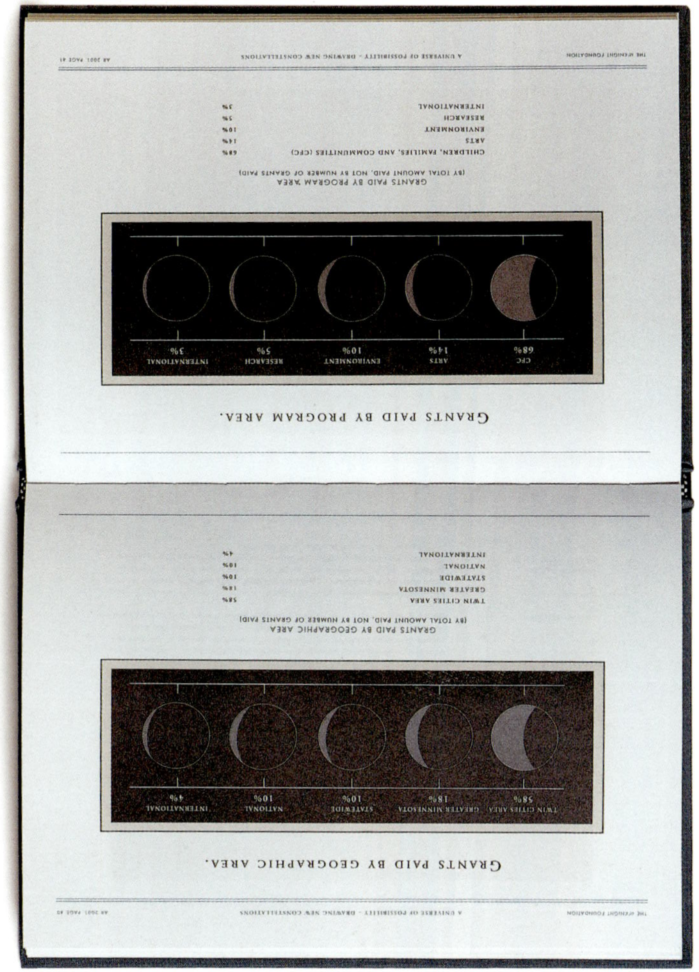

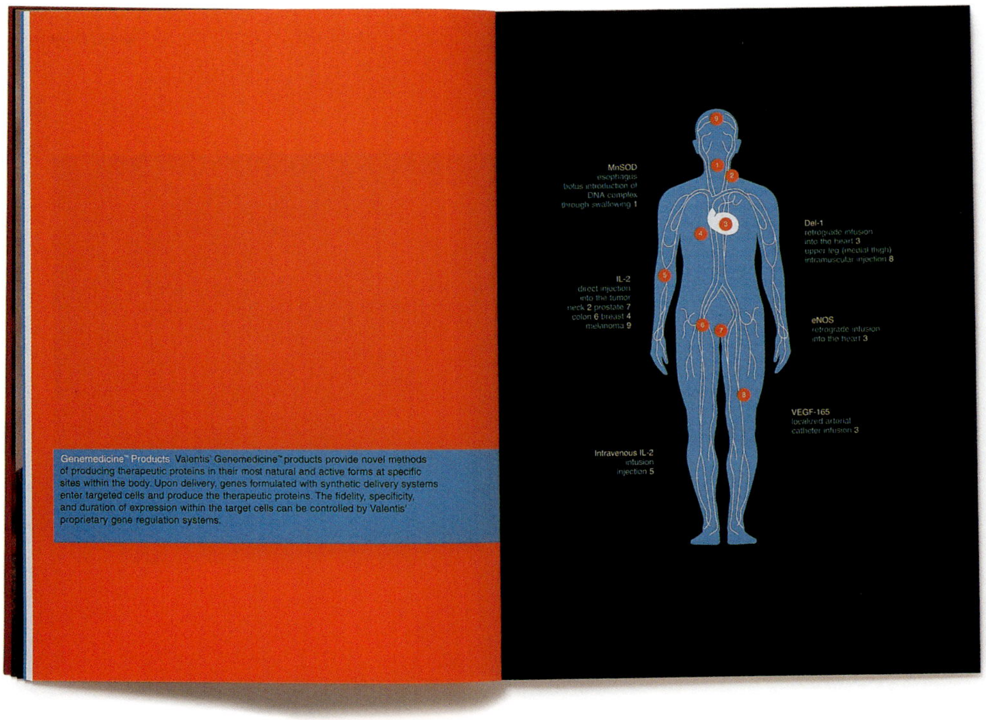

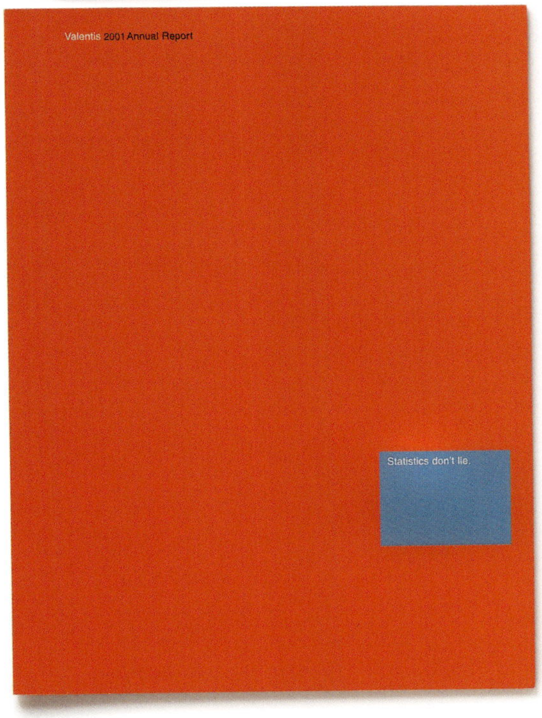

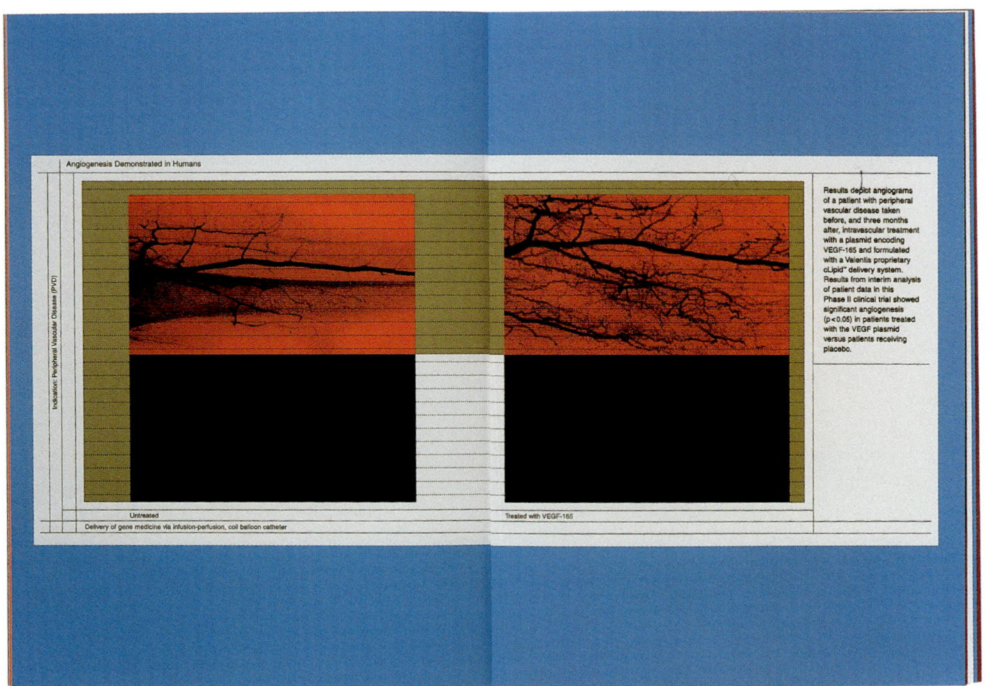

'Valentis 2001 Annual Report' Design Firm: Cahan & Associates Creative Director: Bill Cahan Art Directors: Bill Cahan and Sharrie Brooks Designer: Sharrie Brooks Photographer: Todd Hido Copywriter: Bennet Weintraub Account Coordinator: Nina Howell Client: Valentis

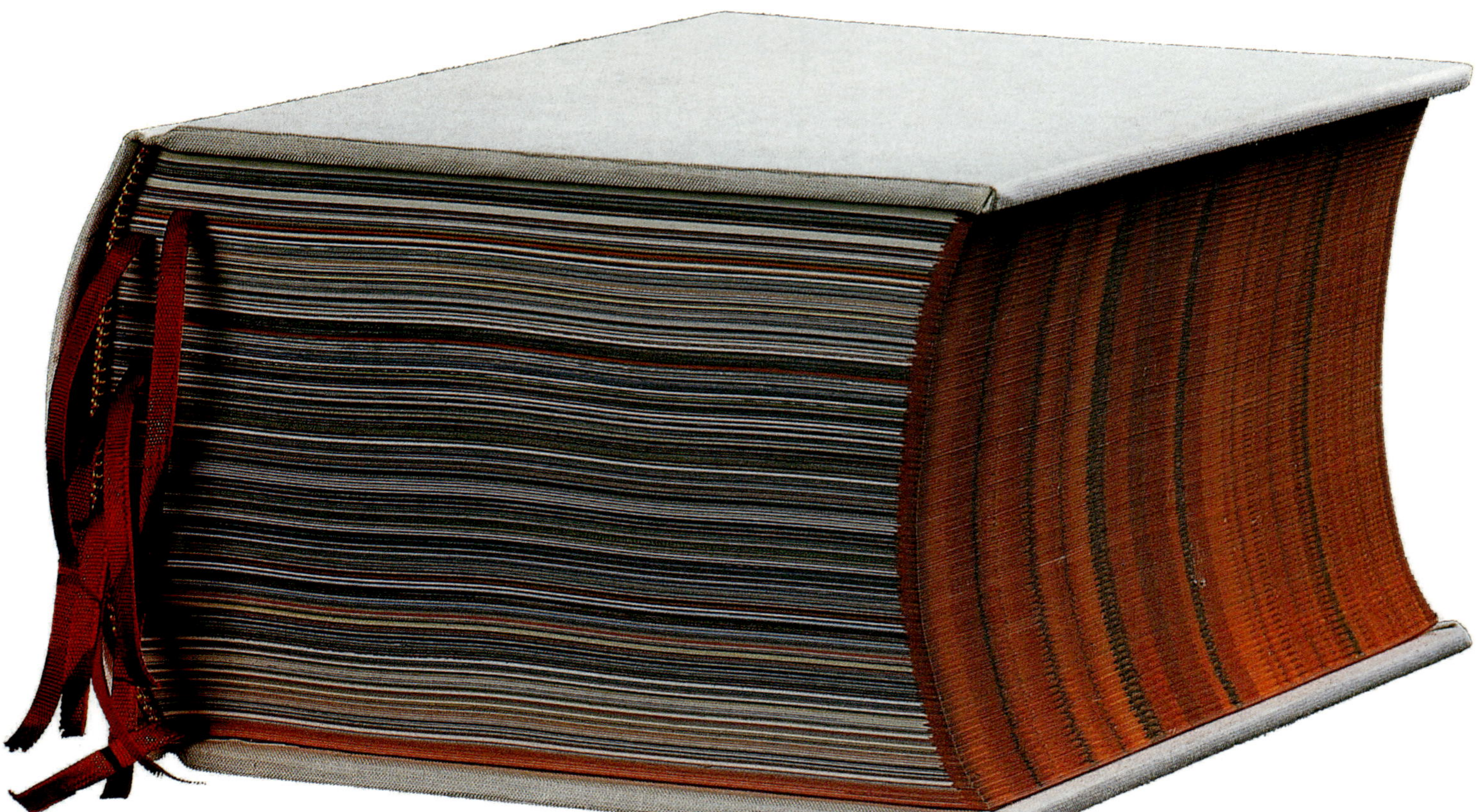

'Jubliee Book (2136 pages)' Designer: Irma Boom Editors: Irma Boom and Johan Pijnappel Client: SHV

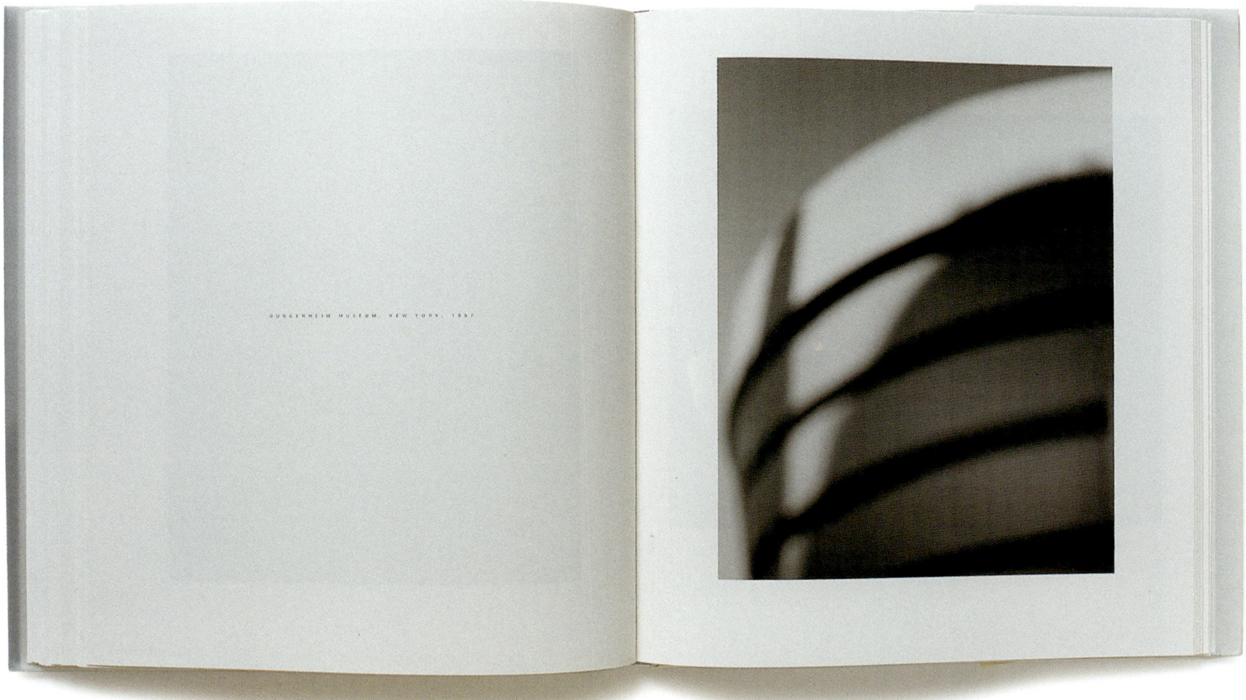

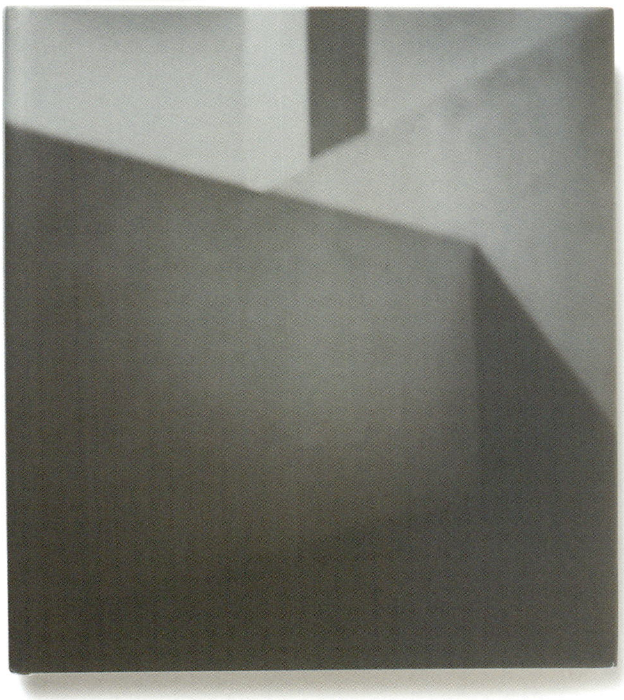

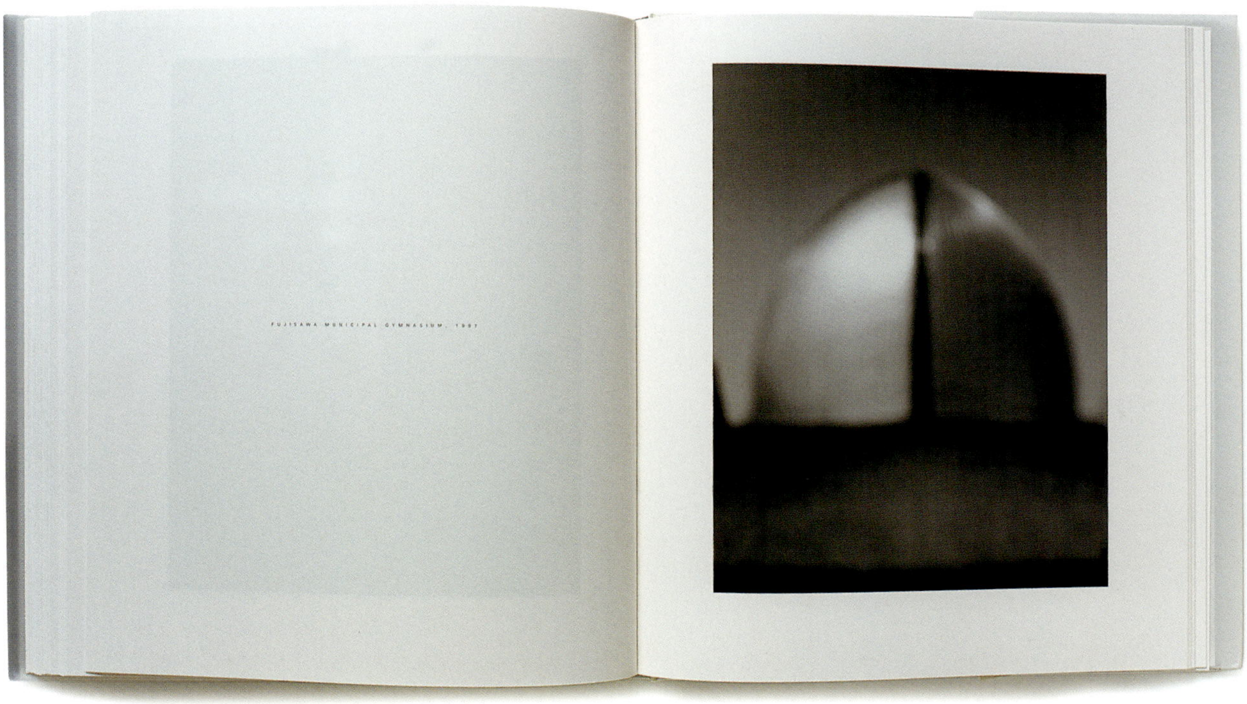

'Sugimoto: Architecture' Design Firm: Matsumoto Incorporated Creative Director: Takaaki Matsumoto Art Director: Takaaki Matsumoto Designer: Takaaki Matsumoto Photographer: Hiroshi Sugimoto Authors: Francesco Bonami, John Yau and Marco DeMichelis Client: Museum of Contemporary Art, Chicago

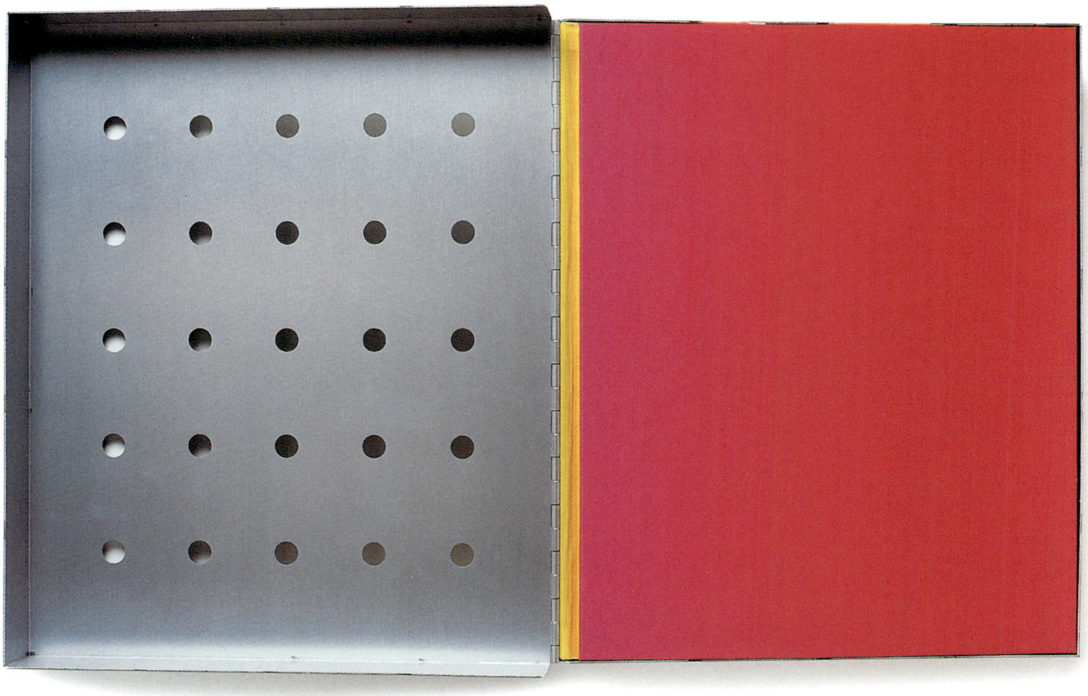

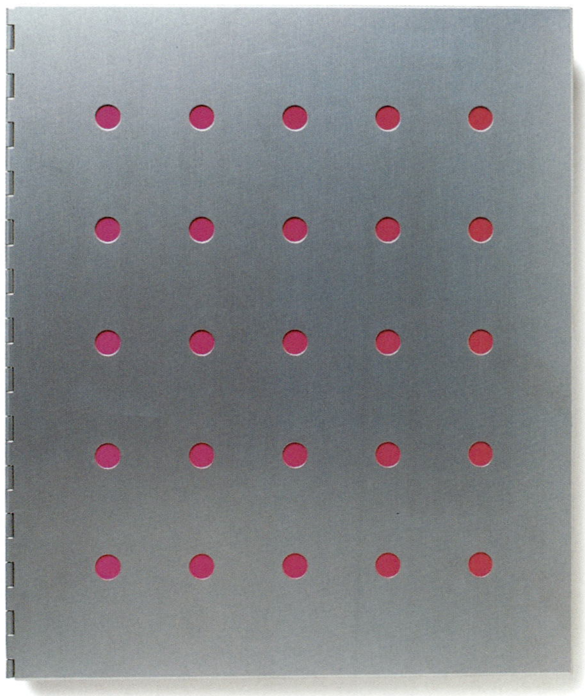

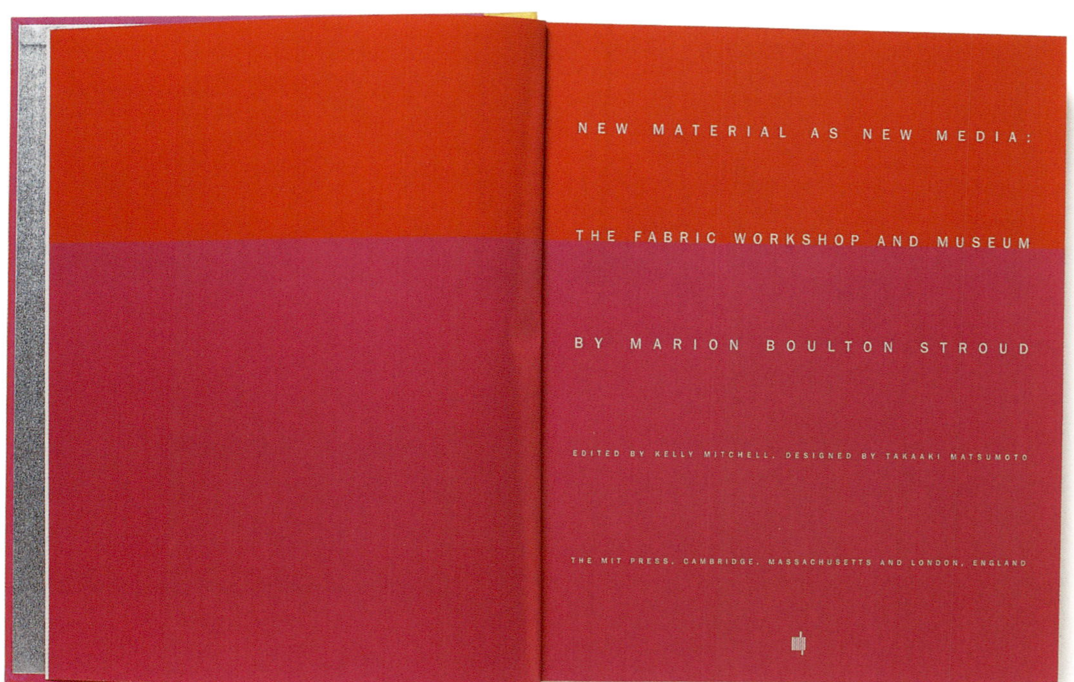

(this spread) 'New Material as New Media' Design Firm: Matsumoto Incorporated Creative Director: Takaaki Matsumoto Art Director: Takaaki Matsumoto
Designers: Takaaki Matsumoto and Than X. Tran Author: Marion Boulton Straud Editor: Kelly Mitchell Client: Fabric Workshop and Museum

Mel Chin

American, born 1951, lives in New York City and Burnsville, North Carolina

Mel Chin was raised in Houston, Texas, the first generation of his family born in the United States. Of Chinese descent, he grew up in a predominantly African American and Latino neighborhood and worked in his family's grocery store. He began making art at an early age and earned his BA from Peabody College in Nashville, Tennessee, in 1975. Chin is best known for undertaking collaborative and cross-disciplinary artistic investigations into political and often ecologically charged topics. For example, in 1991 Chin worked with a group of scientists to create gardens of plants that draw heavy metals from contaminated areas to make *Revival Field*. His numerous one-person exhibitions and innovative projects have been sponsored by List Center for Visual Arts at the Massachusetts Institute of Technology, Cambridge, MA (2000); the Metro Transit Authority, New York City (1995–1997); the Headlands Center for the Arts, Marin County, CA (1994–1999); the Walker Art Center, Minneapolis (1990); and the Hirshhorn Museum and Sculpture Garden, Washington, DC (1989).

During 1991–1992, Mel Chin worked with the FW+M to complete his ambitious installation *Degrees of Paradise*, which was first exhibited at the Storefront for Art and Architecture in New York. As is typical for Chin, the artist worked with a diverse range of collaborators to realize this project, including scientists, computer programmers, and traditional hand-weavers in Turkey. The title references Dante's *Commedia* and the "complex vertical geography of the ascent from earth to heaven . . . [which was] earlier prominent in the Arabic and Persian traditions . . ." (Thomas McEvilley, *Soil and Sky*, The Fabric Workshop and Museum, Philadelphia, 1993).

For the installation, two triangular-shaped rooms were constructed opposite one another. A small drawing on slate of an unfolding lotus serves as the fulcrum between the rooms, in which two divergent yet complementary sculptural installations are suspended from the ceiling. On one side, Chin hung fourteen video monitors that display multi-dimensional fractal images chronicling the world's weather mapped for one full day as recorded by scientists at McGill University. The images appear in a triangular format on the monitors, a looped display of clouds moving across a blue sky. On the ceiling of the other room hangs a hand-knotted Kurdish wool carpet made by women in Damlacik, Turkey, during the beginning of the Gulf War—the influence of which can be detected in a helicopter form hidden in the design. The carpet depicts the women's interpretation of the scientific satellite mappings, samples of which were given to them in still format.

The elements of *Degrees of Paradise* represent Mel Chin's first explorations into the subject of ozone depletion, and provided the basis for a larger installation called *The State of Heaven*. *Degrees of Paradise* was included in an exhibition of Chin's work, co-sponsored by the FW+M and Swarthmore College in 1992.

Installation of *Degrees of Paradise* at The Fabric Workshop and Museum, 1992 (right).
Following pages: *Degrees of Paradise* (video), 1991 (left). Video monitors and computers. 96 x 276 x 144 inches (243.84 x 701.04 x 365.76 cm) and *Degrees of Paradise* (carpet), 1991 (right).
Wool and cotton. 96 x 276 x 144 inches (243.84 x 701.04 x 365.76 cm). Collection of the artist.

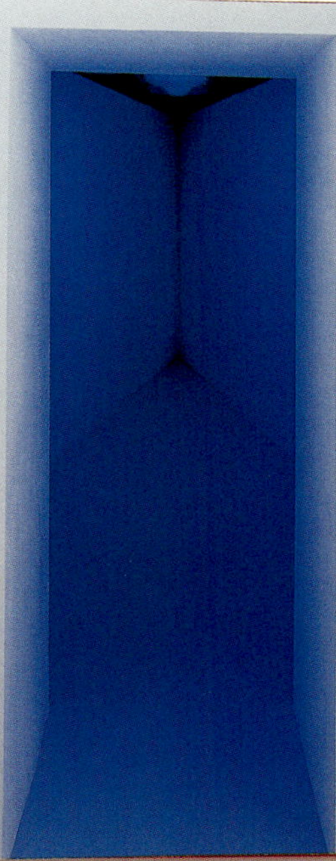

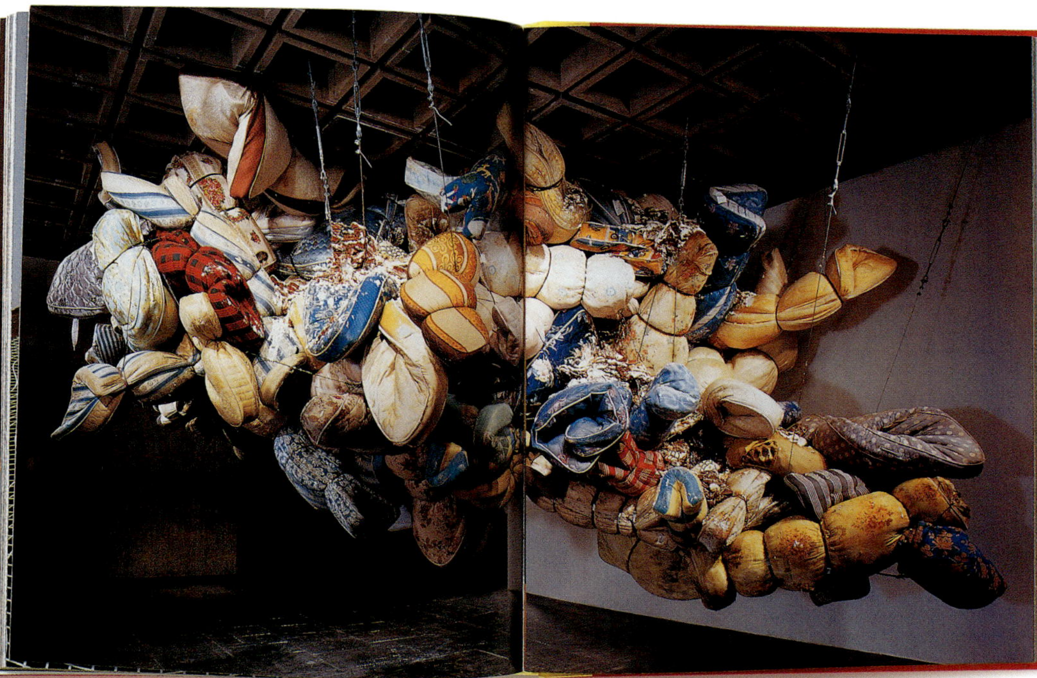

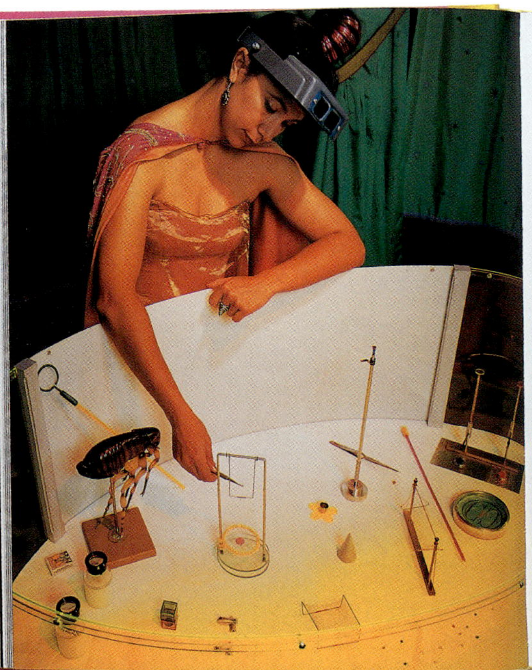

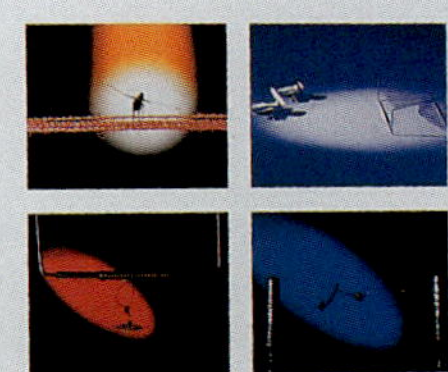

Maria Fernanda Cardoso performing *Cardoso Flea Circus* at The Fabric Workshop and Museum, 6 December 1996 (preceding pages).
Still images from the performance of *Cardoso Flea Circus* (above).

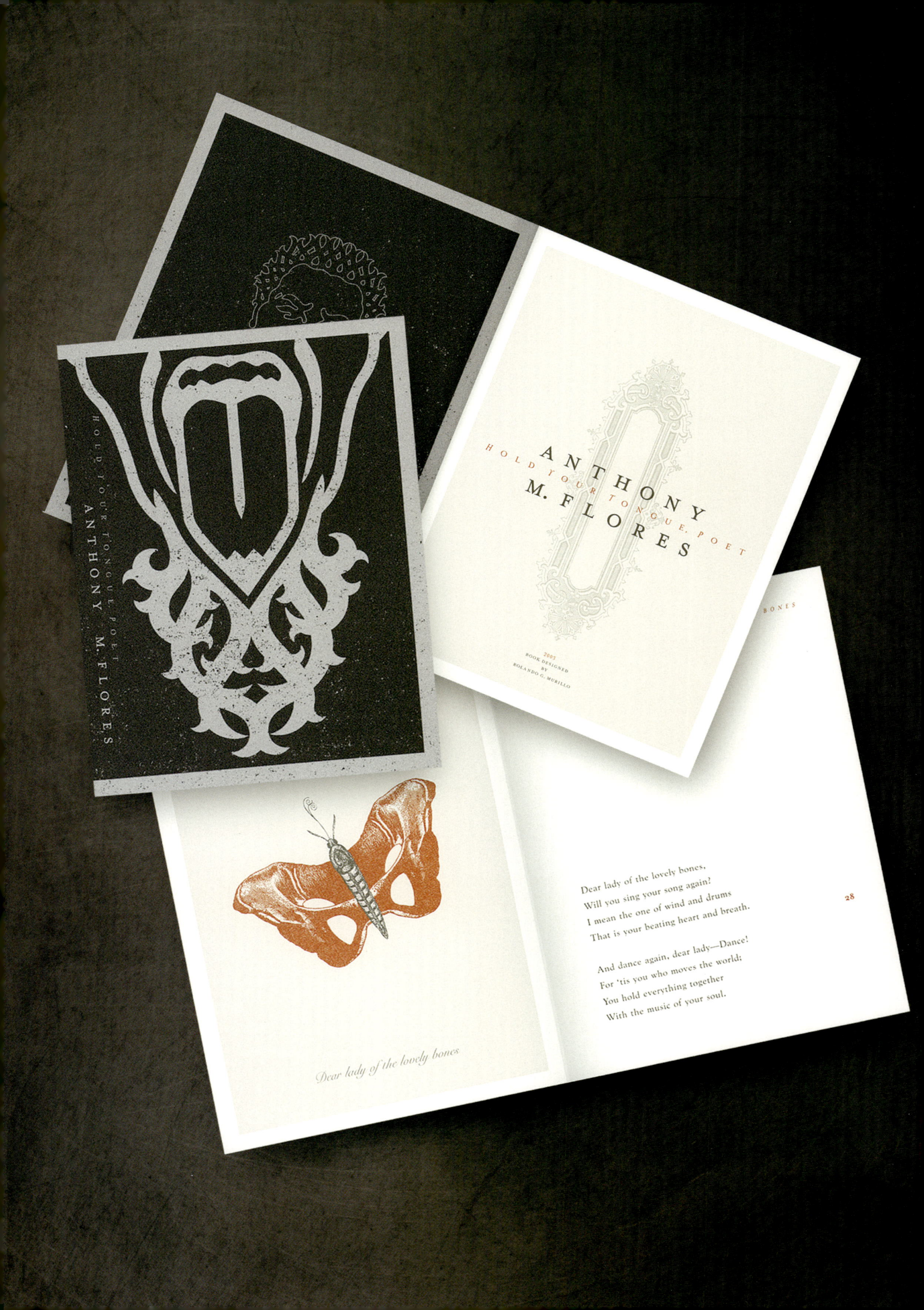
HOLD YOUR TONGUE, POET
ANTHONY M. FLORES
ANTHONY M. FLORES
HOLD YOUR TONGUE, POET
2005
BOOK DESIGNED
BY
ROLANDO G. MURILLO
BONES
Dear lady of the lovely bones
Dear lady of the lovely bones,
Will you sing your song again?
I mean the one of wind and drums
That is your beating heart and breath.
And dance again, dear lady—Dance!
For 'tis you who moves the world;
You hold everything together
With the music of your soul.
28

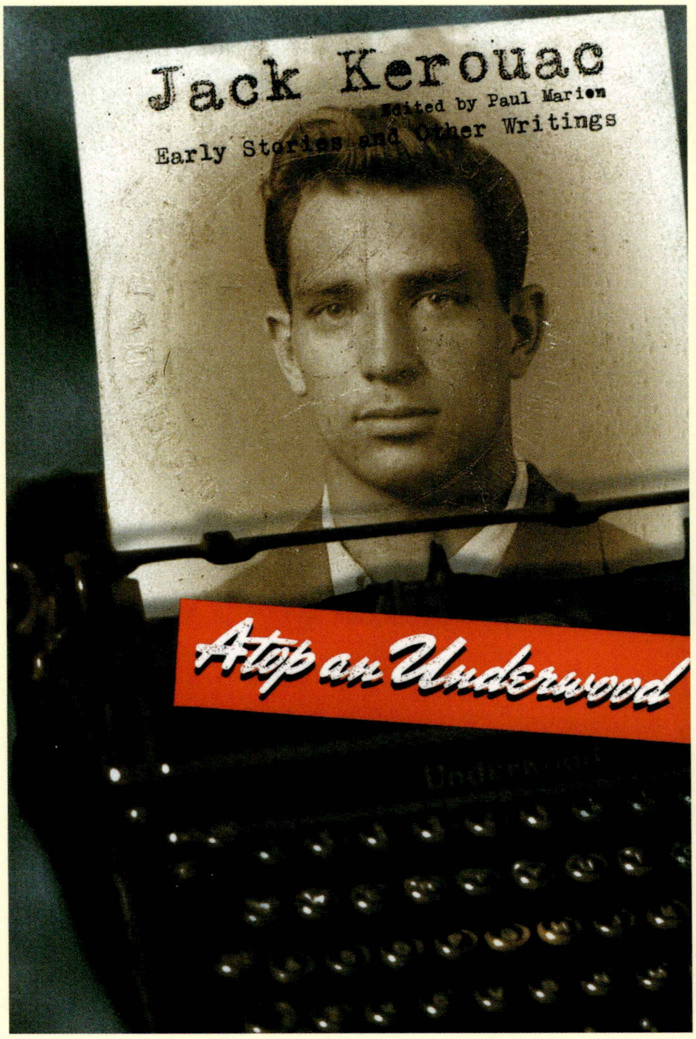

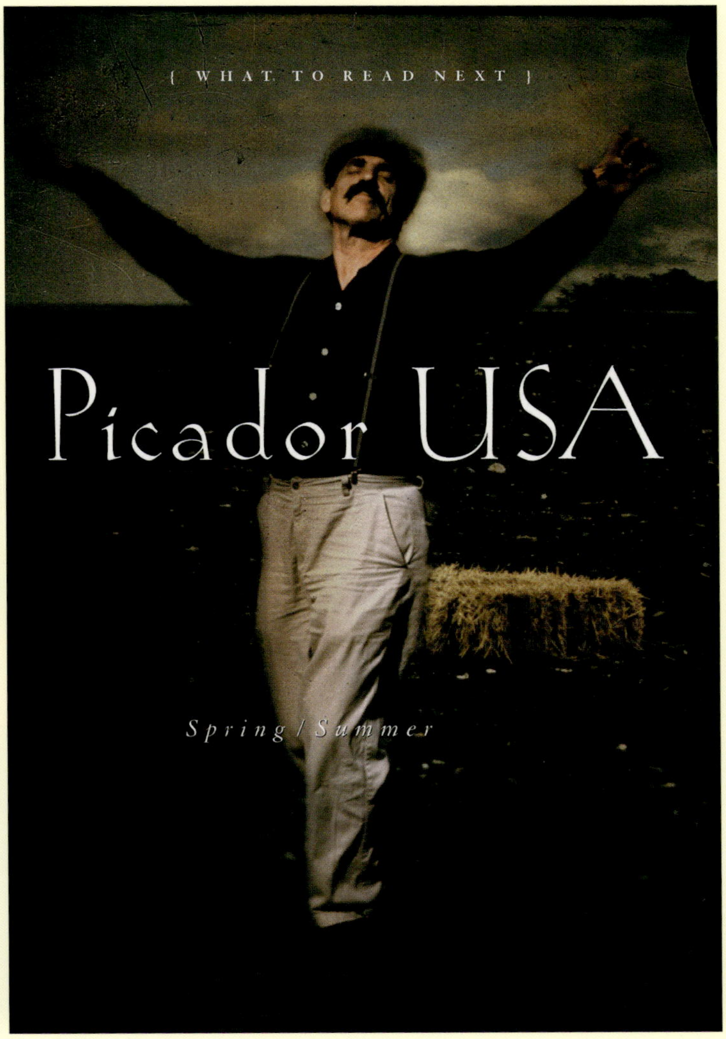

(left) 'Jack Kerouac Early stories and Other Writings' Art Director: Jesse Reyes Photographer: Marc Yankus Illustrator: Marc Yankus Client: Viking Books (right) 'Picador USA (What to Read Next)' Art Director: Henry Sene Yee Photographer: Marc Yankus Illustrator: Marc Yankus Client: Picador USA and (opposite spread) 'Hold Your Tongue Poet' Design Firm: Murillo Design Creative Director: Rolando Murillo Art Director: Rolando Murillo Designer: Rolando Murillo Illustrator: Rolando Murillo Author: Anthony M. Flores Client: MiLenguas Press

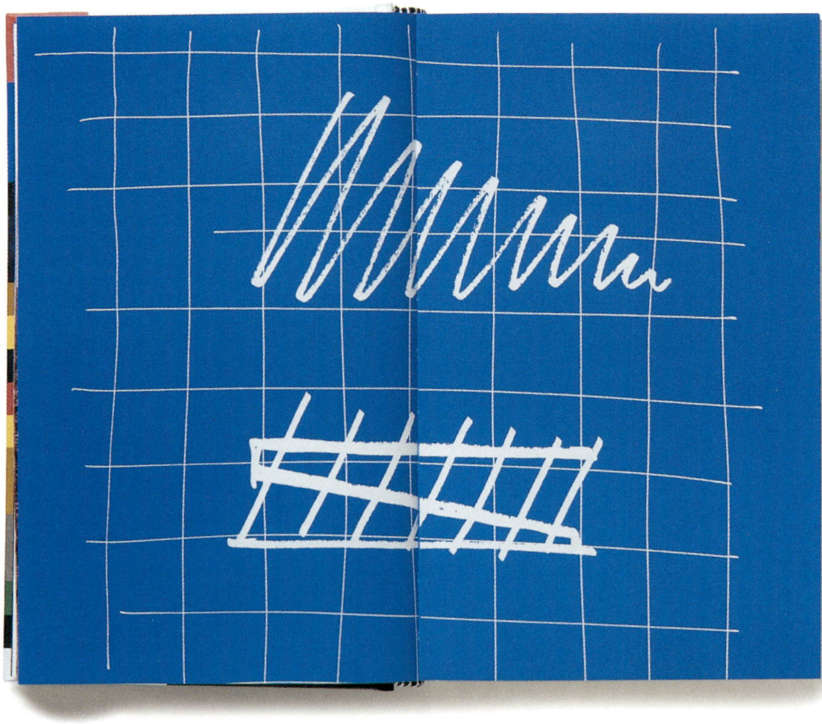

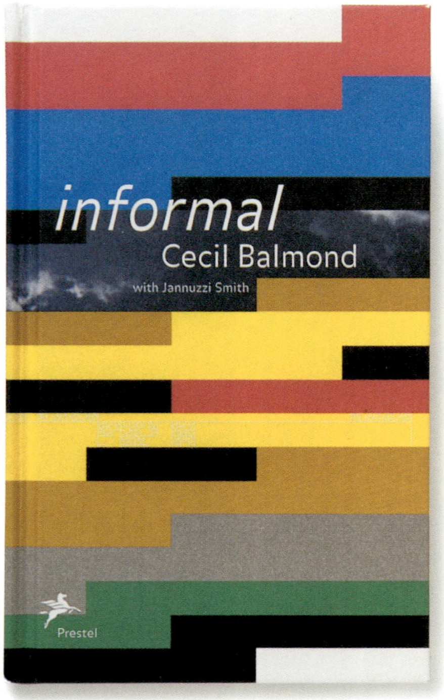

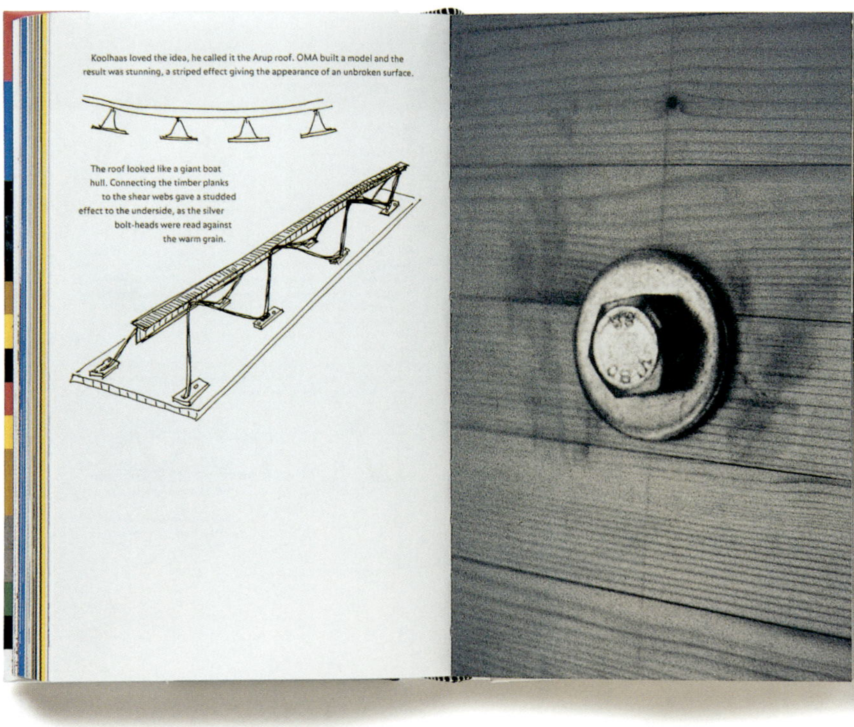

(this spread) 'Informal' Design Firm: Jannuzzi Smith Creative Director: Richard Smith Art Director: Michele Jannuzzi Designers: Michele Jannuzzi and Richard Smith Author: Cecil Balmond Client: Prestel

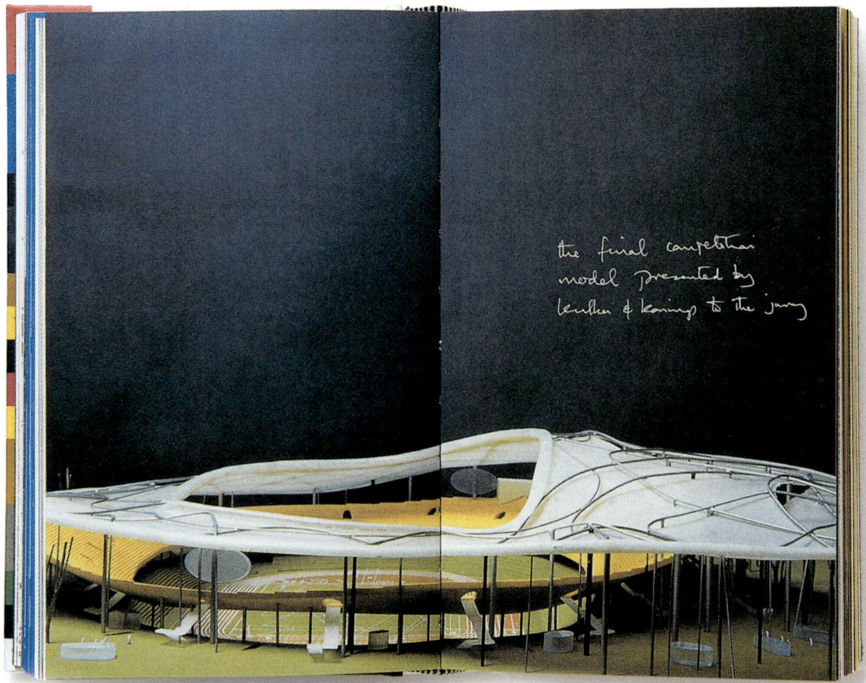
the final competition
model presented by

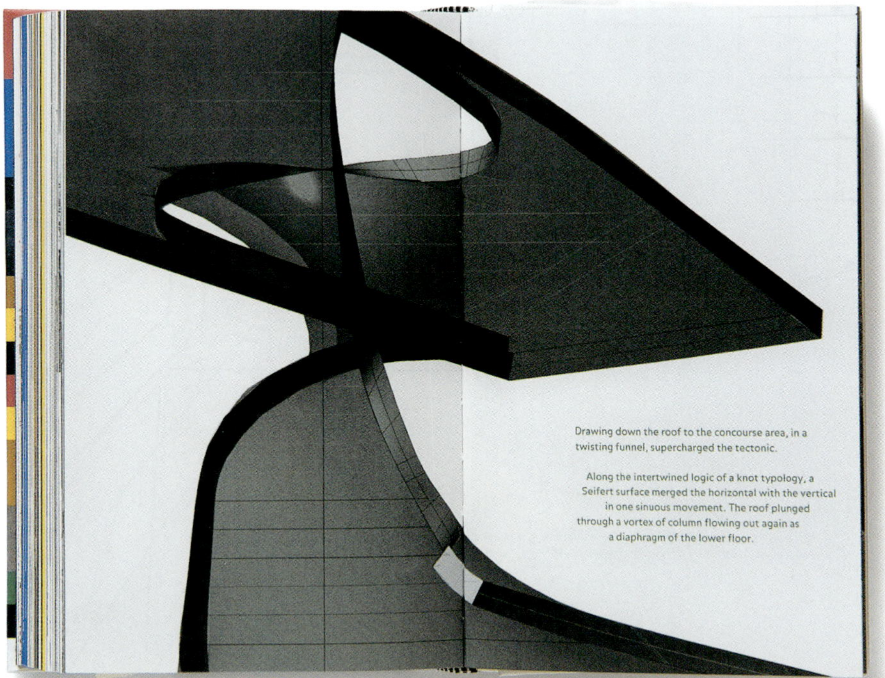
Drawing down the roof to the concourse area, in a twisting funnel, supercharged the tectonic.
Along the intertwined logic of a knot typology, a Seifert surface merged the horizontal with the vertical in one sinuous movement. The roof plunged through a vortex of column flowing out again as a diaphragm of the lower floor.

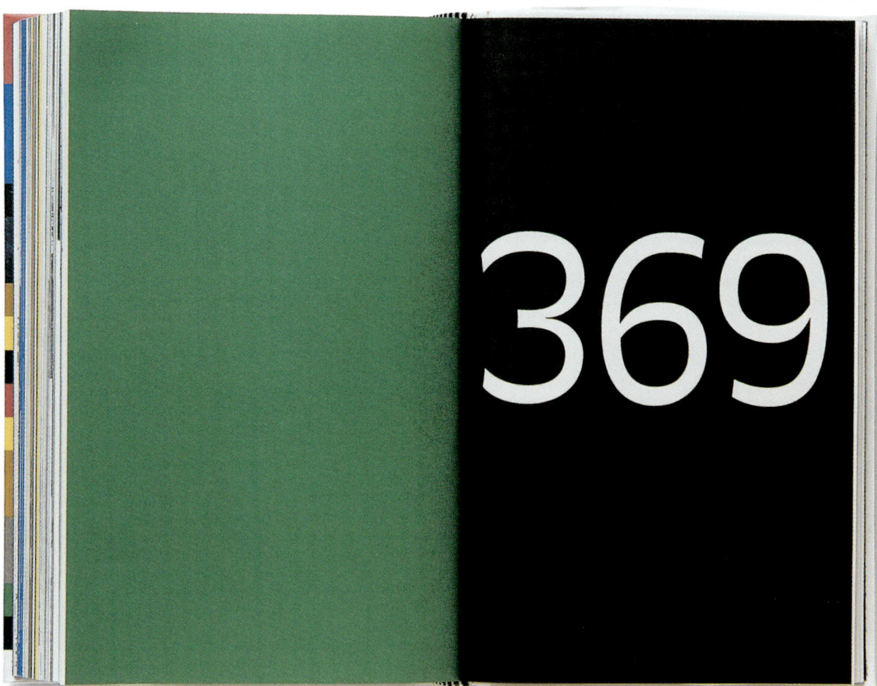
369

'Mica Prospectus' Design Firm: Rutka Weadock Design Creative Director: Anthony Rutka Art Director: Anthony Rutka Designer: Ally Weiner Photographers: Bruce Weller and Others Client: Maryland Institute College of Art

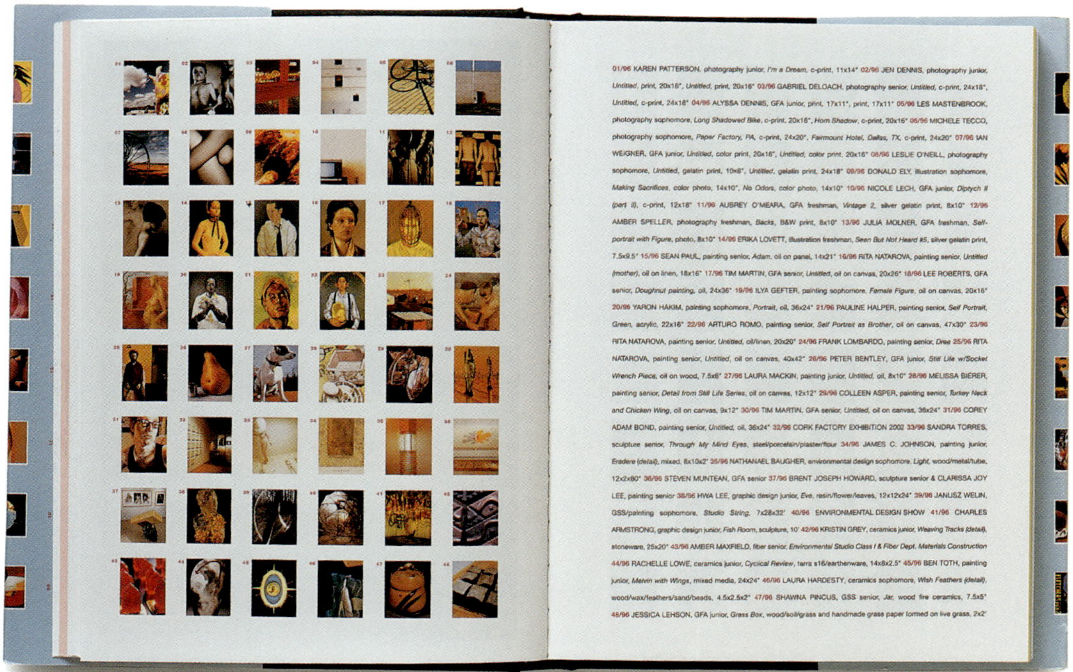

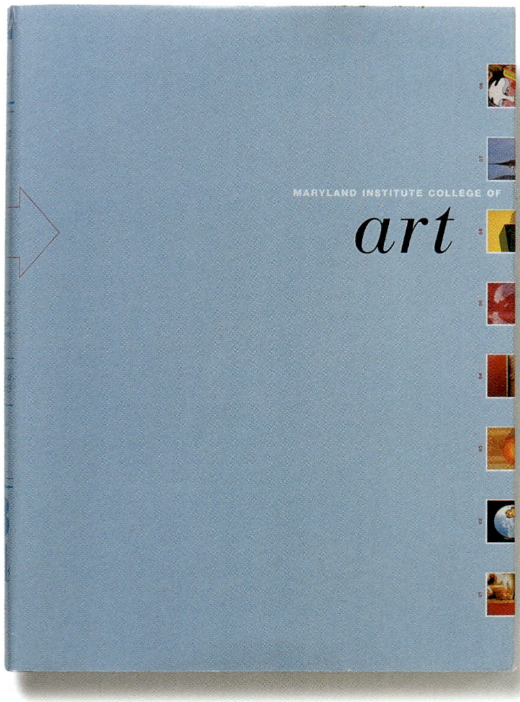

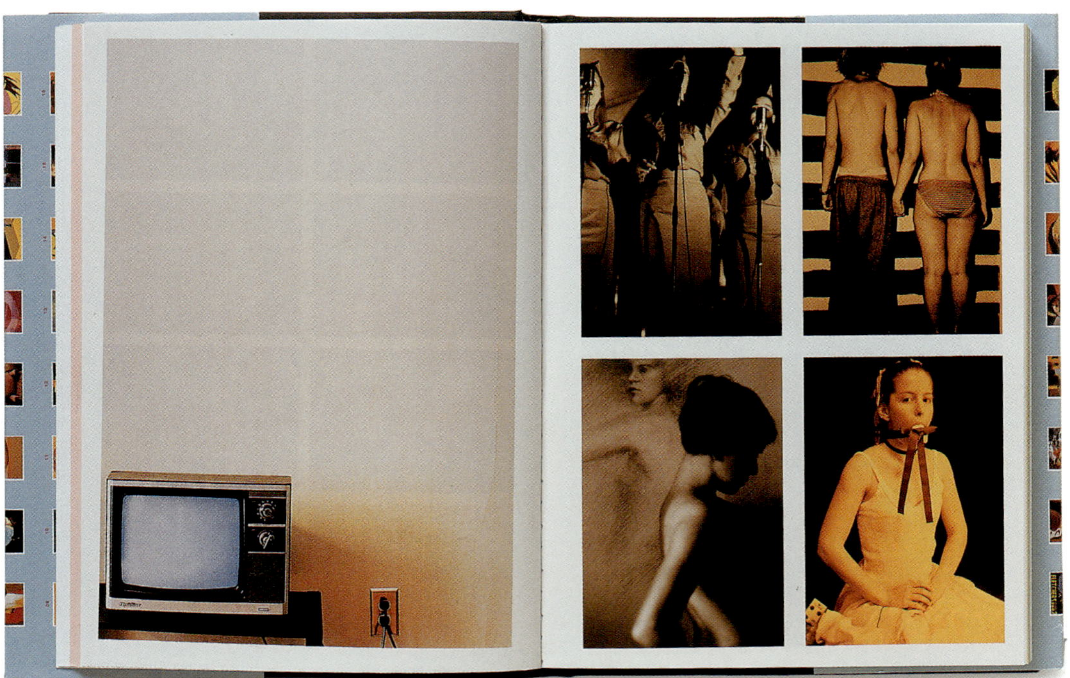

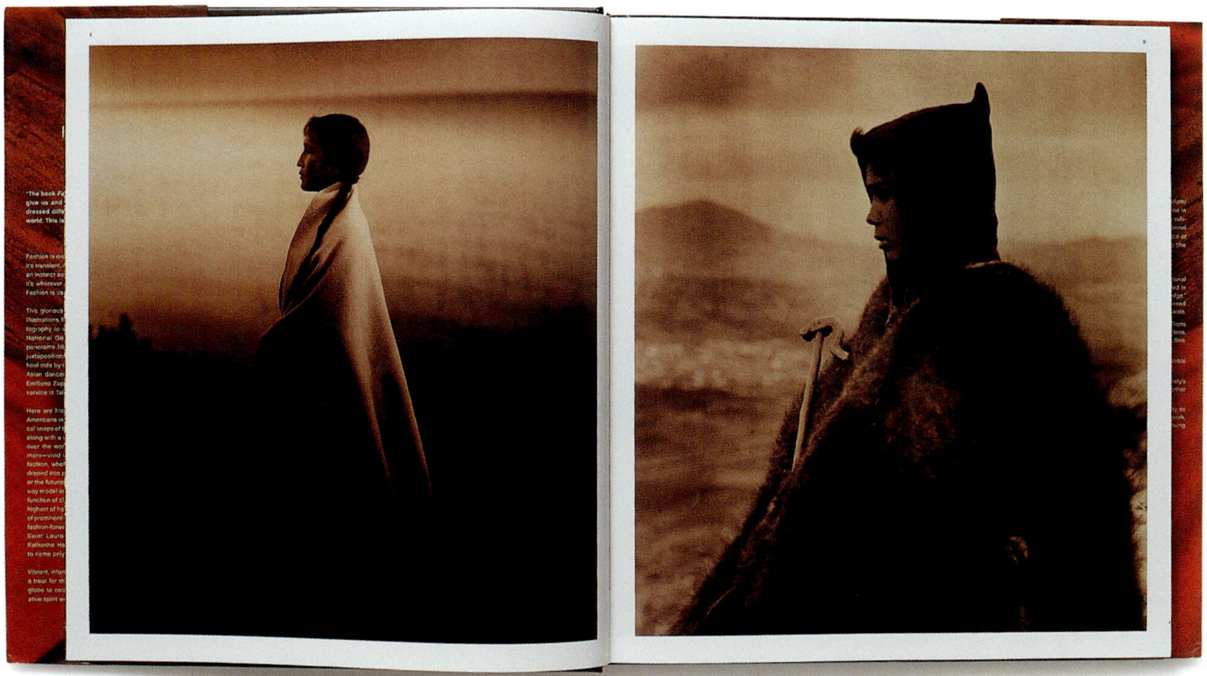

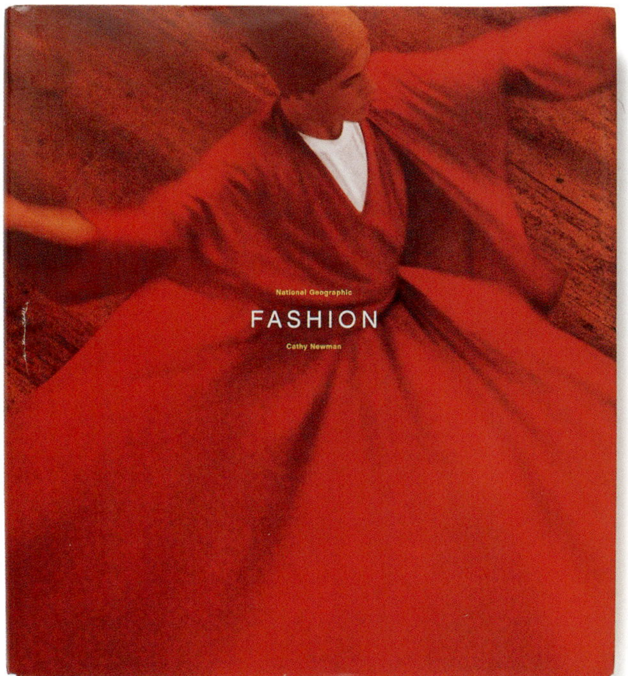

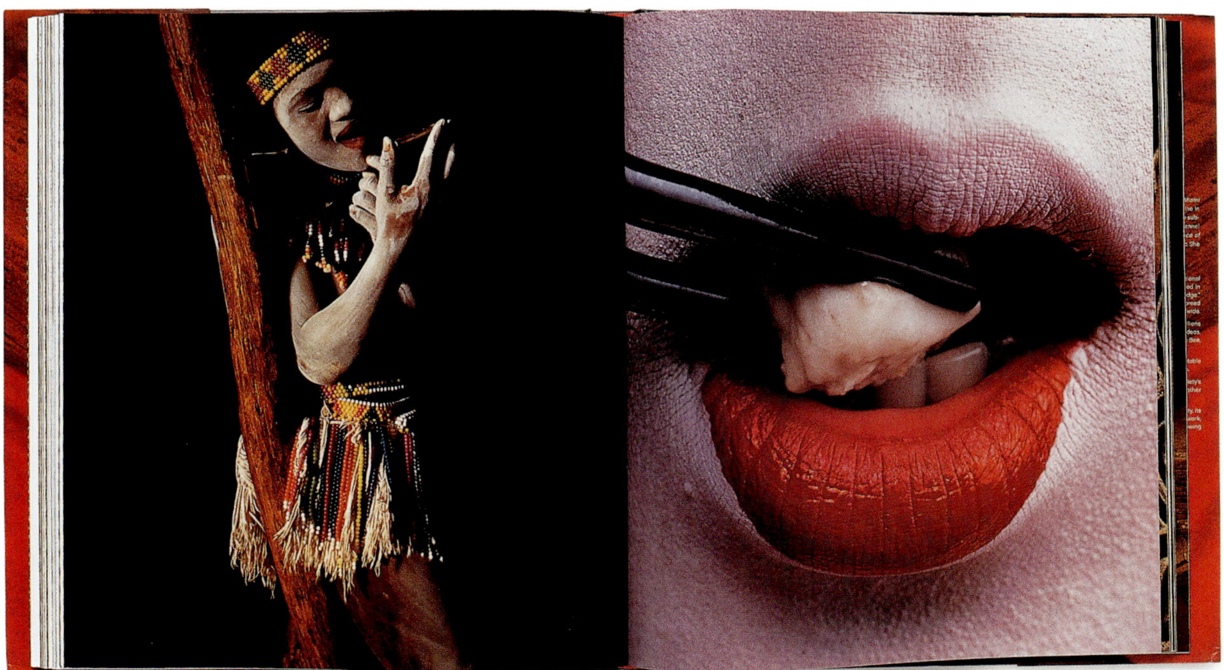

'National Geographic: Fashion' Design Firm: Character Creative Directors: Benjamin Pham, Patricia Evangelista and Rishi Shourie Art Directors: Benjamin Pham, Patricia Evangelista and Rishi Shourie Designers: Benjamin Pham, Patricia Evangelista and Rishi Shourie Client: National Geographic Society

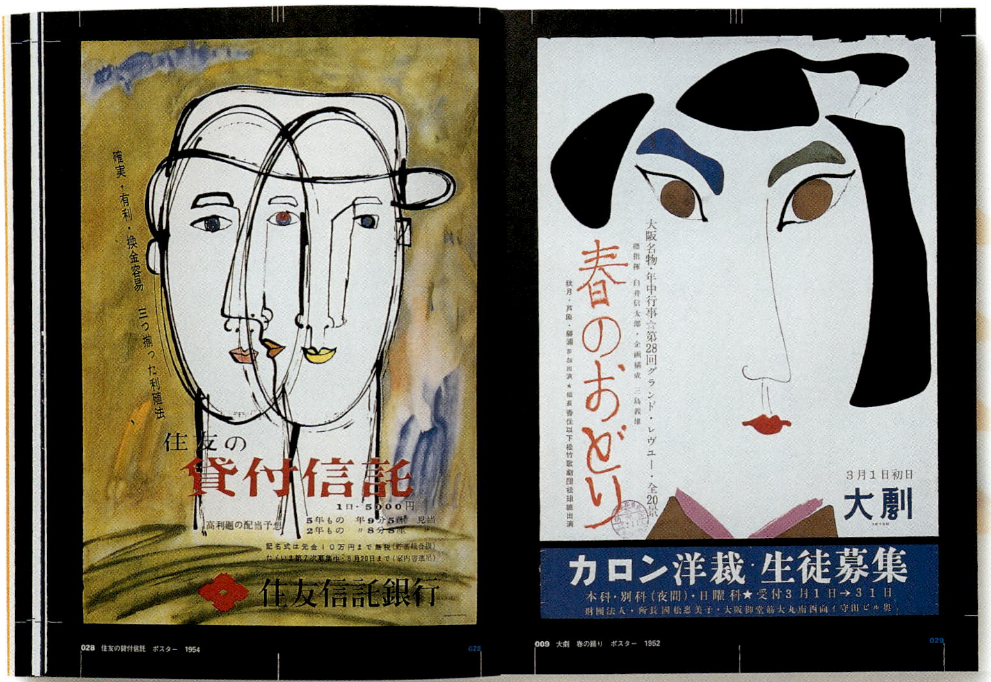

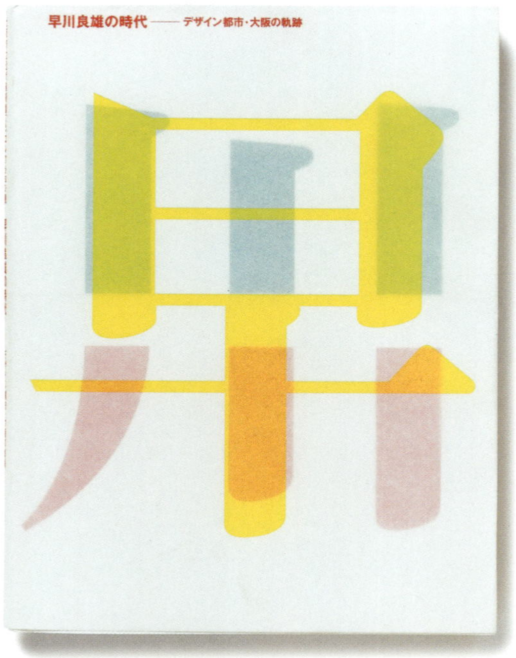

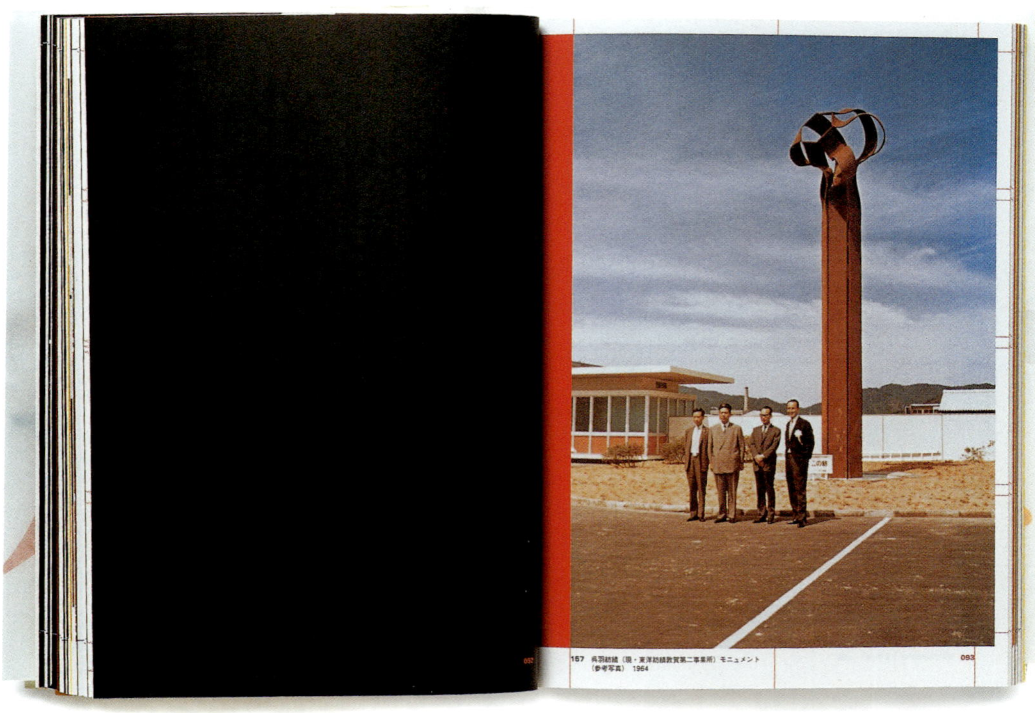

(this spread) 'Yoshio Hayakawa: His Design, Times and Osaka' Design Firm: Shinnoske Inc. Creative Director: Tomio Sugaya Art Director: Shinnoske Sugisaki
Designers: Shinnoske Sugisaki and Chiaki Okuno Photographer: Taku Fukuda Printer: Nissha Printing Co., Ltd Client: Osaka City Museum of Modern Art

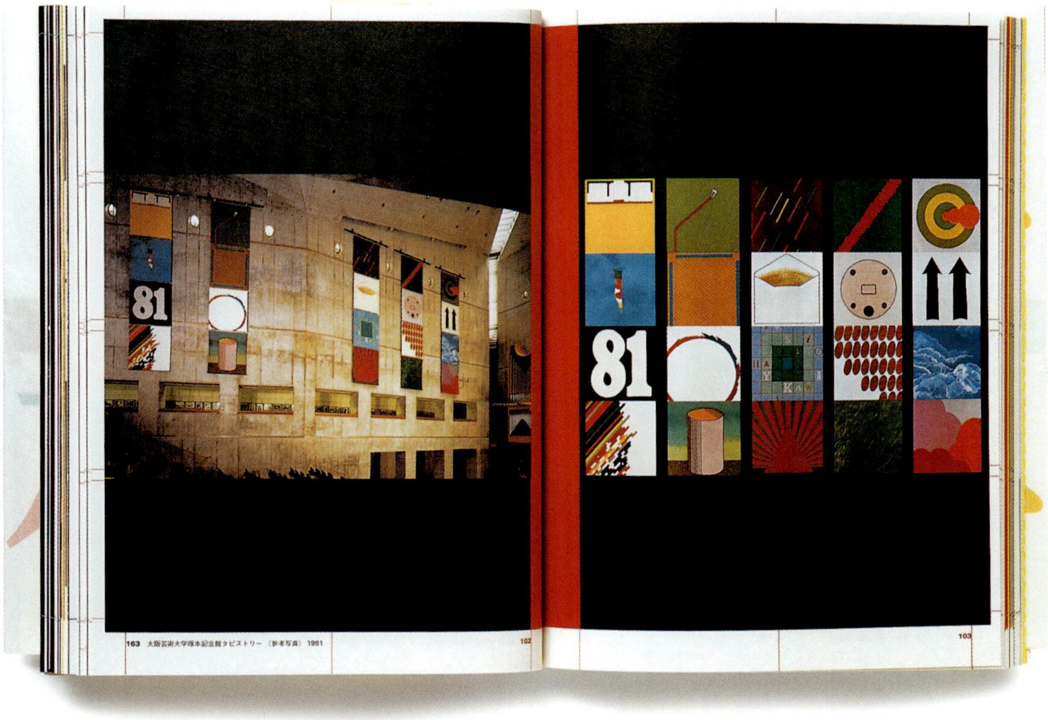

163 大阪芸術大学塚本記念館タピストリー （参考写真） 1981

102

103

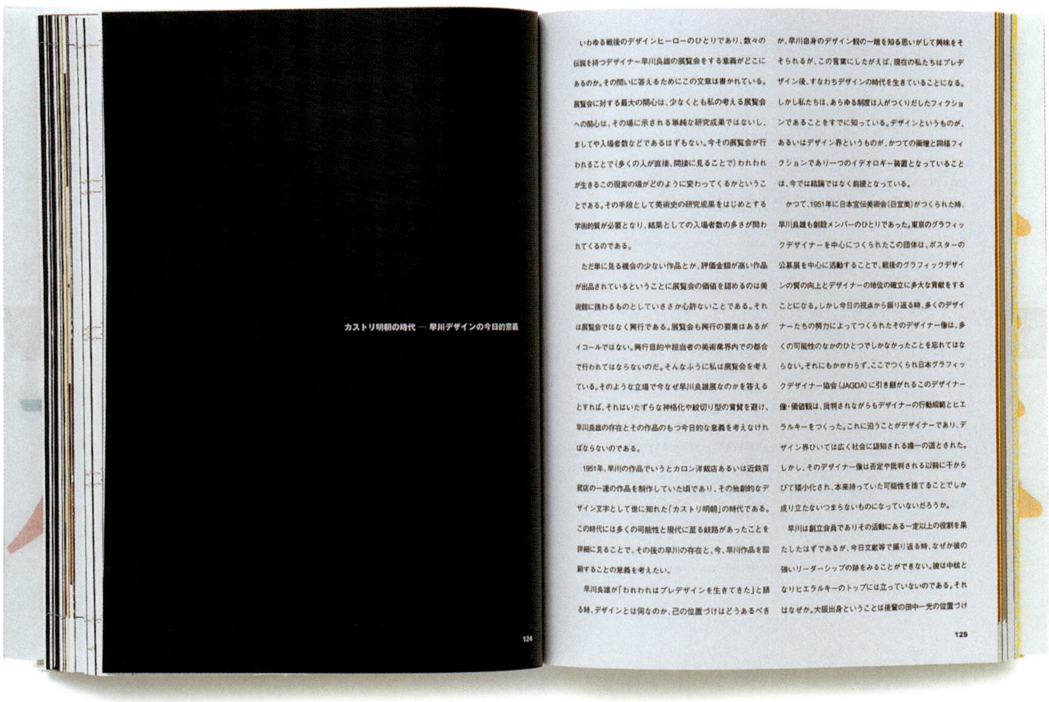

カストリ明朝の時代 — 早川デザインの今日的意義

124

いわゆる戦後のデザインヒーローのひとりであり、数々の伝説を持つデザイナー早川良雄の展覧会をする意義がどこにあるのか。その問いに答えるためにこの文章は書かれている。展覧会に対する最大の関心は、少なくとも私の考える展覧会への関心は、その場に示される単純な研究成果ではないし、ましてや入場者数などであるはずもない。今その展覧会が行われることで（多くの人が直接、間接に見ることで）われわれが生きるこの現実の場がどのように変わってくるかということである。その手段として美術史の研究成果をはじめとする学術的質が必要となり、結果としての入場者数の多さが問われてくるのである。

ただ単に見る機会の少ない作品とか、評価金額が高い作品が出品されているということに展覧会の価値を認めるのは美術館に携わるものとしていささか心許ないことである。それは展覧会ではなく興行である。展覧会も興行の要素はあるがイコールではない。興行目的や担当者の美術業界内での都合で行われてはならないのだ。そんなふうに私は展覧会を考えている。そのような立場で今なぜ早川良雄展なのかを答えるとすれば、それはいたずらな神格化や紋切り型の賞賛を避け、早川良雄の存在とその作品のもつ今日的な意義を考えなければならないのである。

1951年、早川の作品でいうとカロン洋裁店あるいは近鉄百貨店の一連の作品を制作していた頃であり、その独創的なデザイン文字として世に知れた「カストリ明朝」の時代である。この時代には多くの可能性と現代に至る岐路があったことを詳細に見ることで、その後の早川の存在と、今、早川作品を回顧することの意義を考えたい。

早川良雄が「われわれはプレデザインを生きてきた」と語る時、デザインとは何なのか、己の位置づけはどうあるべきか、早川自身のデザイン観の一端を知る思いがして興味をそそられるが、この言葉にしたがえば、現在の私たちはプレデザイン後、すなわちデザインの時代を生きていることになる。しかし私たちは、あらゆる制度は人がつくりだしたフィクションであることをすでに知っている。デザインというものが、あるいはデザイン界というものが、かつての画壇と同様フィクションであり一つのイデオロギー装置となっていることは、今では結論ではなく前提となっている。

かつて、1951年に日本宣伝美術会（日宣美）がつくられた時、早川良雄も創設メンバーのひとりであった。東京のグラフィックデザイナーを中心につくられたこの団体は、ポスターの公募展を中心に活動することで、戦後のグラフィックデザインの質の向上とデザイナーの地位の確立に多大な貢献をすることになる。しかし今日の視点から振り返る時、多くのデザイナーたちの努力によってつくられたそのデザイナー像は、多くの可能性のなかのひとつでしかなかったことを忘れてはならない。それにもかかわらず、ここでつくられ日本グラフィックデザイナー協会（JAGDA）に引き継がれるこのデザイナー像・価値観は、批判されながらもデザイナーの行動規範とヒエラルキーをつくった。これに沿うことがデザイナーであり、デザイン界ひいては広く社会に認知される唯一の道とされた。しかし、そのデザイナー像は否定や批判される以前に干からびて矮小化され、本来持っていた可能性を捨てることでしか成り立たないつまらないものになっていないだろうか。

早川は創立会員でありその活動にある一定以上の役割を果たしたはずであるが、今日文献等で振り返る時、なぜか彼の強いリーダーシップの跡をみることができない。彼は中核となりヒエラルキーのトップには立っていないのである。それはなぜか。大阪出身ということは後輩の田中一光の位置づけ

125

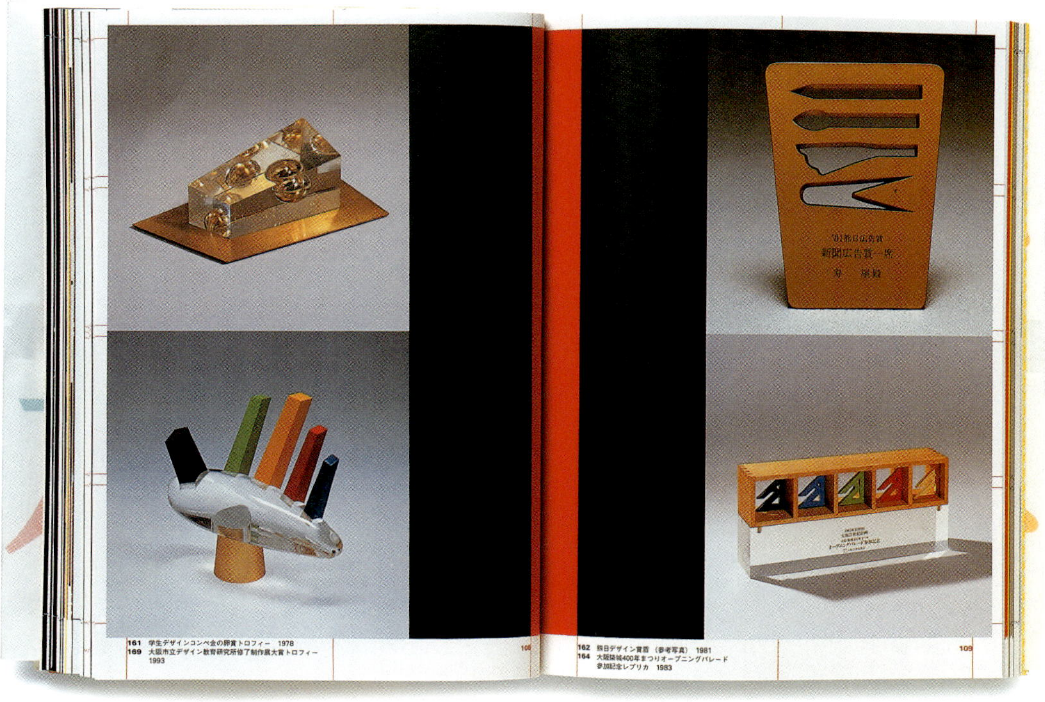

161 学生デザインコンペ金の卵賞トロフィー 1978
169 大阪市立デザイン教育研究所修了制作展大賞トロフィー 1993

108

162 毎日デザイン賞盾 （参考写真） 1981
164 大阪築城400年まつりオープニングパレード参加記念レプリカ 1983

109

'Takashimaya NY Volume Ten' Design Firm: design: mw Creative Director: Allison Williams Art Directors: Allison Williams and Yael Eisele Designer: Yael Eisele Photographer: Martyn Thompson Copywriter: Laura Silverman Client: Takashimaya New York

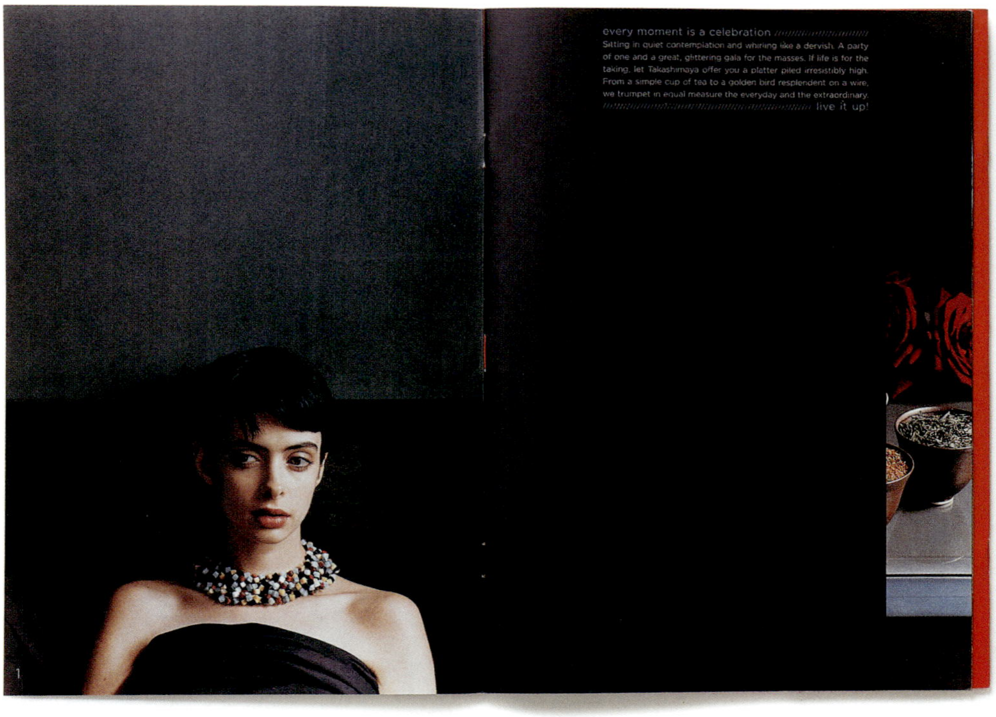

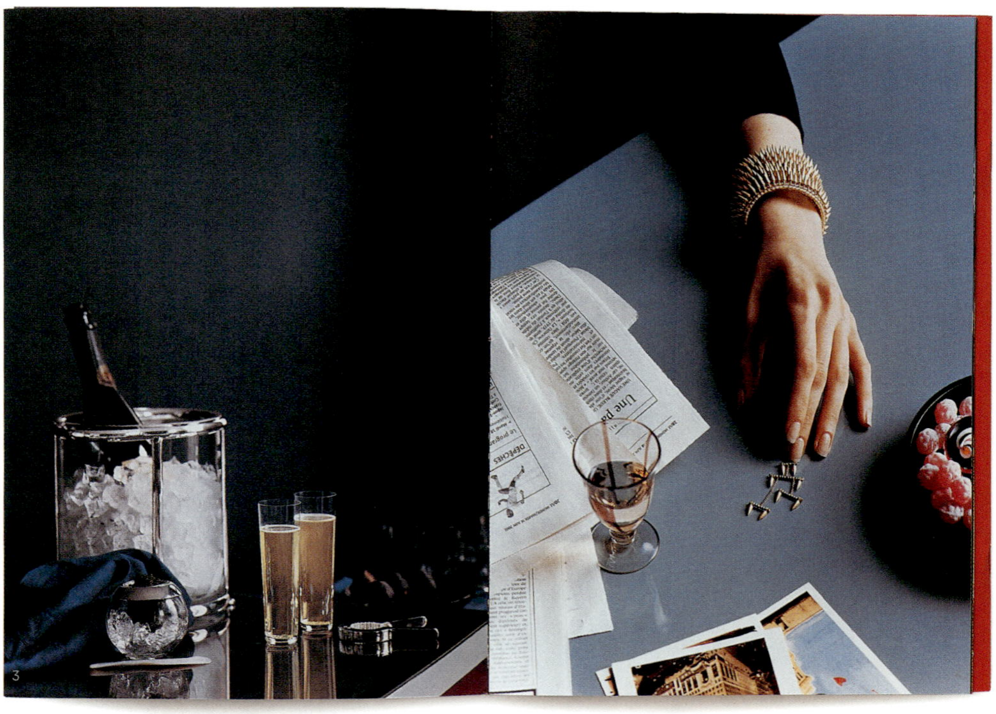

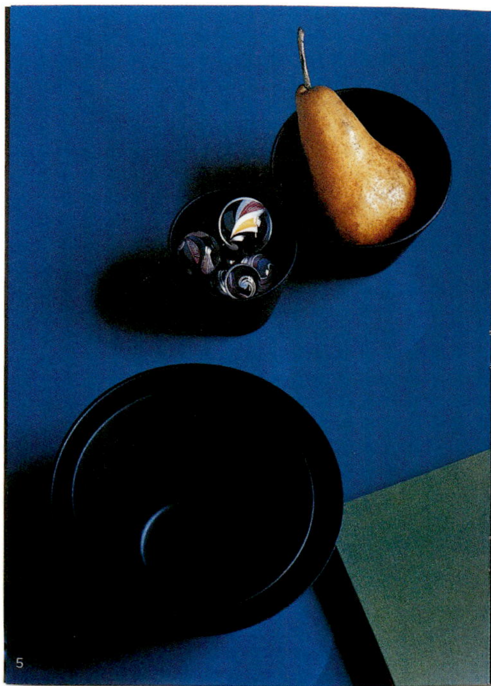

1/800/753/2038

Alone or part of a pair?

Either way, the symmetry is perfect. An amusing thought can sometimes be company enough. But when romance is in the air, things heat up twice as fast. Keep them on ice.

previous spread

LEFT To be the toast of the town, entertain in style. Ercuis has been offering exquisite accoutrements since the 19th century, perpetuating its heritage of French craftsman traditions and luxurious design. The CHAMPAGNE BUCKET has a silver-plated frame with a removable glass insert. 9"x10" /3A $255/ The matching CAVIAR BOWL with silver-plated rim contains a smaller glass bowl which can be insulated with ice. 3"x3.5" /3B $98/ Our hand finished mother of pearl CAVIAR SPREADER resists the salt like silver can't. /3C $25/ When these bottoms go up, so does your stock. Deborah Ehrlich, whose eclectic experience includes a stint restoring stained glass in Viennese cathedrals, brings an artist's eye to her hand-blown glass. These perfectly tapered CHAMPAGNE FLUTES are cut and polished in Sweden, land of perfectionists. 6.5oz /3D $35/ The silver-plated champagne bottle opener combines elegant form and efficient function in one sleek stroke. /3E $77/ 3/4

RIGHT Love is a moving target. Be prepared with a wristful of ammunition. One well-placed bullet can change the course of history. The designs of Jessica Rose display a rare fluidity, as if she leaves gravity to do some of the sculpting. Her bold CUFF BRACELET with its gold-plated bullets and golden glass beads is at once come-hither and invulnerable. /4A $1,295/ Coordinating CHANDELIER EARRINGS with gold-plated bullets and glass beads dangling from gold-plated chain. /4B $225/ SAKE GLASS with amber stripes, sold on page 12.

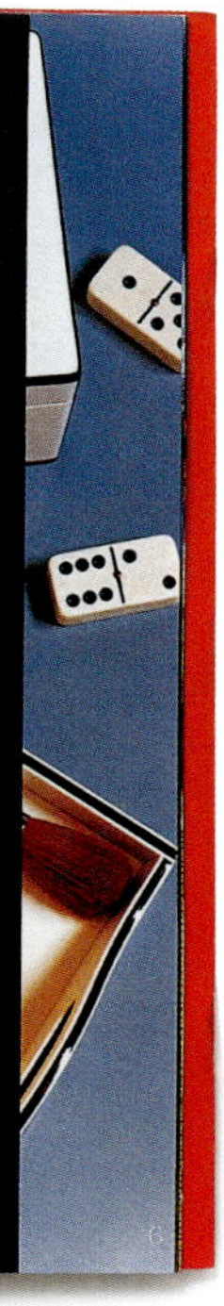

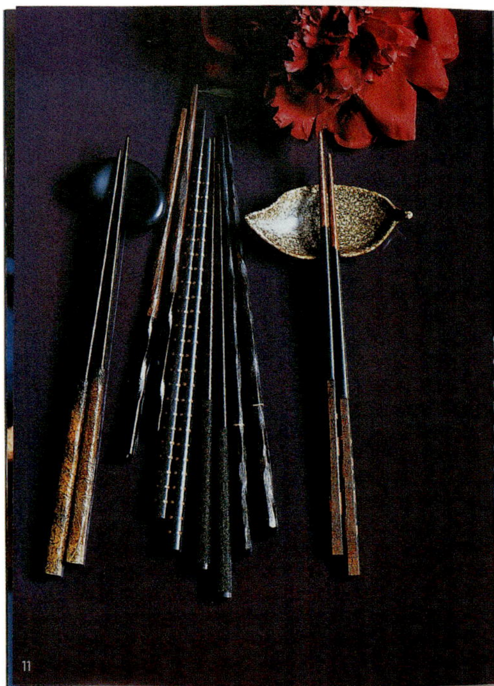

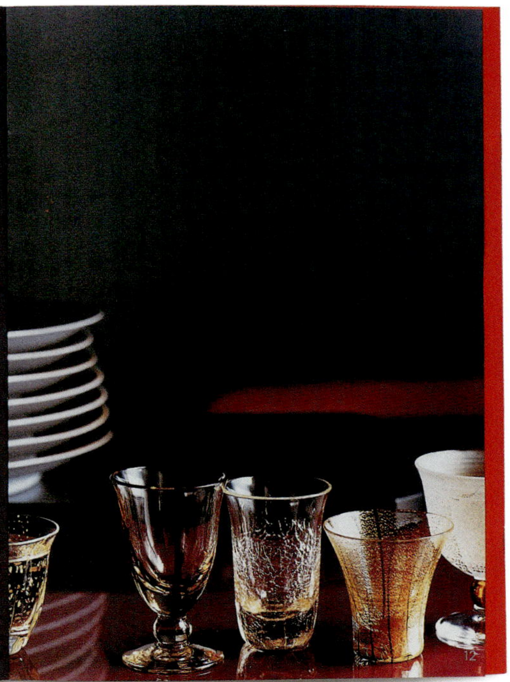

1/800/753/2038

What are the tools of seduction?

They range from sultry stares to Lear jets. In the right hands, dinner is the ultimate foreplay. (Remember Tom Jones.) Set a beautiful table and whip up something to set the senses a-tingle.

previous spread

LEFT Chopsticks make the fork seem crude. Next to their spare elegance, its stabbing tines are artless. Their skillfully orchestrated duet is both simple and sublime. Left to right: Ebony with natural line leaf (lacquered), 9" /11A $45/ Black-tipped, 9" /11B $38/ Textured, 9" /11C $45/ Black fabric, 9.5" /11D $28/ Ebony with gold, 9.25" /11E $40/ Brown-tipped, 9" /11F $25/ All hand carved and lacquered in Japan. "Soramame" ceramic CHOPSTICK REST, shaped like a broad bean, 2" /11G $8/ Ceramic LEAF CHOPSTICK REST, hand finished in Japan, 3.5" /11H $8.50/ 11/12

RIGHT Sake-to-me. Serve it cold in small GLASSES that make a big impact. All hand finished in Japan. Gold leaf, 2oz /12A $35/ Amber with stripes, 2oz /12B $55/ Crackle, 2oz /12C $25/ Gold with blue stripes, 2oz /12D $50/ Frosted with gold ball, 2.5oz /12E $85/

LEFT Spices, once prized for masking foods' undesirable flavors, are now used to enhance and underscore. Their unique pungency is matched by their rich and powerful colors. Clockwise from top left: SANSHO, a hot and spicy pepper with a strong herb-like fragrance. Use in place of traditional pepper. 3oz /13A $28/ WASABI, a Japanese root similar to horseradish, has a light fruity smell and a tingling heat that goes straight to the sinus. It is the traditional condiment for sushi and sashimi. Simply add water to create a paste-like consistency. 2.8oz /13B $8.30/ SHICHIMI, a seven-spice chili mix, combines sansho (Japanese pepper), shiso (perilla), aonori (seaweed), onomi (hemp seed), sesame and chinpi (dried orange skin). Superb on grilled foods, it is used traditionally on Japanese noodles or yakitori. 3.2oz /13C $14/ KARASHI is Japanese mustard, and it's even hotter than the English variety! Eat it and weep. Add water to make a paste. 2.9oz /13D $7/ Lacquer SPOON, hand finished in Japan, 6.5" /13E $18/ Black lacquer SAKE CUP, hand finished in Japan, 2.5" /13F $8/ 13

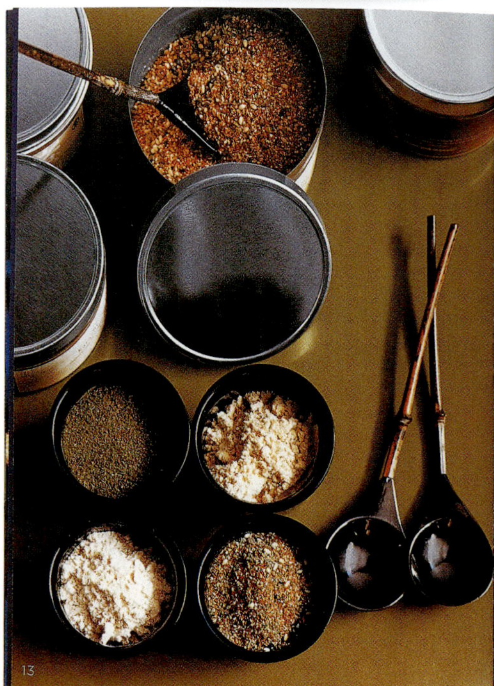

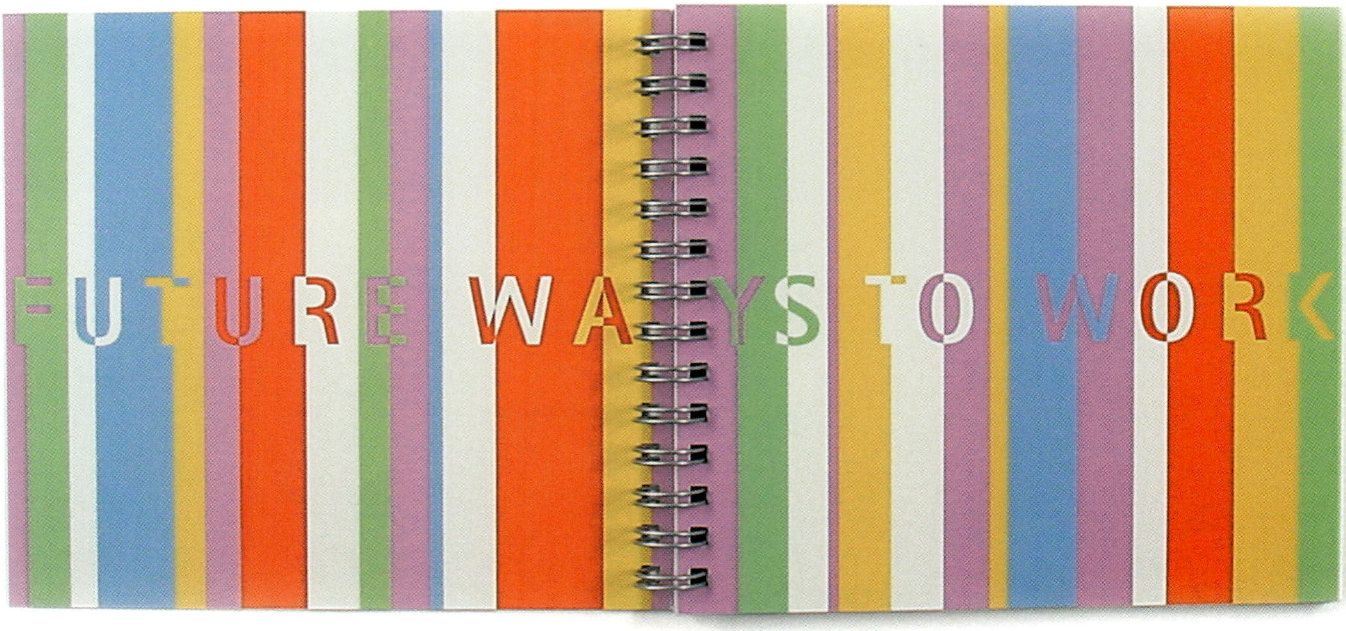

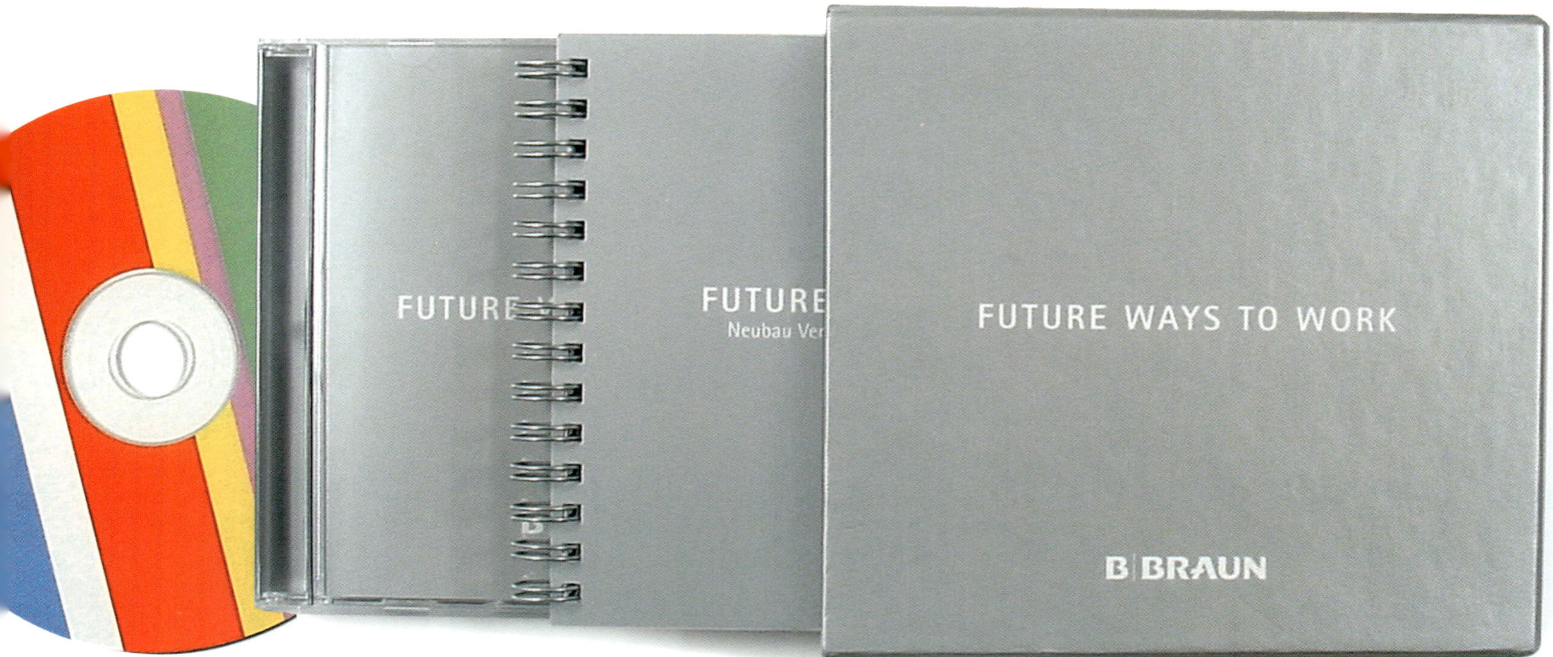

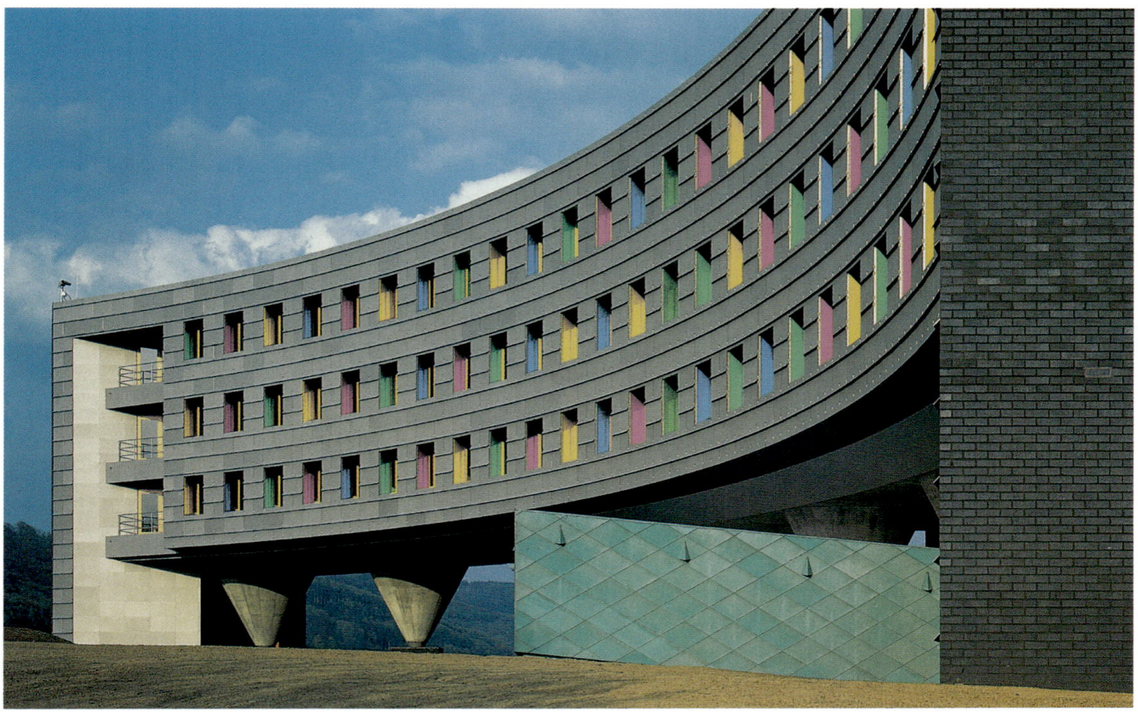

'Future Ways to Work' Design Firm: Design Hoch Drei Creative Director: Diethard Keppler Art Director: Susanne Wacker Designer: Bettina Geist Photographers: Marco Moog and Thurston Ovendt Illustrator: Michael Wilford Copywriter: Christian Marquart Client: B. Braun Melsungen AG

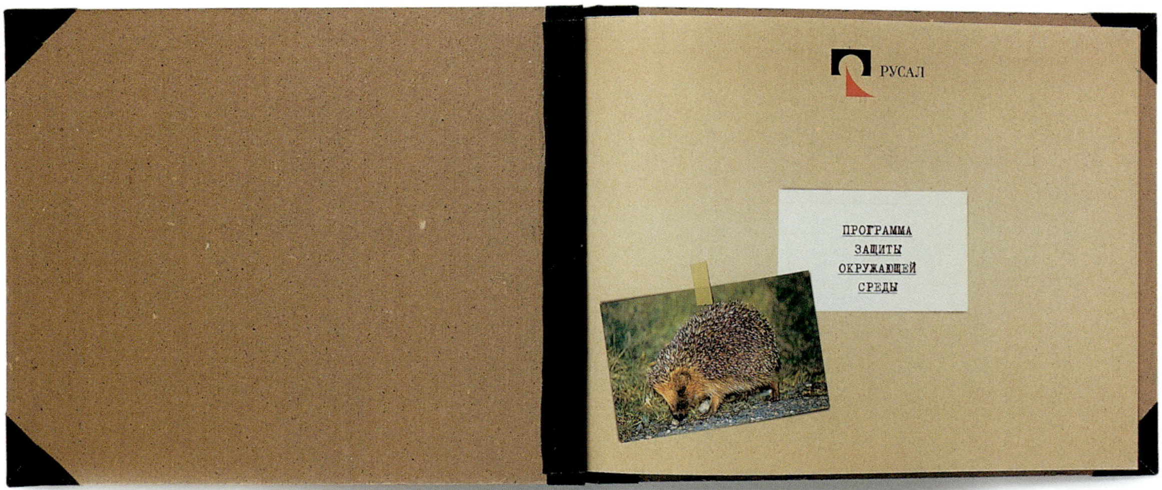

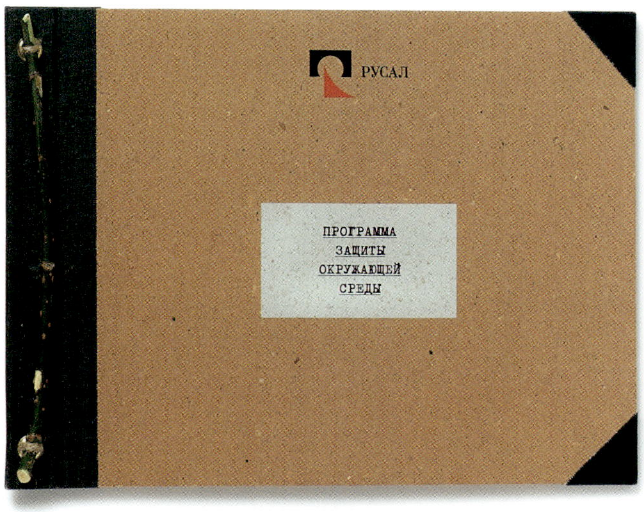

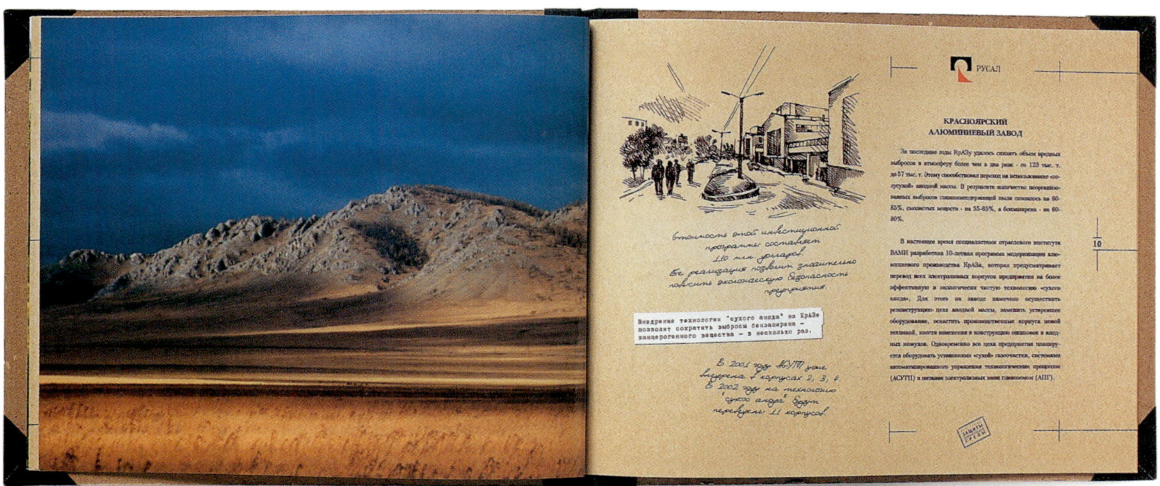

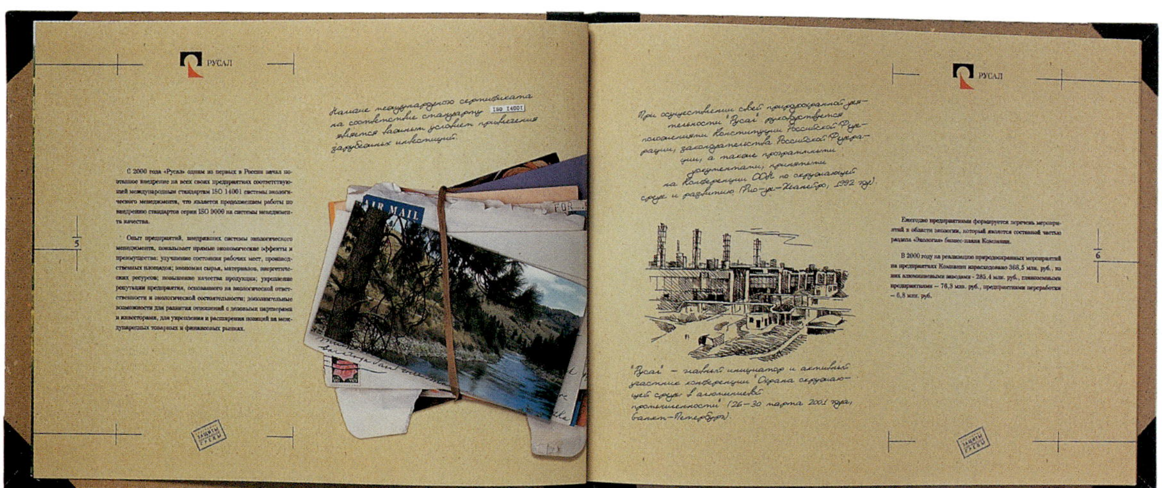

'RusAl Ecology' Design Firm: Direct Design Studio Creative Directors: D. Peryshkov and L. Feigin Art Directors: D. Peryshkov and L. Feigin Designer: K. Tarosova Client: RusAl Company

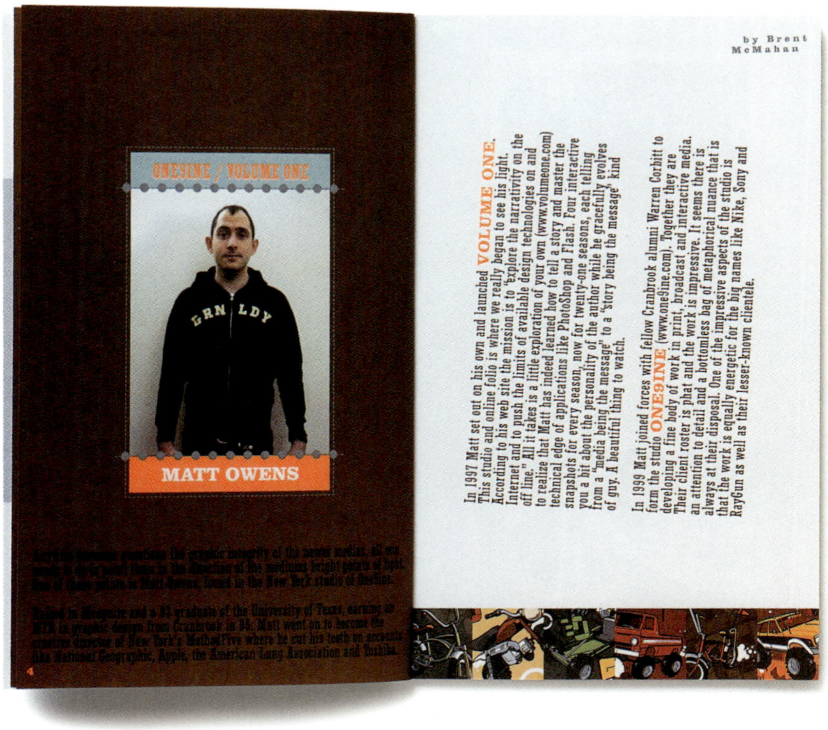

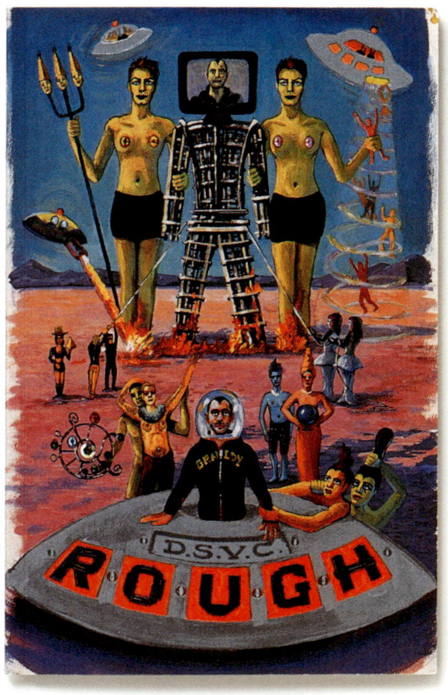

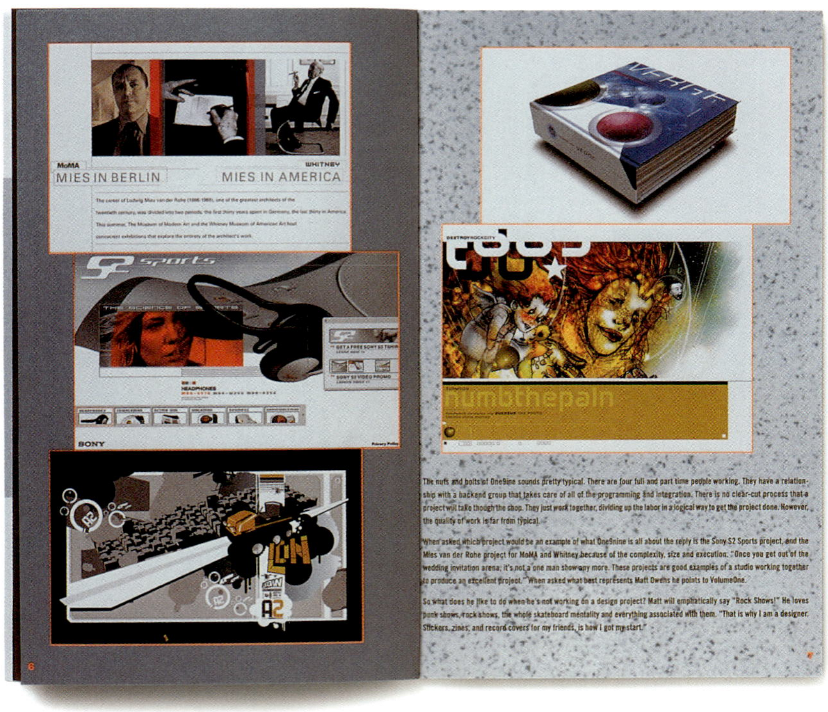

(this spread) 'Rough/October' Design Firm: Squires and Company Creative Director: Brandon Murphy Designers: Brandon Murphy, Adam Hallmark and Bret Sano Photographers: Phil Hollenbeck, Kent Kirkly and Andy Bennett Illustrators: Linda Helton, Ellen Tanner and Cathey Miller Copywriters: Phil Hollenbeck and Brani Knox Client: Dallas Society of Visual Communication

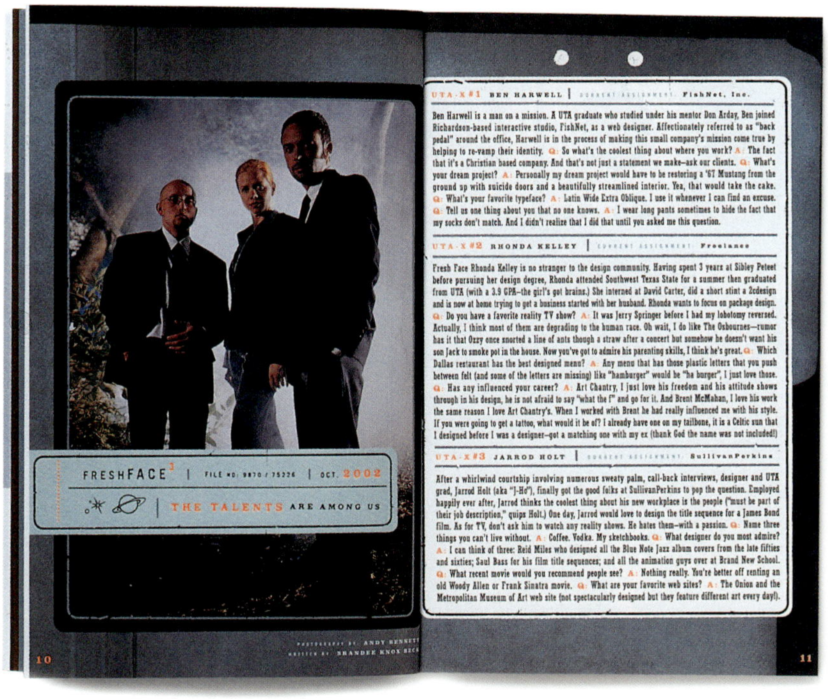
FRESHFACE 3 | FILE NO: 9870 / 75226 | OCT. 2002
THE TALENTS ARE AMONG US
UTA-X #1 BEN HARWELL | CURRENT ASSIGNMENT: FishNet, Inc.
Ben Harwell is a man on a mission. A UTA graduate who studied under his mentor Don Arday, Ben joined Richardson-based interactive studio, FishNet, as a web designer. Affectionately referred to as "back pedal" around the office, Harwell is in the process of making this small company's mission come true by helping to re-vamp their identity. Q: So what's the coolest thing about where you work? A: The fact that it's a Christian based company. And that's not just a statement we make–ask our clients. Q: What's your dream project? A: Personally my dream project would have to be restoring a '67 Mustang from the ground up with suicide doors and a beautifully streamlined interior. Yea, that would take the cake. Q: What's your favorite typeface? A: Latin Wide Extra Oblique. I use it whenever I can find an excuse. Q: Tell us one thing about you that no one knows. A: I wear long pants sometimes to hide the fact that my socks don't match. And I didn't realize that I did that until you asked me this question.
UTA-X #2 RHONDA KELLEY | CURRENT ASSIGNMENT: Freelance
Fresh Face Rhonda Kelley is no stranger to the design community. Having spent 3 years at Sibley Peteet before pursuing her design degree, Rhonda attended Southwest Texas State for a summer then graduated from UTA (with a 3.9 GPA–the girl's got brains.) She interned at David Carter, did a short stint a 2cdesign and is now at home trying to get a business started with her husband. Rhonda wants to focus on package design. Q: Do you have a favorite reality TV show? A: It was Jerry Springer before I had my lobotomy reversed. Actually, I think most of them are degrading to the human race. Oh wait, I do like The Osbournes—rumor has it that Ozzy once snorted a line of ants though a straw after a concert but somehow he doesn't want his son Jack to smoke pot in the house. Now you've got to admire his parenting skills, I think he's great. Q: Which Dallas restaurant has the best designed menu? A: Any menu that has those plastic letters that you push between felt (and some of the letters are missing) like "hamburger" would be "ha burger", I just love those. Q: Has any influenced your career? A: Art Chantry, I just love his freedom and his attitude shows through in his design, he is not afraid to say "what the f" and go for it. And Brent McMahan, I love his work the same reason I love Art Chantry's. When I worked with Brent he had really influenced me with his style. If you were going to get a tattoo, what would it be of? I already have one on my tailbone, it is a Celtic sun that I designed before I was a designer–got a matching one with my ex (thank God the name was not included!)
UTA-X #3 JARROD HOLT | CURRENT ASSIGNMENT: SullivanPerkins
After a whirlwind courtship involving numerous sweaty palm, call-back interviews, designer and UTA grad, Jarrod Holt (aka "J-Ho"), finally got the good folks at SullivanPerkins to pop the question. Employed happily ever after, Jarrod thinks the coolest thing about his new workplace is the people ("must be part of their job description," quips Holt.) One day, Jarrod would love to design the title sequence for a James Bond film. As for TV, don't ask him to watch any reality shows. He hates them–with a passion. Q: Name three things you can't live without. A: Coffee. Vodka. My sketchbooks. Q: What designer do you most admire? A: I can think of three: Reid Miles who designed all the Blue Note Jazz album covers from the late fifties and sixties; Saul Bass for his film title sequences; and all the animation guys over at Brand New School. Q: What recent movie would you recommend people see? A: Nothing really. You're better off renting an old Woody Allen or Frank Sinatra movie. Q: What are your favorite web sites? A: The Onion and the Metropolitan Museum of Art web site (not spectacularly designed but they feature different art every day!).
10
11

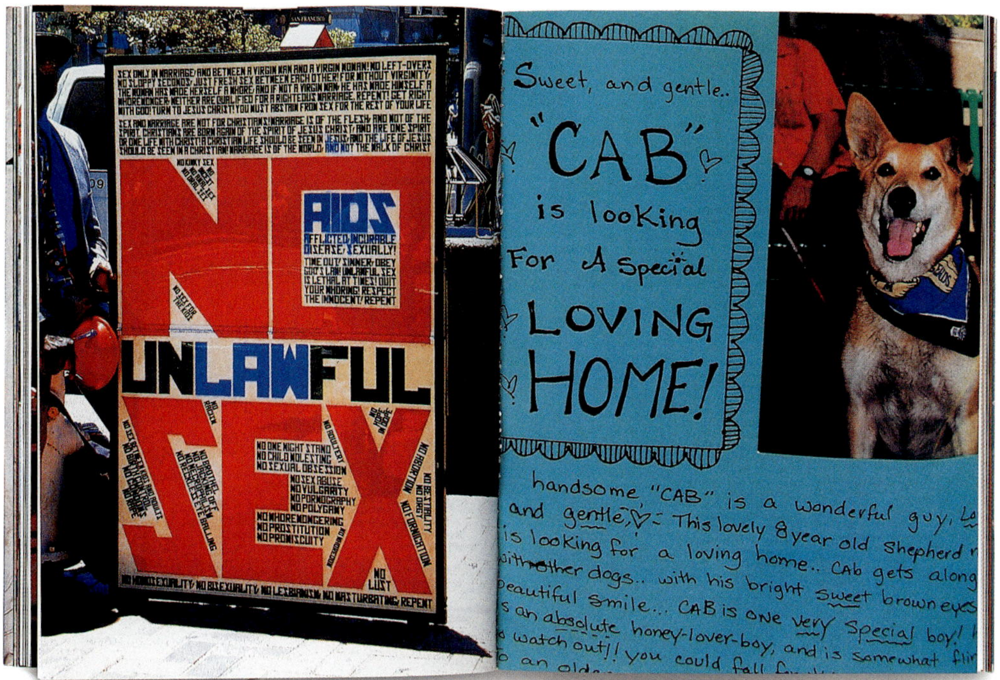
NO
AIDS
UNLAWFUL
SEX
Sweet, and gentle..
"CAB"
is looking
For A Special
LOVING
HOME!
handsome "CAB" is a wonderful guy,
and gentle. This lovely 8 year old shepherd
is looking for a loving home.. Cab gets along
with other dogs.. with his bright sweet brown eyes
beautiful smile... CAB is one very special boy!
is an absolute honey-lover-boy, and is somewhat
watch out!! you could fall

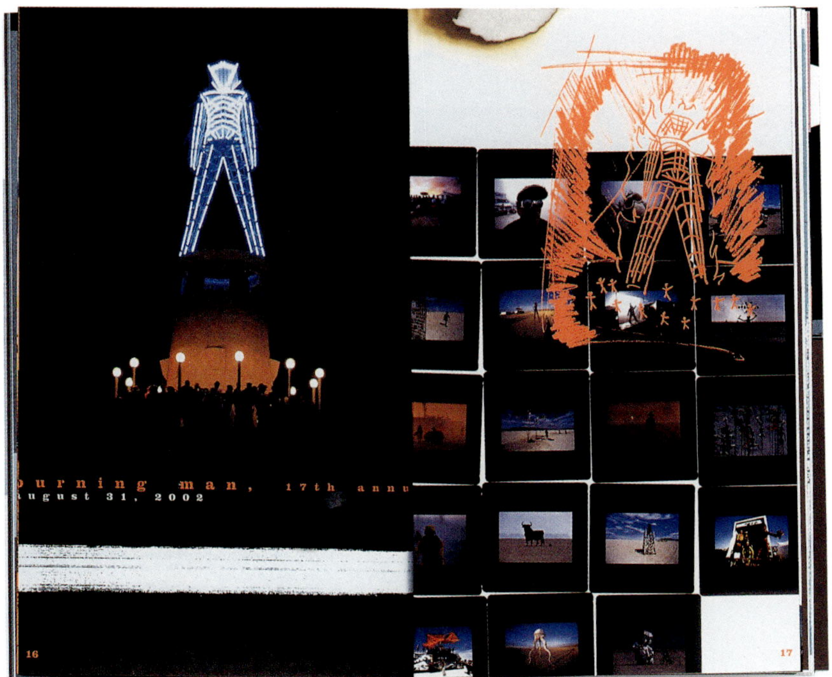
burning man, 17th annu
ugust 31, 2002
16
17

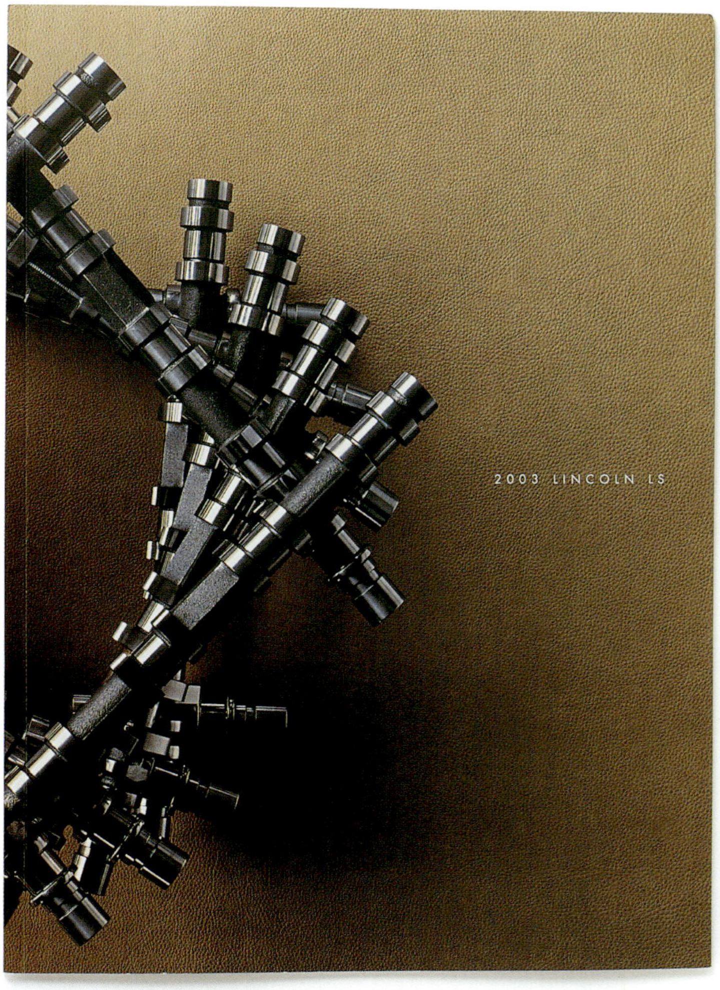

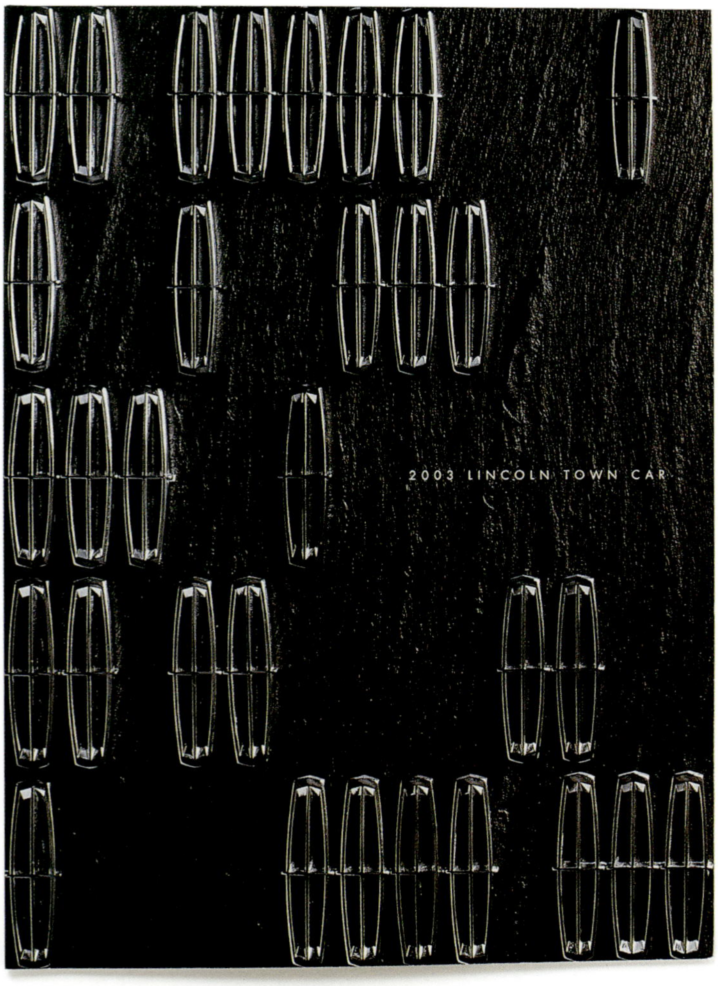

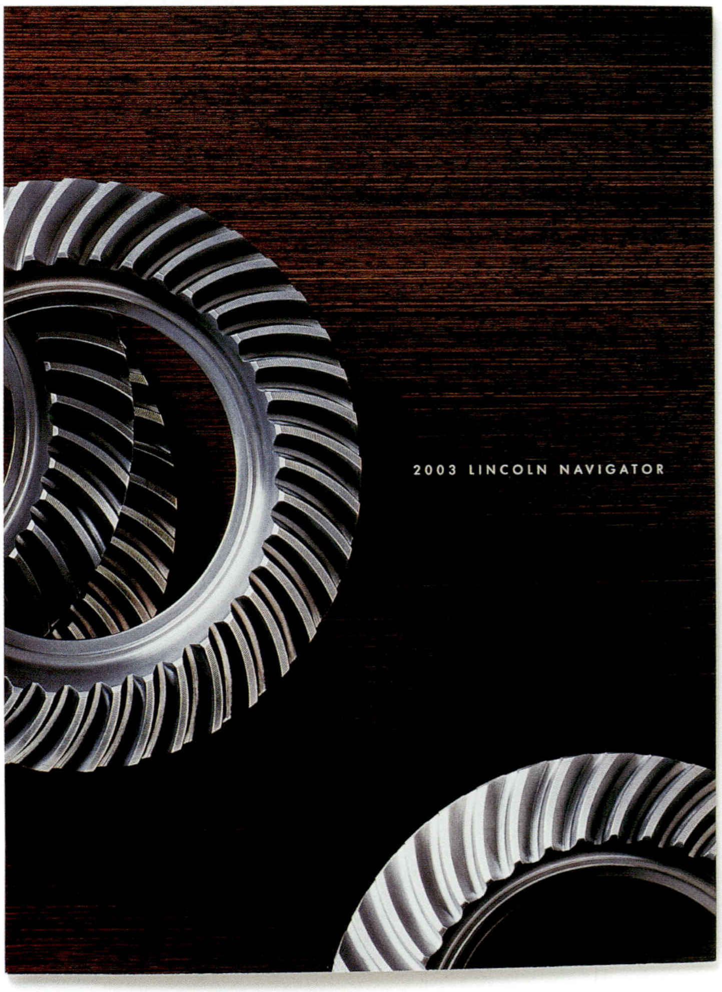

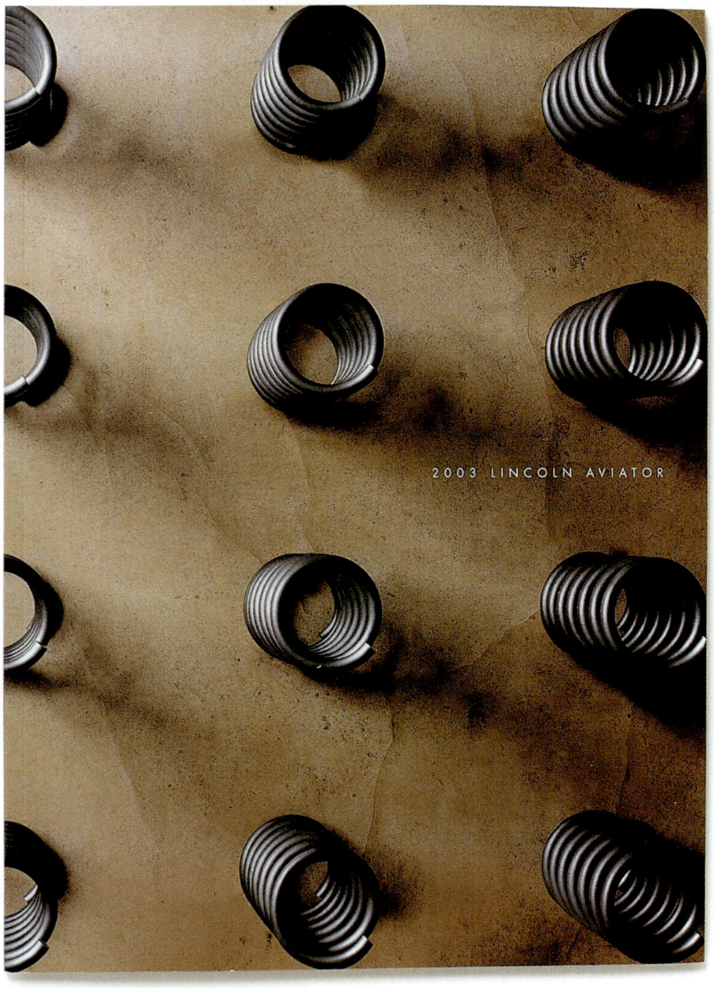

(this spread) '2003 Lincoln LS' Design Firm: Landor Associates Art Directors: Dennis Merritt and Parinaz Zamani Designers: Mike Barton and Scott Bremner Photographers: David Lebon, Rodney Rascona and Abrams Lacagnina Copywriter: Beau Elwell Client: Lincoln Mercury

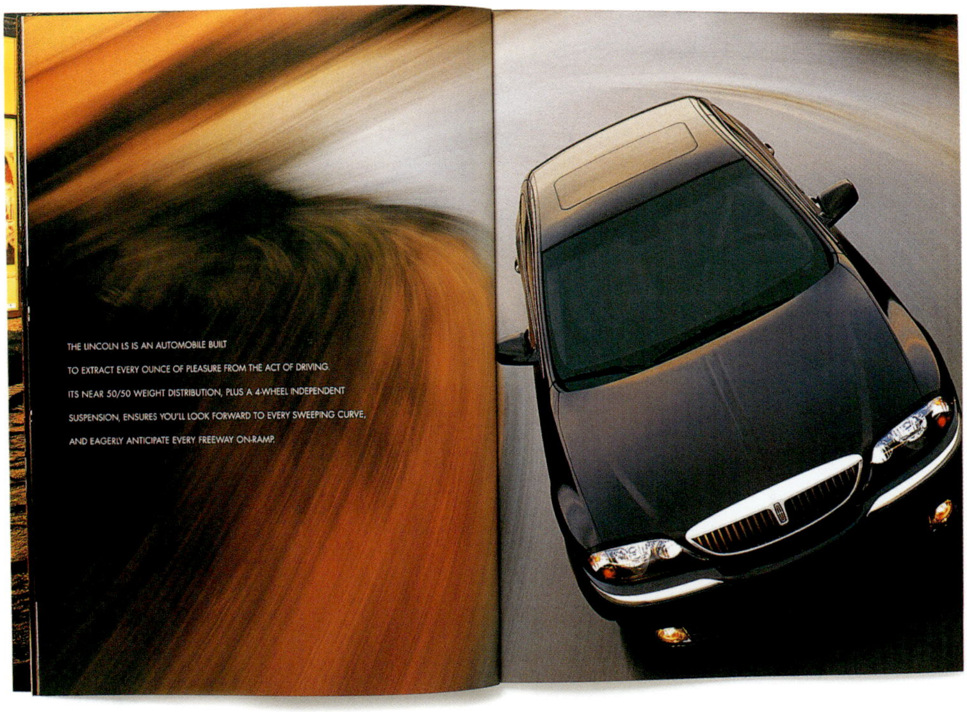
THE LINCOLN LS IS AN AUTOMOBILE BUILT
TO EXTRACT EVERY OUNCE OF PLEASURE FROM THE ACT OF DRIVING.
ITS NEAR 50/50 WEIGHT DISTRIBUTION, PLUS A 4-WHEEL INDEPENDENT
SUSPENSION, ENSURES YOU'LL LOOK FORWARD TO EVERY SWEEPING CURVE,
AND EAGERLY ANTICIPATE EVERY FREEWAY ON-RAMP.

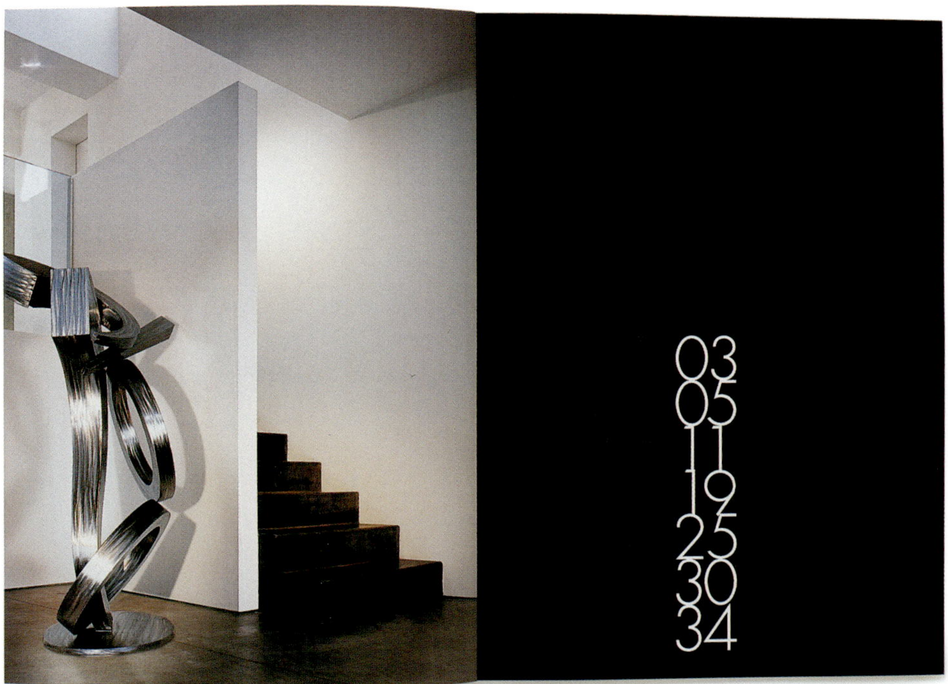
03
05
11
19
25
30
34

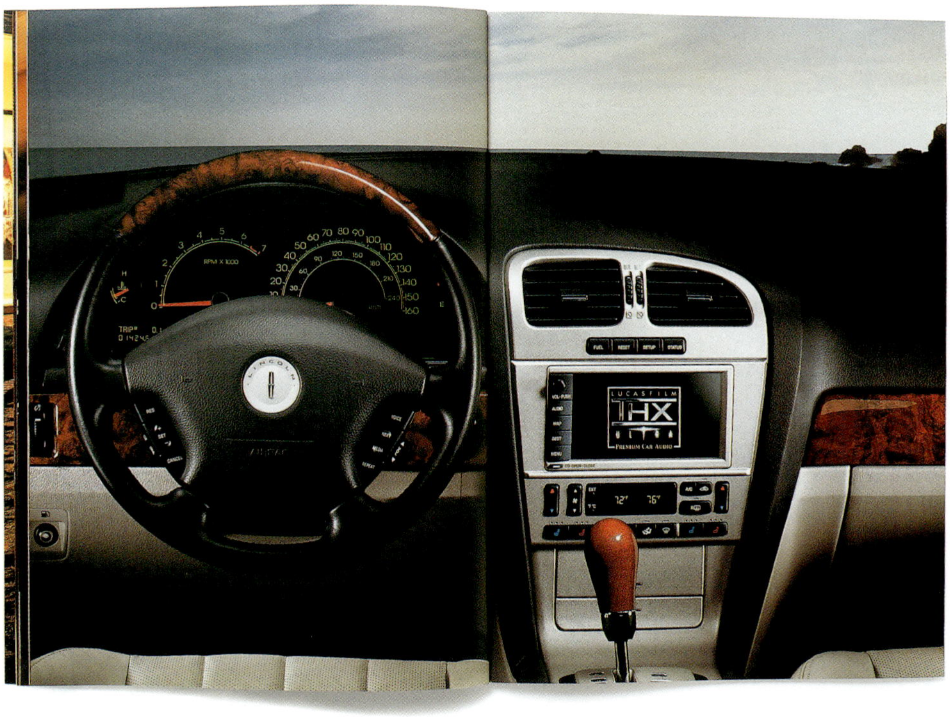
THX

(this spread) Design Firm: Cahan & Associates Creative Director: Bill Cahan Art Director: Bill Cahan Designers: Kevin Roberson, Sharrie Brooks, Gary Williams, Michael Braley and Bob Dinetz
Photographers: Bob Dinetz and Kevin Roberson Illustrators: Gary Williams and Bob Dinetz Copywriters: Gary Williams, Kevin Roberson and Bob Dinetz Account Coordinator: Gwendolyn Rogers Client: AIGA

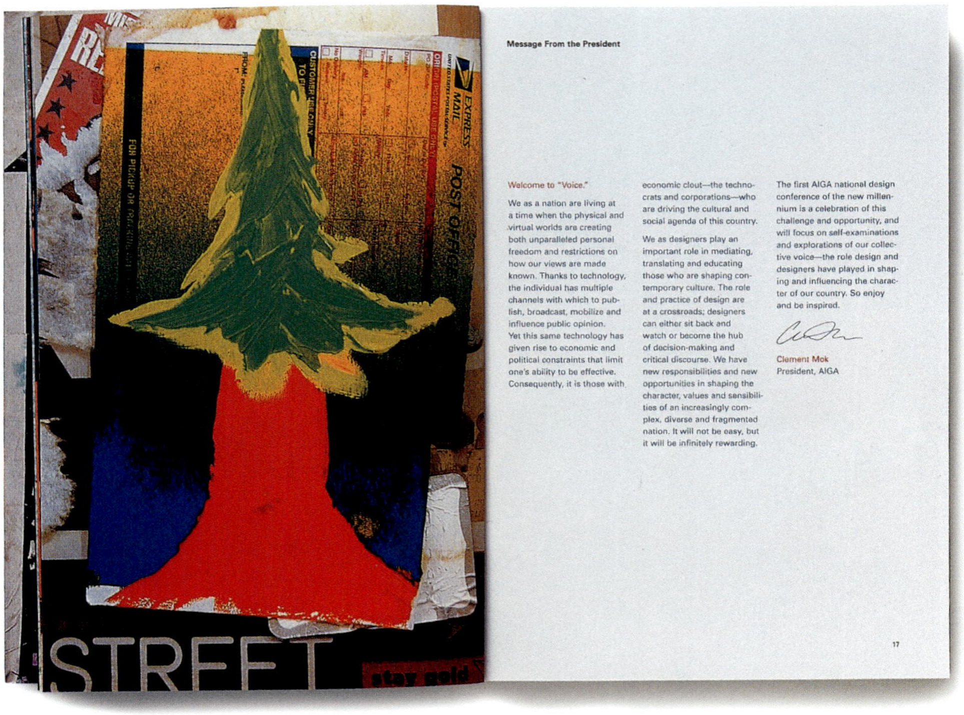

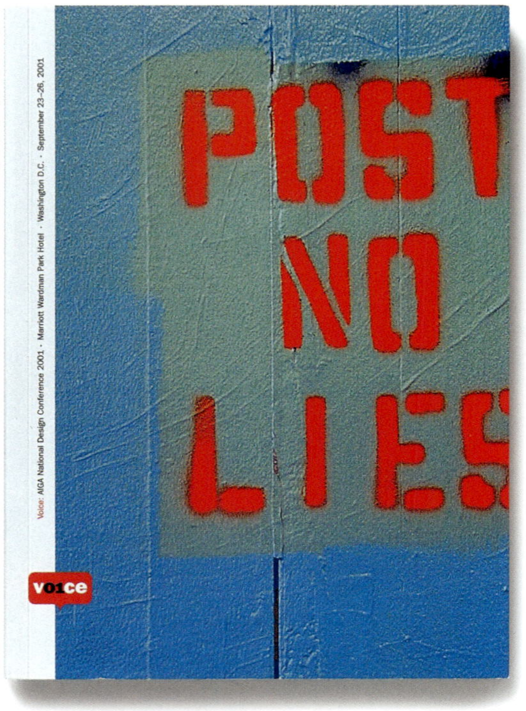

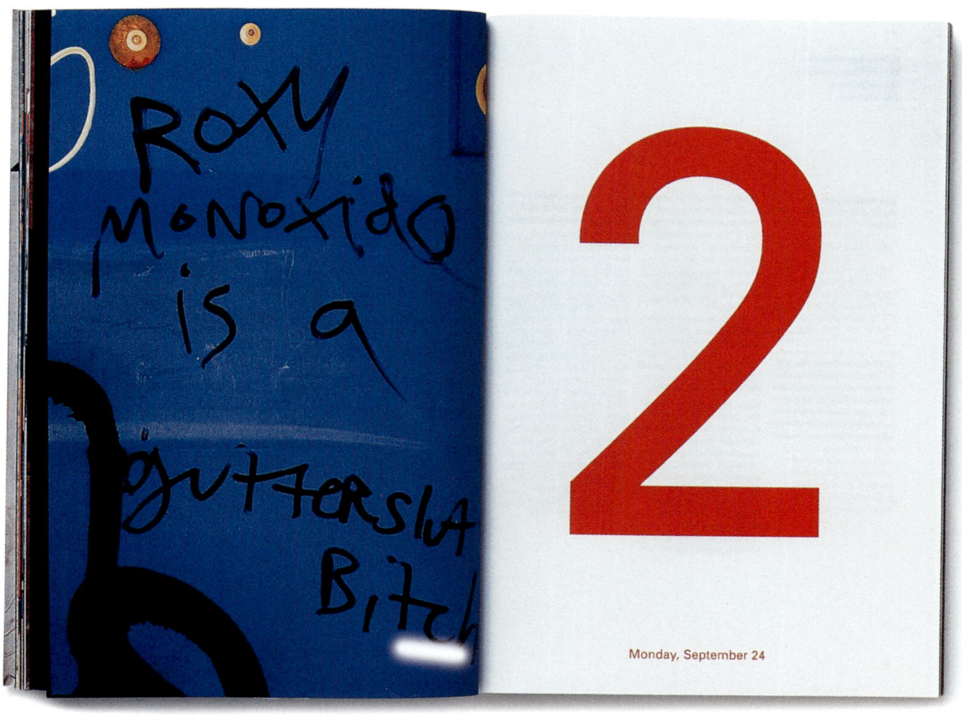

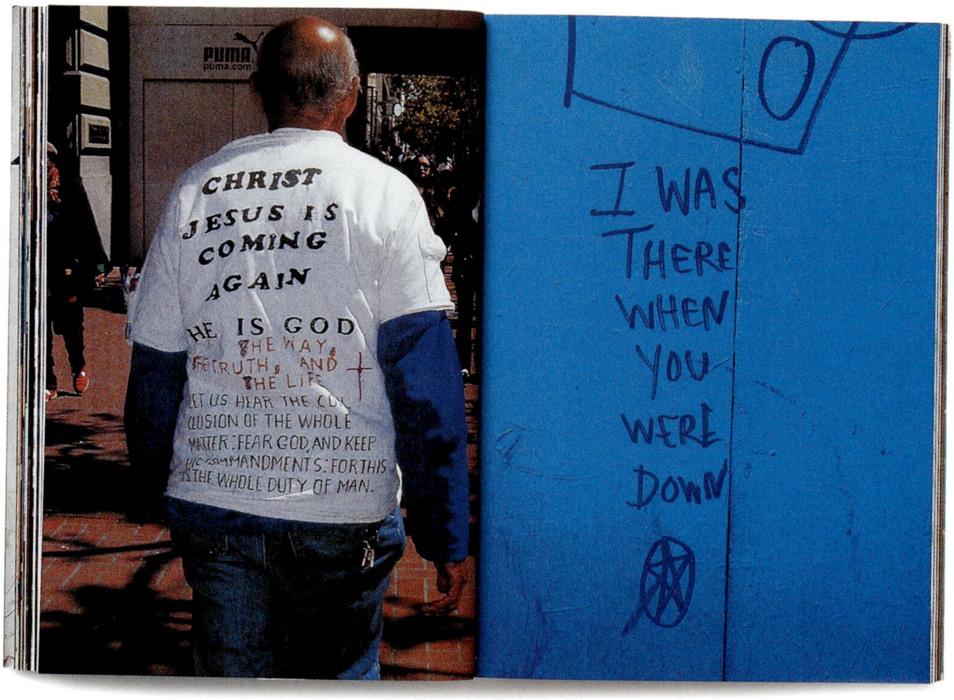
CHRIST JESUS IS COMING AGAIN
HE IS GOD
I WAS THERE WHEN YOU WERE DOWN

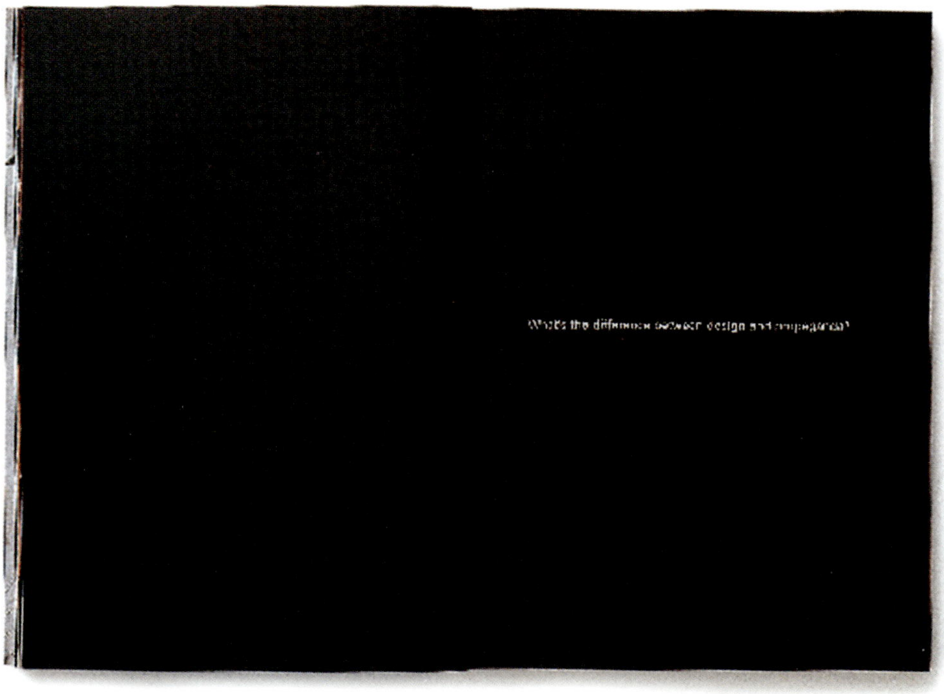

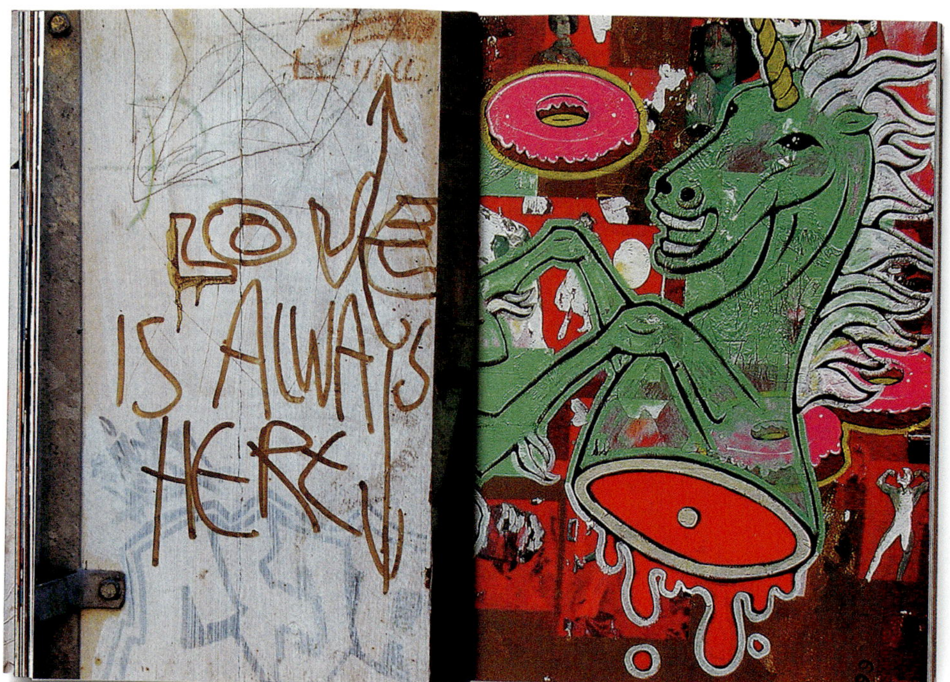
LOVE IS ALWAYS HERE

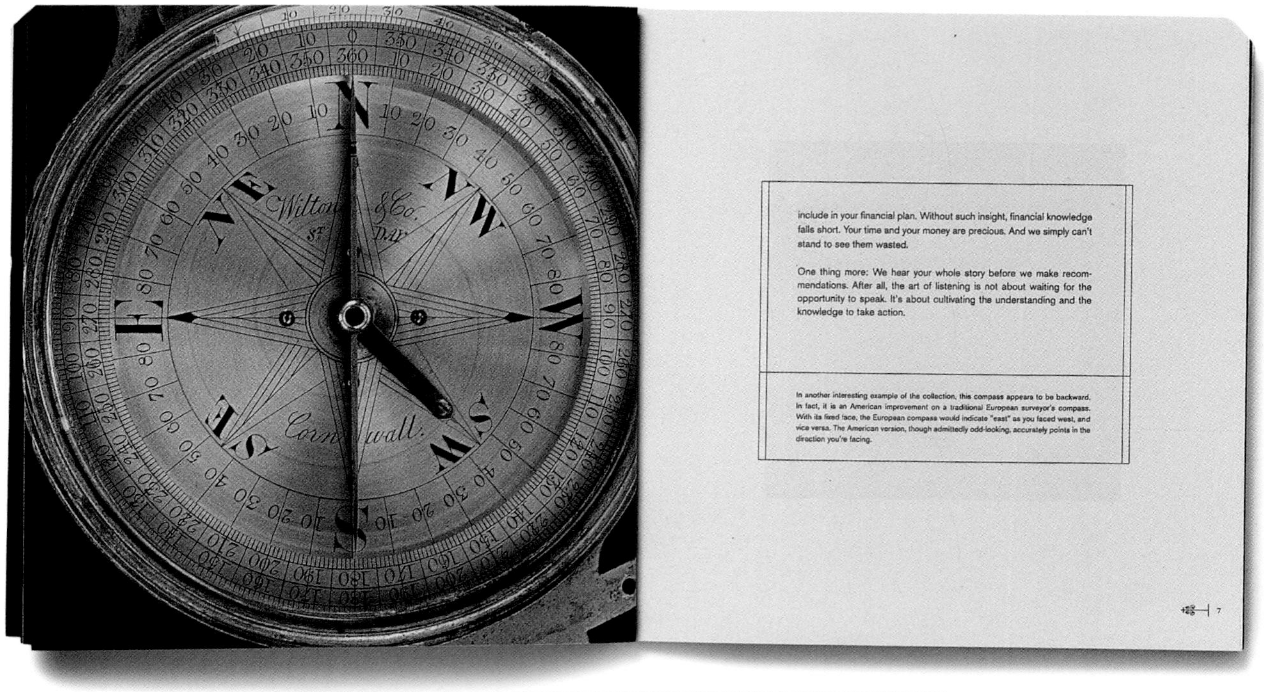

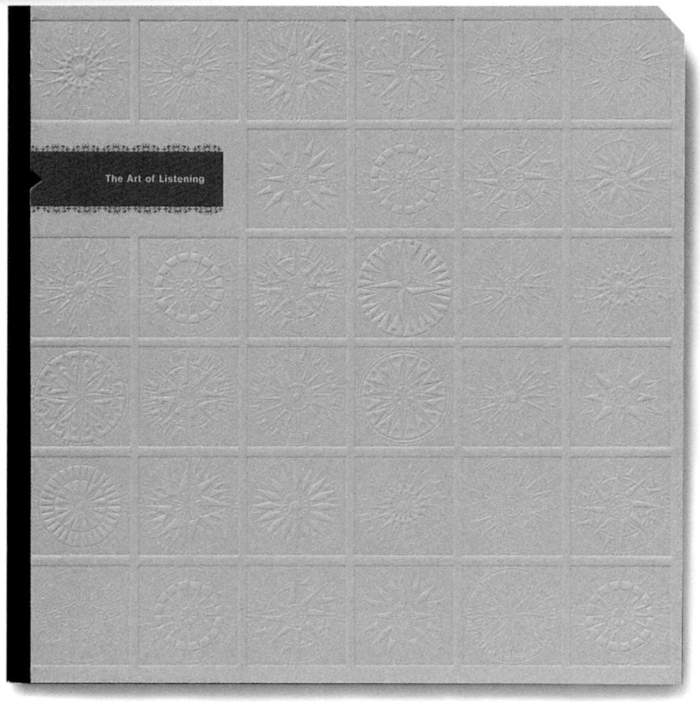

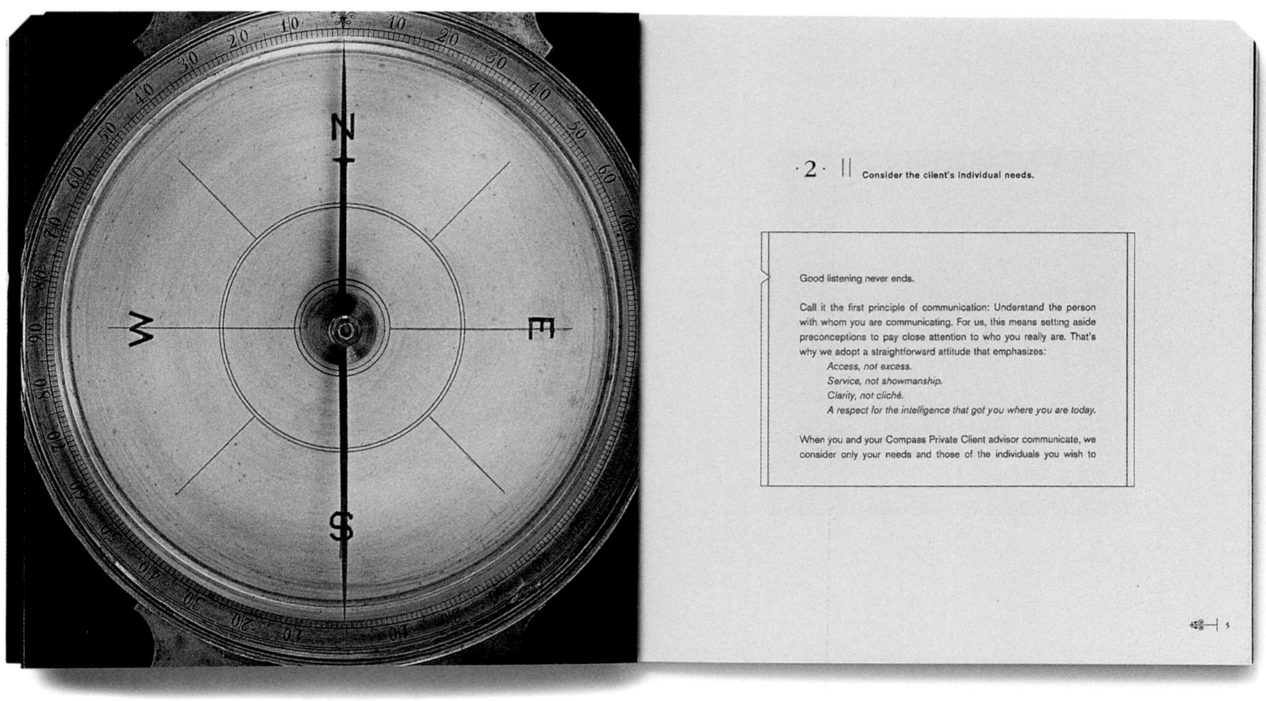

'AMG Brochure' Design Firm: Th Designers: Blake Tannery and Clark Hook Client: Compass Bank

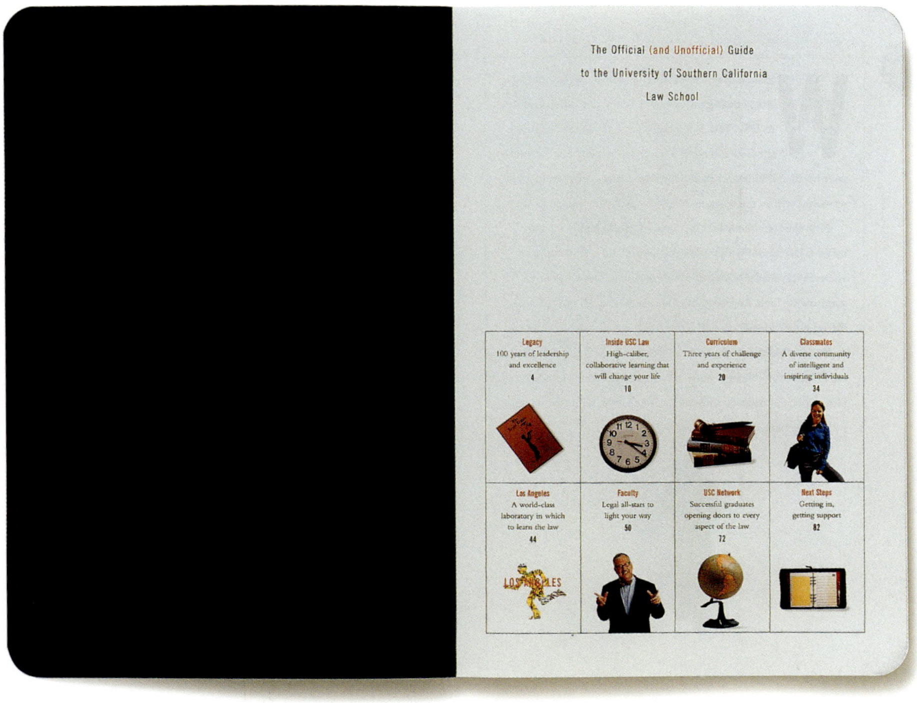

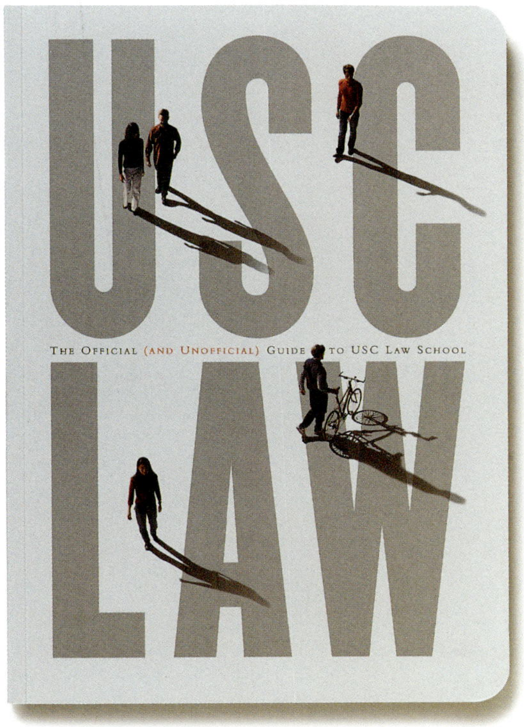

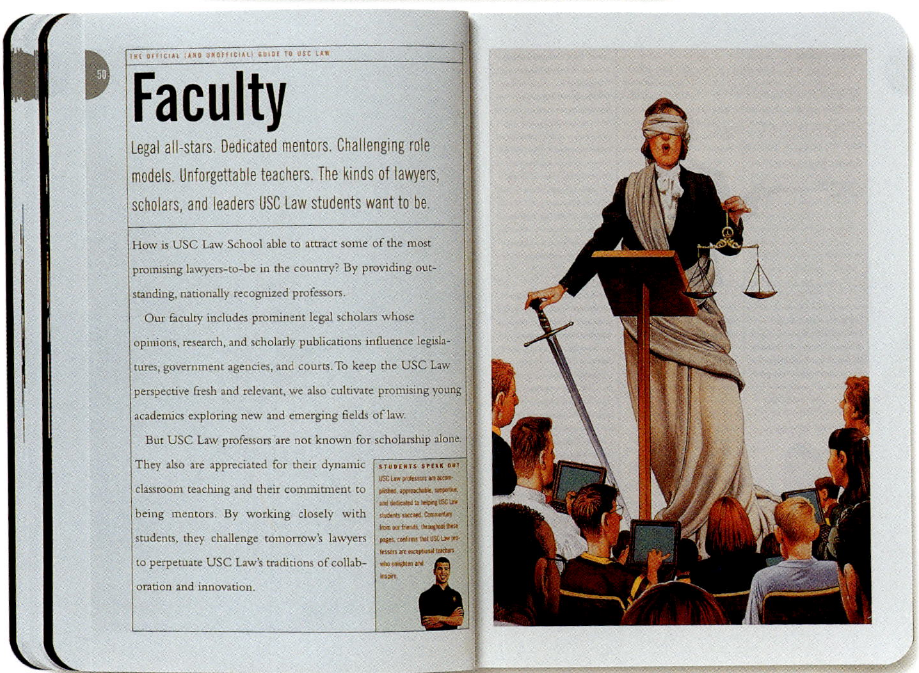

'USC Law School Brochure' Design Firm: Pentagram SF Creative Director: Kit Hinrichs Art Director: Belle How Designers: Belle How and Takayo Muroga Copywriter: Peterson, Skolnick & Dodge Project Manager: Christy Brand Client: University of Southern California

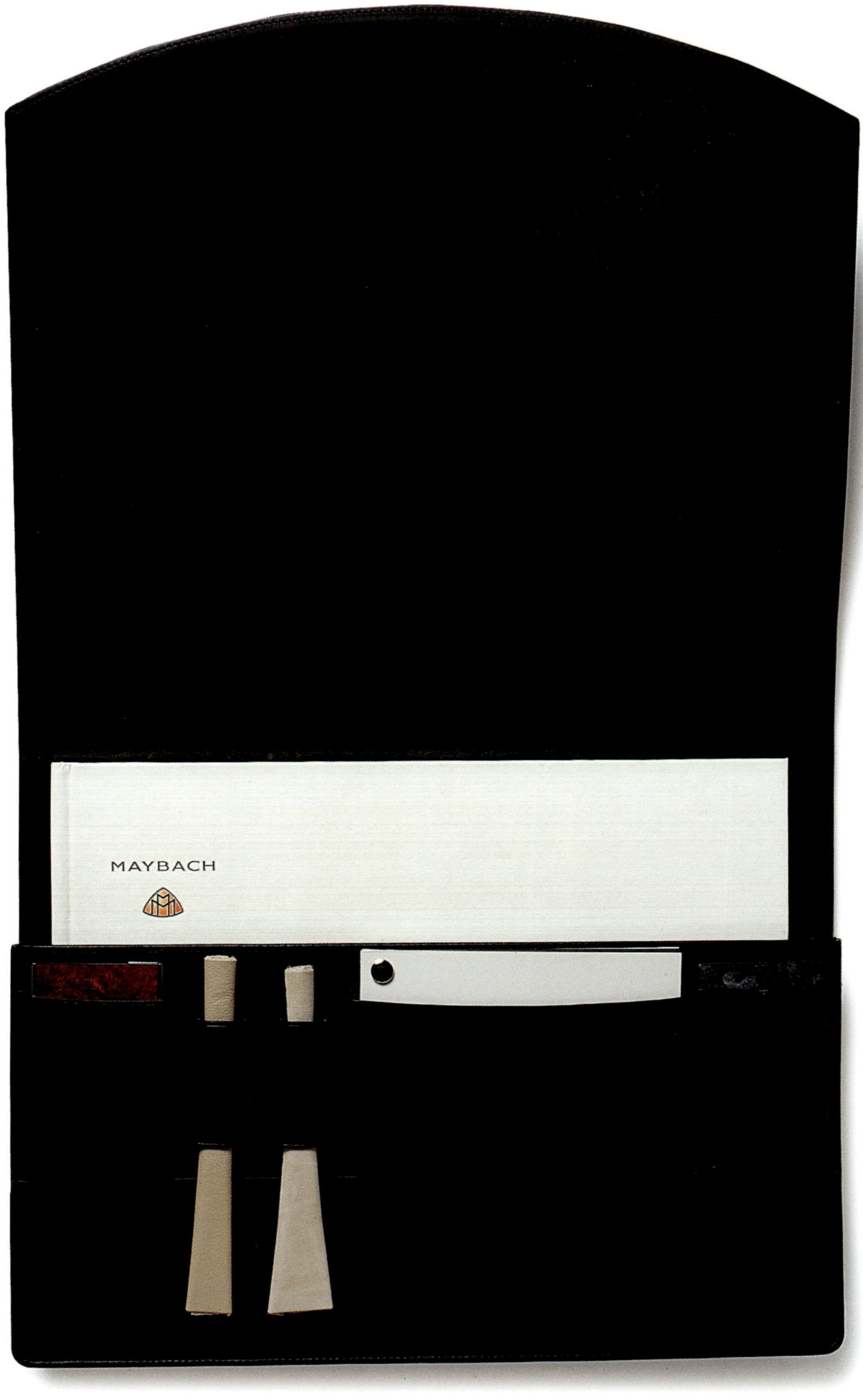

(this spread) 'Maybach Materials' Design Firm: TC Gruppe GmbH, Target Communications Creative Director: Christian Croemer Art Director: Daniela Deeg
Photographers: Bletz & Pixel, Martin Schoeuble, René Staud Studios GmbH and Vàclav Reischel Copywriter: Bettina Lehmann Client: Daimler Chrysler AG

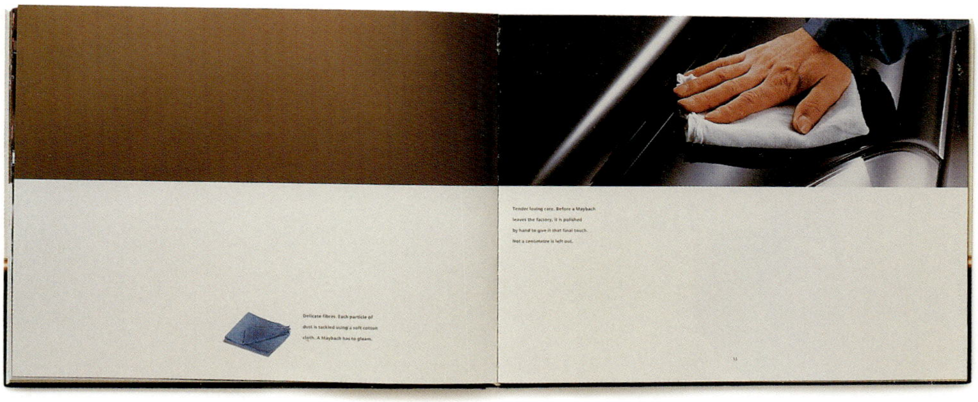
Delicate fibres. Each particle of
dust is tackled using a soft cotton
cloth. A Maybach has to gleam.
Tender loving care. Before a Maybach
leaves the factory, it is polished
by hand to give it that final touch.
Not a centimetre is left out.

MAYBACH
MAYBACH MATERIALS

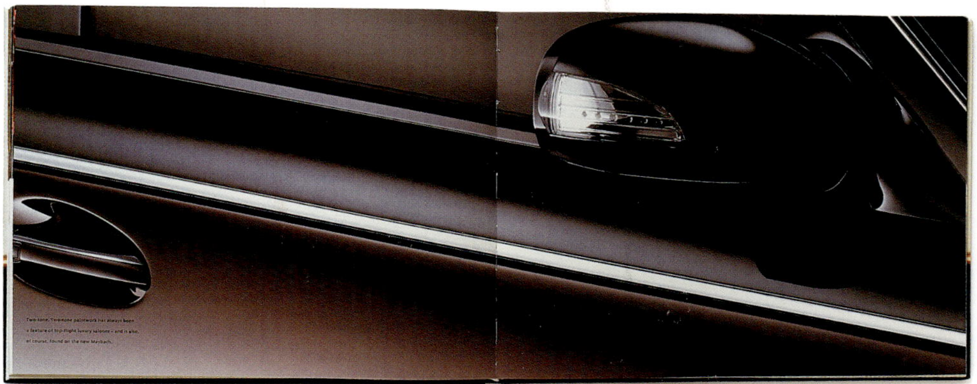
Two-tone. Two-tone paintwork has always been
a feature of top-flight luxury saloons – and it is also,
of course, found on the new Maybach.

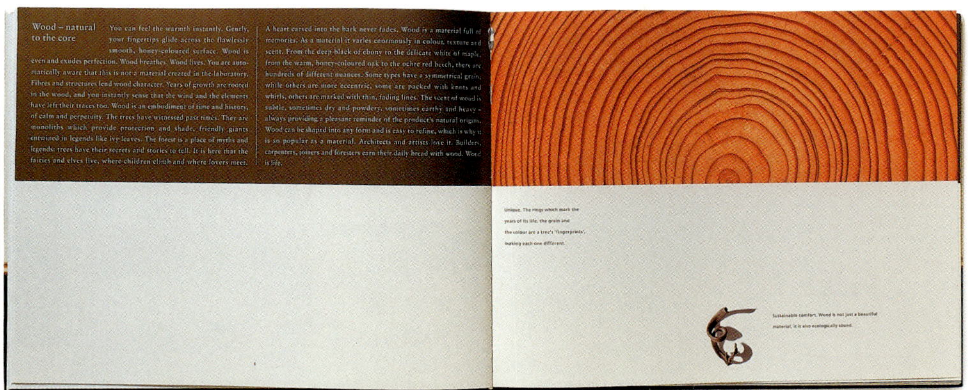
Wood – natural to the core
You can feel the warmth instantly. Gently, your fingertips glide across the flawlessly smooth, honey-coloured surface. Wood is even and exudes perfection. Wood breathes. Wood lives. You are automatically aware that this is not a material created in the laboratory. Fibres and structures lend wood character. Years of growth are rooted in the wood, and you instantly sense that the wind and the elements have left their traces too. Wood is an embodiment of time and history, of calm and perpetuity. The trees have witnessed past times. They are monoliths which provide protection and shade, friendly giants entwined in legends like ivy leaves. The forest is a place of myths and legends: trees have their secrets and stories to tell. It is here that the fairies and elves live, where children climb and where lovers meet.
A heart carved into the bark never fades. Wood is a material full of memories. As a material it varies enormously in colour, texture and scent. From the deep black of ebony to the delicate white of maple, from the warm, honey-coloured oak to the ochre red beech, there are hundreds of different nuances. Some types have a symmetrical grain, while others are more eccentric, some are packed with knots and whirls, others are marked with thin, fading lines. The scent of wood is subtle, sometimes dry and powdery, sometimes earthy and heavy – always providing a pleasant reminder of the product's natural origins. Wood can be shaped into any form and is easy to refine, which is why it is so popular as a material. Architects and artists love it. Builders, carpenters, joiners and foresters earn their daily bread with wood. Wood is life.
Unique. The rings which mark the
years of its life, the grain and
the colour are a tree's 'fingerprints',
making each one different.
Sustainable comfort. Wood is not just a beautiful
material, it is also ecologically sound.

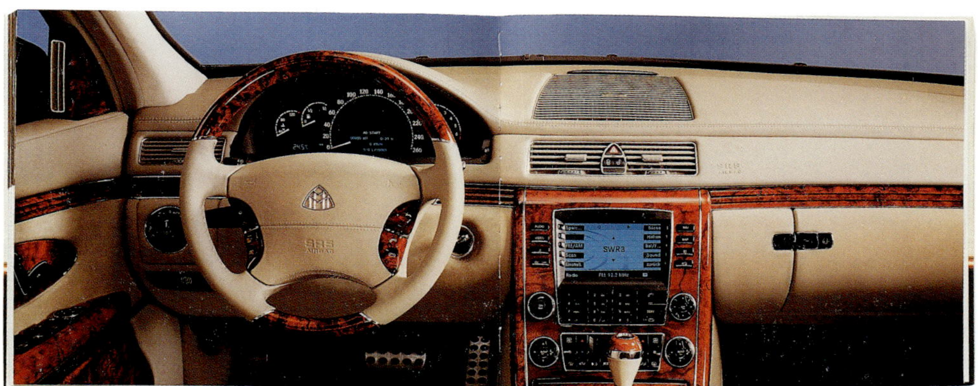
SWR3

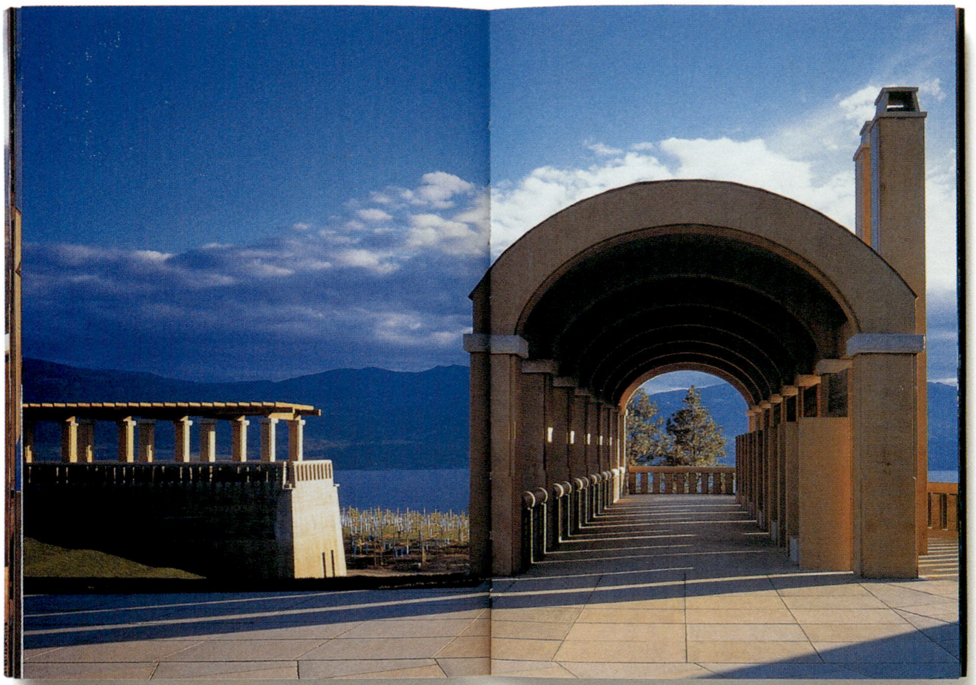

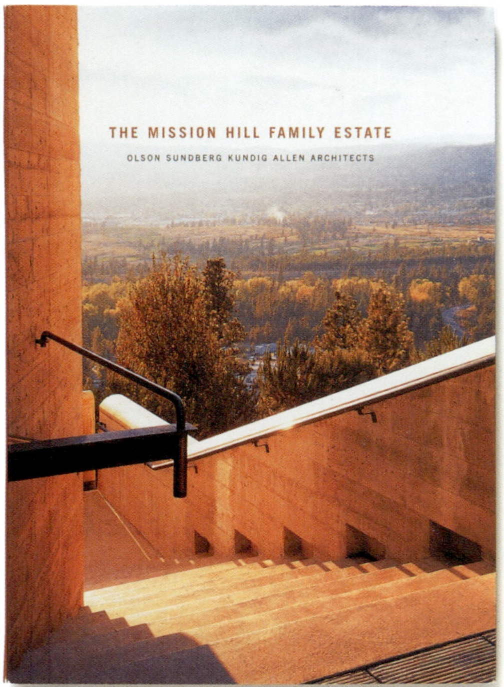

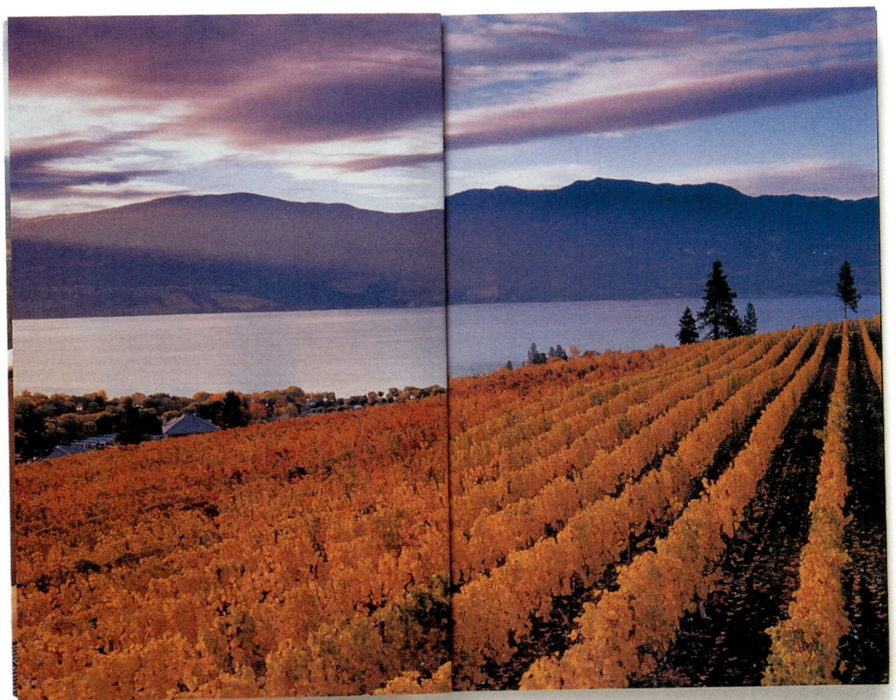

(this spread) Design Firm: Jon Cannell Design Art Director: Jon Cannell Designer: Jon Cannell Photographer: Nancy Levine Illustrator: Jon Cannell

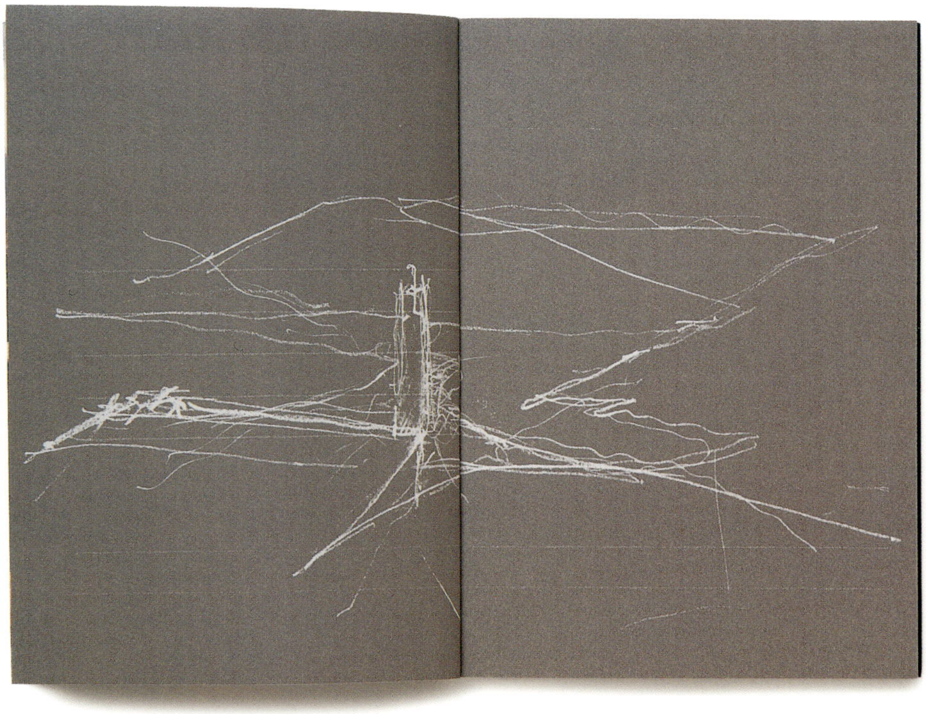

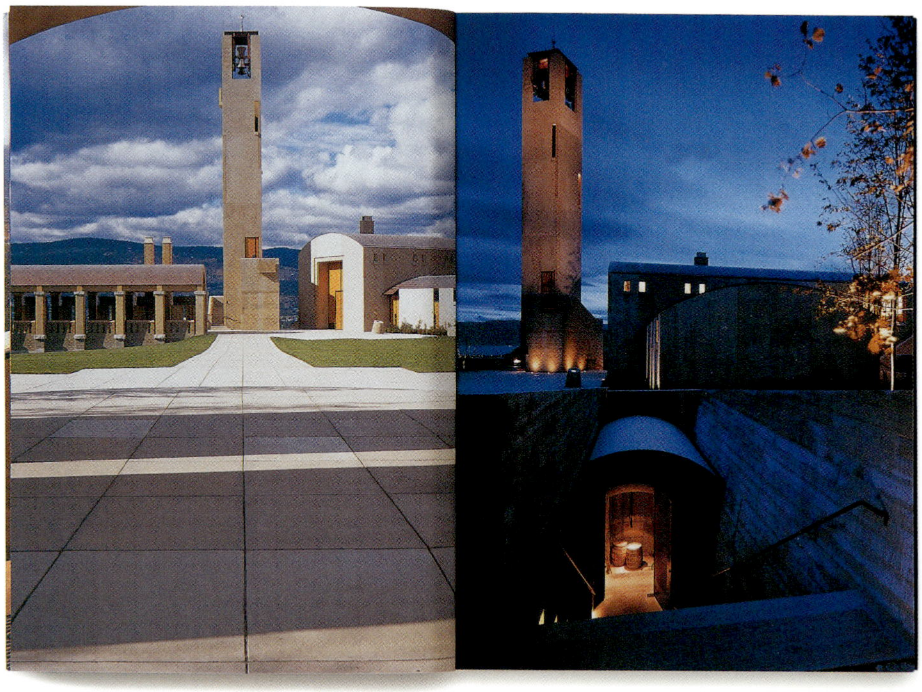

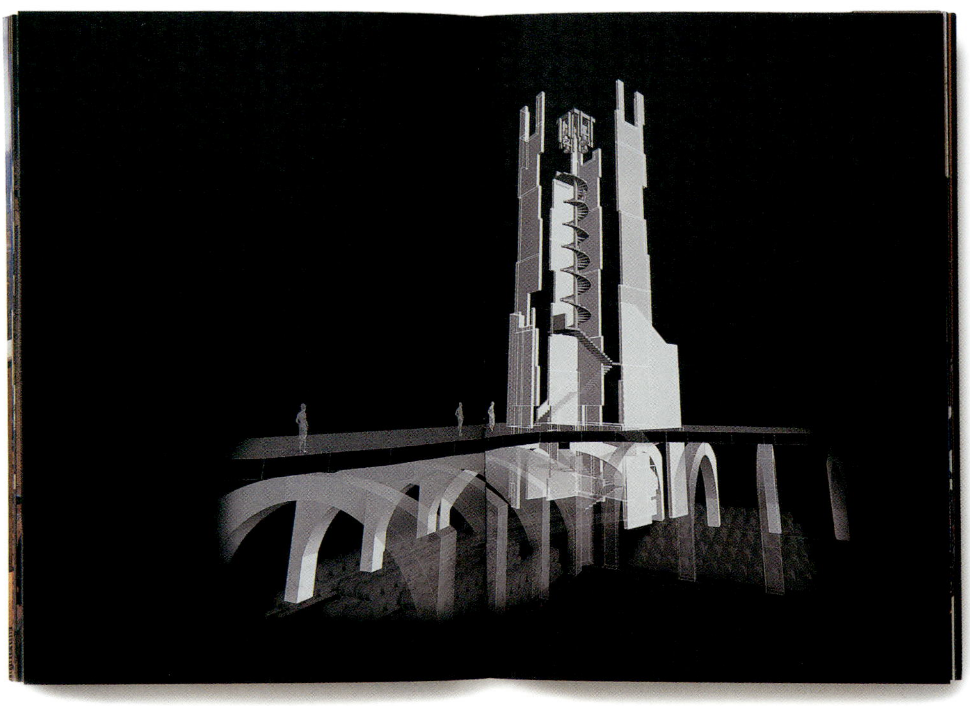

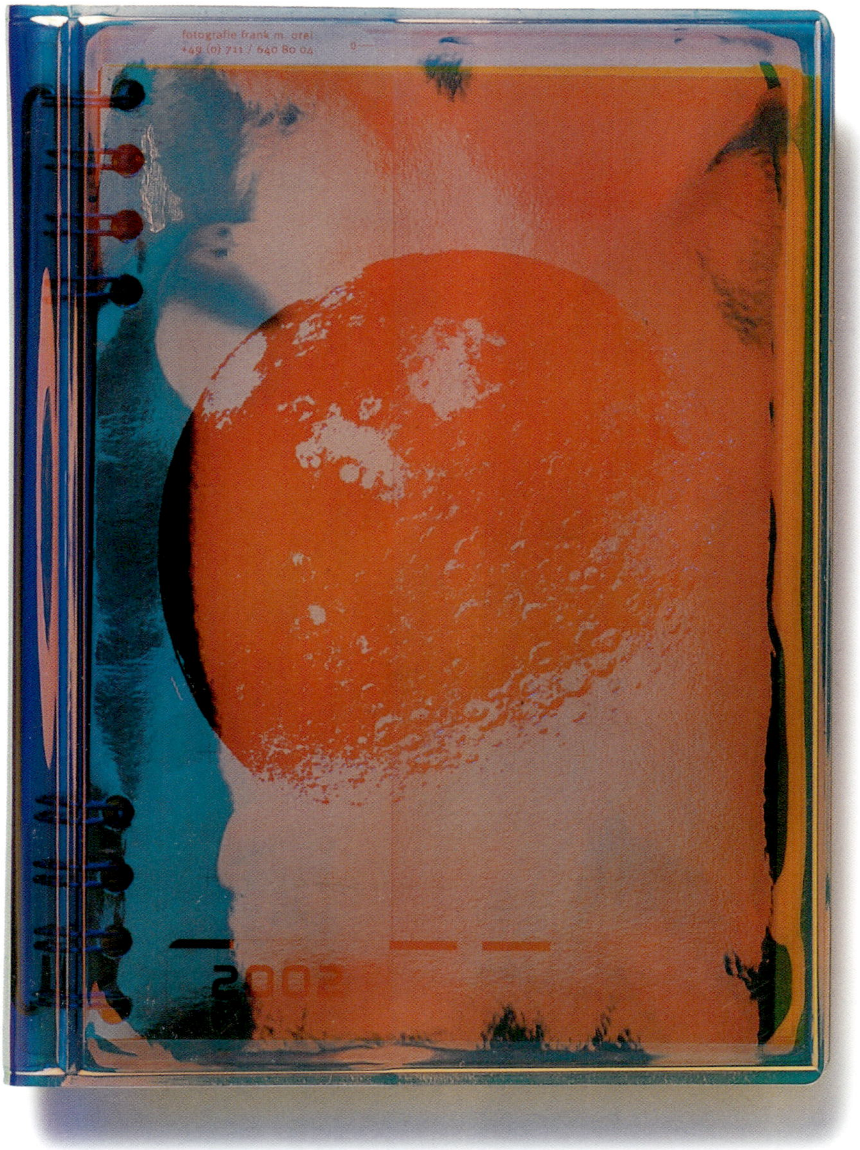

(this spread) 'Lebensart' Design Firm: Fotografie Frank M. Orel Creative Director: Frank M. Orel Art Director: Ingeborg Orel Photographers: Mike Nanz, Volker Hink and Frank M. Orel Copywriter: Goddy Buehler Client: Fotografie Frank M. Orel

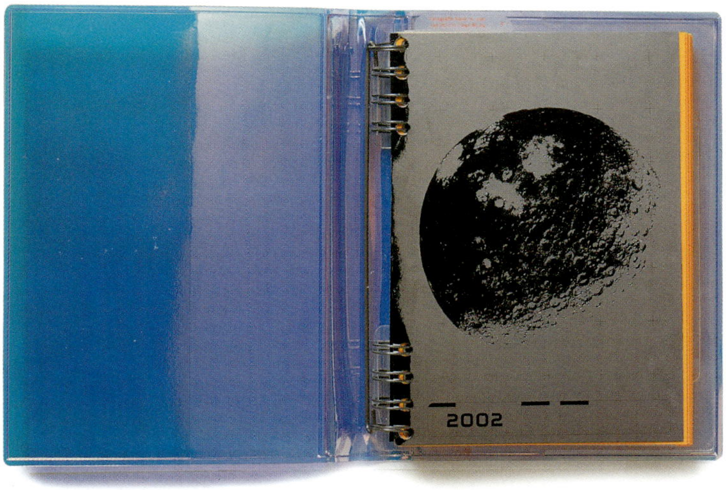
2002

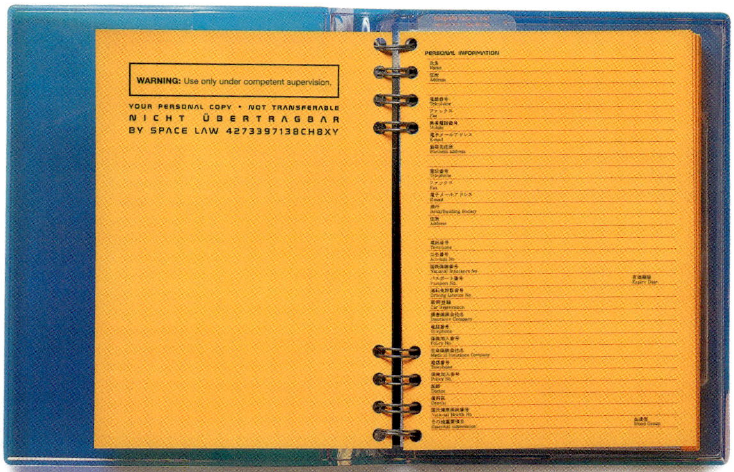
WARNING: Use only under competent supervision.
YOUR PERSONAL COPY · NOT TRANSFERABLE
NICHT ÜBERTRAGBAR
BY SPACE LAW 427339713BCH8XY
PERSONAL INFORMATION

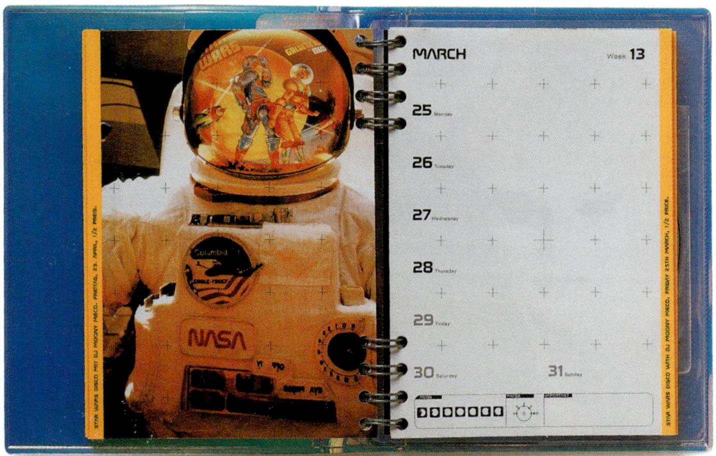
MARCH
Week 13
25
26
27
28
29
30
31
NASA

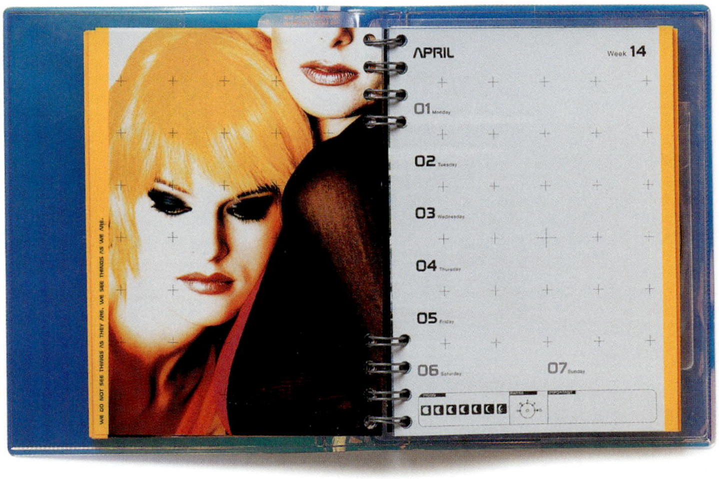
APRIL
Week 14
01
02
03
04
05
06
07

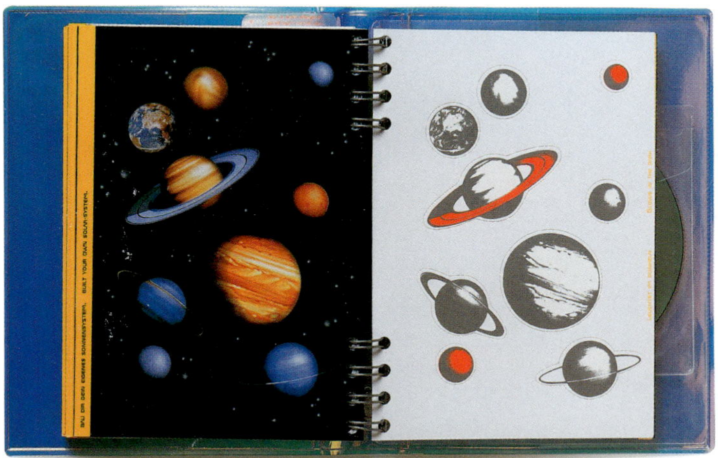

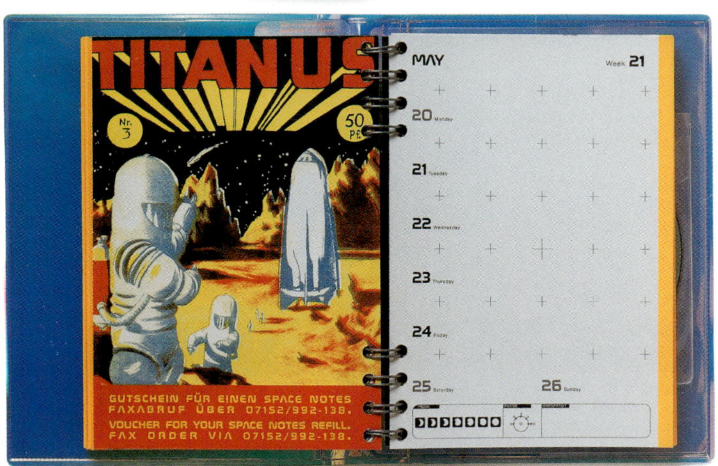
TITANUS
Nr. 3
50
MAY
Week 21
20
21
22
23
24
25
26
GUTSCHEIN FÜR EINEN SPACE NOTES
FAXABRUF ÜBER 07152/992-138.
VOUCHER FOR YOUR SPACE NOTES REFILL.
FAX ORDER VIA 07152/992-138.

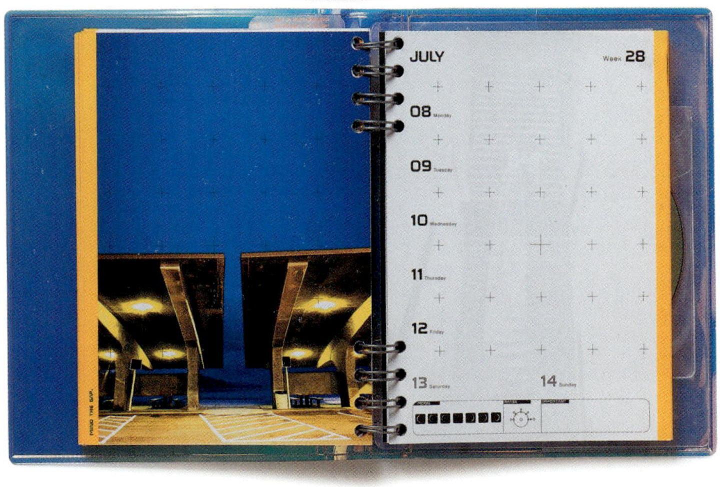
JULY
Week 28
08
09
10
11
12
13
14

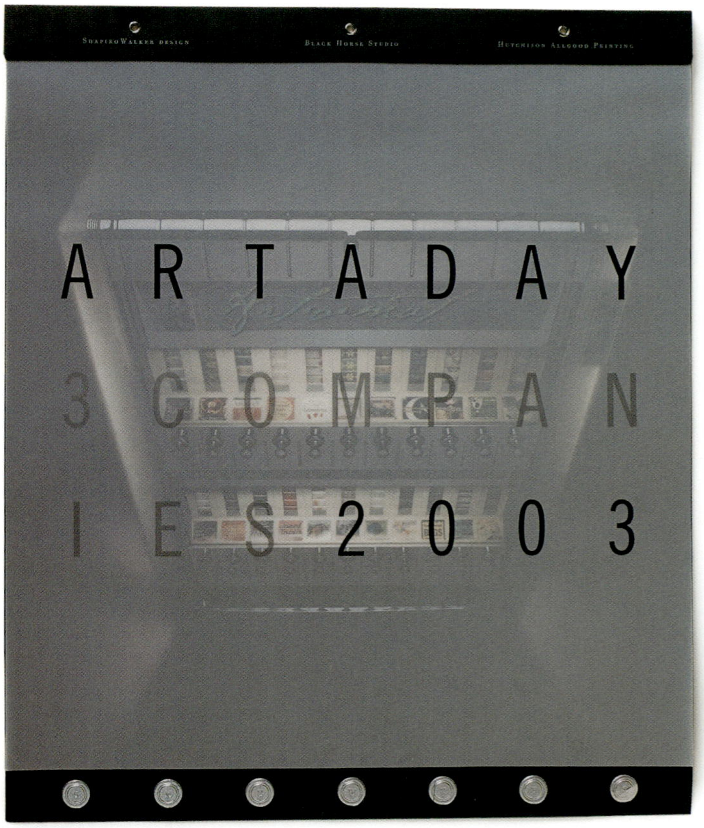

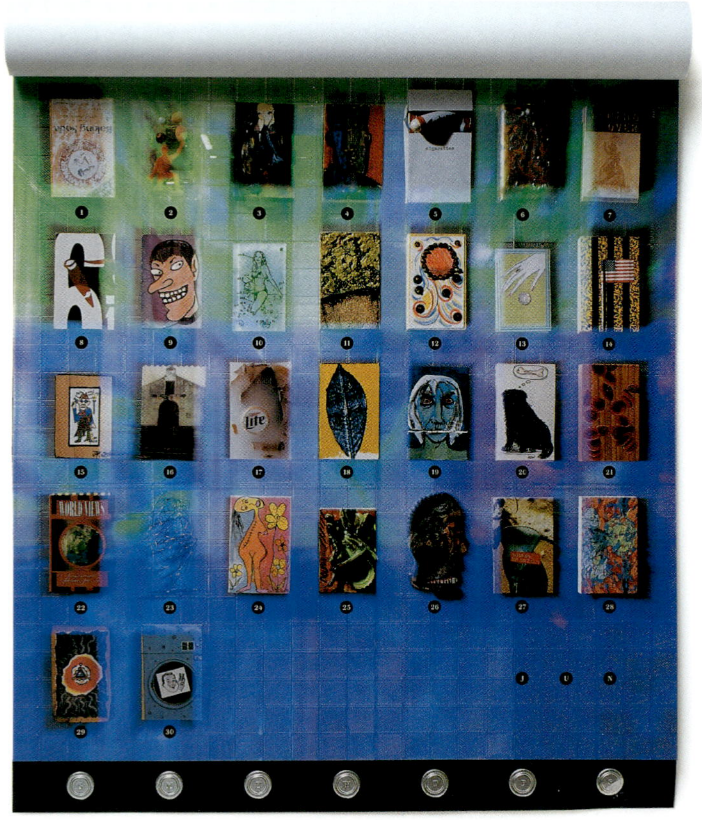

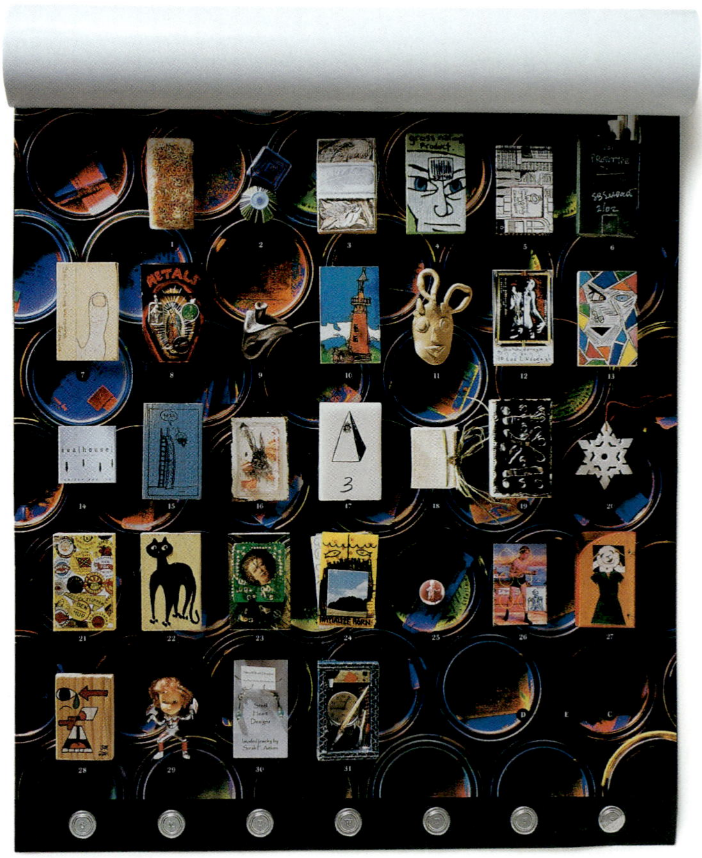

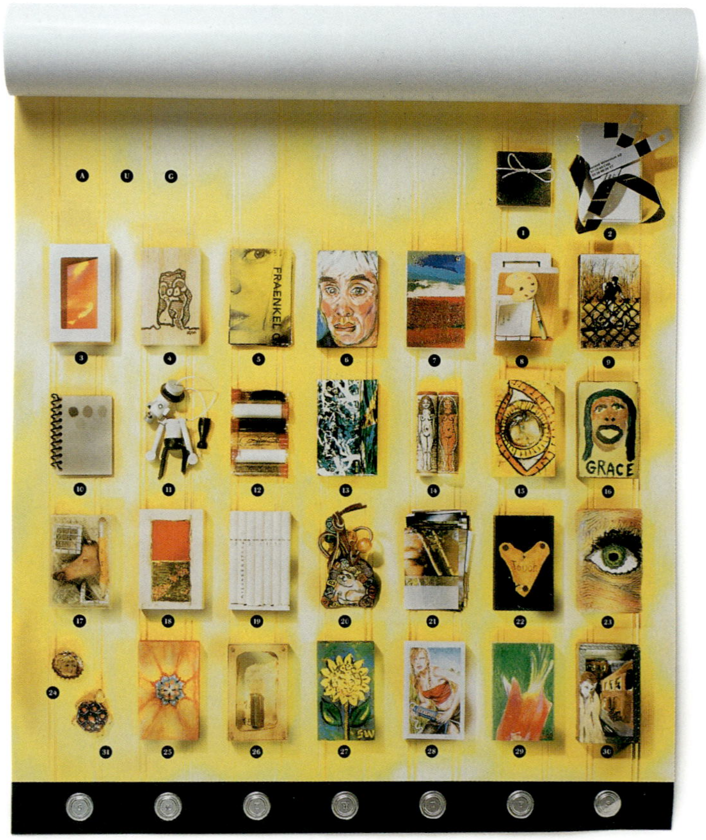

'Art a Day 3 Companies 2003' Design Firm: Shapiro Walker Design Creative Directors: David Shapiro and John Walker Art Directors: David Shapiro and John Walker Designers: David Shapiro and John Walker Photographer: Black Horse Studio Printer: Hutchison Allgood Printing Client: 3 Companies

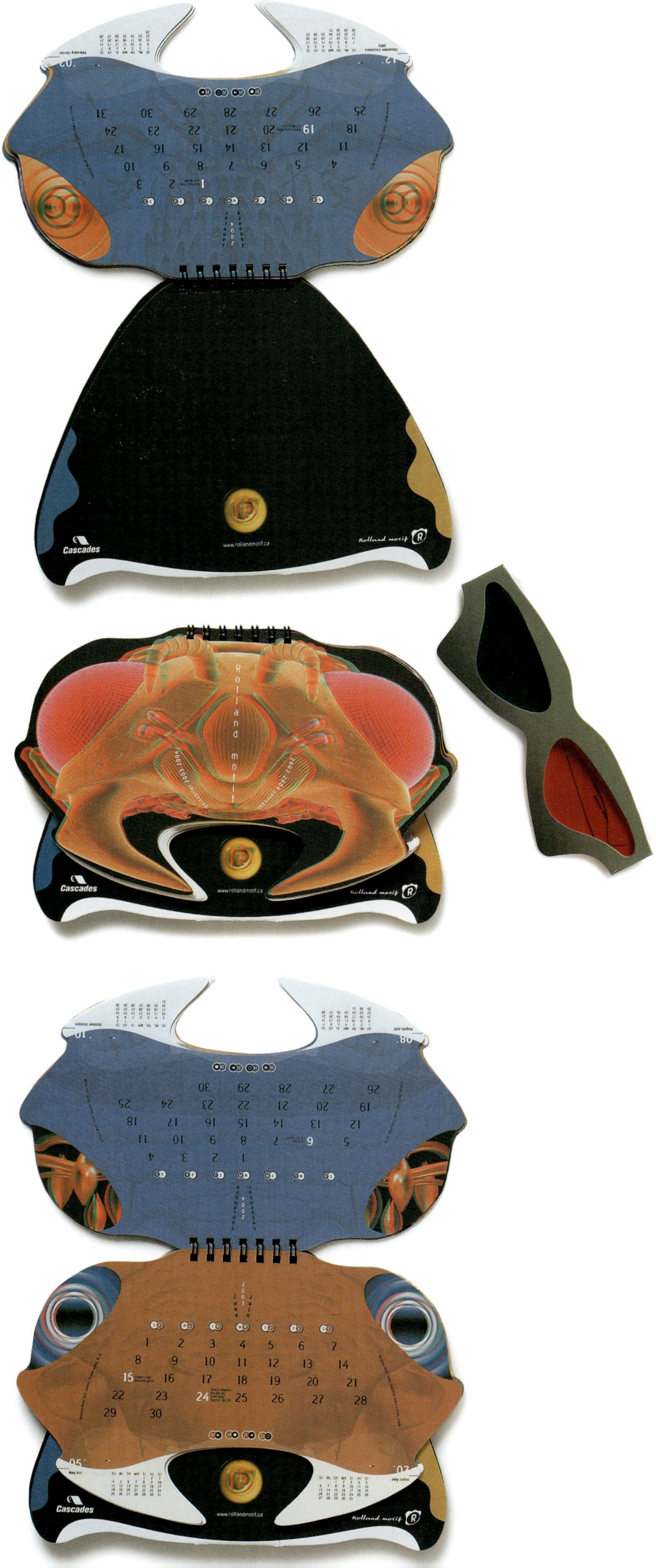

'Bug 3D' Design Firm: Epoxy Communications Creative Directors: Daniel Fortin and George Fok Art Directors: Stephanie Legault and David Kessous Designers: Stephanie Legault and David Kessous Illustrators: Gunner Hansen, Jonathan Legris and Luke McLellan Copywriters: Michelle Fairfield and Spiro Rondos Client: Cascades Groupe Papiers Fins

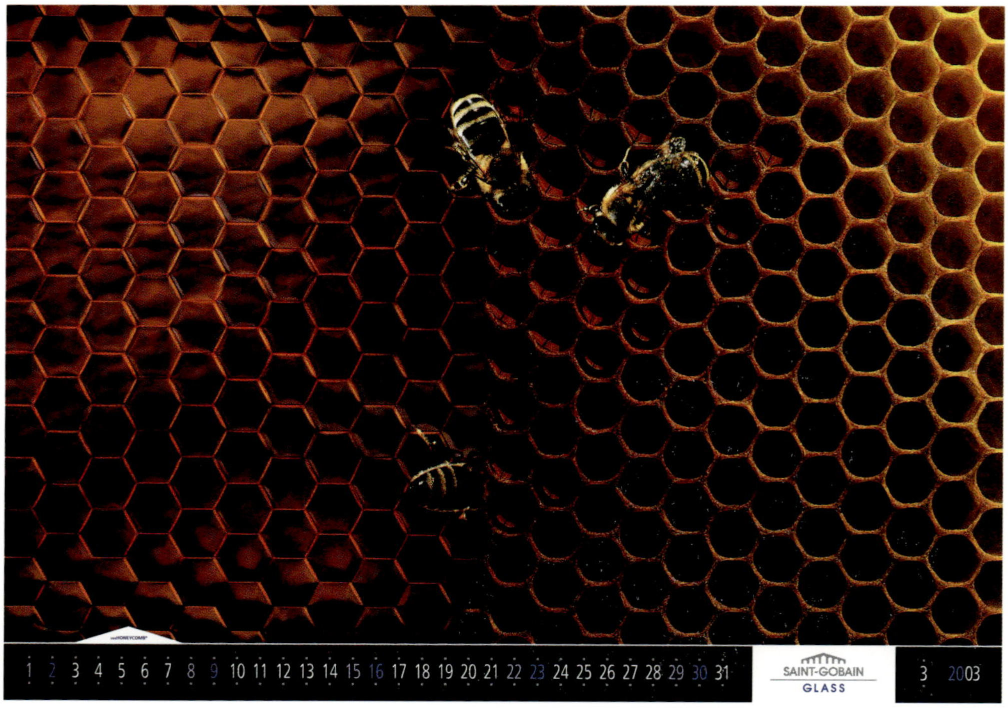

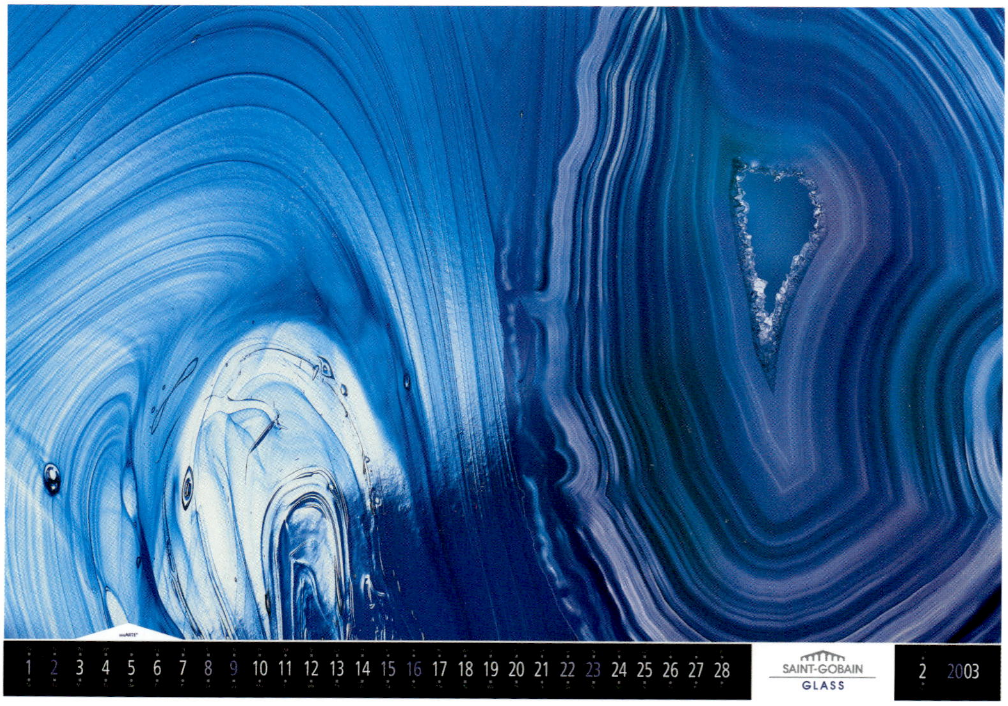

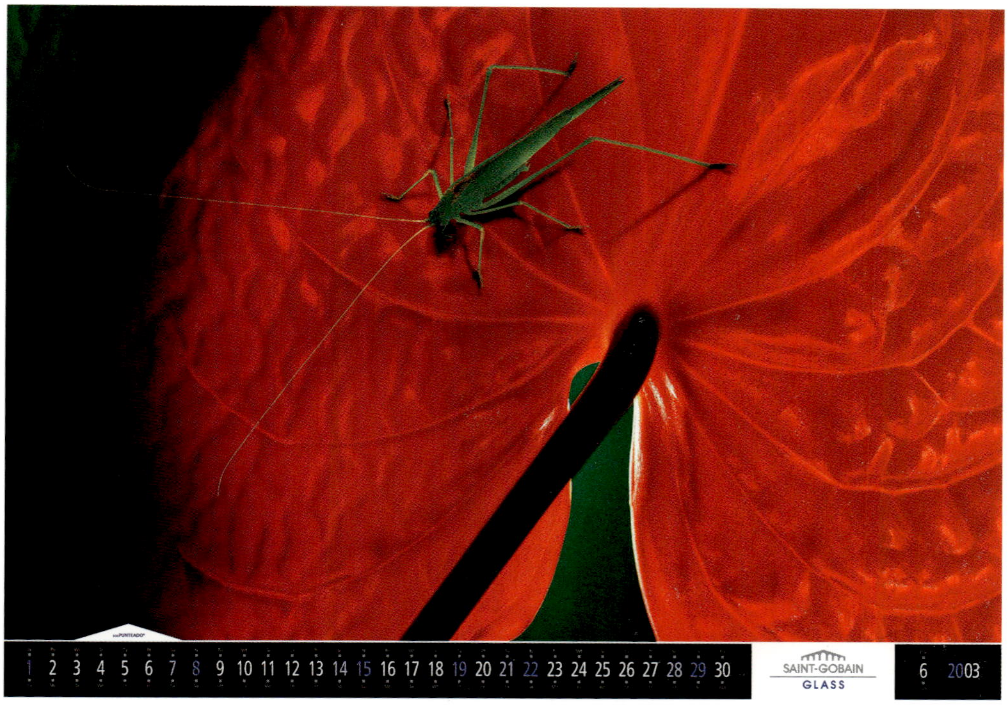

'Nature Begins, Art Directs and Usage Completes' Design Firm: Bilbo Creative Directors: Jarosław Kaczmarski and Artur Nyk Art Director: Jarosław Kaczmarski Designer: Jarosław Kaczmarski Photographers: Artur Nyk and Jarosław Kaczmarski Client: Saint-Gobain Glass (opposite page) 'Waterwheel' Design Firm: good morning inc. Art Director: Katsumi Tamura Designers: Hiroyuki Fukazu and Akira Katagiri

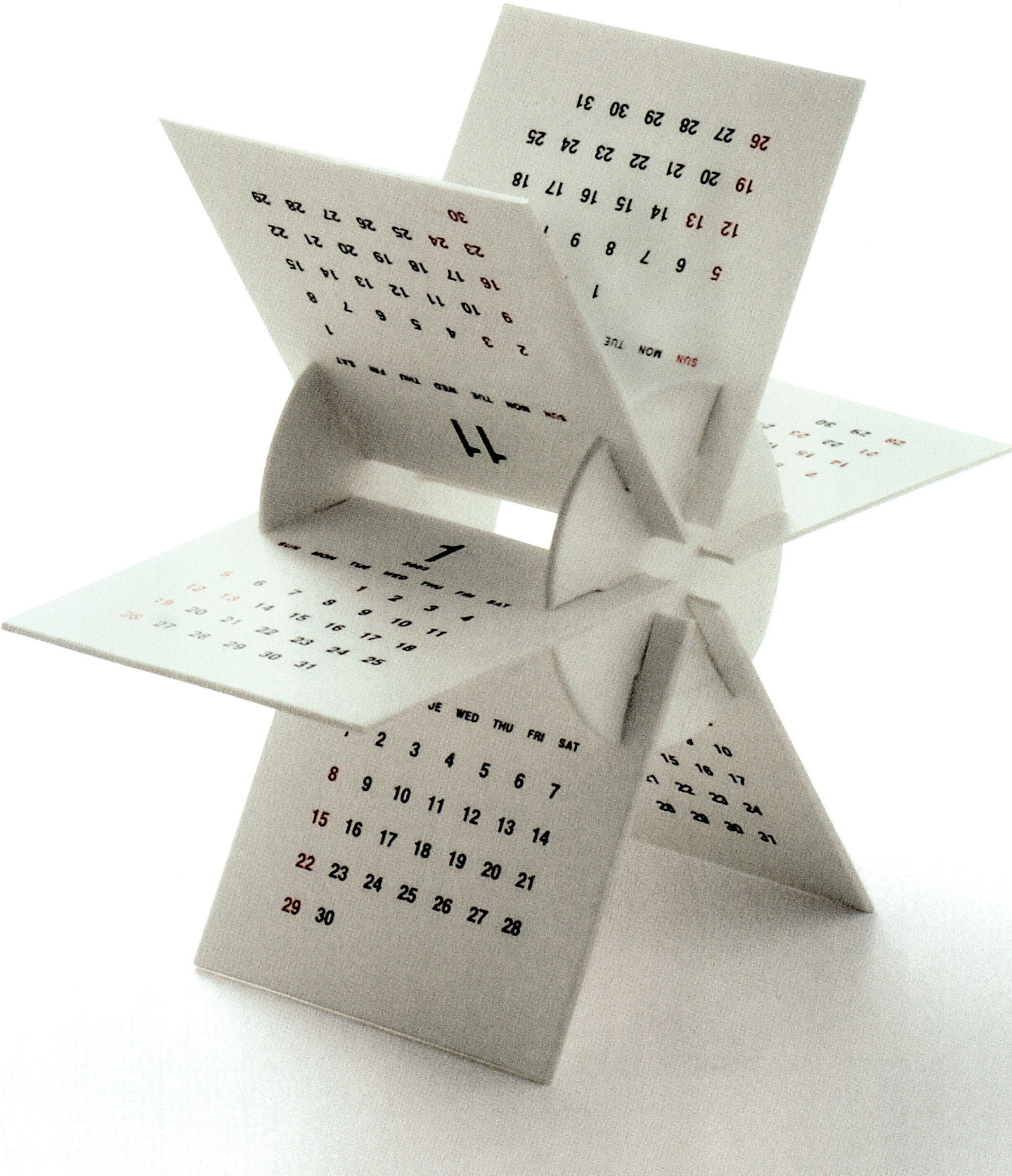
WED THU FRI SAT
2 3 4 5 6 7
8 9 10 11 12 13 14
15 16 17 18 19 20 21
22 23 24 25 26 27 28
29 30

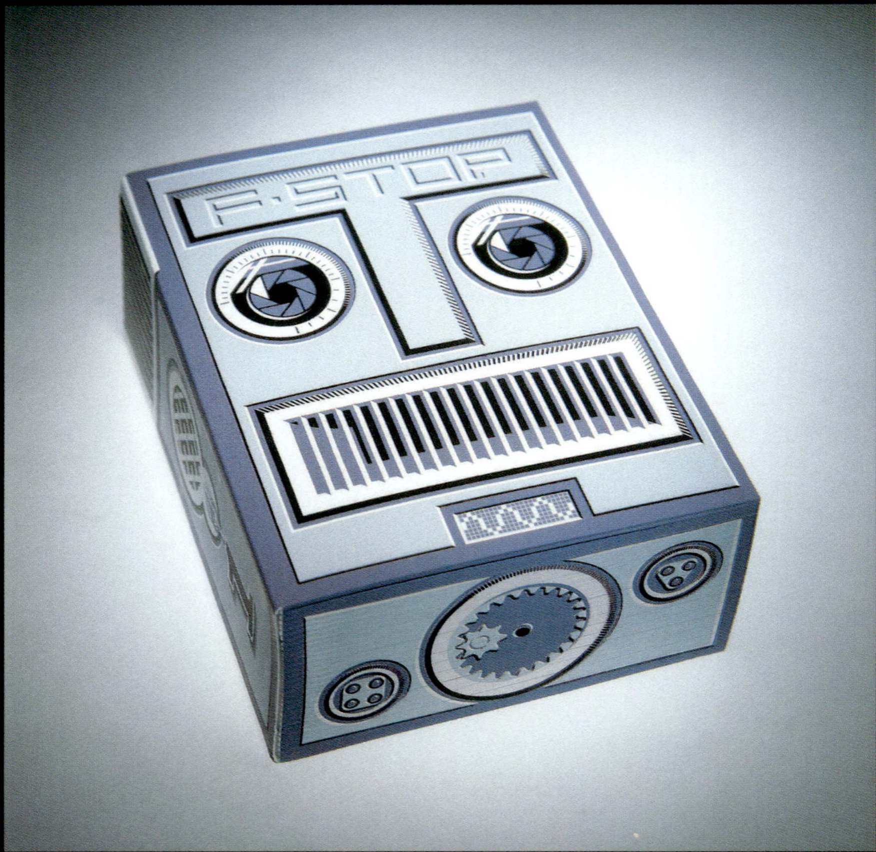

F-Stop' Design Firm: Sagmeister Inc. Creative Director: Stefan Sagmeister Art Director: Stefan Sagmeister Designer: Matthias Ernstberger Illustrator: Matthias Ernstberger Copywriter: Eric Spiekermann

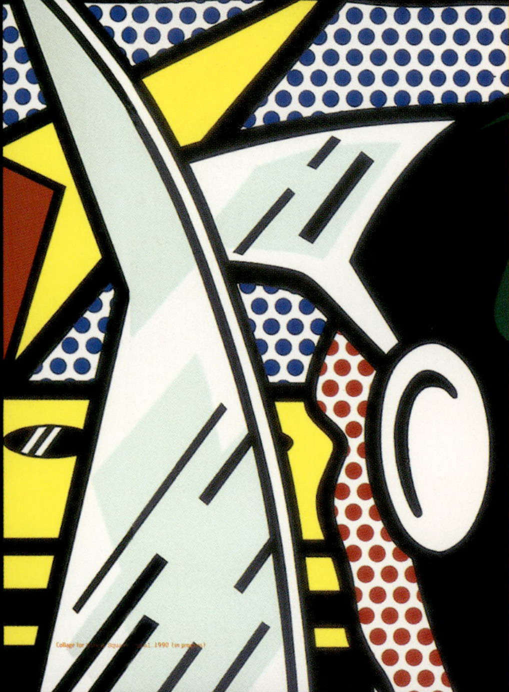

Collage for Times Square Mural, 1990 (in progress)

Roy Lichtenstein

Times Square Mural

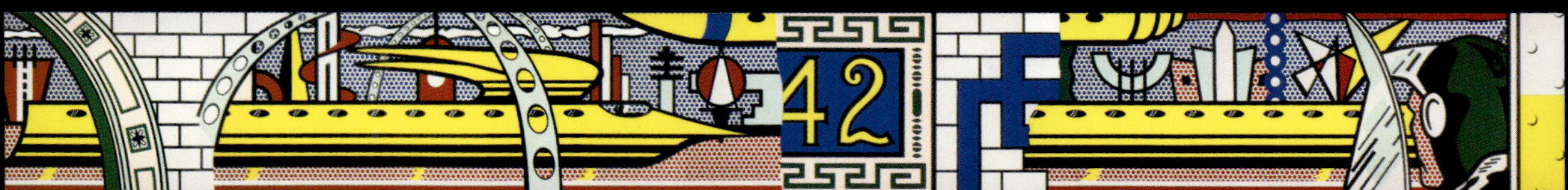

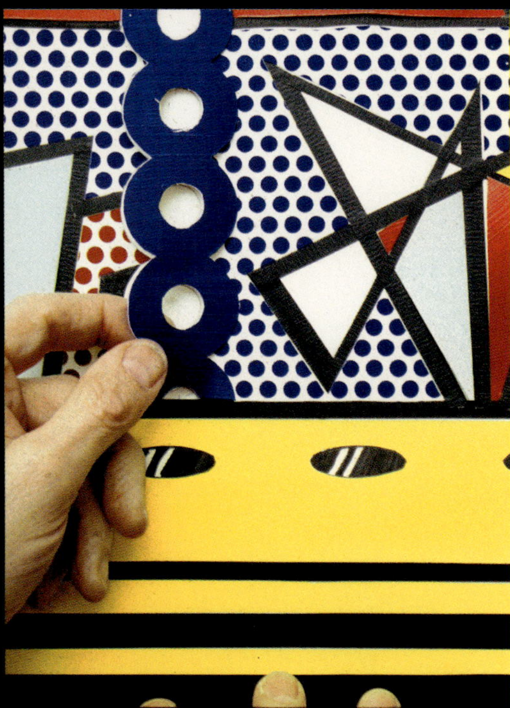

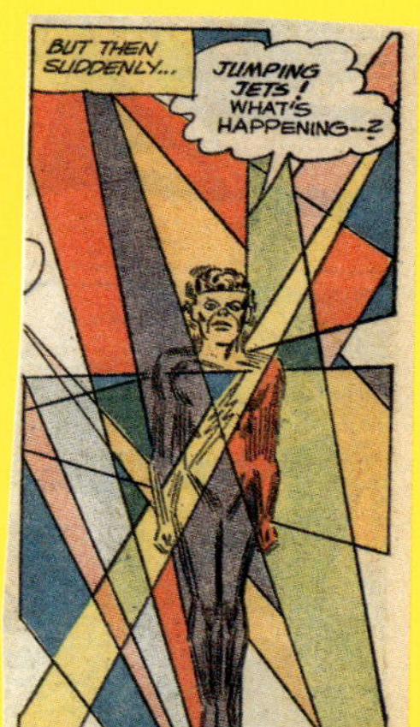

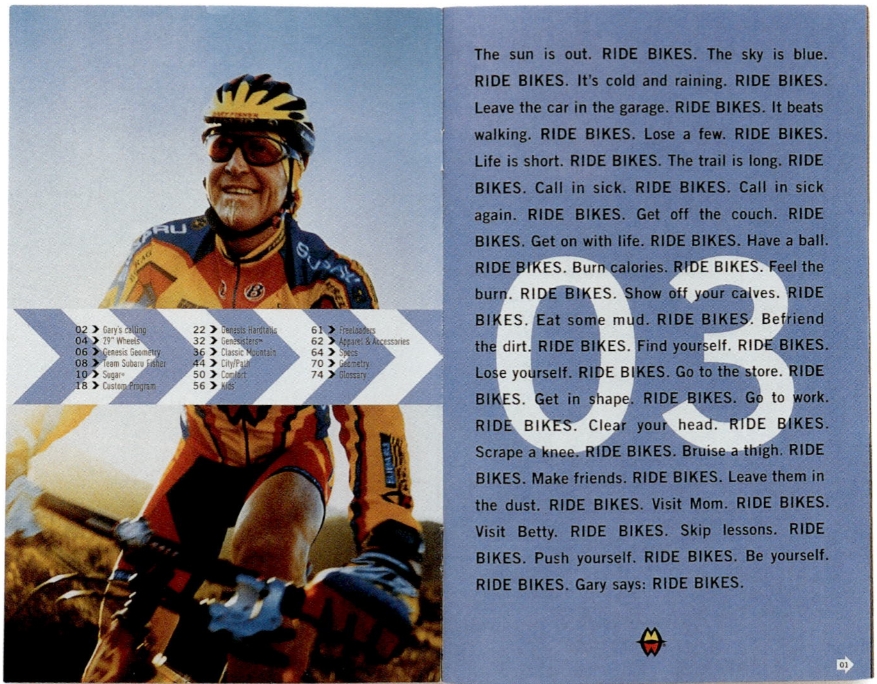

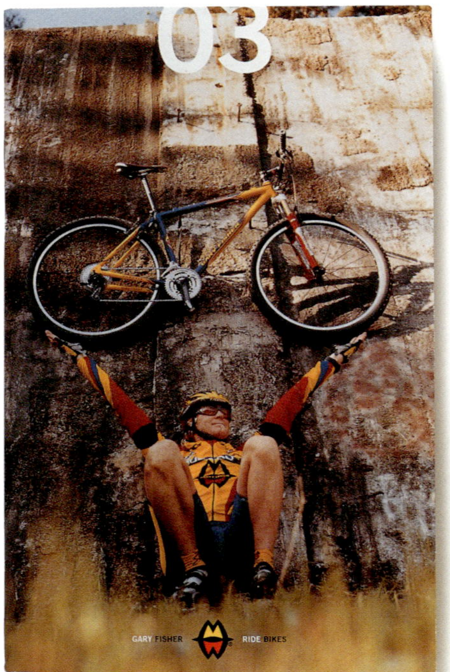

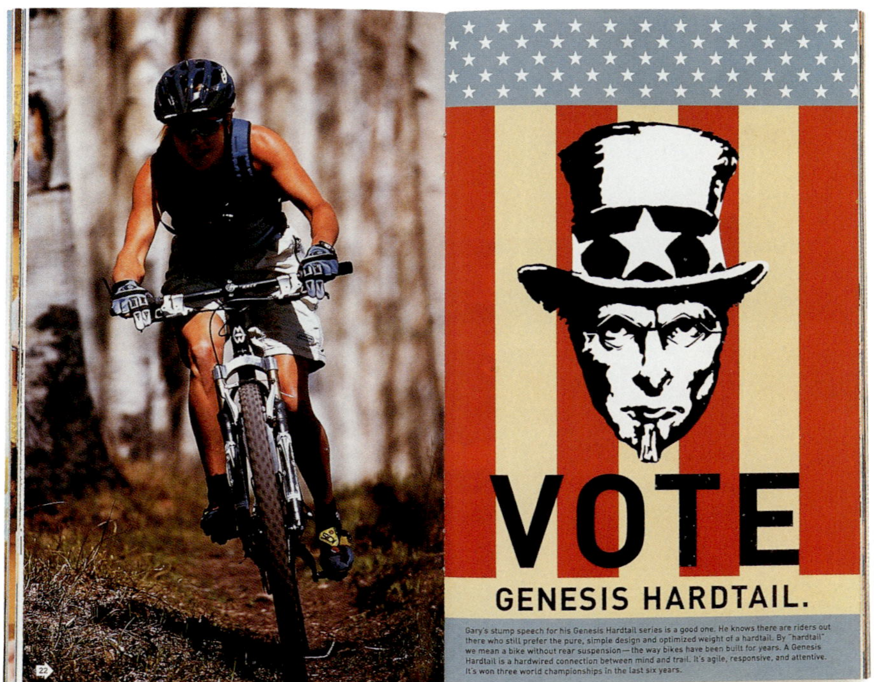

(this spread) Design Firm: Planet Propaganda Creative Director: Dana Lytle Designer: Michael Byzewski Copywriter: James Breen Client: Gary Fisher Bikes

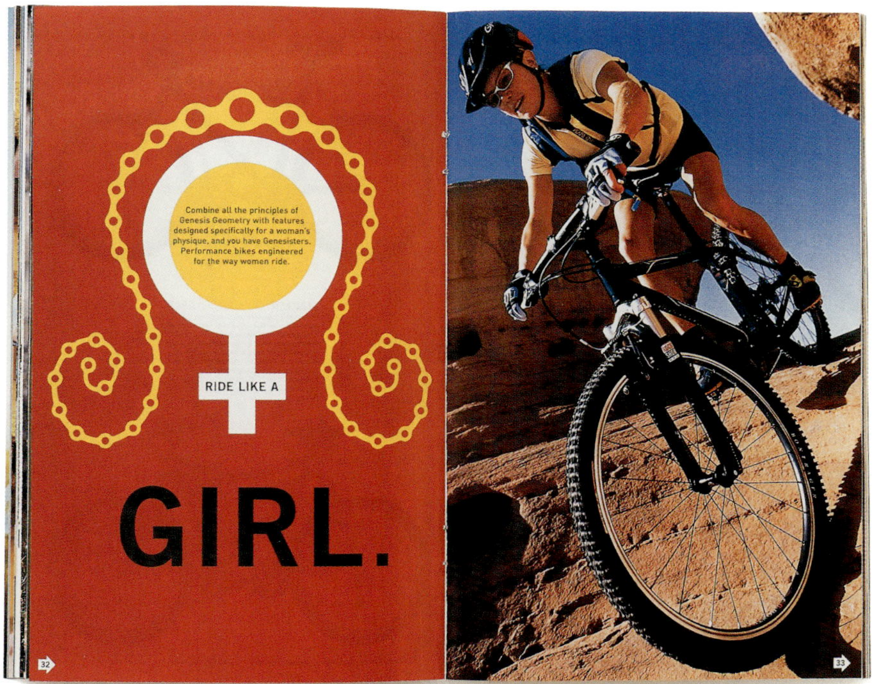
Combine all the principles of Genesis Geometry with features designed specifically for a woman's physique, and you have Genesisters. Performance bikes engineered for the way women ride.
RIDE LIKE A
GIRL.
32
33

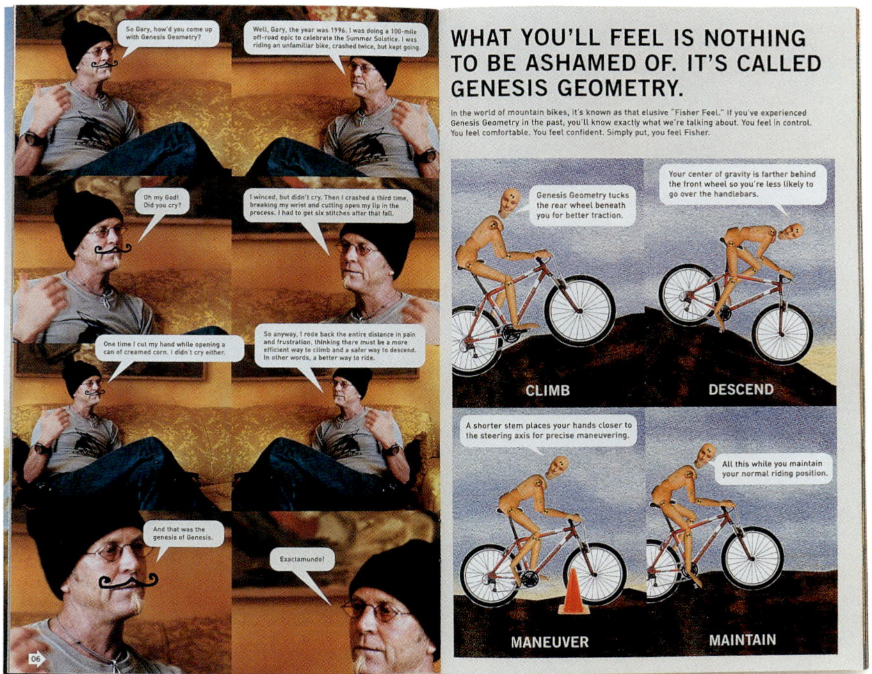
So Gary, how'd you come up with Genesis Geometry?
Well, Gary, the year was 1996. I was doing a 100-mile off-road epic to celebrate the Summer Solstice. I was riding an unfamiliar bike, crashed twice, but kept going.
Oh my God! Did you cry?
I winced, but didn't cry. Then I crashed a third time, breaking my wrist and cutting open my lip in the process. I had to get six stitches after that fall.
One time I cut my hand while opening a can of creamed corn. I didn't cry either.
So anyway, I rode back the entire distance in pain and frustration, thinking there must be a more efficient way to climb and a safer way to descend. In other words, a better way to ride.
And that was the genesis of Genesis.
Exactamundo!
06
WHAT YOU'LL FEEL IS NOTHING TO BE ASHAMED OF. IT'S CALLED GENESIS GEOMETRY.
In the world of mountain bikes, it's known as that elusive "Fisher Feel." If you've experienced Genesis Geometry in the past, you'll know exactly what we're talking about. You feel in control. You feel comfortable. You feel confident. Simply put, you feel Fisher.
Genesis Geometry tucks the rear wheel beneath you for better traction.
Your center of gravity is farther behind the front wheel so you're less likely to go over the handlebars.
CLIMB
DESCEND
A shorter stem places your hands closer to the steering axis for precise maneuvering.
All this while you maintain your normal riding position.
MANEUVER
MAINTAIN

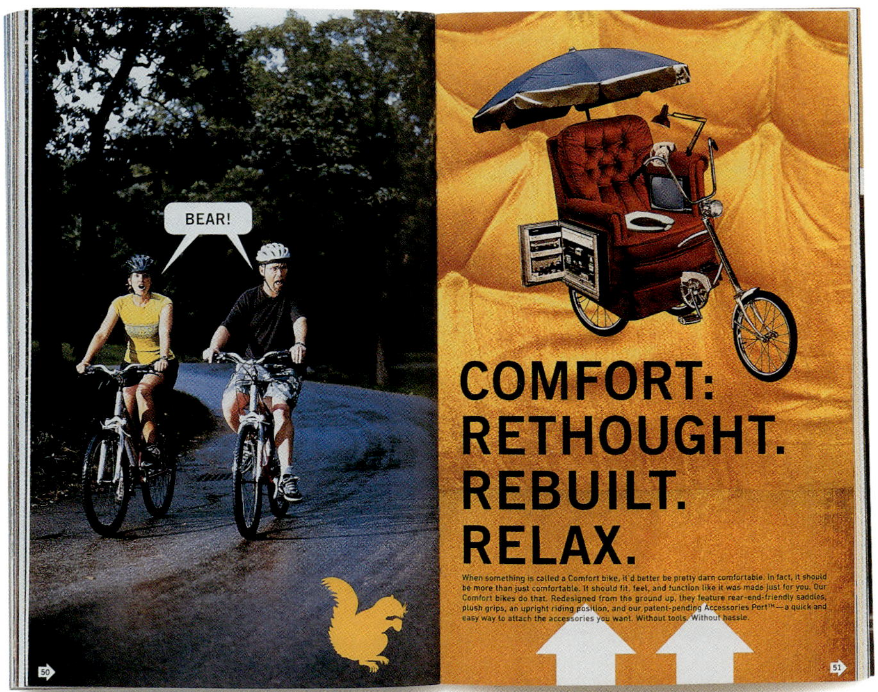
BEAR!
COMFORT: RETHOUGHT. REBUILT. RELAX.
When something is called a Comfort bike, it'd better be pretty darn comfortable. In fact, it should be more than just comfortable. It should fit, feel, and function like it was made just for you. Our Comfort bikes do that. Redesigned from the ground up, they feature rear-end-friendly saddles, plush grips, an upright riding position, and our patent-pending Accessories Port™—a quick and easy way to attach the accessories you want. Without tools. Without hassle.
50
51

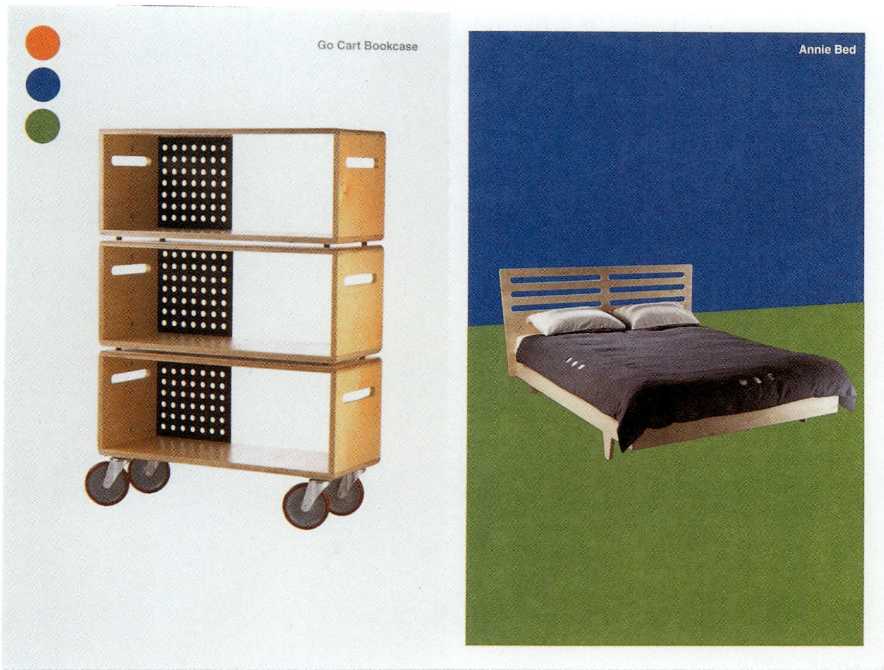

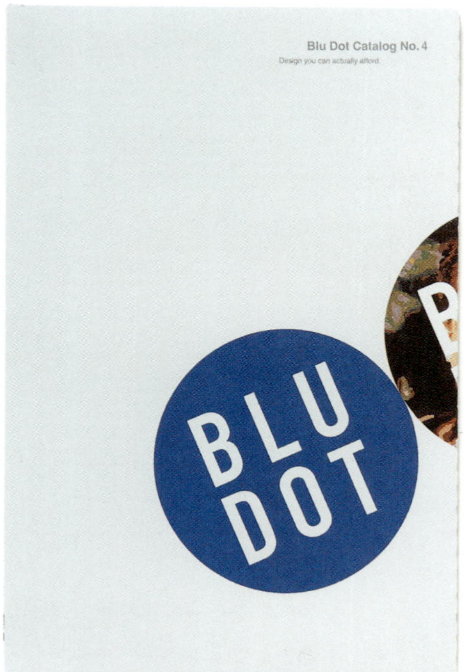

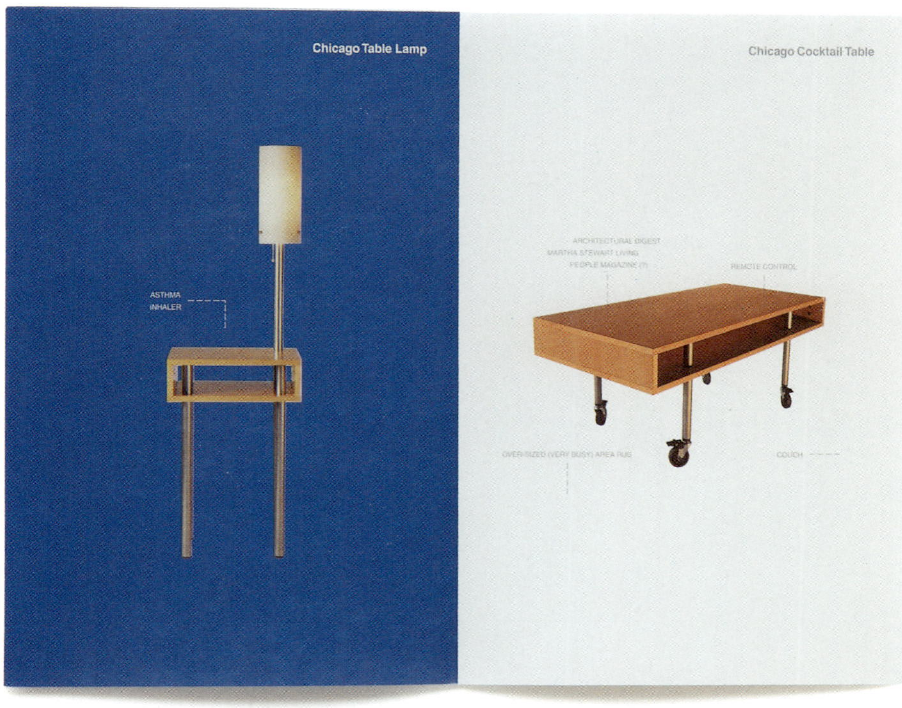

(this spread) Design Firm: Wink Creative Directors: Richard Boynton and Scott Thares Designers: Richard Boynton and Scott Thares Photographer: Visko Hatfield Illustrators: Richard Boynton and Scott Thares Copywriters: Richard Boynton and Scott Thares Client: Blu Dot

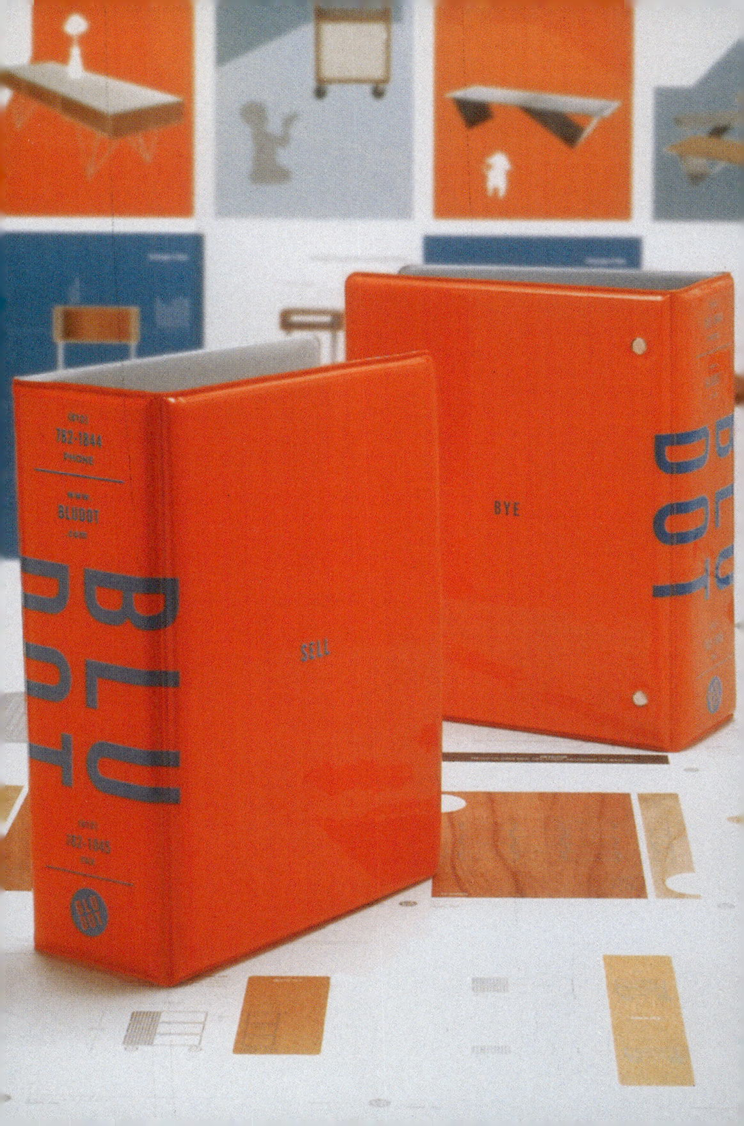
BLU
DOT
SELL
BYE
BLU
DOT

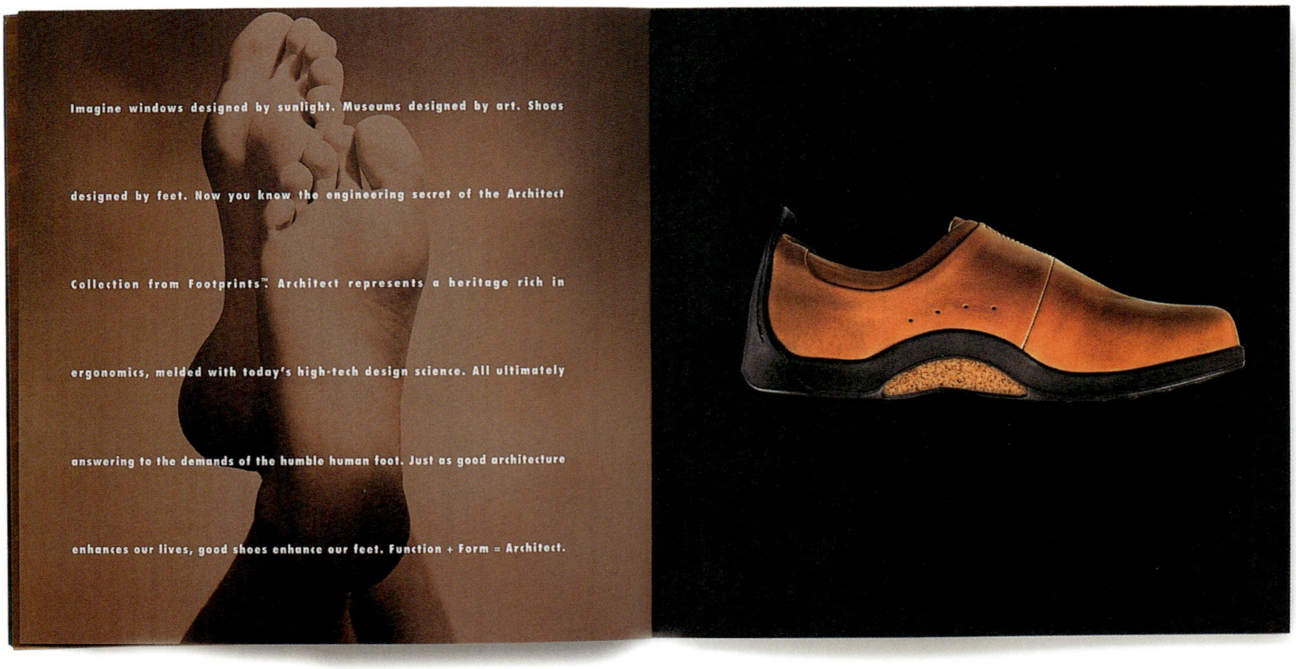

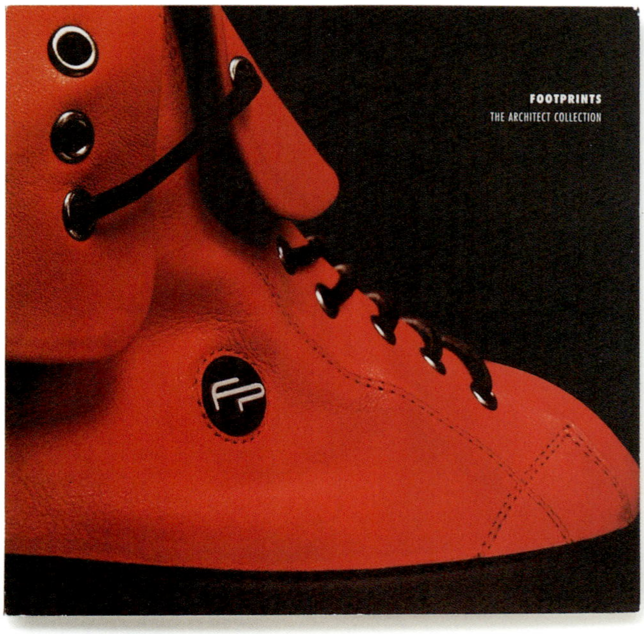

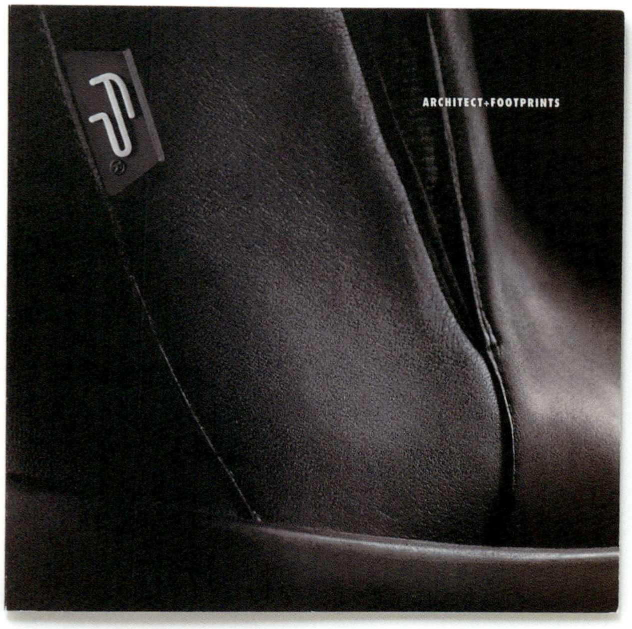

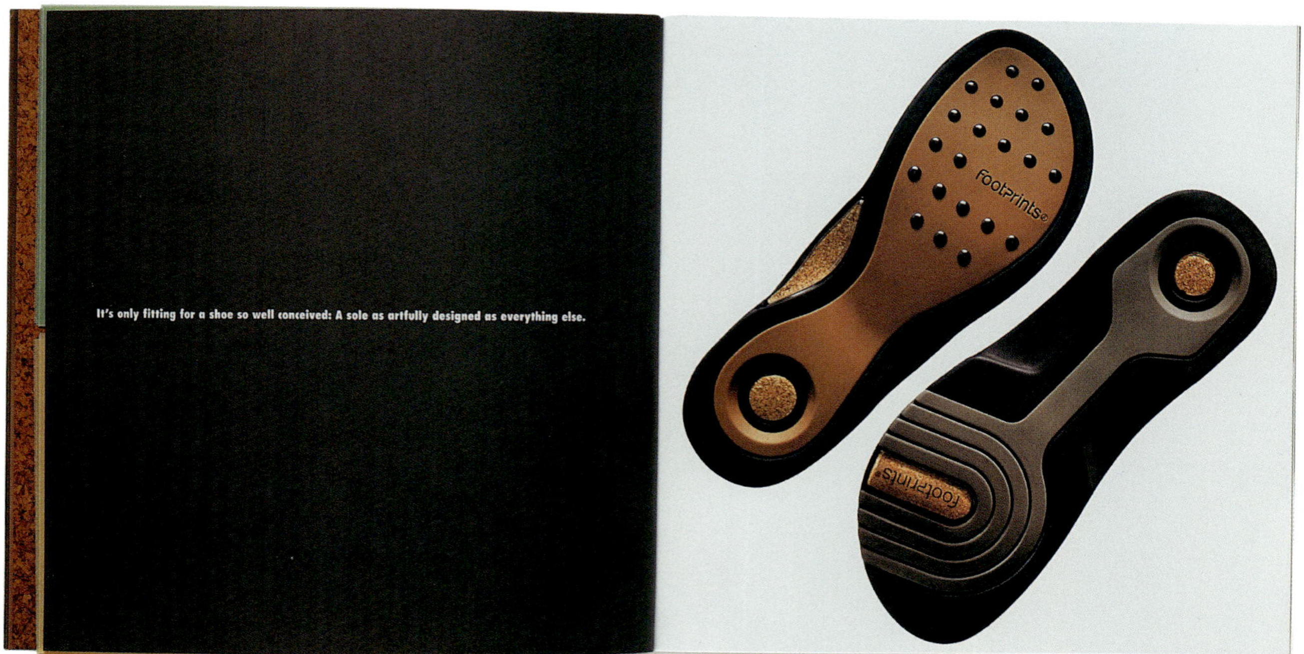

'Architect Collection 2' Creative Director: Steve Fehler Art Director: Richard Garnas Designer: Richard Garnas Photographers: Sandbox and David Roth Copywriter: Carol Bousson Client: Birkenstock

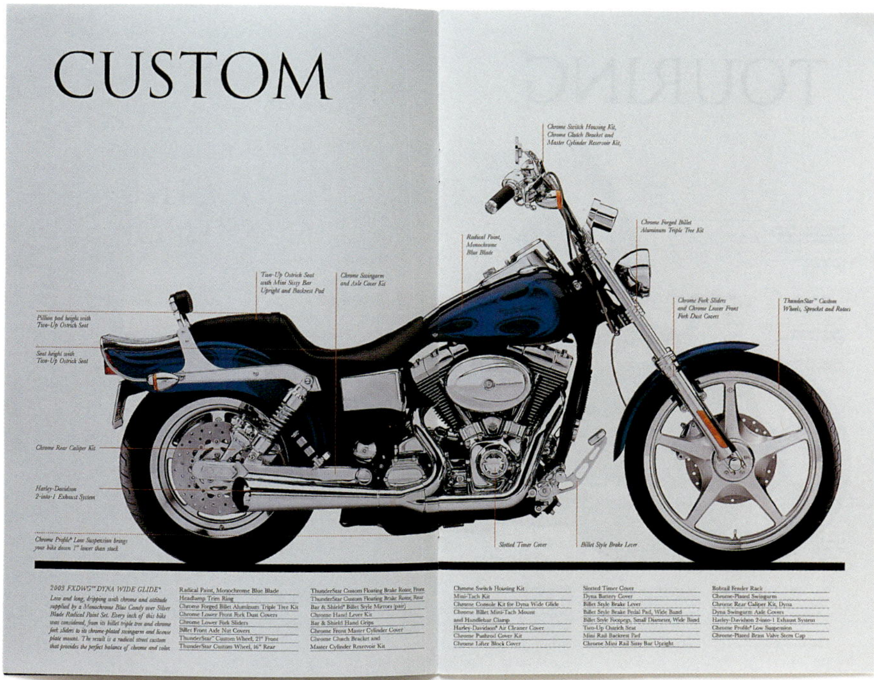

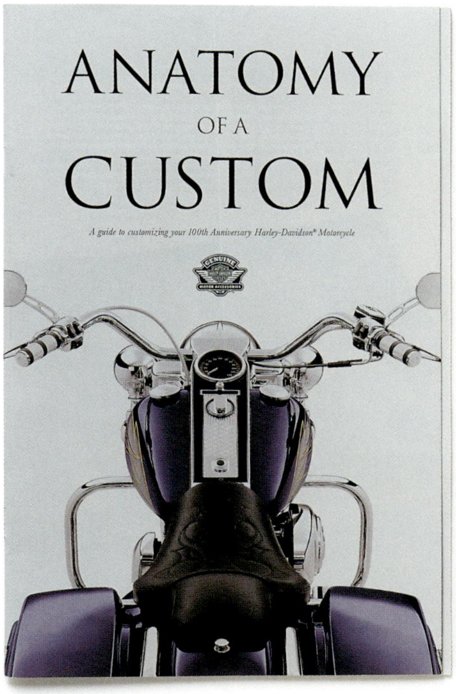

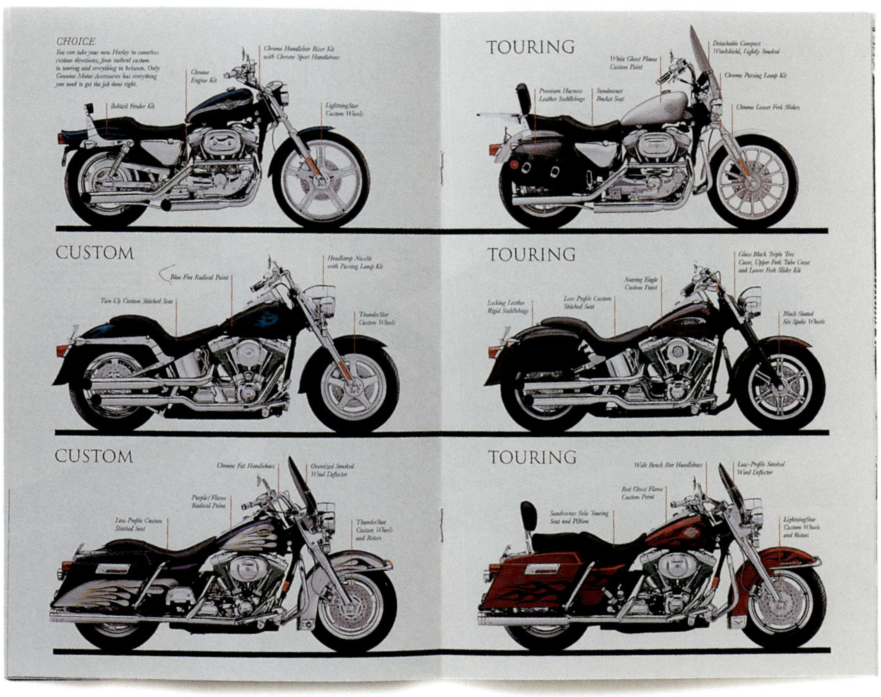

'Anatomy of a Custom' Design Firm: 50,000 Feet Inc. Creative Directors: Michael Petersen, Jack Sichterman and Ken Fox
Designers: Michael Petersen and Ken Fox Photographers: Phil Greatorex and Mid Coast Studio Copywriter: Jack Sichterman Client: Harley-Davidson

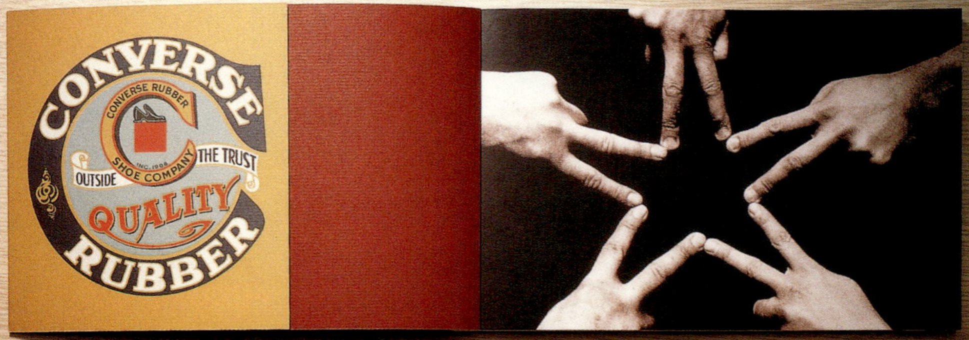
CONVERSE
CONVERSE RUBBER
INC. 1908
SHOE COMPANY
OUTSIDE
THE TRUST
QUALITY
RUBBER

BUS
51

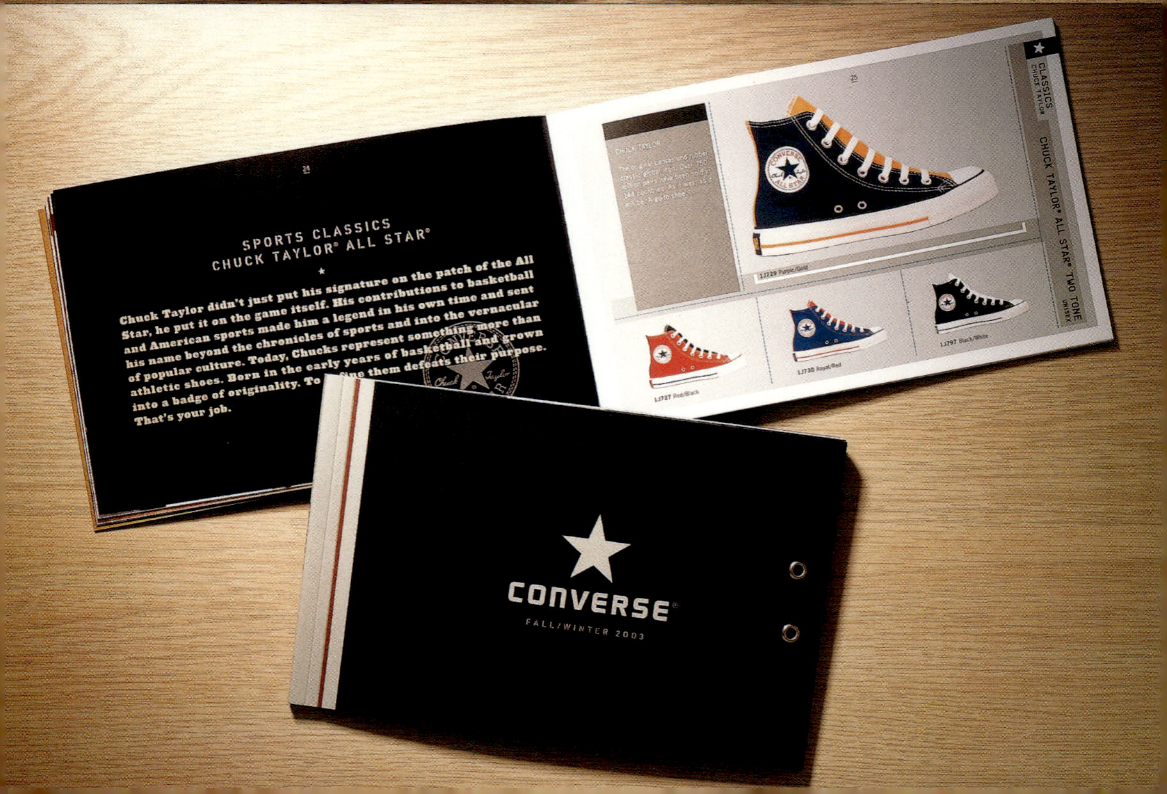
24
SPORTS CLASSICS
CHUCK TAYLOR® ALL STAR®
Chuck Taylor didn't just put his signature on the patch of the All
Star, he put it on the game itself. His contributions to basketball
and American sports made him a legend in his own time and sent
his name beyond the chronicles of sports and into the vernacular
of popular culture. Today, Chucks represent something more than
athletic shoes. Born in the early years of basketball and grown
into a badge of originality. To
them defeats their purpose.
That's your job.
25
CLASSICS
CHUCK TAYLOR®
CHUCK TAYLOR
CHUCK TAYLOR® ALL STAR® TWO TONE
UNISEX
CONVERSE ALL STAR
1J729 Purple/Gold
1J727 Red/Black
1J730 Royal/Red
1J797 Black/White
CONVERSE®
FALL/WINTER 2003

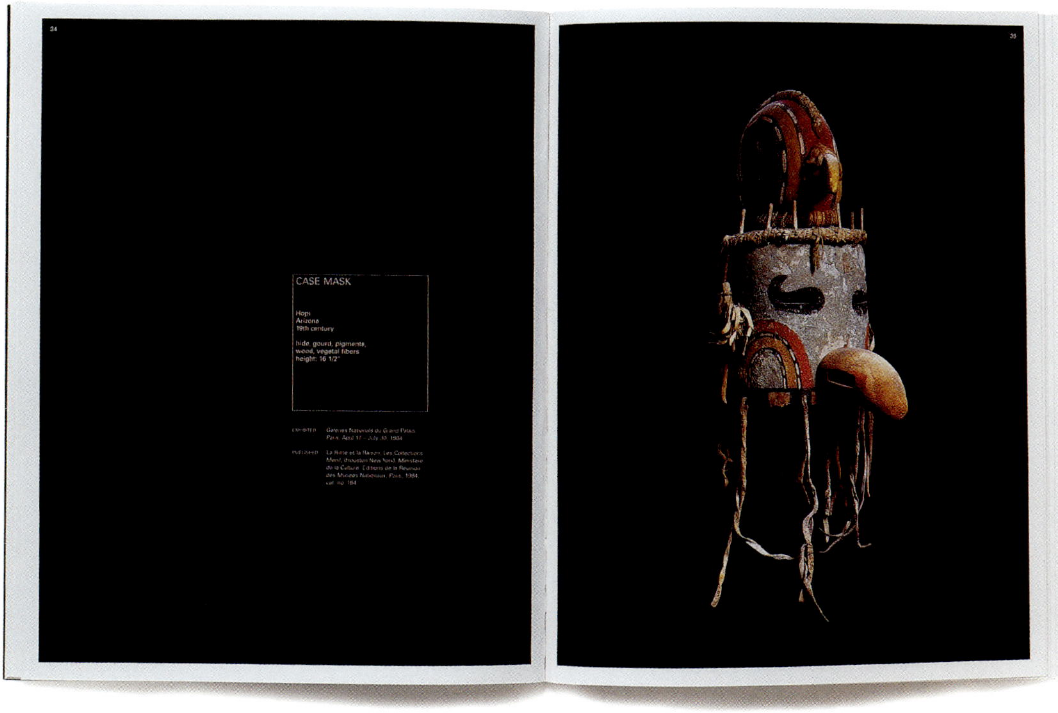

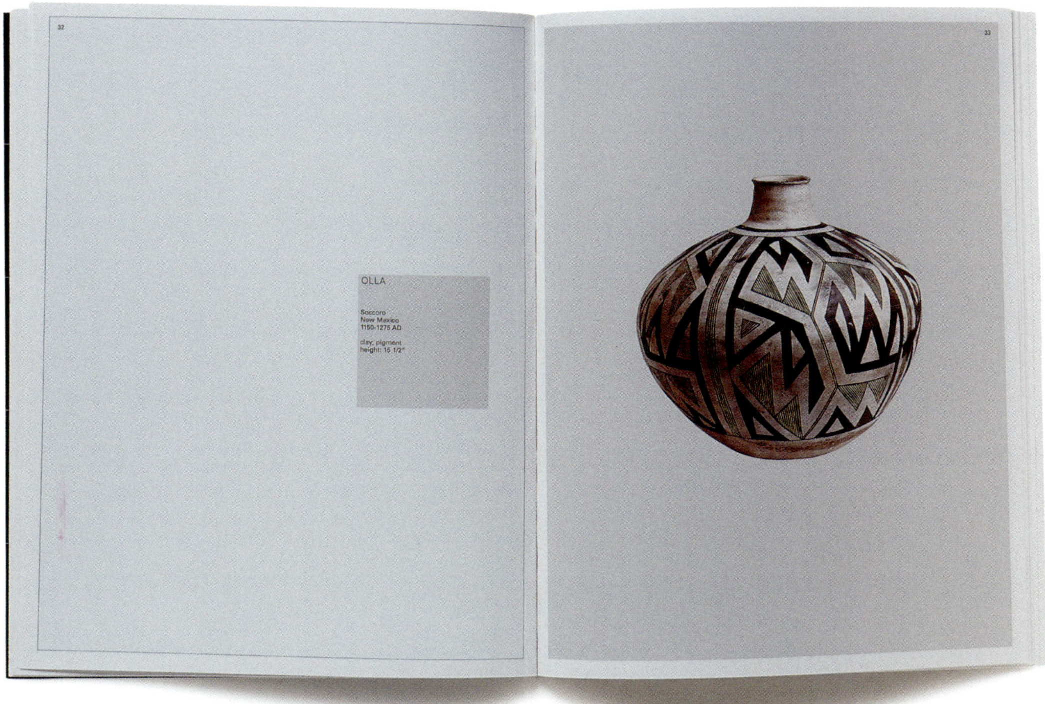

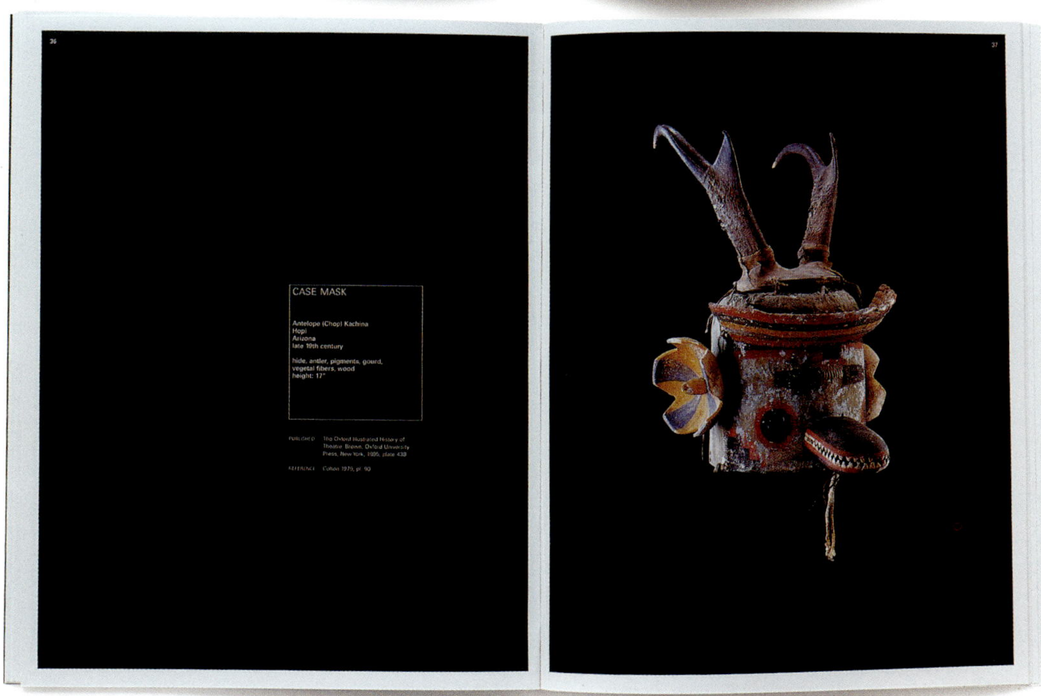

Design Firm: Hambly & Woolley Inc. Creative Director: Barb Wolley Designer: Barb Woolley Photographers: Frank Tancredi and John Bigelo Taylor Client: Donald Ellis Gallery

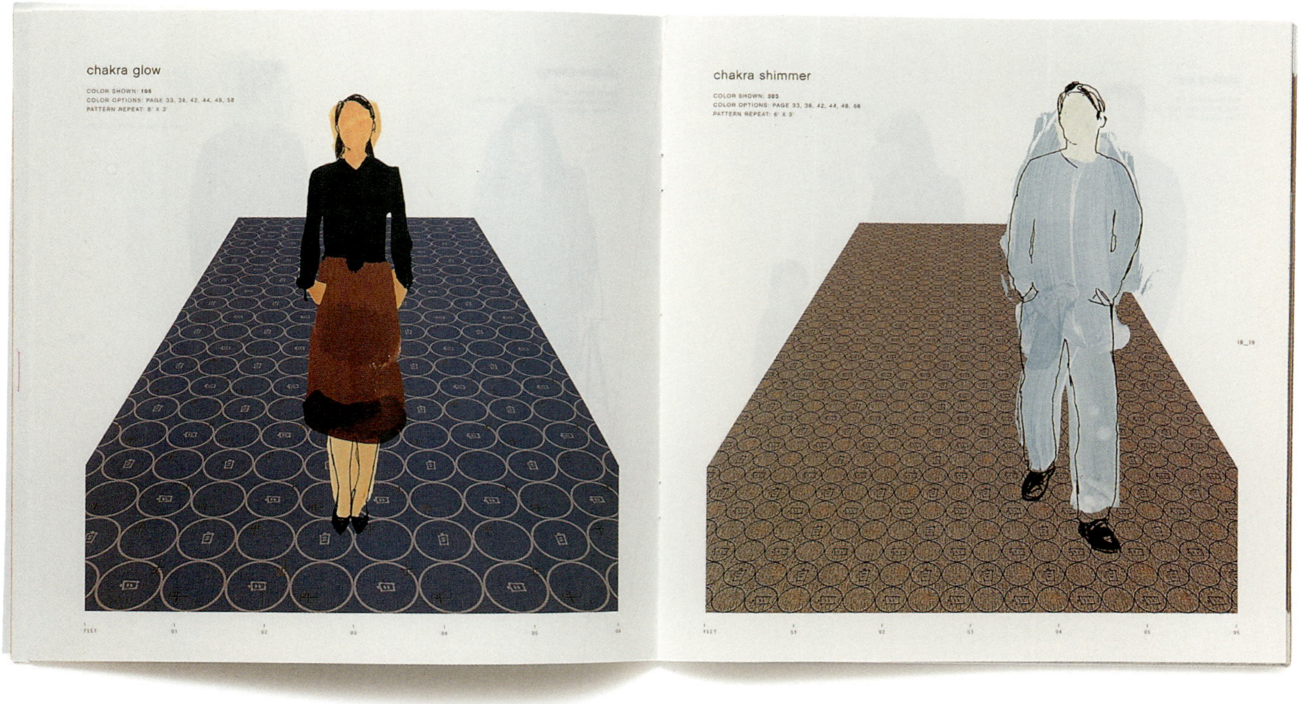

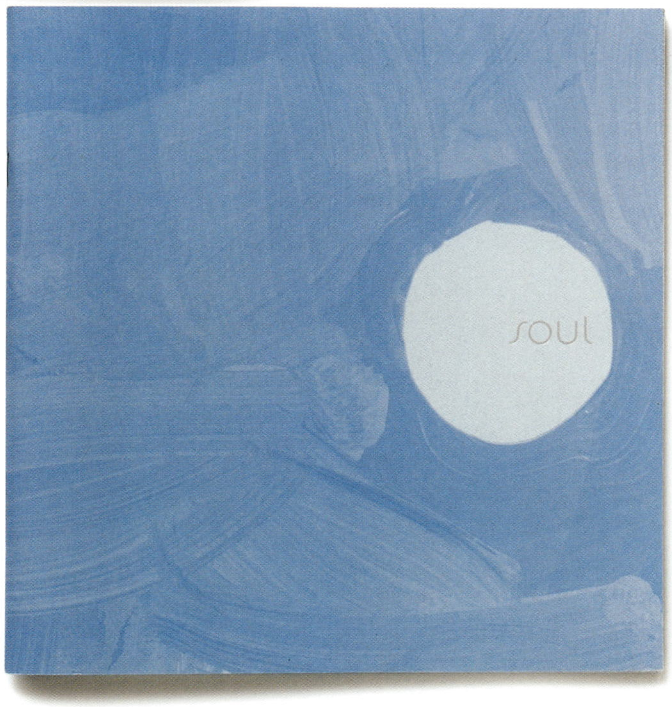

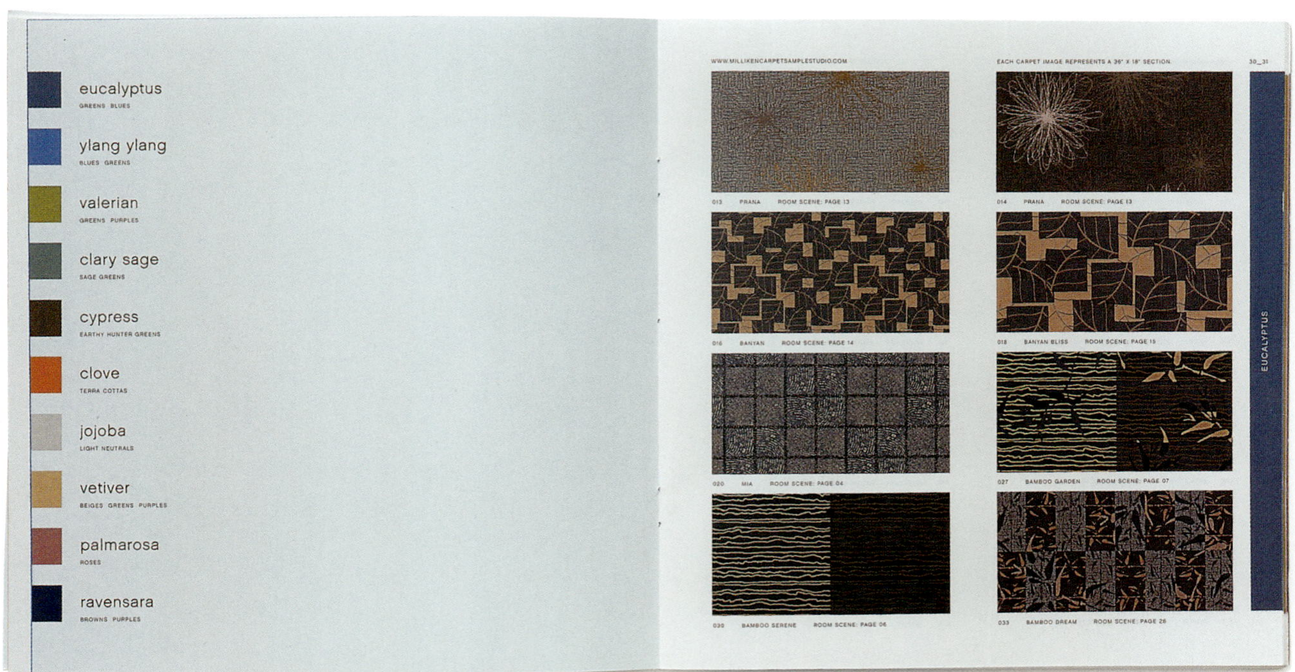

'Soul' Design Firm: Iconologic Designer: Lionel Ferreira Illustrator: Michael Gillette Copywriter: Juliet D'ambrosio Client: Milliken Carpet

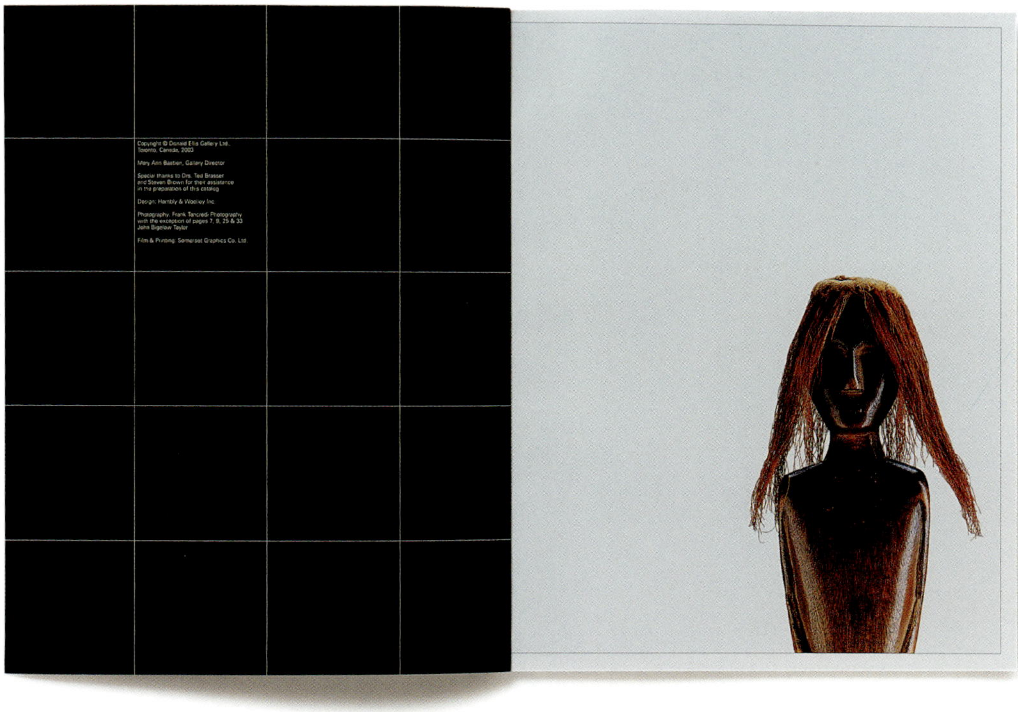

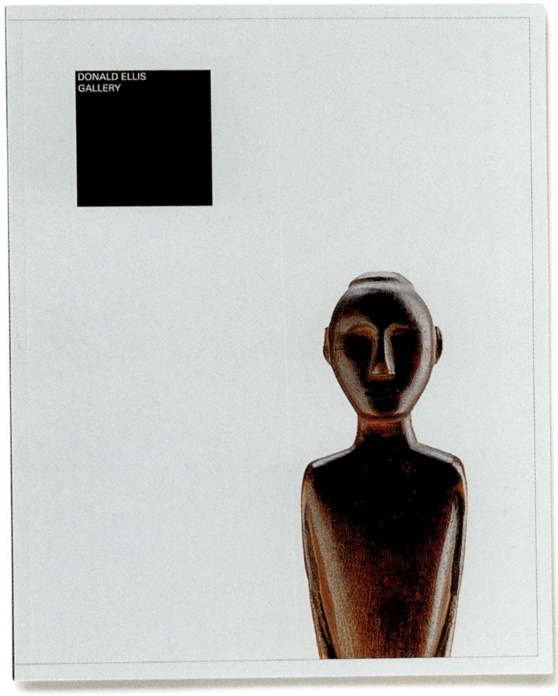

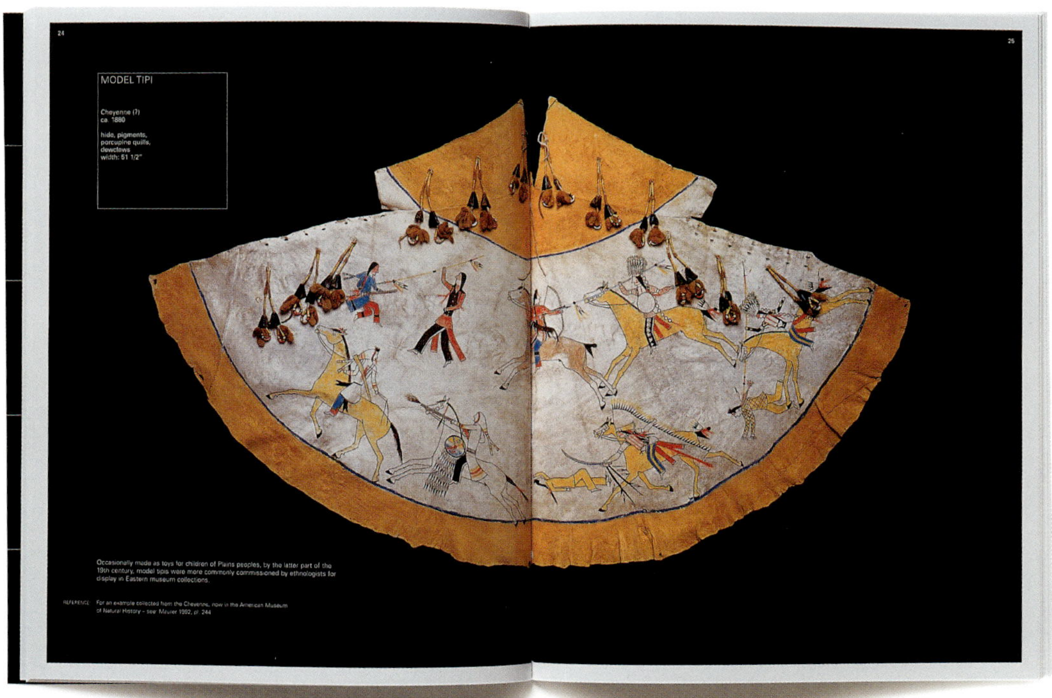

Design Firm: Hambly & Woolley Inc. Creative Director: Barb Woolley Designer: Barb Wolley Photographers: Frank Tancredi and John Bigelo Taylor Client: Donald Ellis Gallery

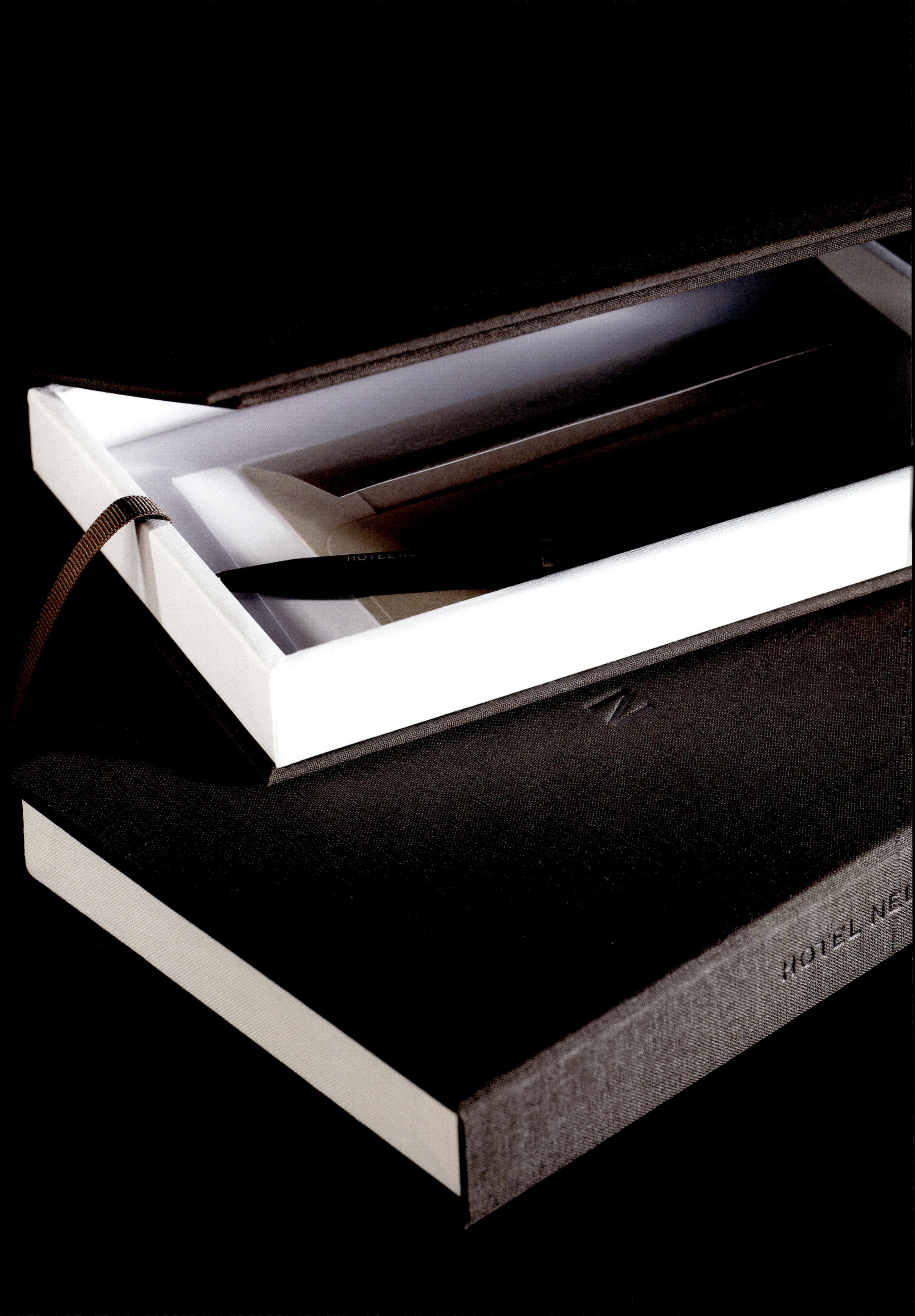

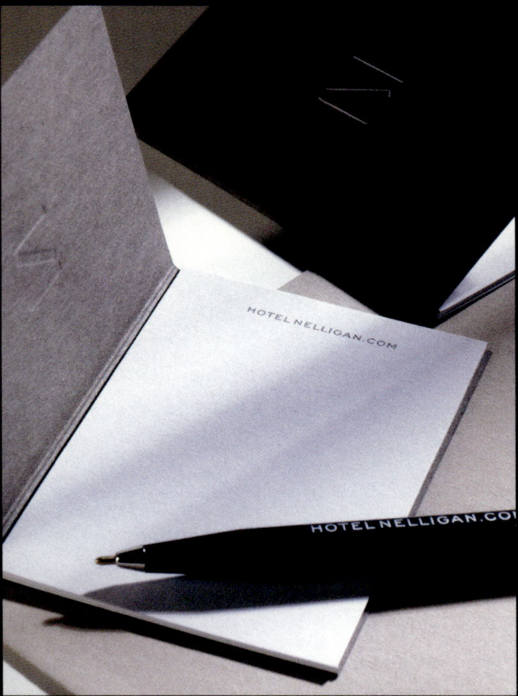

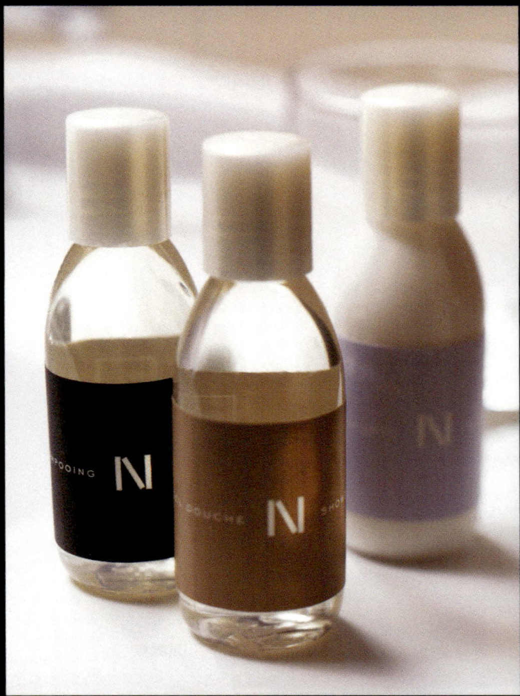

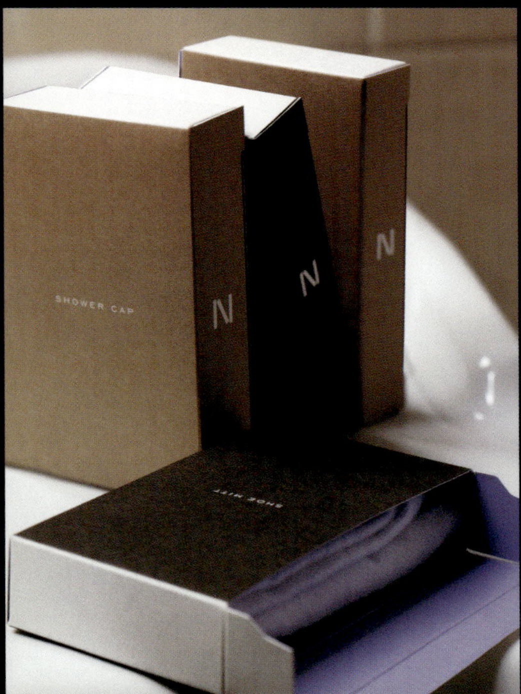

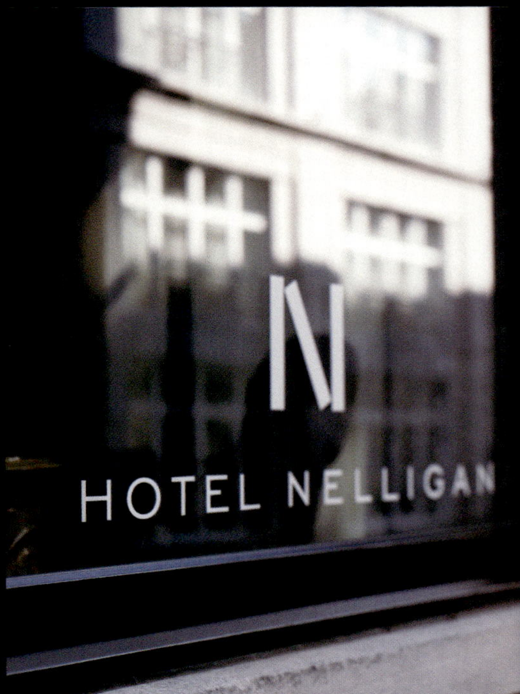

pread) Design Firm: Paprika Creative Director: Louis Gagnon Art Director: Louis Gagnon Designer: René Clément Photographer: Michel Touchette Client: Hotel NelliganDesigners Association Inc.

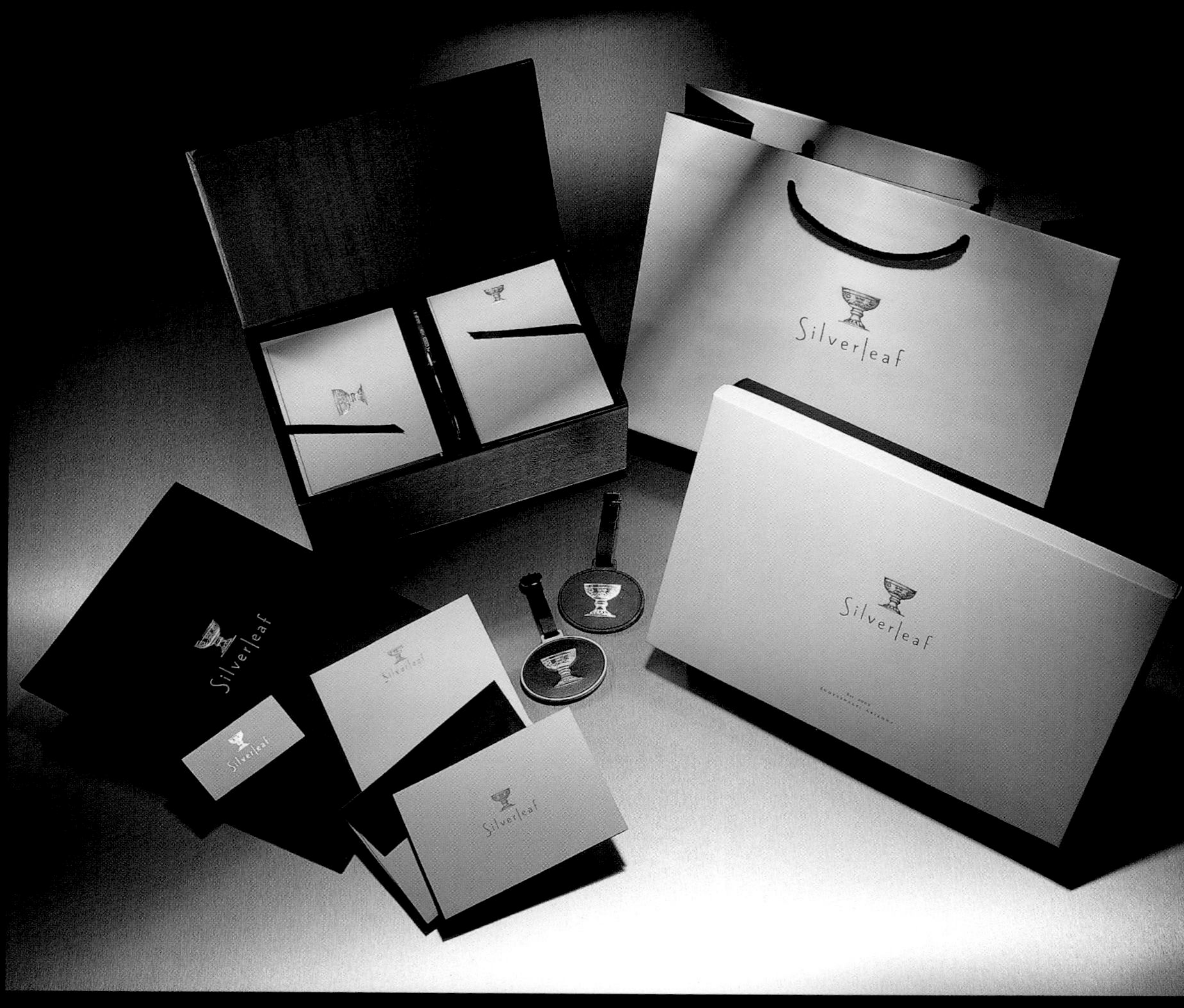

'Silverleaf Corporate Identity' Design Firm: SHR Perceptual Management Creative Director: Barry Shepard Art Director: Miles E. Abernethy Designer: Brad Jones Illustrator: Robert Case Printer: Ponté Client: DMB Realty

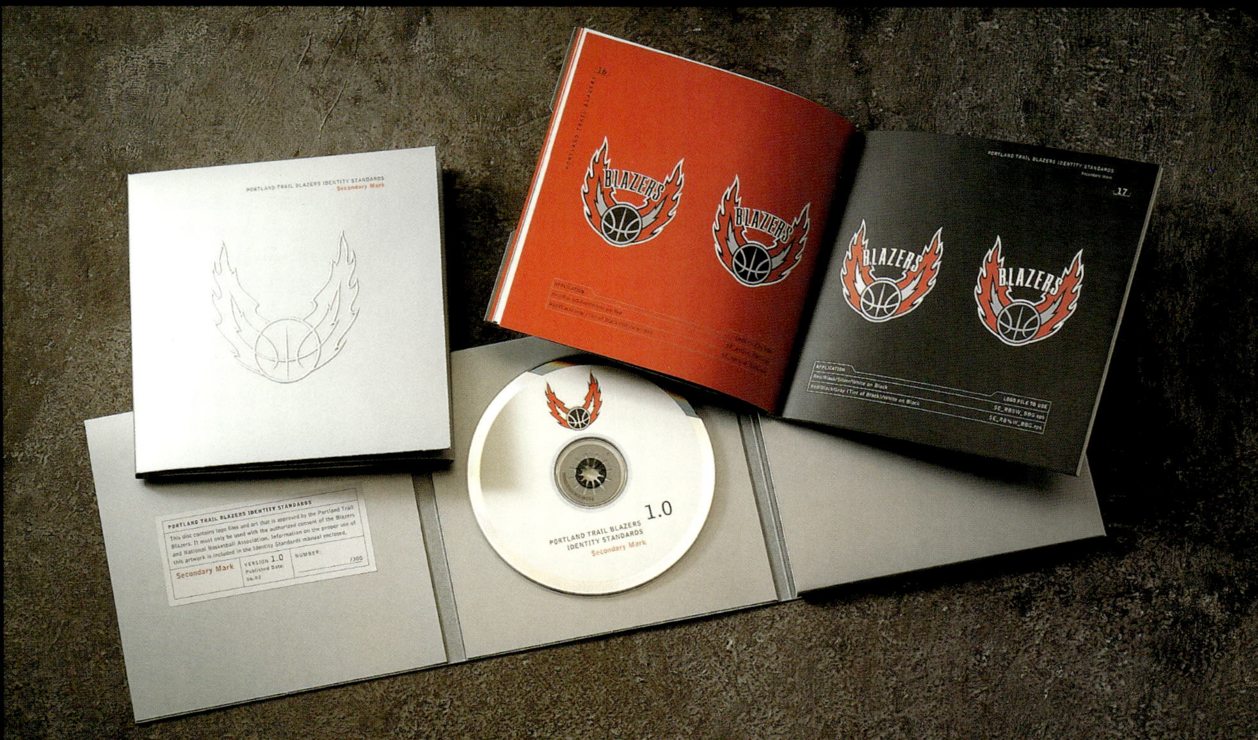

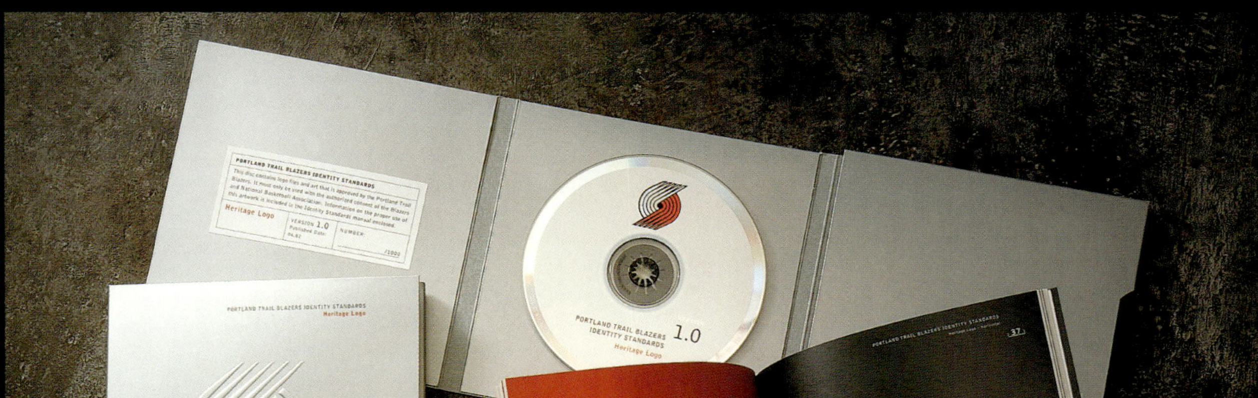

Sandstrom Design Creative Director: Steve Sandstrom Art Director: Steve Sandstrom Designers: Steve Sandstrom and James Parker Illustrator: James Parker Copywriter: Neil Webster Client: Portland Trailblazers

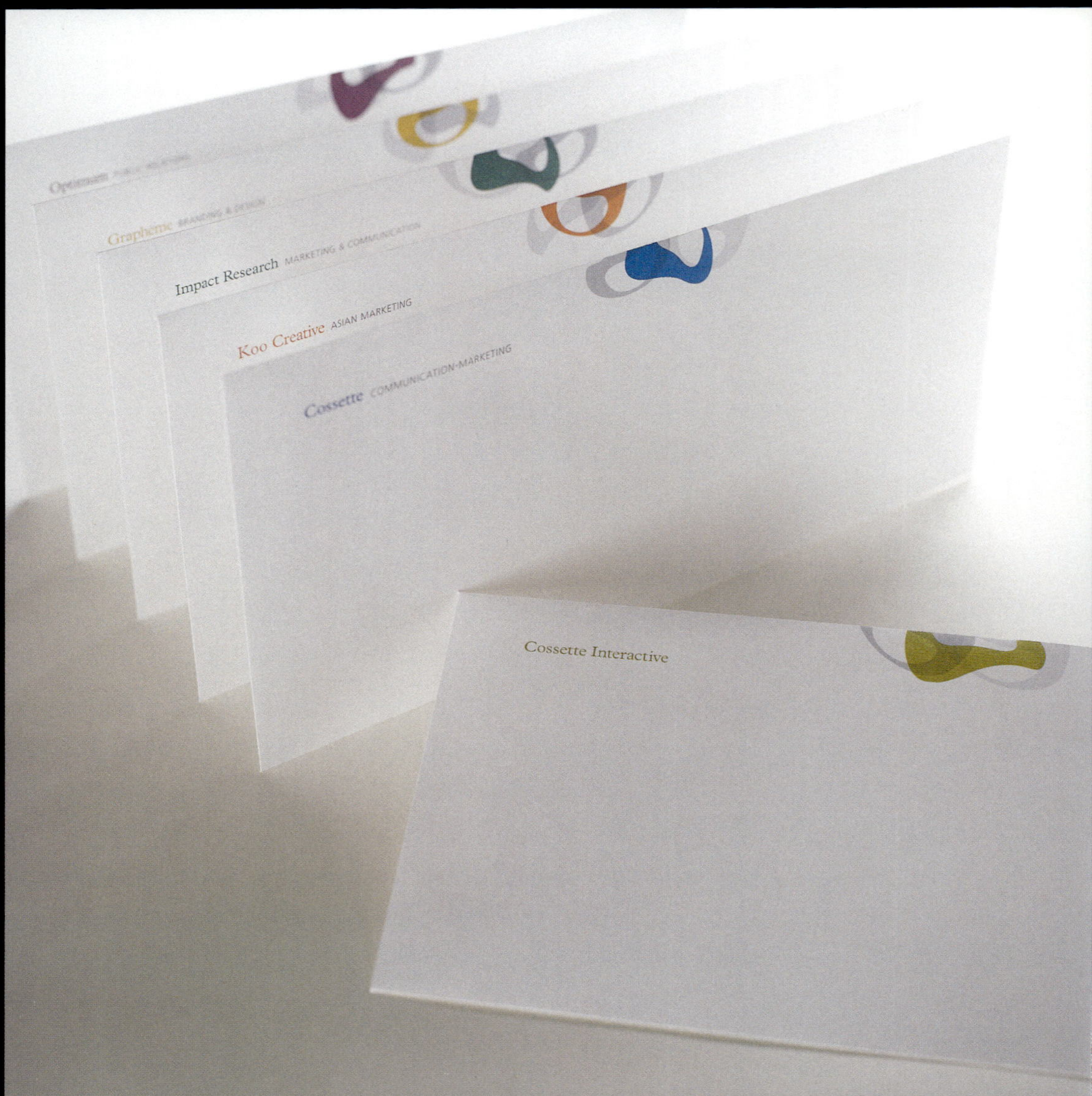

(this spread) Design Firm: Graphème Branding & Design Creative Director: Pierre Léonard Art Directors: Pierre Léonard and Sylvie Turcotte Designers: Sébastien Bisson and François Théorêt Print producer: Sylvie Ouzilleau Client: Cossette

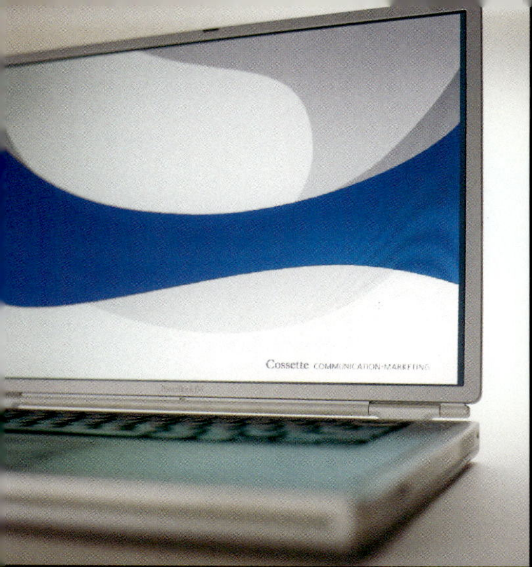
Cossette COMMUNICATION-MARKETING

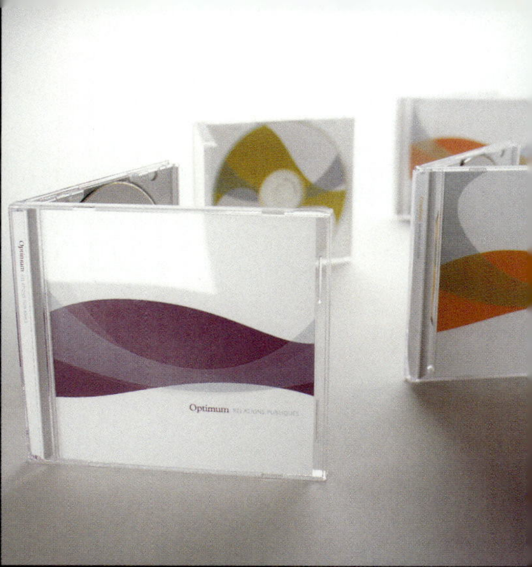
Optimum

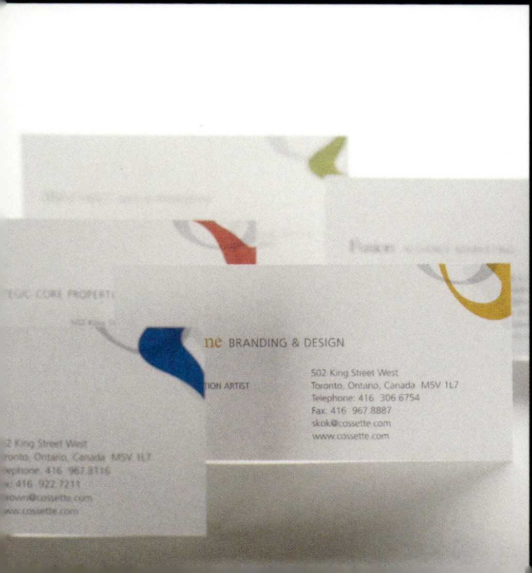
ne BRANDING & DESIGN
TION ARTIST
502 King Street West
Toronto, Ontario, Canada M5V 1L7
Telephone: 416 306.6754
Fax: 416 967.8887
skok@cossette.com
www.cossette.com
2 King Street West
ronto, Ontario, Canada M5V 1L7
ephone: 416 967.8116
: 416 922.7211
rovn@cossette.com
ww.cossette.com

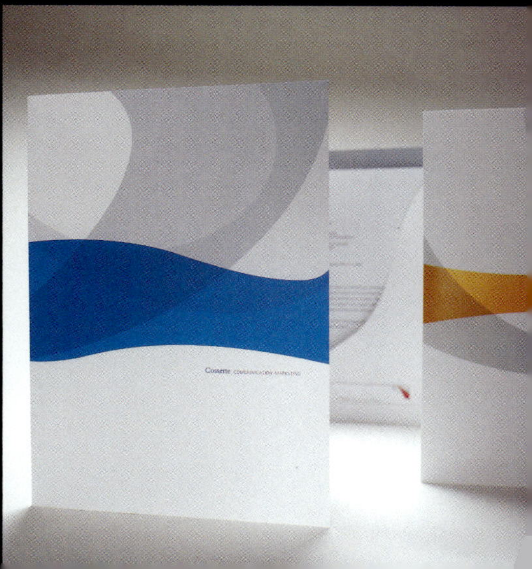
Cossette

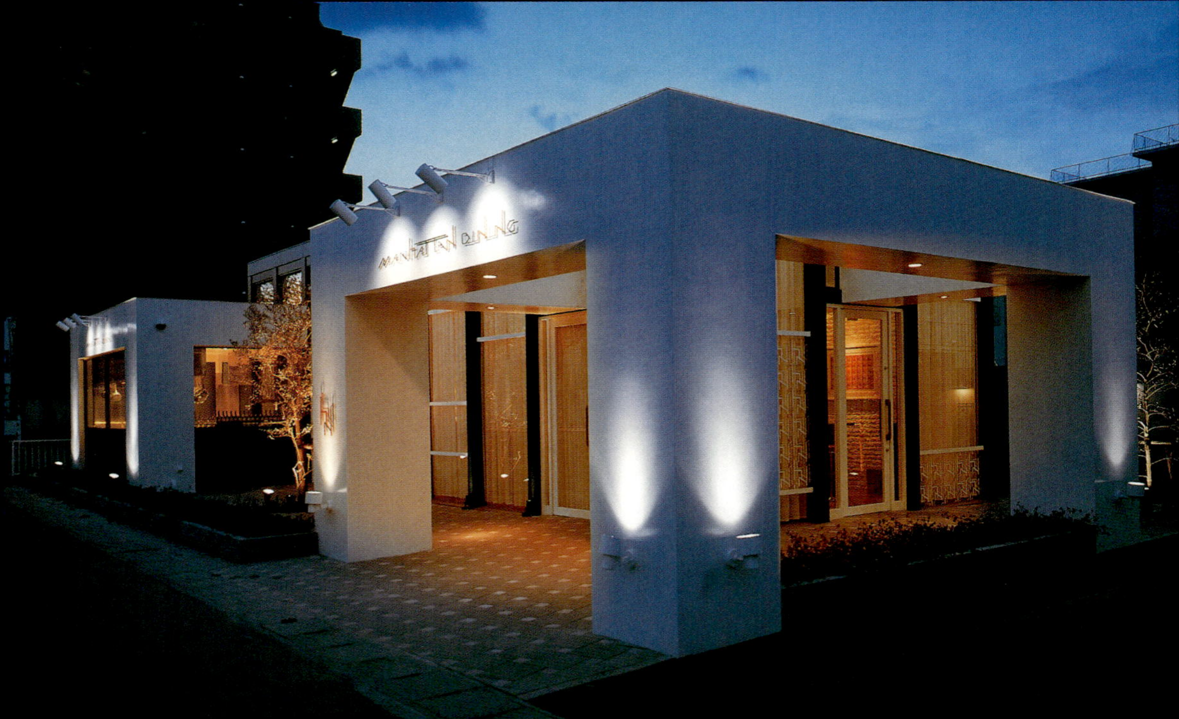

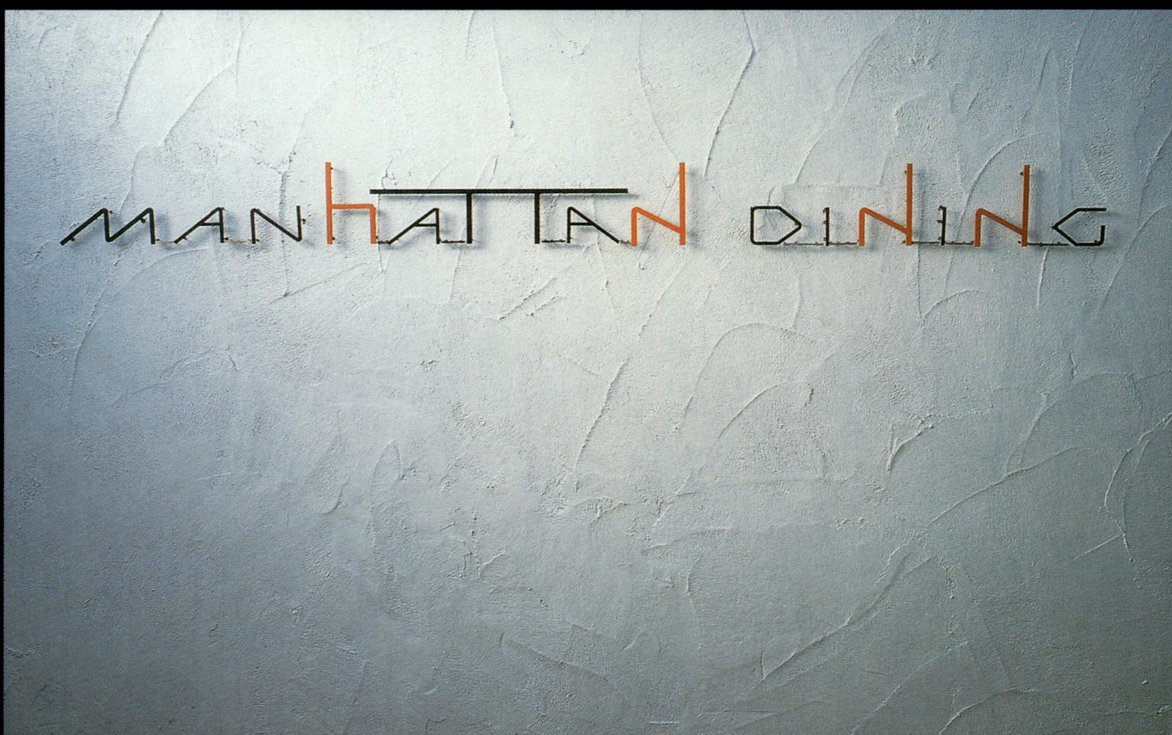

(this spread) 'Manhattan Dining' Design Firm: Graphics & Designing Inc. Creative Director: Takanori Aiba Art Director: Toshihiro Onimaru Designer: Toshihiro Onimaru Client: Will Planning Inc.

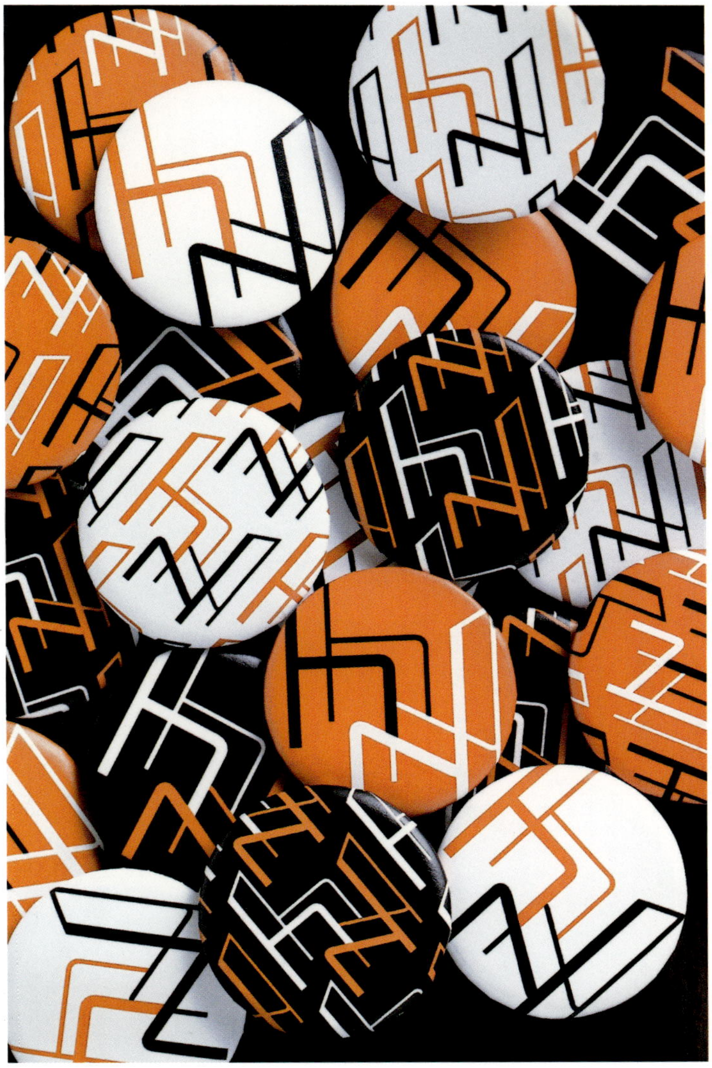

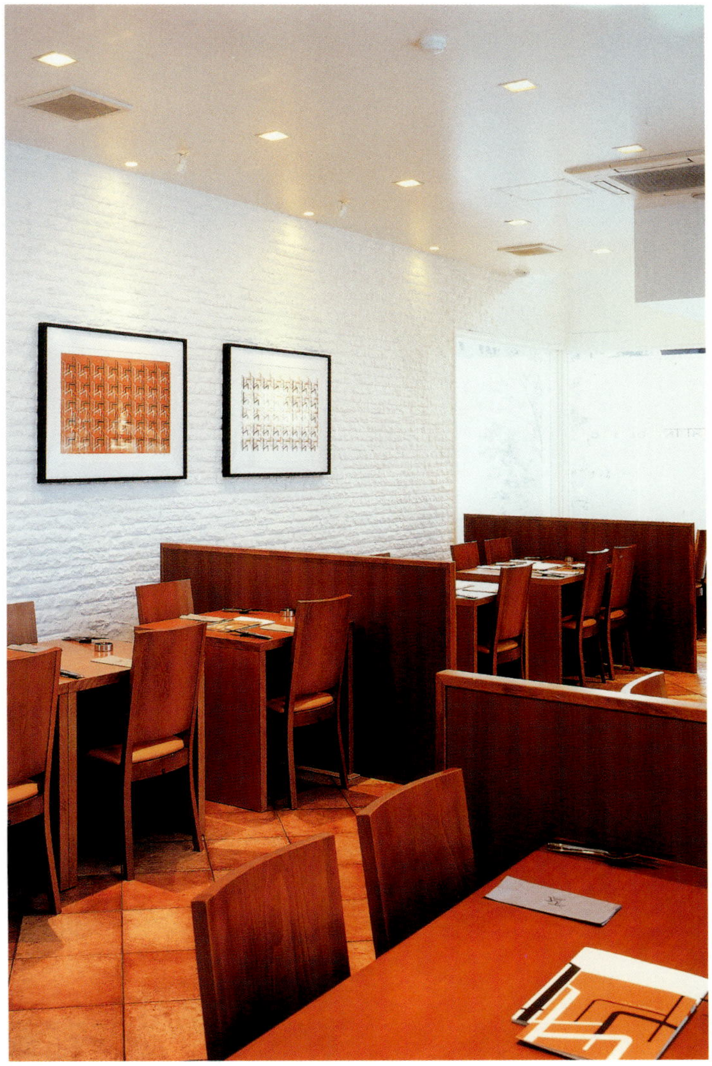

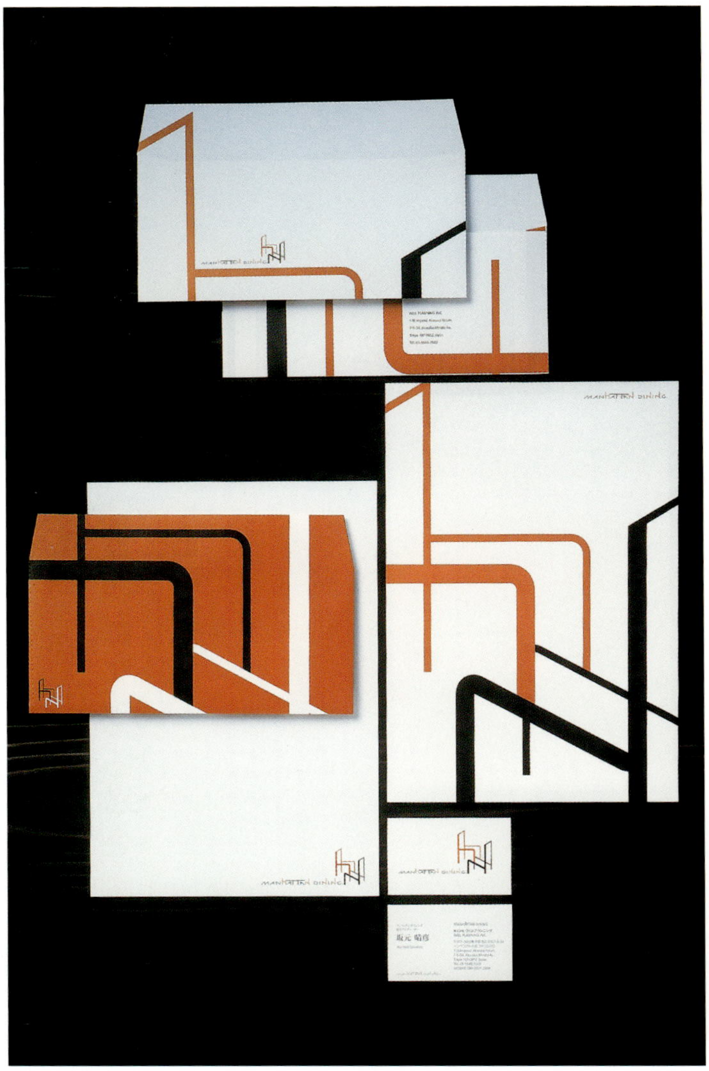

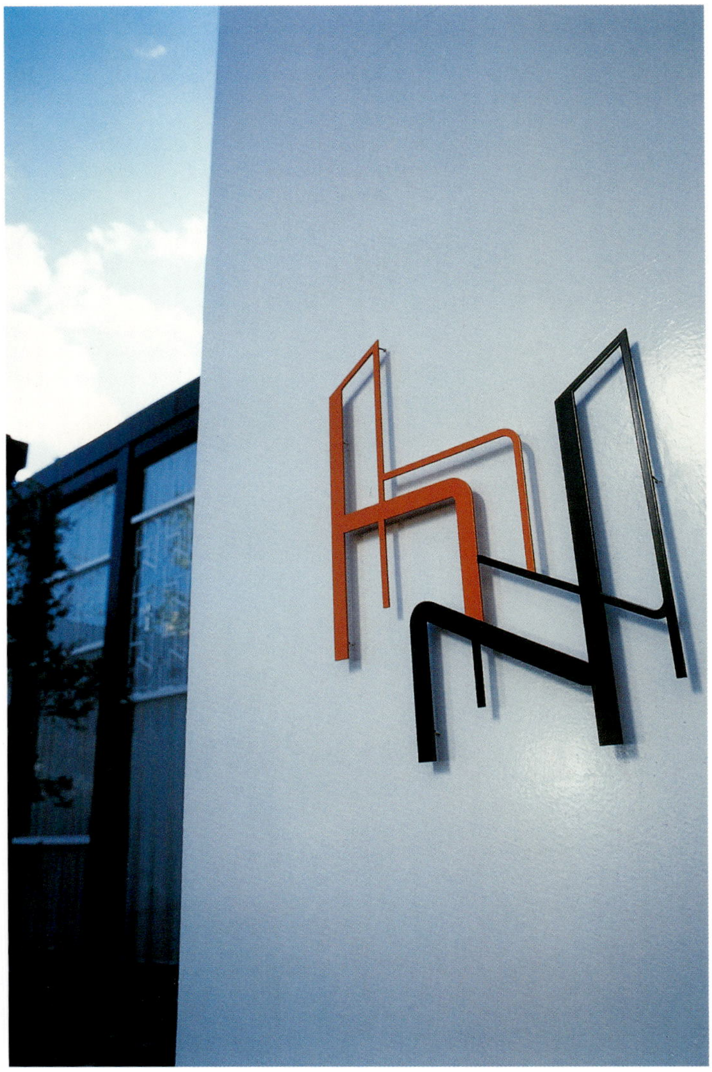

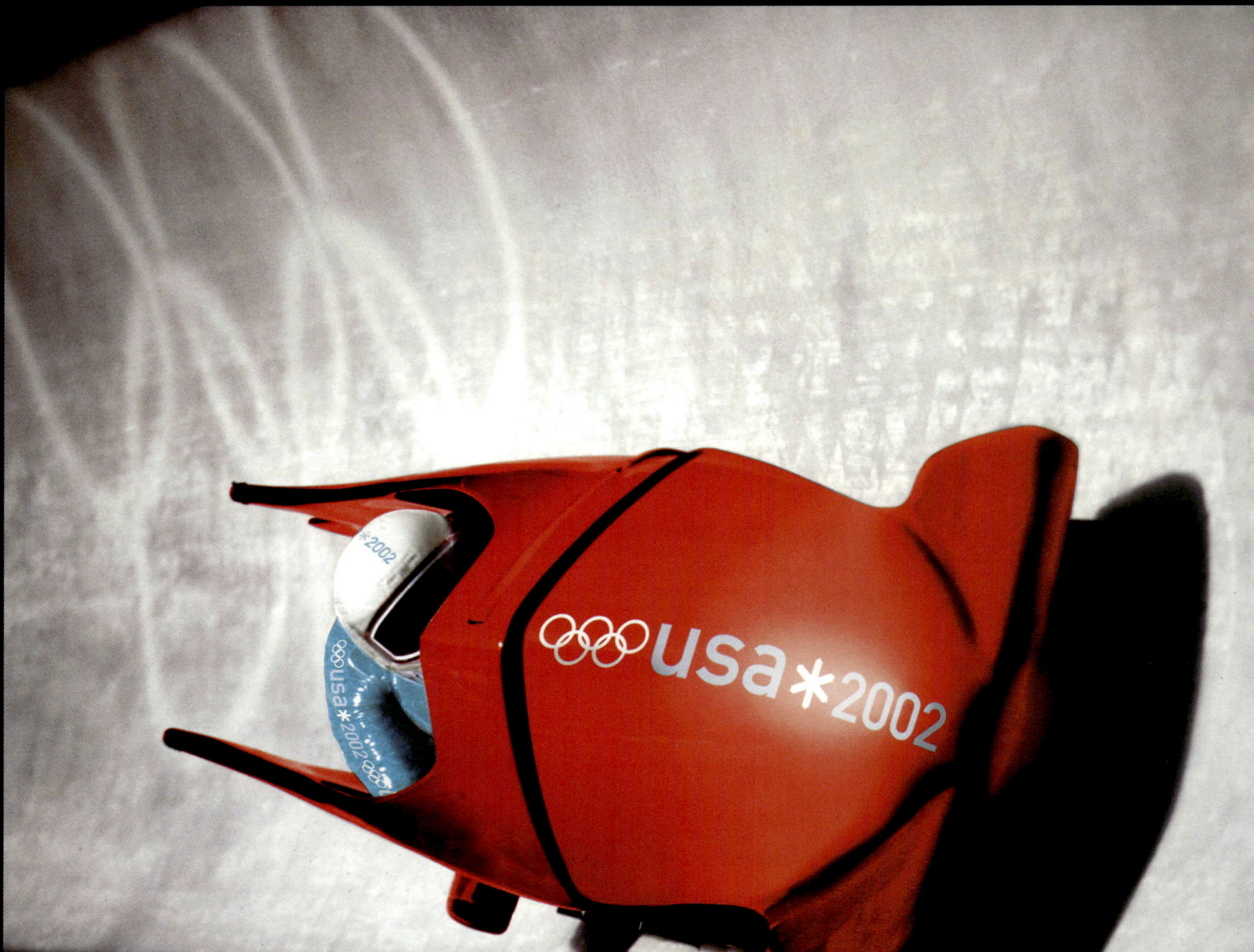

(this spread) 'Olympic Uniform Program' Design Firm: Landor Associates Creative Director: Margaret Youngblood Art Director: Eric Scott Designer: Tina Schoepflin Client Lead: Susie Ivelich Client: US Olympic Committee

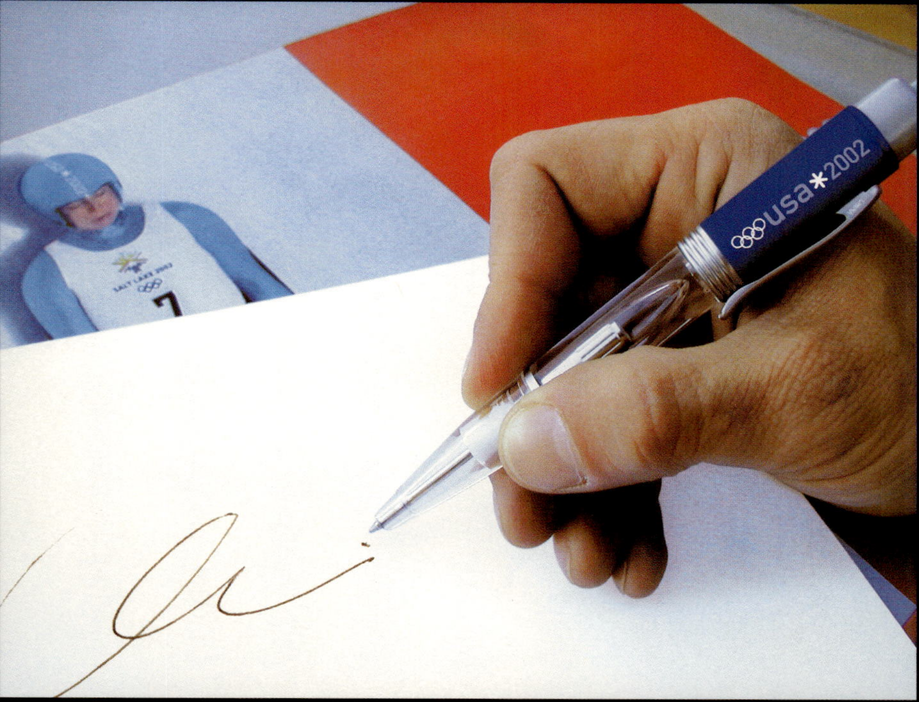
usa*2002
SALT LAKE 2002
7

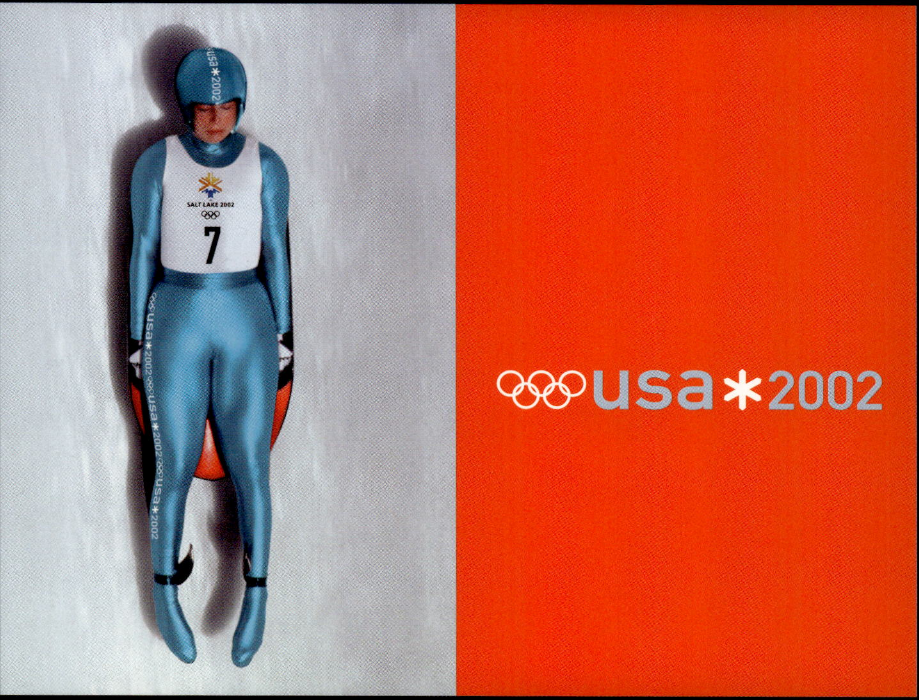
usa*2002
SALT LAKE 2002
7
usa*2002

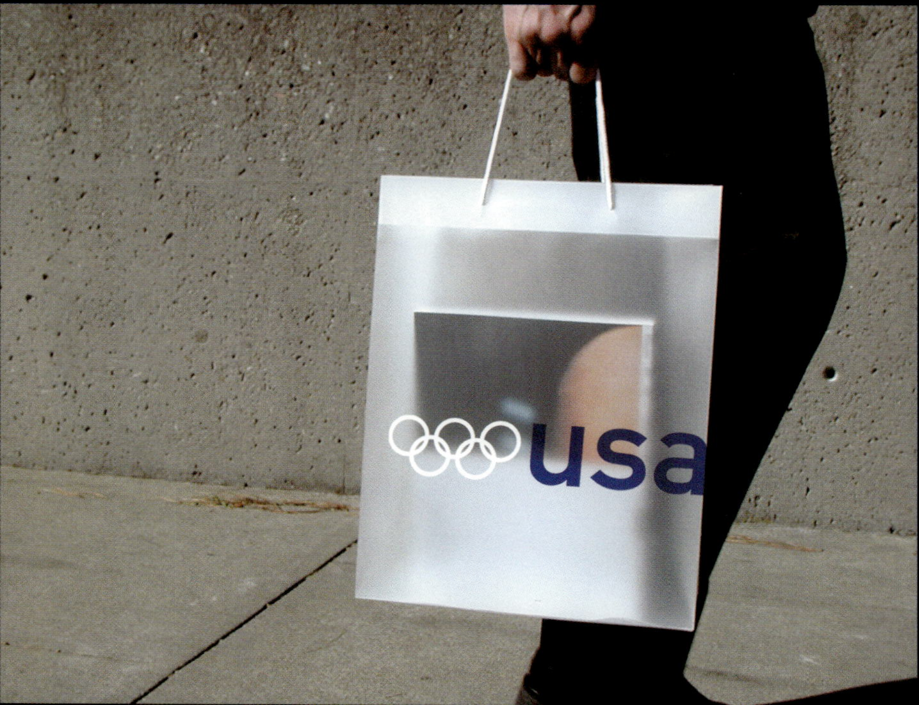
usa

LAB 1
.COMMUNICATION

1.1 als die bilder sprechen lernten
Seit Urzeiten arbeiten die Menschen mit Bildsprachen. Nun gibt es neue kommunikationstechnische Mittel dazu

1.2 icons of information
Iconic communication has distinct advantages for some people and in some situations

1.3 handy? logo!
In Ungarn ist mit dem Handy eine neue Volkskunst entstanden: Handybesitzer kreieren eigene Logos

1.4 sag's mit einem bild
Ein Porträt Otto Neuraths, des Begründers der modernen Bildsprache

1.5 stone people
The Esselen way to make stones into people in a ceremony called sweatlodge

1.6 .copy.digest Wichtige Infos auf einen Blick

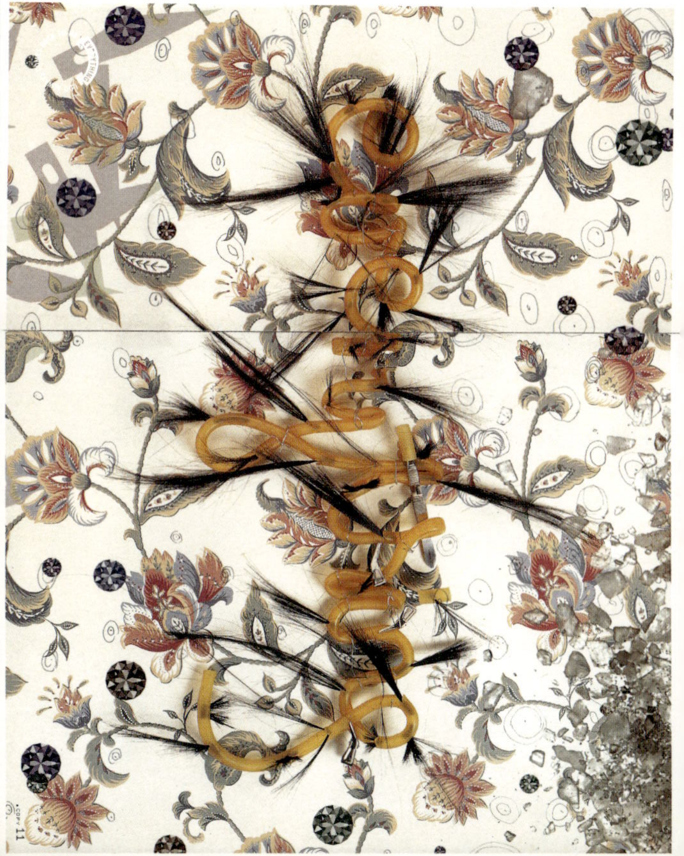

LAB 2
.CYBERNETICS

2.1 bilder der zukunft
Breitbandtechnologien ermöglichen neue Formen der Bildsprache

2.2 mp3 war erst der anfang
MP3-Erfinder Karlheinz Brandenburg entwickelt neue Technologien für perfekte Klangerlebnisse

2.3 .copy.digest Wichtige Infos auf einen Blick

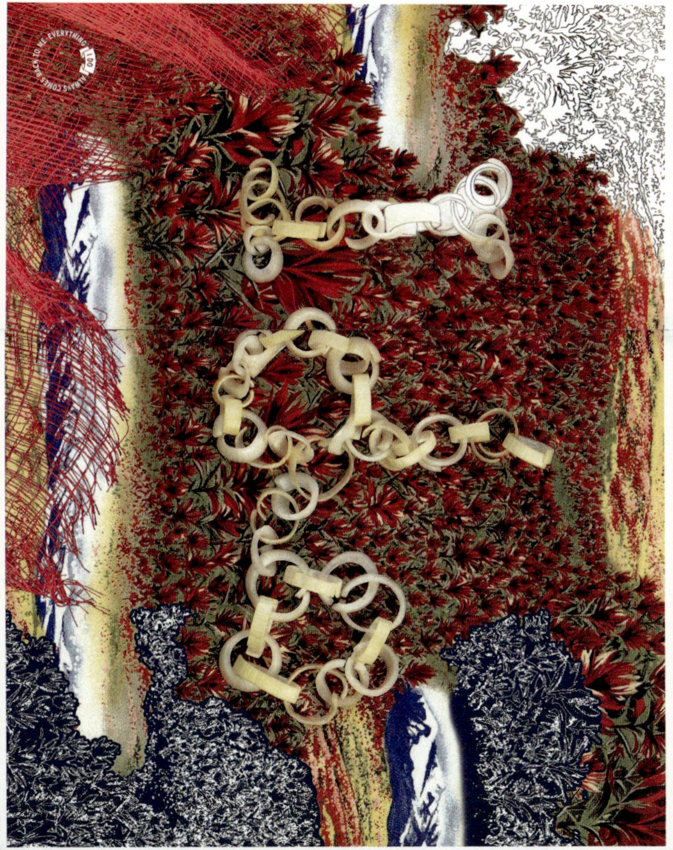

LAB 3
.CONVENIENCE

3.1 entspannung nach bildern
Wie Bilder zu körperlichem Wohlbefinden führen: eine Anleitung zu entspannenden Shiatsu-Übungen

3.2 internetmission bei nomaden
Trotz Skepsis und Armut beginnen die Tuaregs, sich mit Handy und Internet vertraut zu machen

3.3 bild: reporter
Was schleppt ein Reporter bei seinen Auslandseinsätzen mit? Ein Suchbild mit Thomas Seifert

3.4 was, bitte, ist myanmar?
Hinter dem Namen verbirgt sich Burma, ein Land, in dem Internetsurfen und Fahrradfahren verboten sind

3.5 wirft große bilder
Videobeamer sorgen für Kinopalastgefühle in den eigenen vier Wänden

3.6 .copy.digest Wichtige Infos auf einen Blick

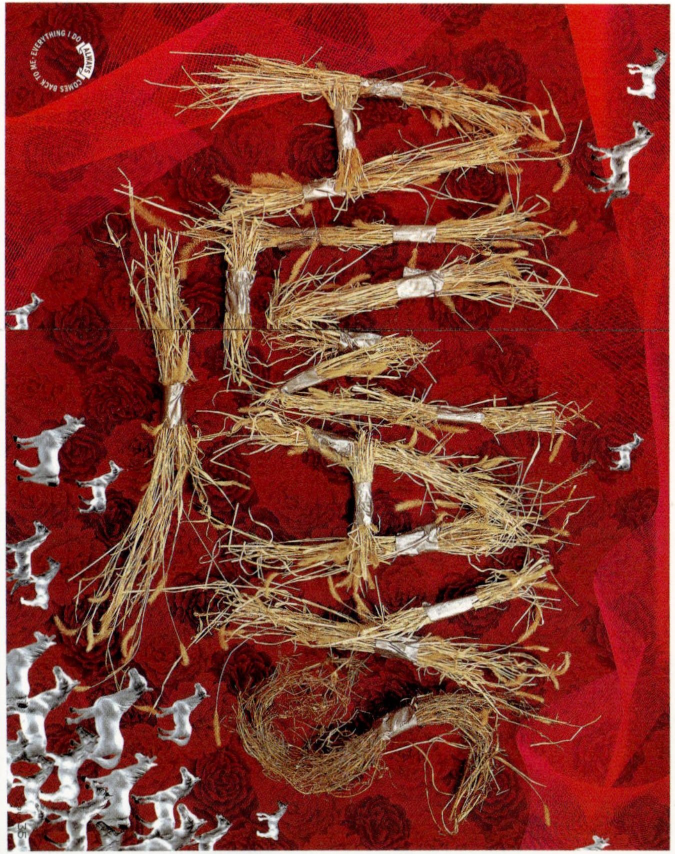

LAB 6
.CULTURE

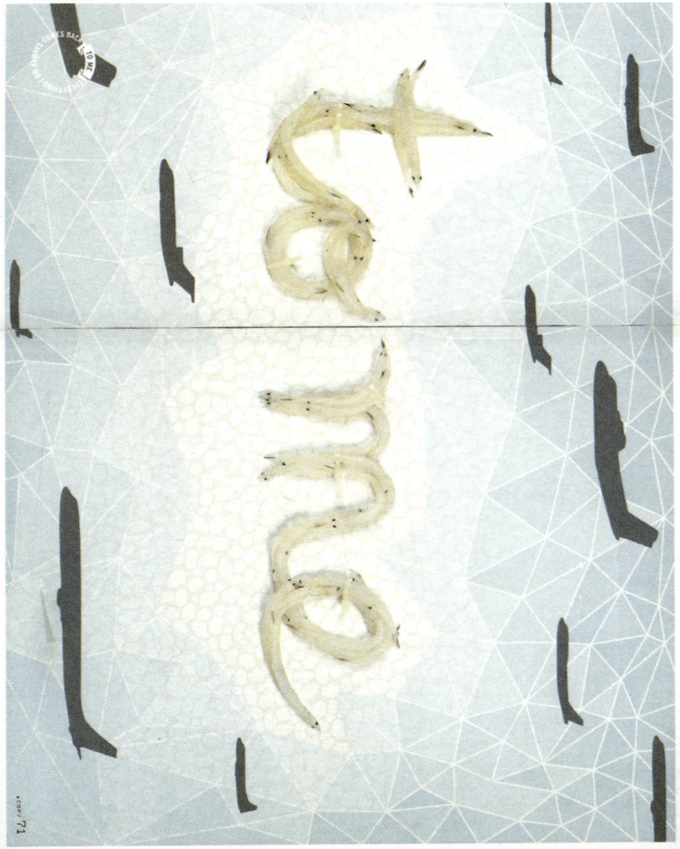

LAB 5
.CHIC

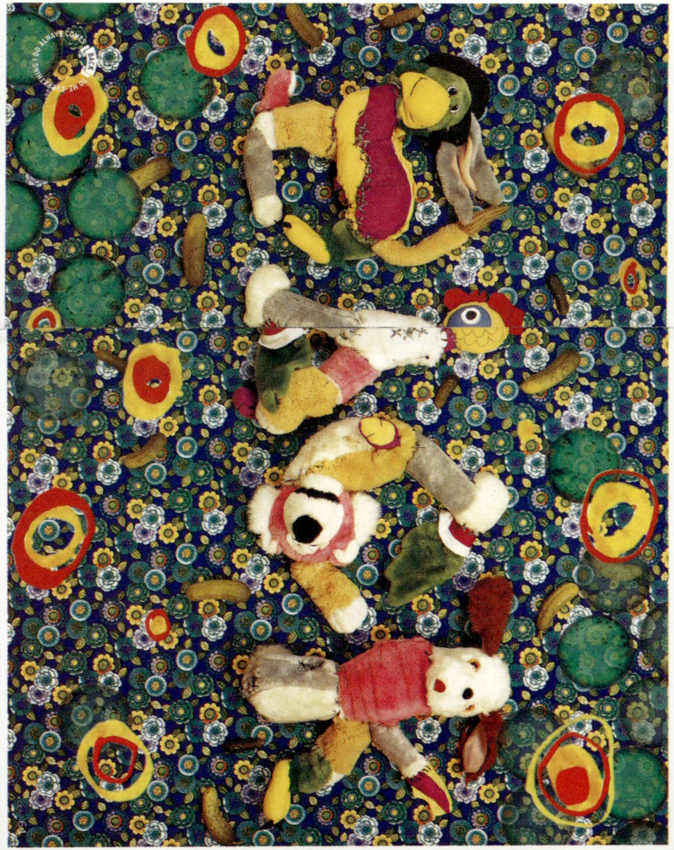

LAB 4
.COMMUNITY

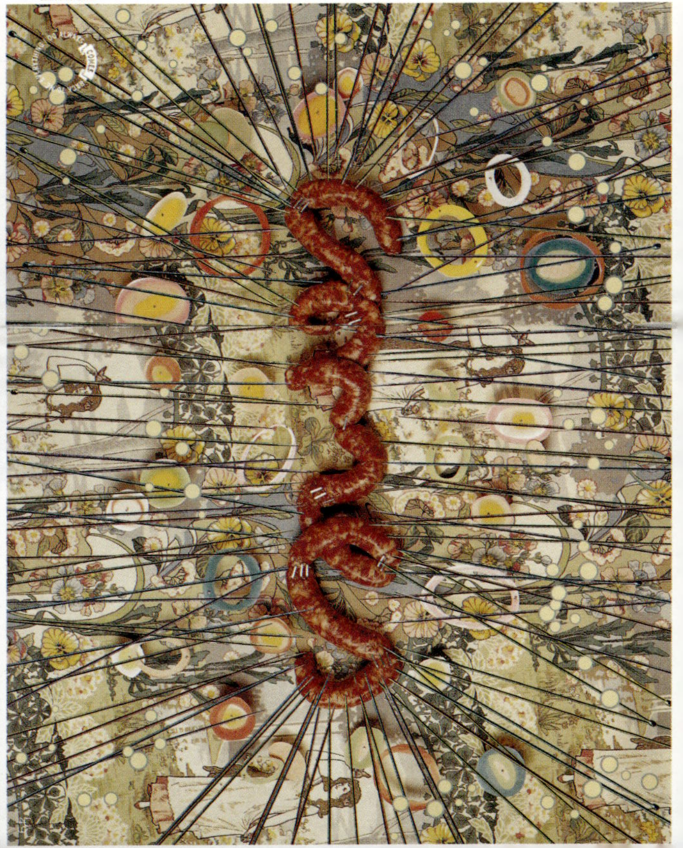

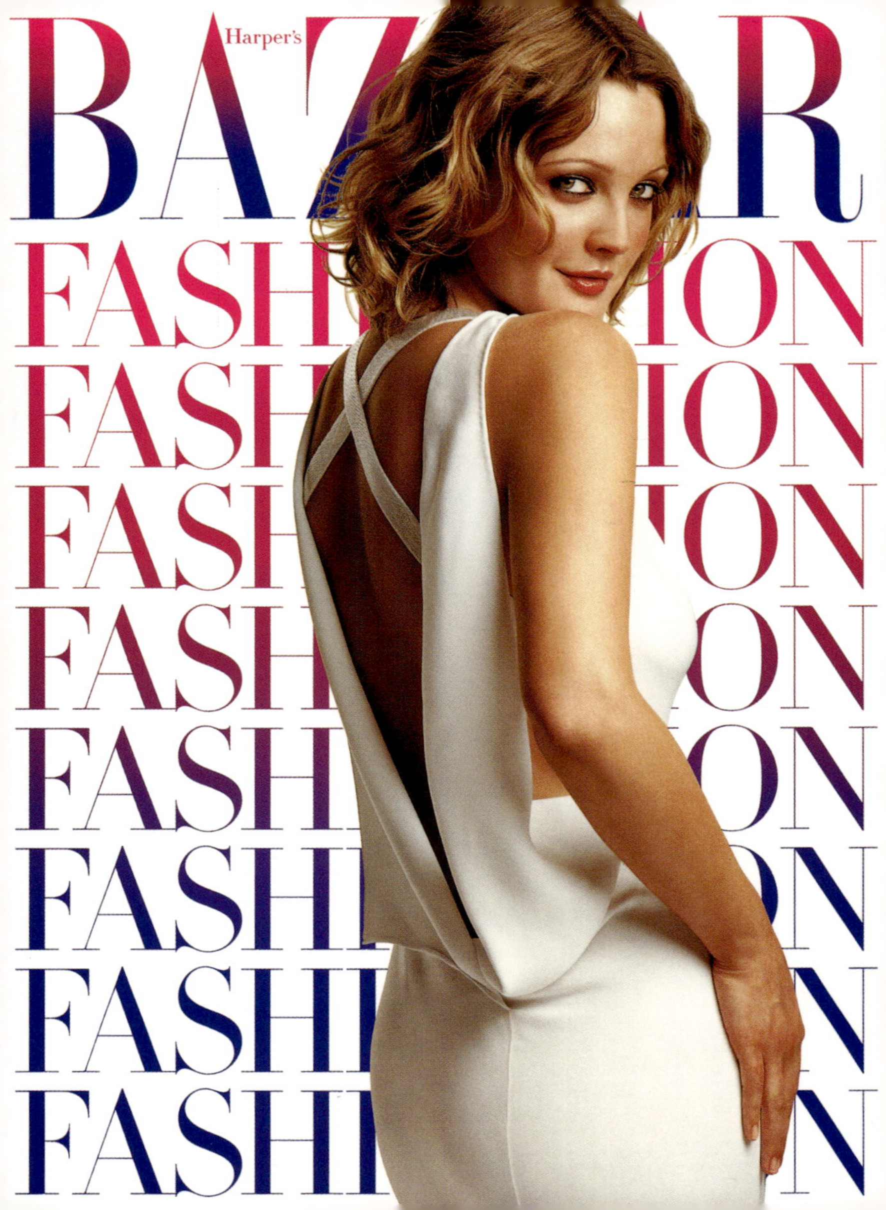
Harper's

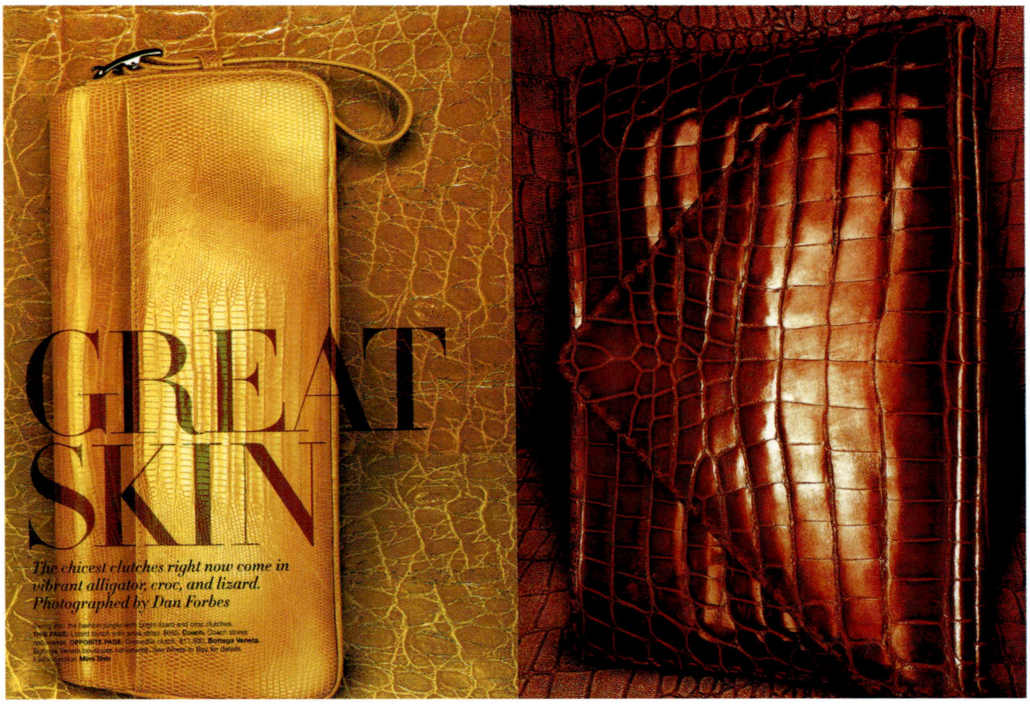
GREAT SKIN
The chicest clutches right now come in vibrant alligator, croc, and lizard. Photographed by Dan Forbes

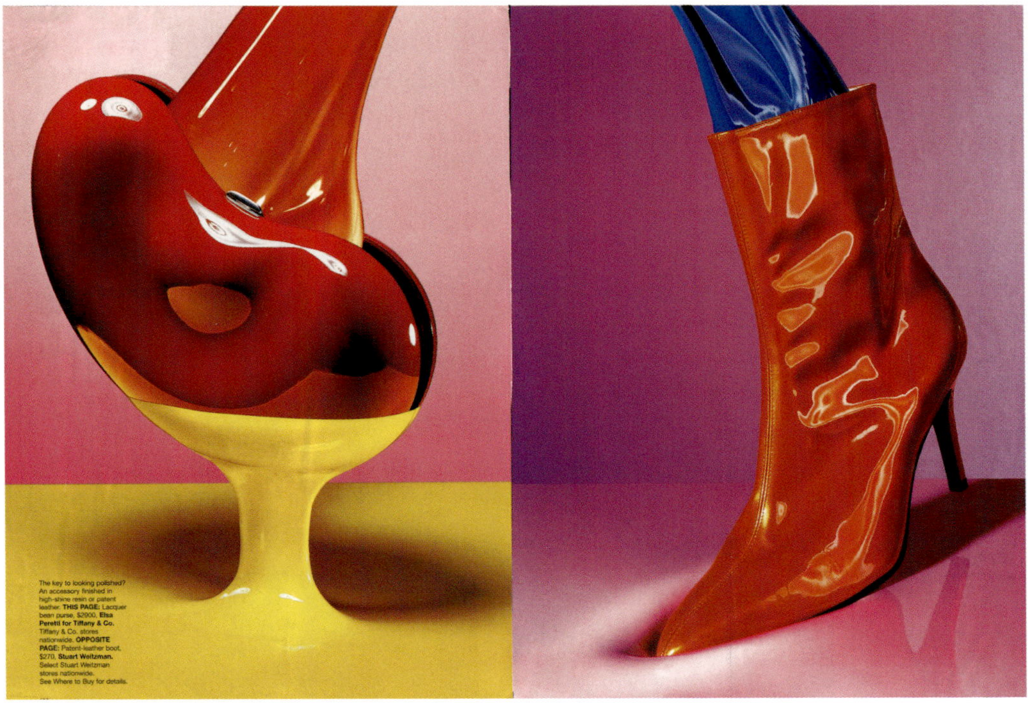
The key to looking polished? An accessory finished in high-shine resin or patent leather. THIS PAGE: Lacquer bean purse, $2900, Elsa Peretti for Tiffany & Co. Tiffany & Co. stores nationwide. OPPOSITE PAGE: Patent-leather boot, $270, Stuart Weitzman. Select Stuart Weitzman stores nationwide. See Where to Buy for details.

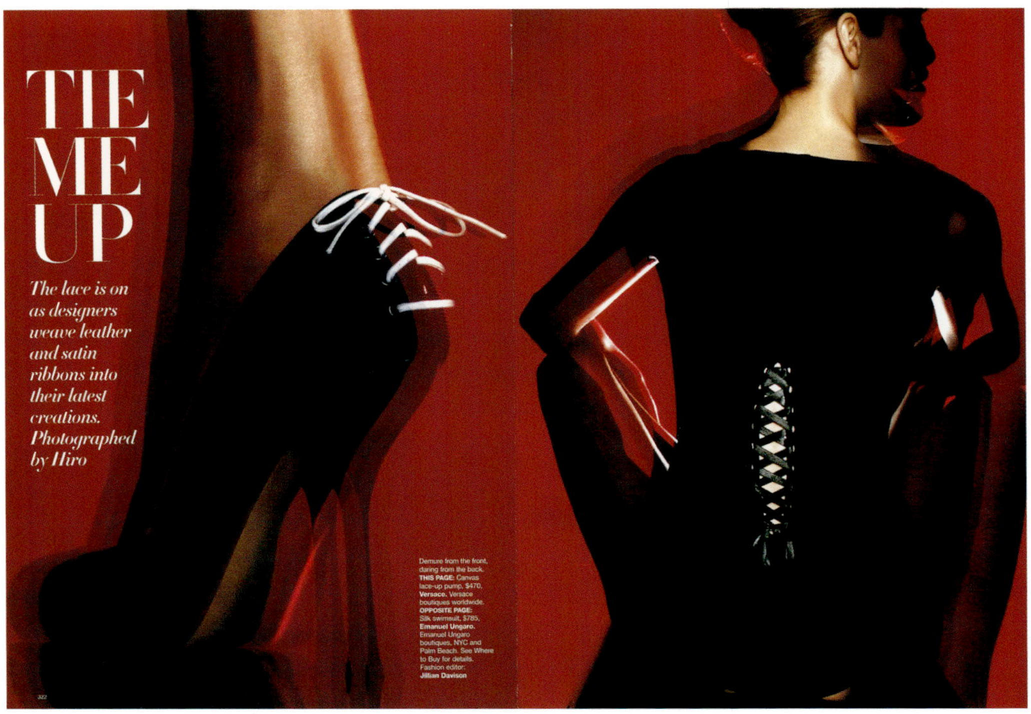
TIE ME UP
The lace is on as designers weave leather and satin ribbons into their latest creations. Photographed by Hiro
Demure from the front, daring from the back. THIS PAGE: Canvas lace-up pump, $470, Versace. Versace boutiques worldwide. OPPOSITE PAGE: Silk swimsuit, $785, Emanuel Ungaro. Emanuel Ungaro boutiques, NYC and Palm Beach. See Where to Buy for details. Fashion editor: Jillian Davison

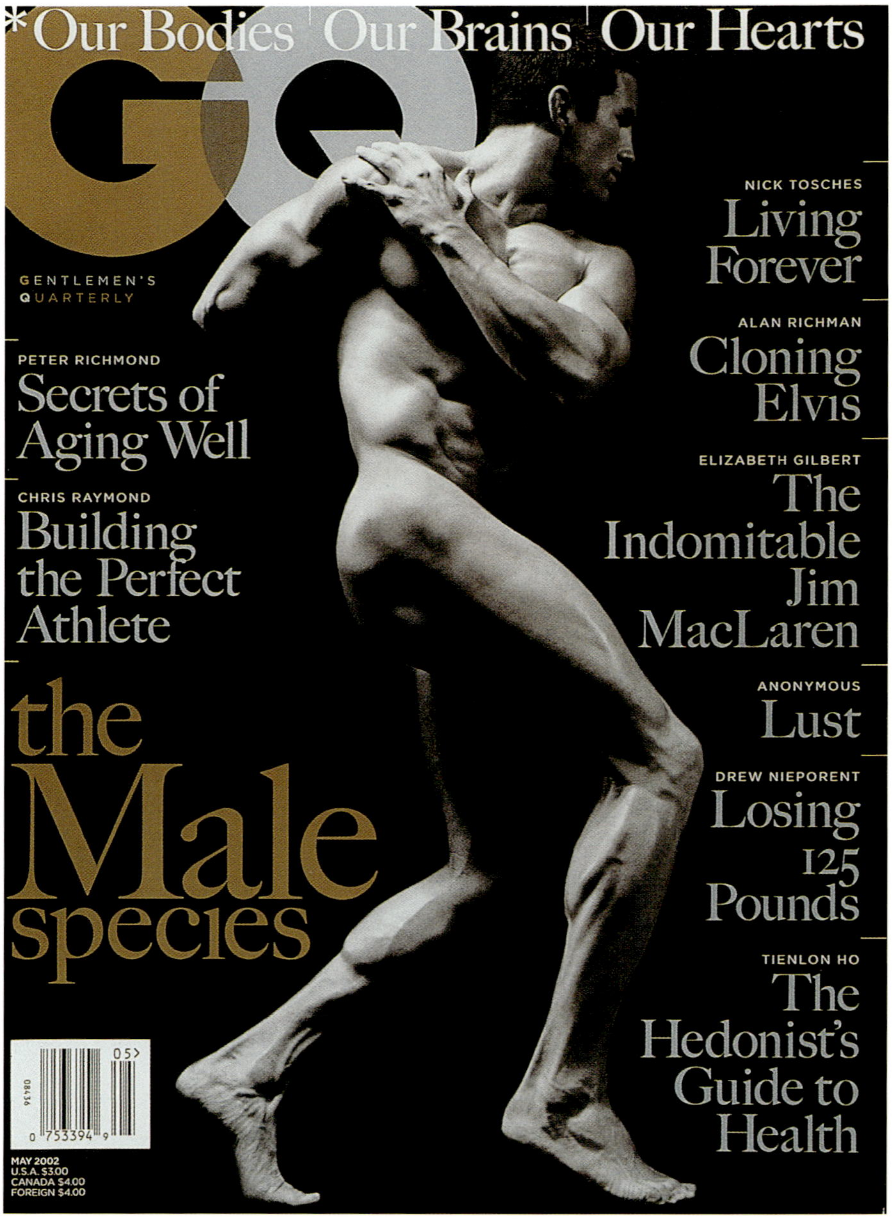

(this spread) Creative Director: Fred Woodward Client: GQ

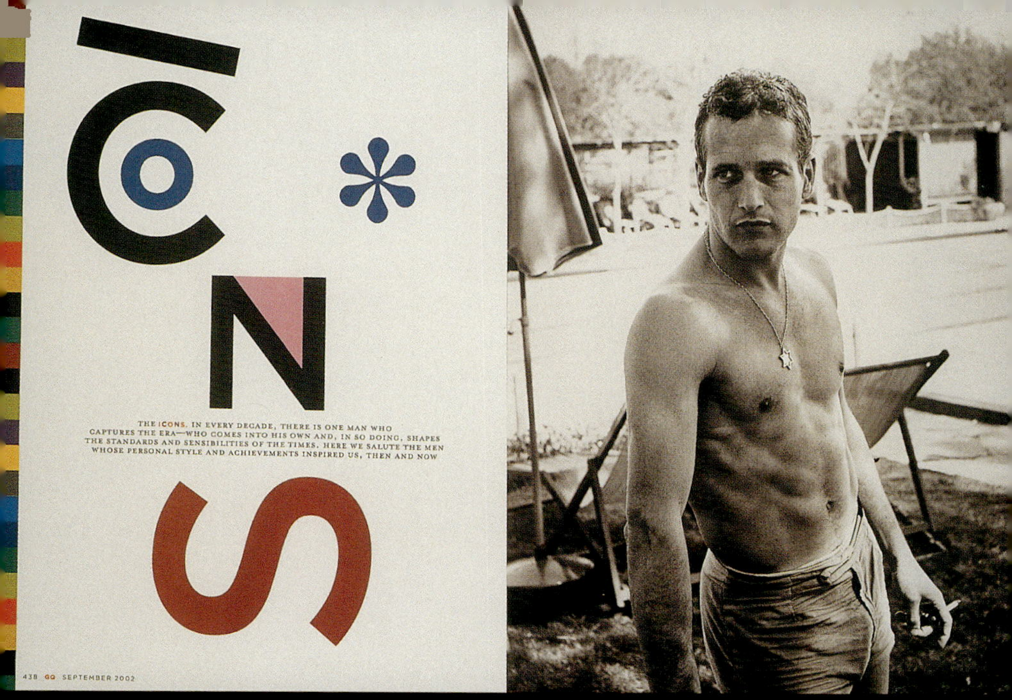
ICONS
THE ICONS. IN EVERY DECADE, THERE IS ONE MAN WHO CAPTURES THE ERA—WHO COMES INTO HIS OWN AND, IN SO DOING, SHAPES THE STANDARDS AND SENSIBILITIES OF THE TIMES. HERE WE SALUTE THE MEN WHOSE PERSONAL STYLE AND ACHIEVEMENTS INSPIRED US, THEN AND NOW
438 GQ SEPTEMBER 2002

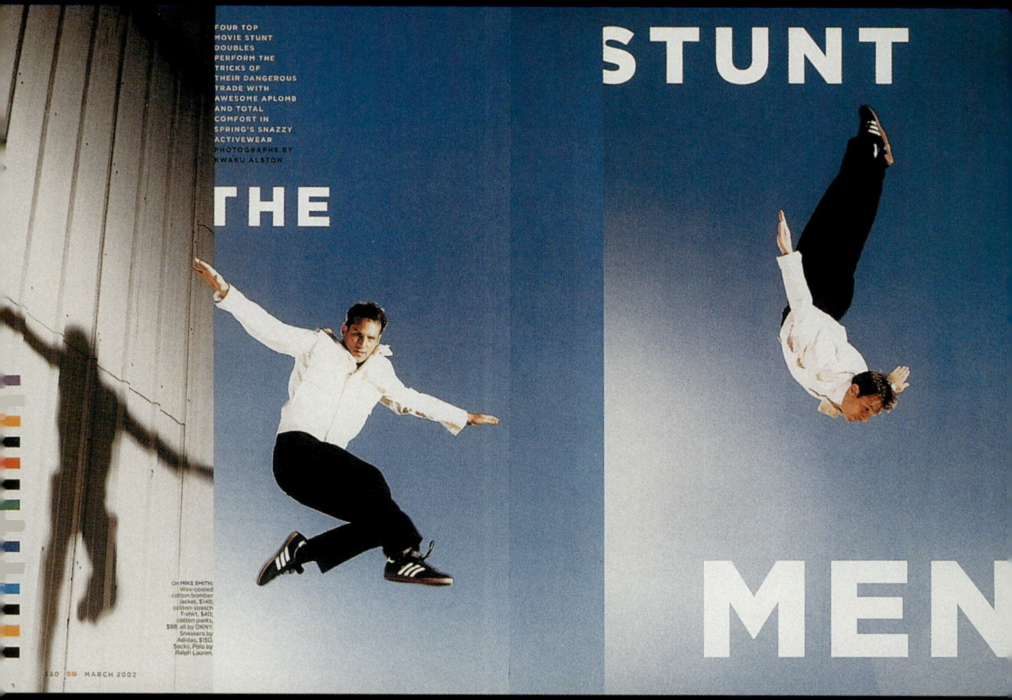
FOUR TOP MOVIE STUNT DOUBLES PERFORM THE TRICKS OF THEIR DANGEROUS TRADE WITH AWESOME APLOMB AND TOTAL COMFORT IN SPRING'S SNAZZY ACTIVEWEAR
PHOTOGRAPHS BY KWAKU ALSTON
THE
STUNT
MEN
On MIKE SMITH: Wax-coated cotton bomber jacket, $148; cotton-stretch T-shirt, $40; cotton pants, $98, all by DKNY. Sneakers by Adidas, $150. Socks, Polo by Ralph Lauren.
GQ MARCH 2002

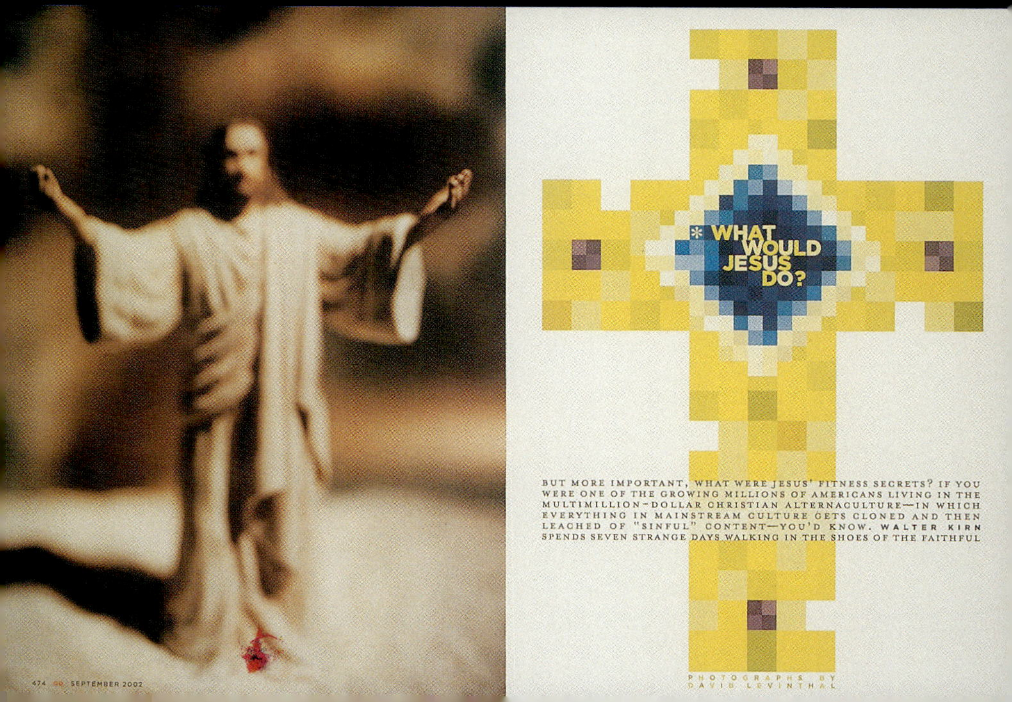
474 GQ SEPTEMBER 2002
WHAT WOULD JESUS DO?
BUT MORE IMPORTANT, WHAT WERE JESUS' FITNESS SECRETS? IF YOU WERE ONE OF THE GROWING MILLIONS OF AMERICANS LIVING IN THE MULTIMILLION-DOLLAR CHRISTIAN ALTERNACULTURE—IN WHICH EVERYTHING IN MAINSTREAM CULTURE GETS CLONED AND THEN LEACHED OF "SINFUL" CONTENT—YOU'D KNOW. WALTER KIRN SPENDS SEVEN STRANGE DAYS WALKING IN THE SHOES OF THE FAITHFUL
PHOTOGRAPHS BY DAVID LEVINTHAL

*THE SEX GODDESSES

*PORTFOLIO BY MARK SELIGER

TWELVE PULCHRITUDINOUS PAGES OF THE WOMEN, FROM MARILYN TO MENA, WHO HAVE MADE OUR HEARTS POUND AND OUR PULSES RACE OVER THE PAST FIVE DECADES. ALL THE ROLES ARE PLAYED BY HEIDI KLUM, WHO CAUSES SERIOUS PALPITATIONS HERSELF

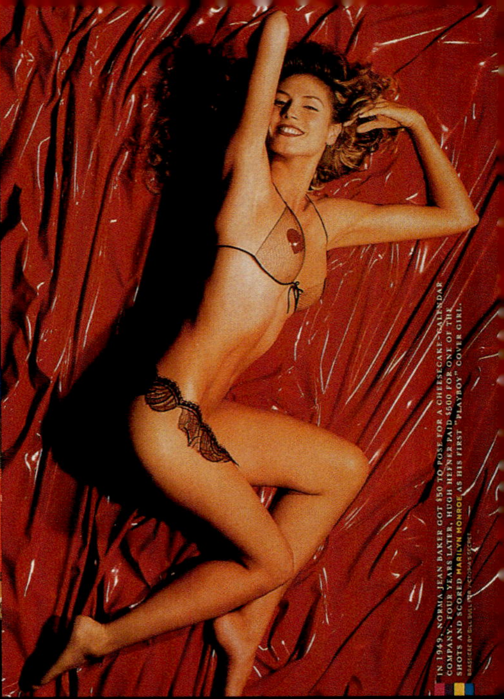

IN 1949, NORMA JEAN BAKER GOT $50 TO POSE FOR A CHEESECAKE-CALENDAR COMPANY. FOUR YEARS LATER, HUGH HEFNER PAID $500 FOR ONE OF THE SHOTS AND SCORED MARILYN MONROE AS HIS FIRST "PLAYBOY" COVER GIRL.

BRASSIERE BY BILL BULL FOR VICTORIA'S SECRET

THE GODDESS*

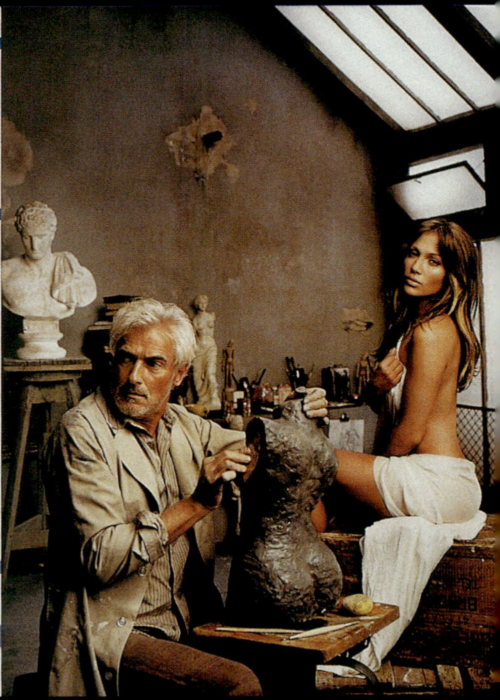

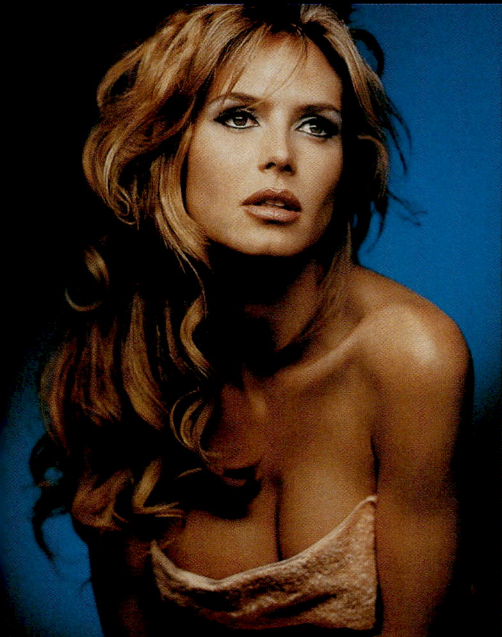

AS HEIDI PROVES AS BRIGITTE BARDOT IN 1956'S "AND GOD CREATED WOMAN," HE DIDN'T STOP THERE.

BATH TOWEL BY CALVIN KLEIN HOME

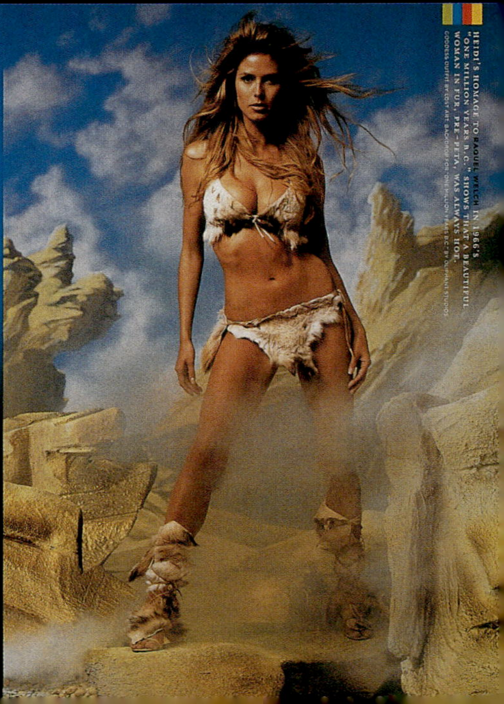

HEIDI'S HOMAGE TO RAQUEL WELCH IN 1966'S "ONE MILLION YEARS B.C." SHOWS THAT A BEAUTIFUL WOMAN IN FUR, PRE-PETA, WAS ALWAYS HOT.

GODDESS OUTFIT BY LOST ART. BACKDROP FOR "ONE MILLION YEARS B.C." BY OLIPHANT STUDIOS.

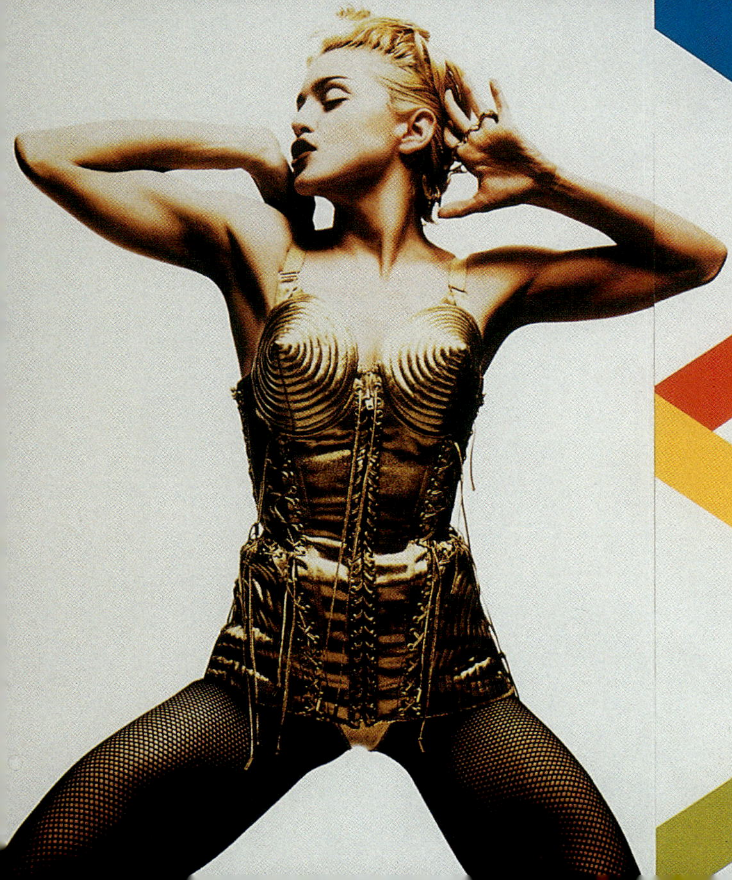

MAD2ONNA

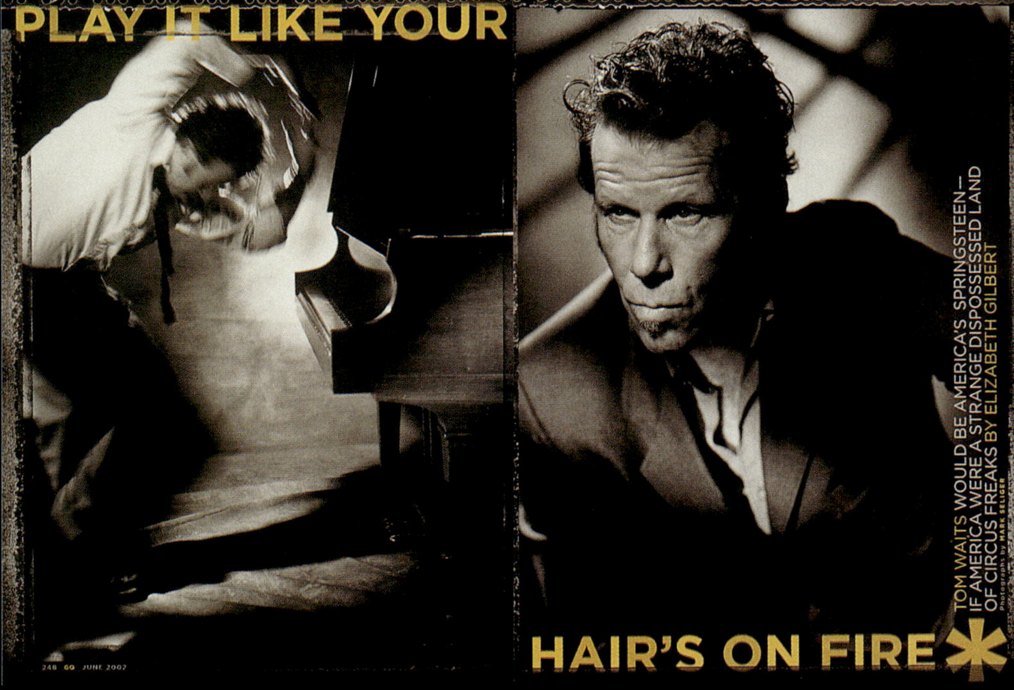

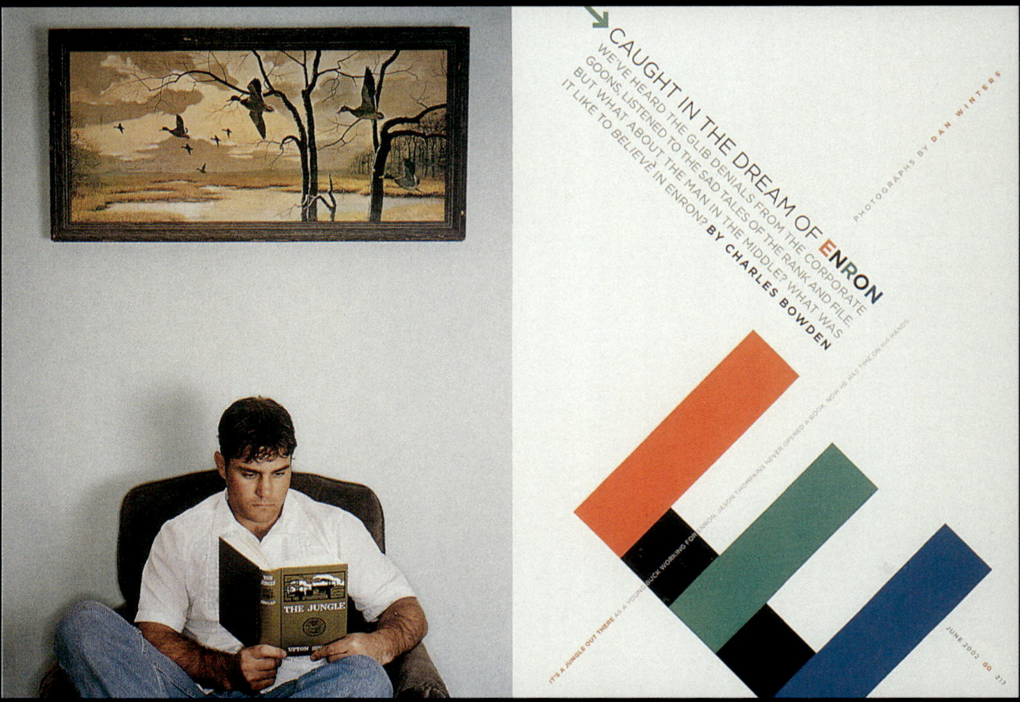

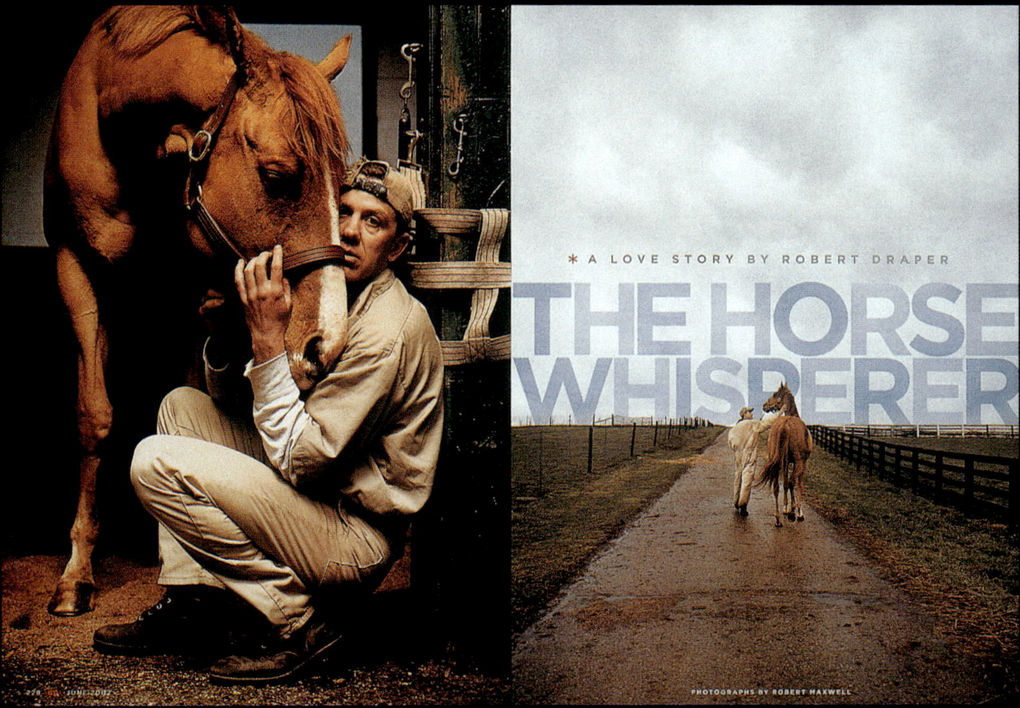

(this spread) Creative Director: Fred Woodward Client: GQ

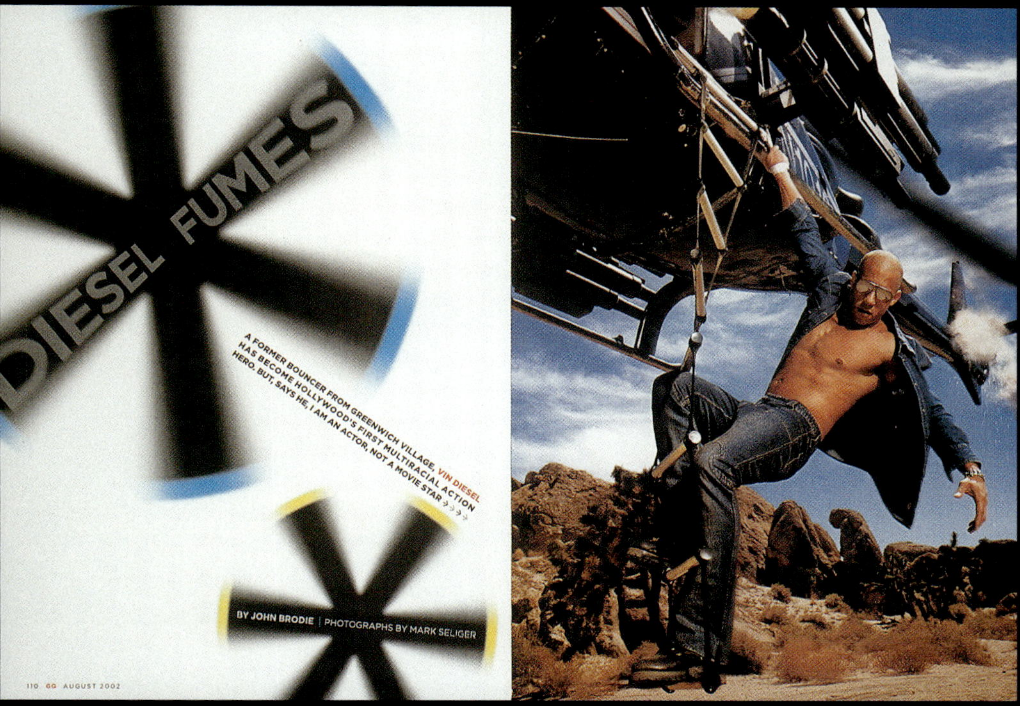
DIESEL FUMES
A FORMER BOUNCER FROM GREENWICH VILLAGE, VIN DIESEL HAS BECOME HOLLYWOOD'S FIRST MULTIRACIAL ACTION HERO. BUT, SAYS HE, I AM AN ACTOR, NOT A MOVIE STAR >>>>
BY JOHN BRODIE | PHOTOGRAPHS BY MARK SELIGER
110 GQ AUGUST 2002

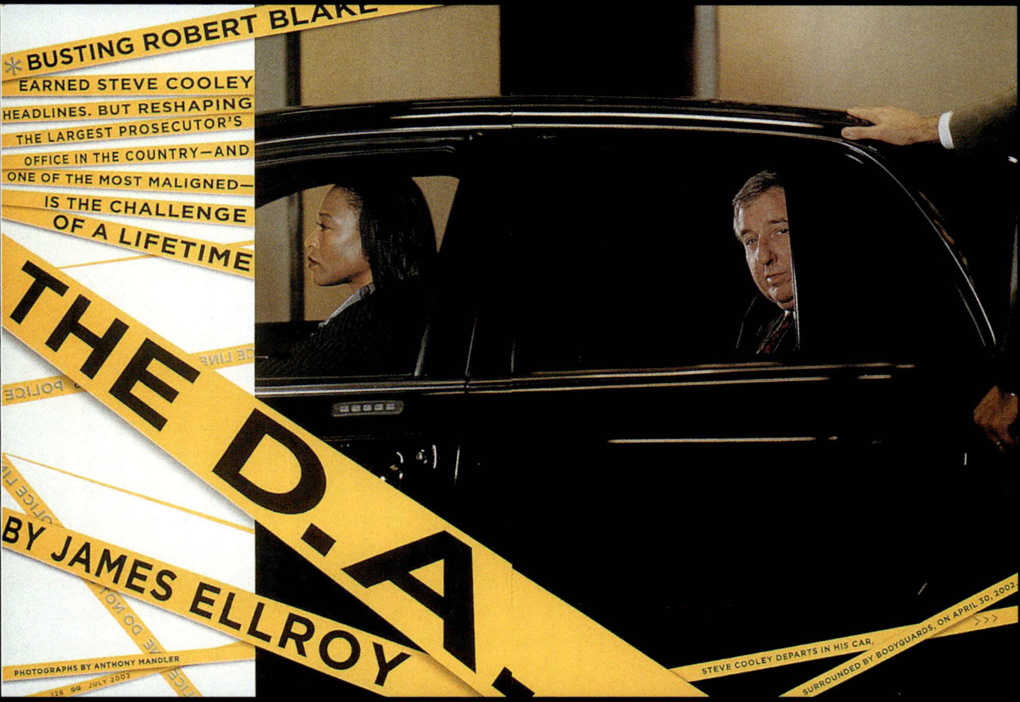
* BUSTING ROBERT BLAKE EARNED STEVE COOLEY HEADLINES. BUT RESHAPING THE LARGEST PROSECUTOR'S OFFICE IN THE COUNTRY—AND ONE OF THE MOST MALIGNED—IS THE CHALLENGE OF A LIFETIME
THE D.A.
BY JAMES ELLROY
PHOTOGRAPHS BY ANTHONY MANDLER
126 GQ JULY 2002
STEVE COOLEY DEPARTS IN HIS CAR, SURROUNDED BY BODYGUARDS, ON APRIL 30, 2002 >>>

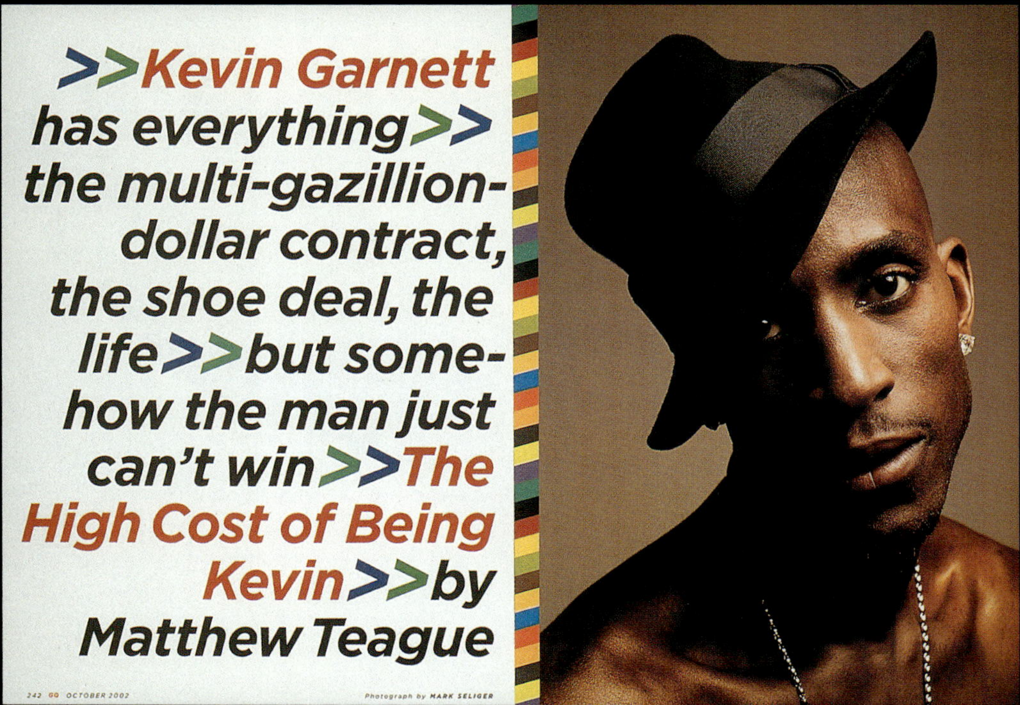
>>Kevin Garnett has everything>> the multi-gazillion-dollar contract, the shoe deal, the life>>but some-how the man just can't win>>The High Cost of Being Kevin>>by Matthew Teague
242 GQ OCTOBER 2002
Photograph by MARK SELIGER

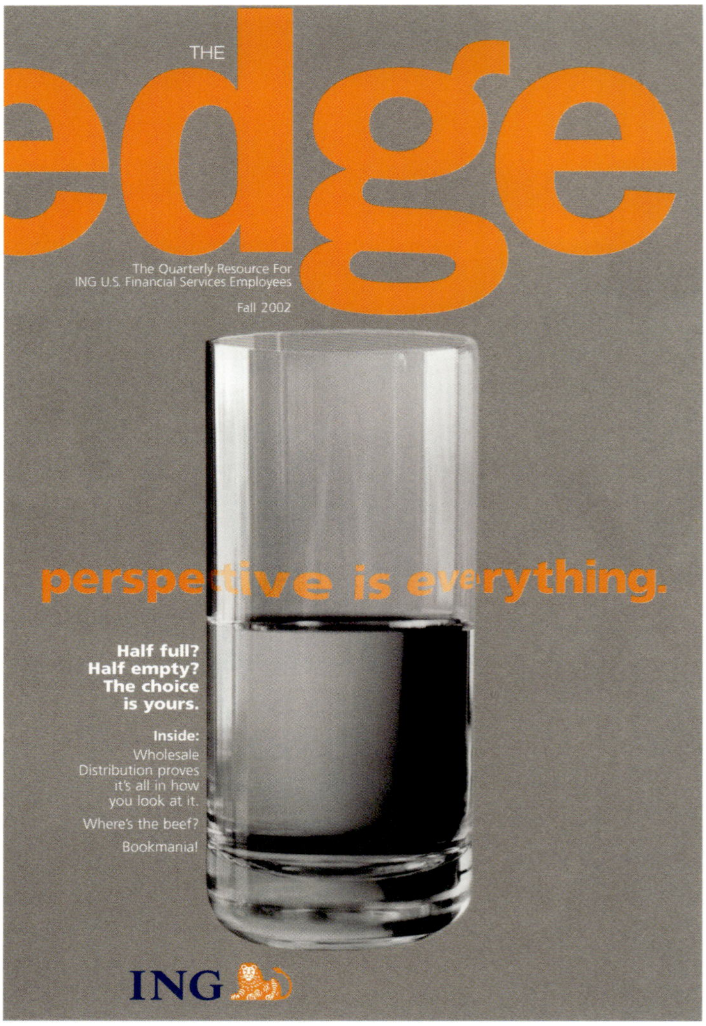

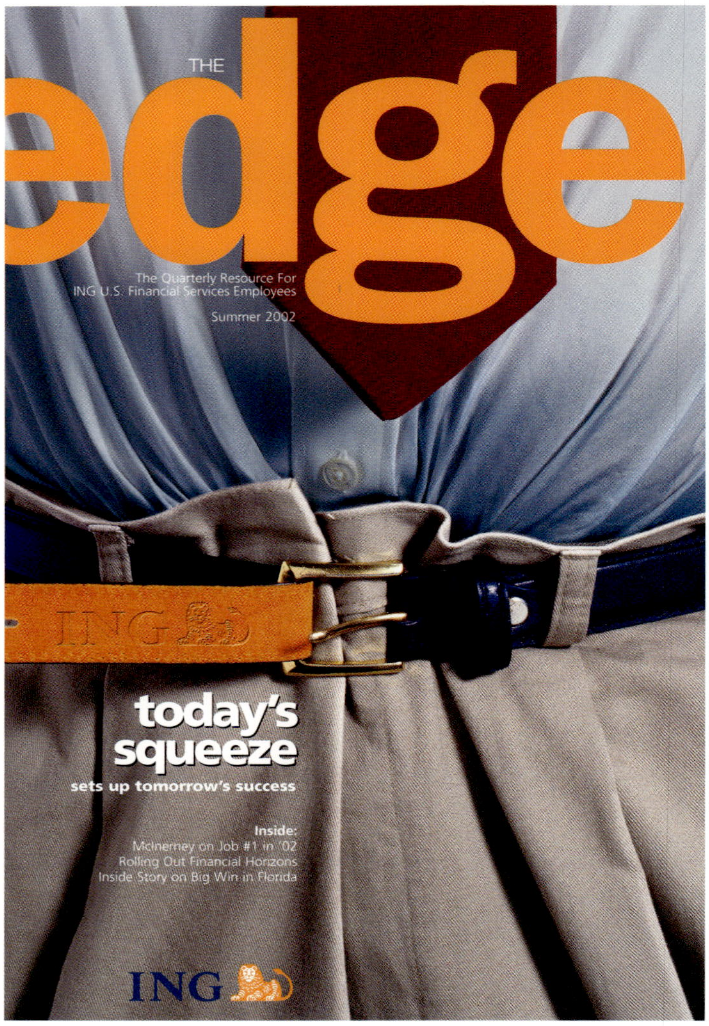

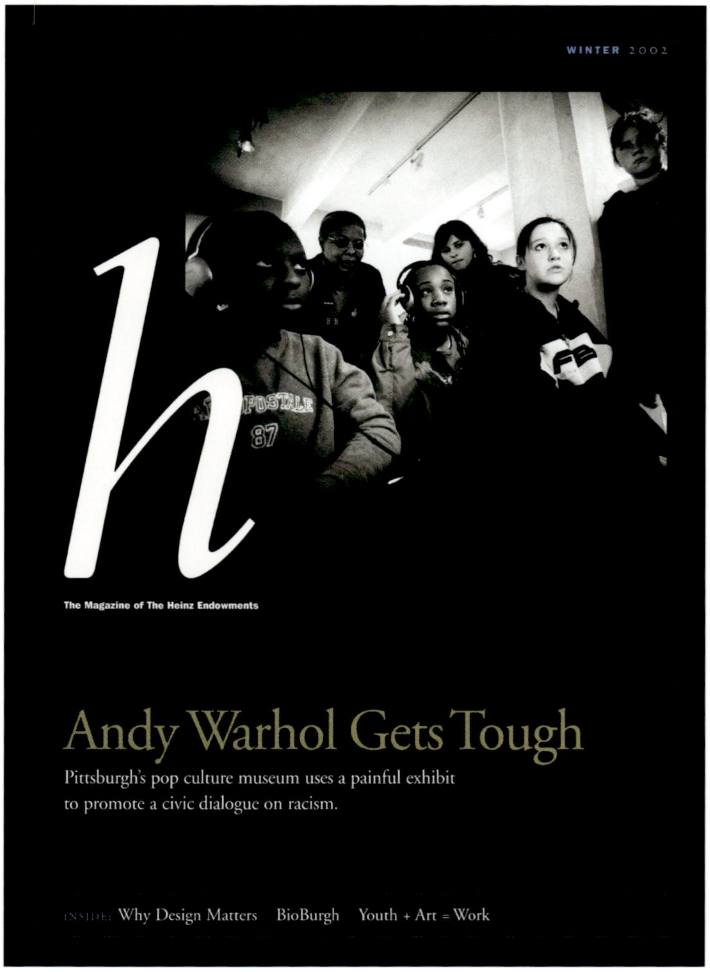

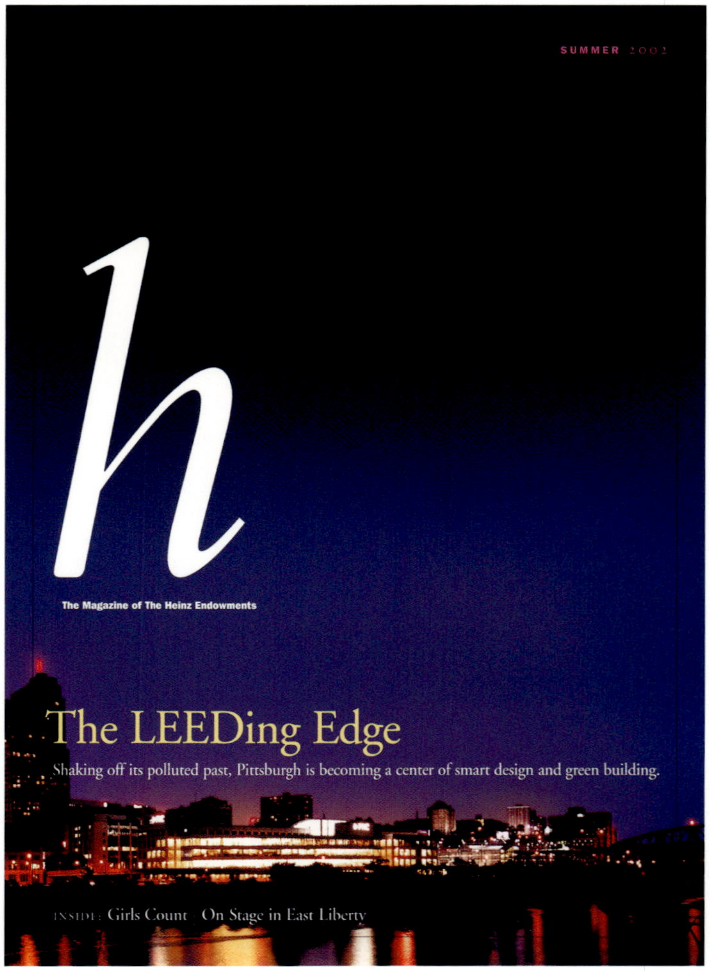

(top) Design Firm: DDB Worldwide - New York Creative Director: John Staffen Photographer: Kate Murphy Account Coordinator: Ty Kendig Client: Ing
(bottom) 'h magazine' Design Firm: Landesberg Design Creative Directors: Rick Landesberg and Kipp Madison Designer: Kipp Madison Client: The Heinz Endowments

MAIA

オッジ増刊2002年11月1日発行第11巻第12号
平成4年12月9日第三種郵便物認可

MY MODE STYLE MAGAZINE

マイア

2002 AUTUMN / WINTER

Oggi SPECIAL ISSUE

¥880

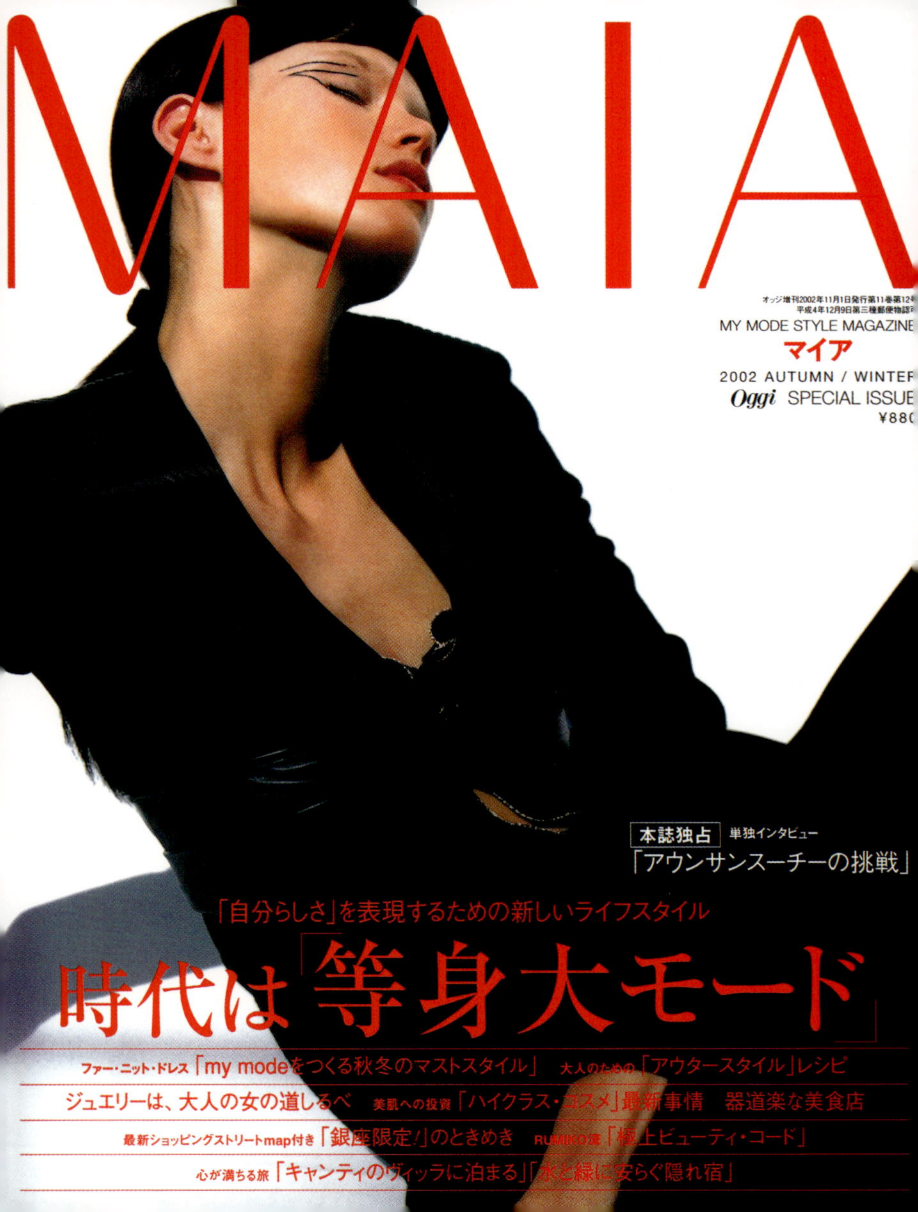

本誌独占 単独インタビュー

「アウンサンスーチーの挑戦」

「自分らしさ」を表現するための新しいライフスタイル

時代は「等身大モード」

ファー・ニット・ドレス「my modeをつくる秋冬のマストスタイル」　大人のための「アウタースタイル」レシピ

ジュエリーは、大人の女の道しるべ　美肌への投資「ハイクラス・コスメ」最新事情　器道楽な美食店

最新ショッピングストリートmap付き「銀座限定!」のときめき　RUMIKO流「極上ビューティ・コード」

心が満ちる旅「キャンティのヴィッラに泊まる」「水と緑に安らぐ隠れ宿」

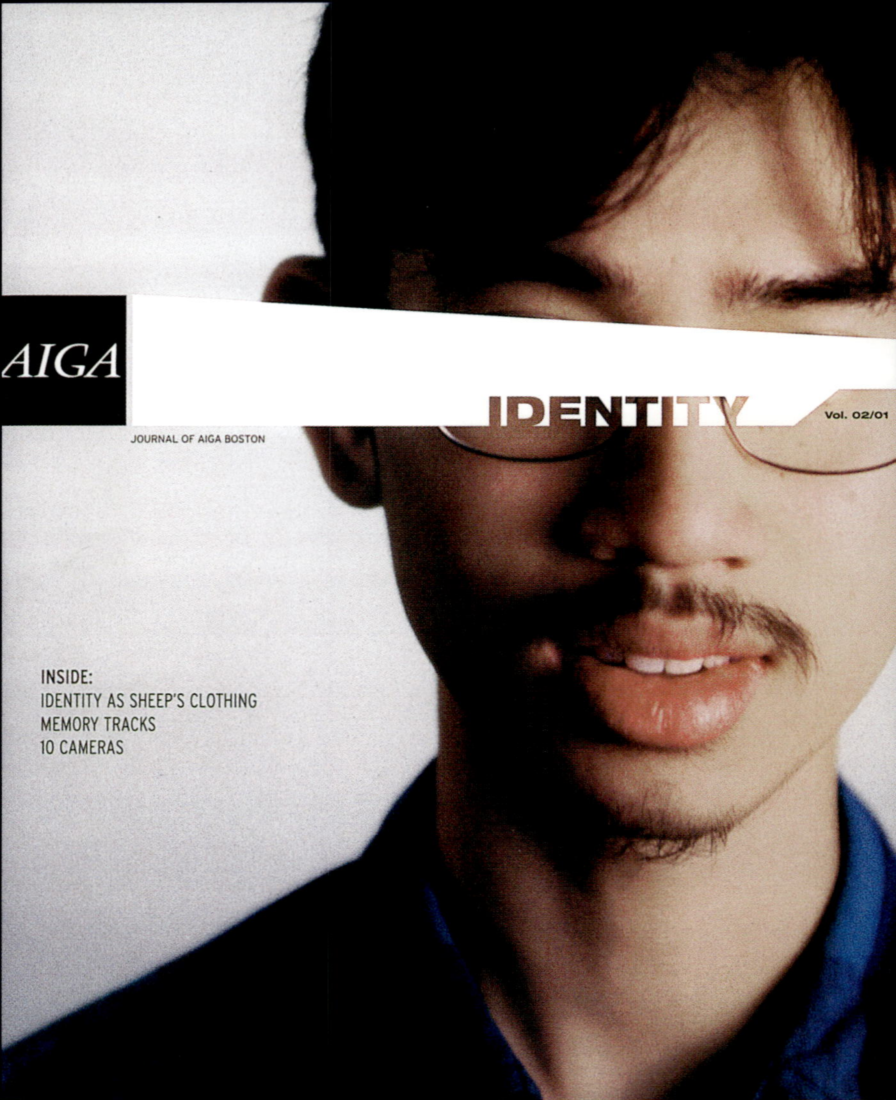
AIGA
IDENTITY
Vol. 02/01
JOURNAL OF AIGA BOSTON
INSIDE:
IDENTITY AS SHEEP'S CLOTHING
MEMORY TRACKS
10 CAMERAS

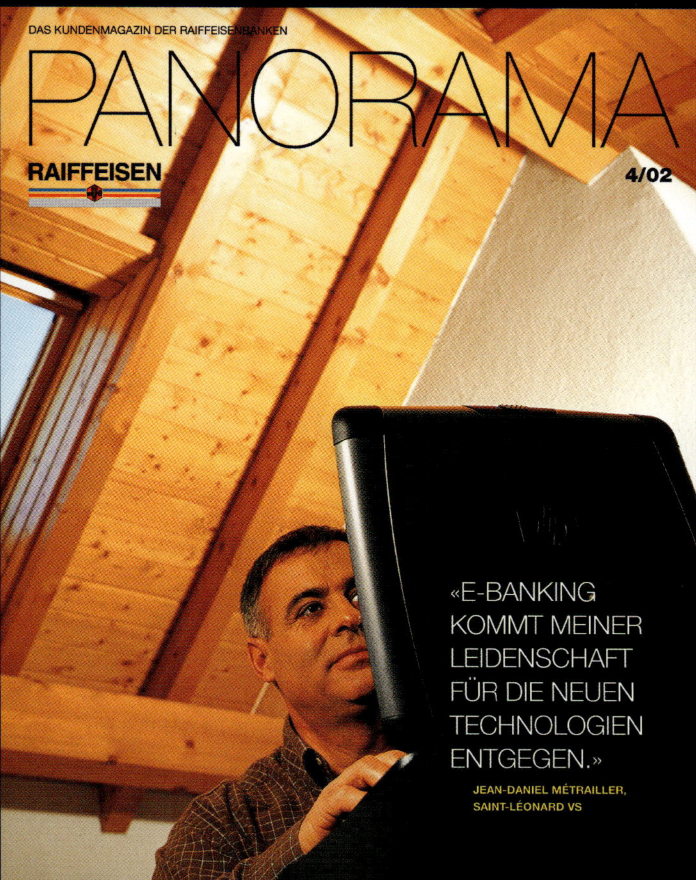

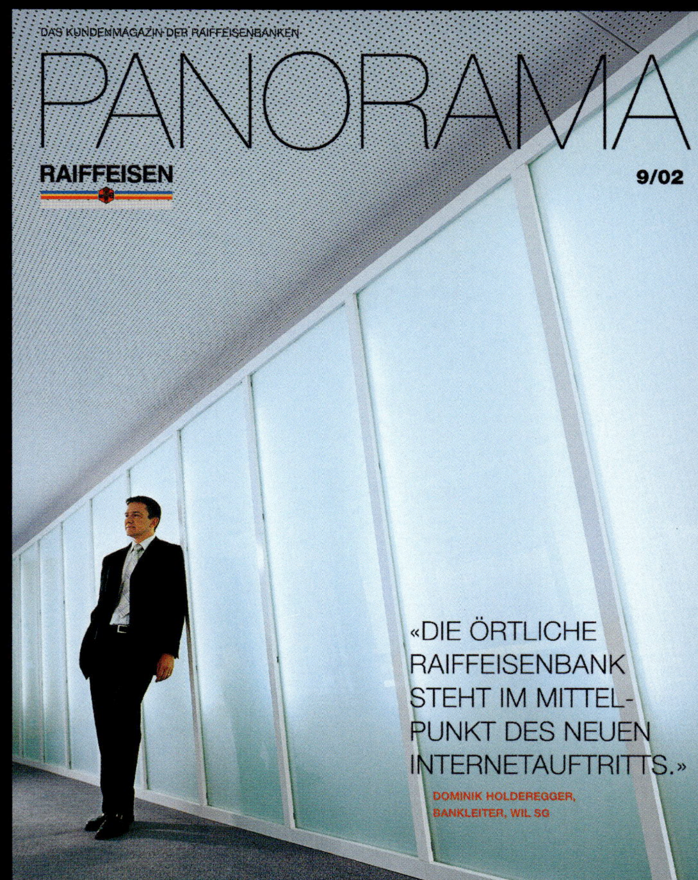

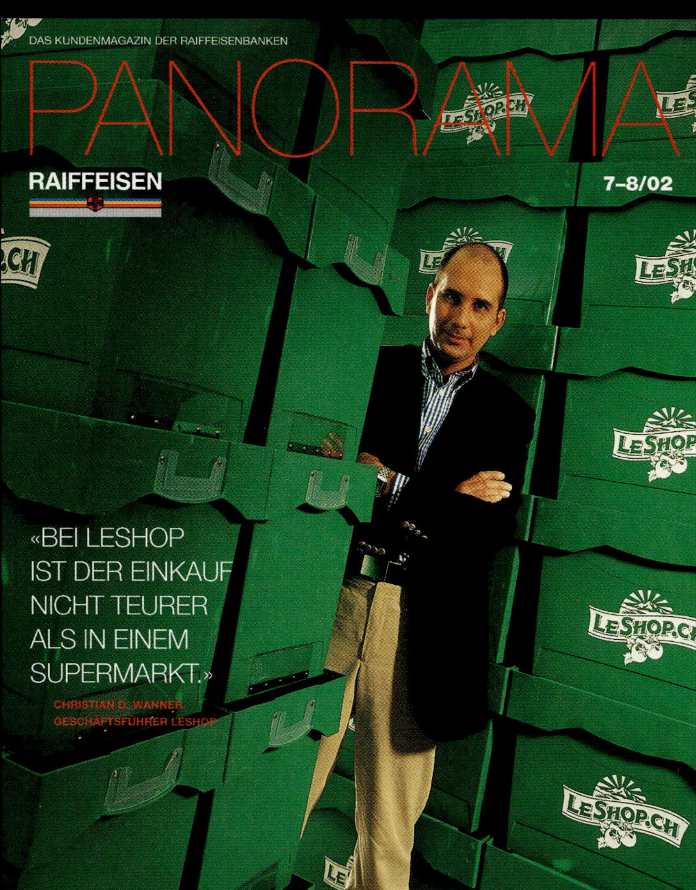

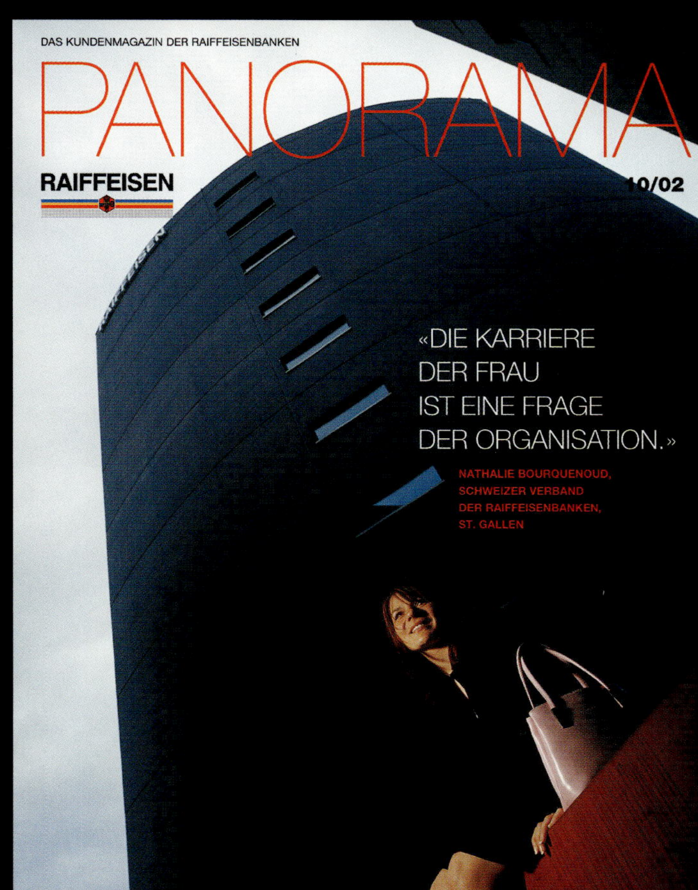

anorama Magazine' Design Firm: Brandl & Scharer AG Creative Directors: Robert Brandl and Kurt Scharer Art Director: Massimo Lansini Designer: Sandra Wyss Photographer: Maja Beck Client: Schweizer Verband der Raiffeis

borah Moses Art Director: Dan Chen Photographer: Ruven Afanador Deputy Art Director: Icarus Leung Client: Elegant Bride Magazine

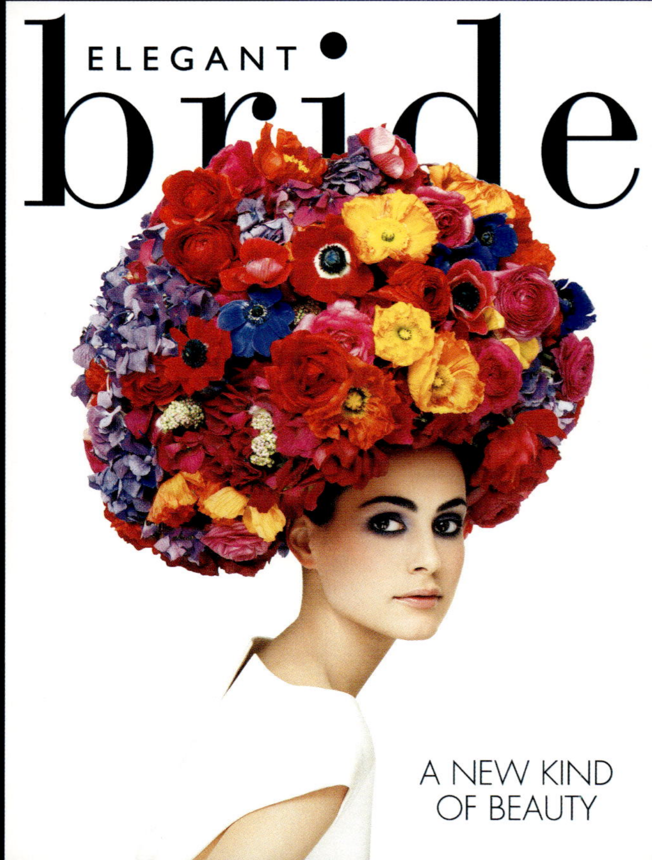

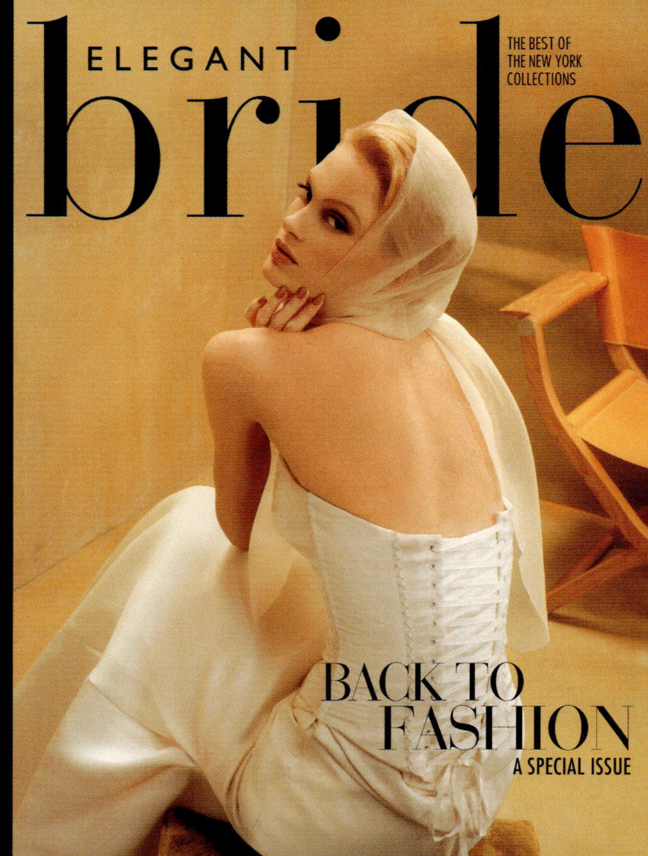

PETAL PUSHERS

Scatter the seeds of heavenly flowers and what do you get?
Beauty that intoxicates both the holder and the beholder.

PHOTOGRAPHED BY TORKIL GUDNASON

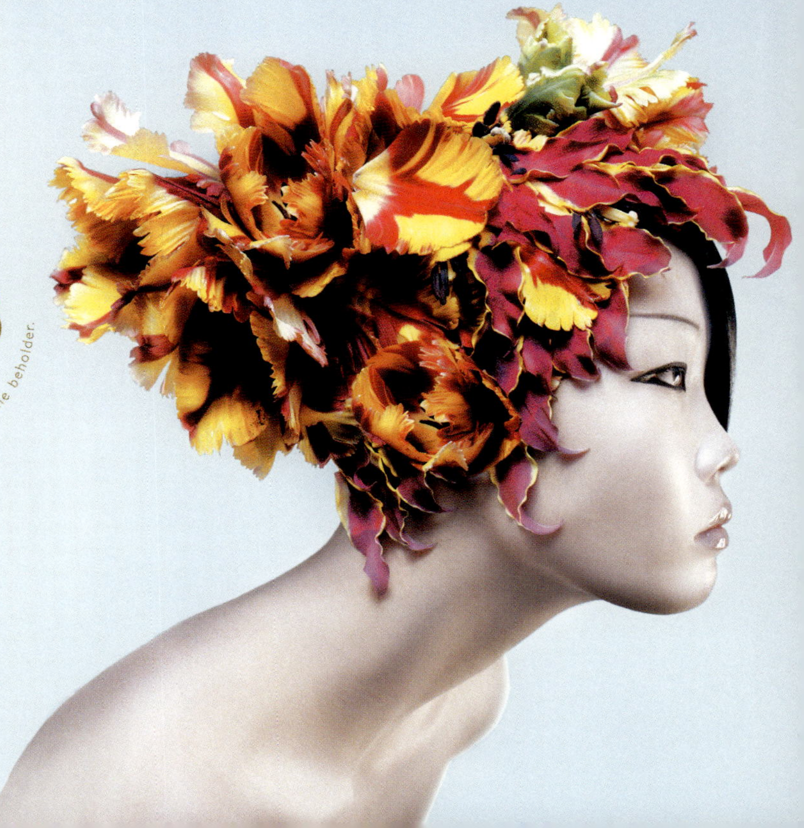

Designers: Anish Kapoor, Zaha Hadid and Mariko Mori Photographers: Red Saunders, Hélène Binet and Gabriele Basilico Editor: Deyan Sudjic Client: Domus

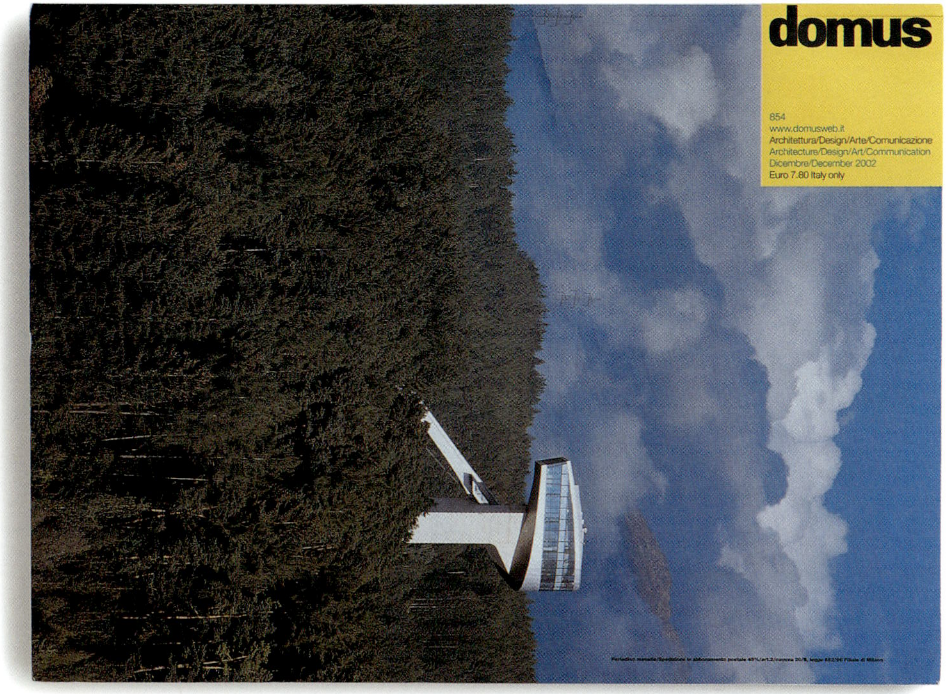

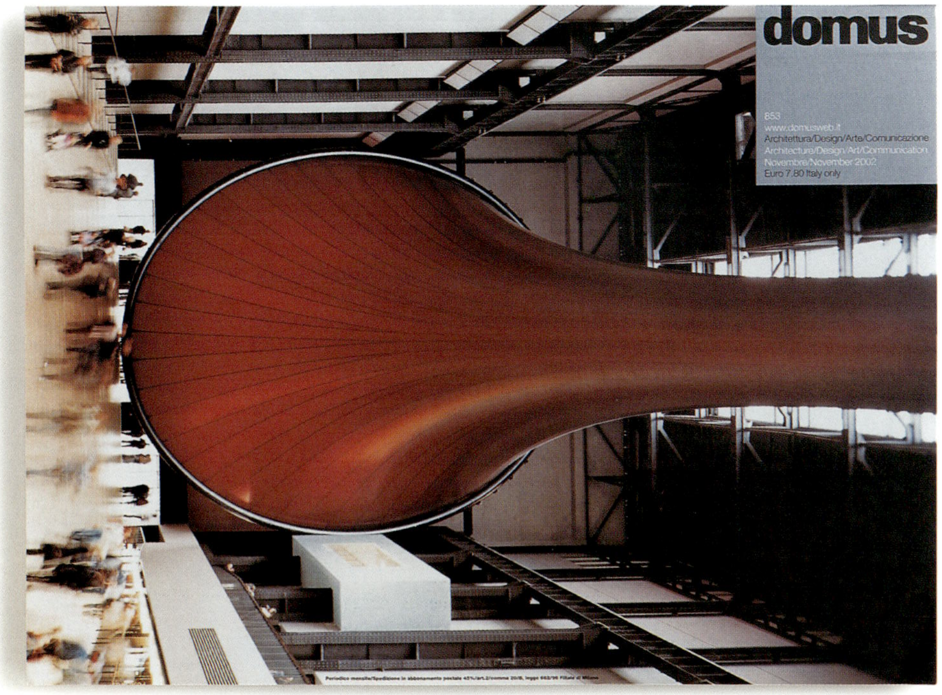

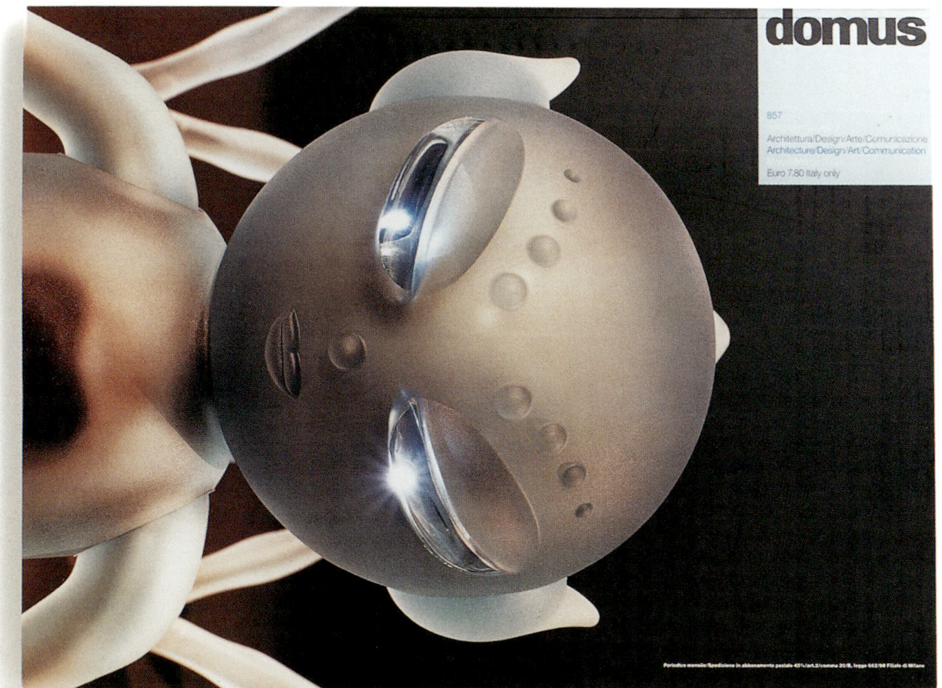

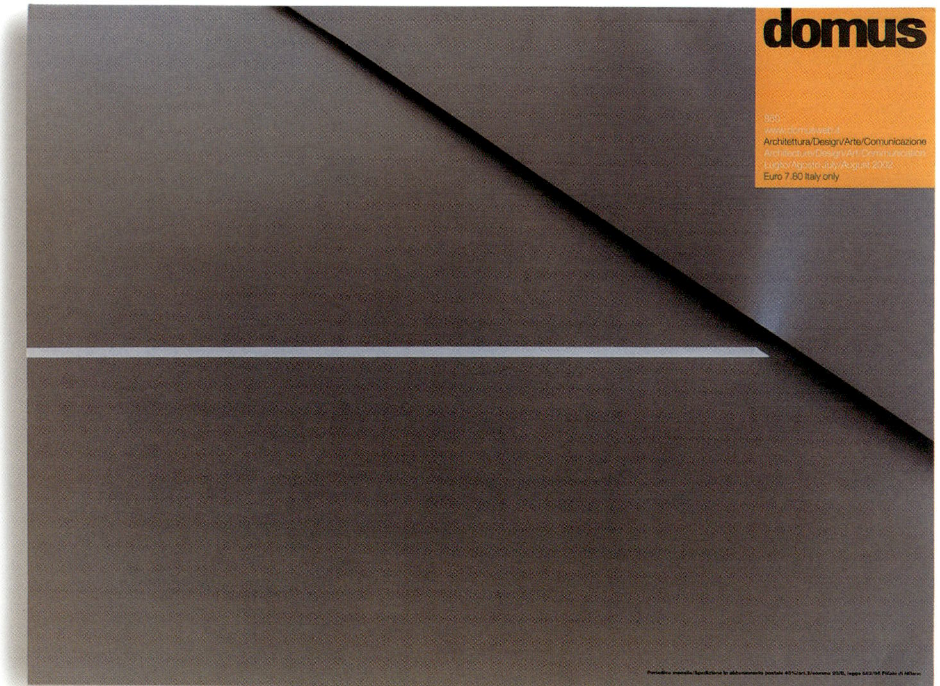

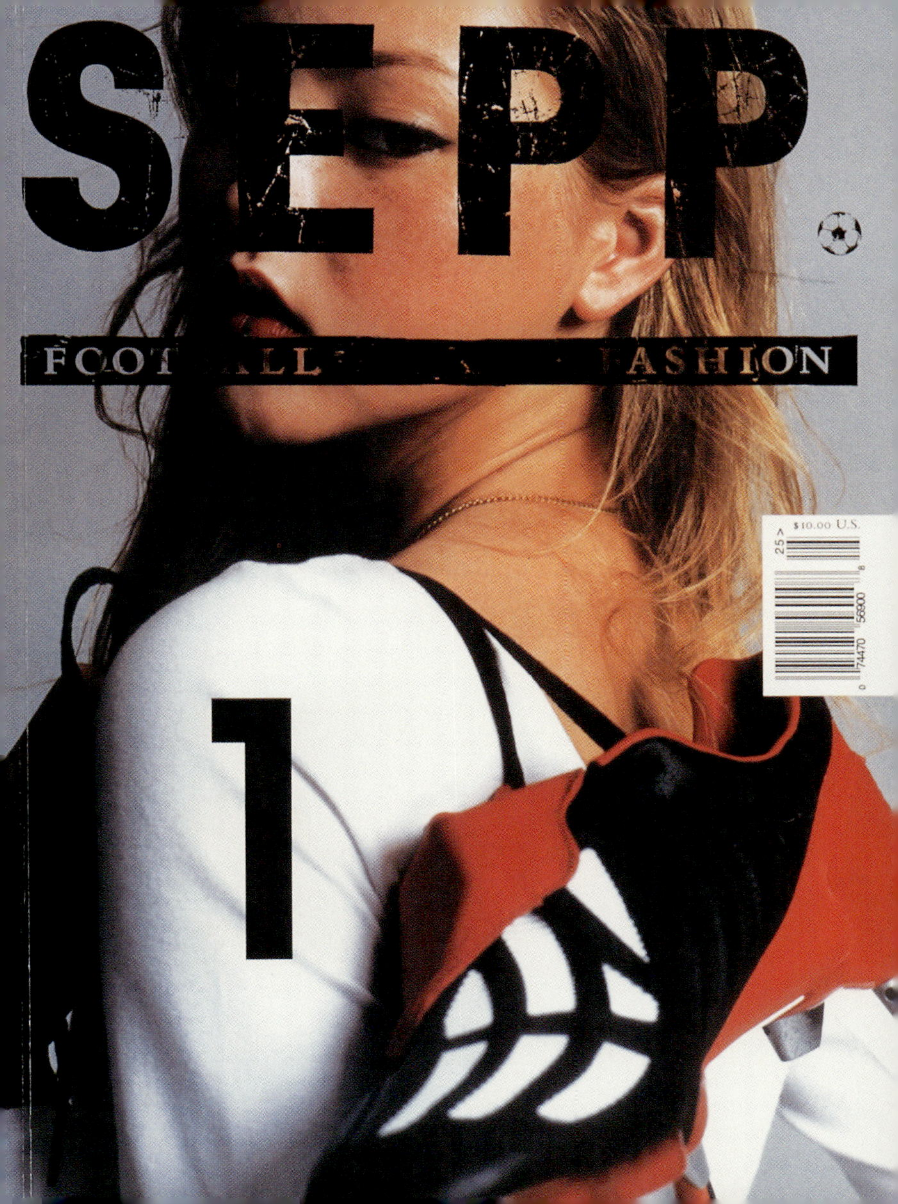
SEPP
$10.00 U.S.
1

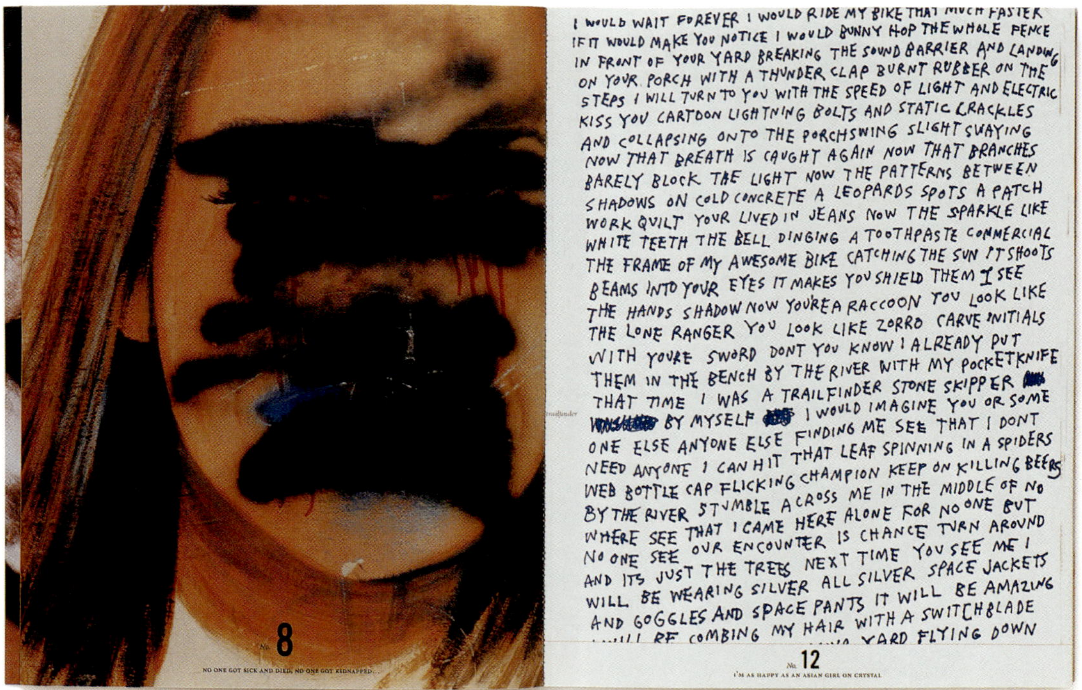

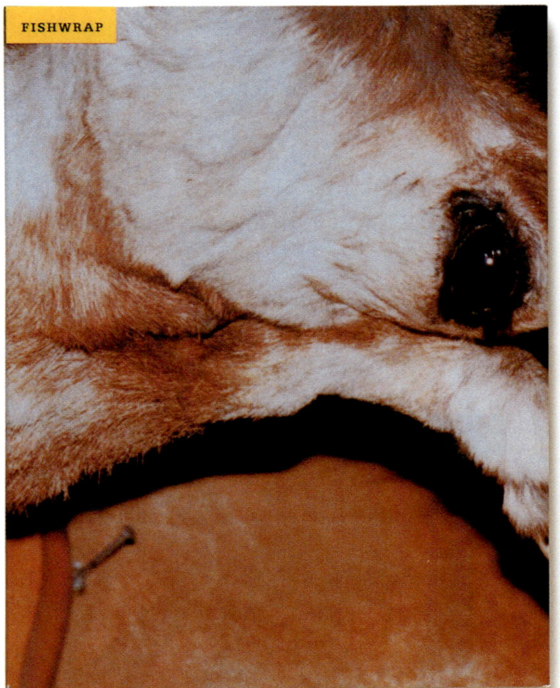

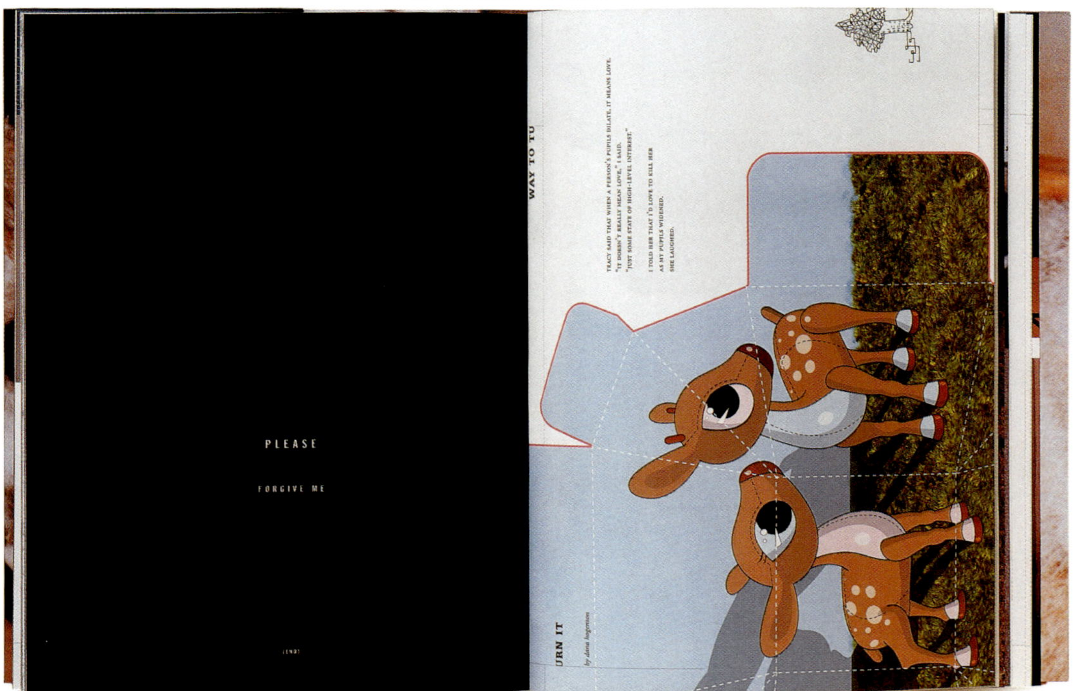

'Fishwrap' Design Firm: Art Center College of Design Student Art Directors: Leigh Okies and Mark Aver Advisors/Teachers: Lisa Wagner-Holley, Jason Holley, Ben Weissman, Chris Clayton Guest Editor: Trinie Dalton Student Designers, Writers, Illustrators, Photographers and Artists: Leigh Okies, Mark Aver, Tracy Johnson, Souther Salazar, Theo Morrisson, Ben Grieme, Rachell Sumpter, Travis Chatham, Oksana Badrak, Paul Yeh, Rene Neri, Jana Haney, Jason Hernandez, Aaron Amaro, Soyoung Kim, Davina Henderson, Christopher Kahl, Hansen Smith and Daniel Chang

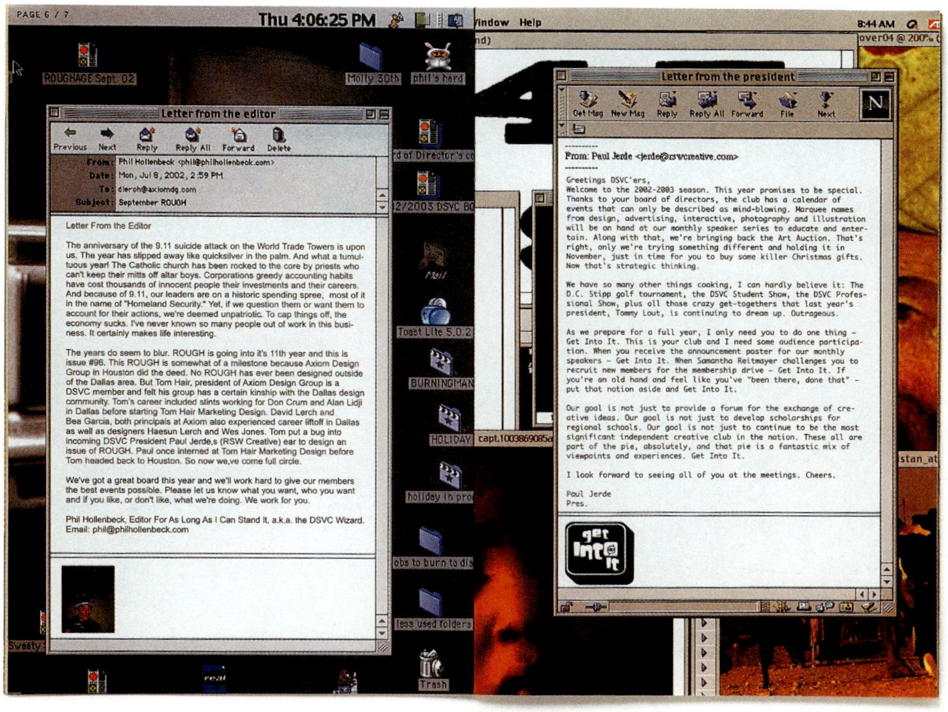

Letter from the editor

From: Phil Hollenbeck <phil@philhollenbeck.com>
Date: Mon, Jul 8, 2002, 2:59 PM
To: dlerch@axiomdg.com
Subject: September ROUGH

Letter From the Editor

The anniversary of the 9.11 suicide attack on the World Trade Towers is upon us. The year has slipped away like quicksilver in the palm. And what a tumultuous year! The Catholic church has been rocked to the core by priests who can't keep their mitts off altar boys. Corporations greedy accounting habits have cost thousands of innocent people their investments and their careers. And because of 9.11, our leaders are on a historic spending spree, most of it in the name of "Homeland Security." Yet, if we question them or want them to account for their actions, we're deemed unpatriotic. To cap things off, the economy sucks. I've never known so many people out of work in this business. It certainly makes life interesting.

The years do seem to blur. ROUGH is going into it's 11th year and this is issue #96. This ROUGH is somewhat of a milestone because Axiom Design Group in Houston did the deed. No ROUGH has ever been designed outside of the Dallas area. But Tom Hair, president of Axiom Design Group is a DSVC member and felt his group has a certain kinship with the Dallas design community. Tom's career included stints working for Don Crum and Alan Lidji in Dallas before starting Tom Hair Marketing Design. David Lerch and Bea Garcia, both principals at Axiom also experienced career liftoff in Dallas as well as designers Haesun Lerch and Wes Jones. Tom put a bug into incoming DSVC President Paul Jerde,s (RSW Creative) ear to design an issue of ROUGH. Paul once interned at Tom Hair Marketing Design before Tom headed back to Houston. So now we,ve come full circle.

We've got a great board this year and we'll work hard to give our members the best events possible. Please let us know what you want, who you want and if you like, or don't like, what we're doing. We work for you.

Phil Hollenbeck, Editor For As Long As I Can Stand It, a.k.a. the DSVC Wizard.
Email: phil@philhollenbeck.com

Letter from the president

From: Paul Jerde <jerde@rswcreative.com>

Greetings DSVC'ers,
Welcome to the 2002-2003 season. This year promises to be special. Thanks to your board of directors, the club has a calendar of events that can only be described as mind-blowing. Marquee names from design, advertising, interactive, photography and illustration will be on hand at our monthly speaker series to educate and entertain. Along with that, we're bringing back the Art Auction. That's right, only we're trying something different and holding it in November, just in time for you to buy some killer Christmas gifts. Now that's strategic thinking.

We have so many other things cooking, I can hardly believe it: The D.C. Stipp golf tournament, the DSVC Student Show, the DSVC Professional Show, plus all those crazy get-togethers that last year's president, Tommy Lout, is continuing to dream up. Outrageous.

As we prepare for a full year, I only need you to do one thing - Get Into It. This is your club and I need some audience participation. When you receive the announcement poster for our monthly speakers - Get Into It. When Samantha Reitmayer challenges you to recruit new members for the membership drive - Get Into It. If you're an old hand and feel like you've "been there, done that" - put that notion aside and Get Into It.

Our goal is not just to provide a forum for the exchange of creative ideas. Our goal is not just to develop scholarships for regional schools. Our goal is not just to continue to be the most significant independent creative club in the nation. These all are part of the pie, absolutely, and that pie is a fantastic mix of viewpoints and experiences. Get Into It.

I look forward to seeing all of you at the meetings. Cheers.

Paul Jerde
Pres.

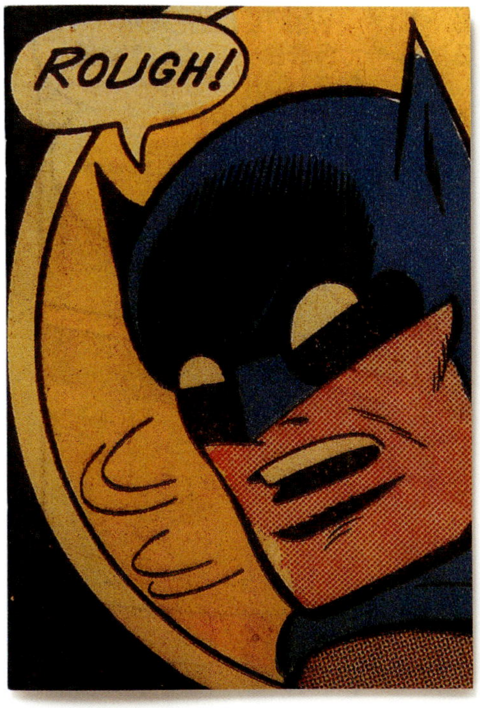

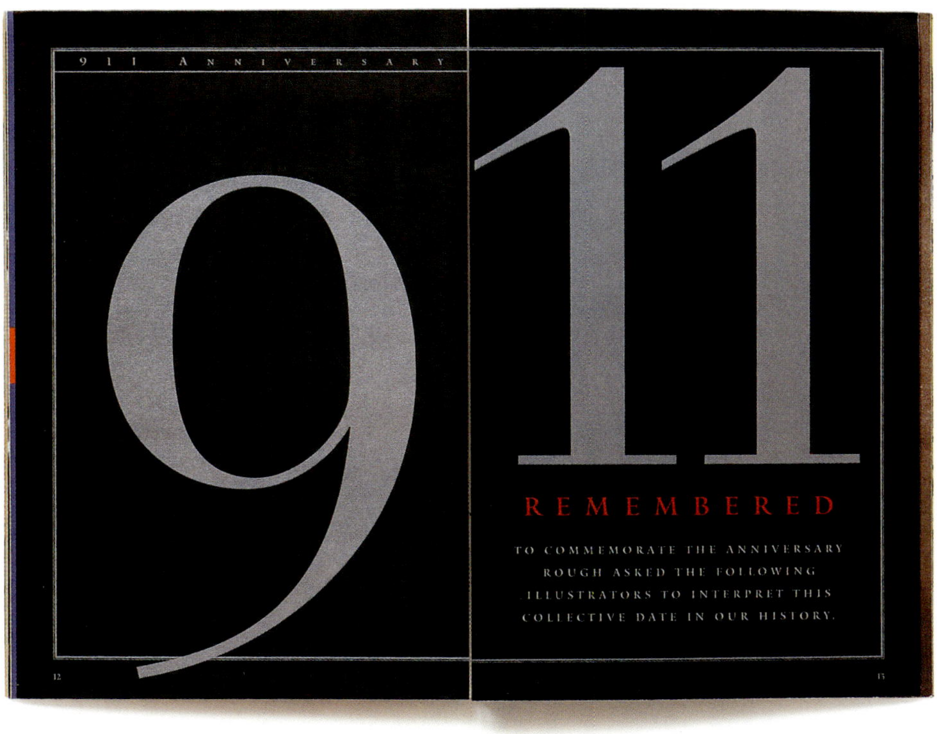

'Rough Magazine' Design Firm: Axiom Design Group Creative Directors: Tom Hair and David Lerch Art Director: David Lerch Designers: David Lerch, Haesun Kim Lerch and Wes Jones
Photographer: Phil Hollenbeck Illustrators: Brad Holland Tim Cook, Sandra Dionisi, Brian Cronin and Mark Burkhardt Copywriter: Phil Hollenbeck Client: Dallas Society of Visual Communications

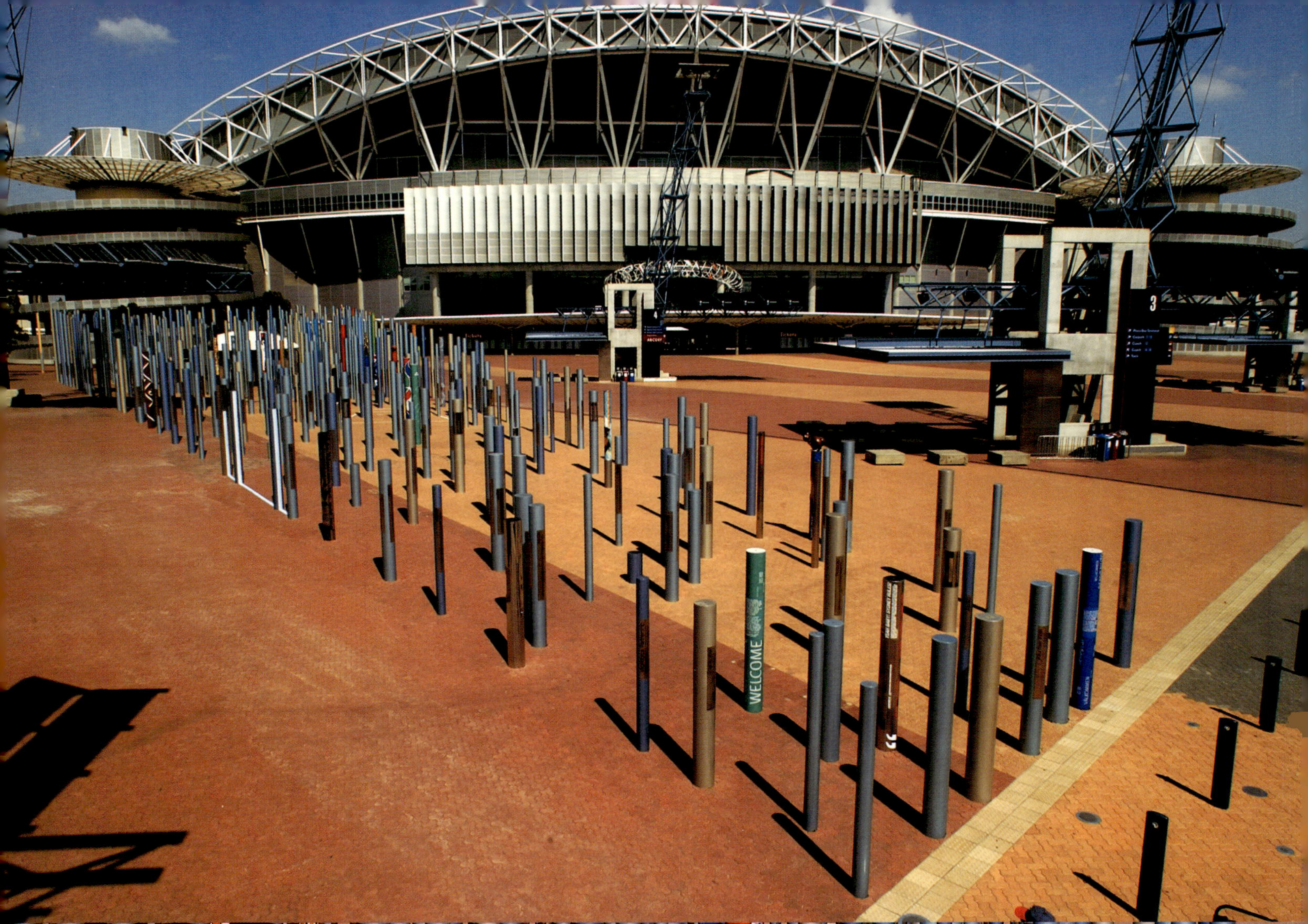
WELCOME

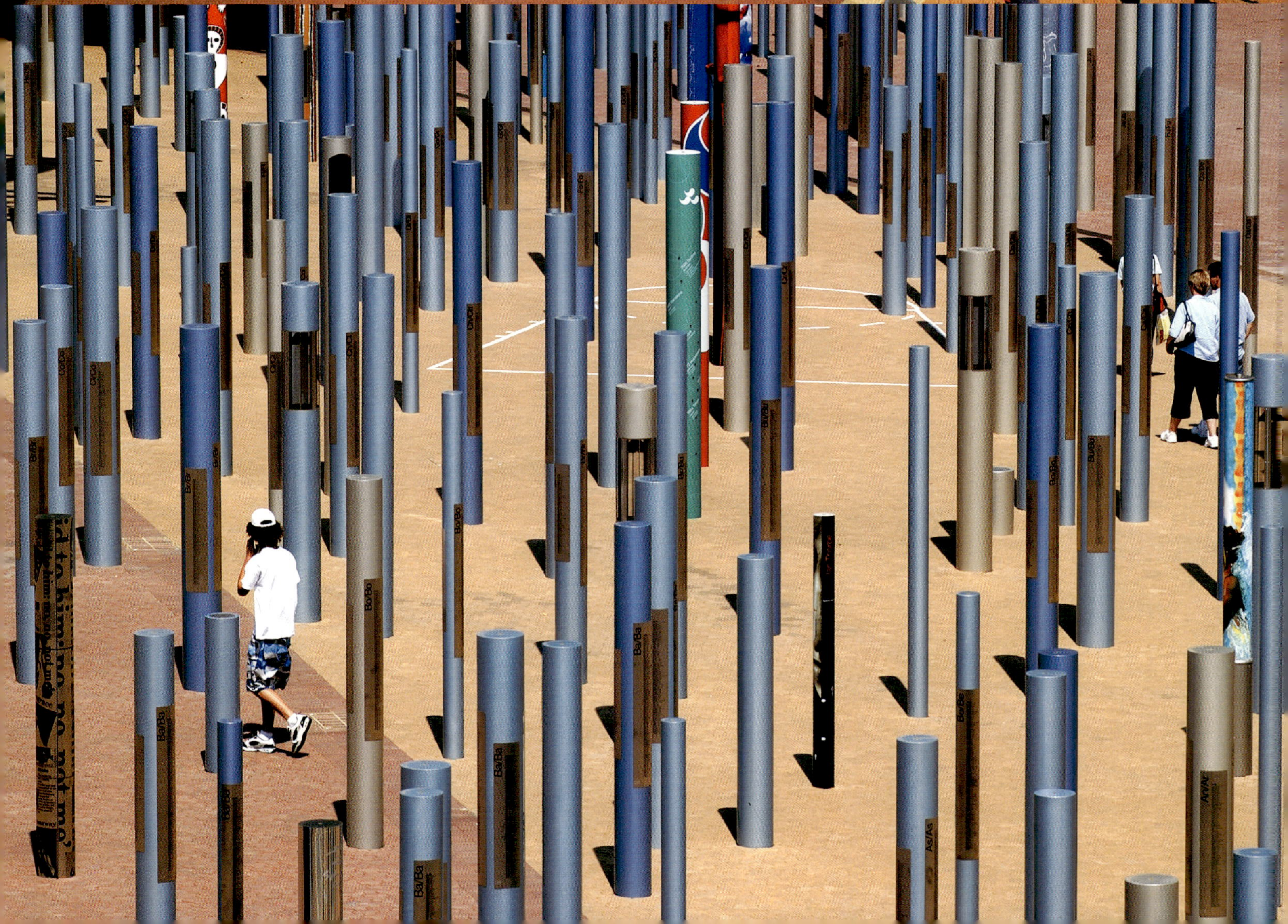

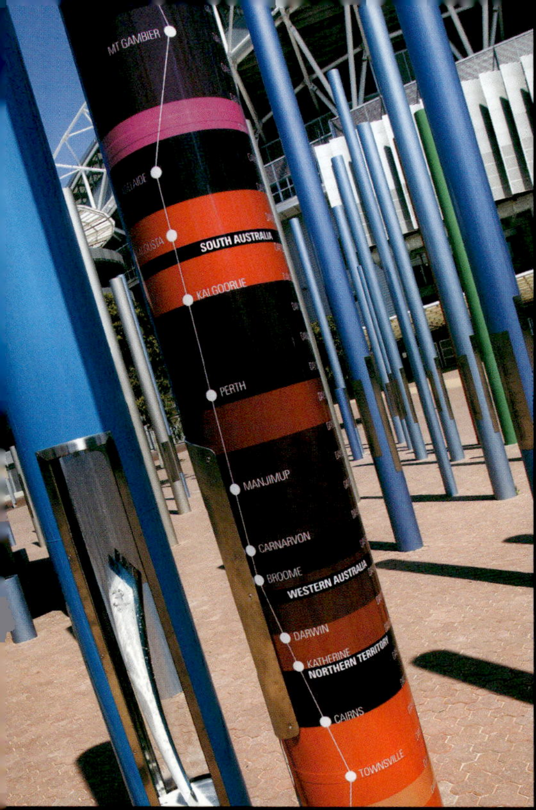
MT GAMBIER
SOUTH AUSTRALIA
KALGOORLIE
PERTH
MANJIMUP
CARNARVON
BROOME
WESTERN AUSTRALIA
DARWIN
KATHERINE
NORTHERN TERRITORY
CAIRNS
TOWNSVILLE

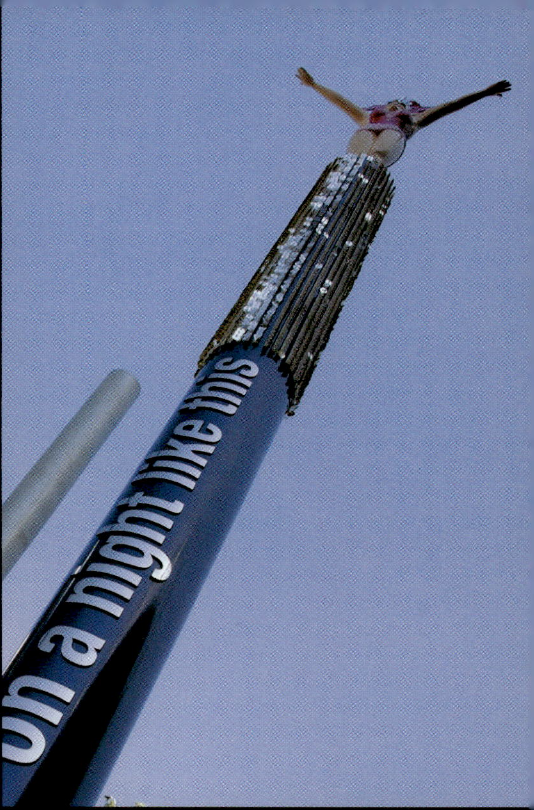
on a night like this

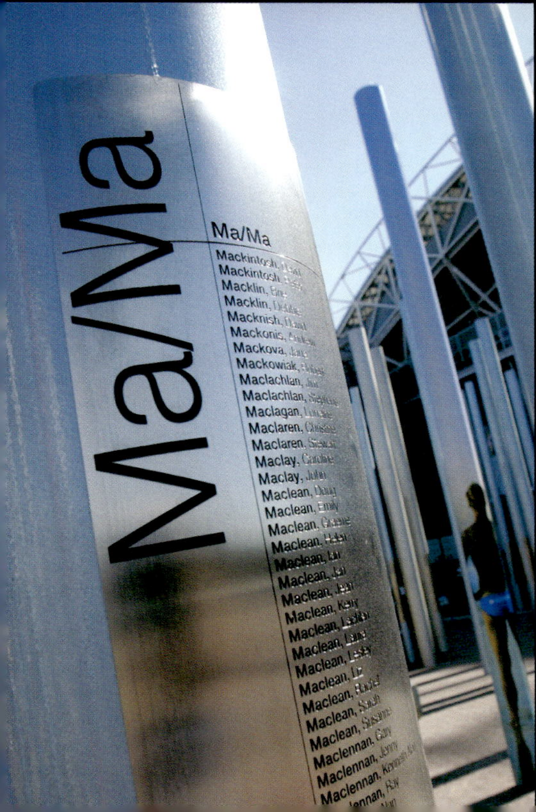
Ma/Ma
Ma/Ma

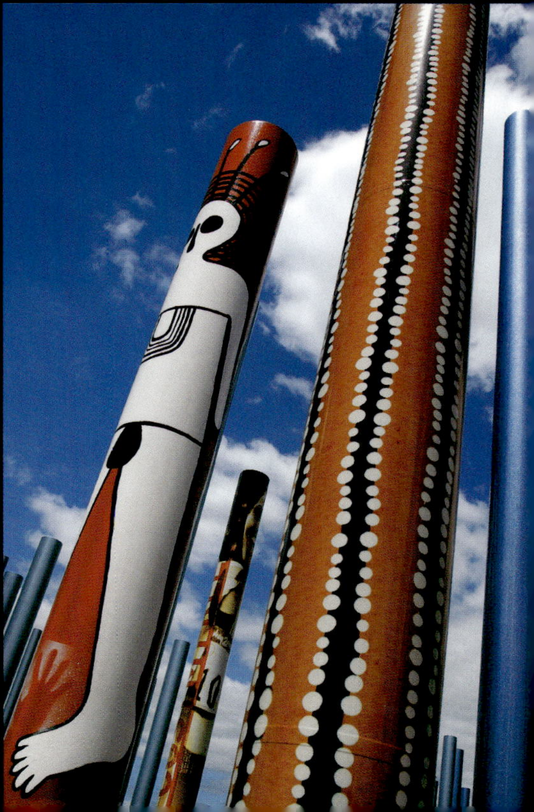

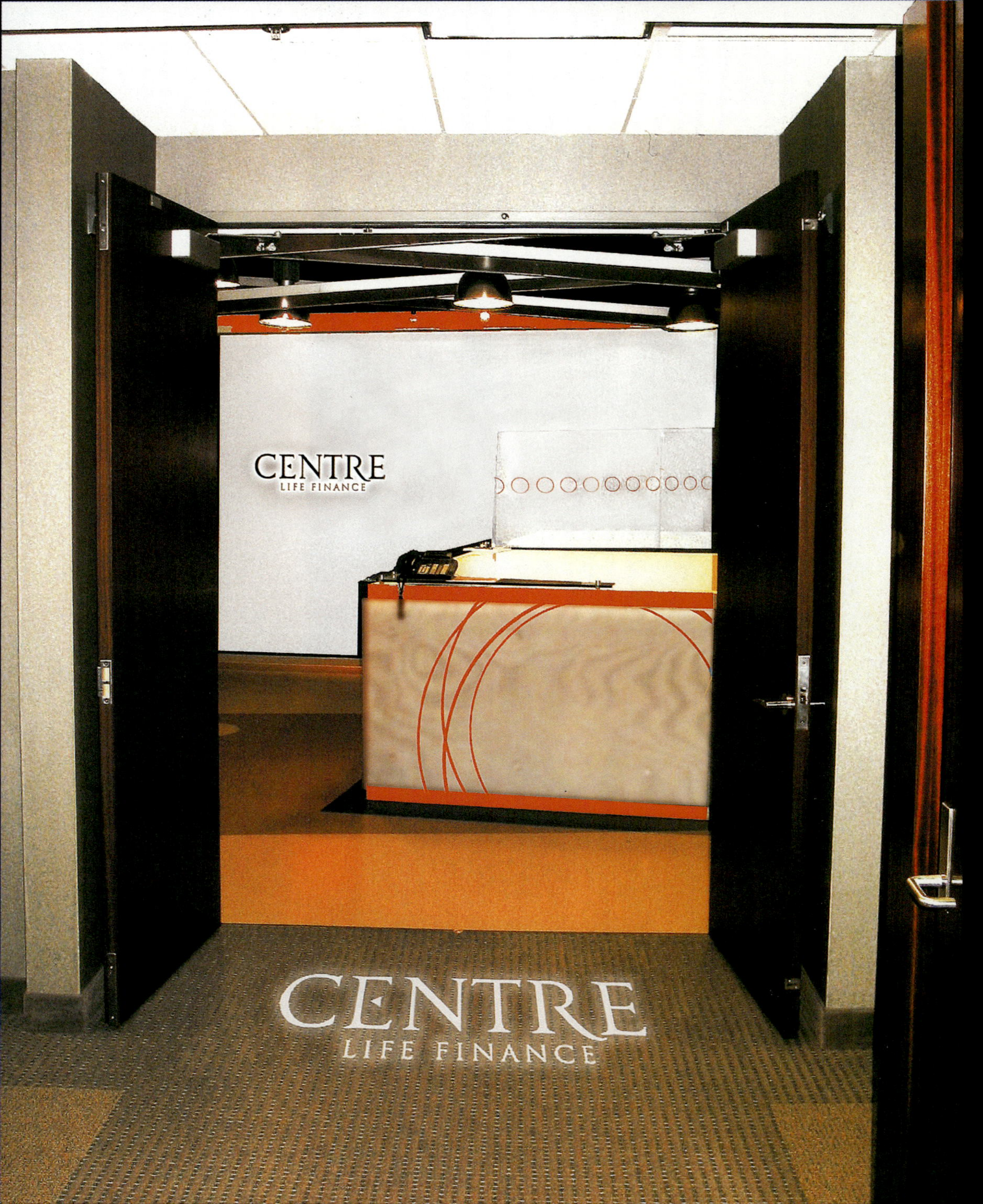
CENTRE
LIFE FINANCE
CENTRE
LIFE FINANCE

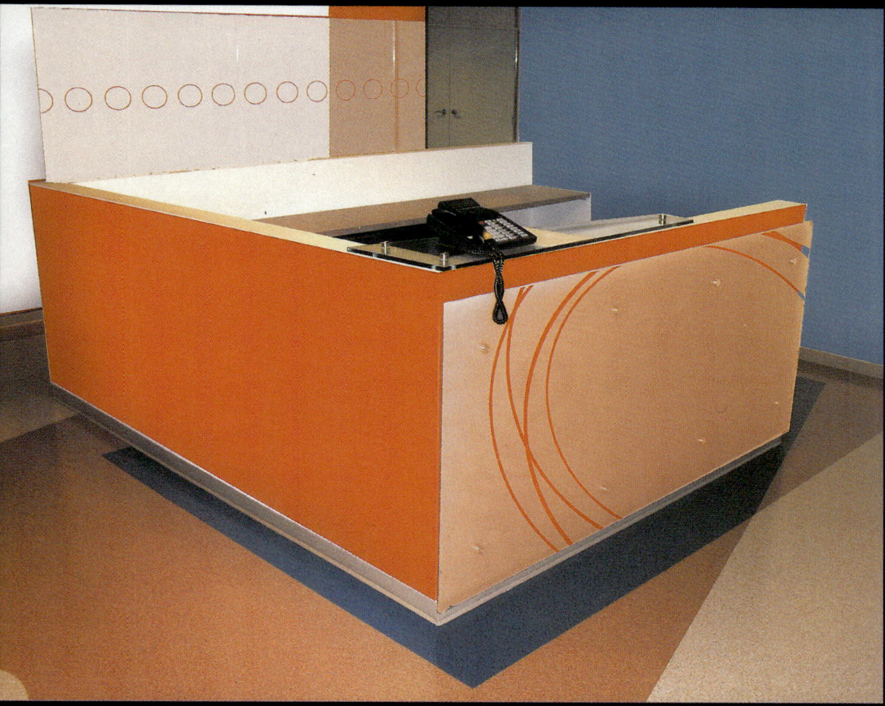

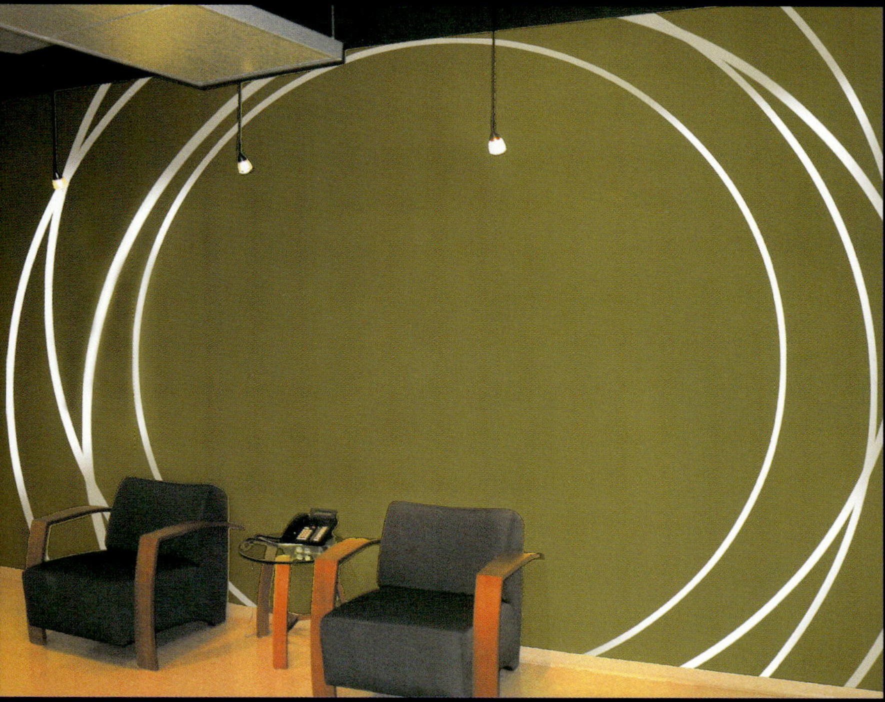

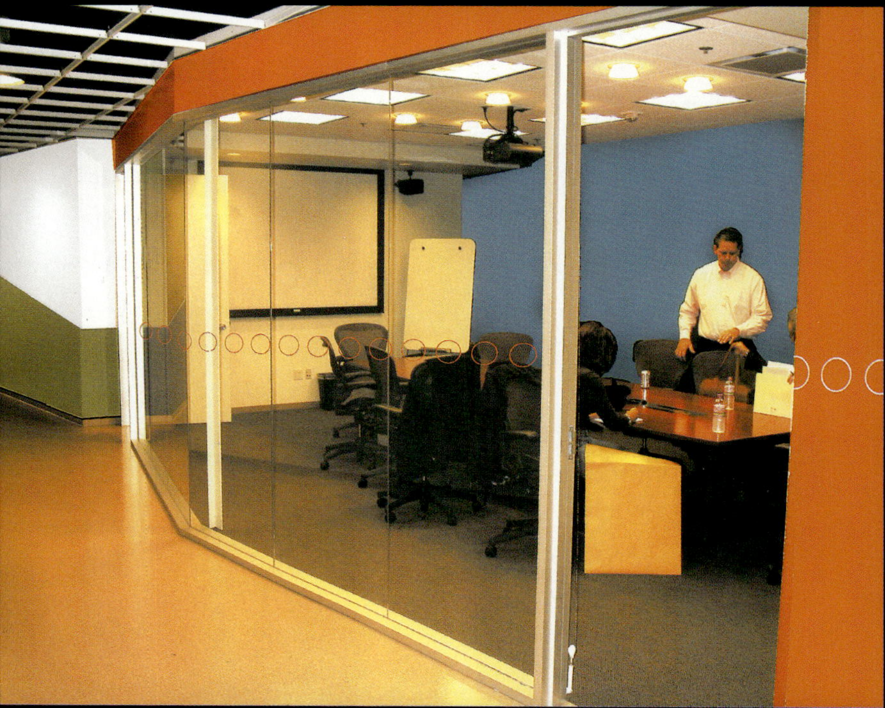

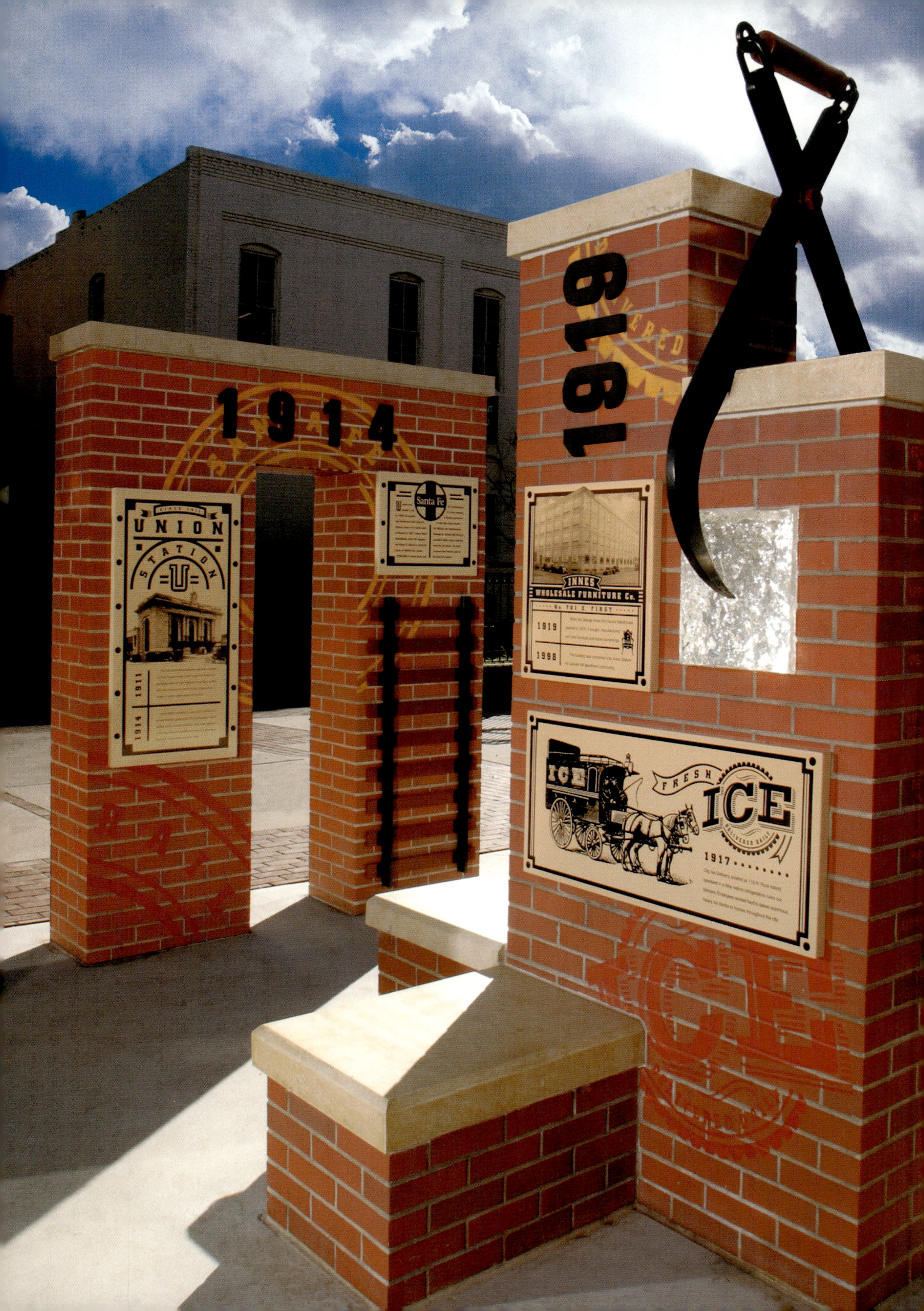
1914
UNION
STATION
U
Santa Fe
1911
1914
1919
INNES
WHOLESALE FURNITURE Co.
No 701 E FIRST
1919
1998
ICE
FRESH
ICE
1917

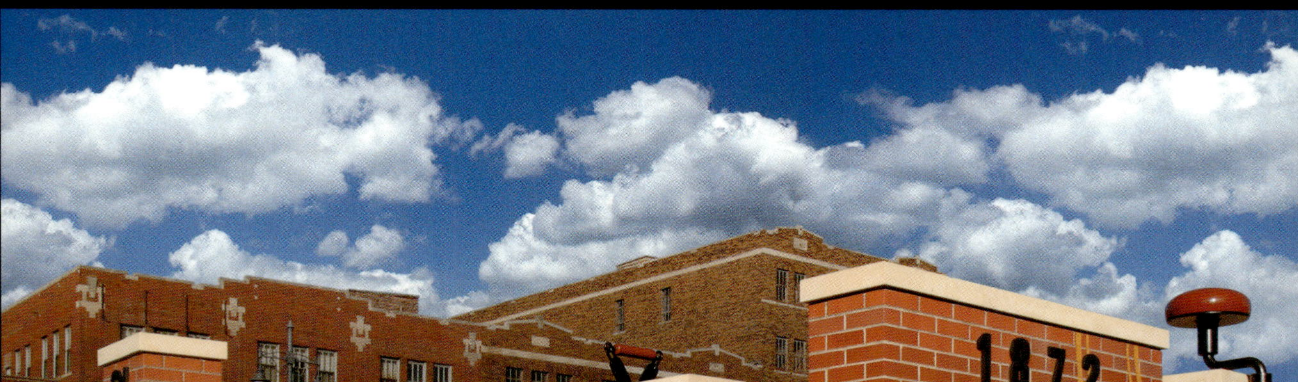

(this spread) Design Firm: Greteman Group Creative Director: Sonia Greteman Art Directors: Garrett Fresh, Sonia Greteman and James Strange Designers: Garrett Fresh, Sonia Greteman and James Strange Client: Arts Council

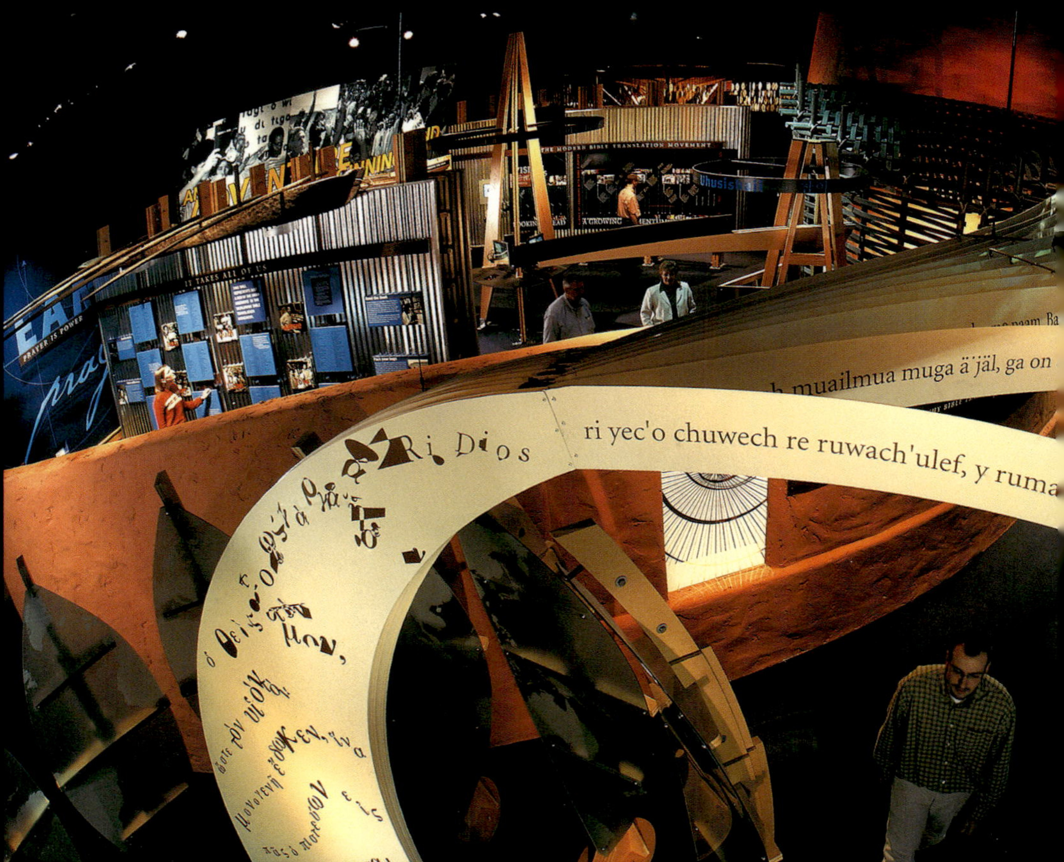

(this spread) Design Firm: Lorenc+Yoo Design Creative Director: Jan Lorenc Designers: Chung Youl Yoo, David Park, Sakchai Rangsiyakorn, Mark Malaer, Ken Boyd, Steve McCall and Gary Flesher Photographer: Lee McKee Graphic Design: Susie Norris Client: Wycliffe

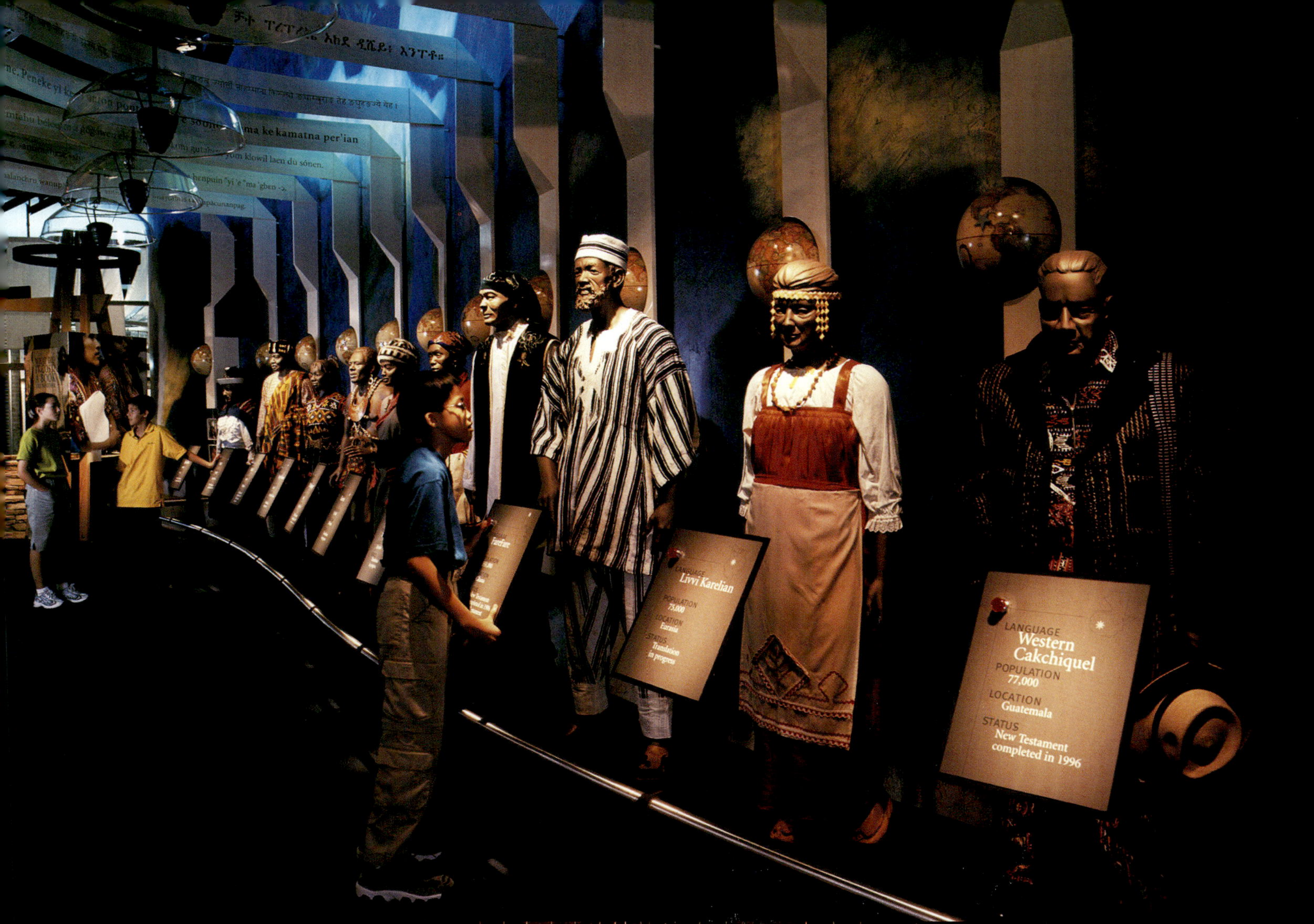
LANGUAGE
Livvi Karelian
POPULATION
75,000
LOCATION
Eurasia
STATUS
Translation in progress
LANGUAGE
Western
Cakchiquel
POPULATION
77,000
LOCATION
Guatemala
STATUS
New Testament
completed in 1996

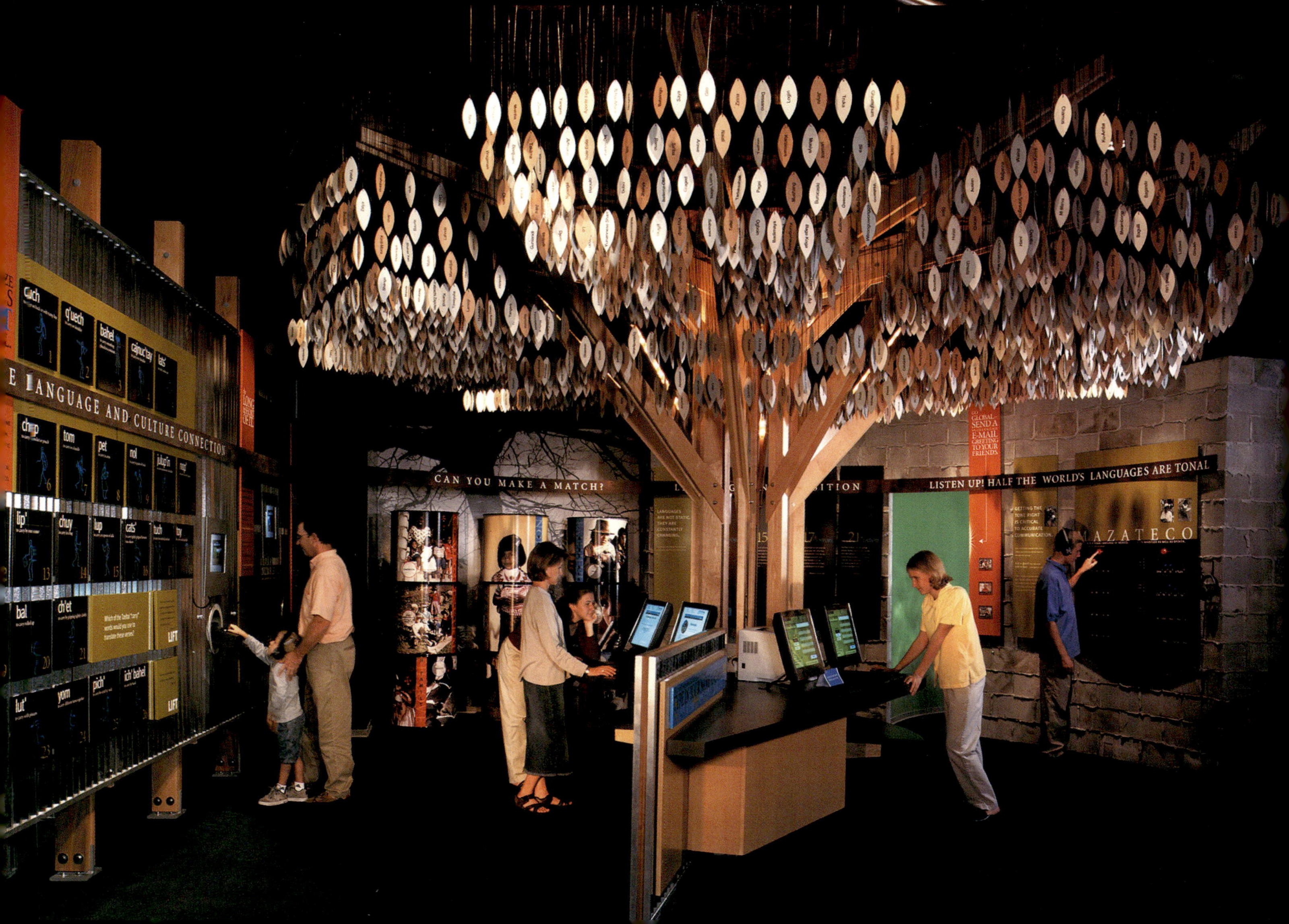
E LANGUAGE AND CULTURE CONNECTION
CAN YOU MAKE A MATCH?
LISTEN UP! HALF THE WORLD'S LANGUAGES ARE TONAL
MAZATECO

(this spread) 'Rewarding Lives: An Exhibition of Timeless Photographs' Design Firm: The Moderns, Ltd. Creative Director: Janine James Art Directors: Sara Mears and Kevin Szell Designers: Janine James and Mark Pedersen Photographers: Annie Leibovitz (artist), Dylan Cross, James Shanks and Paul Warchol Copywriters: Kelly Harrell and Kristen Rumble Curator: Micaela Martegani Scientist: Kristian Bodek Client: American Express

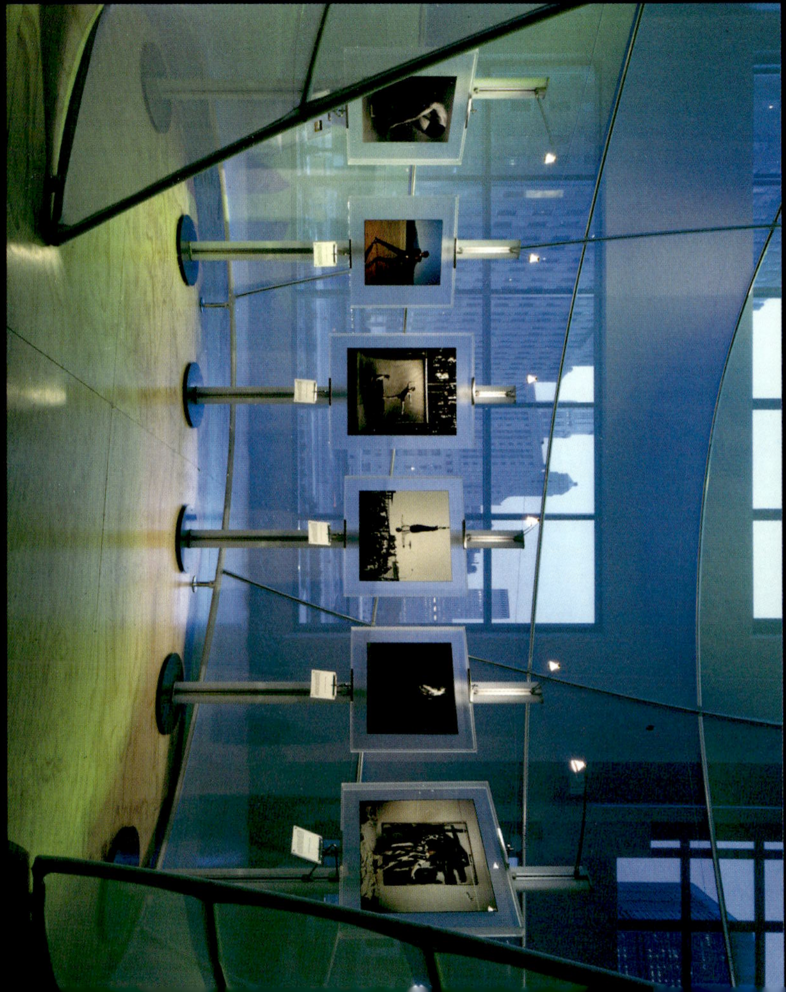

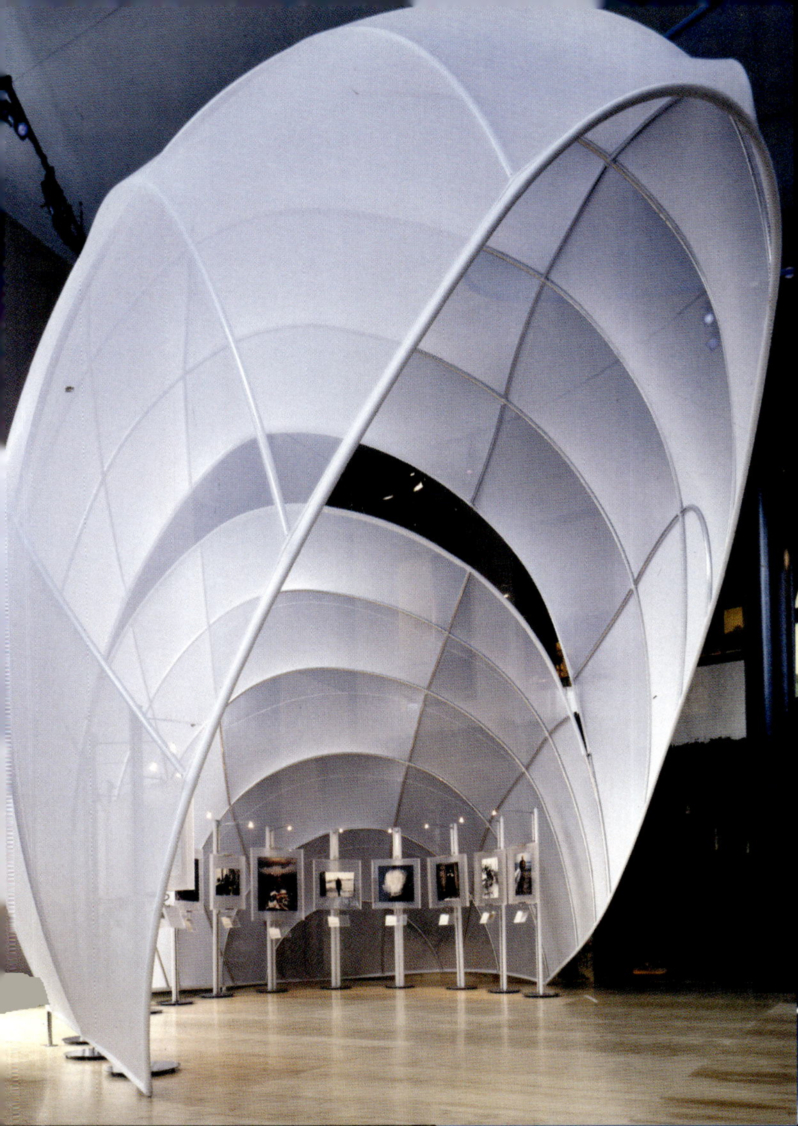
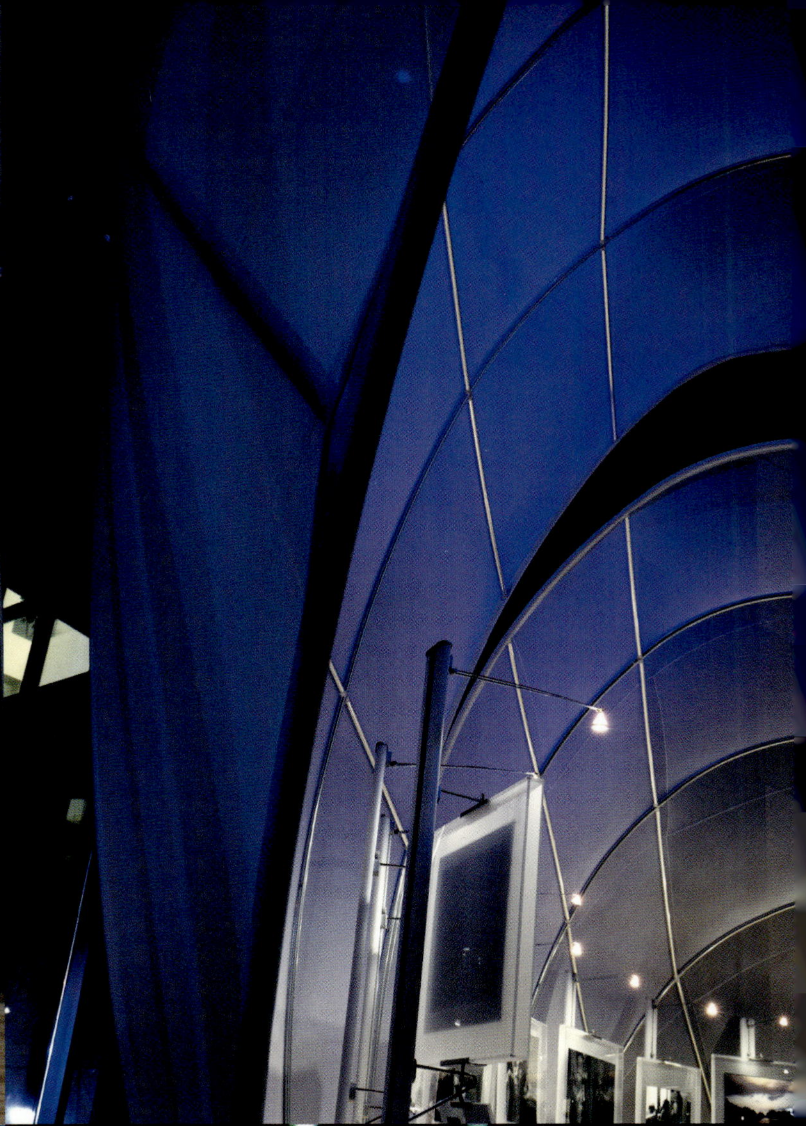
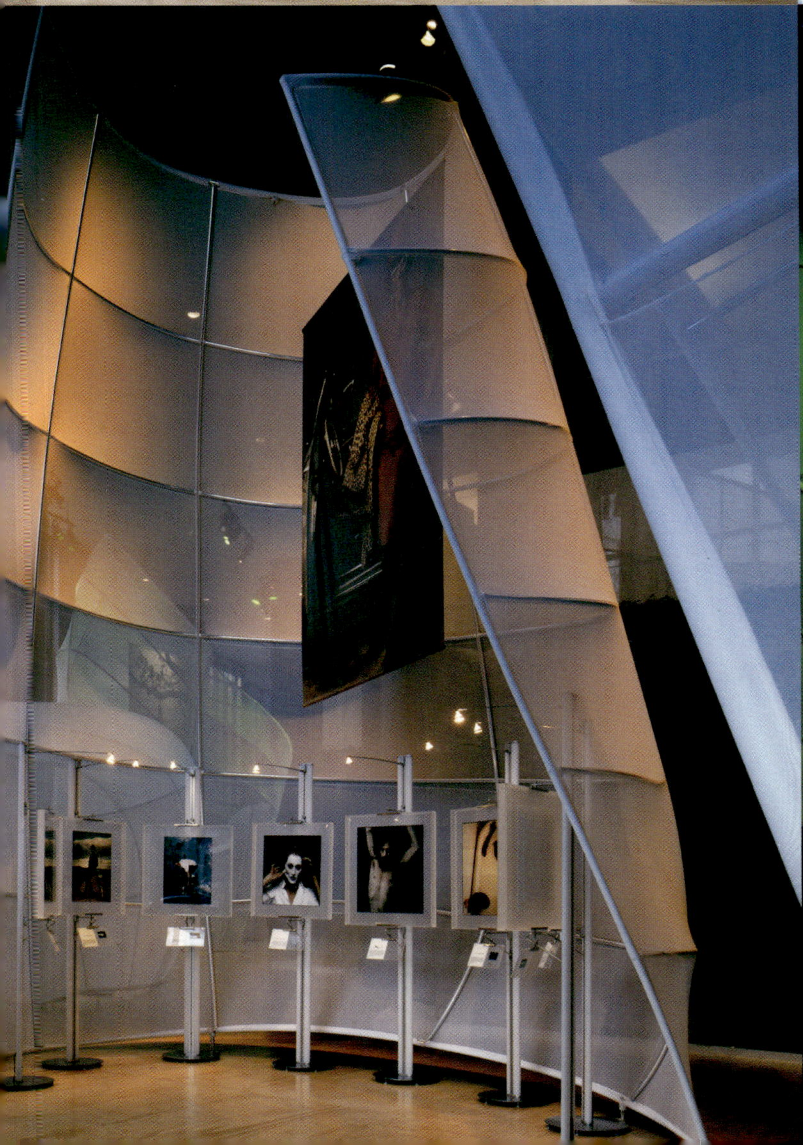
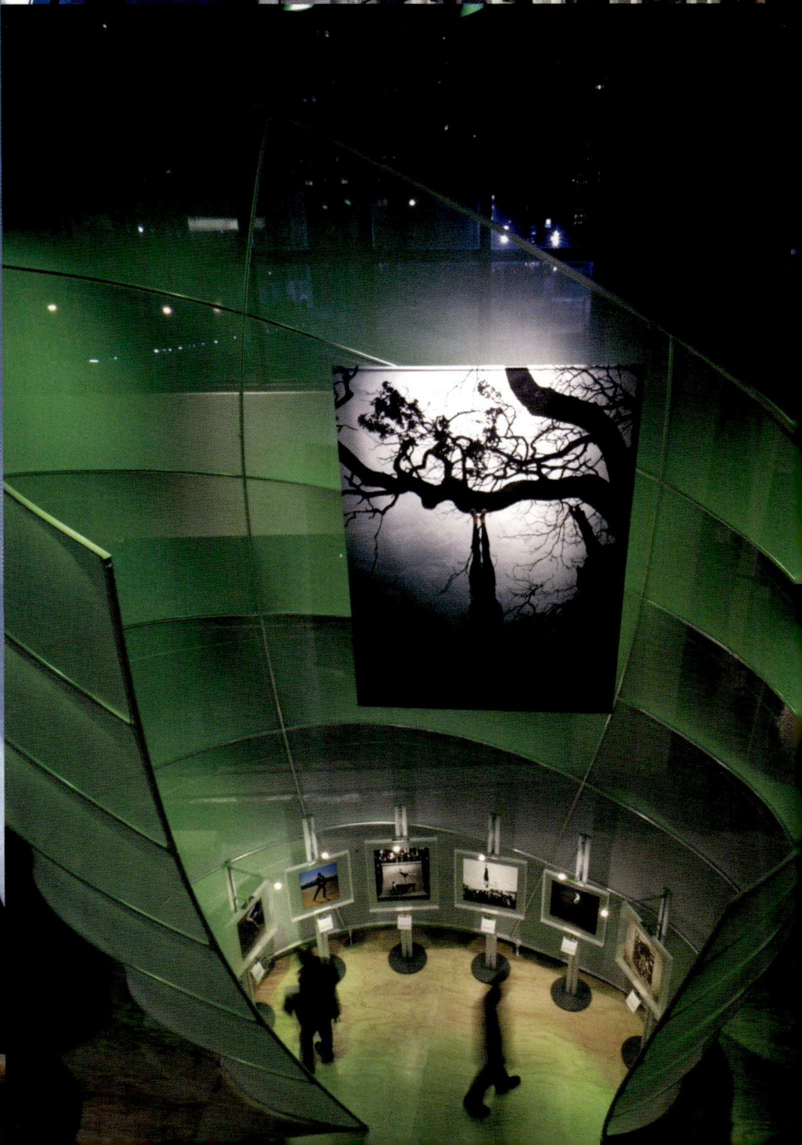

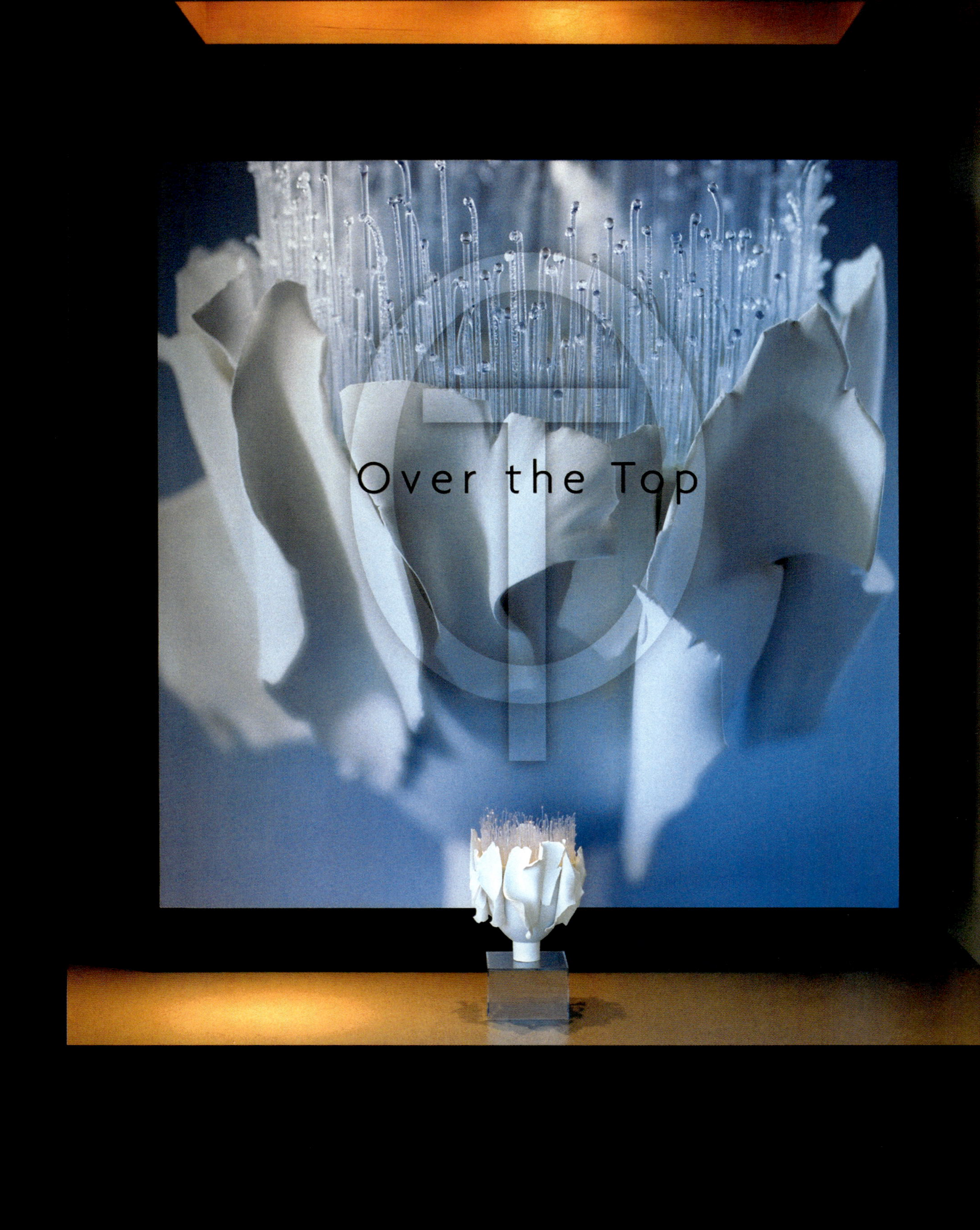

'Over The Top' Ceramic Exhibit Window Posters Design Firm: Hallmark Cards Inc. Creative Director: Patti Streeper Art Director: Dale Forton Designer: Dale Forton Photographer: Scott Gibbons

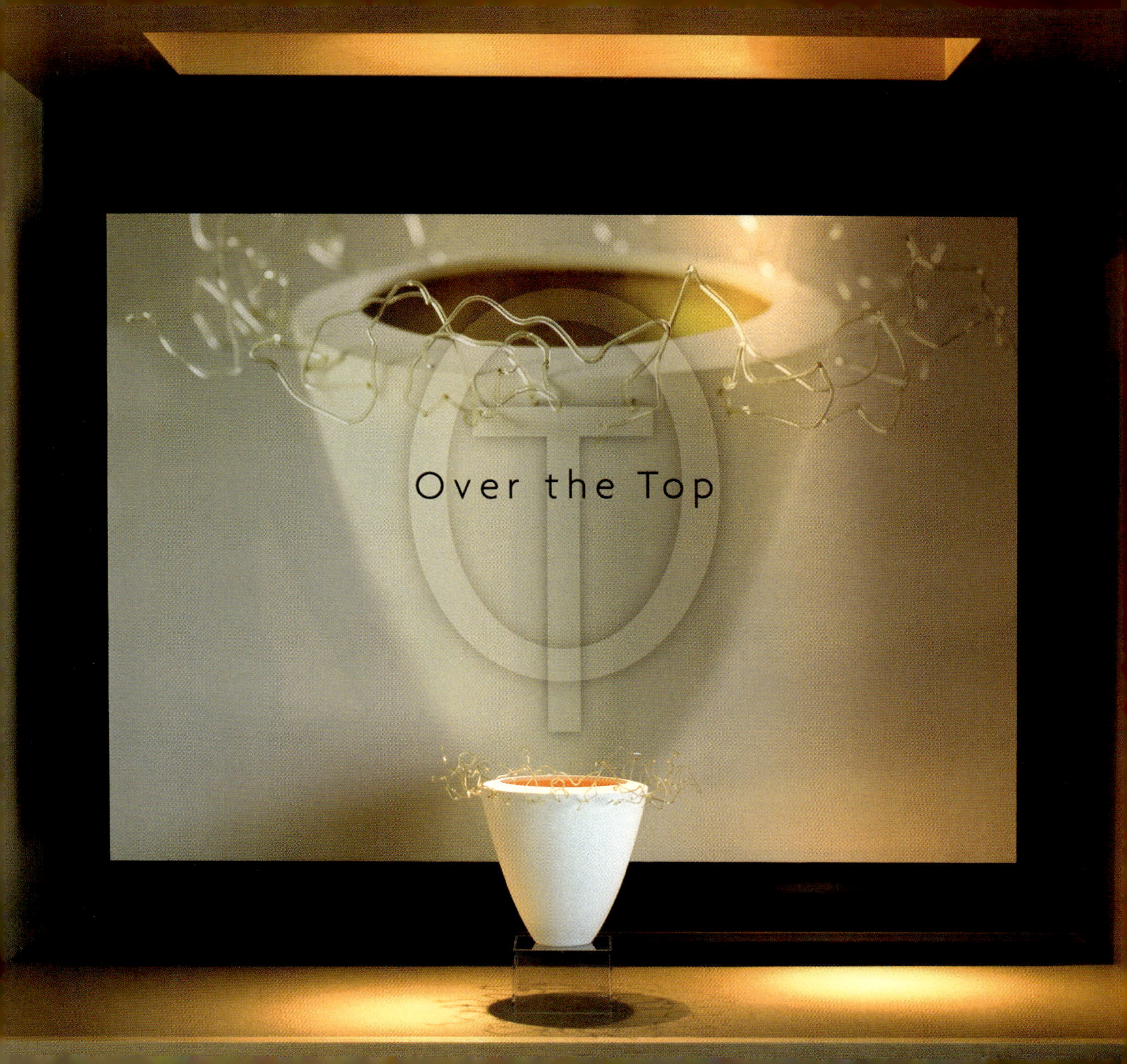
Over the Top

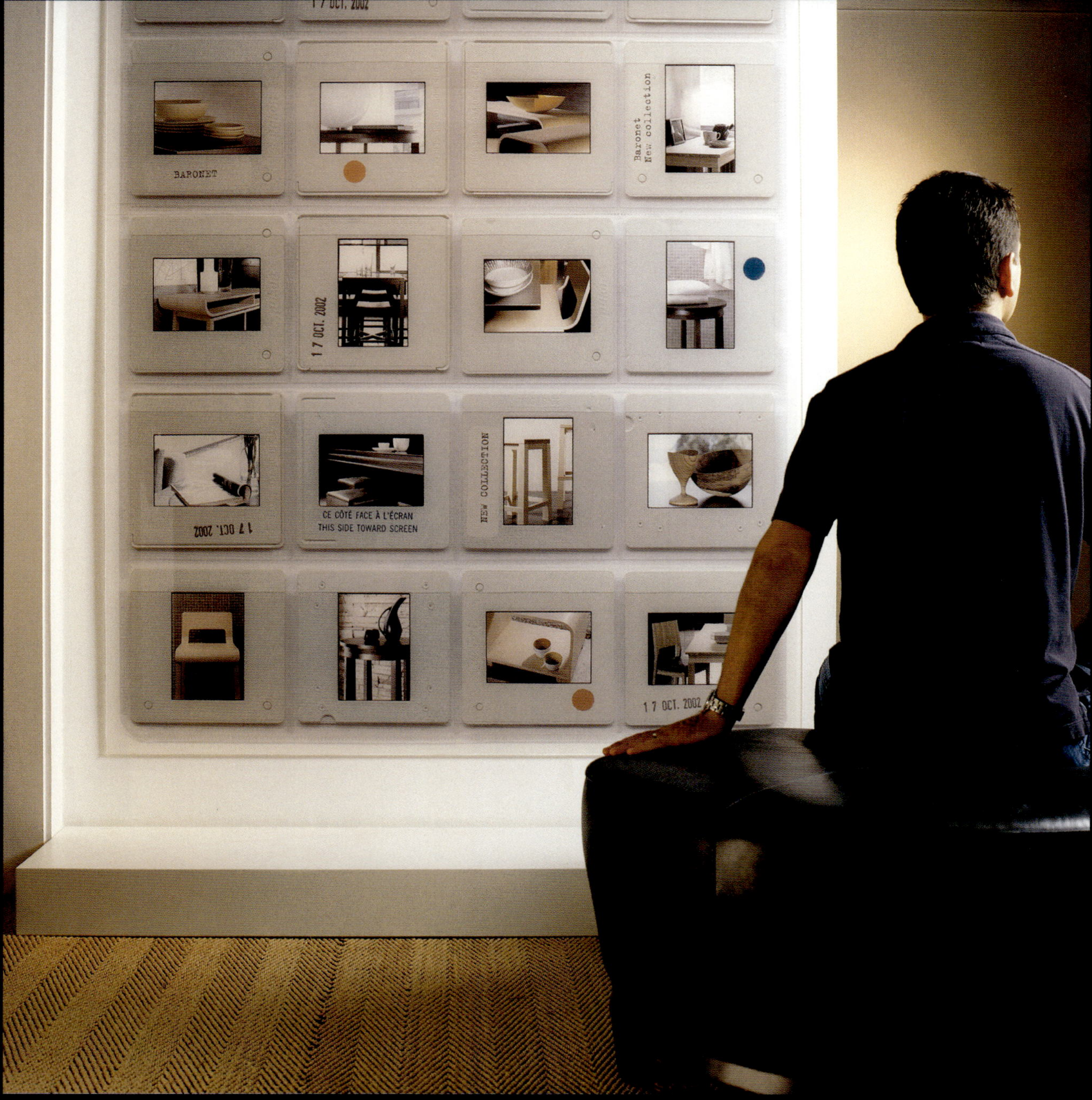

(this spread) 'Fall 2002 Showroom' Design Firm: Paprika Creative Director: Louis Gagnon Art Director: Louis Gagnon Designer: François LeClerc Photographer: William Jarret Client: Baronet

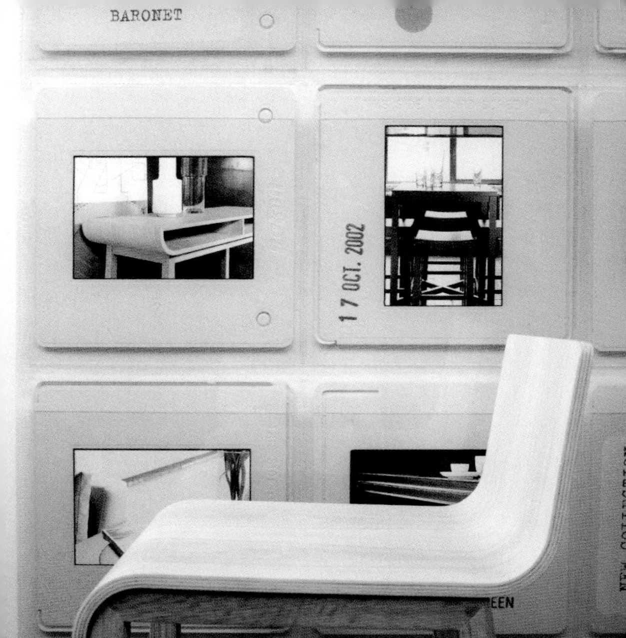
BARONET
17 OCT. 2002
NEW COLLECTION

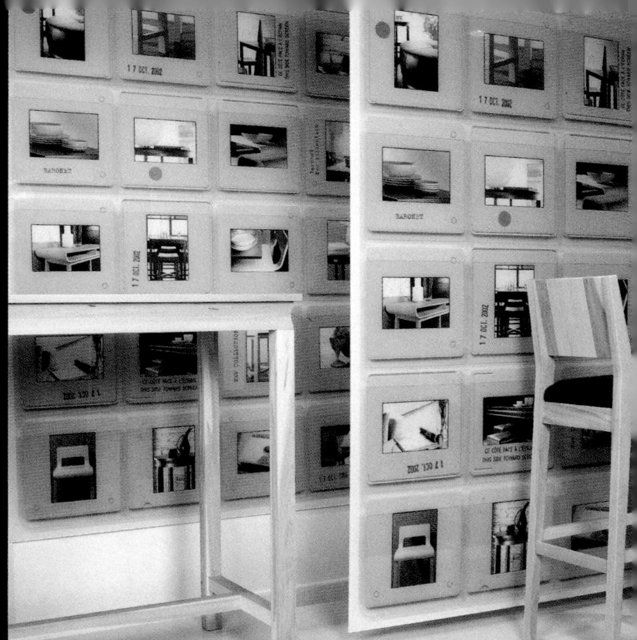
17 OCT. 2002
BARONET

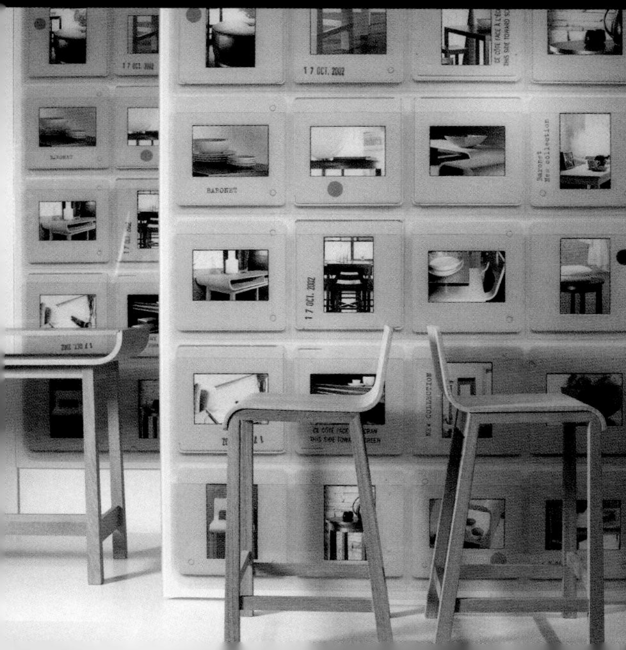
17 OCT. 2002
BARONET
Baronet
New collection

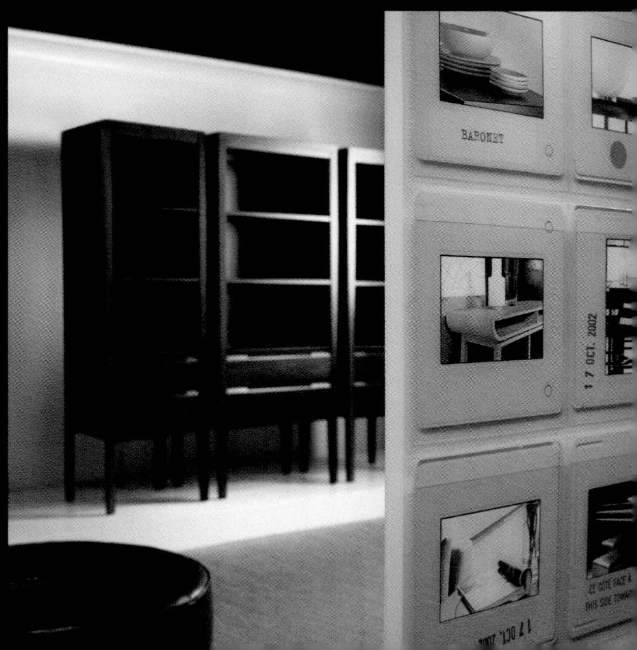
BARONET
17 OCT. 2002

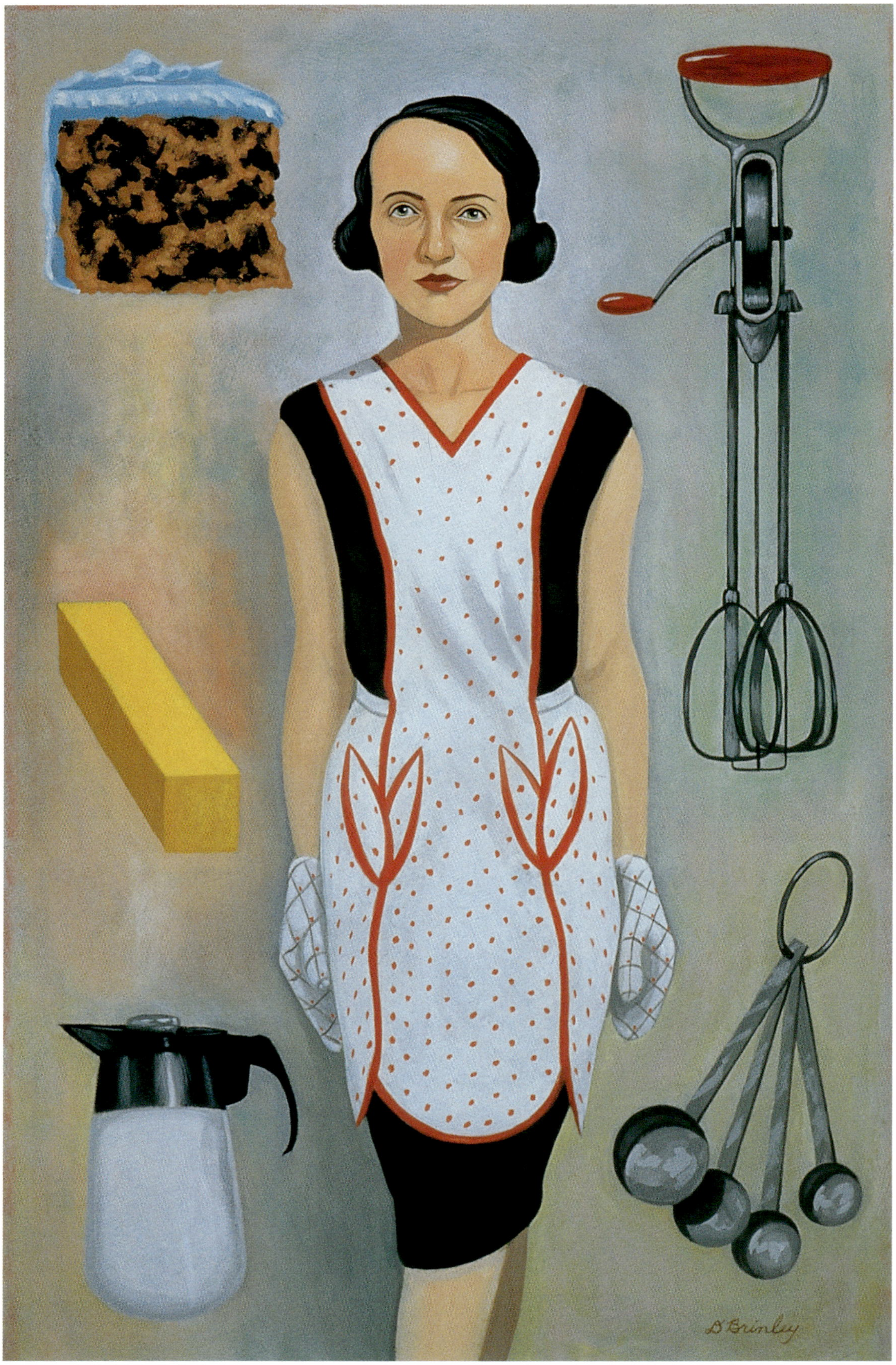

Illustrator: David M. Brinkley (opposite page) Illustrator: John Mattos

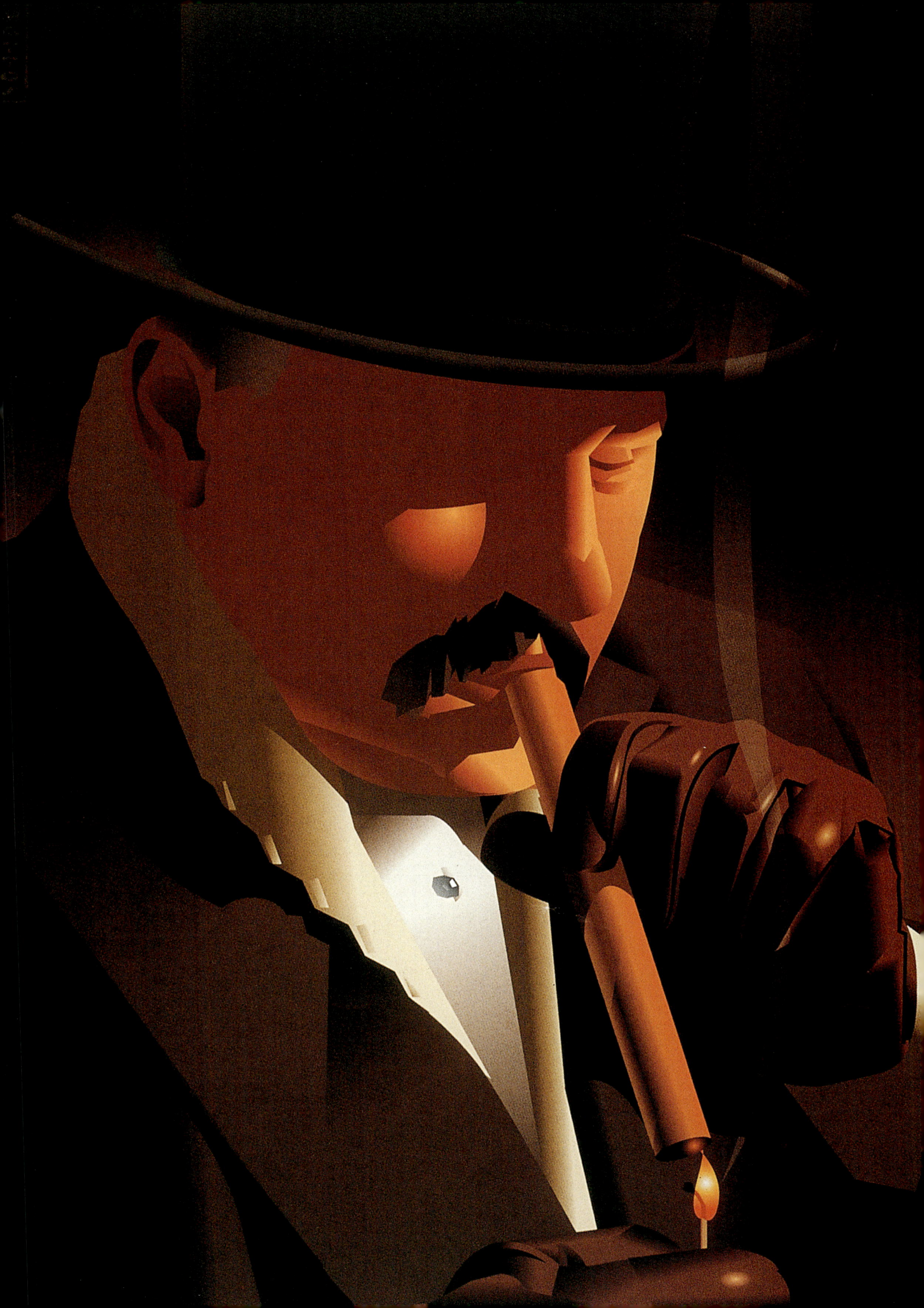

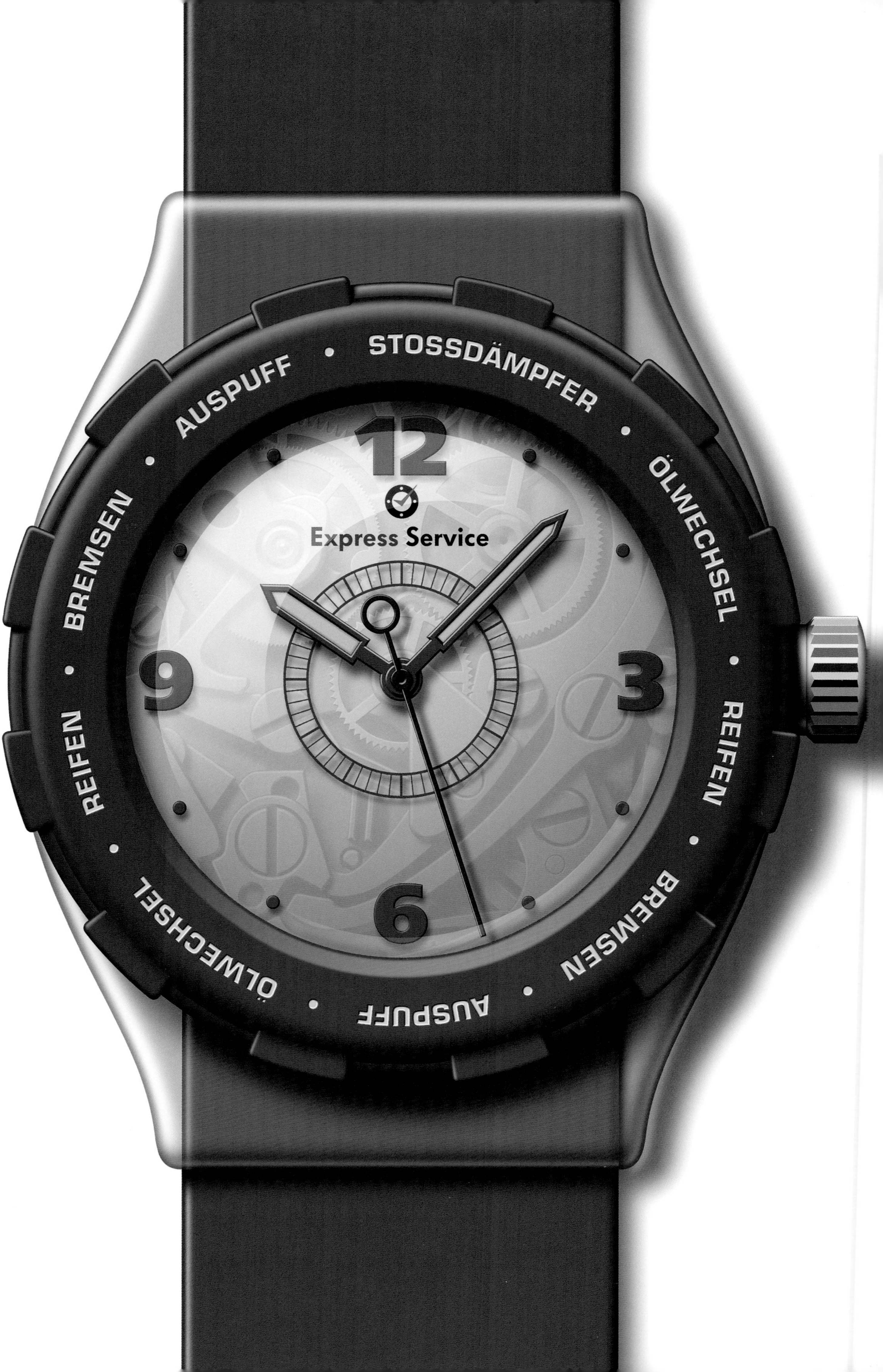

'VW Express Watch' Design Firm: Graf, Bertel, Buczek Werbeagentur GmbH Art Director: Monika Noske Illustrator: Peter Krämer Client: Volkswagen AG

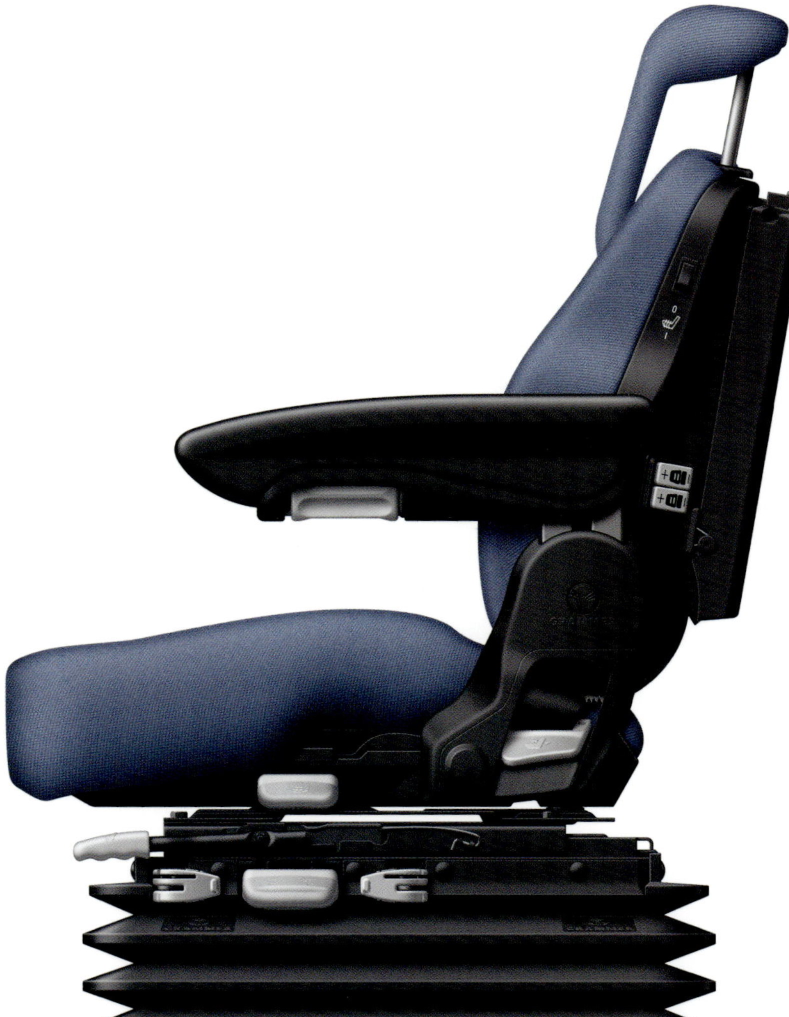

'MaximoXXL' Design Firm: Kuhn, Kammann & Kuhn AG Art Director: Rolf Erbach Illustrator: Peter Krämer Client: Grammer AG

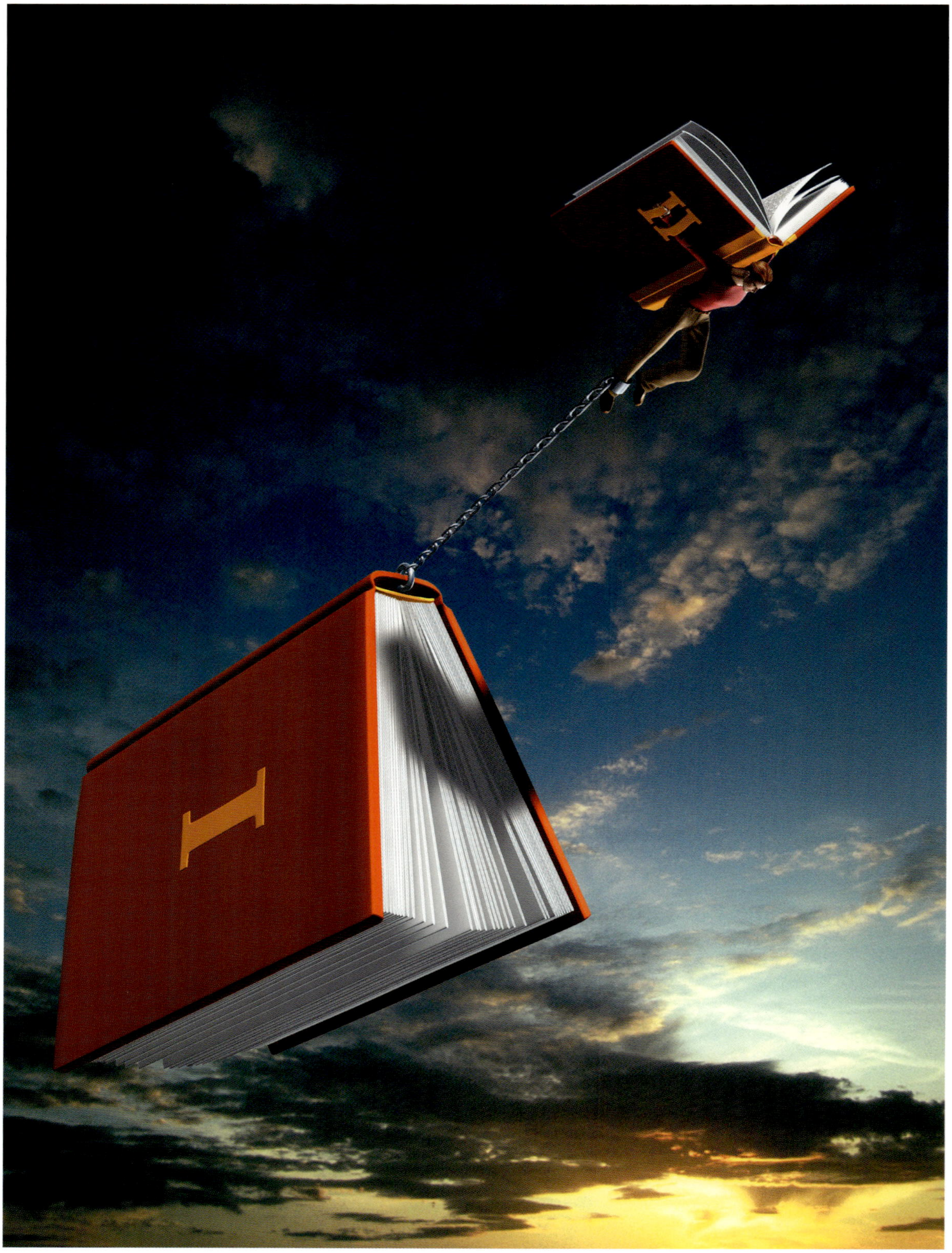

'Sizing Up the New Rep.' Design Firm: Mirko Ilic Corp. Art Director: Steven Heller Illustrator: Mirko Ilic Client: The NY Times Book Review
(opposite page) 'Alexandria Lighthouse' Design Firm: Opto Design Art Director: John Klotnia Illustrator: Peter Krämer Client: Alexandria Real Estate Equities, Inc.

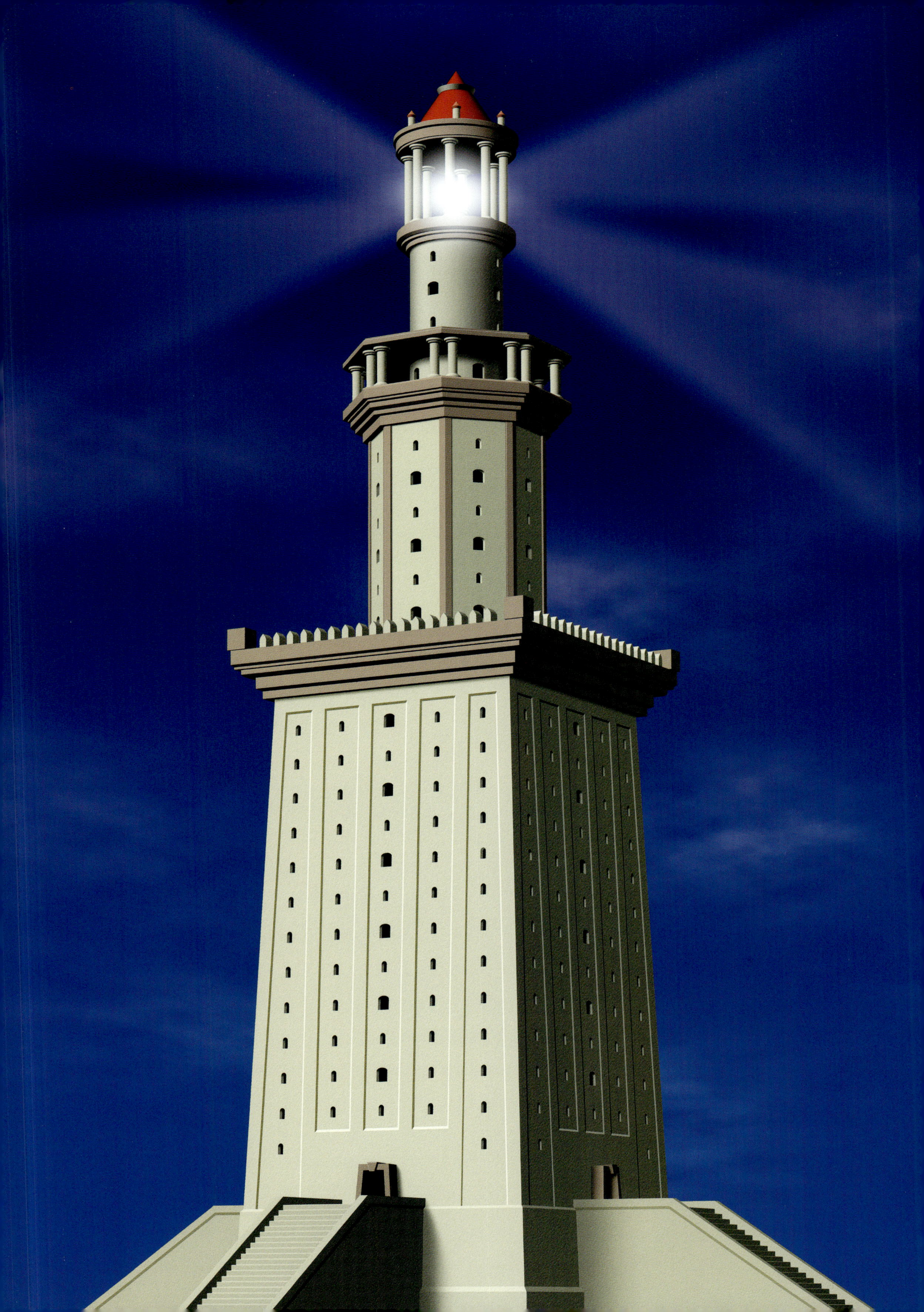

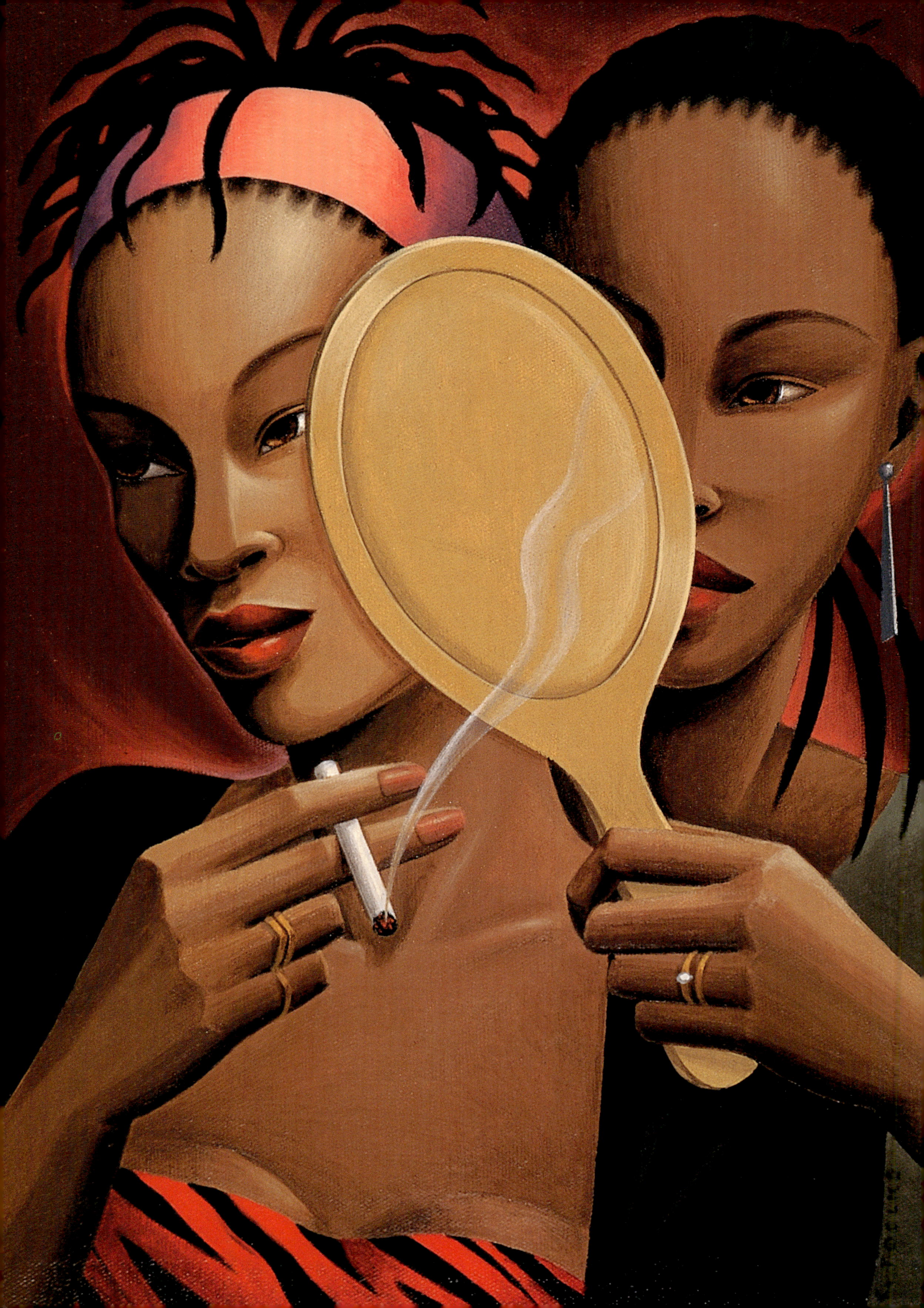

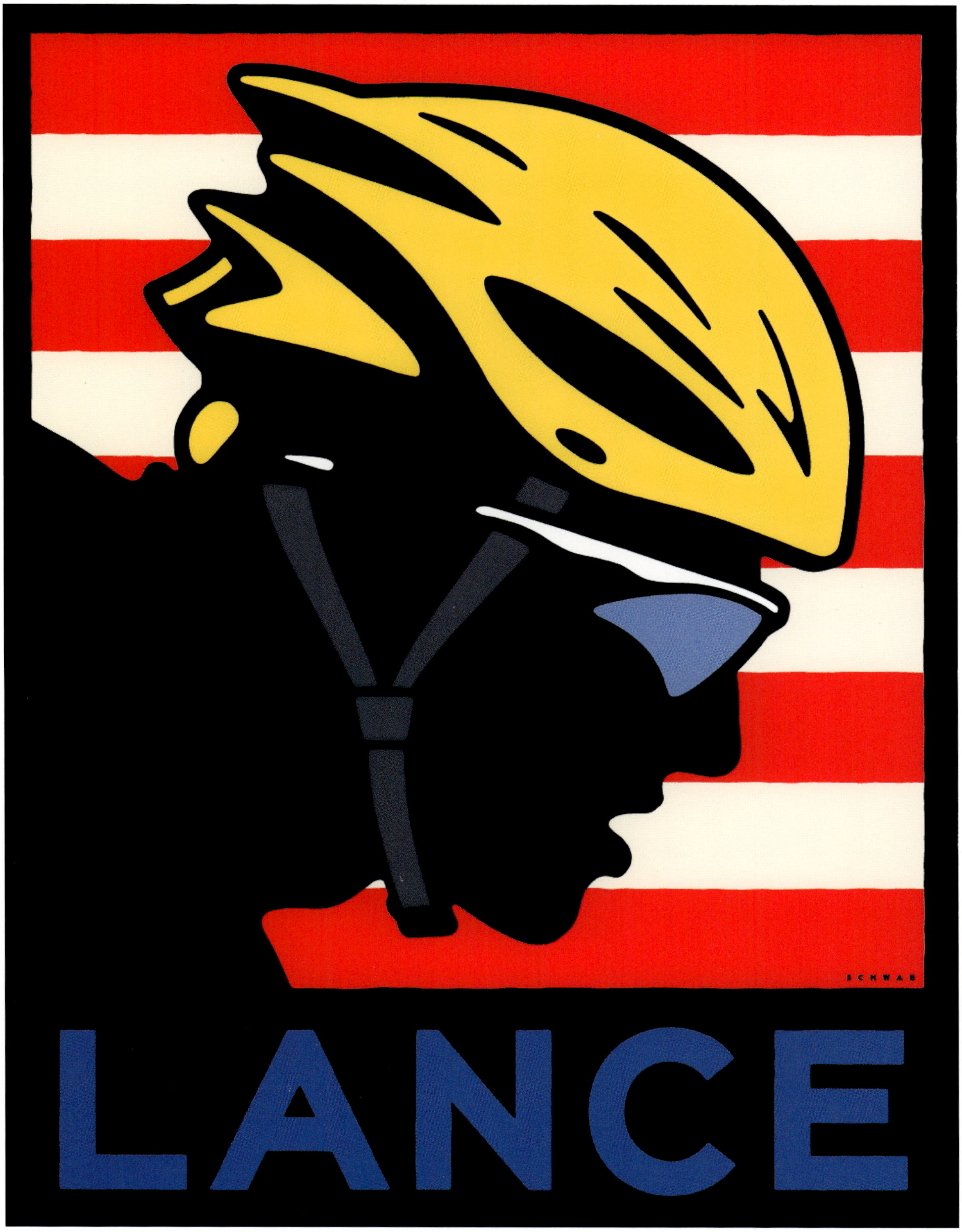

Design Firm: Michael Schwab Studio Art Director: Judi Oyama Designer: Michael Schwab Illustrator: Michael Schwab Client: Giro USA (opposite page) Illustrator: Cathleen Toelke

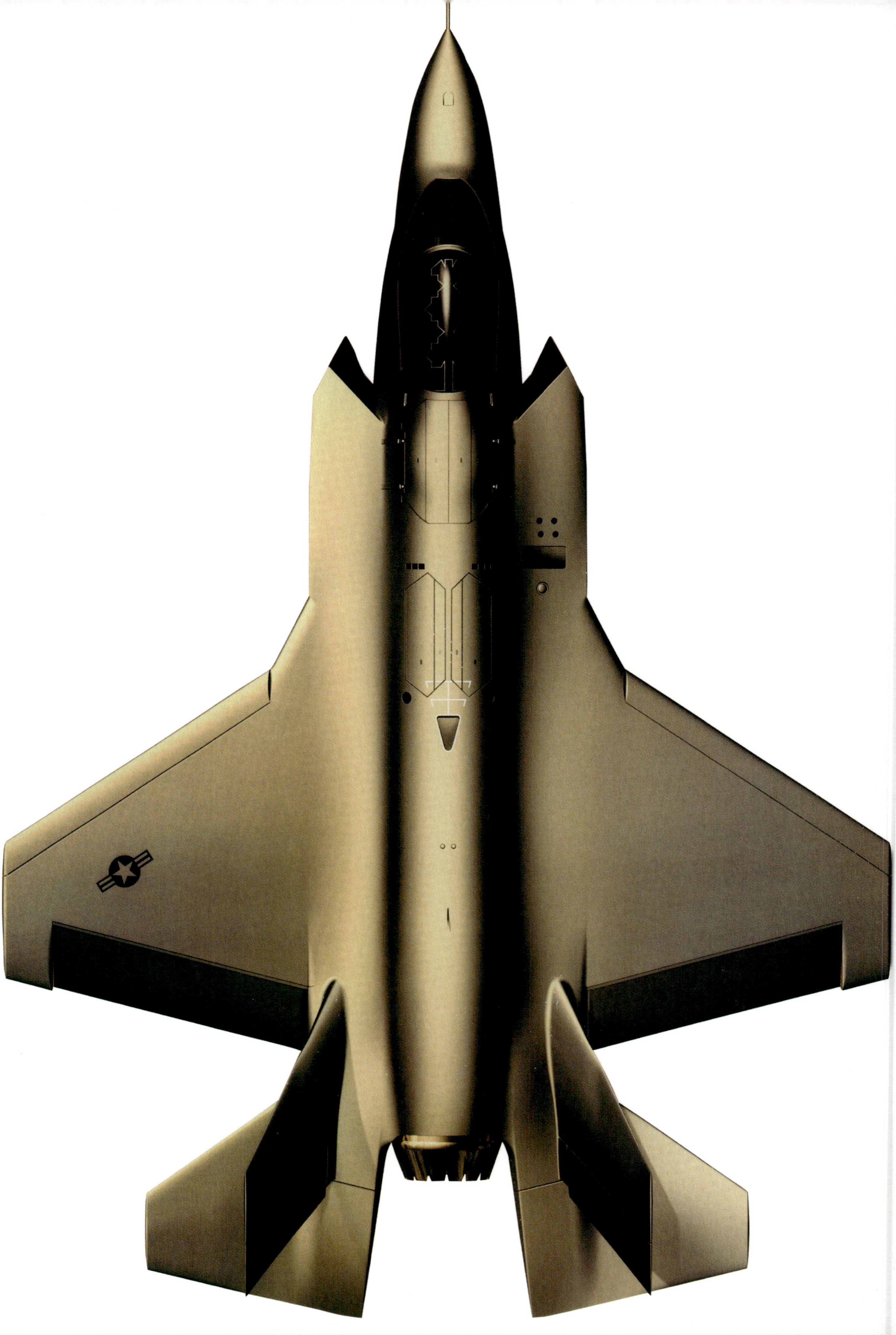

(this spread) '2001 Annual Review' Design Firm: Bertz Design Group Art Directors: Ted Bertz and Richard Uccello Designers: Ted Bertz and Richard Uccello Illustrator: John Harwood Copywriter: Paul Jackson Client: United Technologies Corporation

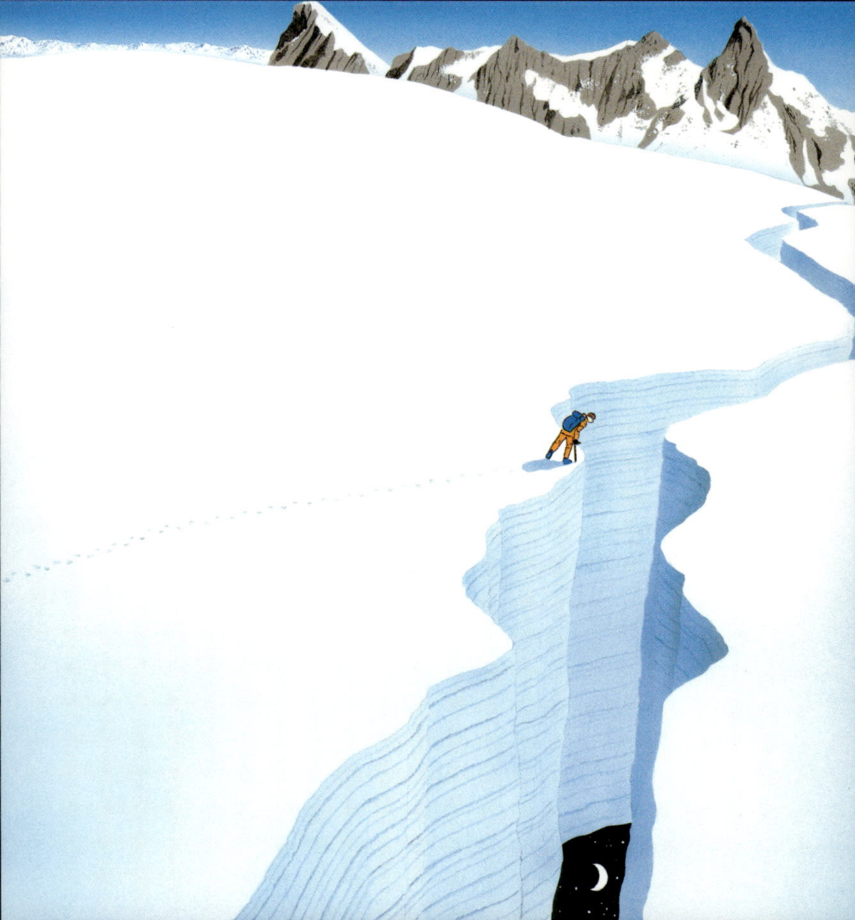

ergy 2001 Annual Report' Design Firm: Benoit Design Inc. Art Directors: Dennis Benoit Designers: Chuck Hodges Illustrator: Guy Billout Copywriter: Bob Collins Client: Entergy Corporation

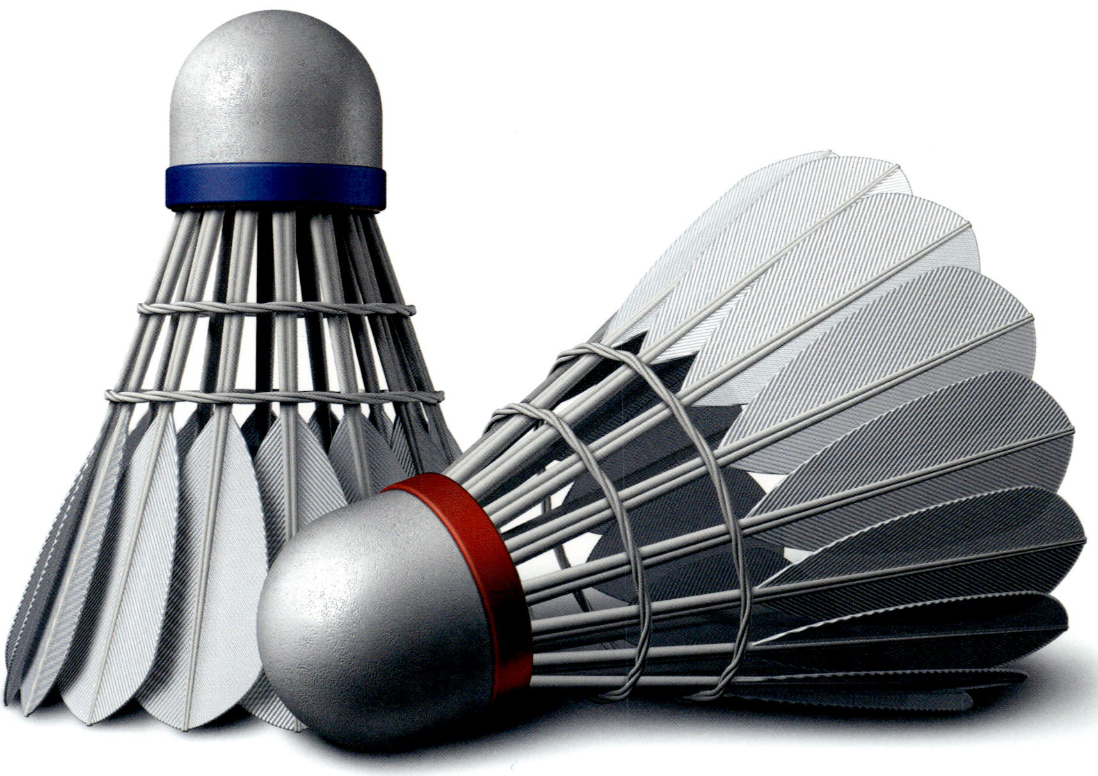

'Shuttlecocks' Design Firm: Peter Krämer Art Director: Peter Krämer Illustrator: Peter Krämer (opposite page) 'Double Digit Growth in No Growth Times' Design Firm: Mirko Ilic Corp. Art Director: Julia Moburg Illustrator: Mirko Ilic Client: Fast Company

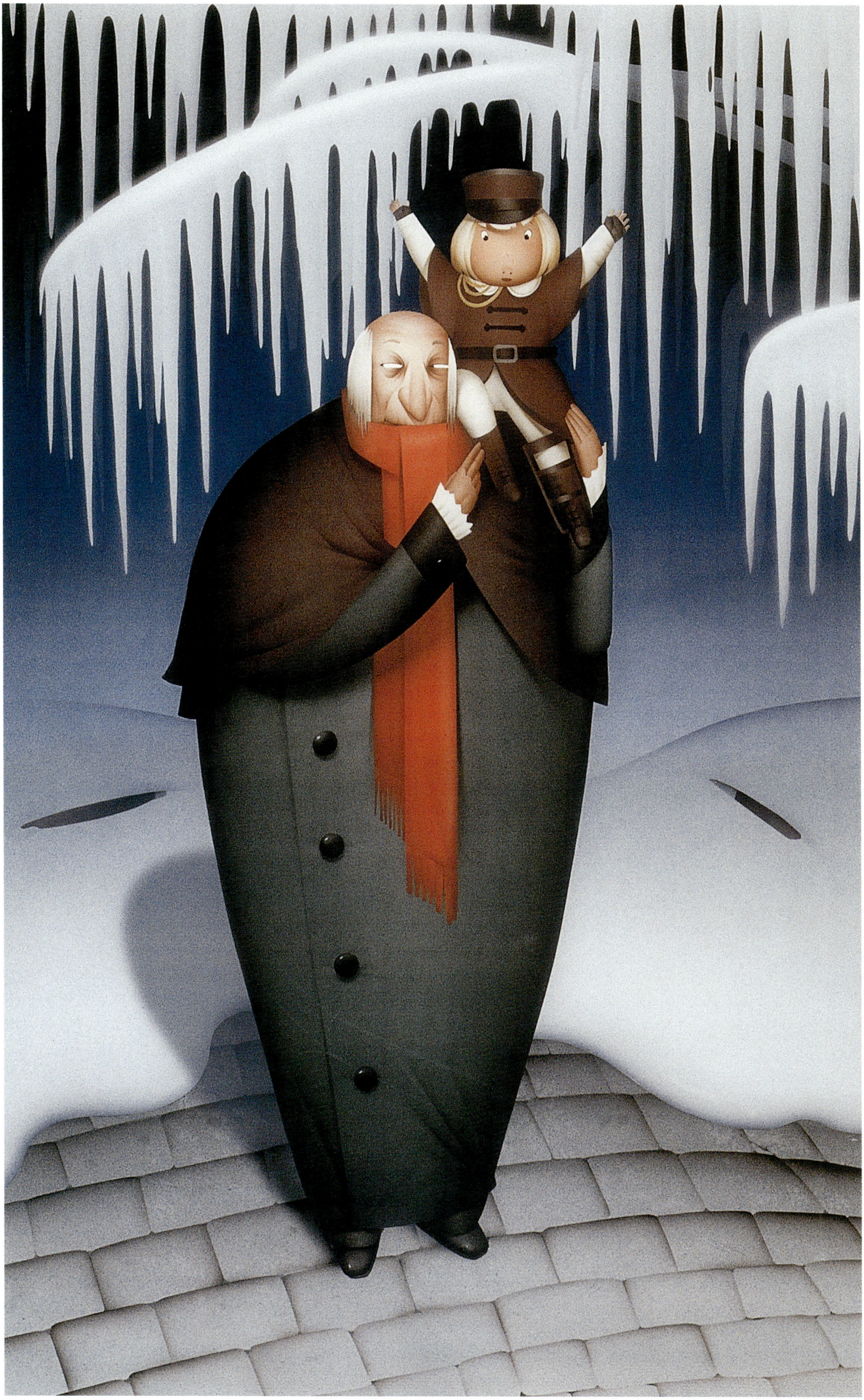

Illustrator: Bill Mayer

2003 Ion Sitelet! Design Firm: Barbarian Group Creative Director: Jamie Barrett Art Directors: Milena Sadee and Jeff Benjamin Copywriter: Aaron Griffiths Design Director: Keith Anderson Producer: Kewan Gregory Client: Saturn

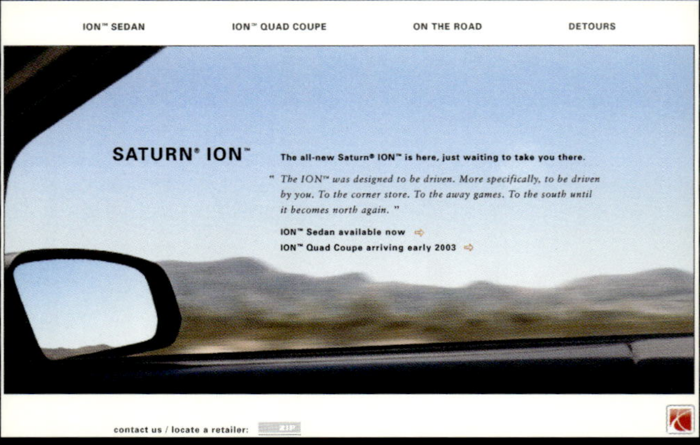

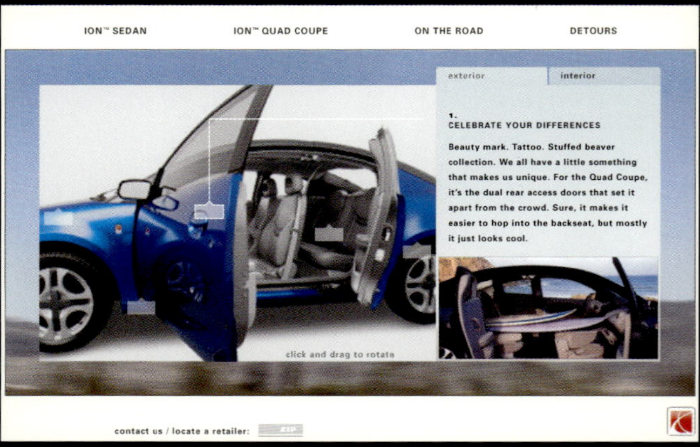

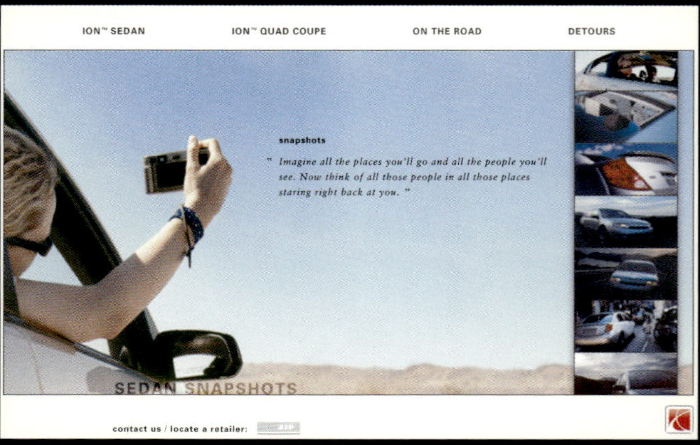

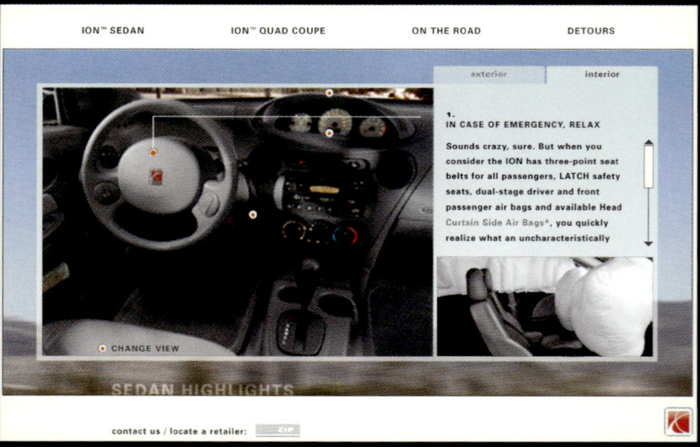

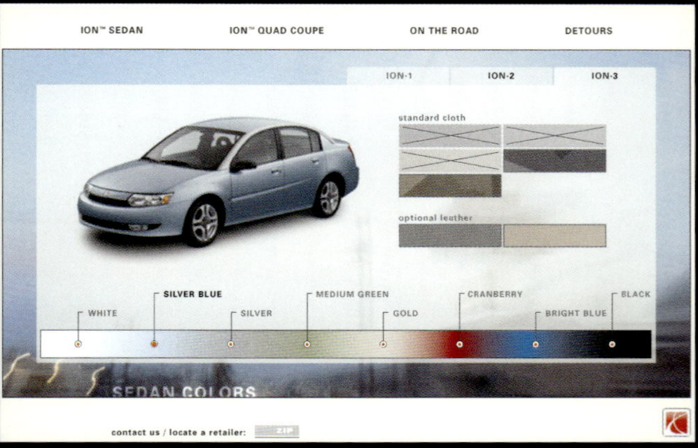

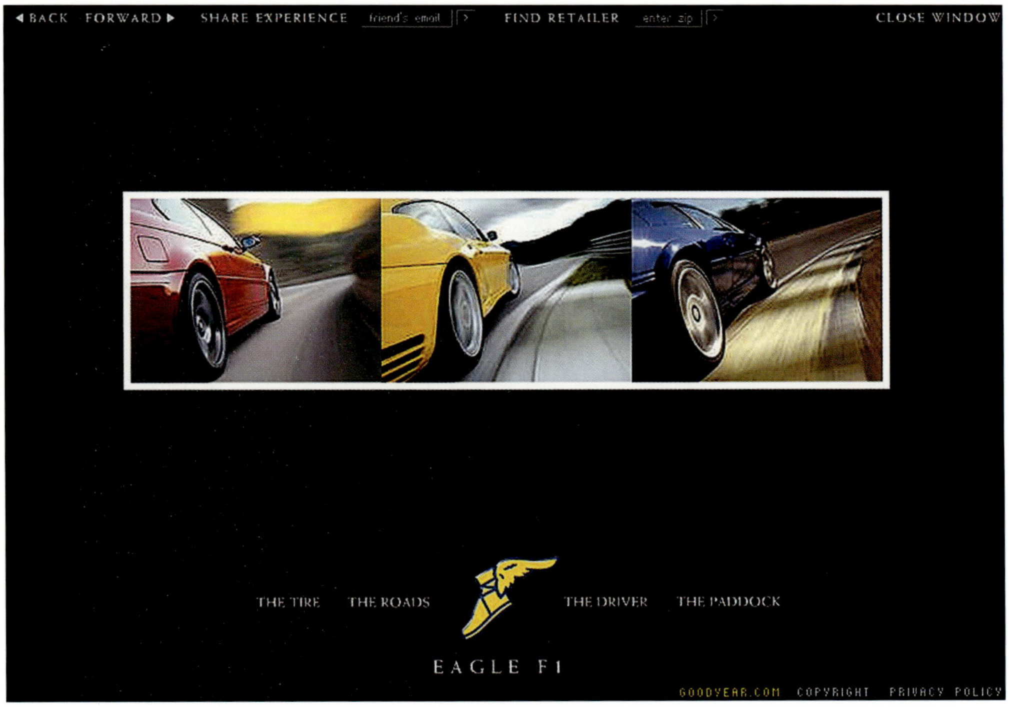

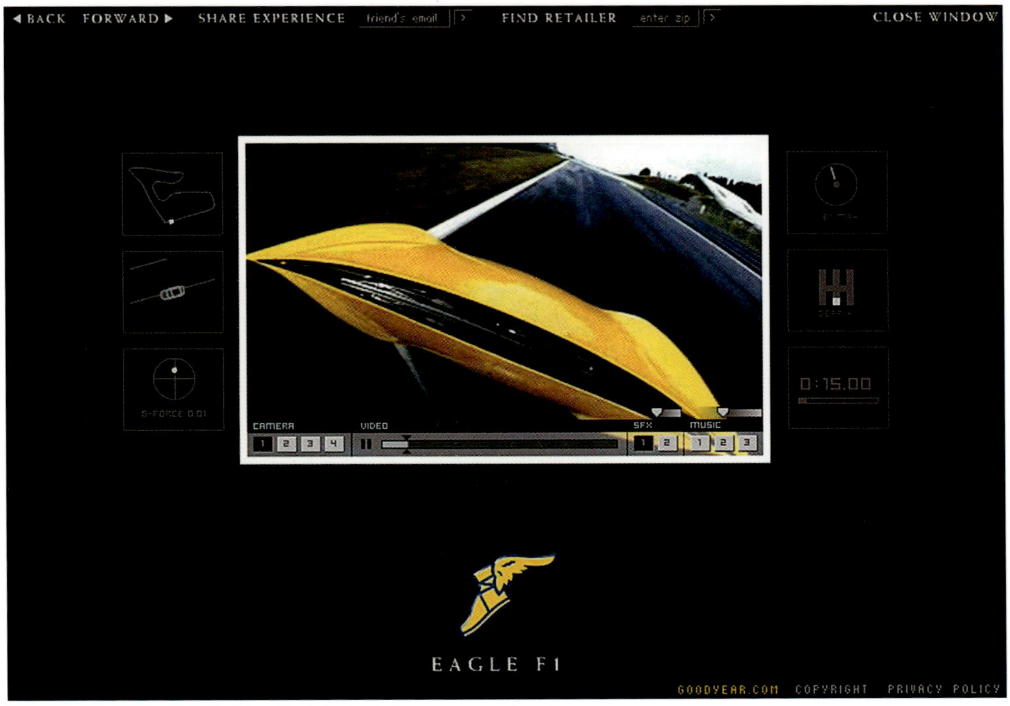

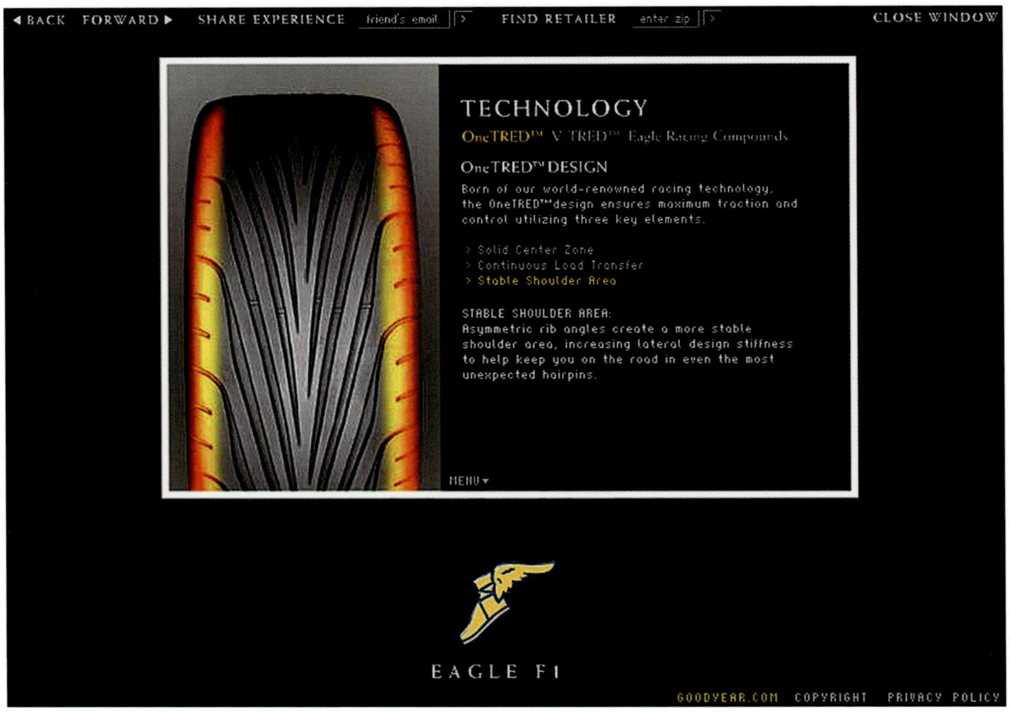

'Eagle F1' Design Firm: Evolution Bureau Creative Director: Dave Gray Copywriter: Aaron Griffiths Design Director: Keith Anderson Producer: Victoria Brown Client: Goodyear

connectingnokia.com

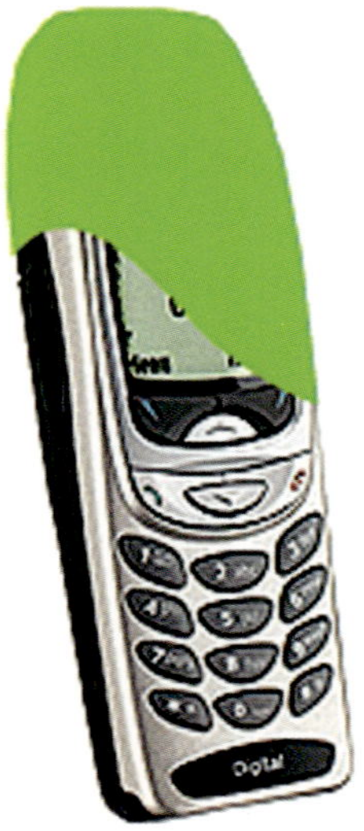

signage

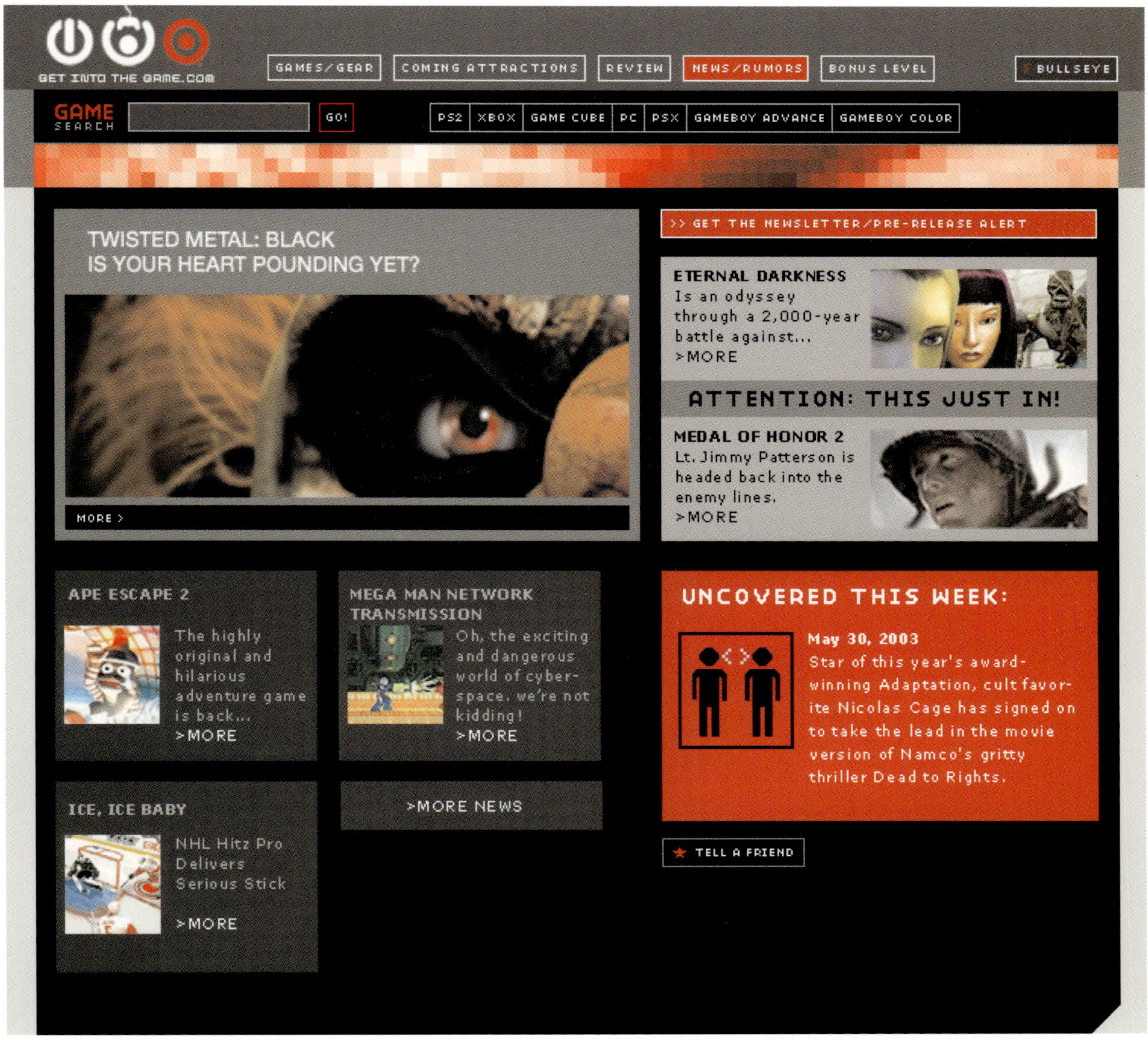

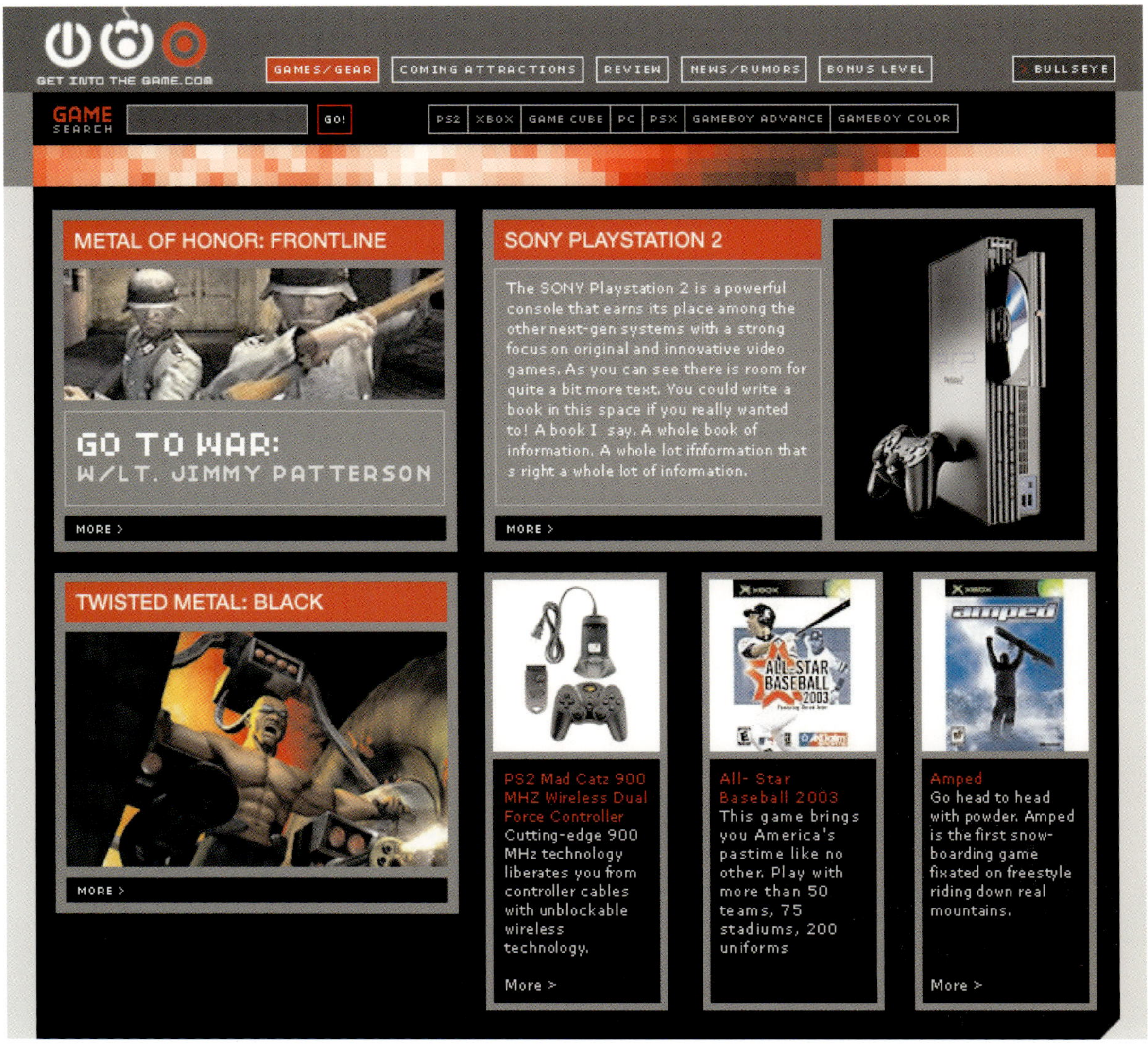

'Get Into The Game Website' Design Firm: Catalyst Studios Client: Target Advertising (this spread) 'Sibley Peteet e-motion' Design Firm: Sibley Peteet Design/Dallas Creative Director: Don Sibley Art Director: Geoff German Client: Sibley Peteet Design

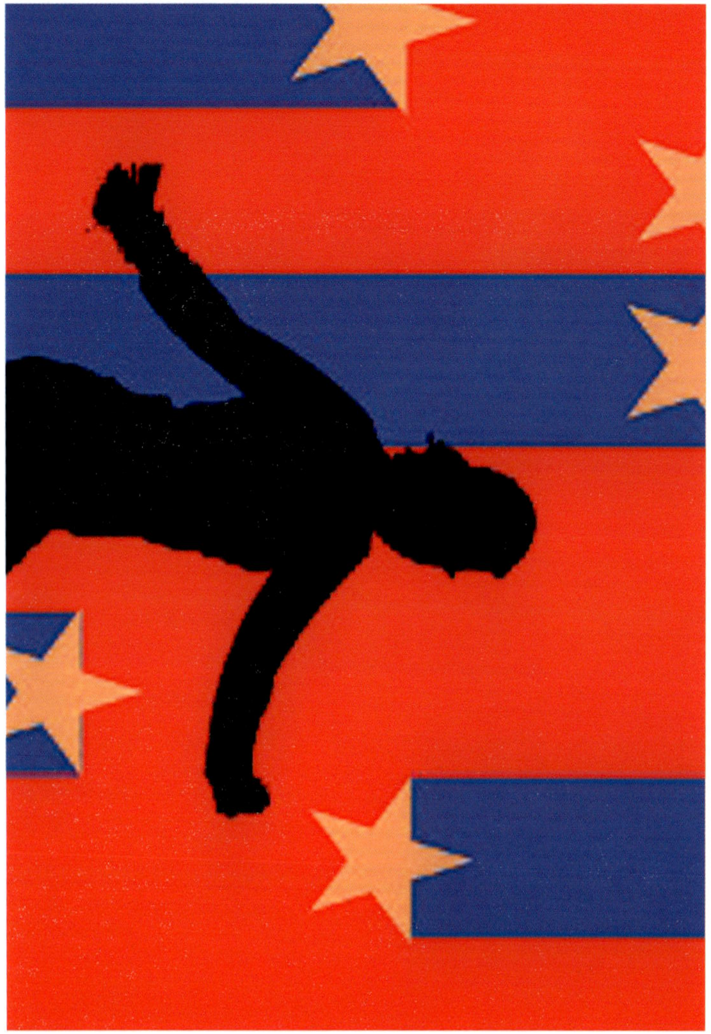

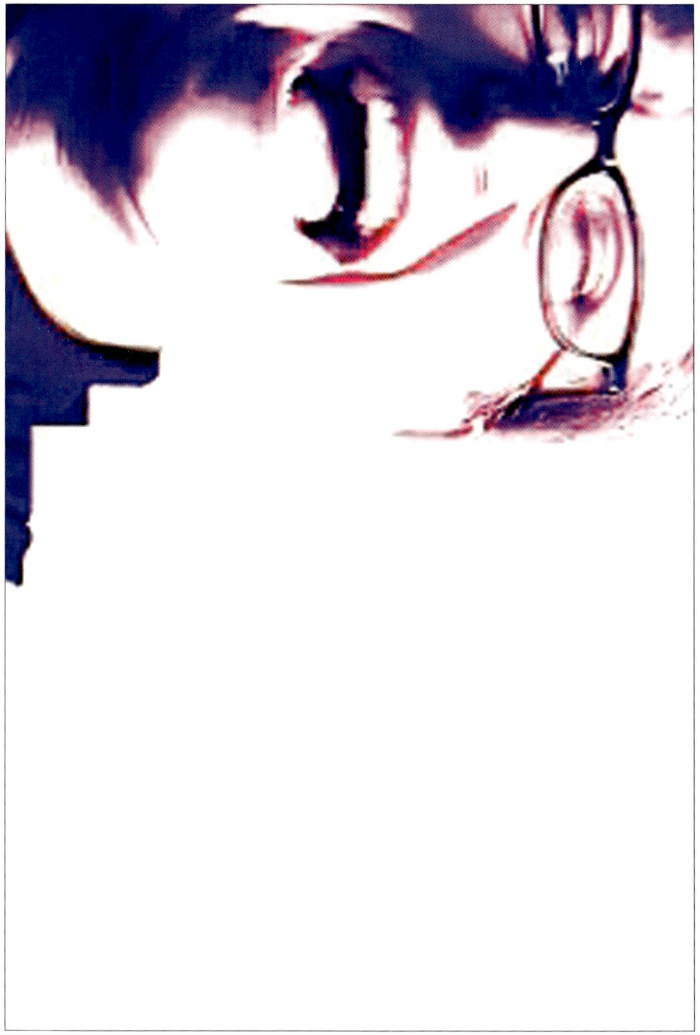

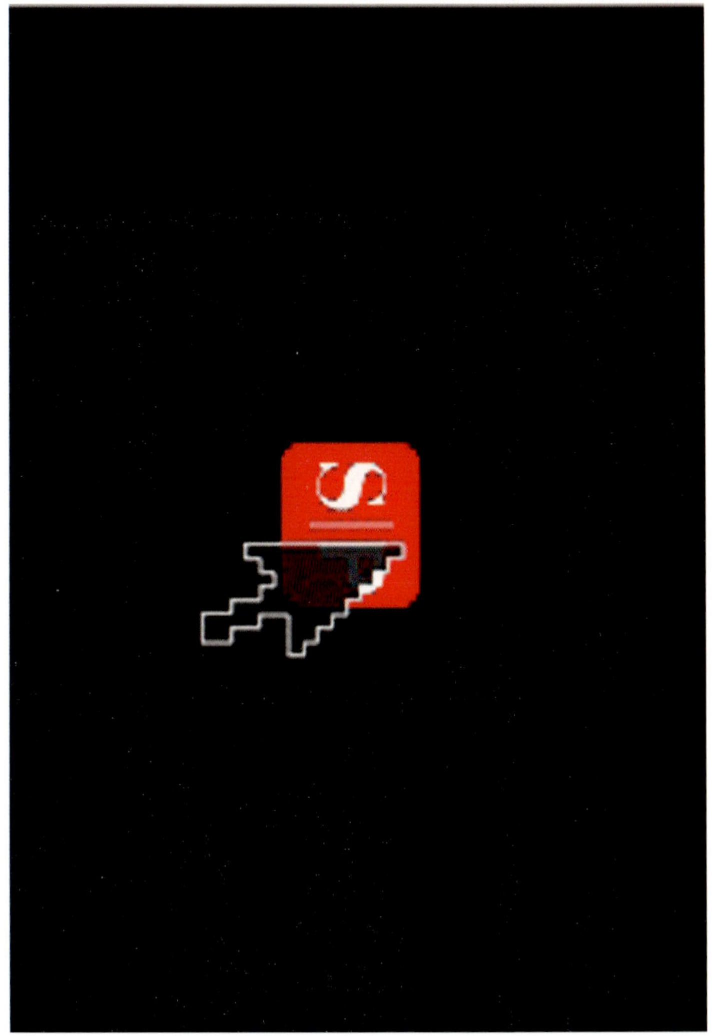

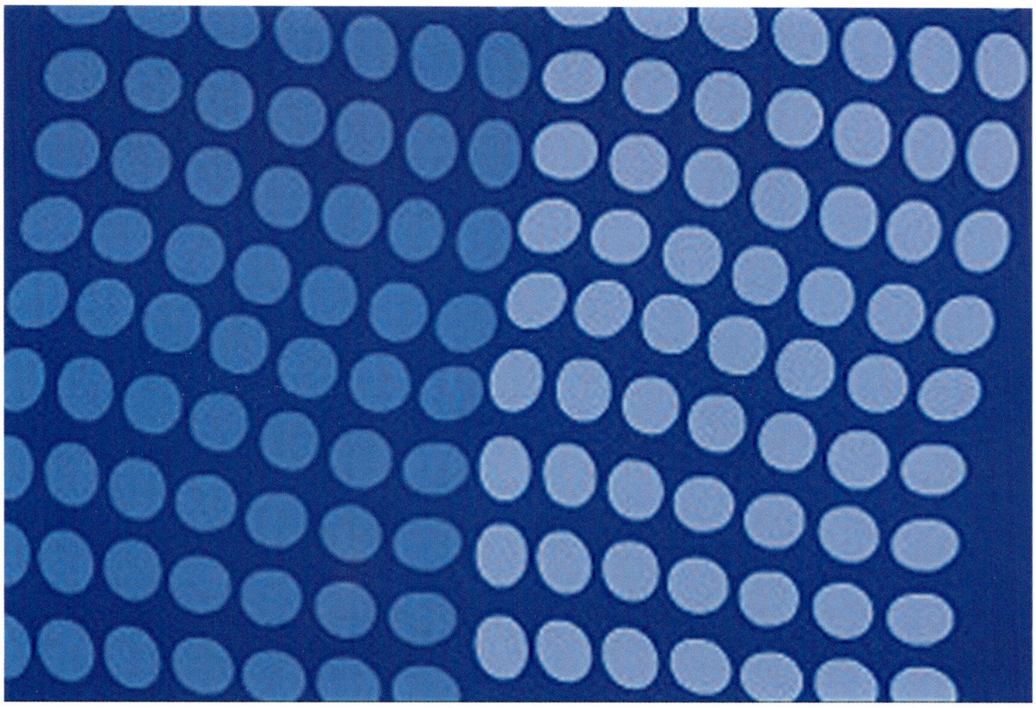

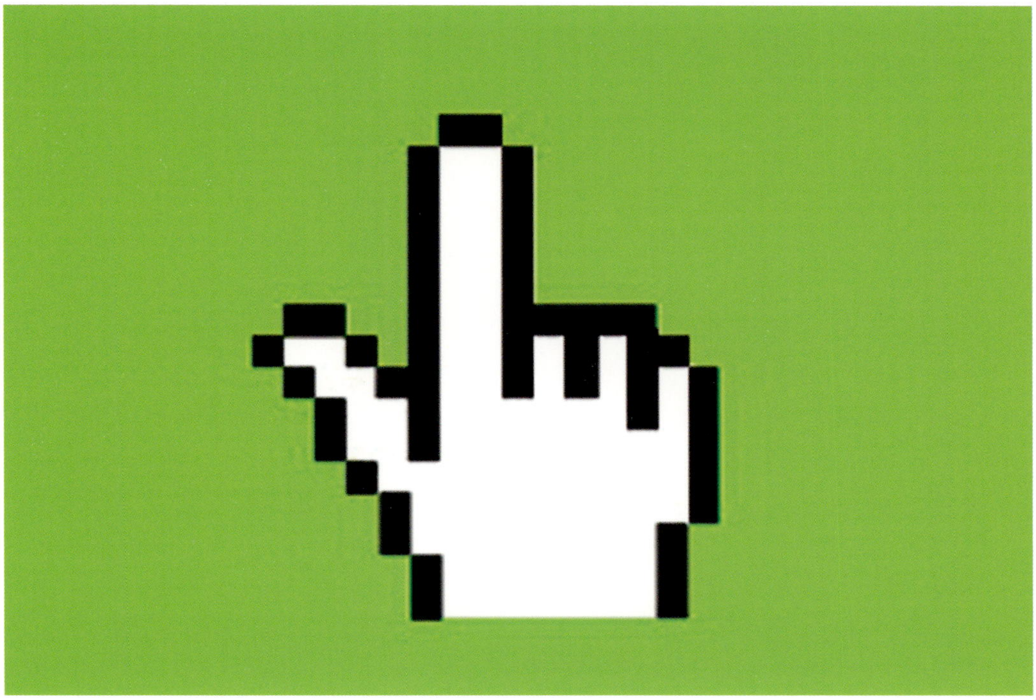

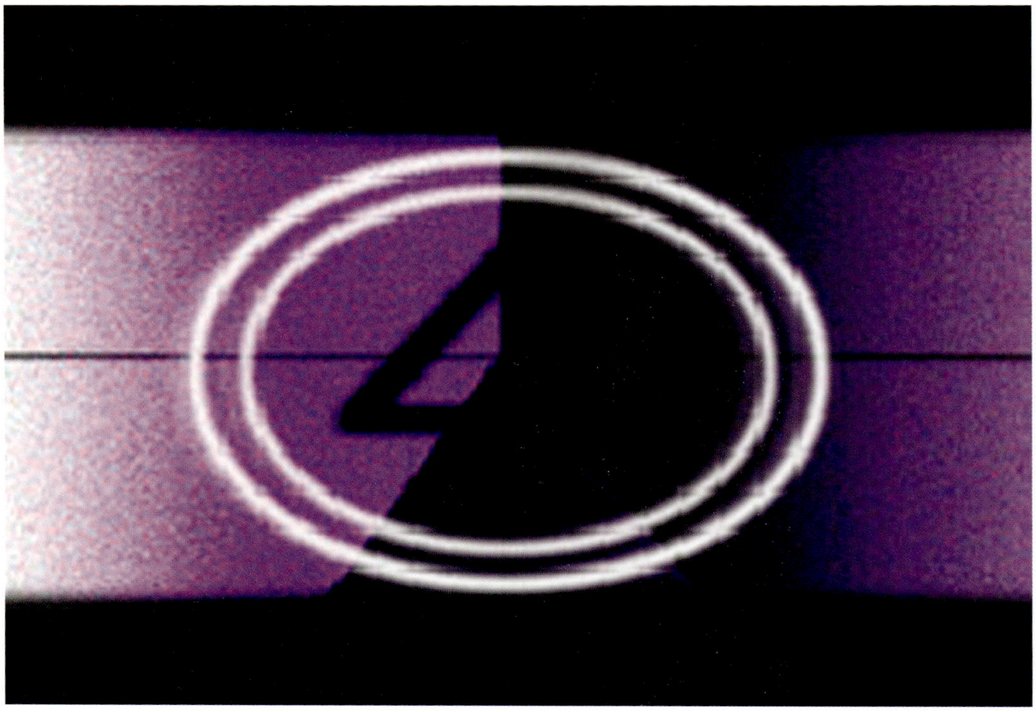

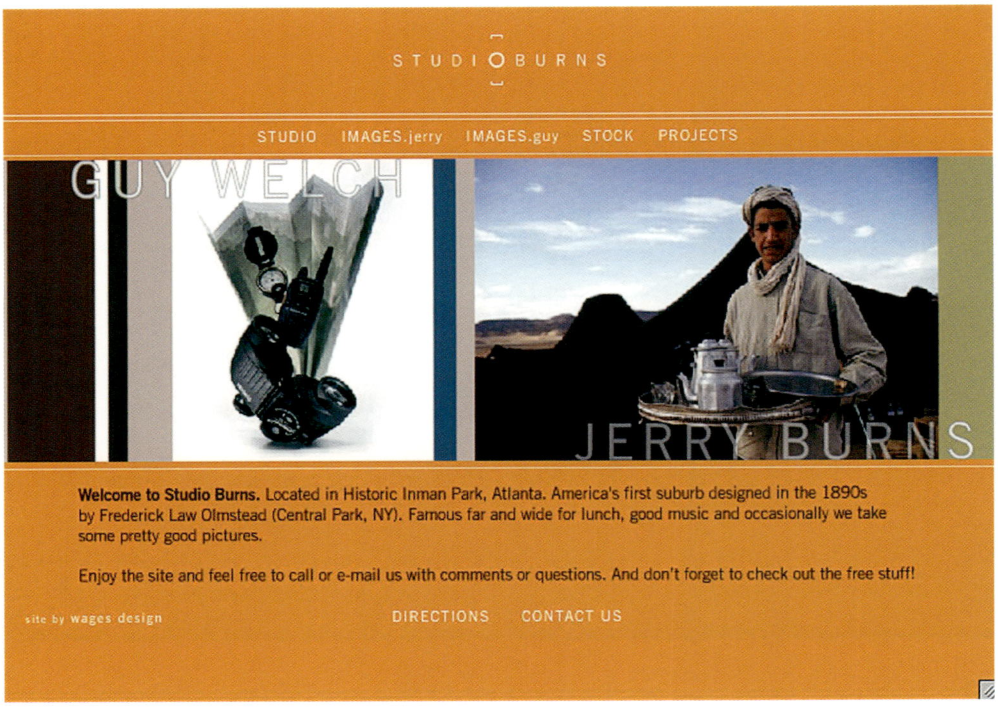

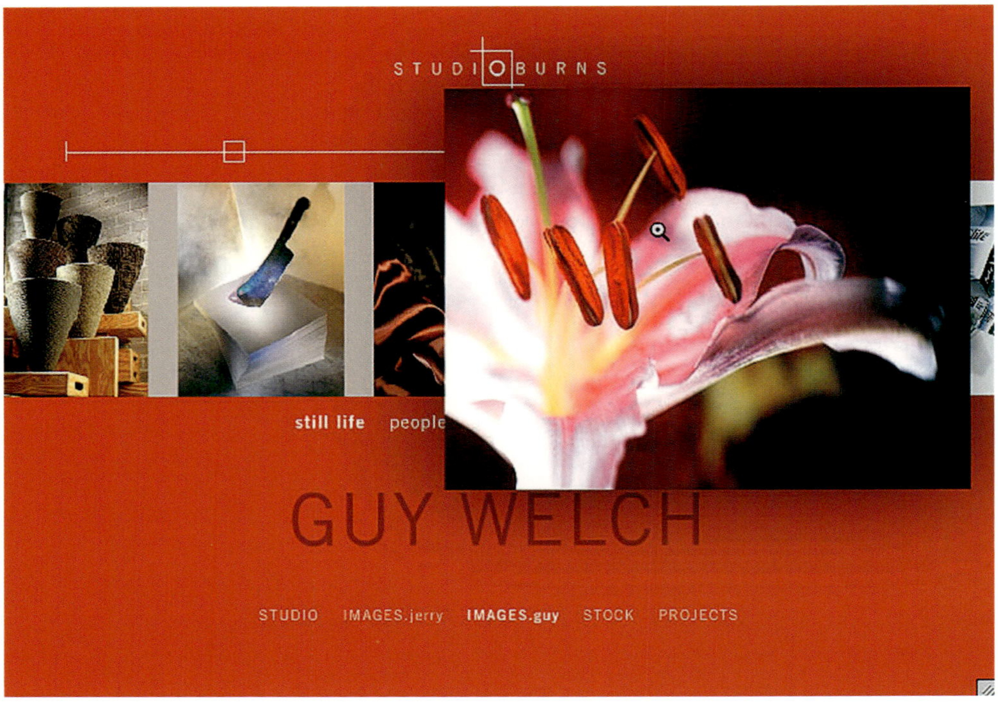

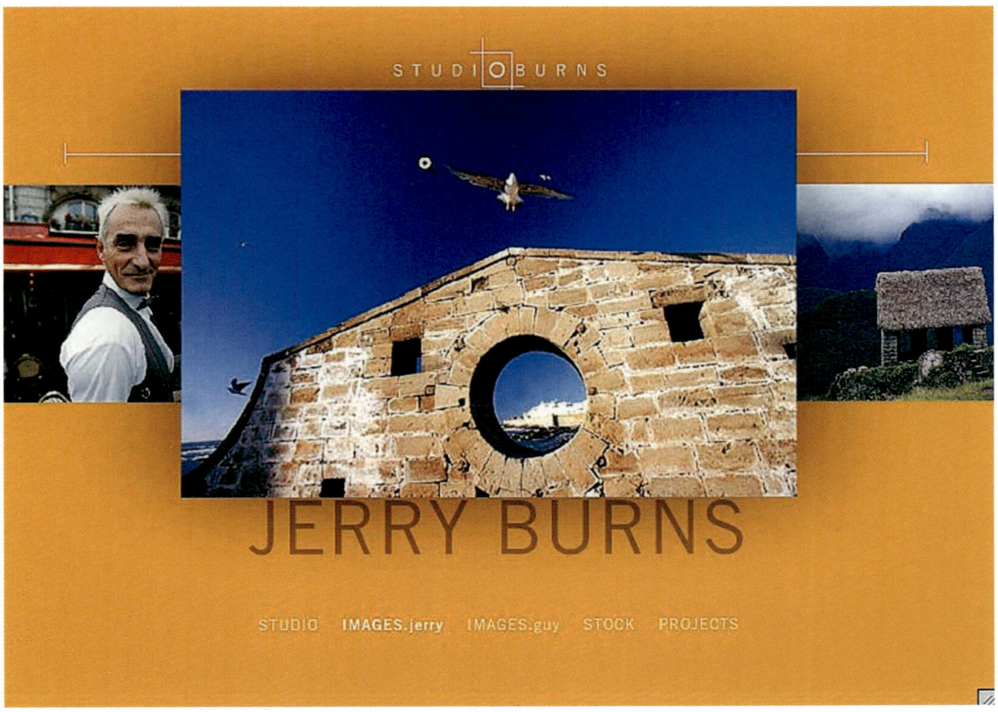

Design Firm: Wages Design, Inc. Art Director: Bob Wages Designers: Dominga Lee, Jimmy Lo and Kevin Kemmerly Photographers: Jerry Burns and Guy Welch Client: Studio Burns

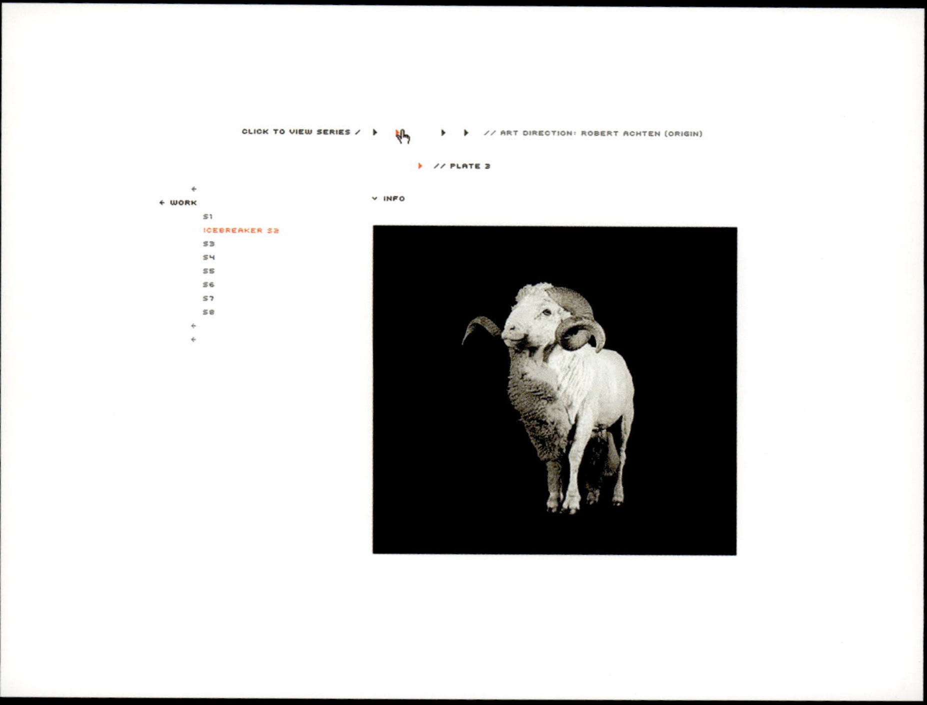

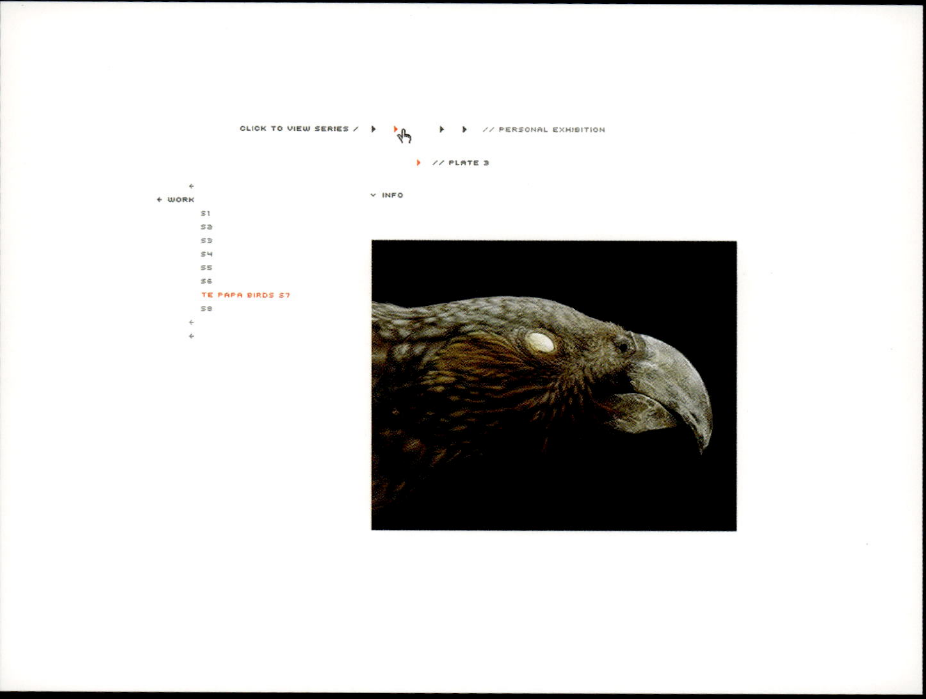

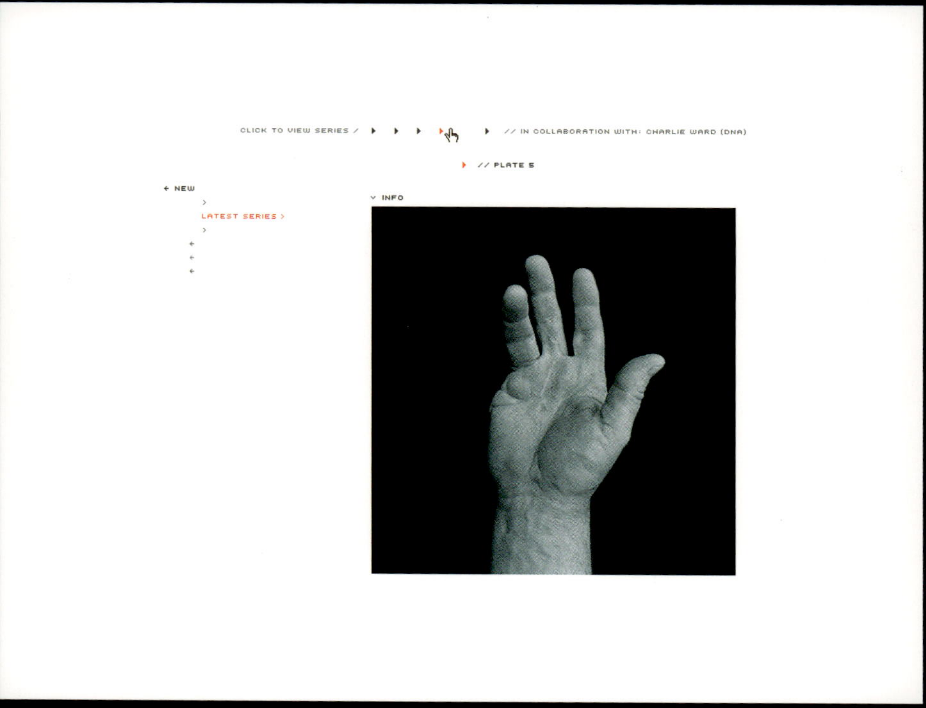

ianrobertson.co.nz Design Firm: DNA Design Creative Director: Charlie Ward Designers: Charlie Ward and Steve LeMarquand Photographers: Matt Barnes and Ian Robertson Copywriter: Charlie Ward Client: Ian Robertson

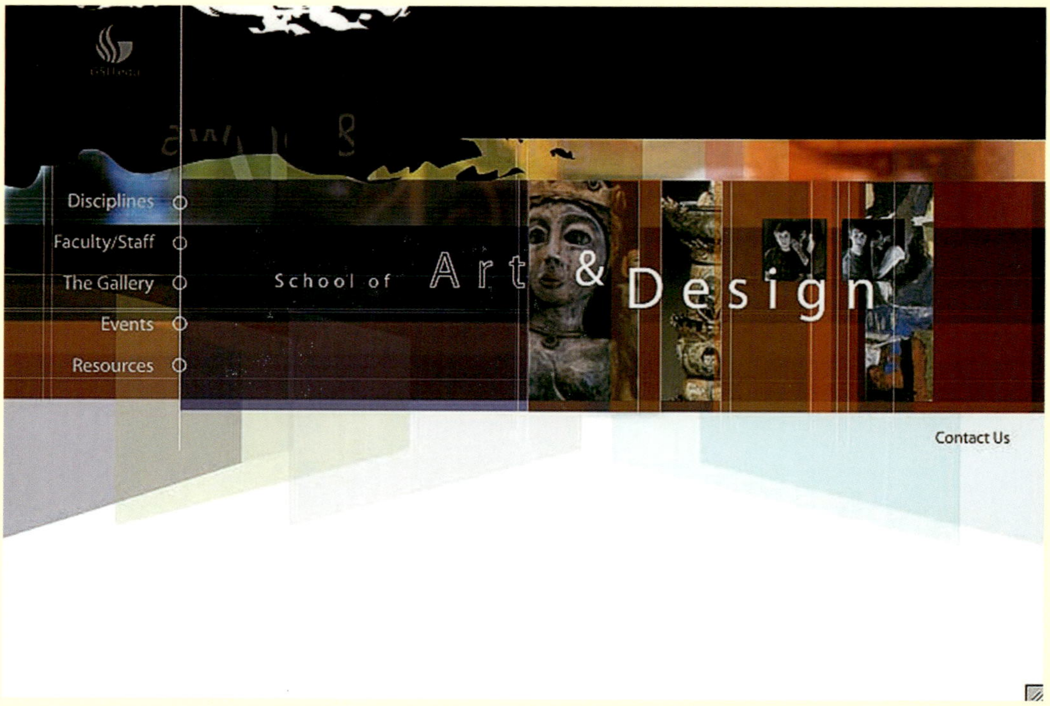

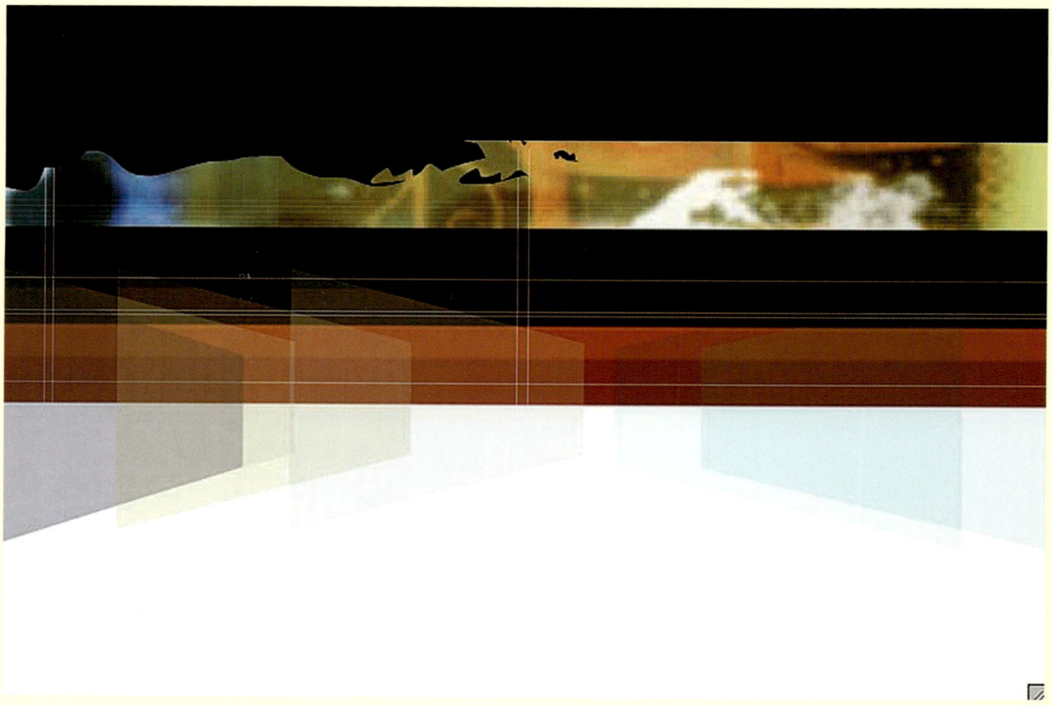

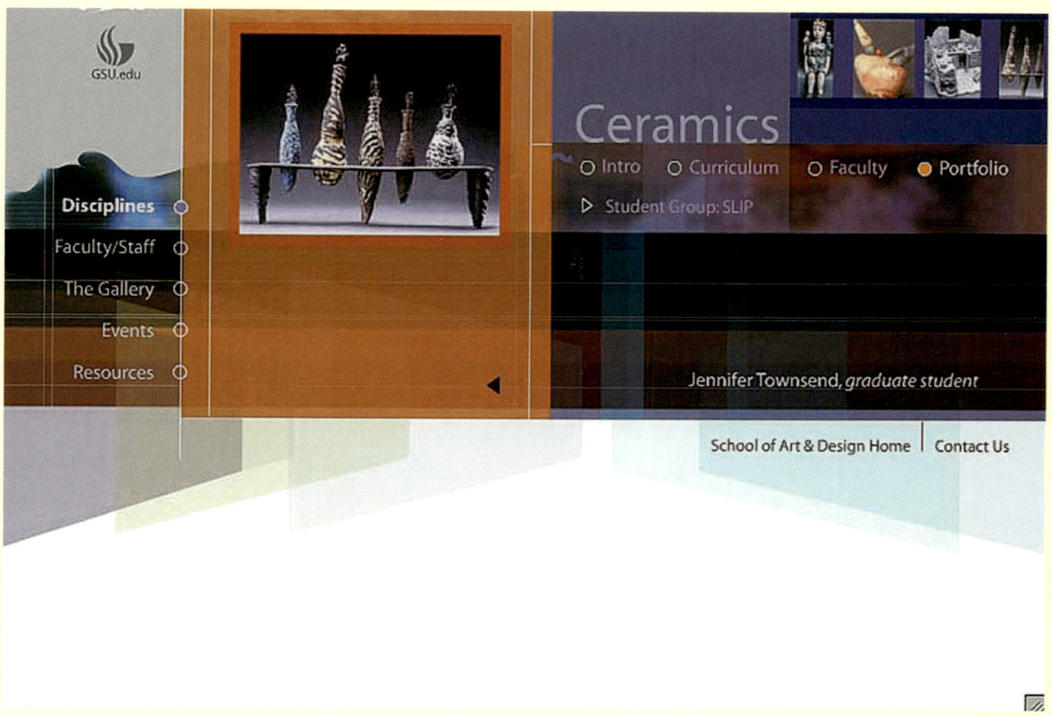

Design Firm: Wages Design, Inc. Art Director: Bob Wages Designers: Joanna Tak, Jimmy Lo and Steven Shinn Client: Georgia State University School of Art and Design

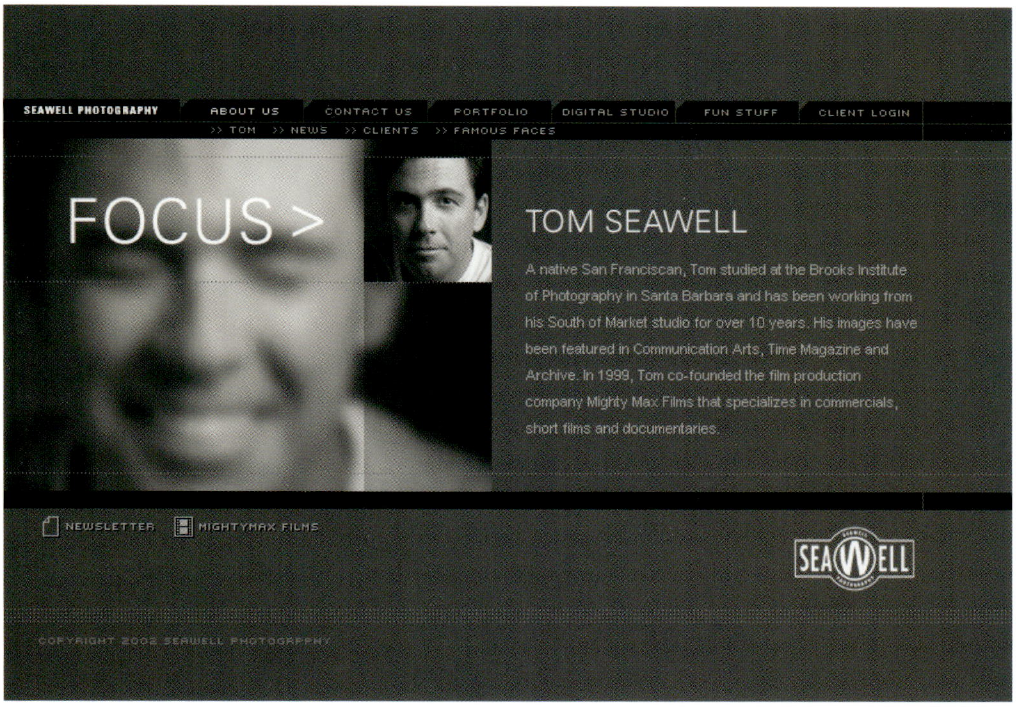

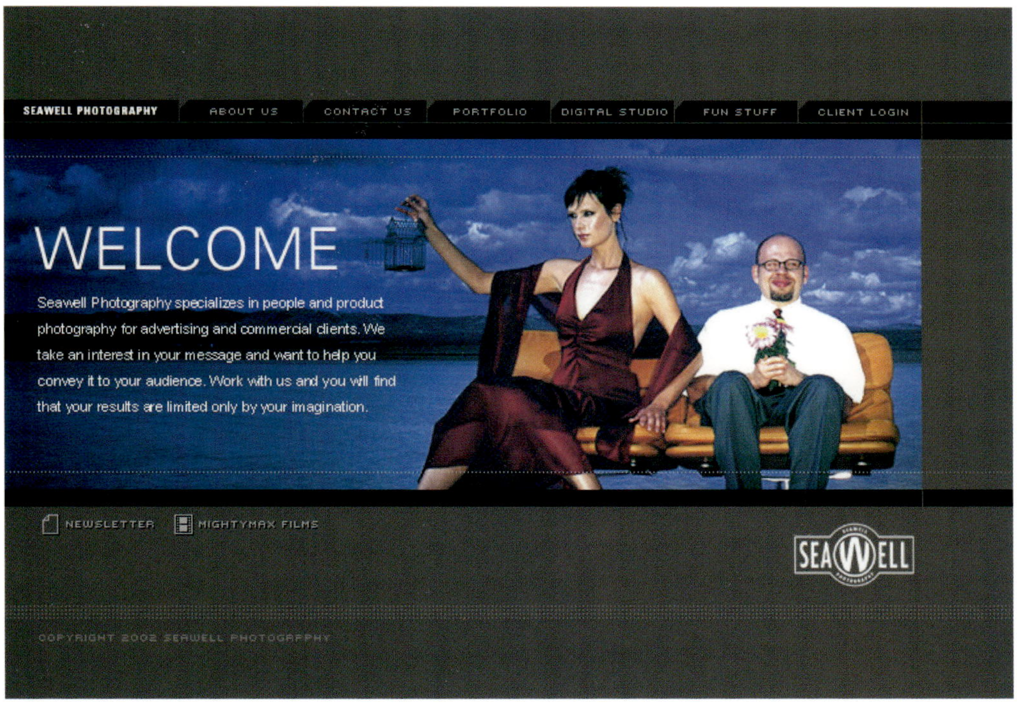

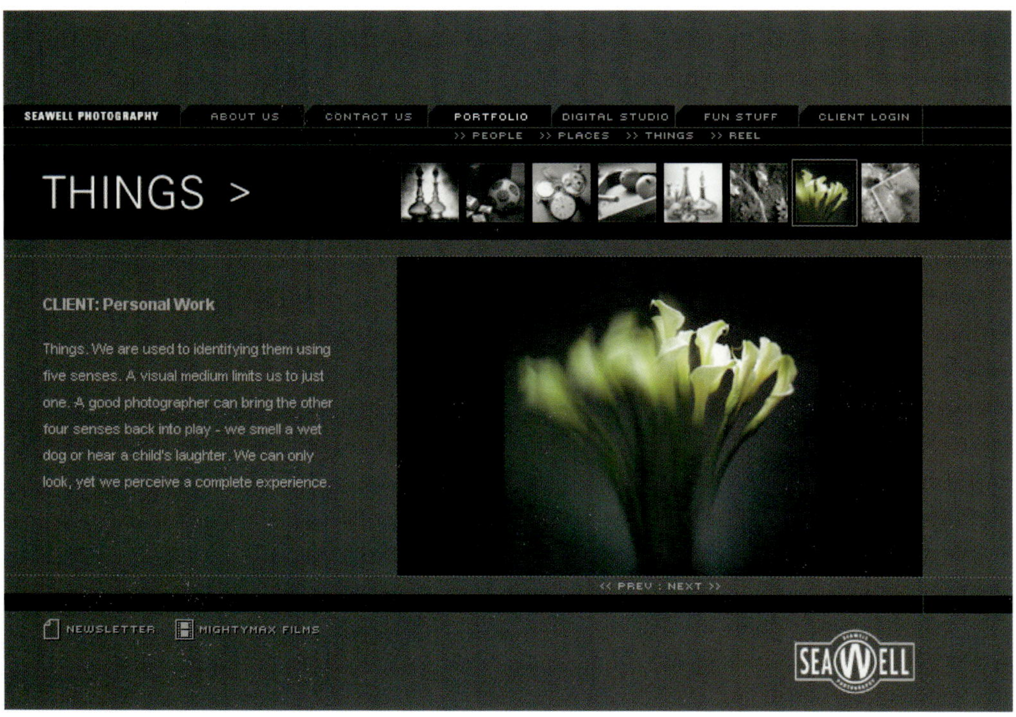

Design Firm: The Engine Room Art Director: Dave Braden Designer: Michael Cotsifas Client: Tom Seawell Photography

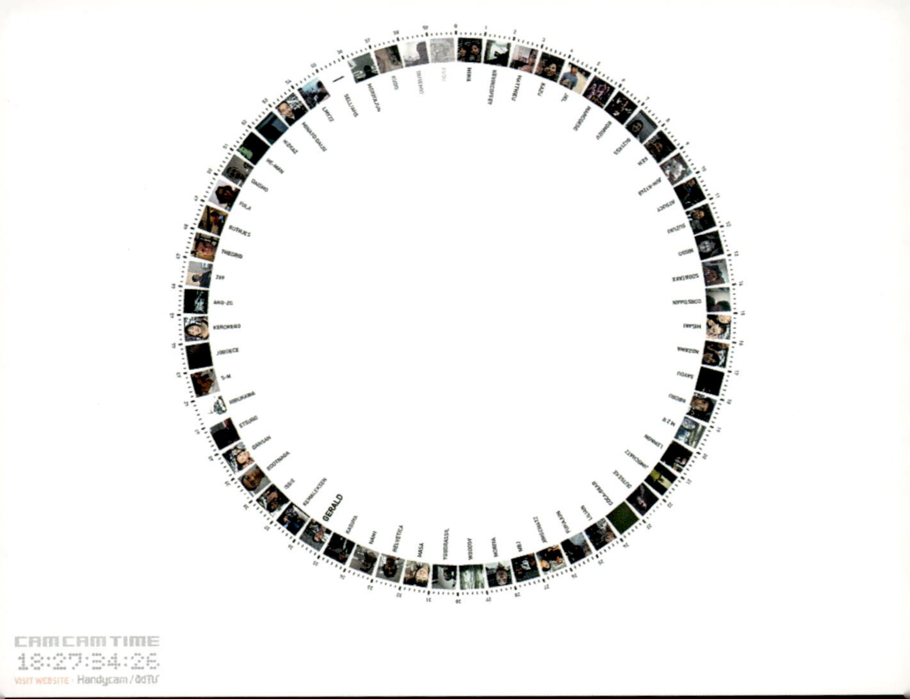
CAMCAMTIME
18:27:34:26
VISIT WEBSITE : Handycam / ddTV
GERALD

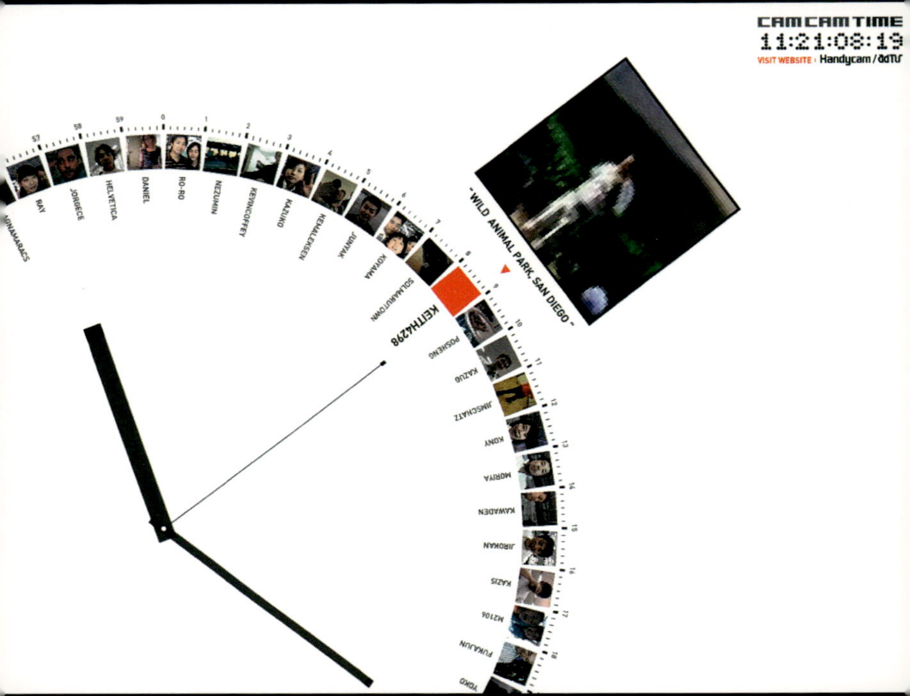
CAMCAMTIME
11:21:08:19
VISIT WEBSITE : Handycam / ddTV
"WILD ANIMAL PARK, SAN DIEGO"
KEITH4298

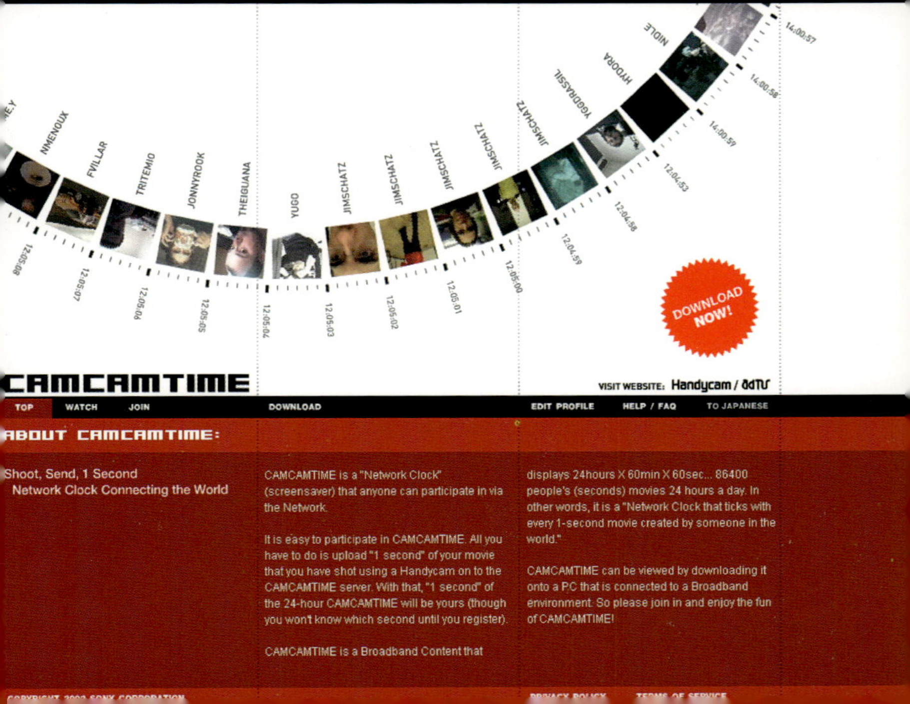
DOWNLOAD NOW!
CAMCAMTIME
VISIT WEBSITE: Handycam / ddTV
TOP
WATCH
JOIN
DOWNLOAD
EDIT PROFILE
HELP / FAQ
TO JAPANESE
ABOUT CAMCAMTIME:
Shoot, Send, 1 Second
Network Clock Connecting the World
CAMCAMTIME is a "Network Clock" (screensaver) that anyone can participate in via the Network.
It is easy to participate in CAMCAMTIME. All you have to do is upload "1 second" of your movie that you have shot using a Handycam on to the CAMCAMTIME server. With that, "1 second" of the 24-hour CAMCAMTIME will be yours (though you won't know which second until you register).
CAMCAMTIME is a Broadband Content that
displays 24hours X 60min X 60sec... 86400 people's (seconds) movies 24 hours a day. In other words, it is a "Network Clock that ticks with every 1-second movie created by someone in the world."
CAMCAMTIME can be viewed by downloading it onto a PC that is connected to a Broadband environment. So please join in and enjoy the fun of CAMCAMTIME!

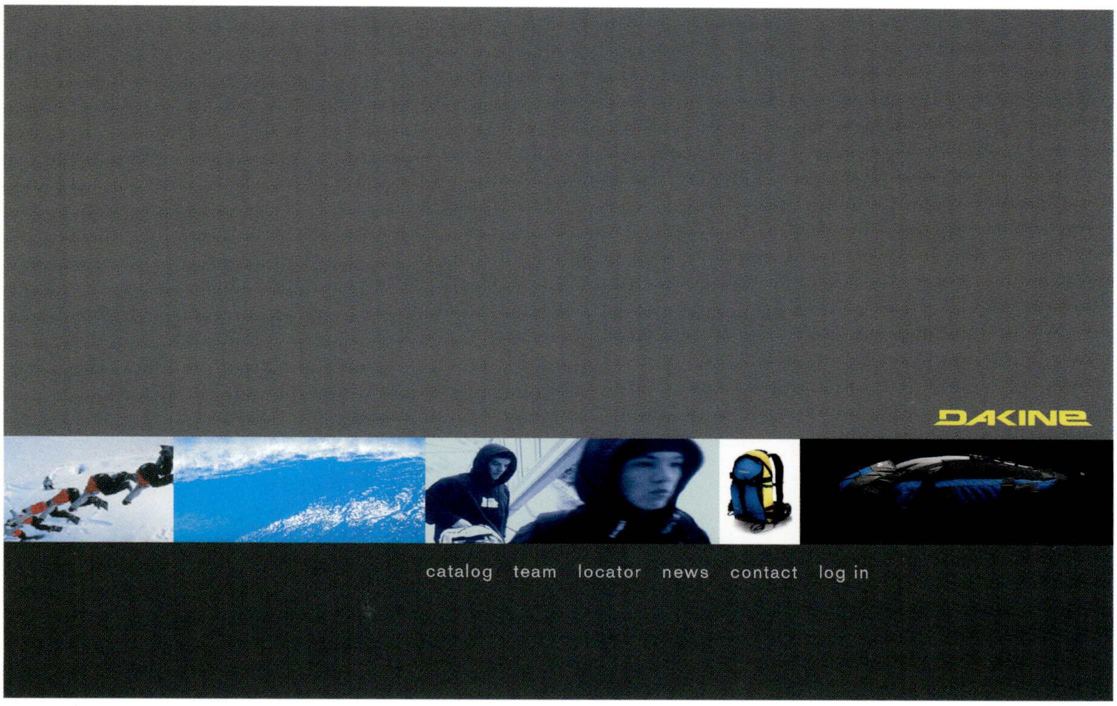

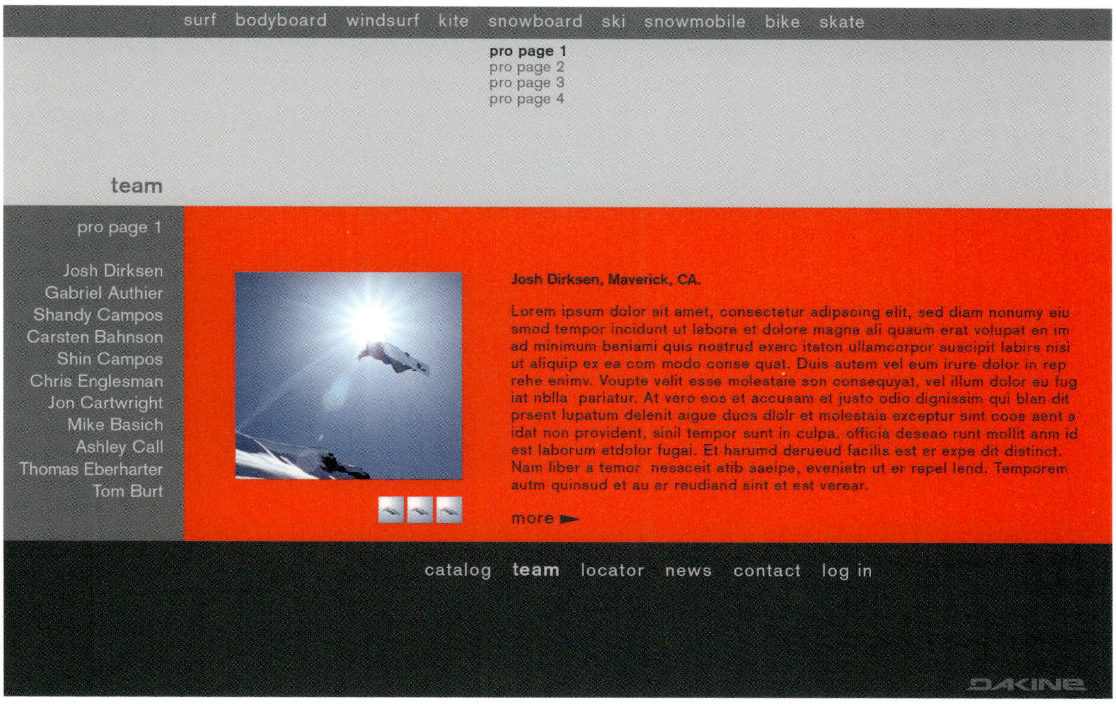

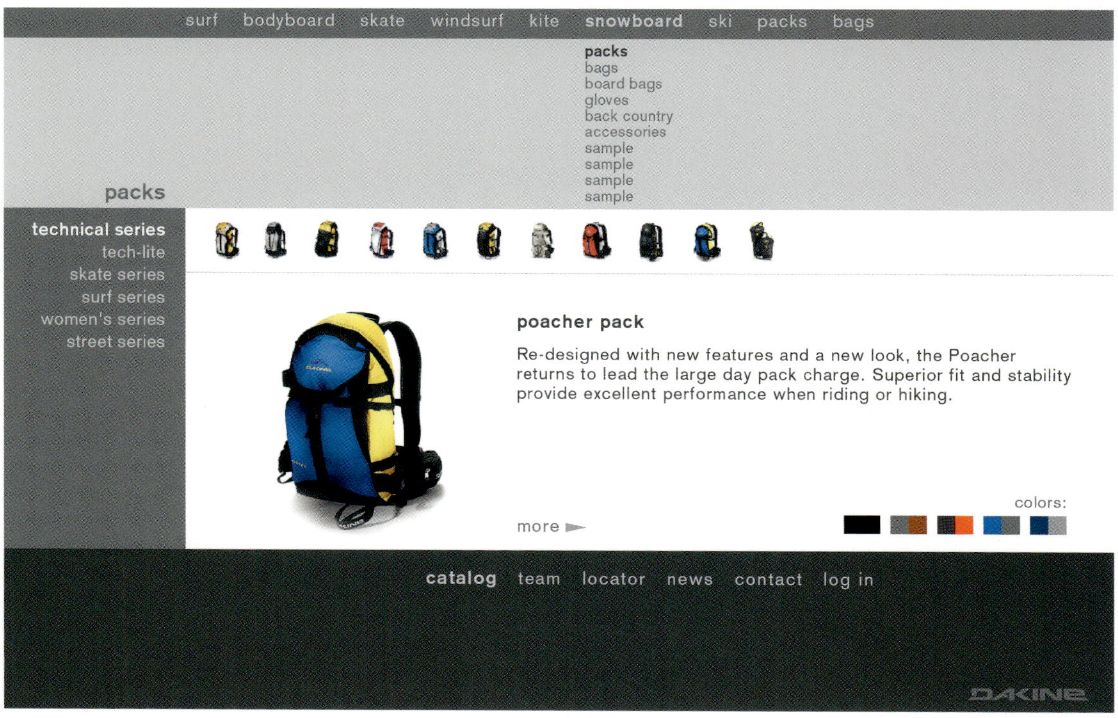

Design Firm: Ford Weithman Design Creative Director: Mark Ford Designers: Mark Ford and Mark Waggoner Client: Dakine Sports Company

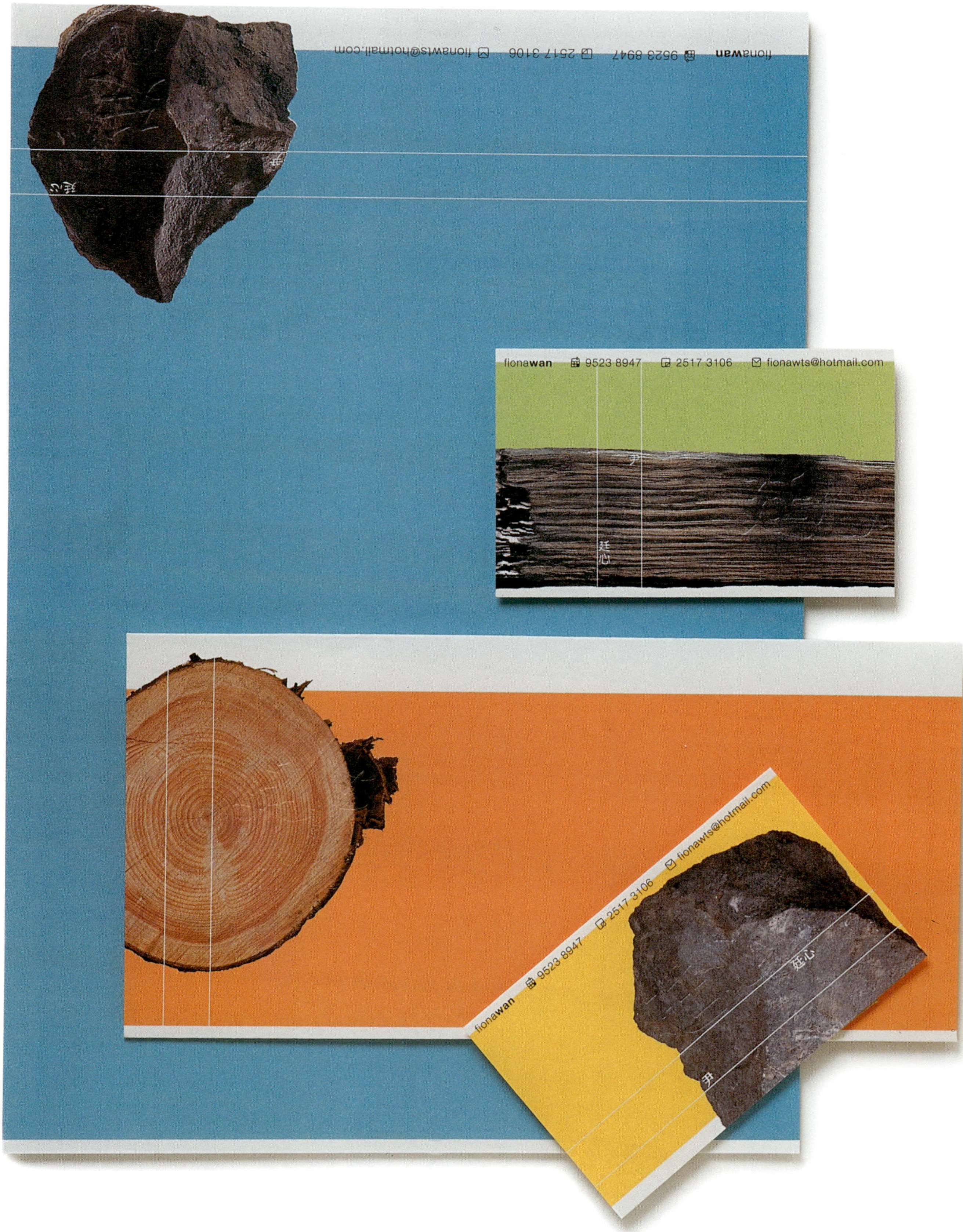

Design Firm: Eric Chan Design Co. Ltd. Creative Director: Eric Chan Art Director: Eric Chan Designer: Eric Chan Illustrator: Francis Lee Client: Fiona Wani

FROM >
>
>
>
> IAN

> > > > > > > > >

A PO BOX 27-352
WELLINGTON
NEW ZEALAND
W WWW.IANROBERTSON.CO.NZ
T +64 4 380 1138
F +64 4 380 1139
M +64 (0) 25 491 489
E HELLO@IANROBERTSON.CO.NZ

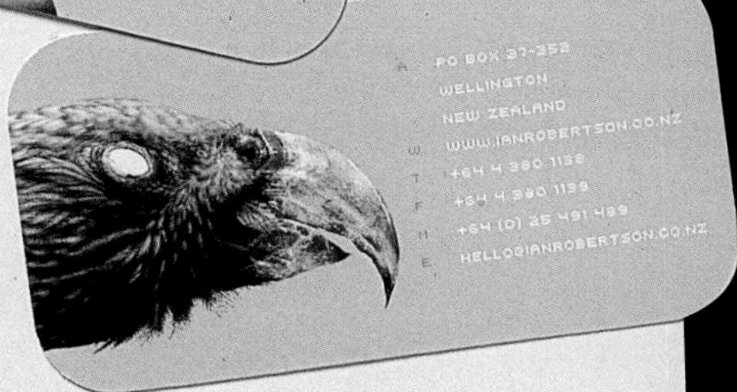

A PO BOX 27-352
WELLINGTON
NEW ZEALAND
W WWW.IANROBERTSON.CO.NZ
T +64 4 380 1138
F +64 4 380 1139
M +64 (0) 25 491 489
E HELLO@IANROBERTSON.CO.NZ

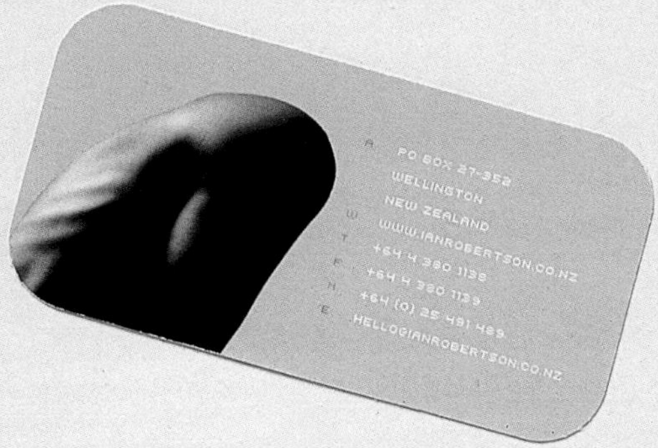

A PO BOX 27-352
WELLINGTON
NEW ZEALAND
W WWW.IANROBERTSON.CO.NZ
T +64 4 380 1138
F +64 4 380 1139
M +64 (0) 25 491 489
E HELLO@IANROBERTSON.CO.NZ

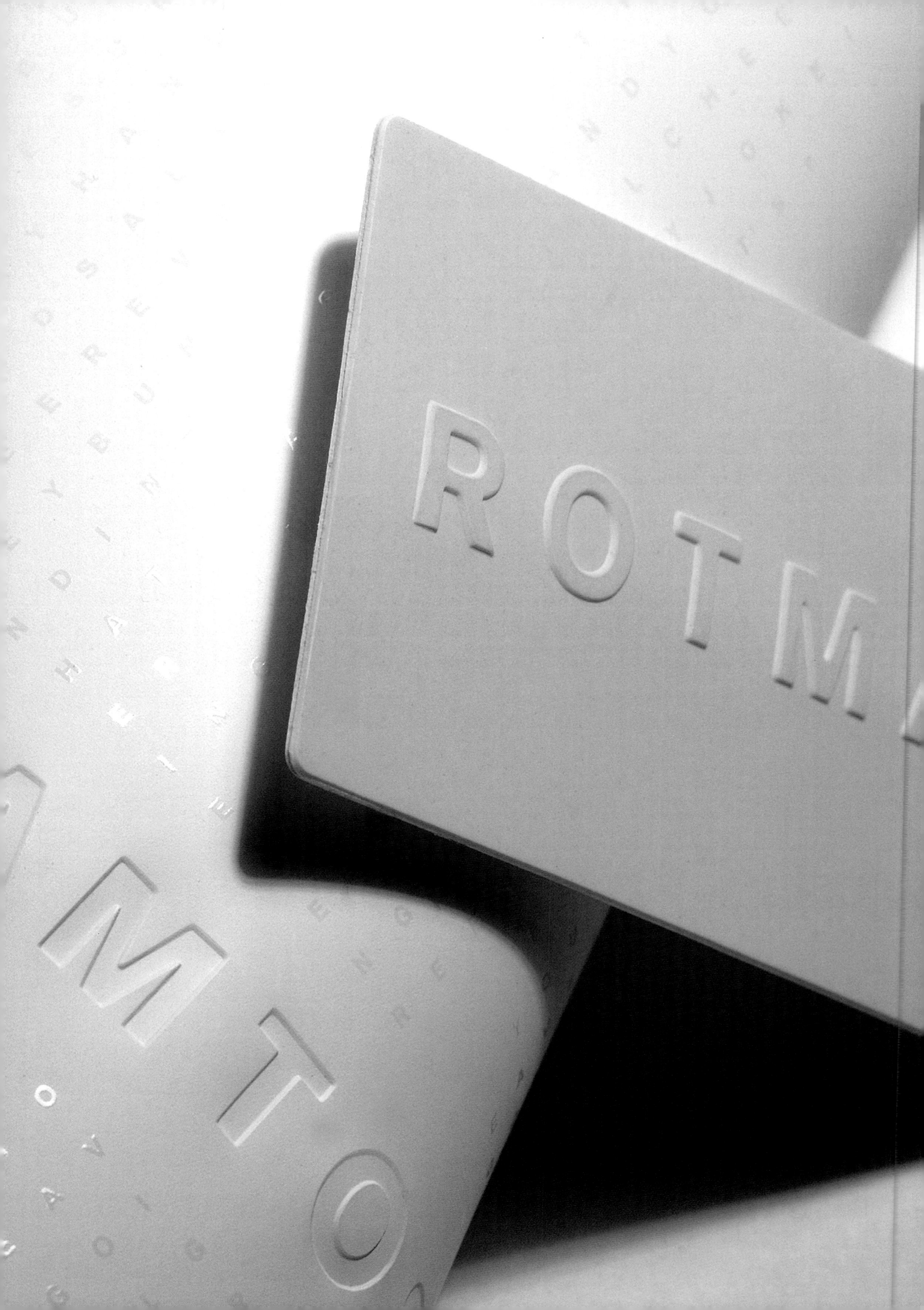
ROTM
MTO

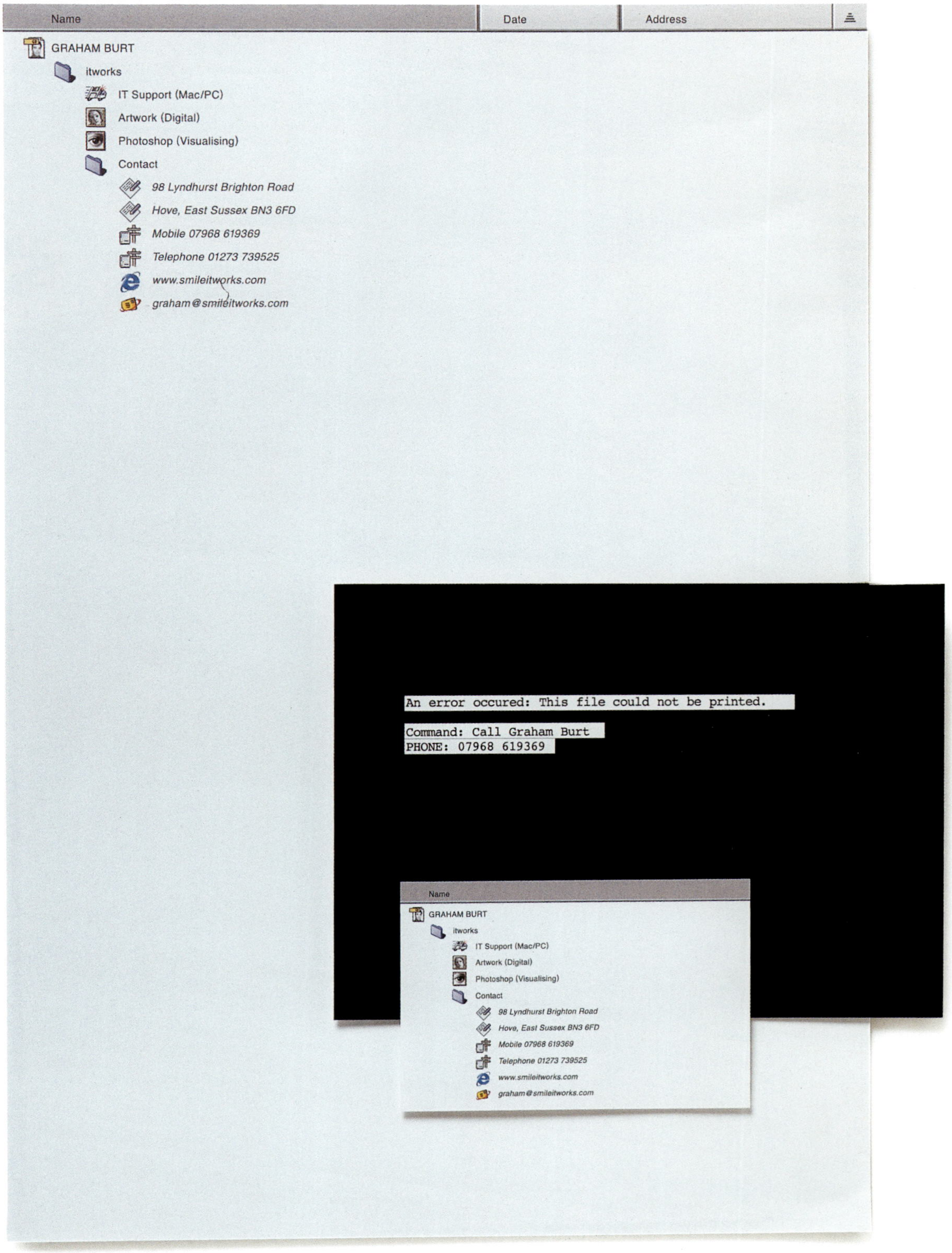

Design Firm: Williams Murray Hamm Creative Director: Garrick Hamm Designers: Garrick Hamm and Gareth Beeson Illustrator: Gareth Beeson Copywriter: Garrick Hamm
Account Coordinator: Garrick Hamm Client: Graham Burt (opposite page) Design Firm: Oxide Design Co. Creative Director: Drew Davies Designer: Drew Davies Client: Oxide Design Co.

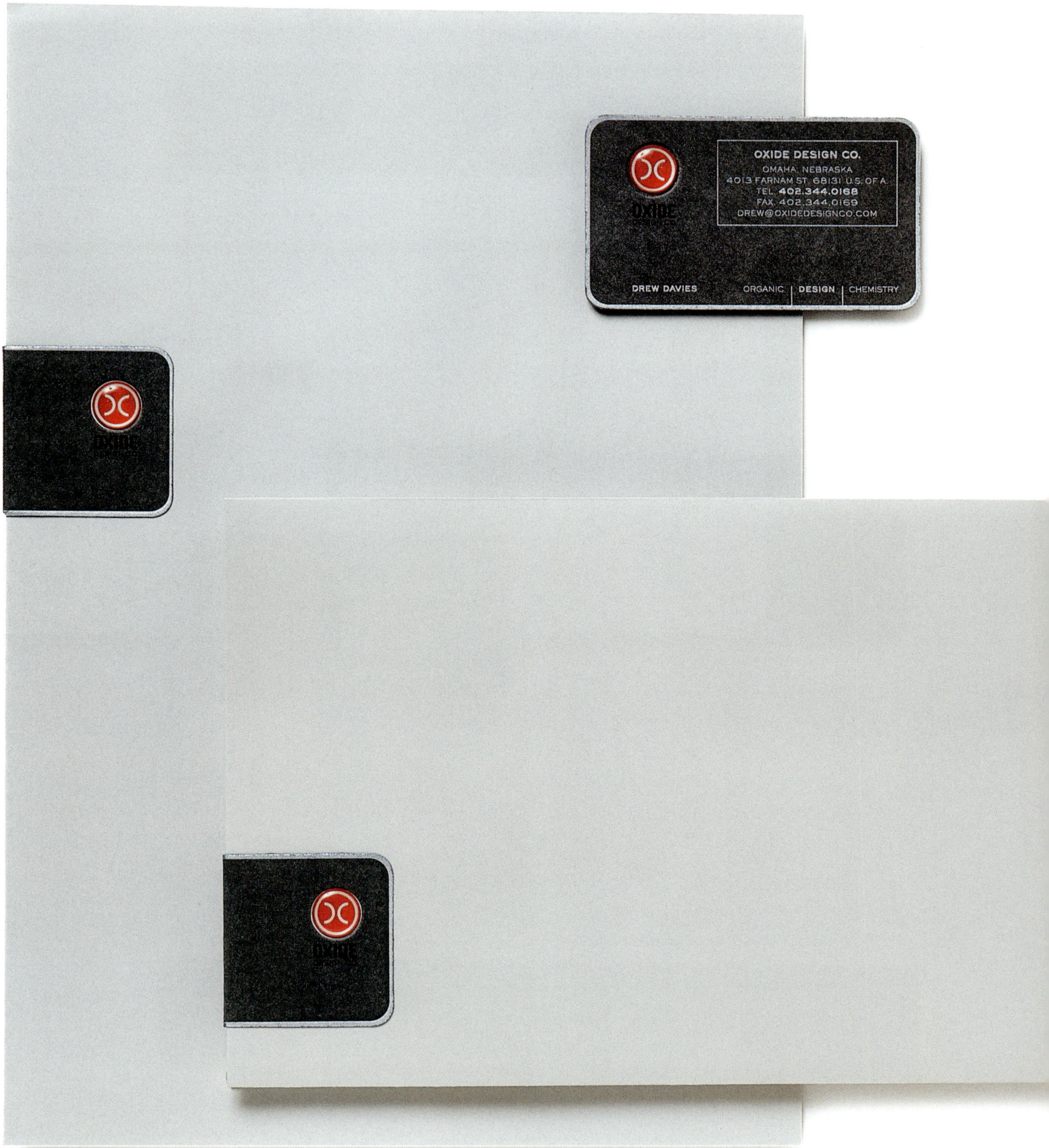
OXIDE DESIGN CO.
OMAHA, NEBRASKA
4013 FARNAM ST. 68131 U.S. OF A.
TEL. 402.344.0168
FAX. 402.344.0169
DREW@OXIDEDESIGNCO.COM
OXIDE
DREW DAVIES
ORGANIC
DESIGN
CHEMISTRY
OXIDE
OXIDE

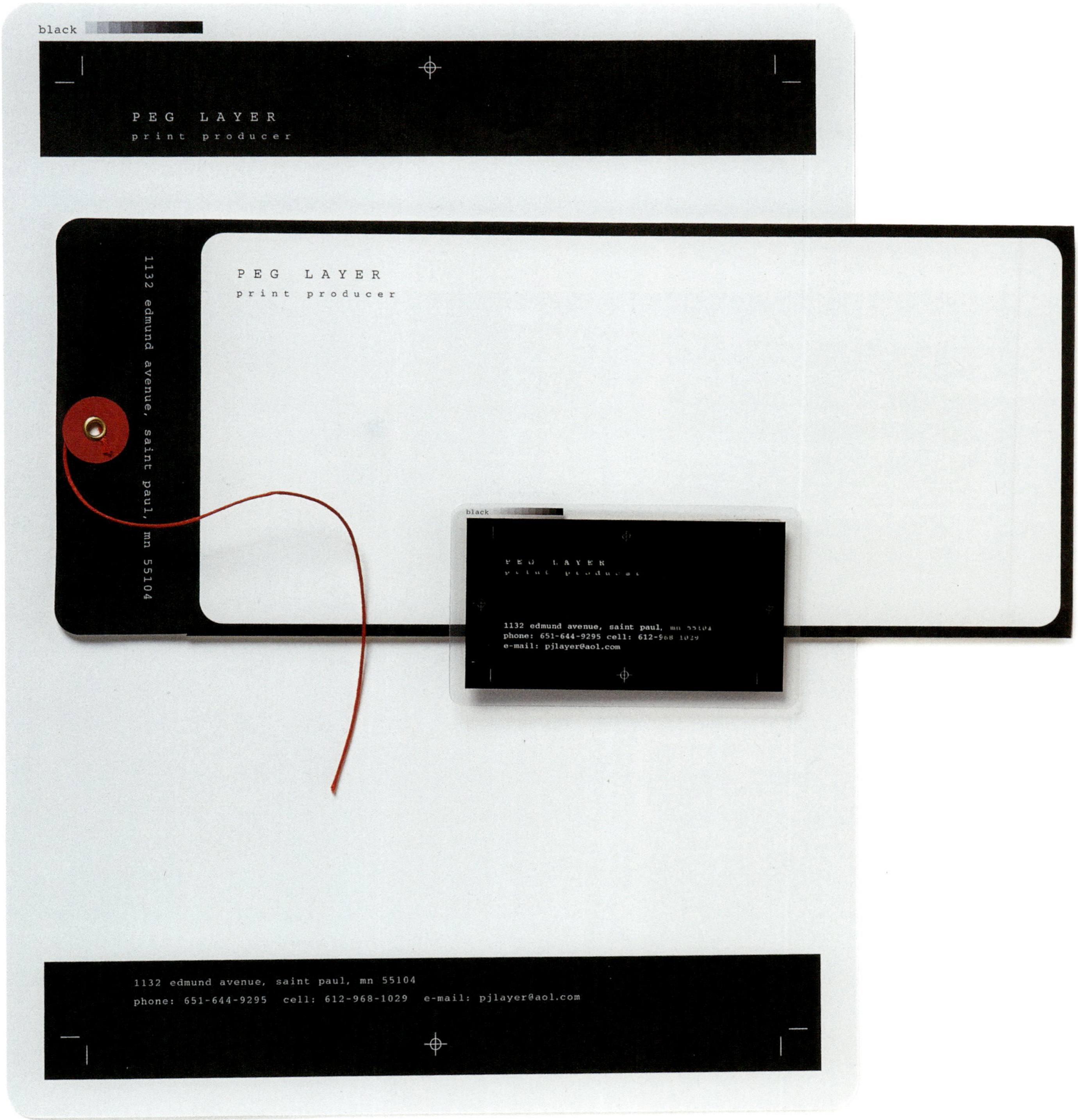

Design Firm: Dalton Advertising Inc. Creative Director: Rob Dalton Designer: Colleen Brown Client: Peg Layer

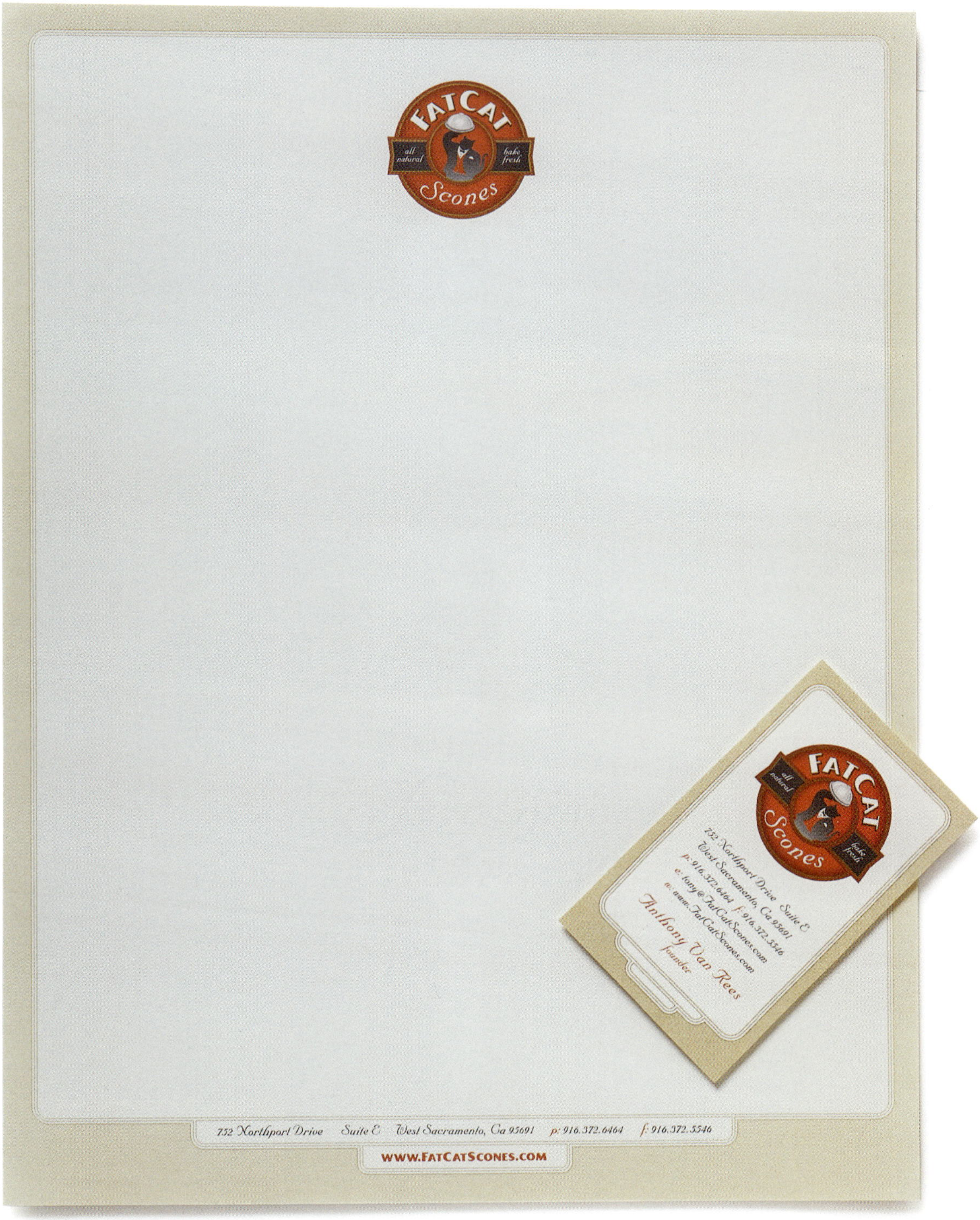

Design Firm: The Engine Room Art Director: Dave Braden Designer: Michael Cotsifas Client: Fat Cat Scones

(1) Design Firm: Sibley Peteet Design/Dallas Designer: Dan Birlew Illustrator: Dan Birlew Client: Santa Fe Satellites (2) Design Firm: Sibley Peteet Design/Dallas Designer: Dan Birlew Illustrator:Dan Birlew Client: Michelson Construction (3) Design Firm: RBMM Art Director: Matt Staab Designer: Matt Staab Client: Brighton Painting (4) Design Firm: RBMM Art Director: Matt Staab Designer: Matt Staab Client: Ellis Construction (5) Design Firm: Sibley Peteet Design Art Directors: Brandon Kirk and Jenny Goodwyn Designer: Brandon Kirk Illustrator: Brandon Kirk Client: Free The Slaves

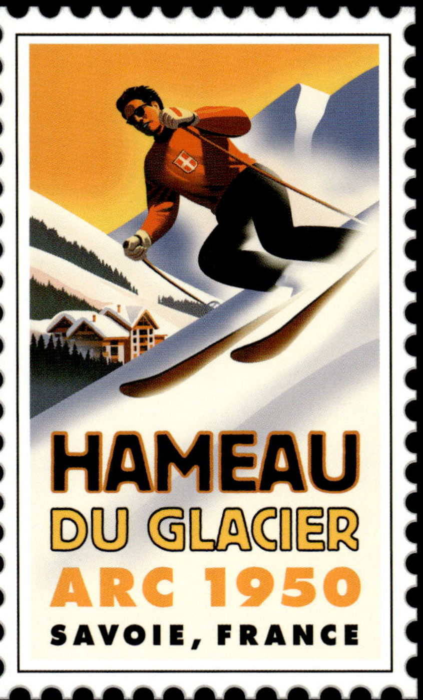

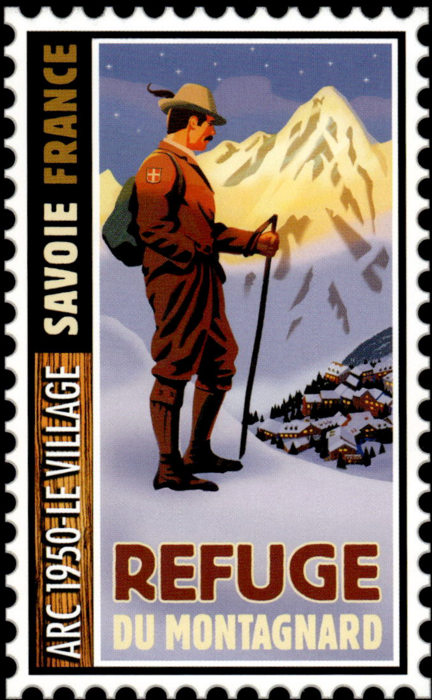

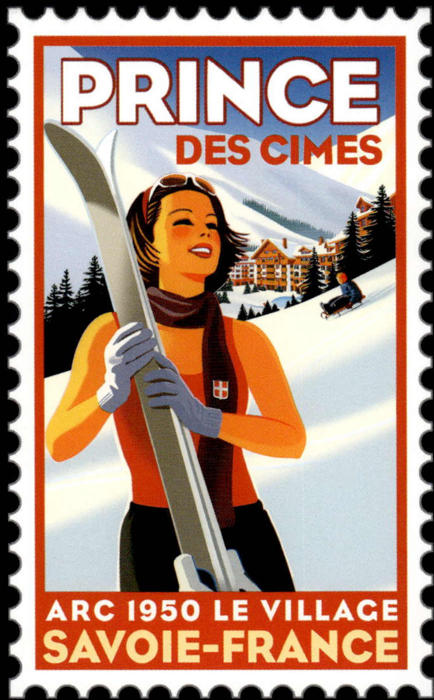

Trio Les Arcs Logos| Design Firm: Ryan & Deslauriers Creative Director: Tom Pedriks Art Director: Sorin Pavelesco Designer: Sorin Pavelesco Illustrator: Maurice Gervais Client: Intrawest

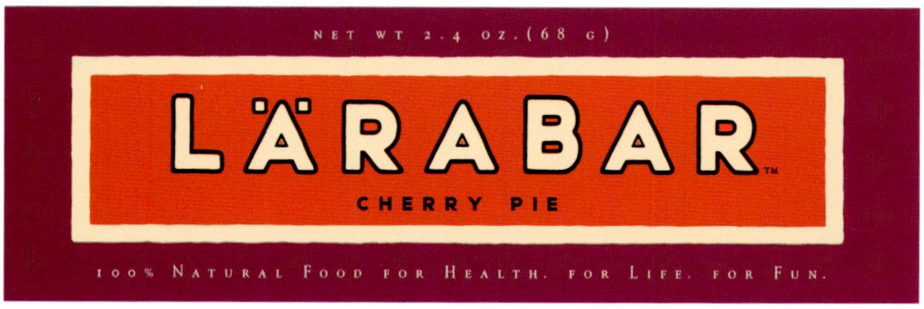

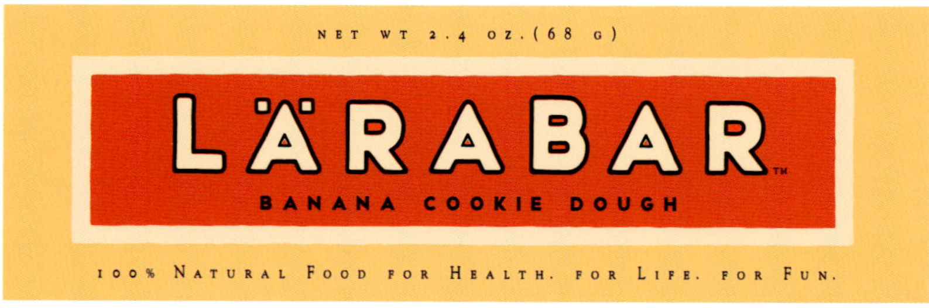

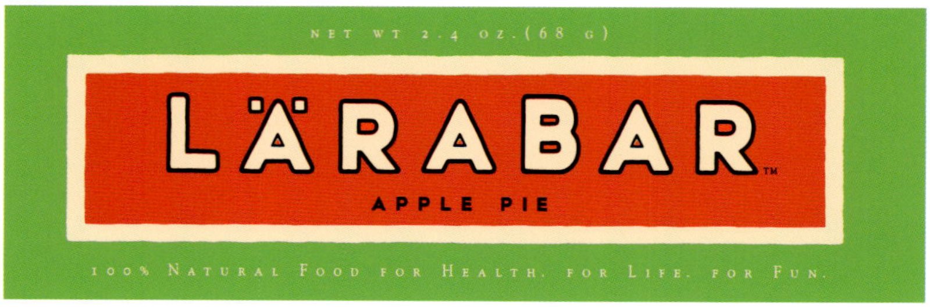

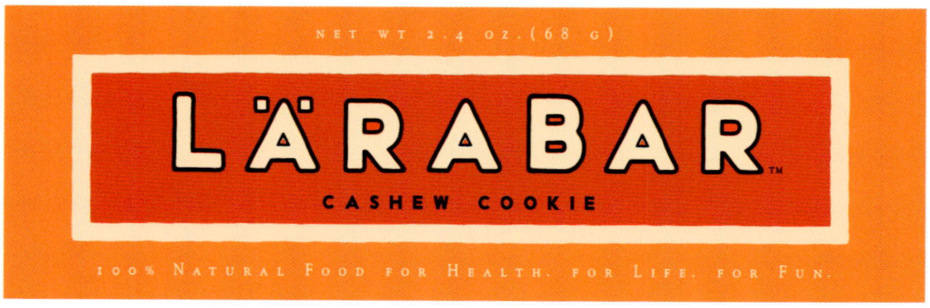

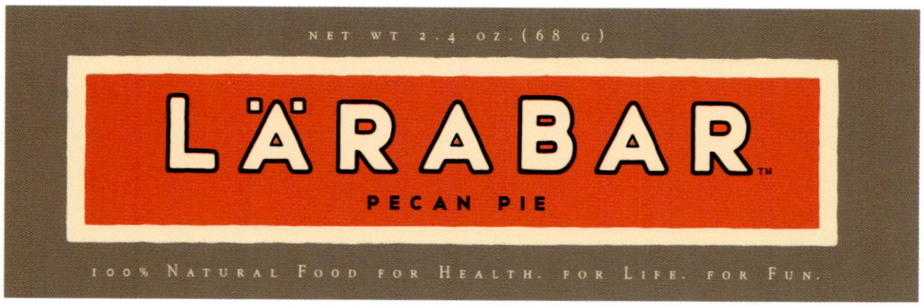

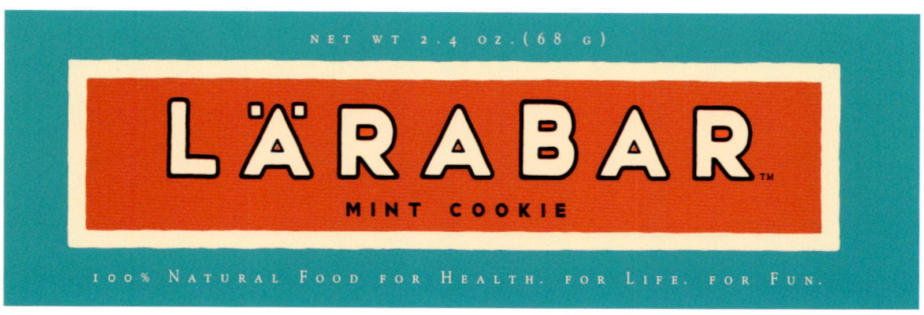

Design Firm: Michael Schwab Studio Designer: Michael Schwab Illustrator: Michael Schwab Client: Larabar

SPREAD

Design Firm: Mirko Ilic Corp. Art Director: Mirko Ilic Designers: Mirko Ilic and Heath Hinegardner Client: Spread Restaurant/Lounge

Design Firm: The Engine Room Art Director: Michael Cotsifas Designer: Dave Braden Client: Global Vegetarian

(from top) (1) 'Ramp Technologies' Design Firm: Edward Walter Design Art Director: Ed Walter Client: Ramp Technologies (2) Design Firm: Sibley Peteet Design/Dallas Designer: Dan Birlew Illustrator: Dan Birlew Client: Sound Bodies (3) Design Firm: DeAngelis Design Art Director: Jean DeAngelis Designer: Jean DeAngelis Client: for a wedding (4) Design Firm: Michael Schwab Studio Art Director: Candra Canning Designer: Michael Schwab Illustrator: Michael Schwab Client: Tahoe Mountain Club (5) Design Firm: Tom Fowler, Inc. Creative Director: Thomas G. Fowler Art Director: Thomas G. Fowler Designer: Thomas G. Fowler Illustrator: Thomas G. Fowler Client: Inua Gallery

(1) '100th Anniversary' Design Firm: Carmichael Lynch Thornburn Creative Director: Bill Thorburn Designer: Travis Olson Client: Harley-Davidson (2) Design Firm: Turner & Associates Art Director: Phil Hamlett Designer: Laura Milton Client: Anderson Lithograph (3) 'Working Man' Design Firm: Kosaka Identity & Design Creative Director: Wayne Kosaka Illustrator: Roger Beerworth Client: Scheid Vineyards (4) Design Firm: i.design Designer: Jonathan Ingram Client: Kessler Venturers (5) Design Firm: Kilmer & Kilmer Creative Director: Richard Kilmer Designer: Travis Driscoll Associate Creative Director: Travis Driscoll Client: Matrix Fitness Systems

Design Firm: Ford Weithman Design Creative Director: Mark Ford Designer: Mark Ford Client: Advanced Cultivation Systems

'Harvard Mentoring Project Logo' Design Firm: Milton Glaser Inc. Designer: Milton Glaser Illustrator: Milton Glaser Client: Harvard School of Public Health

(1) Design Firm: Michael Lee Advertising & Design Art Director: Debby Stasinopoulou Designer: Michael C. Lee Client: Wester Tree Service (2) Design Firm: The Bradford Lawton Design Group Creative Director: Bradford Lawton Designers: Lesile Magee and Bradford Lawton Client: Easy Inch Loss Weight Loss (3) Design Firm: RBMM Art Director: Jacob Ristau Designer: Jacob Ristau Illustrator: Jacob Ristau Client: Button's Cafe (4) Design Firm: Ford Weithman Design Creative Directors: Mark Ford and Jeff Weithman Designers: Mark Ford and Jeff Weithman Client: Tebeau (5) Design Firm: BOWG Creative Director: Jill Bustamante Art Director: Jeremy Oviatt Designer: Jeremy Oviatt Client: Work Activity Center

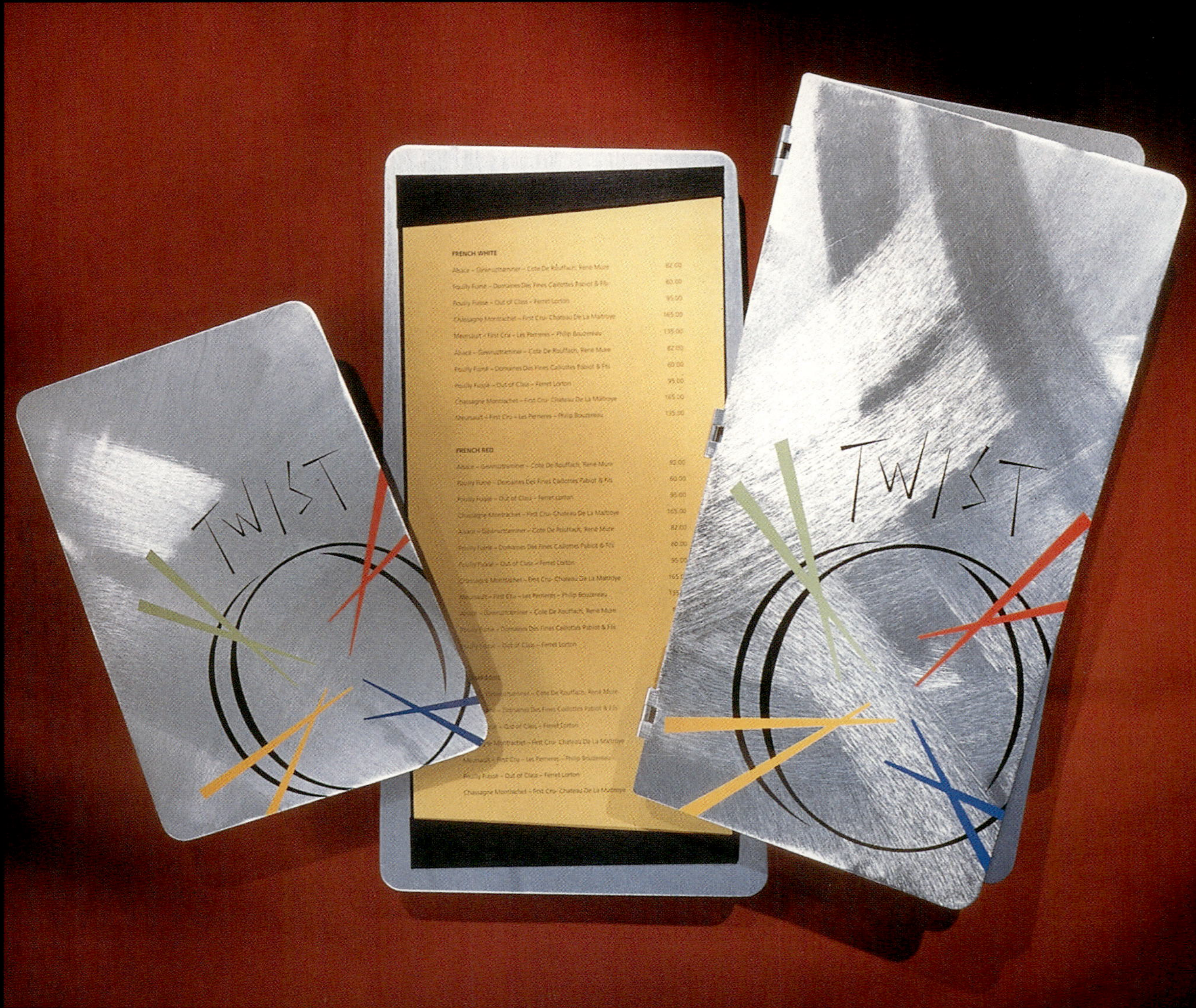

Design Associates Creative Director: Ashley Barron Mattocks Art Director: Donna Aldridge Designer: Rachel Graham Client: Twist

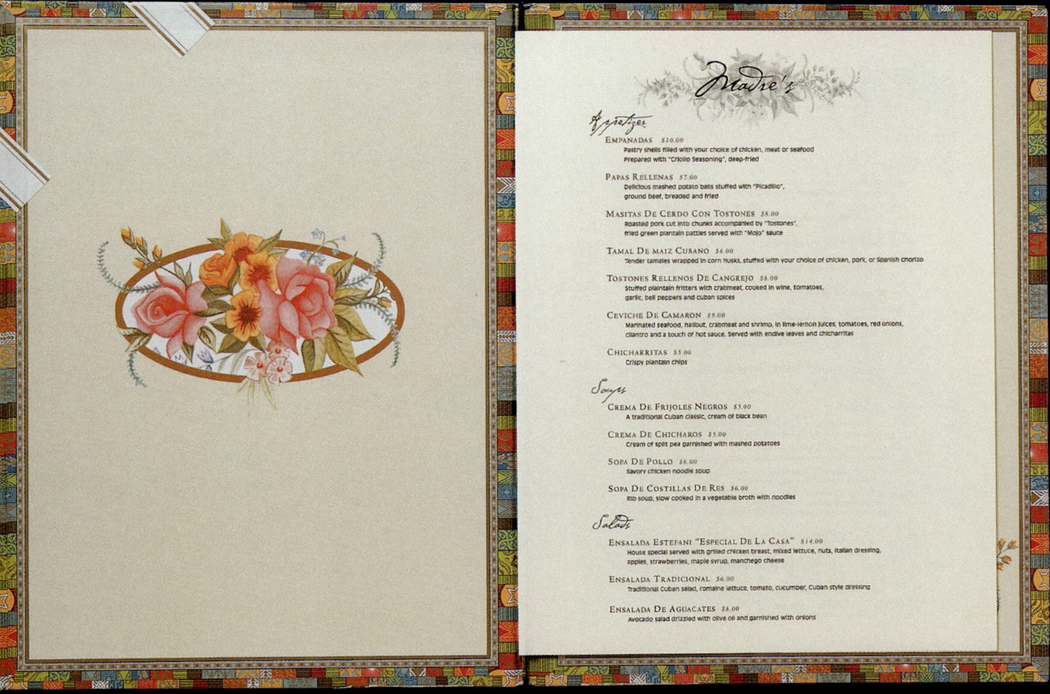

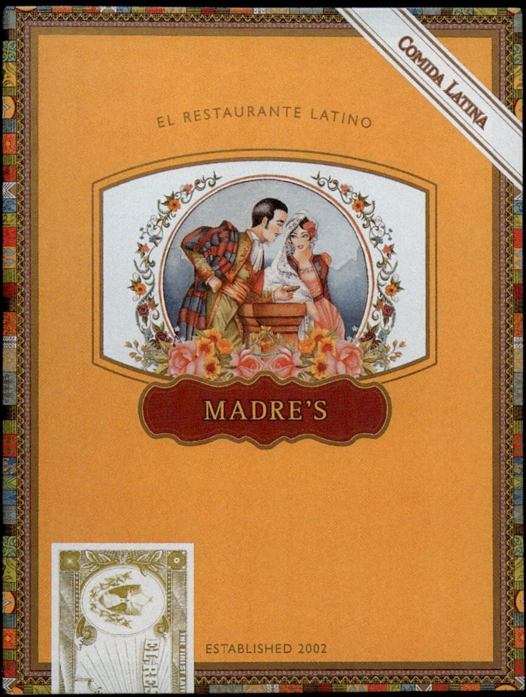

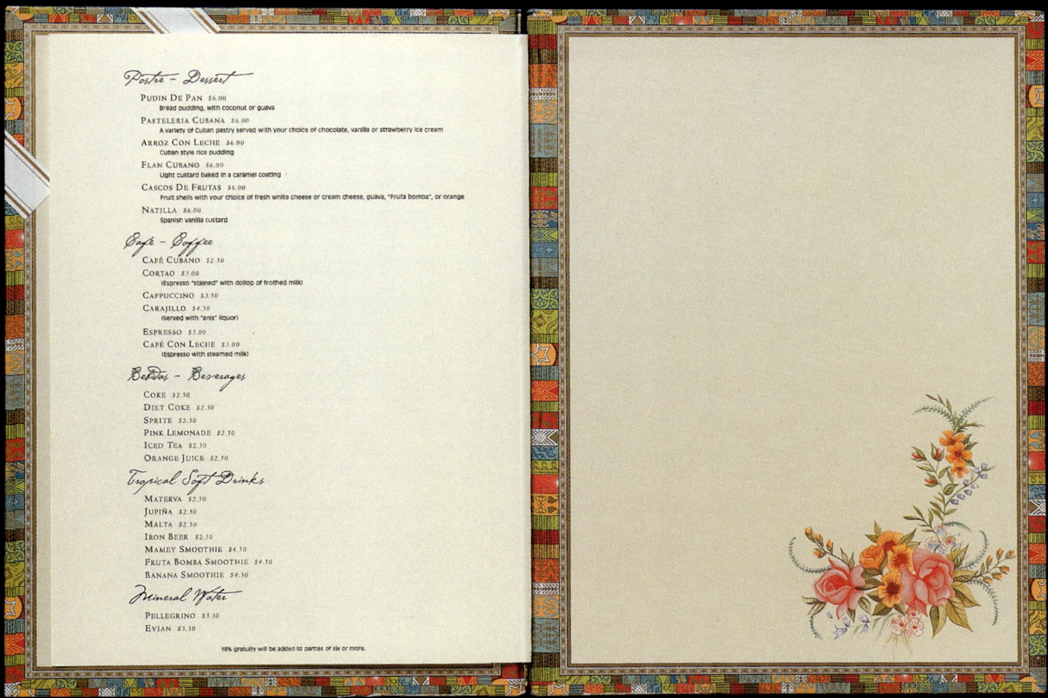

Design Firm: EPOS, Inc. Creative Director: Gabrielle Raumberger Designers: Clifford Singontiko, Eric Martinez, Chad Goodson and Samantha Ahdoot Illustrator: Veronica Palmer Client: Jennifer Lopez/Madre's Restaurant

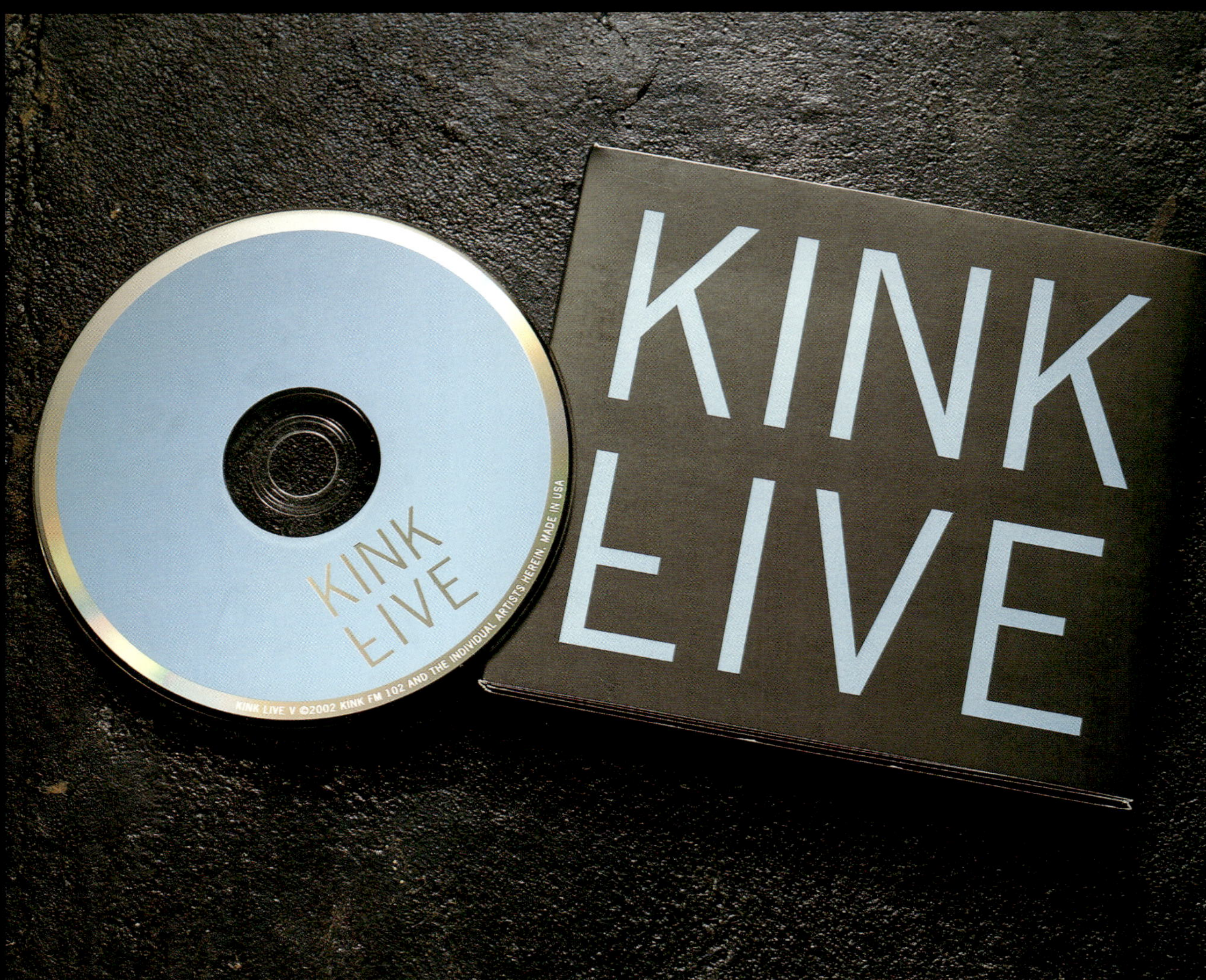

Kink Live V CD Design Firm: Sandstrom Design Creative Director: Steve Sandstrom Art Director: Steve Sandstrom Designer: Steve Sandstrom Copywriter: Dave Scott Production Designer: Greg Parra

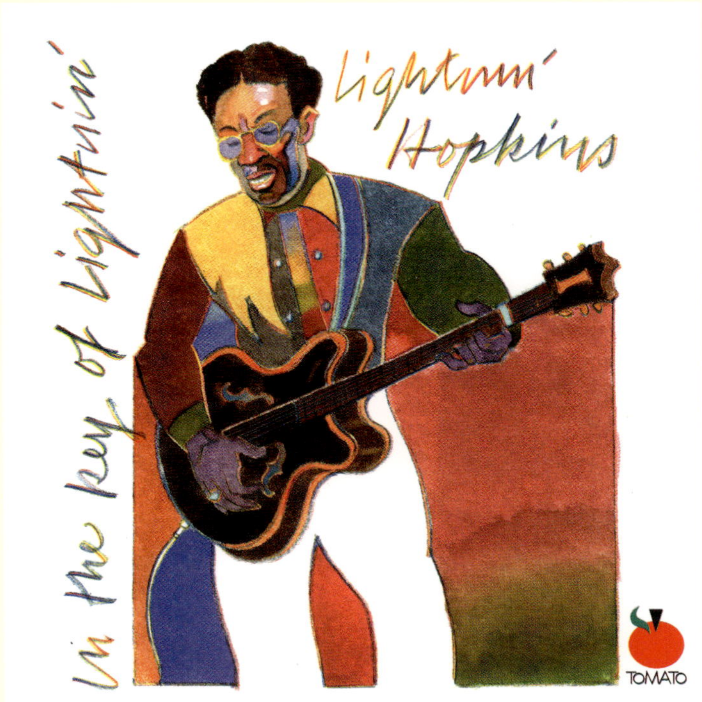

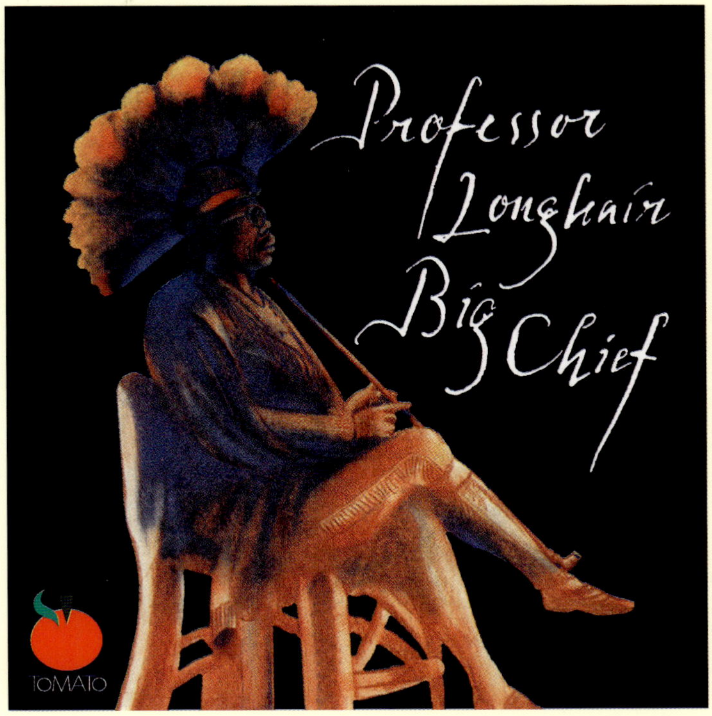

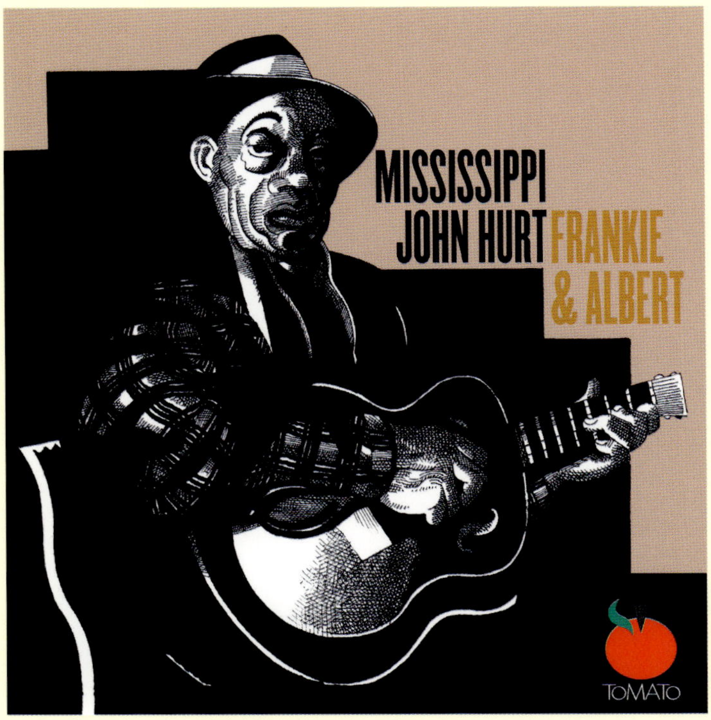

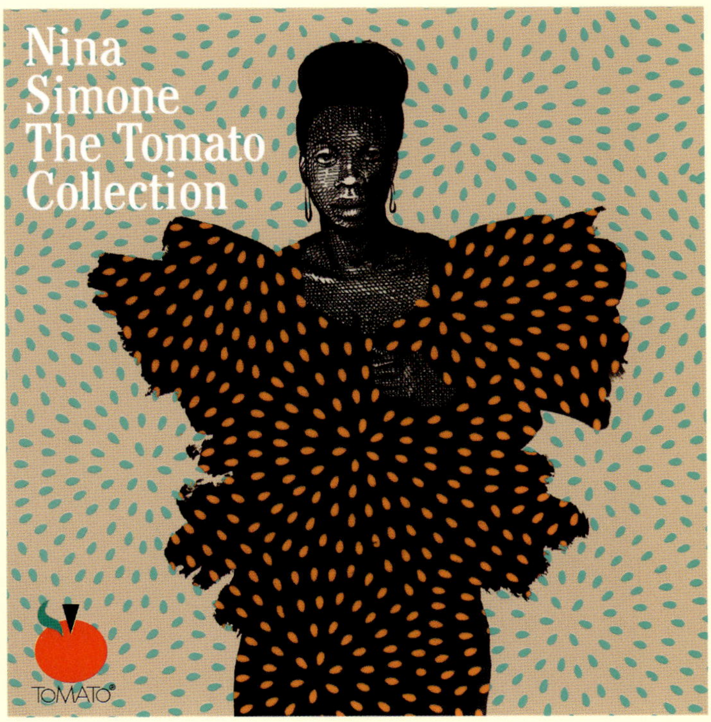

Design Firm: Milton Glaser Inc. Designer: Milton Glaser Illustrator: Milton Glaser Client: Tomato Records

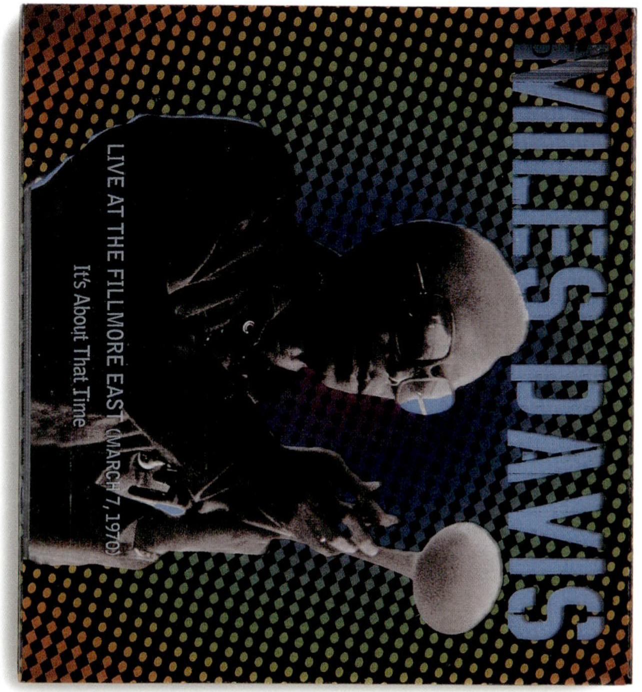

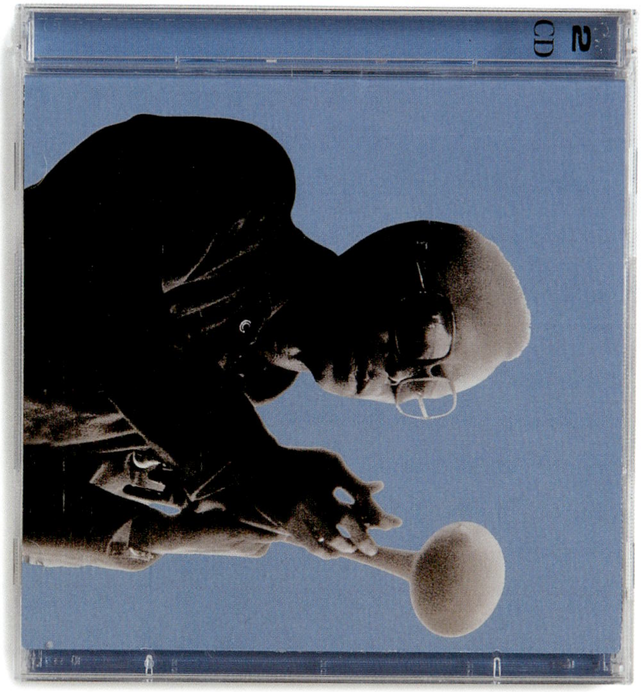

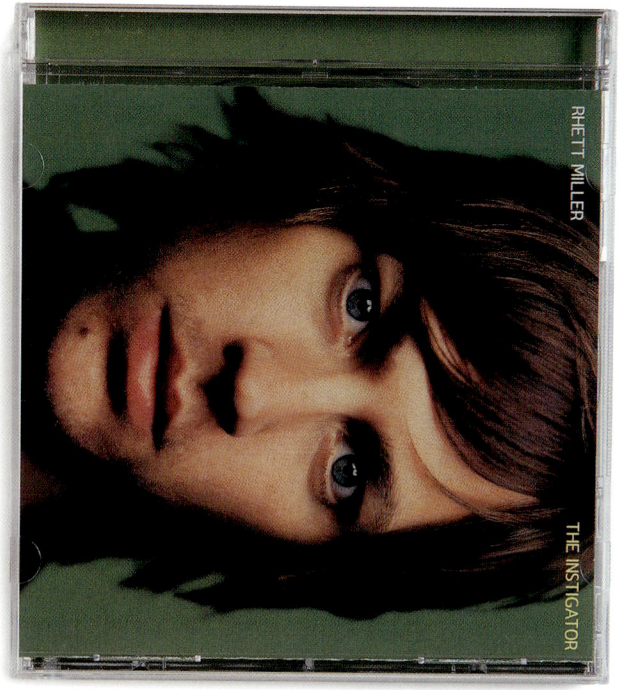

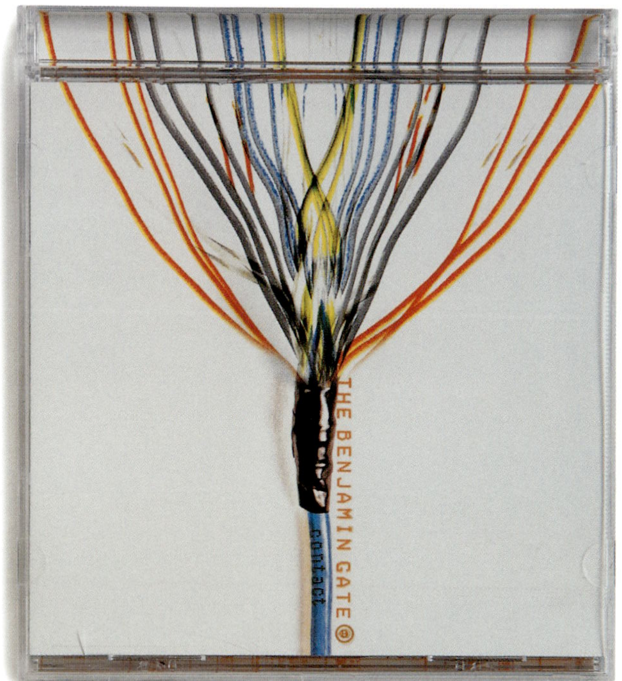

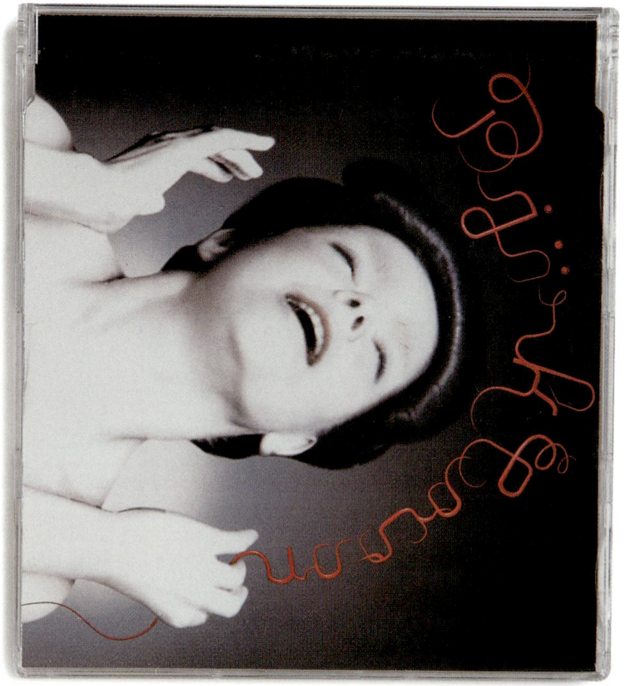

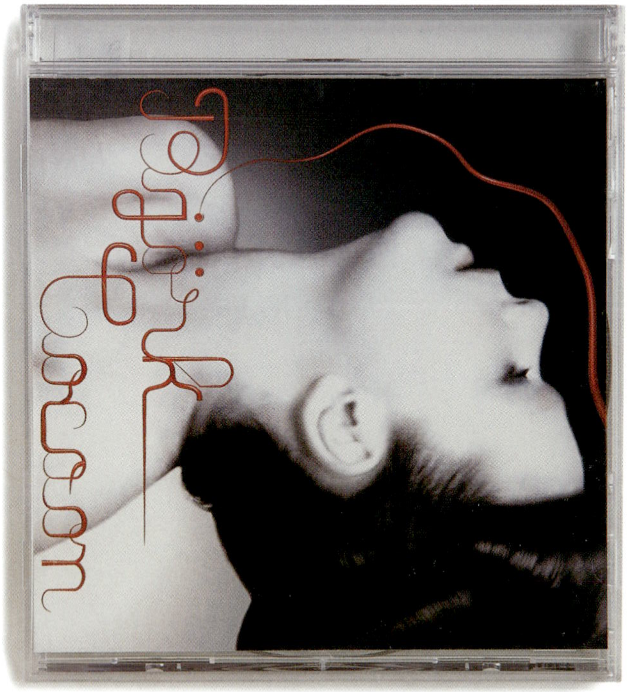

(clockwise from top left) (1, 6) 'Miles Davis' Design Firm: Sony Music Entertainment Art Director: Alice V. Butts Designer: Alice V. Butts Photographer: Amaille R. Rothschild (2) 'The Instigator' Design Firm: Elektra Records Art Director: Lili Picou Designer: Lili Picou Photographer: Mark Seliger Client: Rhett Miller (2, 4) 'Cocoon' Design Firm: Radical Media Art Director: Eiko Ishioka Designer: Rafael Esquer CG Artist: Tim Wilder Client: Björk and One Little Indian Records (5) 'Contact Cd Packaging' Design Firm: Th Designers: Blake Tannery and Clark Hook Client: Forefront Records

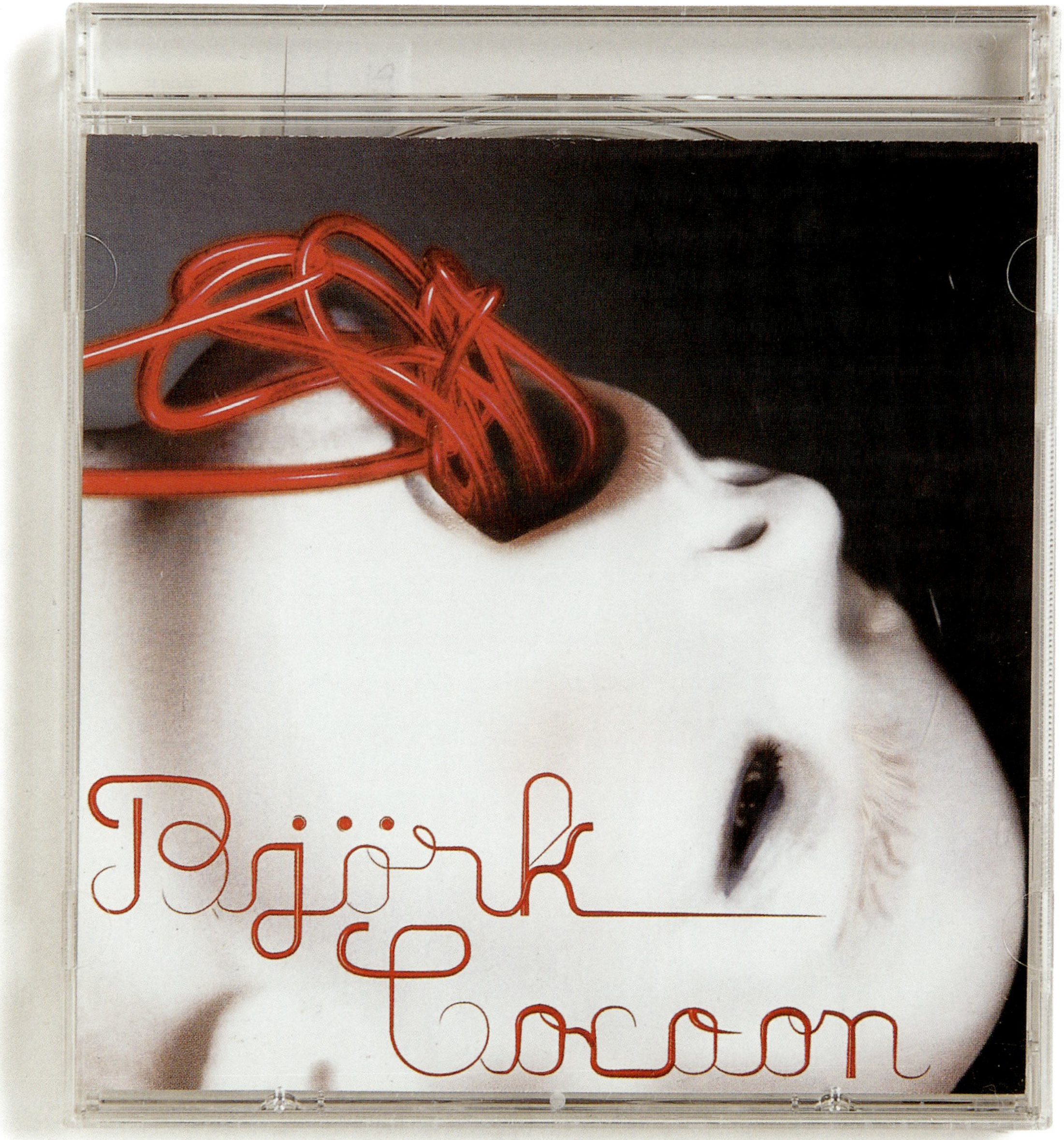

'Cocoon' **Design Firm:** Radical Media **Art Director:** Eiko Ishioka **Designer:** Rafael Esquer **CG Artist:** Tim Wilder **Client:** Björk and One Little Indian Records

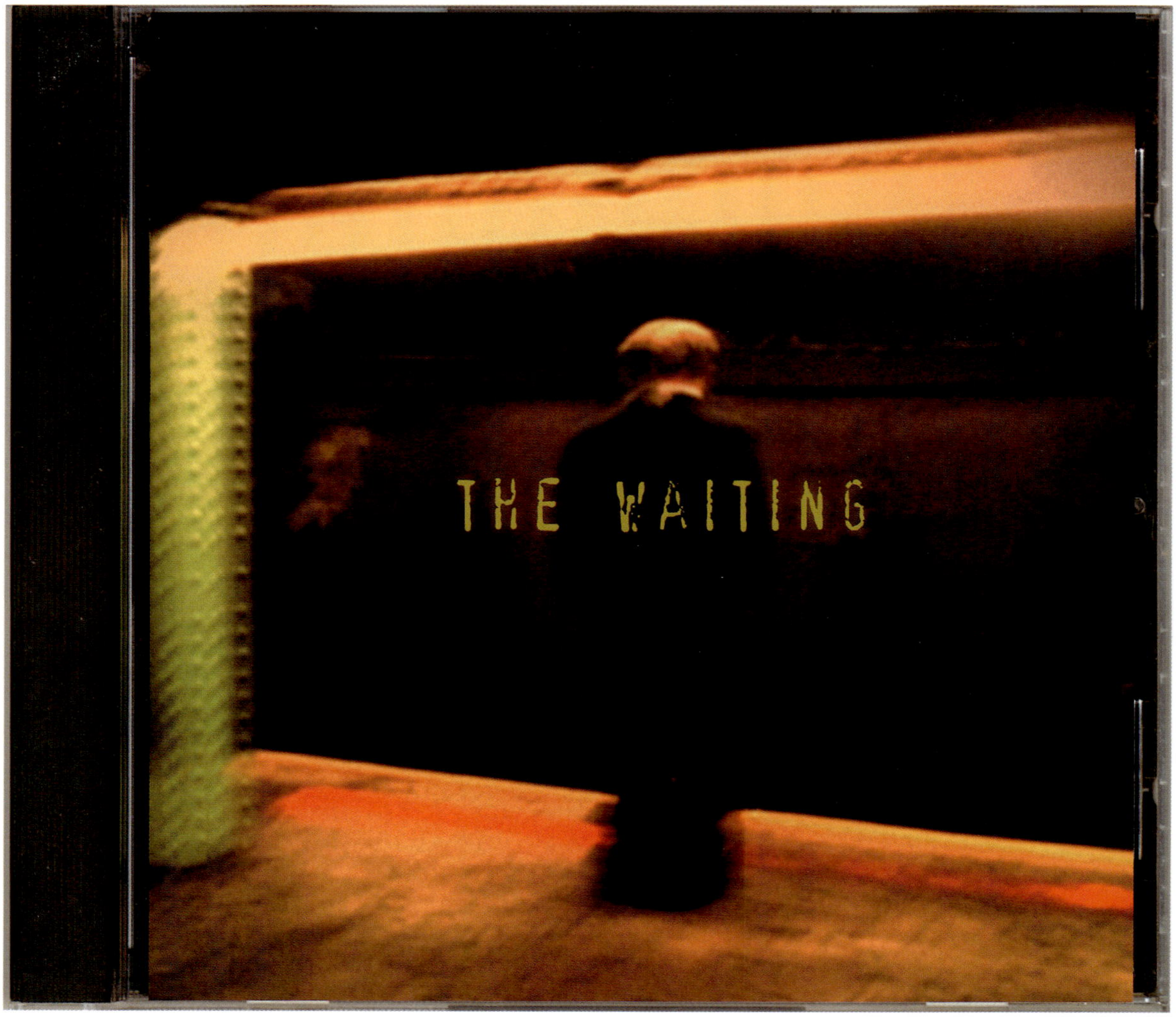

'The Waiting' Art Director: Joyce Revoir Photographer: Marc Yankus Client: Sparrow Records

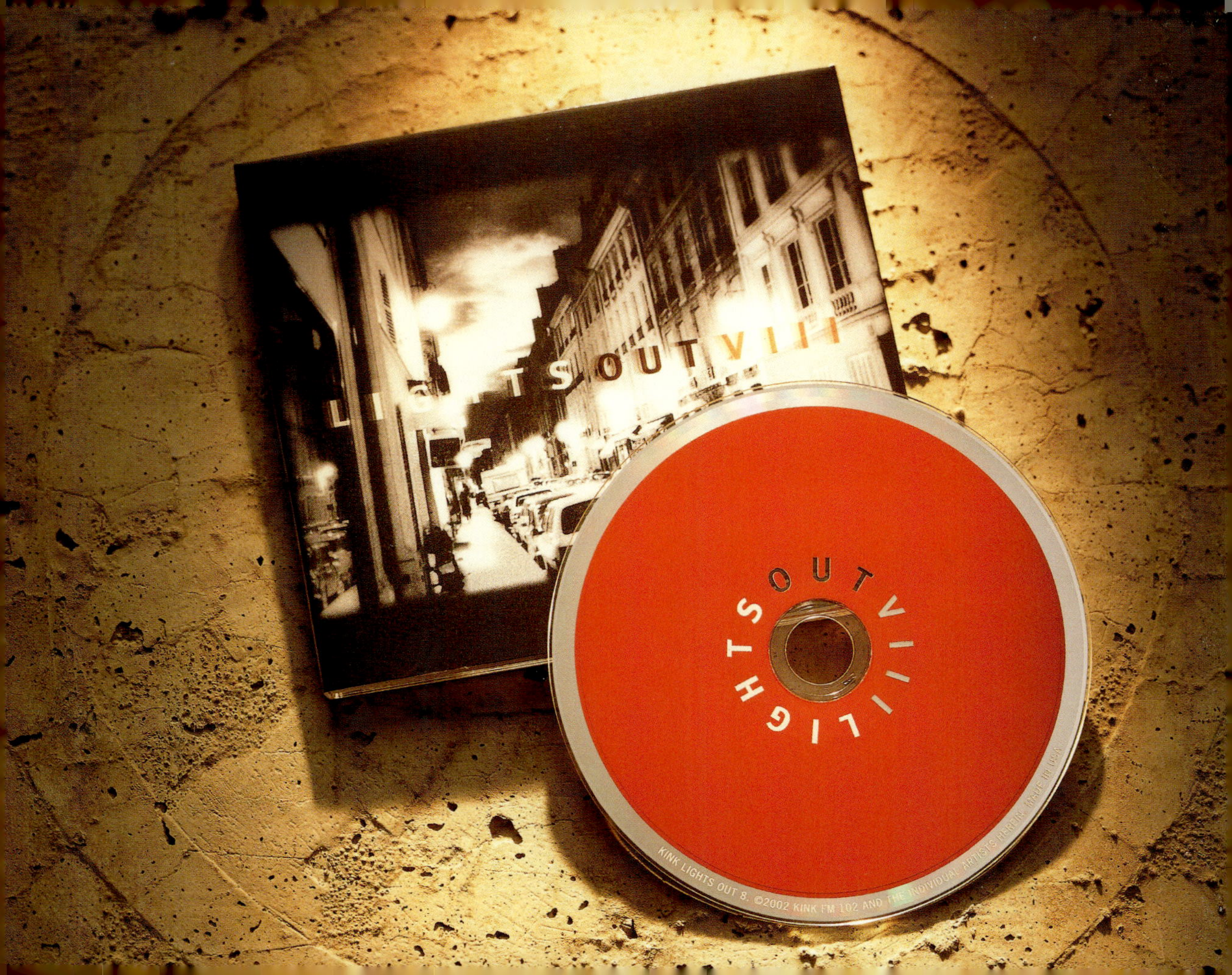
LIGHTS OUT VIII
KINK LIGHTS OUT 8. ©2002 KINK FM 102 AND THE INDIVIDUAL ARTISTS HEREIN. MADE IN USA

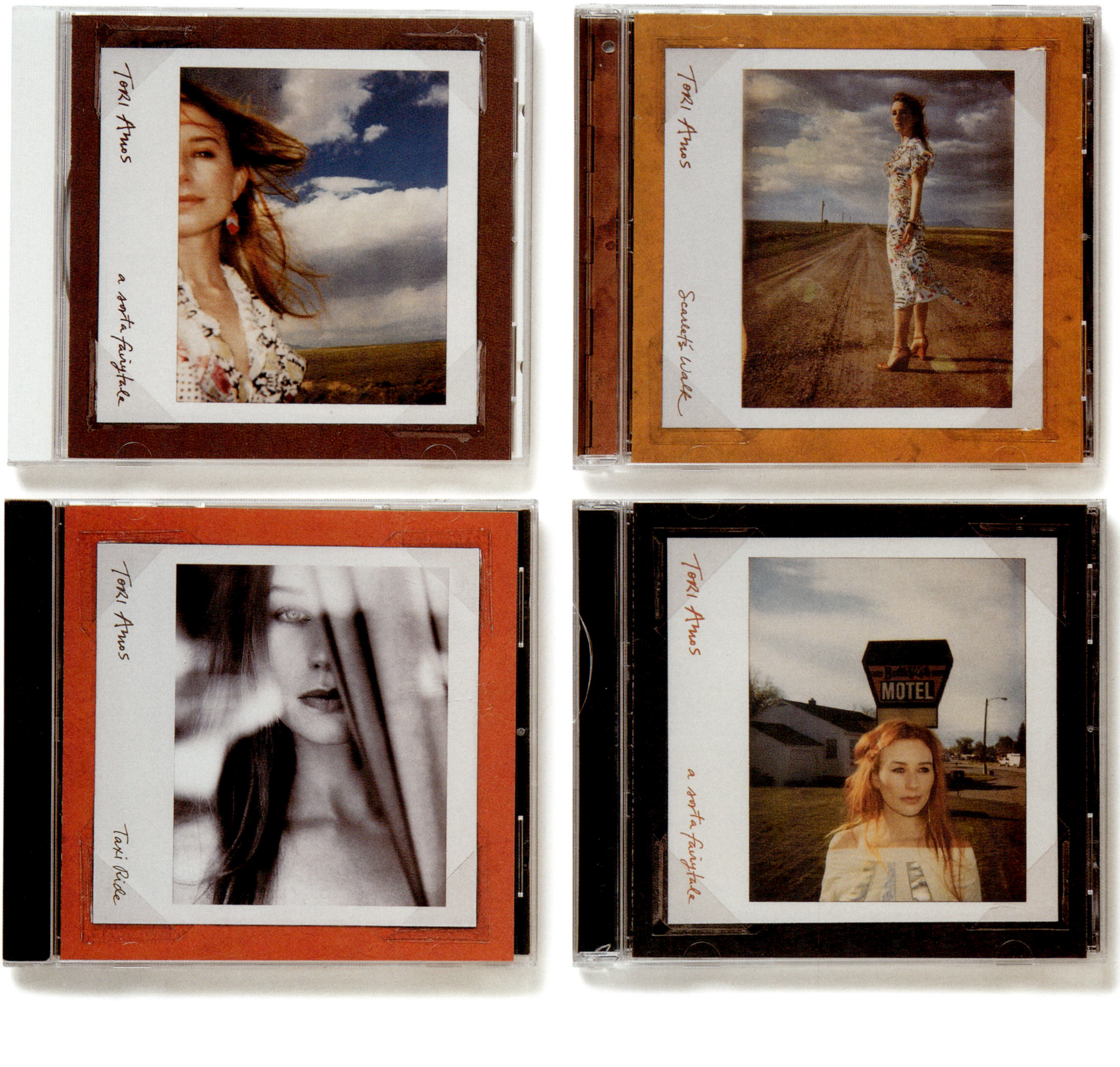

'Tori Amos: Scarlet's Walk Series' Design Firm: Sony Music Creative Services Creative Director: Chris Austopchuk Art Directors: Sheri Lee and Dave Bett Designers: Sheri Lee and Dave Bett Photographer: Kurt Markus Illustrator: Jeffrey Fulvimari Client: Epic Records

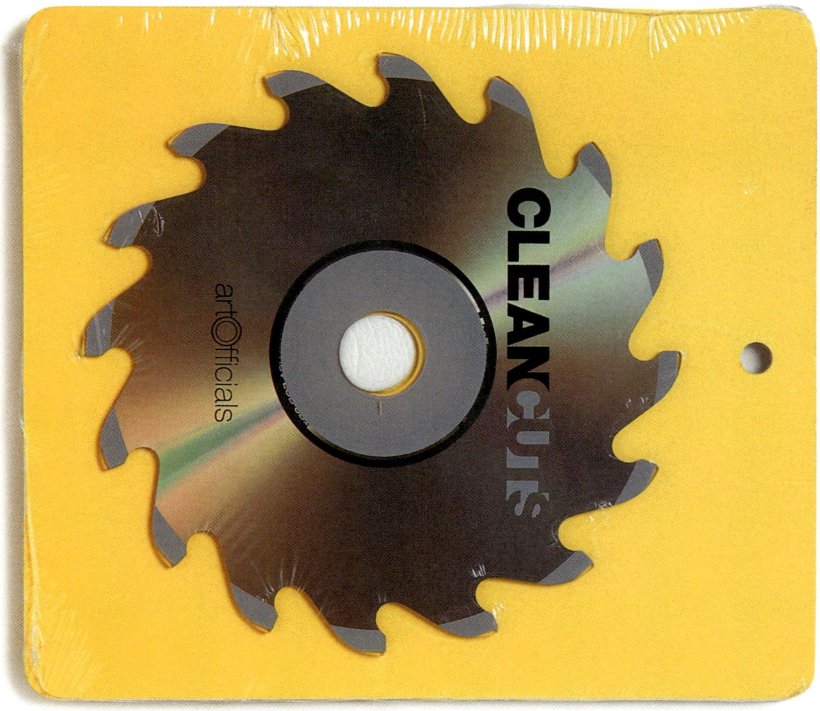

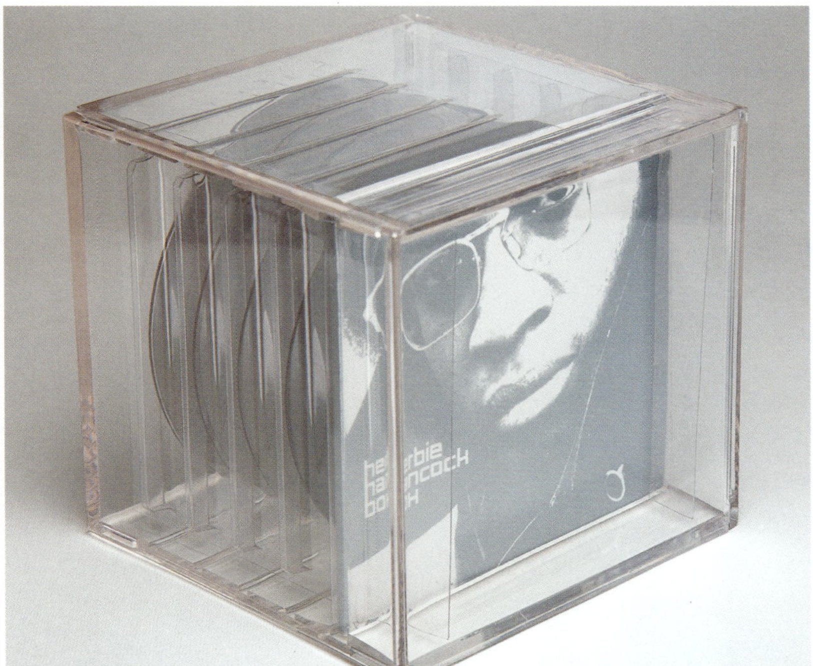

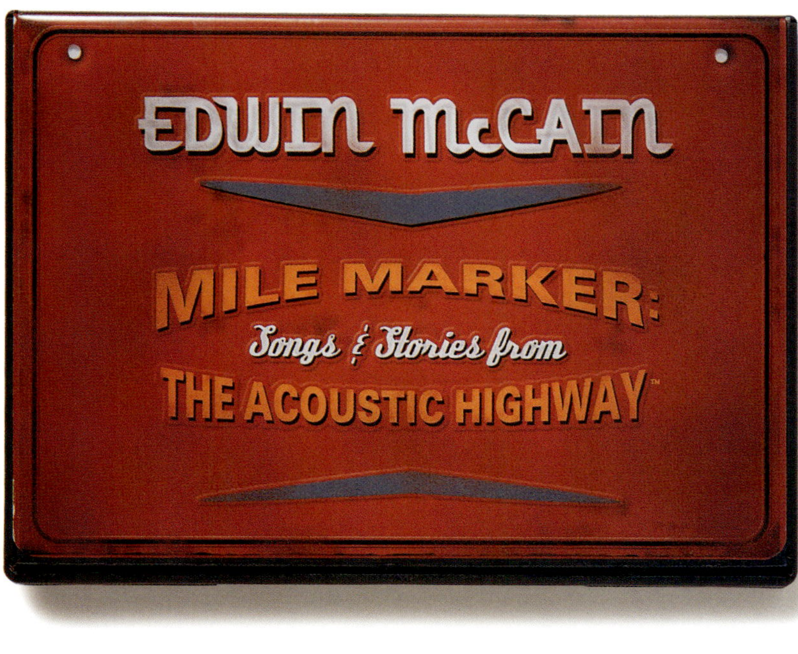

(from top) (1) 'Clean Cuts' Design Firm: Bozell Creative Director: Greg Crossley Art Director: Greg Crossley Designer: Greg Crossley Client: ArtOfficials
(2) 'The Herbie Hancock Box' Design Firm: Sony Music Art Directors: Rance Brown, Seth Rothstein and Howard Fritzson Designer: Rance Brown Client: Columbia/Legacy Records
(3) 'Mile Marker' Design Firm: ComGroup Creative Director: Jim Newbury Art Director: Justin Harris Designer: Justin Harris Client: ATM Records/Edwin McCain

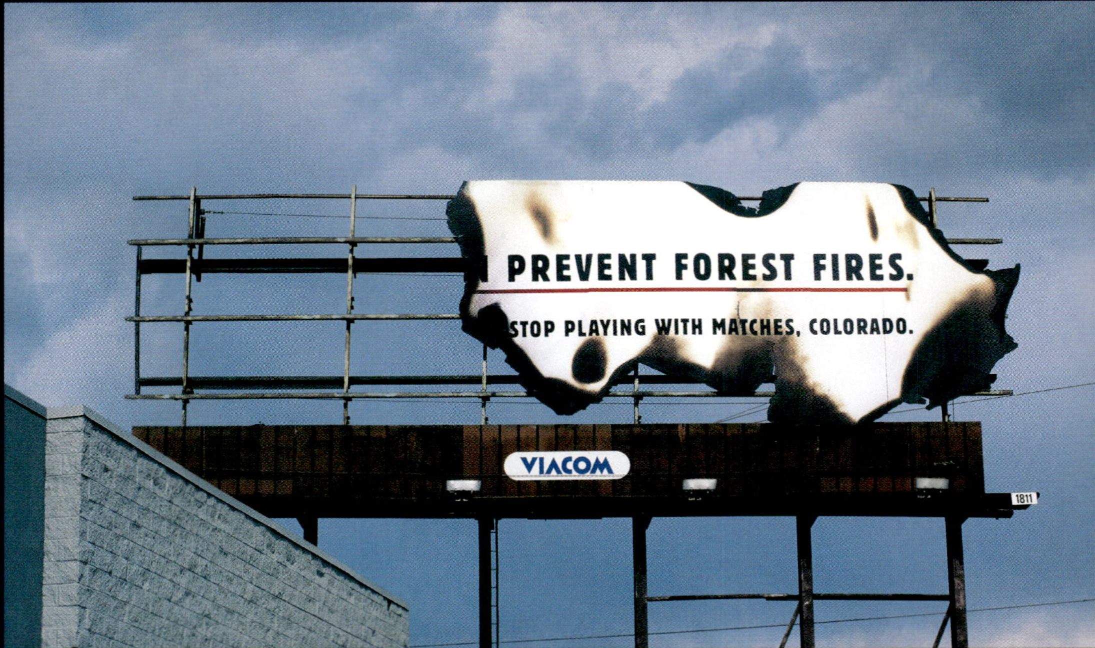

Fire Billboard' Design Firm: Cultivator Advertising & Design Creative Directors: Tim Abare and Chris Beatty Designers: Chris Beatty and August Sandberg Copywriter: Tim Abare
Client: Colorado Wildlands (opposite page) '340 Banners' Design Firm: Graham Hanson Design Designer: Graham Hanson Client: Macklowe Properties

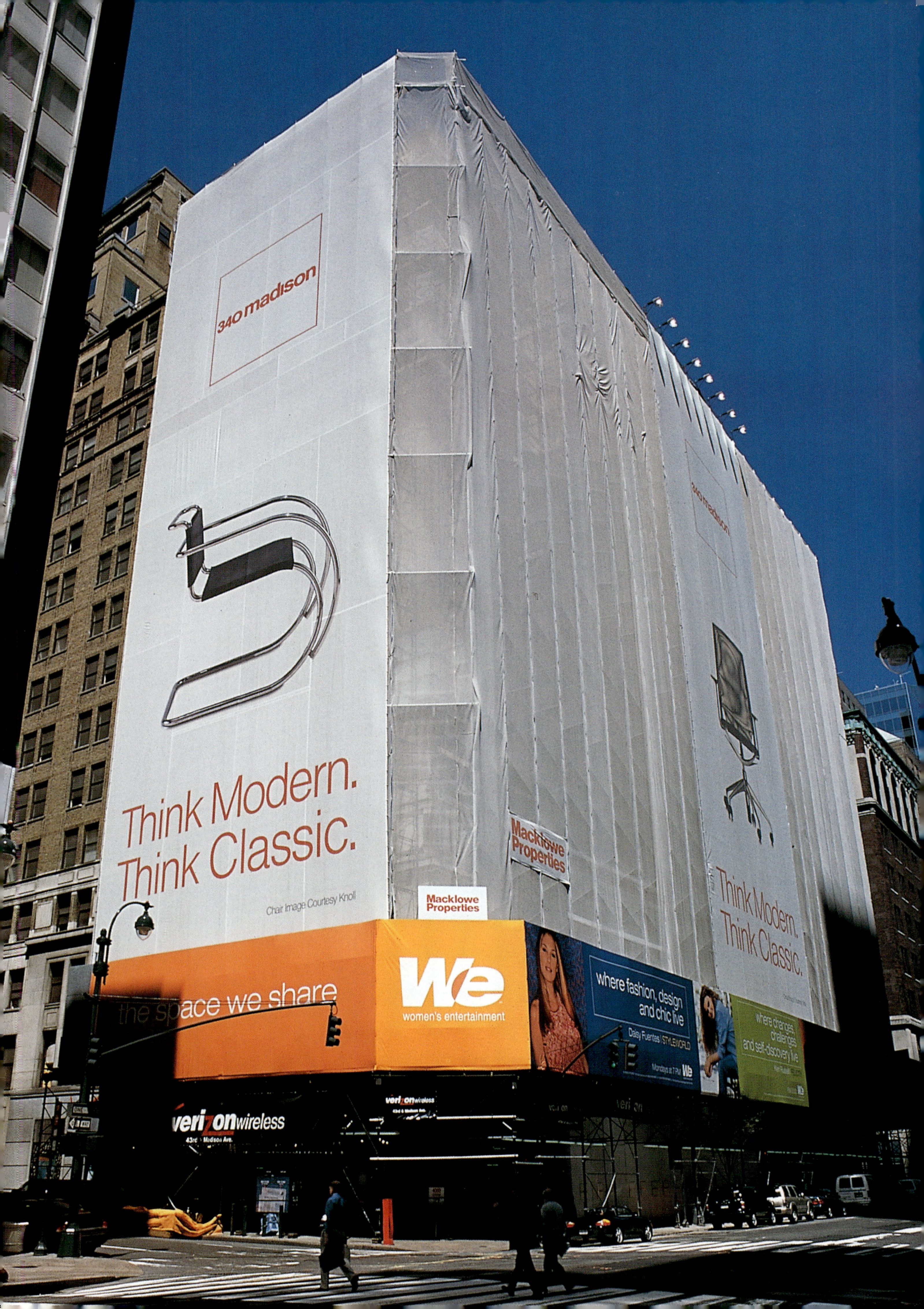
340 madison
Think Modern.
Think Classic.
Chair Image Courtesy Knoll
Macklowe Properties
Macklowe Properties
340 madison
Think Modern.
Think Classic.
the space we share
We
women's entertainment
where fashion, design and chic live
Daisy Fuentes | STYLEWORLD
where changes, challenges and self-discovery live
verizonwireless

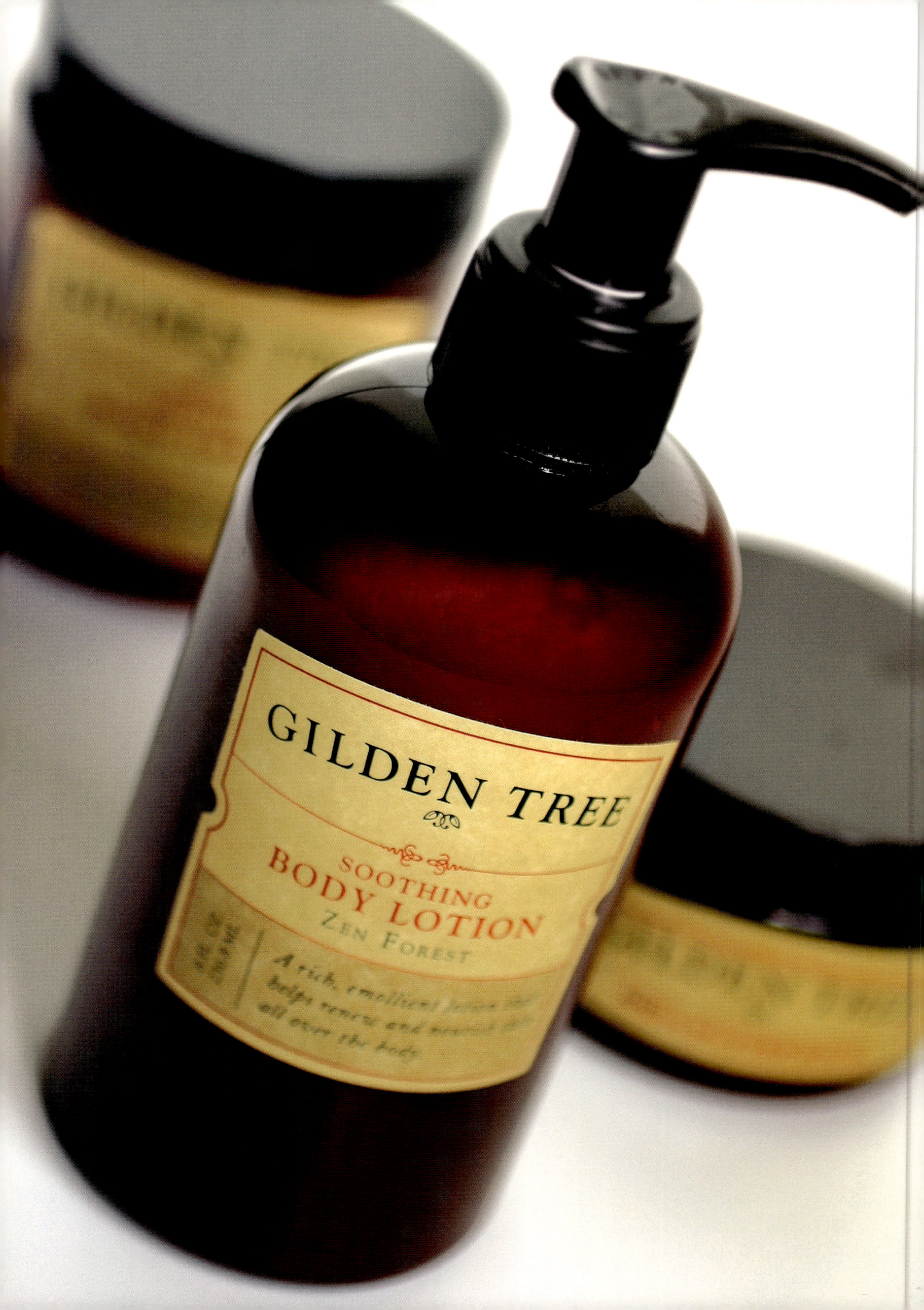
GILDEN TREE
SOOTHING
BODY LOTION
ZEN FOREST

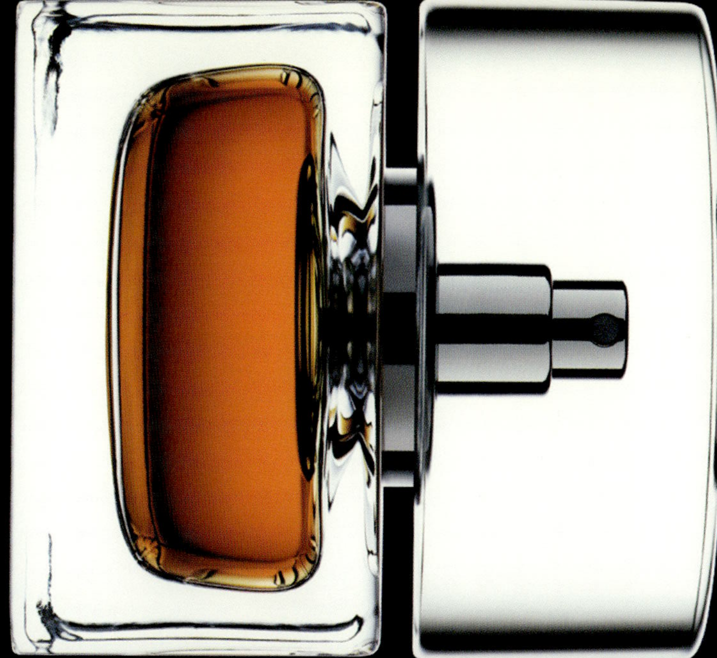

Design Firm: Lloyd & Co. Creative Director: Douglas Lloyd Art Director: Alfredo Castro Client: Gucci Parfum
(previous page) 'Gilden Tree Pack' Design Firm: Webster Design Associates Creative Director: Dave Webster Art Director: Derek McClure Client: Gilden Tree

Design Firm: Turner Duckworth Creative Directors: Bruce Duckworth and David Turner Designer: Anthony Biles Photographer: Peter Ruane Account Manager: Moira Riddell Client: Marks & Spencer PLC (opposite page) Design Firm: Twist Inc.
Creative Director: Kristine Anderson Dahms Art Director: Kristine Anderson Dahms Designer: Kristine Anderson Dahms Photographer: Rick Dahms Illustrator: Kristine Anderson Dahms Copywriter: Mustapha Haddouch Client: Mustapha's Argan Oil

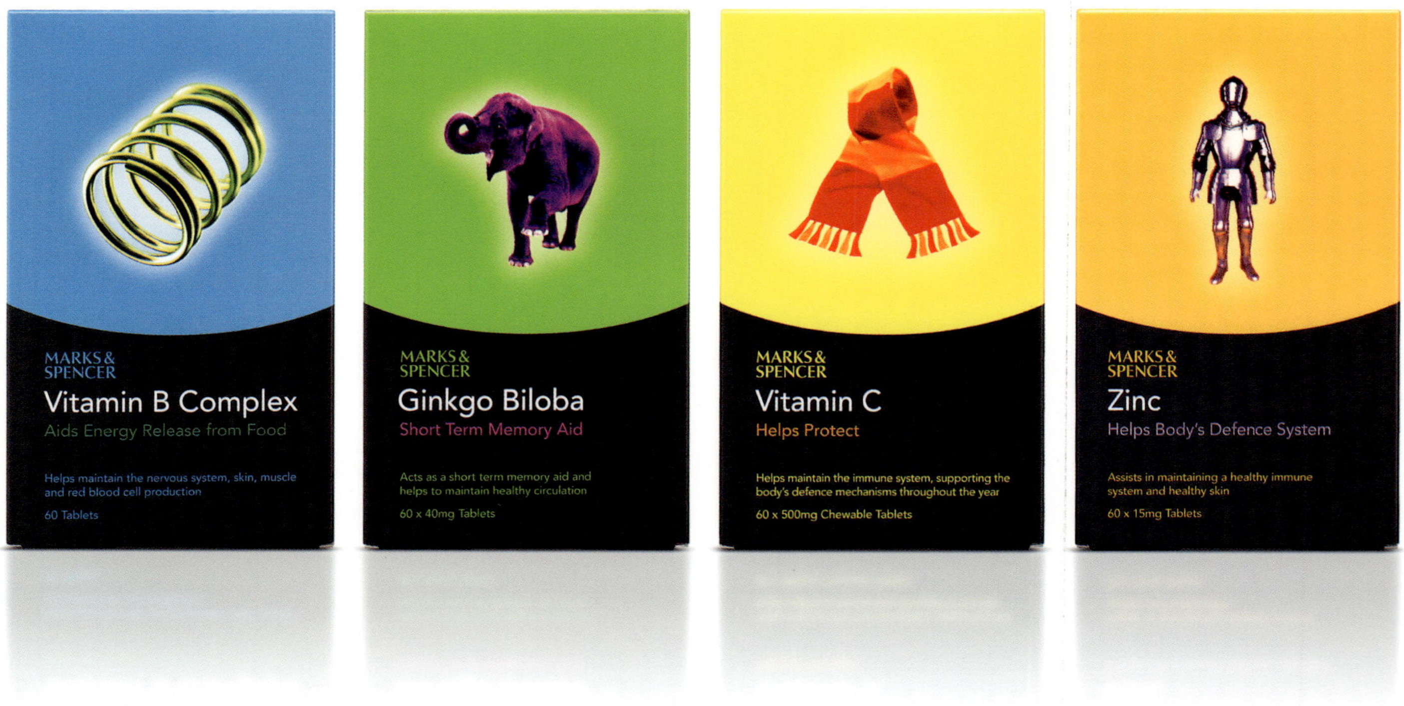

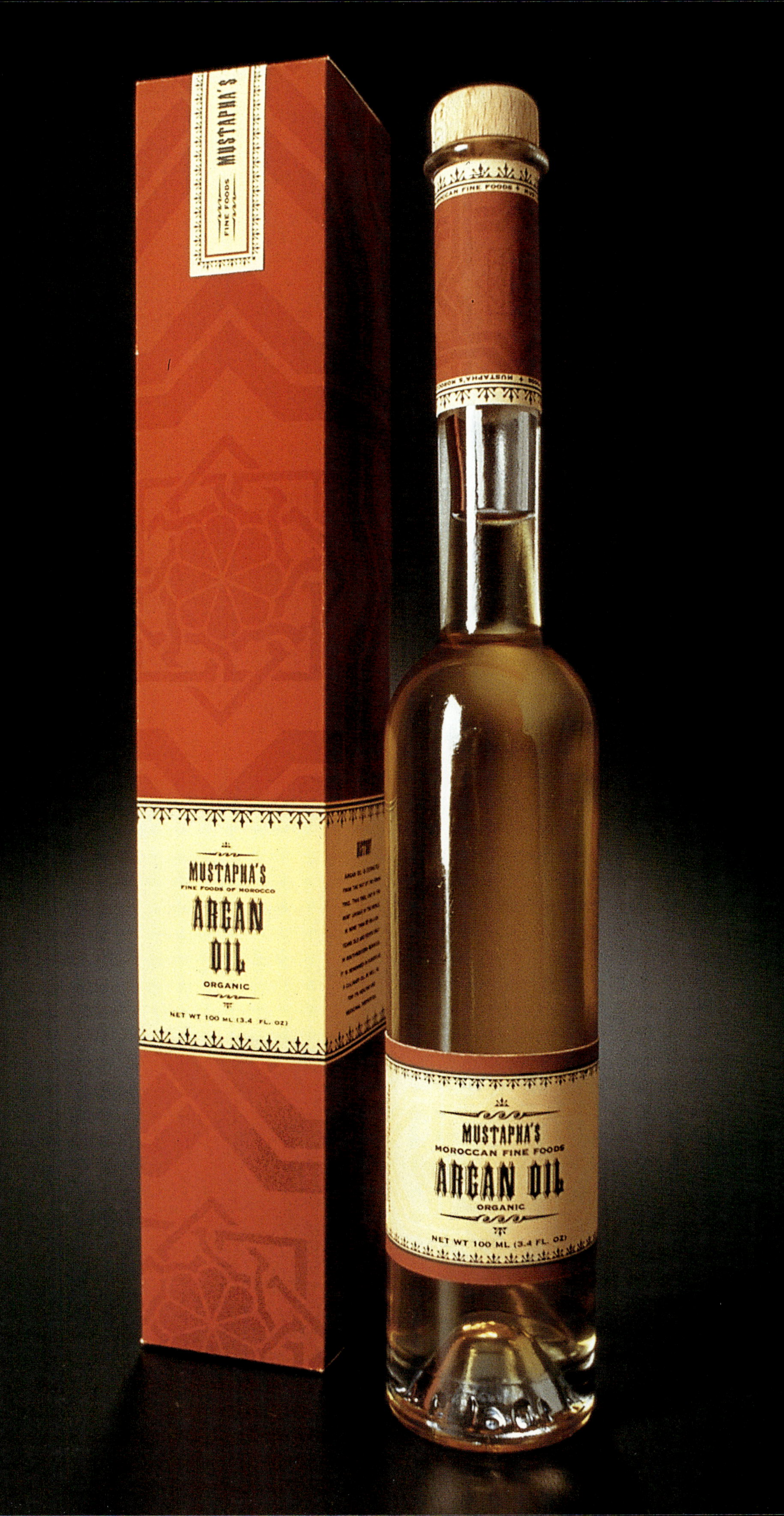
MUSTAPHA'S
FINE FOODS
MUSTAPHA'S
FINE FOODS OF MOROCCO
ARGAN
OIL
ORGANIC
NET WT 100 ML (3.4 FL. OZ)
MUSTAPHA'S
MOROCCAN FINE FOODS
ARGAN OIL
ORGANIC
NET WT 100 ML. (3.4 FL. OZ)

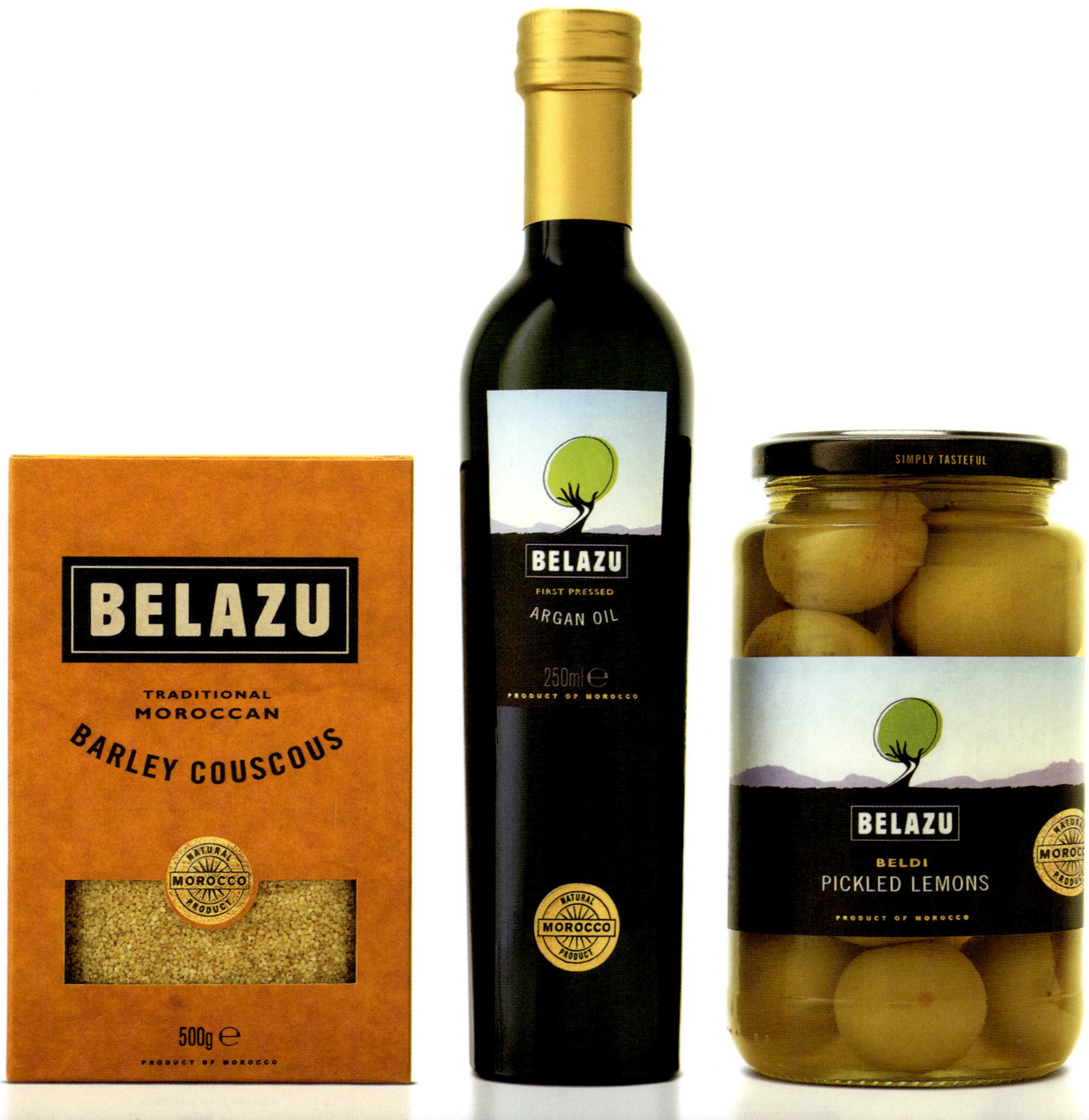

'Belazu Moroccan Range' Design Firm: Turner Duckworth Creative Directors: Bruce Duckworth and David Turner Designer: Janice Davison Illustrator: John Seary Account Manager: Alex Bennett Client: The Fresh Olive Company

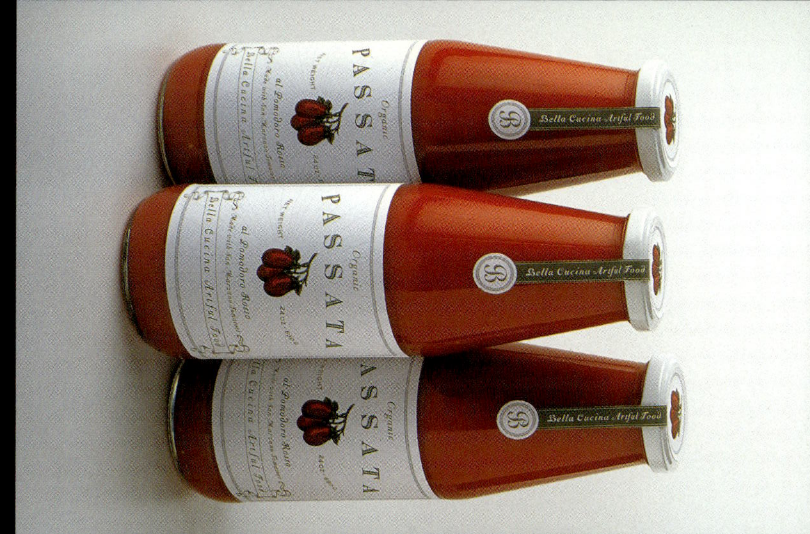

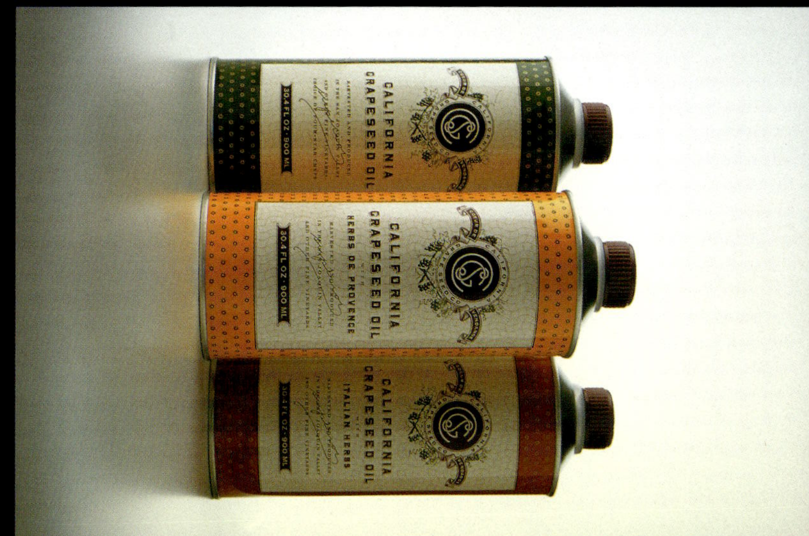

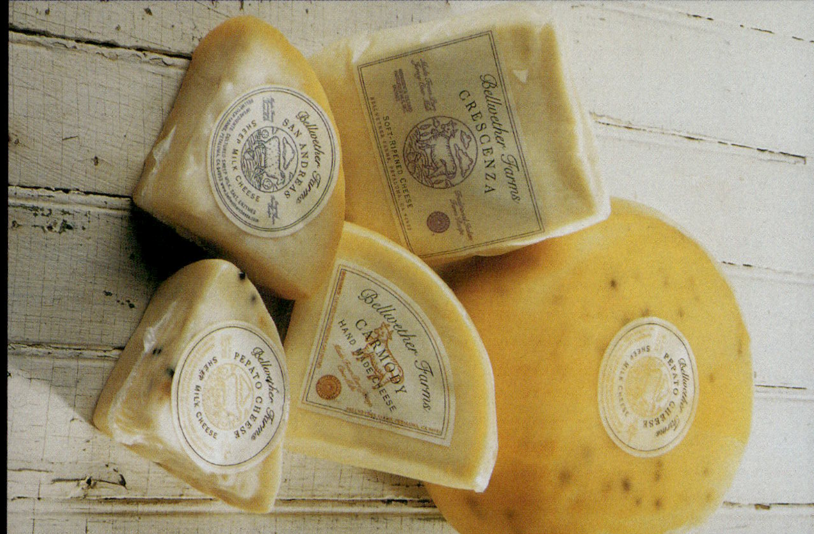

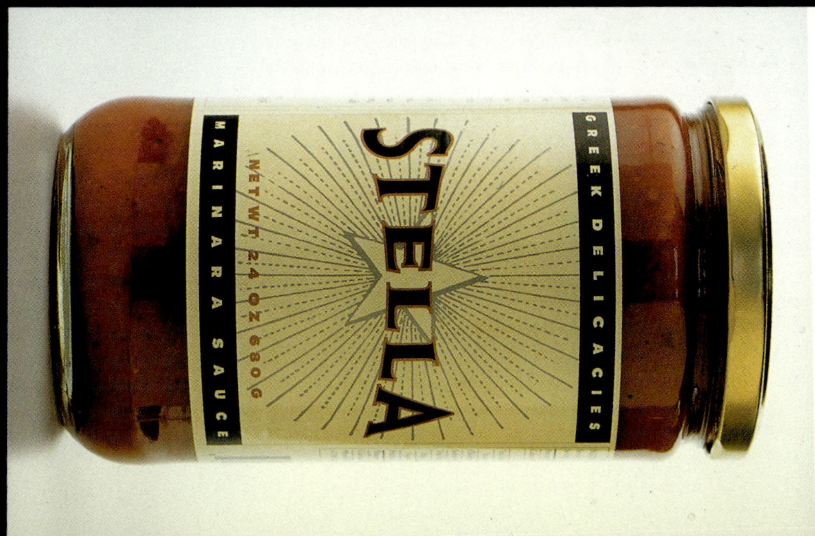

(clockwise from top left) (1) 'Bella Cucina Organic Passata' Design Firm: Louise Fili Ltd. Creative Director: Louise Fili Art Director: Louise Fili Designer: Louise Fili Client: Bella Cucina (2) 'California Grapeseed Oil' Design Firm: Louise Fili Ltd. Creative Director: Louise Fili Art Director: Louise Fili Designers: Louise Fili and Mary Jane Callister Client: Jean-Georges Vongerichten (3) 'Stella Marinara Sauce' Design Firm: Louise Fili Ltd. Creative Director: Louise Fili Art Director: Louise Fili Designers: Louise Fili and Mary Jane Callister (4) Design Firm: Mark Oliver, Inc. Art Director: Mark Oliver Designers: Mark Oliver and Patty Devlin-Driskel Illustrator: Sudi McCollum Client: Bellwether Farms

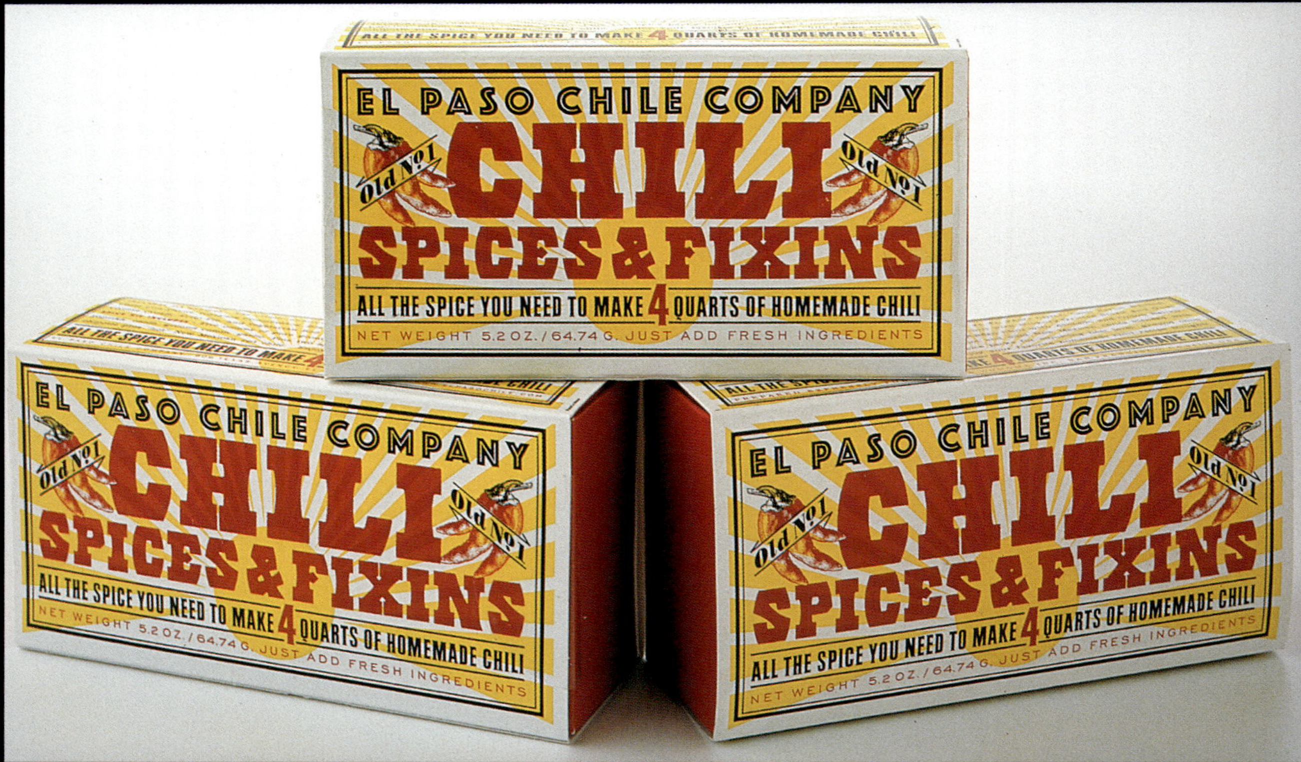

El Paso Chile 'Spices & Fixins' Design Firm: Louise Fili Ltd. Creative Director: Louise Fili Art Director: Louise Fili Designer: Chad Roberts Client: El Paso Chile Company

(opposite page) 'Caviar Bar Packaging' Design Firm: Graphics & Designing Inc. Art Director: Toshihiro Onimaru Designers: Toshihiro Onimaru and Hiroki Ariyoshi Client: Will Planning Inc.

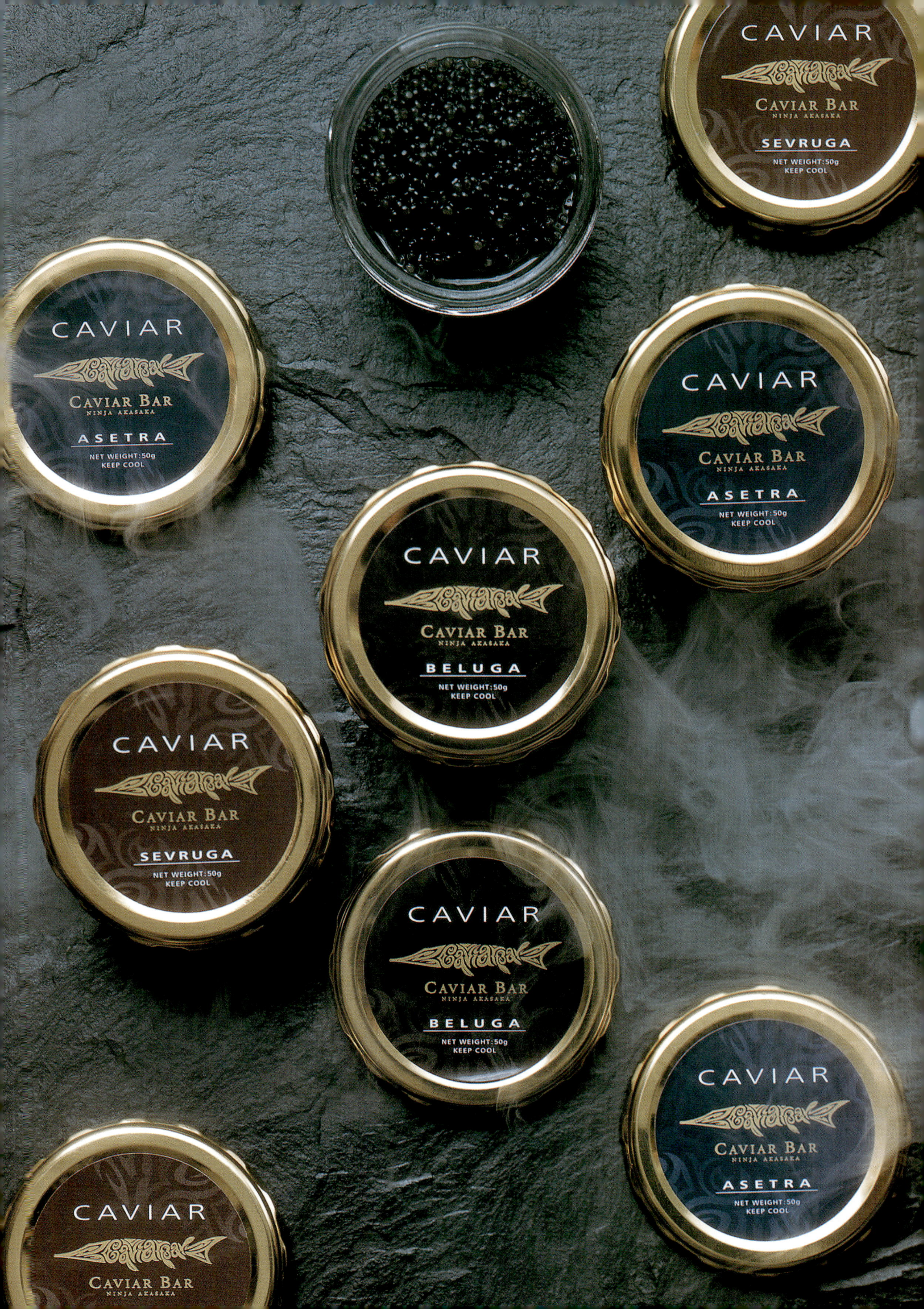
CAVIAR
CAVIAR BAR
NINJA AKASAKA
SEVRUGA
NET WEIGHT:50g
KEEP COOL
CAVIAR
CAVIAR BAR
NINJA AKASAKA
ASETRA
NET WEIGHT:50g
KEEP COOL
CAVIAR
CAVIAR BAR
NINJA AKASAKA
ASETRA
NET WEIGHT:50g
KEEP COOL
CAVIAR
CAVIAR BAR
NINJA AKASAKA
BELUGA
NET WEIGHT:50g
KEEP COOL
CAVIAR
CAVIAR BAR
NINJA AKASAKA
SEVRUGA
NET WEIGHT:50g
KEEP COOL
CAVIAR
CAVIAR BAR
NINJA AKASAKA
BELUGA
NET WEIGHT:50g
KEEP COOL
CAVIAR
CAVIAR BAR
NINJA AKASAKA
ASETRA
NET WEIGHT:50g
KEEP COOL
CAVIAR
CAVIAR BAR
NINJA AKASAKA

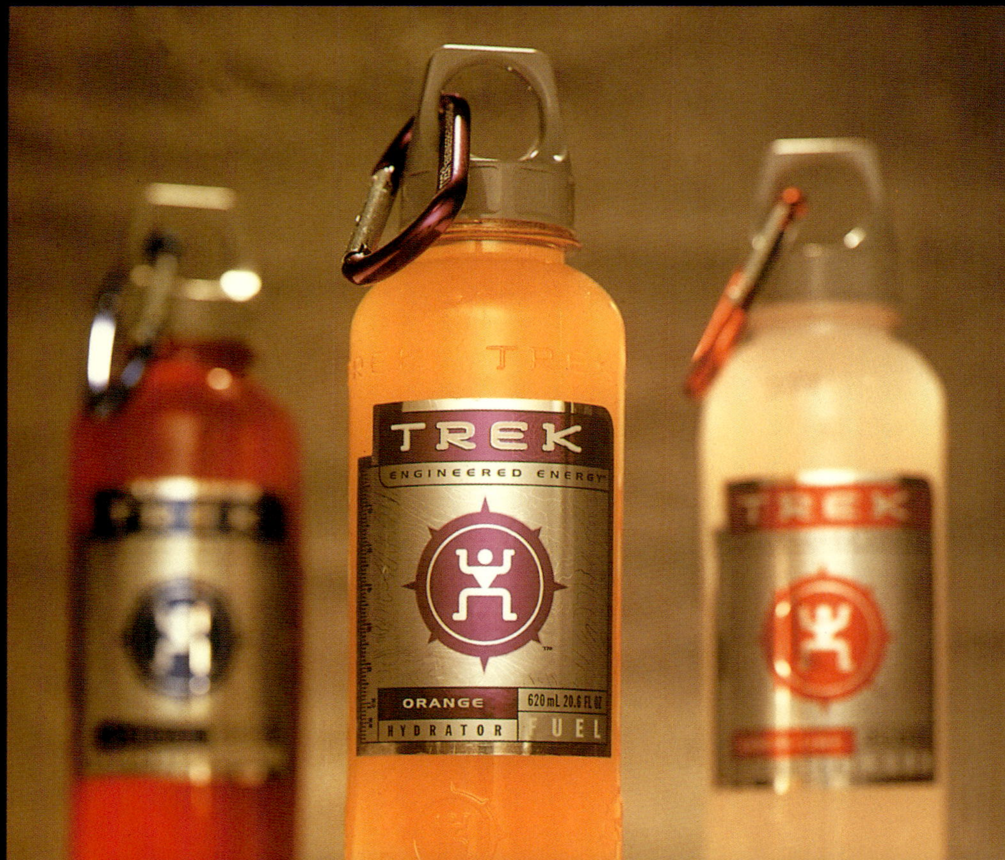

Trek Optimized Performance Beverage' Design Firm: Ryan & Deslauriers Creative Director: Tom Pedriks Art Director: Tom Pedriks Designer: Tom Pedriks Copywriter: Dianna Carr Client: Leading Brands, Inc
(opposite page) Design Firm: Sandstrom Design Creative Director: Steve Sandstrom Art Director: Steve Sandstrom Designer: Steve Sandstrom Copywriter: Steve Sandoz Client: Tazo

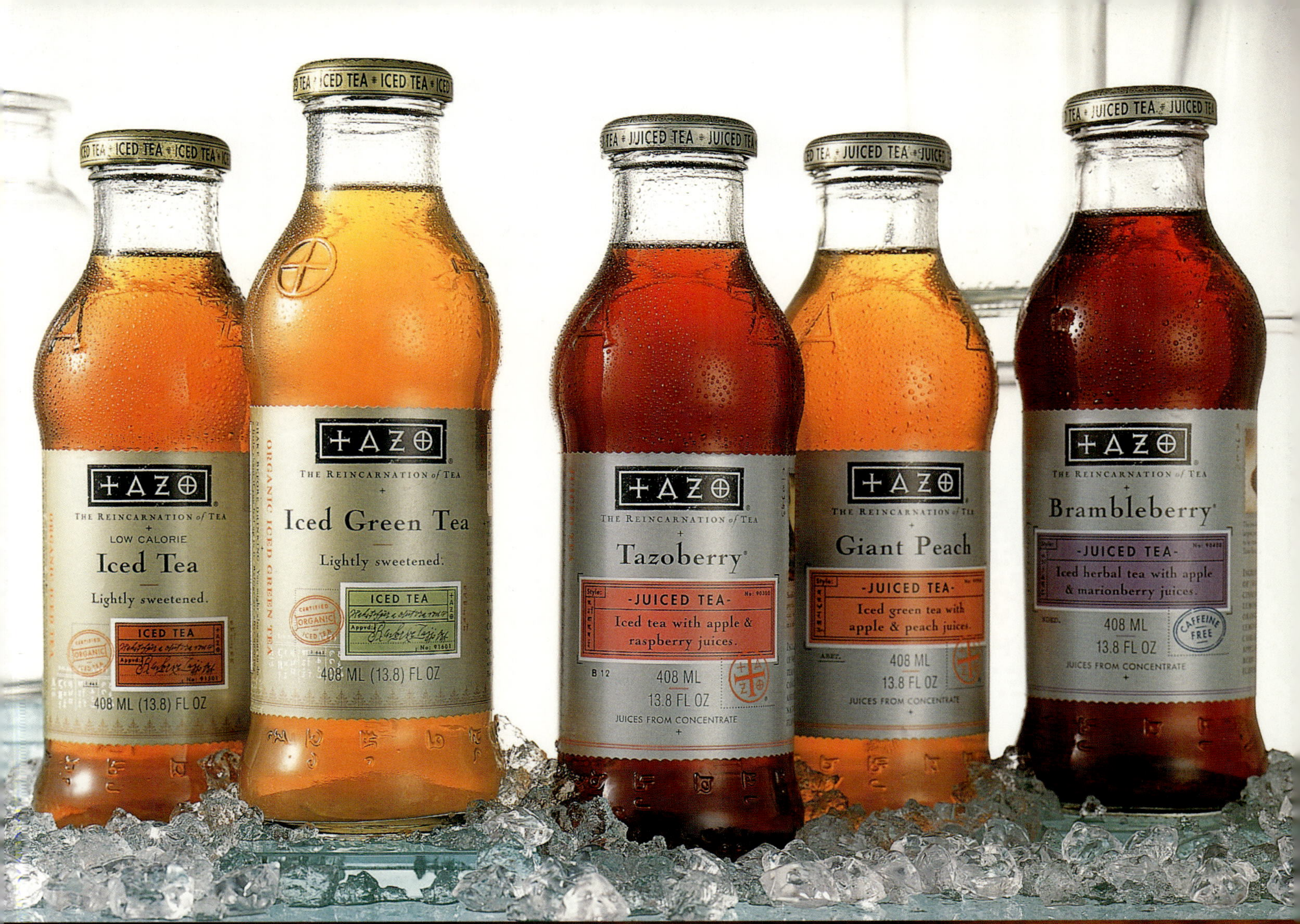
ICED TEA
JUICED TEA
TAZO
THE REINCARNATION of TEA
LOW CALORIE
Iced Tea
Lightly sweetened.
ICED TEA
408 ML (13.8) FL OZ
Iced Green Tea
Lightly sweetened.
ICED TEA
ORGANIC ICED GREEN TEA
408 ML (13.8) FL OZ
Tazoberry
-JUICED TEA-
Iced tea with apple & raspberry juices.
408 ML
13.8 FL OZ
JUICES FROM CONCENTRATE
Giant Peach
-JUICED TEA-
Iced green tea with apple & peach juices.
408 ML
13.8 FL OZ
JUICES FROM CONCENTRATE
Brambleberry
-JUICED TEA-
Iced herbal tea with apple & marionberry juices.
408 ML
13.8 FL OZ
CAFFEINE FREE
JUICES FROM CONCENTRATE

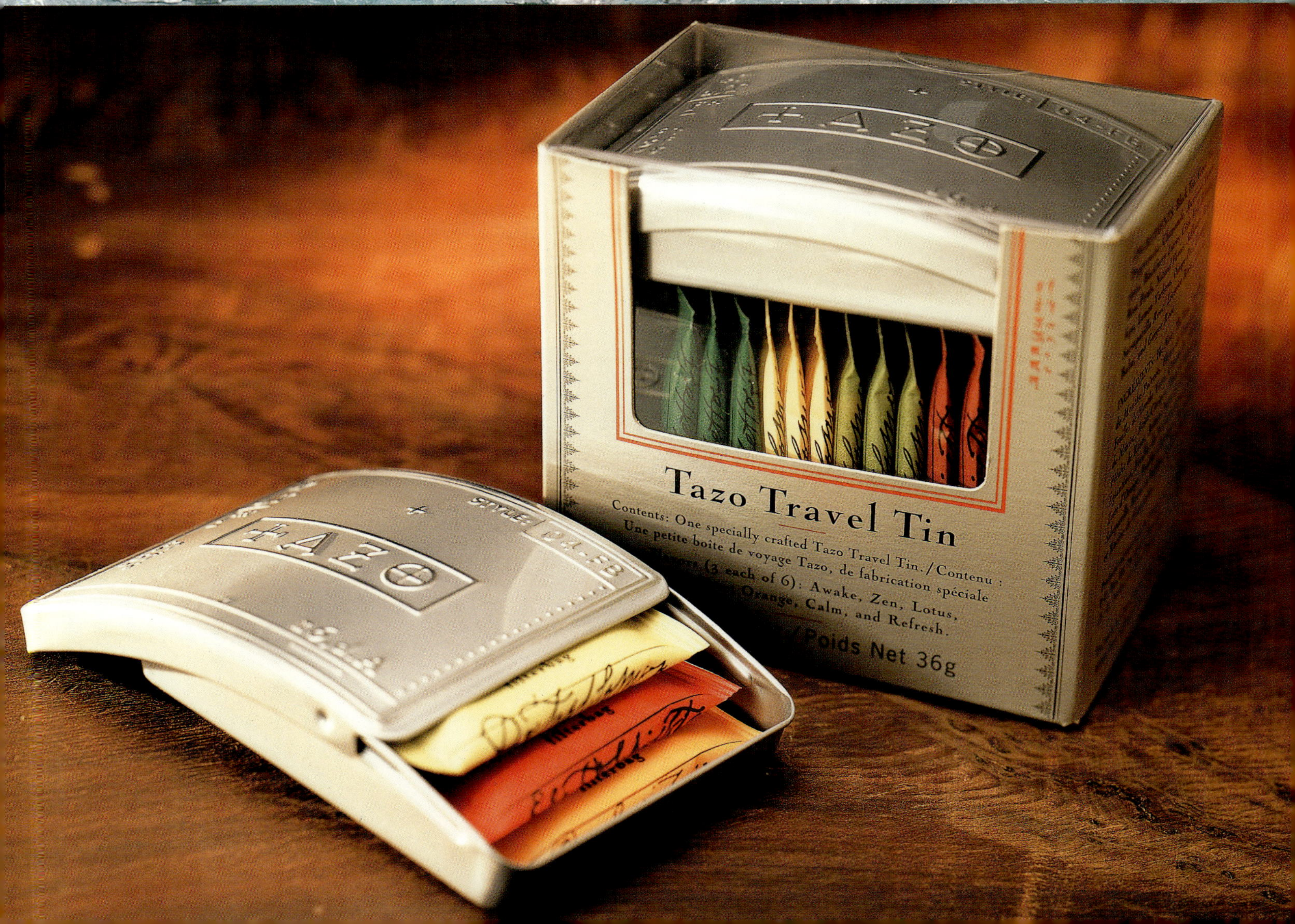
TAZO
Tazo Travel Tin
Contents: One specially crafted Tazo Travel Tin./Contenu :
Une petite boite de voyage Tazo, de fabrication spéciale
(3 each of 6): Awake, Zen, Lotus,
Orange, Calm, and Refresh.
Poids Net 36g

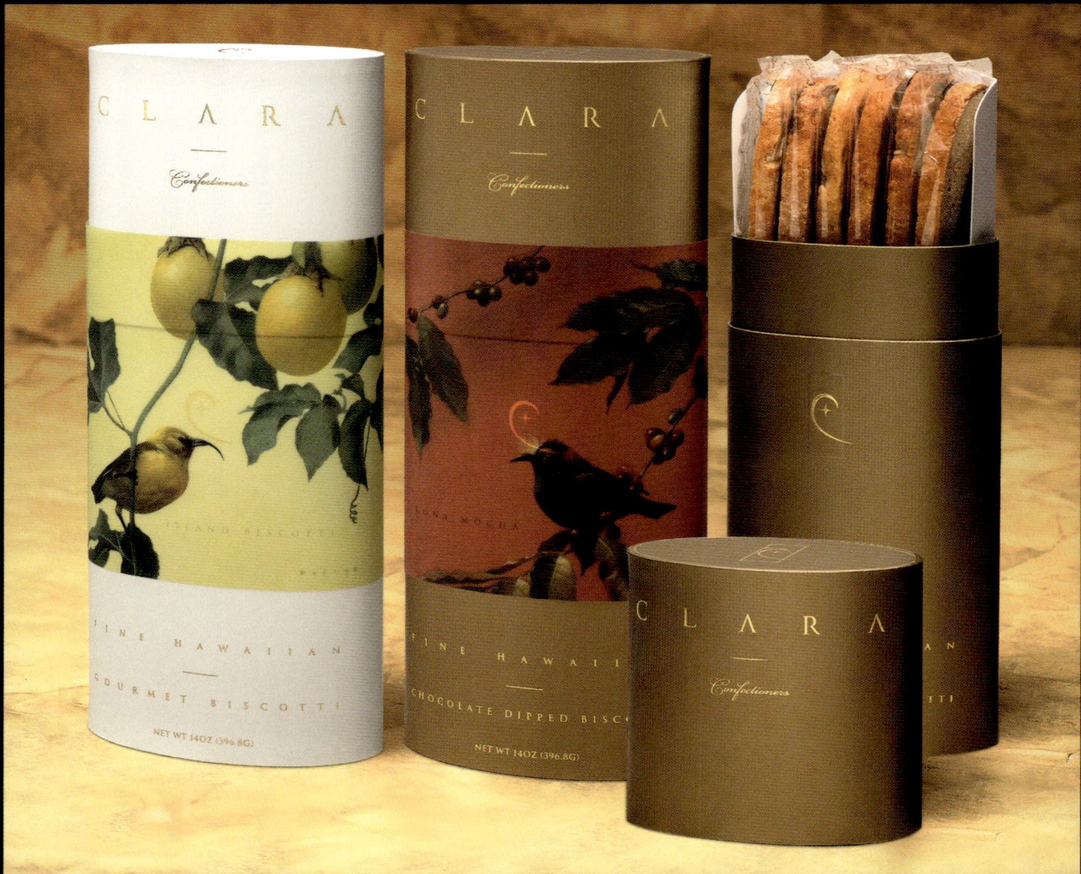

ead) 'Biscotti Packages' Design Firm: Studio Ignition Art Director: Stephen Goss Designers: Stephen Goss, Noah Tom and Donald Cheung Illustrator: Michael Furhya Client: Clara Confectioners

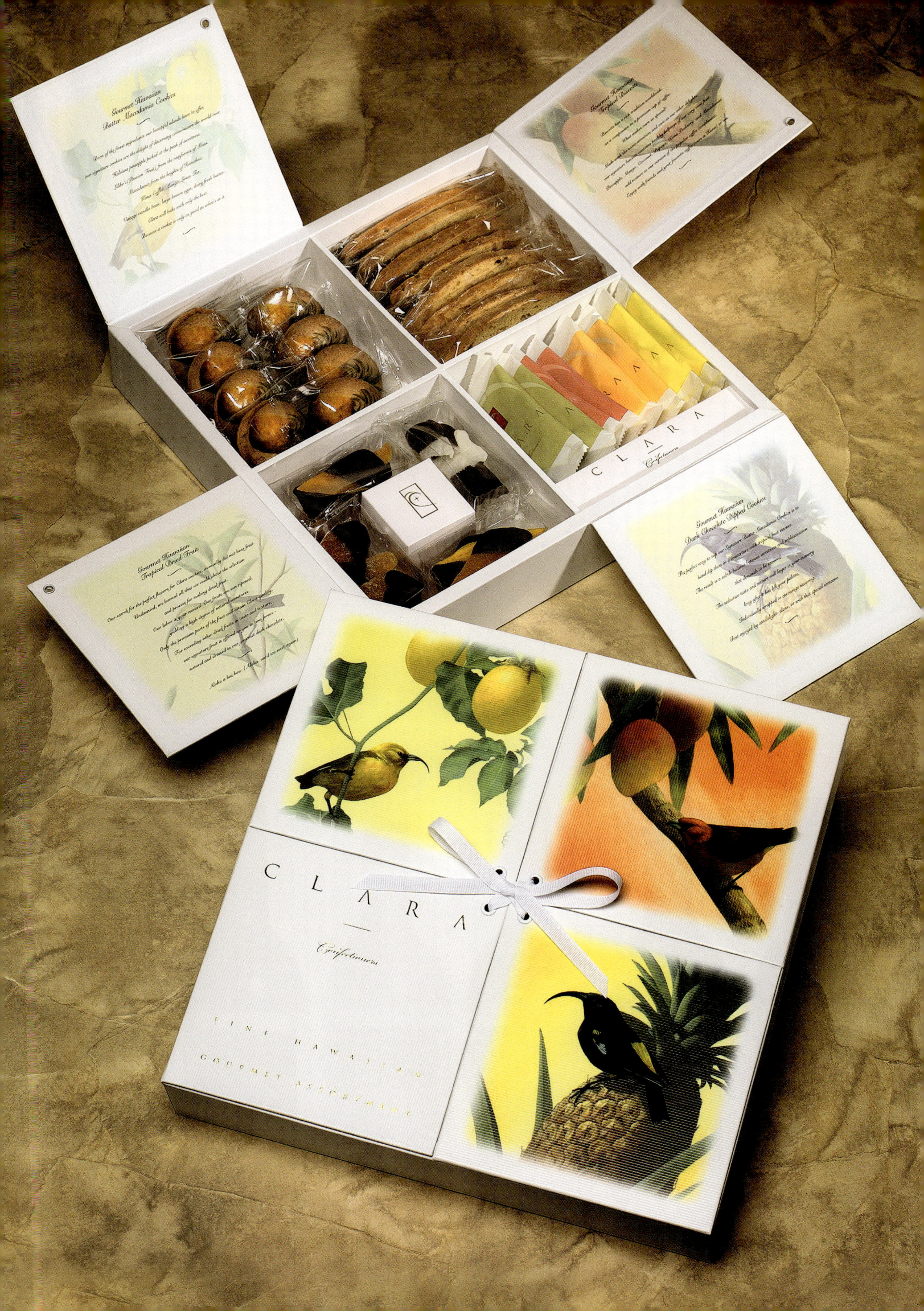
CLARA
Confectioners
FINE HAWAIIAN
GOURMET ASSORTMENTS

'Barsquare Winelabels' Design Firm: Intellecta Branding & Design Art Director: Anders Schmidt Designer: Anders Schmidt Client: Intellecta Corporate (opposite page) Designer: Marina Drukman

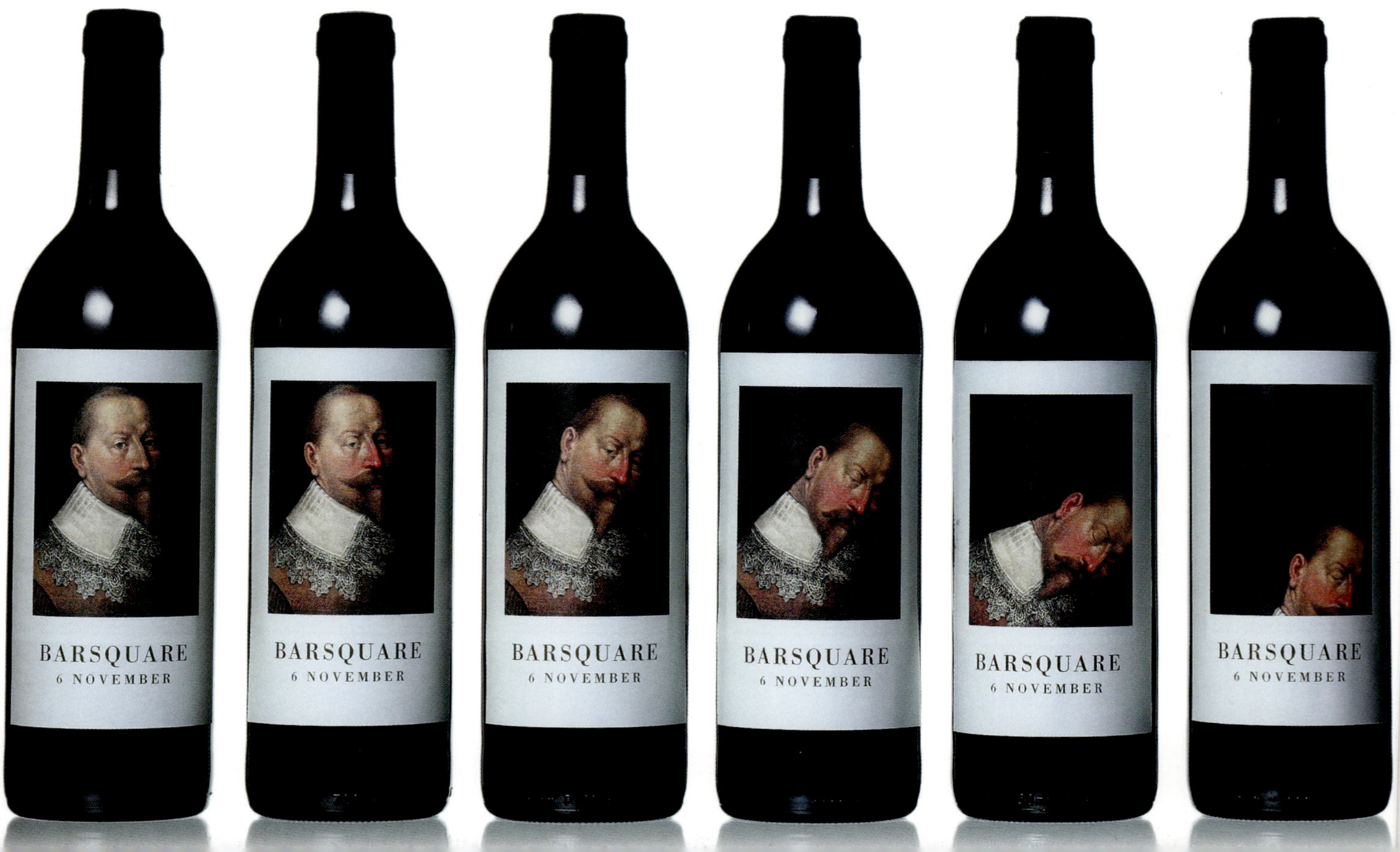

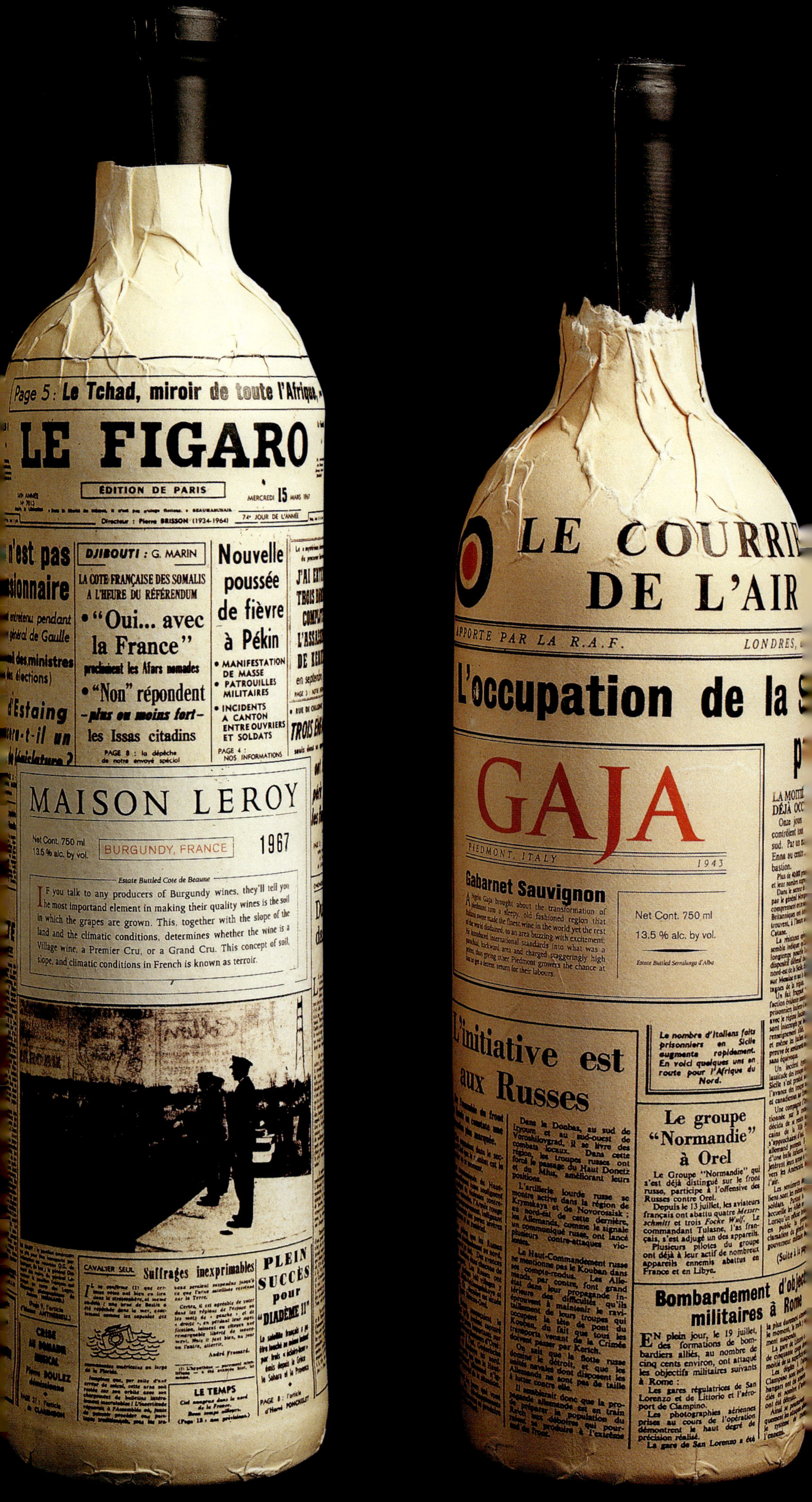
Page 5: Le Tchad, miroir de toute l'Afrique
LE FIGARO
ÉDITION DE PARIS
MERCREDI 15 MARS 1967
74e JOUR DE L'ANNÉE
Directeur : Pierre BRISSON (1934-1964)
DJIBOUTI : G. MARIN
LA COTE FRANÇAISE DES SOMALIS A L'HEURE DU RÉFÉRENDUM
• "Oui... avec la France"
• "Non" répondent
les Issas citadins
Nouvelle poussée de fièvre à Pékin
• MANIFESTATION DE MASSE
• PATROUILLES MILITAIRES
• INCIDENTS A CANTON ENTRE OUVRIERS ET SOLDATS
MAISON LEROY
Net Cont. 750 ml
13.5 % alc. by vol.
BURGUNDY, FRANCE
1967
Estate Bottled Cote de Beaune
If you talk to any producers of Burgundy wines, they'll tell you the most importand element in making their quality wines is the soil in which the grapes are grown. This, together with the slope of the land and the climatic conditions, determines whether the wine is a Village wine, a Premier Cru, or a Grand Cru. This concept of soil, slope, and climatic conditions in French is known as terroir.
Suffrages inexprimables
PLEIN SUCCÈS pour "DIADÈME II"
LE TEMPS
LE COURRIER DE L'AIR
APPORTE PAR LA R.A.F.
LONDRES
L'occupation de la
GAJA
PIEDMONT, ITALY
1943
Cabernet Sauvignon
Net Cont. 750 ml
13.5 % alc. by vol.
L'initiative est aux Russes
Le groupe "Normandie" à Orel
Bombardement d'objectifs militaires à Rome

'Zygo Vodka' Design Firm: Wallace Church, Inc. Creative Director: Stan Church Art Director: Lawrence Haggerty Designer: Lawrence Haggerty Client: Icon Brands (opposite page) (clockwise from top left) (1) 'Anime Wine' Design Firm: Louise Fili Ltd. Creative Director: Louise Fili Art Director: Louise Fili Designers: Louise Fili and Mary Jane Callister Client: Matt Brothers (2) 'Christiana Vodka' Design Firm: Deutsch Design Works Creative Director: Bruce Campbell Art Director: Barry Deutsch Designer: Lori Wynn Illustrator: Mark Summers Client: Nordic Beverages (3) 'SFiDA' Design Firm: Louise Fili Ltd. Creative Director: Louise Fili Art Director: Louise Fili Designers: Louise Fili and Mary Jane Callister Client: Matt Brothers (4) 'Sauza Diablo' Design Firm: Primo Angeli Fitch Creative Directors: Richard Scheve and Aaron Stapley Art Directors: Richard Scheve and Aaron Stapley Designer: Toby Sudduth Illustrators: Toby Sudduth and Matthew Holmes Client: Allied Domecq

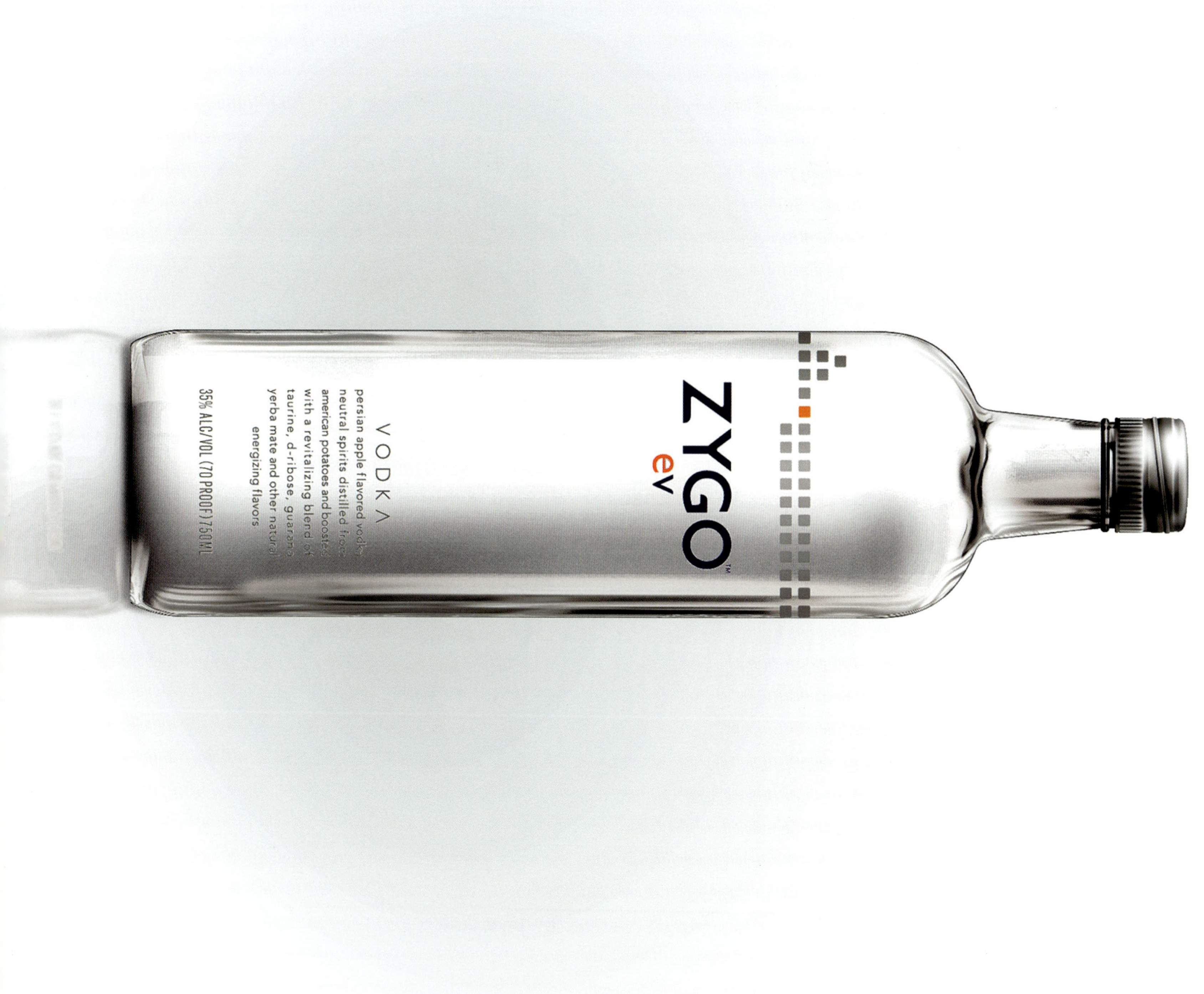

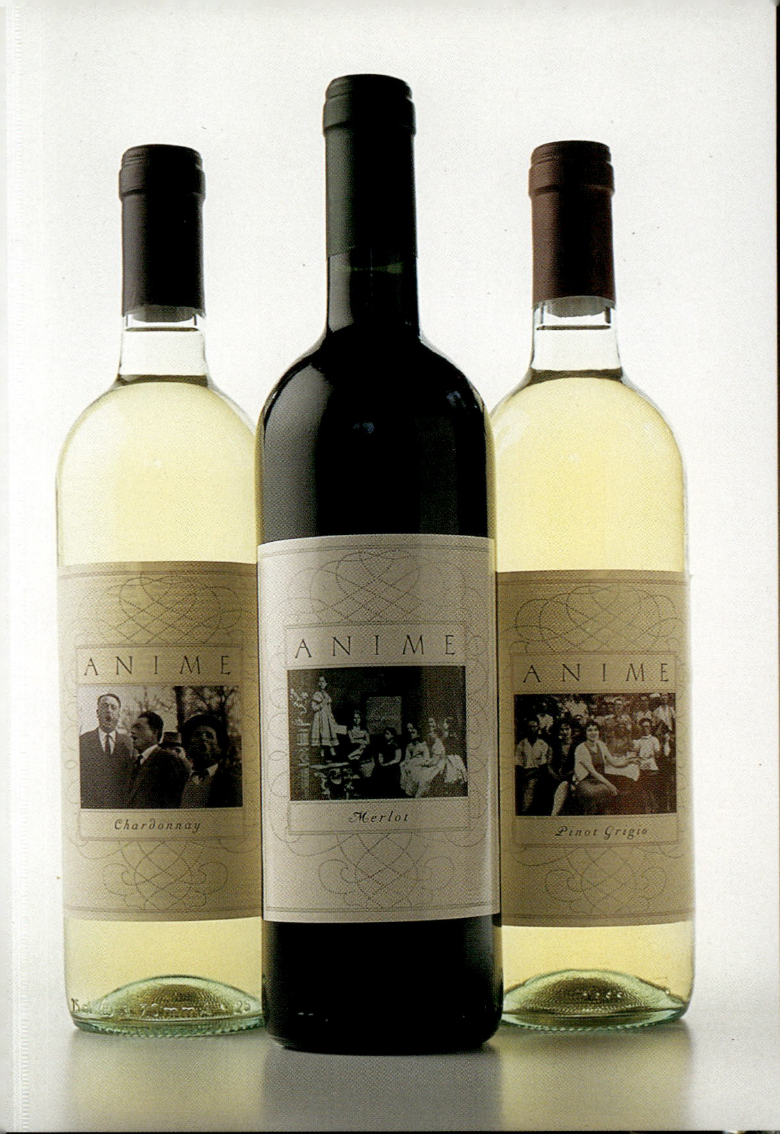
ANIME
Chardonnay
ANIME
Merlot
ANIME
Pinot Grigio

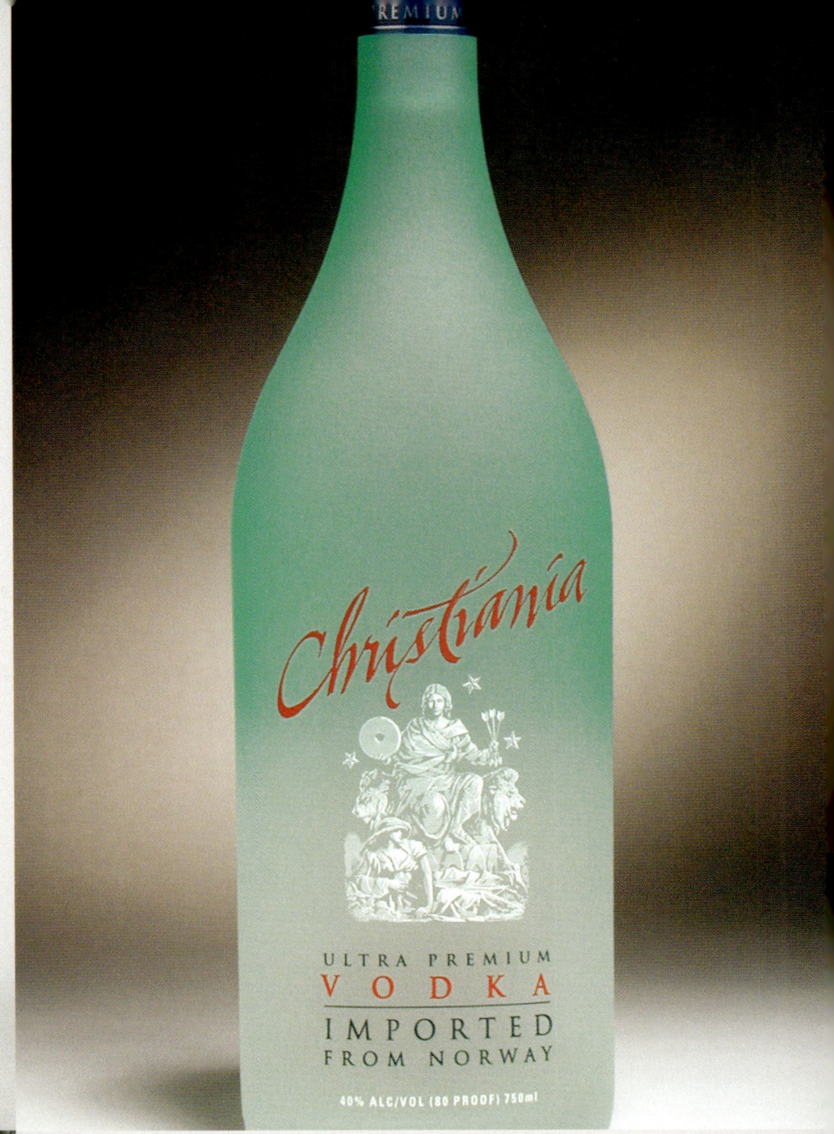
Christiania
ULTRA PREMIUM
VODKA
IMPORTED
FROM NORWAY
40% ALC/VOL (80 PROOF) 750ml

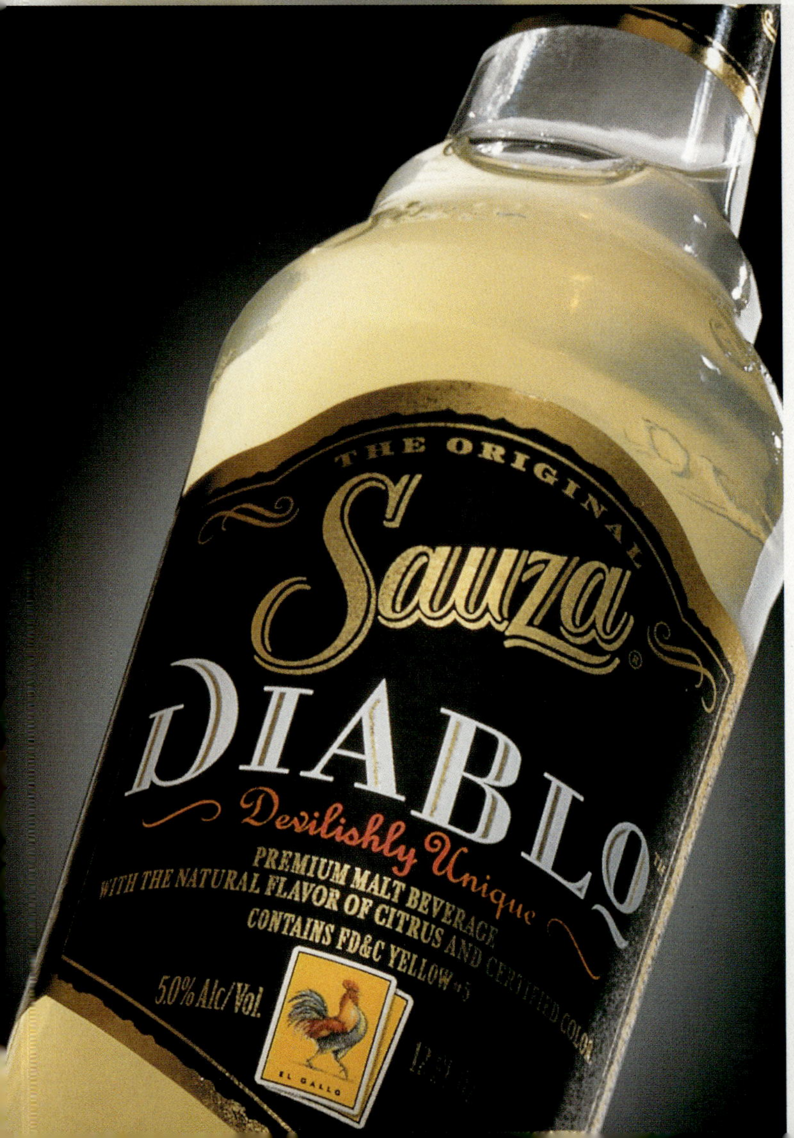
THE ORIGINAL
Sauza
DIABLO
Devilishly Unique
PREMIUM MALT BEVERAGE
WITH THE NATURAL FLAVOR OF CITRUS AND CERTIFIED COLOR
CONTAINS FD&C YELLOW #5
5.0% Alc/Vol.
EL GALLO

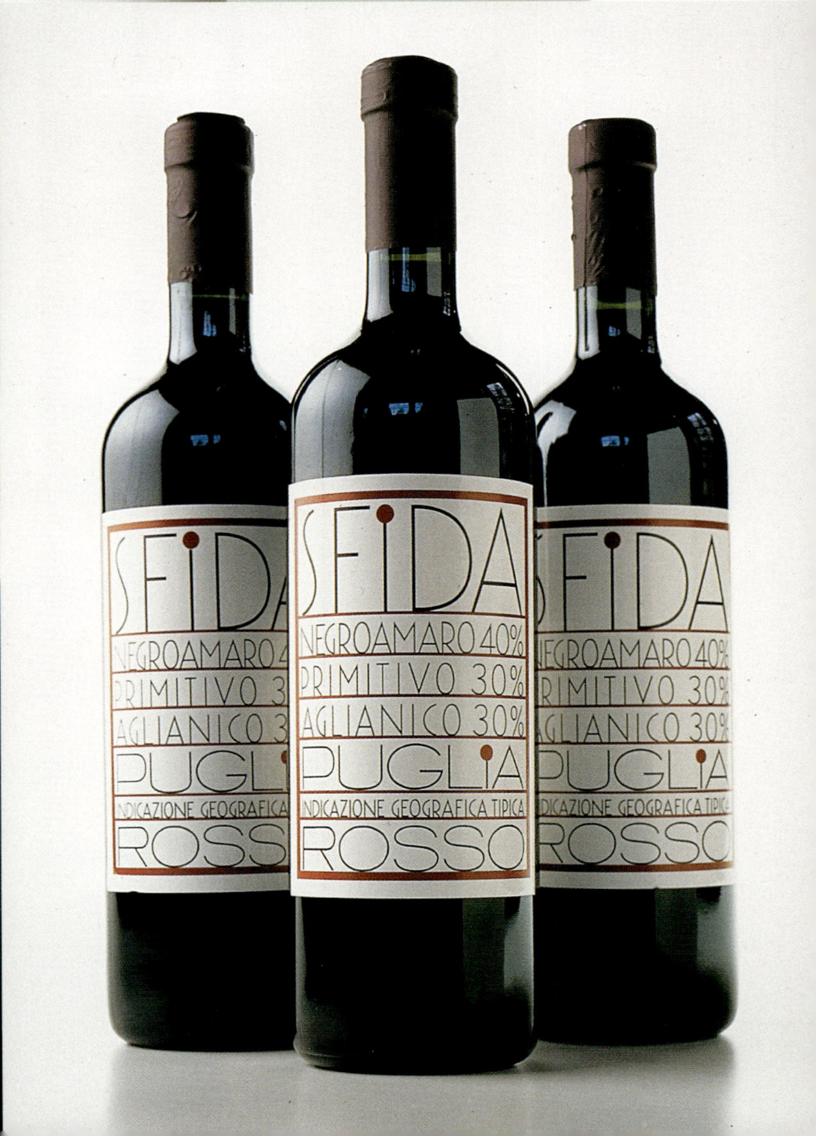
SFIDA
NEGROAMARO 40%
PRIMITIVO 30%
AGLIANICO 30%
PUGLIA
INDICAZIONE GEOGRAFICA TIPICA
ROSSO

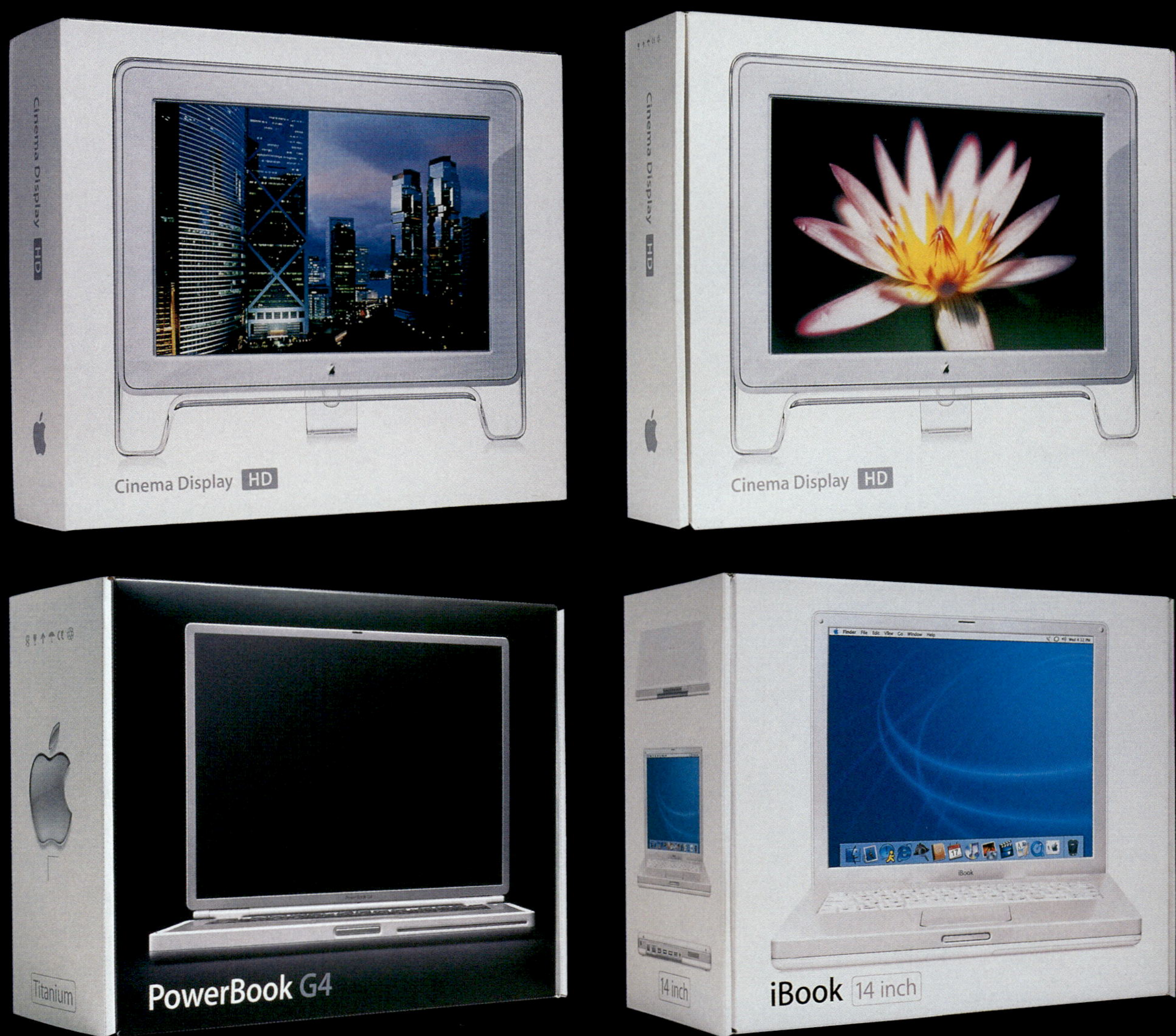

(clockwise from top left) (1, 2) Design Firm: Apple Computers Designers: Hiroki Asai, Josh Distler, Peggy Jensen, Steve Jobs and Mee-Soo Kim Photographer: Hunter Freeman Client: Apple Computers (3) Design Firm: Apple Computers Designers: Mike Abbink, Hiroki Asai, Peggy Jensen and Jeff Zwerner Photographer: Hunter Freeman Client: Apple Computers (4) Design Firm: Apple Computers Designers: Mike Abbink, Hiroki Asai, Gabe Campodonico, Sam Davy, Peggy Jensen, Steve Jobs, Meng Mantasoot, Emma Webb and Jeff Zwerner Photographer: Hunter Freeman Client: Apple Computers (opposite page) Design Firm: Apple Computers Designers: Mike Abbink, Hiroki Asai, Peggy Jensen and Jeff Zwerner Photographer: Hunter Freeman Client: Apple Computers

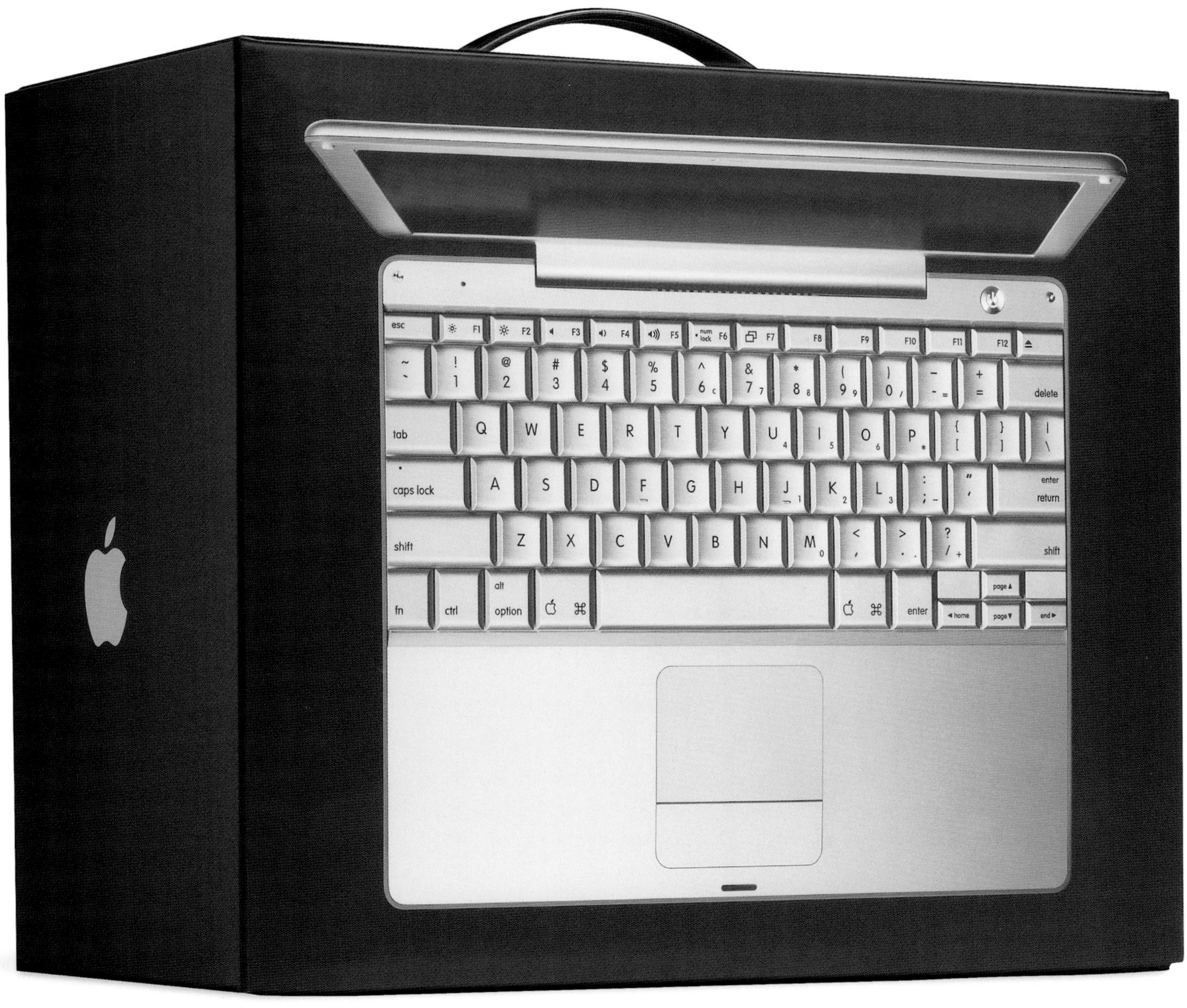

'Canpull' Design Firm: Turner Duckworth Creative Directors: Bruce Duckworth and David Turner Designer: Anthony Biles Account Manager: Moira Riddell Typographers: Jeremy Tankard and Anthony Biles Client: Boa Housewares (opposite page) 'Senior Solutions Dog Food' Design Firm: Out of the Box Creative Director: Rick Schneider Art Directors: Rick Schneider and Paul Porot Designers: Rick Schneider and Paul Porot Photographer: Tom Vogt Copywriter: James Lincoln Client: 4 Square Pet Products

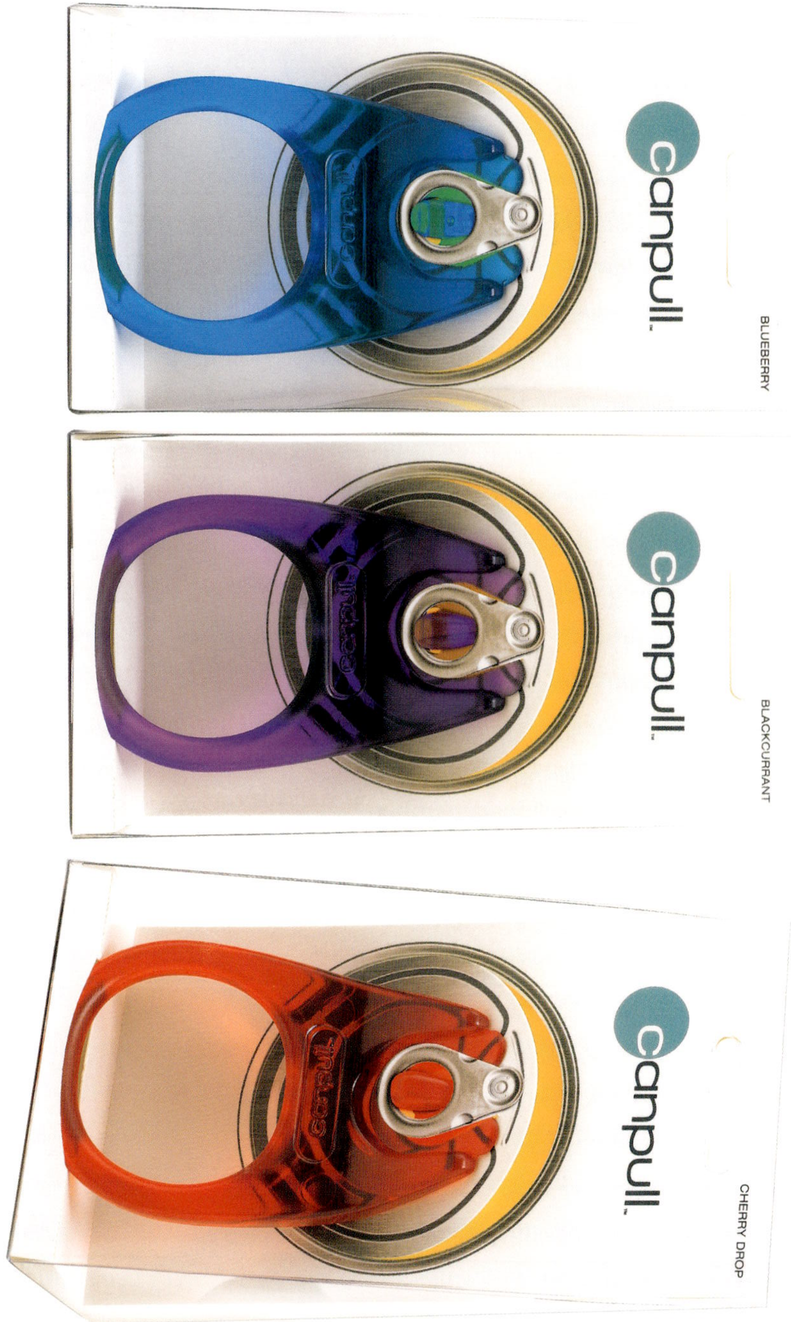

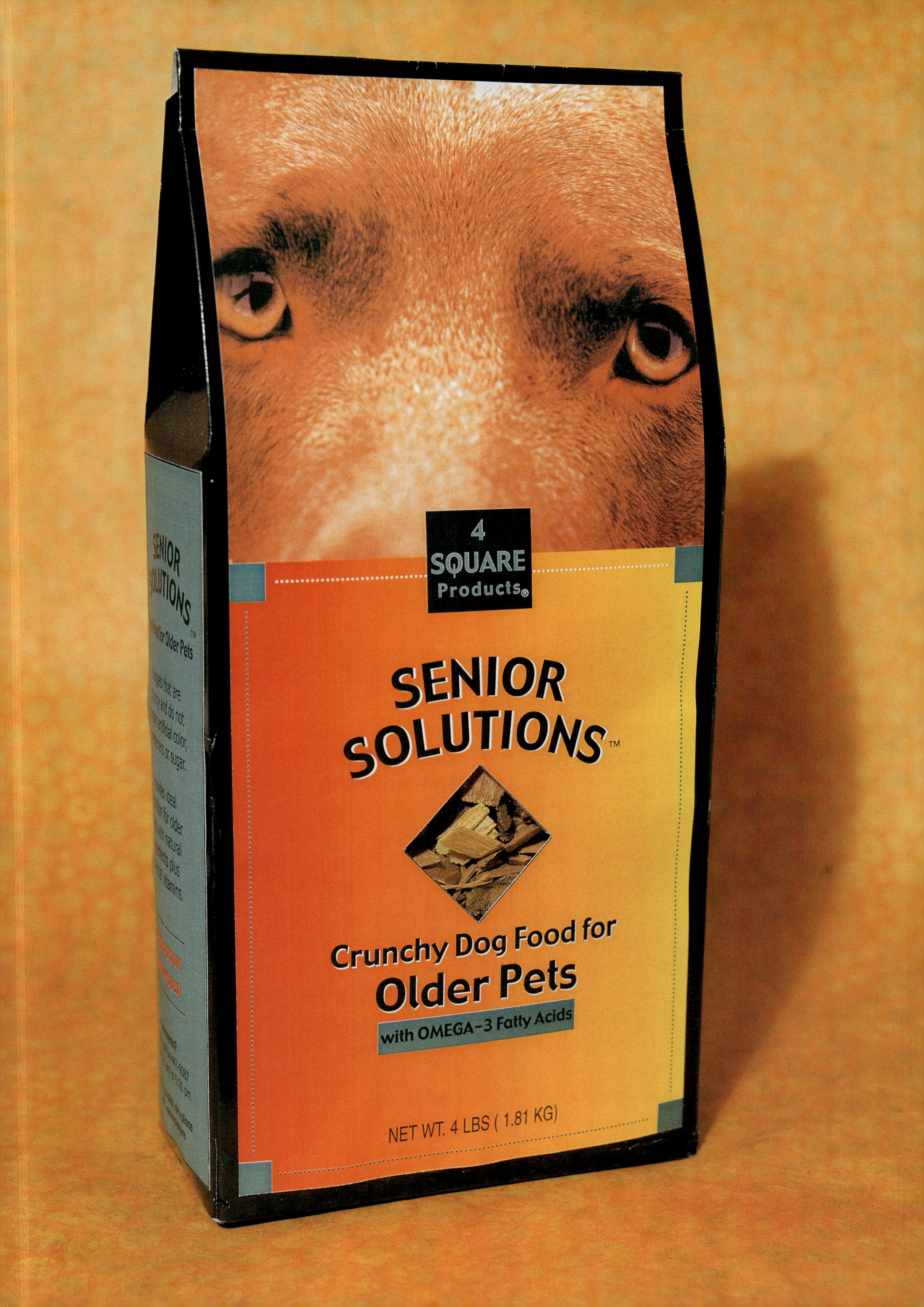
4
SQUARE
Products®
SENIOR
SOLUTIONS™
Crunchy Dog Food for
Older Pets
with OMEGA-3 Fatty Acids
NET WT. 4 LBS (1.81 KG)

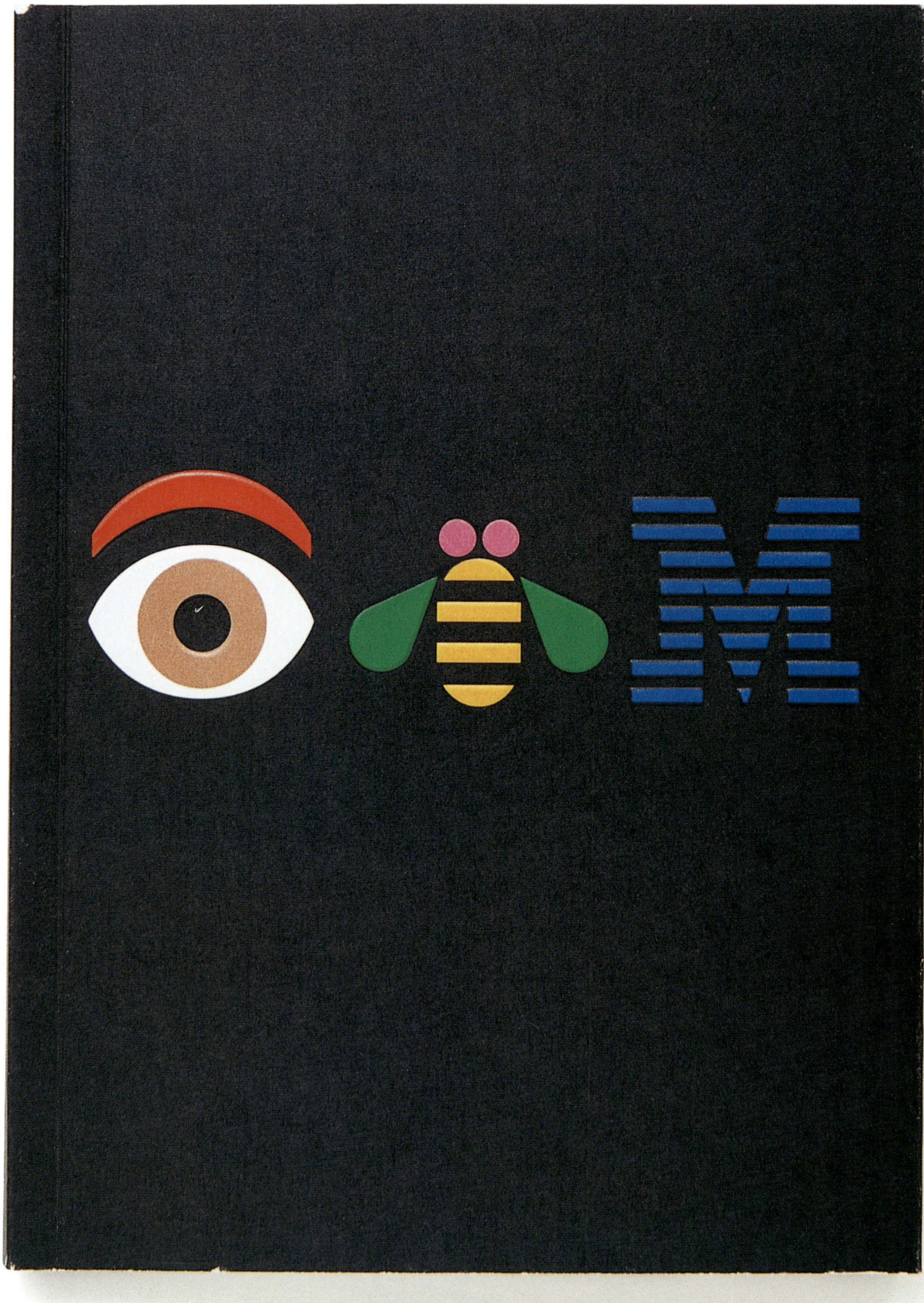

(this spread) 'Icons of Design' Design Firm: Sibley Peteet Design/Dallas Art Director: Don Sibley Designer: Don Sibley Illustrator: Various Legends Copywriter: Don Sibley Client: Weyerhaeuser Paper

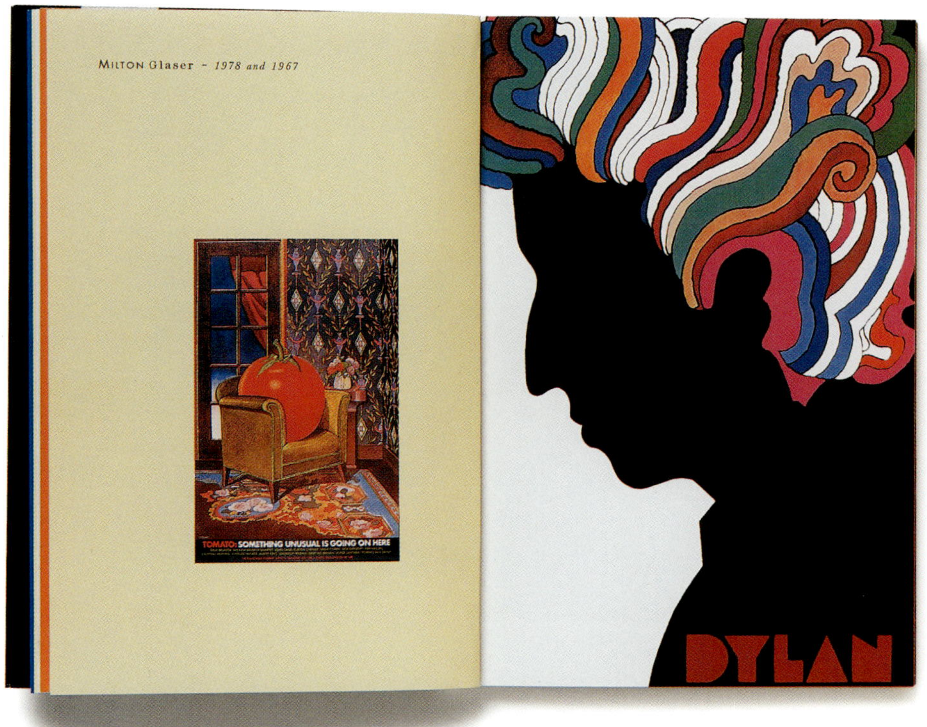
MILTON Glaser - 1978 and 1967
TOMATO: SOMETHING UNUSUAL IS GOING ON HERE
DYLAN

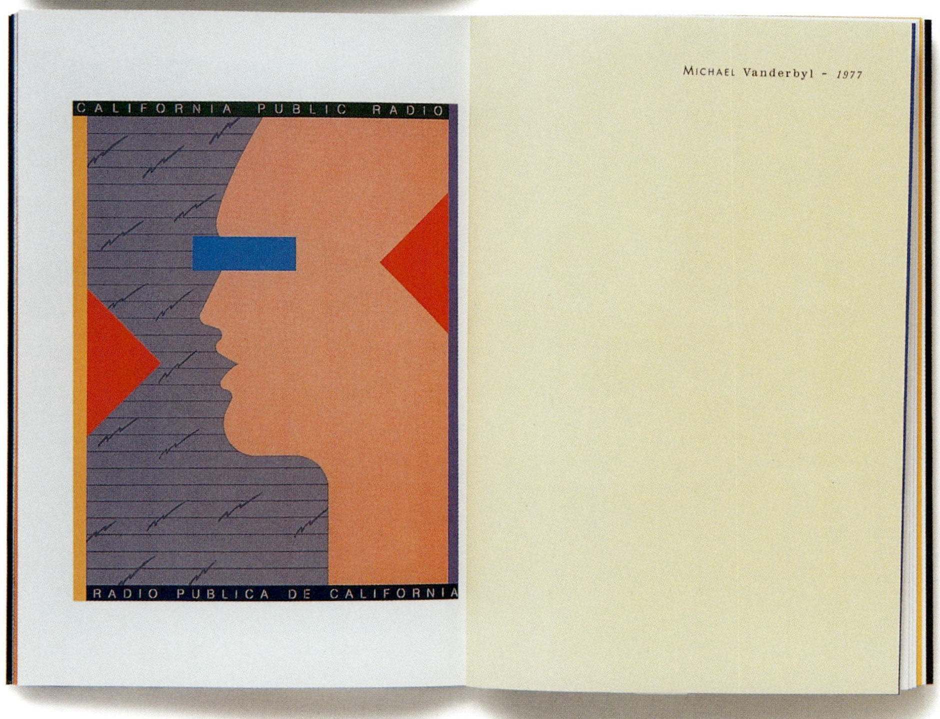
MICHAEL Vanderbyl - 1977
CALIFORNIA PUBLIC RADIO
RADIO PUBLICA DE CALIFORNIA

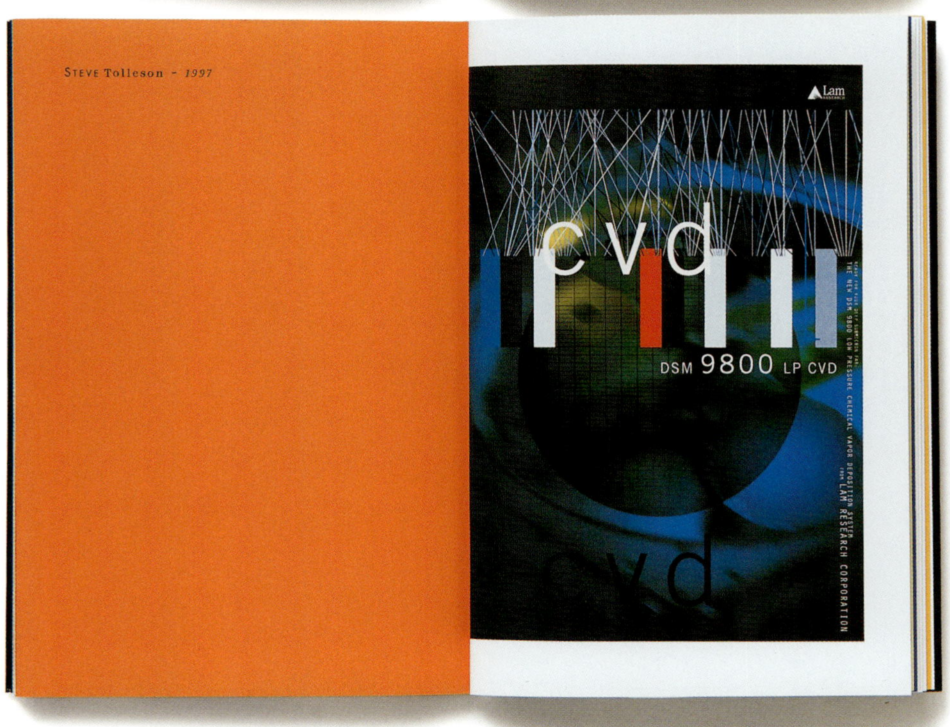
STEVE Tolleson - 1997
Lam
cvd
DSM 9800 LP CVD
LAM RESEARCH CORPORATION
cvd

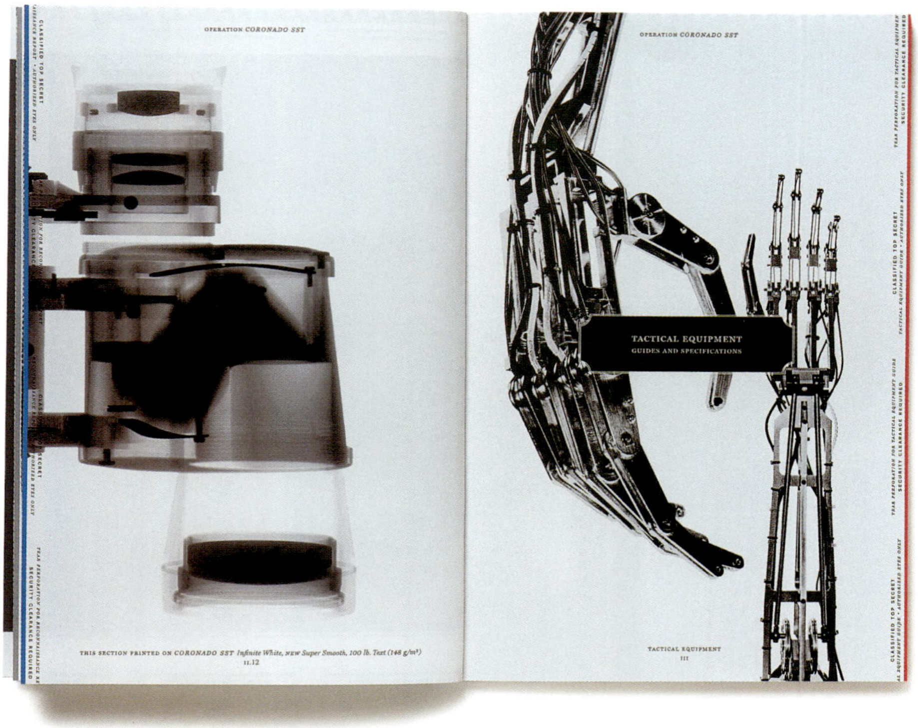

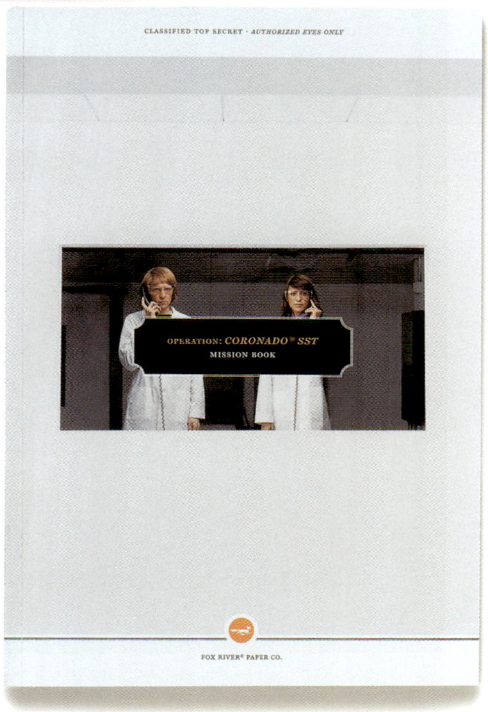

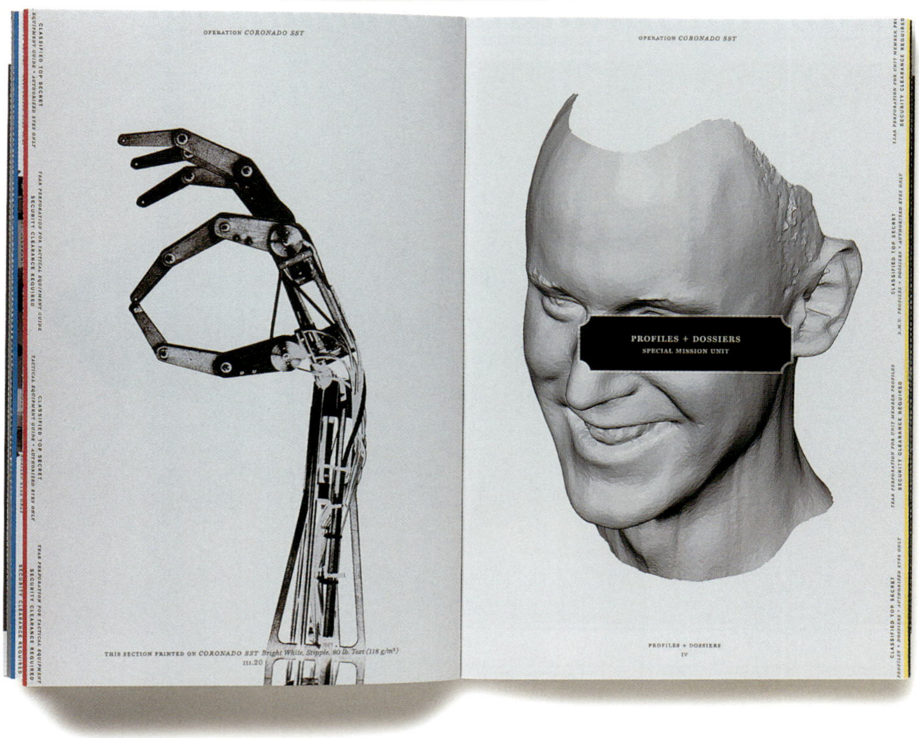

Design Firm: VSA Partners Art Director: Thom Wolfe Client: Fox River

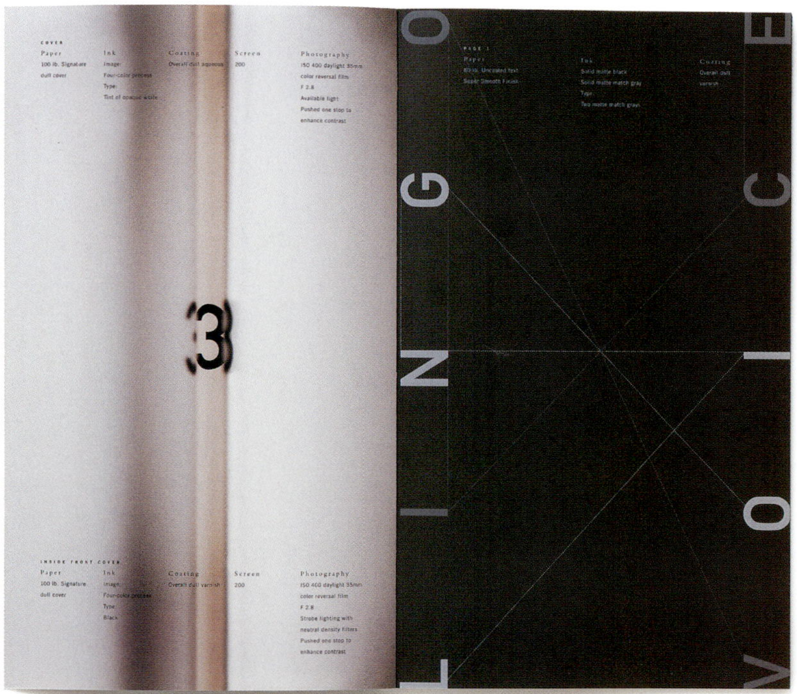

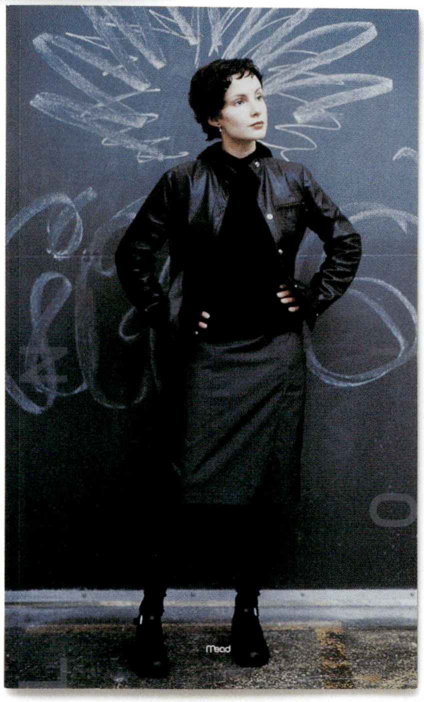

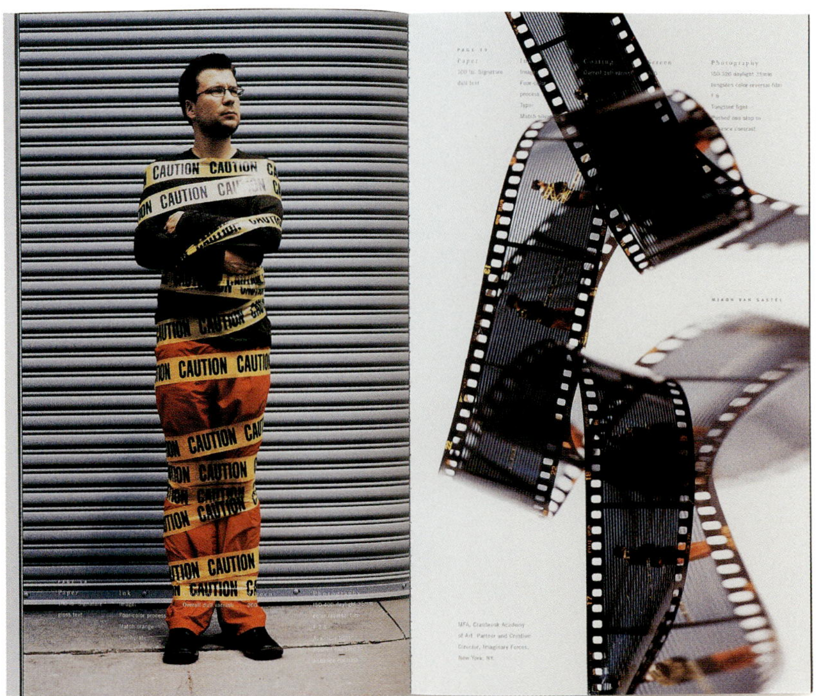

'Lingo 3' Design Firm: Weymouth Design Art Director: Tom Laidlaw Designers: Robert Krivicich and Brad Lewthwaite Photographer: Michael Weymouth Copywriters: Tom Laidlaw and Julie Davis Client: Mead Coated Papers

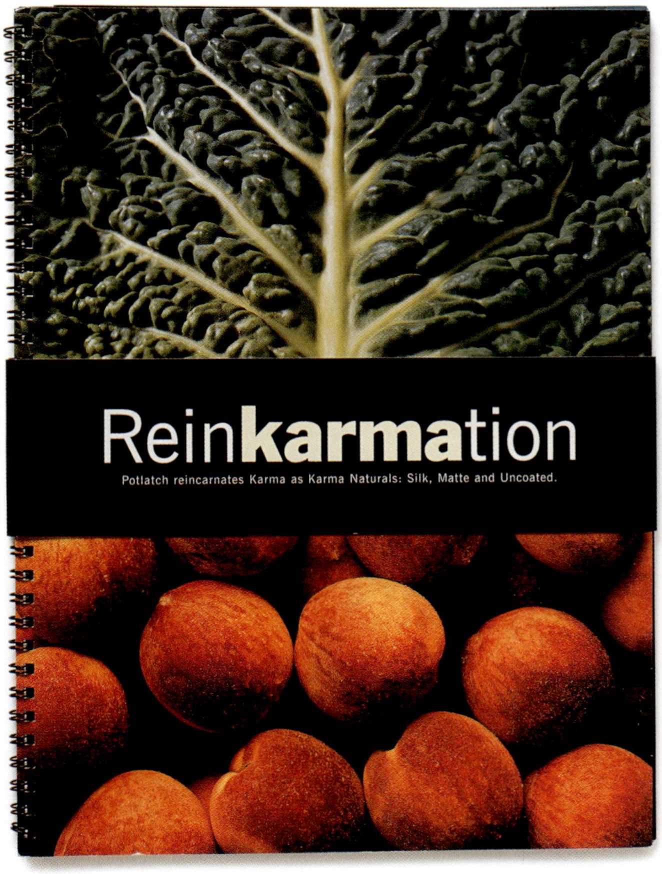

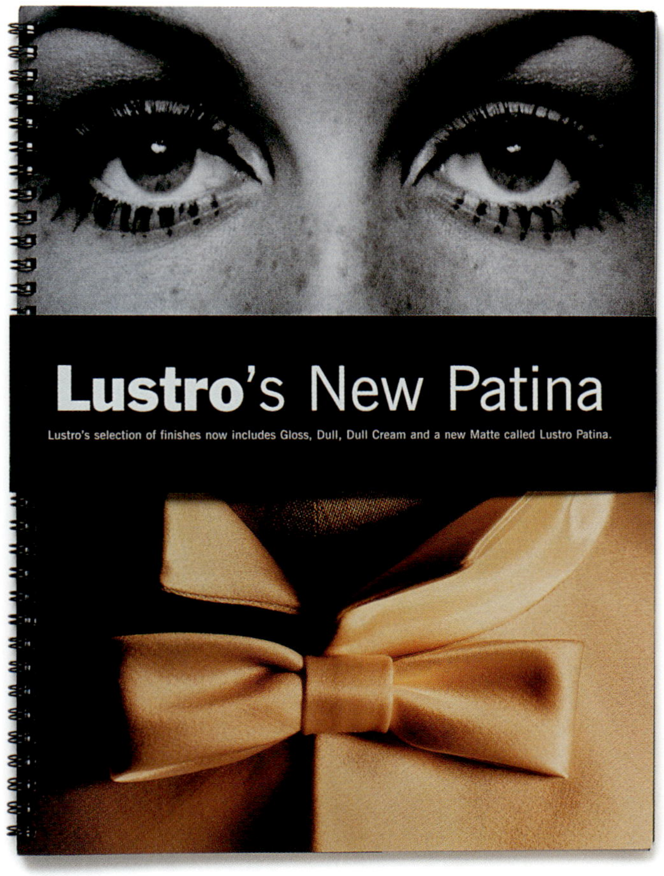

(this and following spread) 'Reinkarmation' Design Firm: Pentagram SF Creative Director: Kit Hinrichs Designers: Belle How and Takayo Muroga Photographers: Skip Barton, Terry Heffernan, Barry Robinson, Laurie Rubin and Tom Tracy Illustrators: Karen Montgomery, Takayo Muroga, Will Nelson, Nancy Stahl and Maria Wenzel Copywriter: Delphine Hirasuna Client: Potlatch Paper Company 'Lustro's New Patina' Design Firm: Pentagram SF Creative Director: Kit Hinrichs Designers: Belle How and Takayo Muroga Photographers: Alex Ardenti, Erwin Blumenfeld, John Casado, Michelle Clement, Clifford Coffin, Terry Heffernan, Frank Horvat, Geoge Hoyningen-Huene, Barry Lategan Man Ray , Barry Robinson, Rico Schwarzberg and Edward Steichen Illustrators: John J. Audobon, Rene Gruau, John Peacock and Everett Peck Copywriter: Delphine Hirasuna Client: Potlatch Paper Company

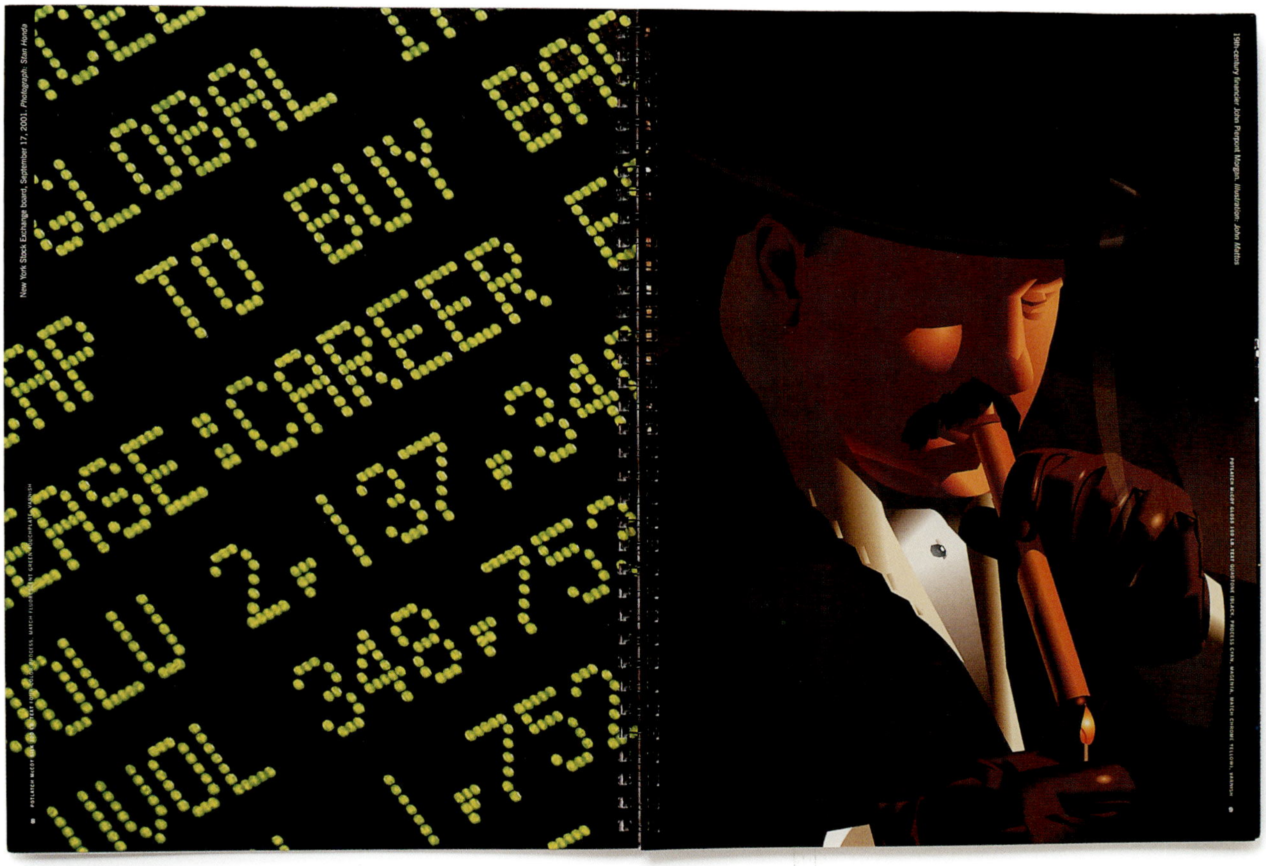
GLOBAL
TO BUY
CAREER
2,137.34
348.75
New York Stock Exchange board, September 17, 2001. Photograph: Stan Honda
19th-century financier John Pierpont Morgan. Illustration: John Mattos

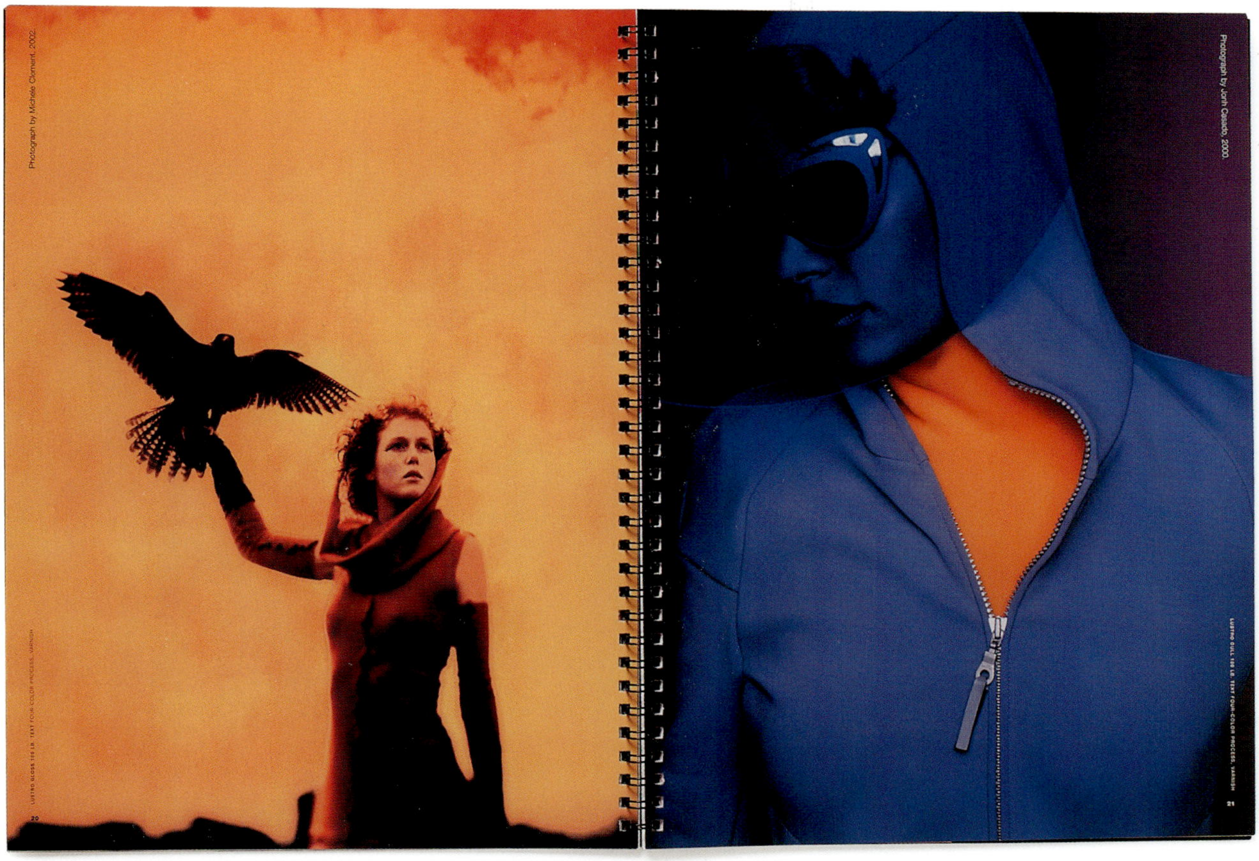
Photograph by Michele Clement, 2002.
Photograph by Jonh Casado, 2000.

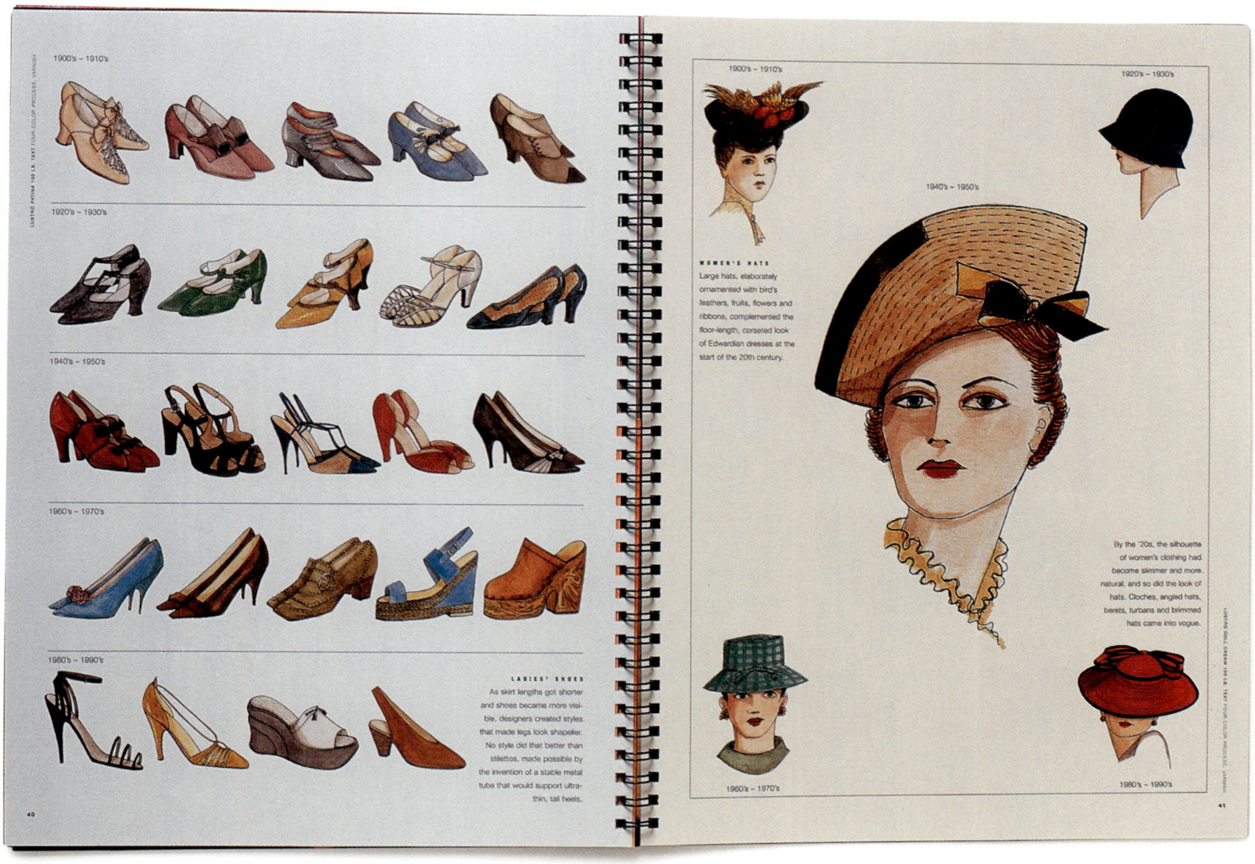
1900's – 1910's
1920's – 1930's
1940's – 1950's
1960's – 1970's
1980's – 1990's
LADIES' SHOES
As skirt lengths got shorter and shoes became more visible, designers created styles that made legs look shapelier. No style did that better than stilettos, made possible by the invention of a stable metal tube that would support ultra-thin, tall heels.
40
1900's – 1910's
1920's – 1930's
1940's – 1950's
WOMEN'S HATS
Large hats, elaborately ornamented with bird's feathers, fruits, flowers and ribbons, complemented the floor-length, corseted look of Edwardian dresses at the start of the 20th century.
By the '20s, the silhouette of women's clothing had become slimmer and more natural, and so did the look of hats. Cloches, angled hats, berets, turbans and brimmed hats came into vogue.
1960's – 1970's
1980's – 1990's
41

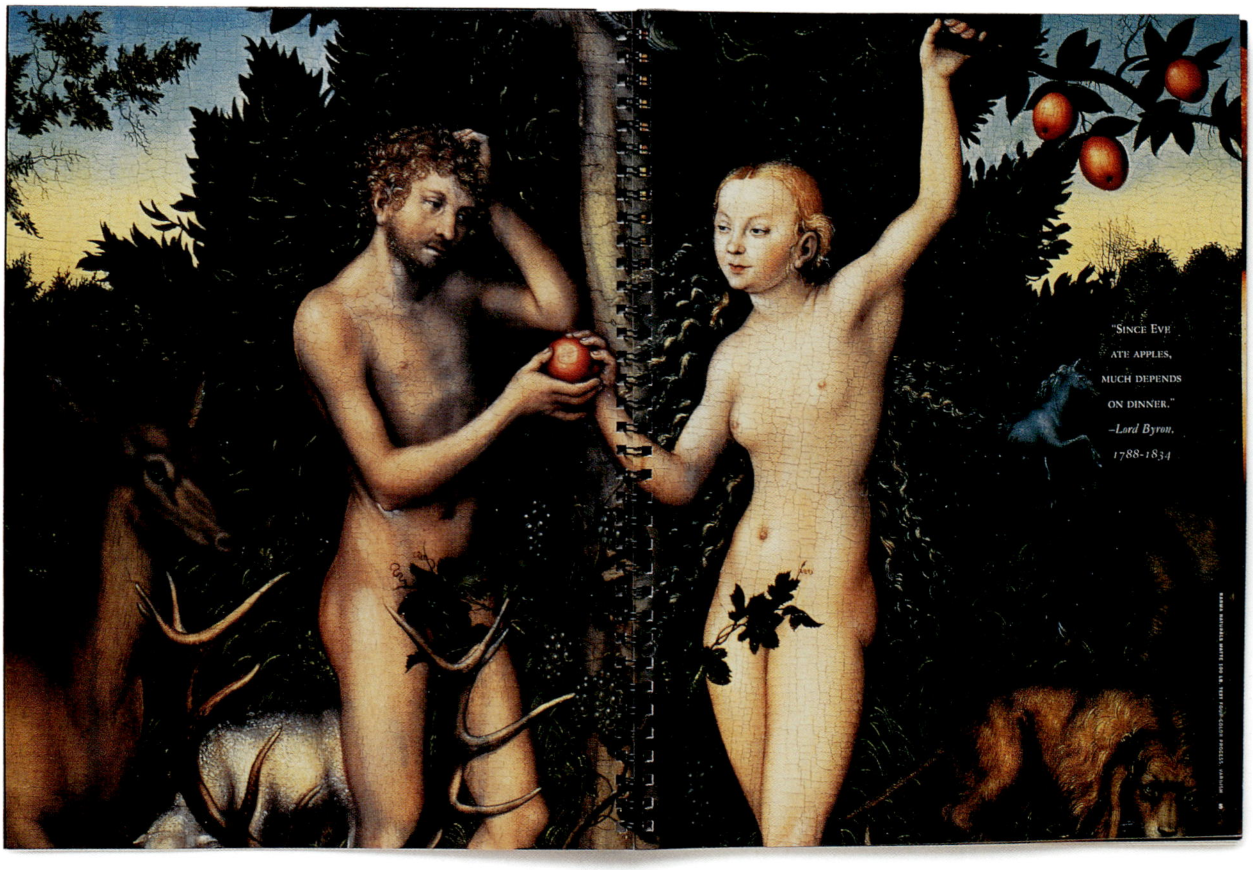
"SINCE EVE ATE APPLES, MUCH DEPENDS ON DINNER."
–Lord Byron, 1788-1834

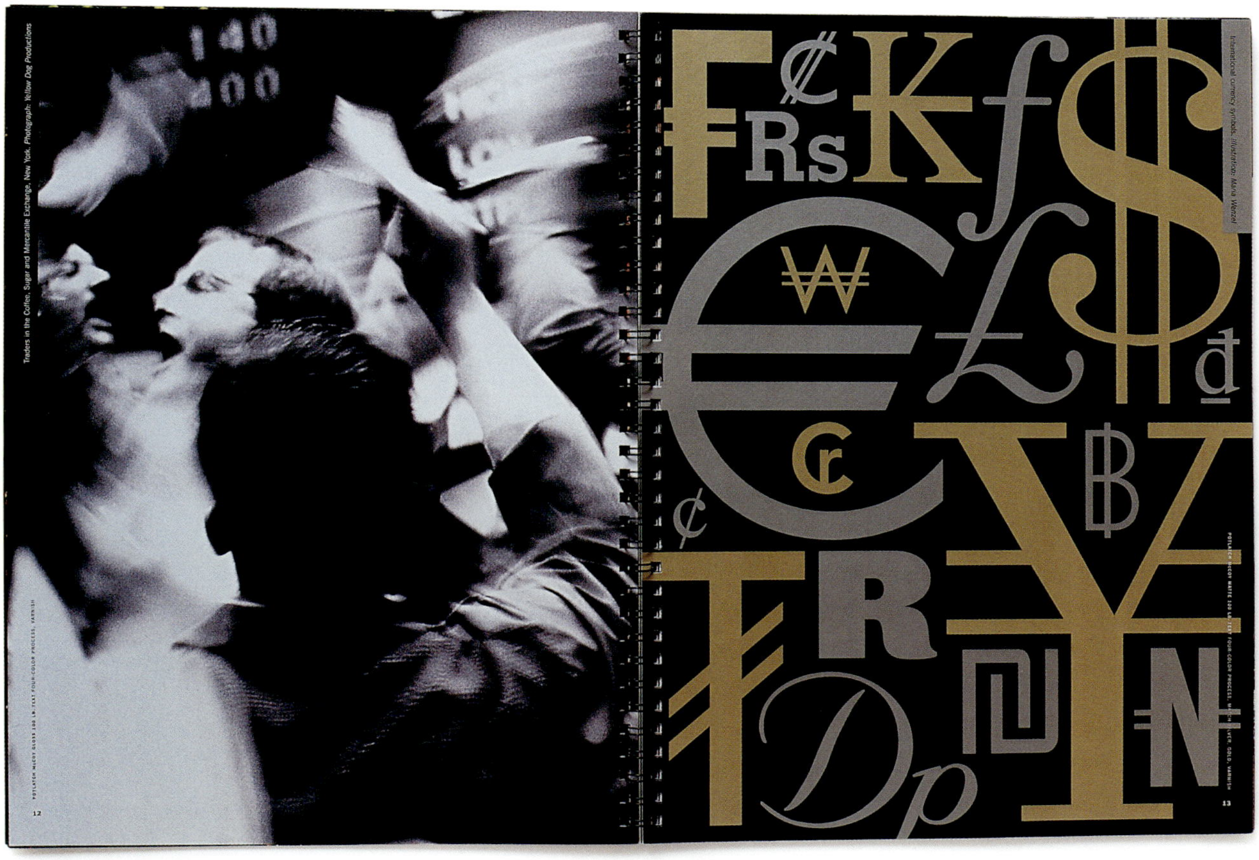
Traders in the Coffee, Sugar and Mercantile Exchange, New York. *Photograph: Yellow Dog Productions*
International currency symbols. *Illustration: Maria Wenzel*

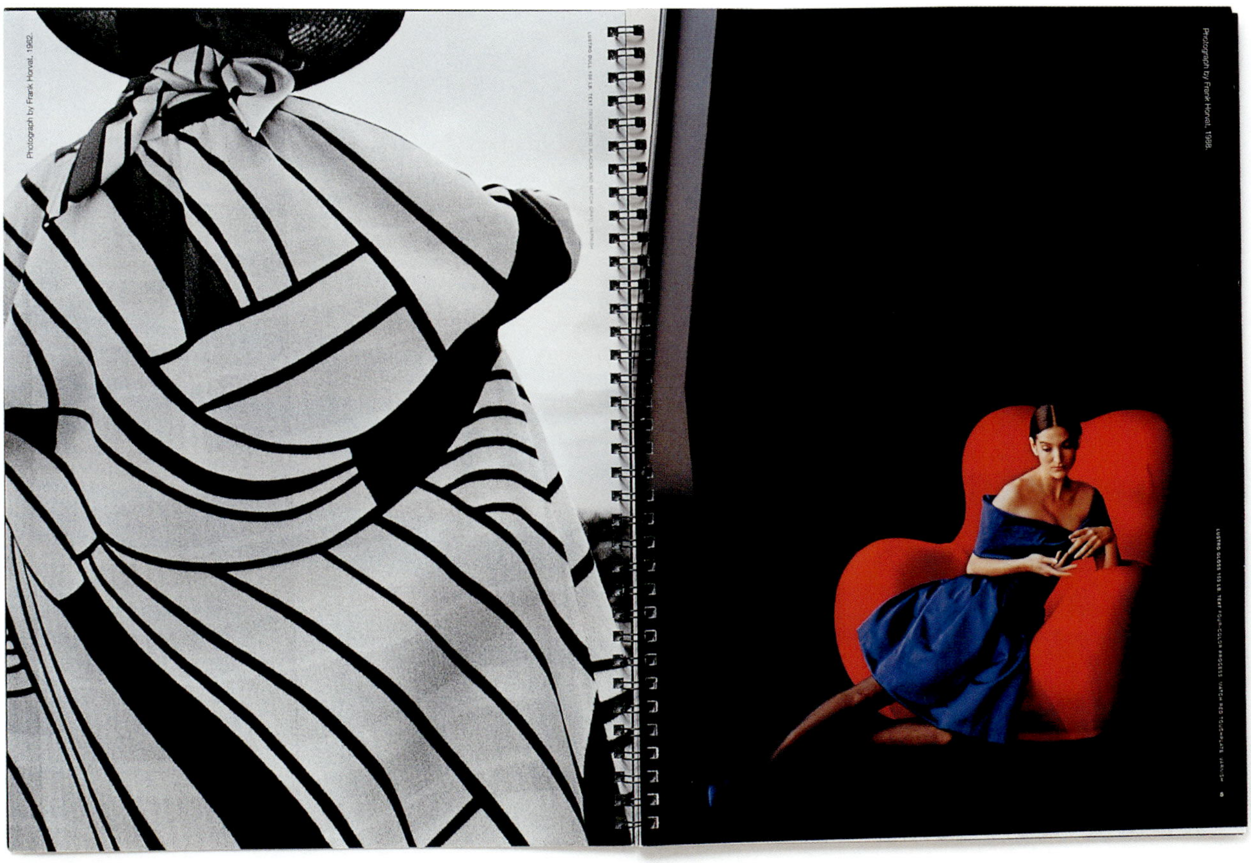
Photograph by Frank Horvat, 1962.
Photograph by Frank Horvat, 1986.

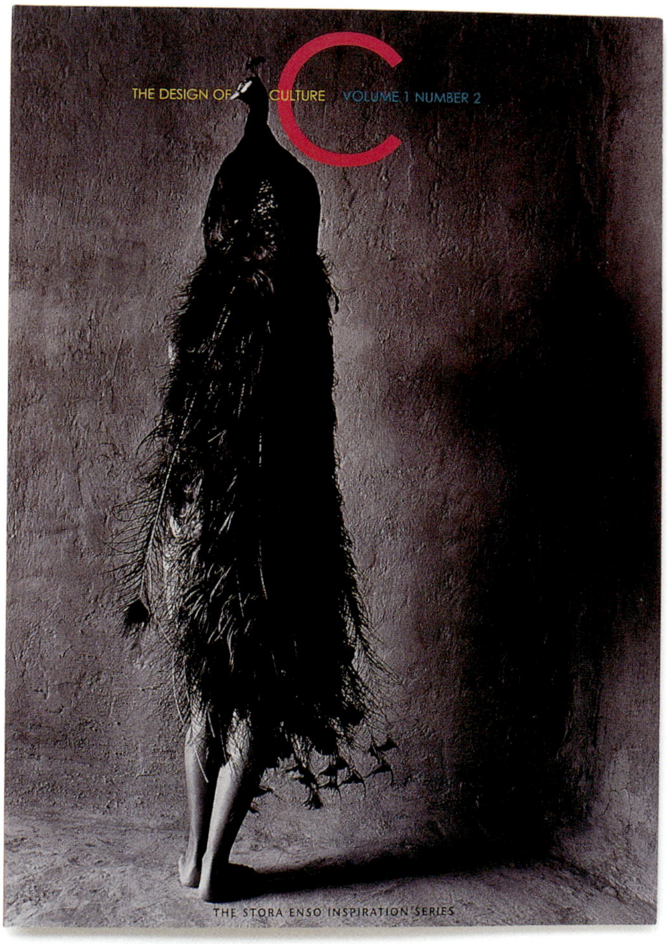

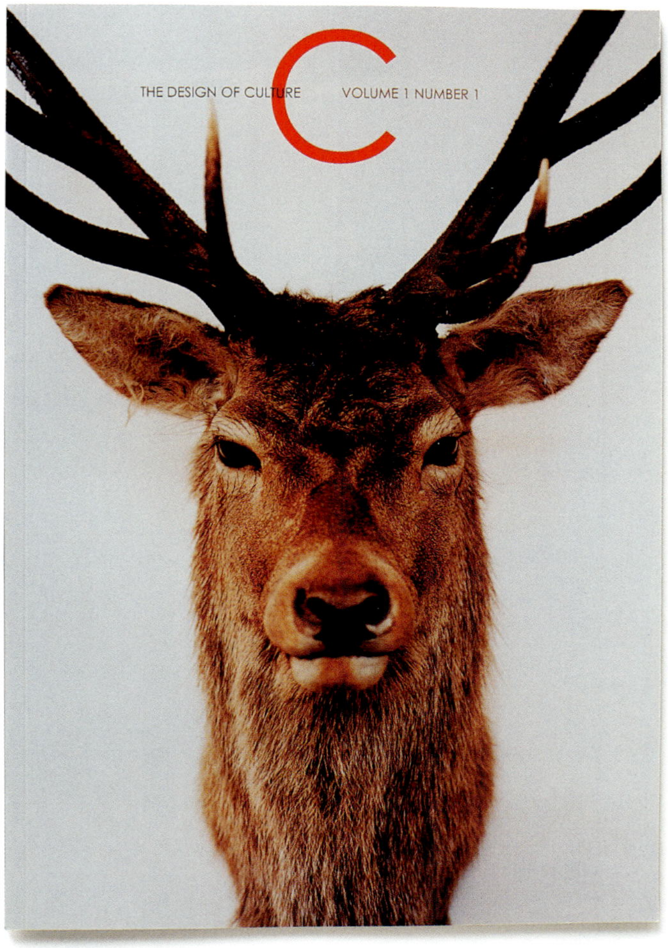

(this spread) '"C" The Design of Culture Vol. 1 and 2' Design Firm: Heller Communications Creative Director: Cheryl Heller Designer: Cheryl Heller Client: Stora Enso North America

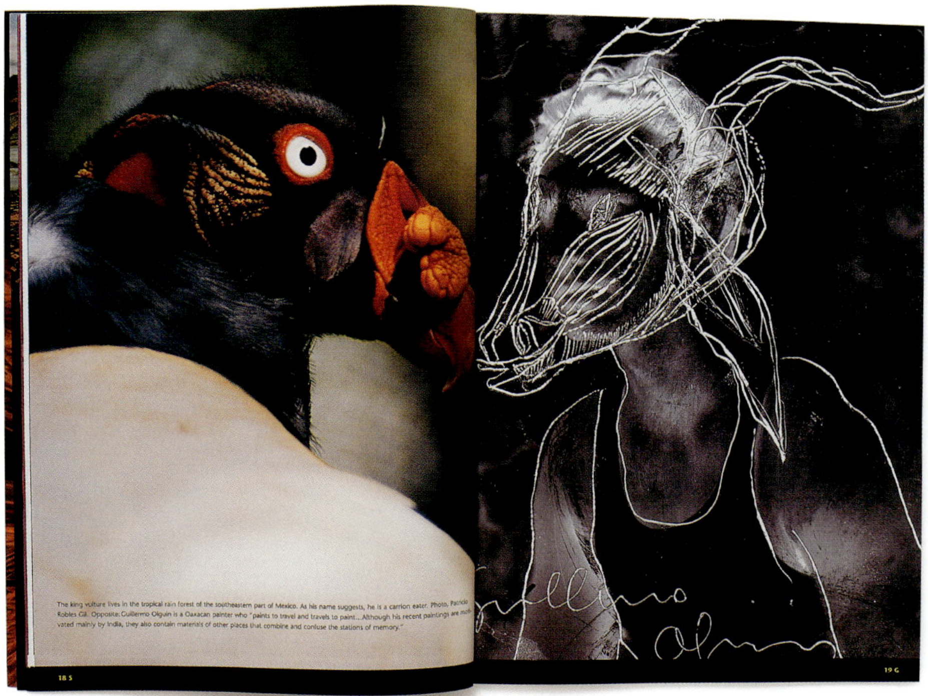
The king vulture lives in the tropical rain forest of the southeastern part of Mexico. As his name suggests, he is a carrion eater. Photo, Patricio
Robles Gil. Opposite: Guillermo Olguin is a Oaxacan painter who "paints to travel and travels to paint....Although his recent paintings are moti-
vated mainly by India, they also contain materials of other places that combine and confuse the stations of memory."
18 S
19 G

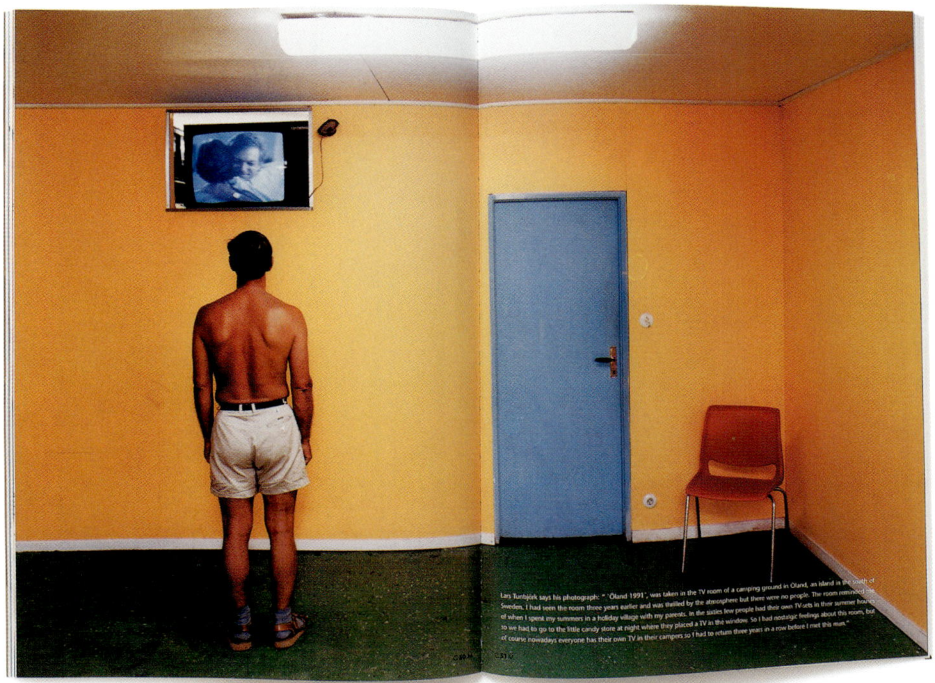
Lars Tunbjörk says his photograph: " 'Öland 1991', was taken in the TV room of a camping ground in Öland, an island in the south of
Sweden. I had seen the room three years earlier and was thrilled by the atmosphere but there were no people. The room reminded me
of when I spent my summers in a holiday village with my parents. In the sixties few people had their own TV-sets in their summer houses
so we had to go to the little candy store at night where they placed a TV in the window. So I had nostalgic feelings about this room, but
of course nowadays everyone has their own TV in their campers so I had to return three years in a row before I met this man."

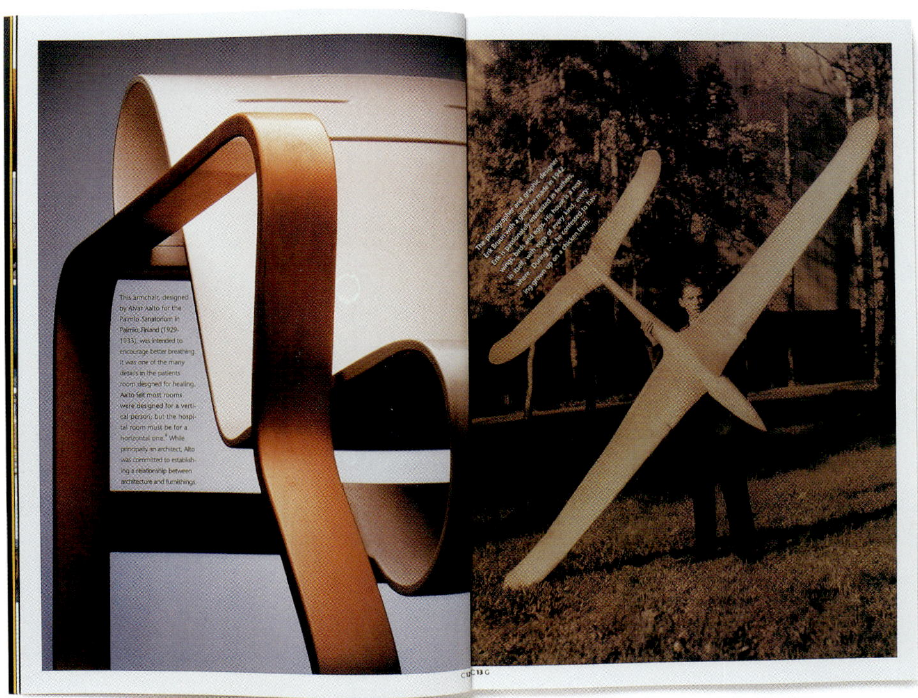
This armchair, designed
by Alvar Aalto for the
Paimio Sanatorium in
Paimio, Finland (1929-
1933), was intended to
encourage better breathing.
It was one of the many
details in the patients
room designed for healing.
Aalto felt most rooms
were designed for a verti-
cal person, but the hospi-
tal room must be for a
horizontal one.[4] While
principally an architect, Alto
was committed to establish-
ing a relationship between
architecture and furnishings.

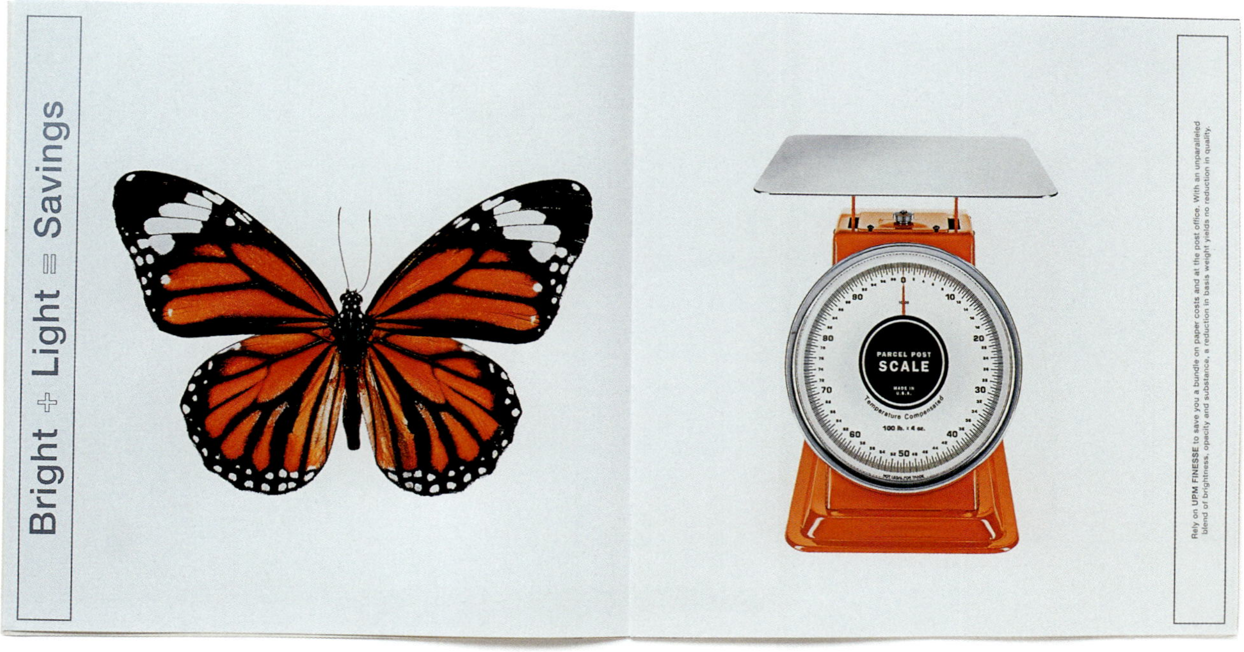

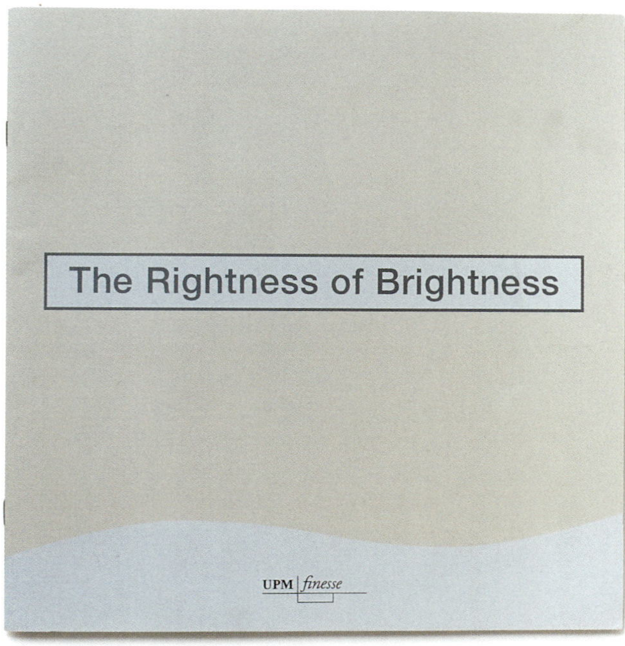

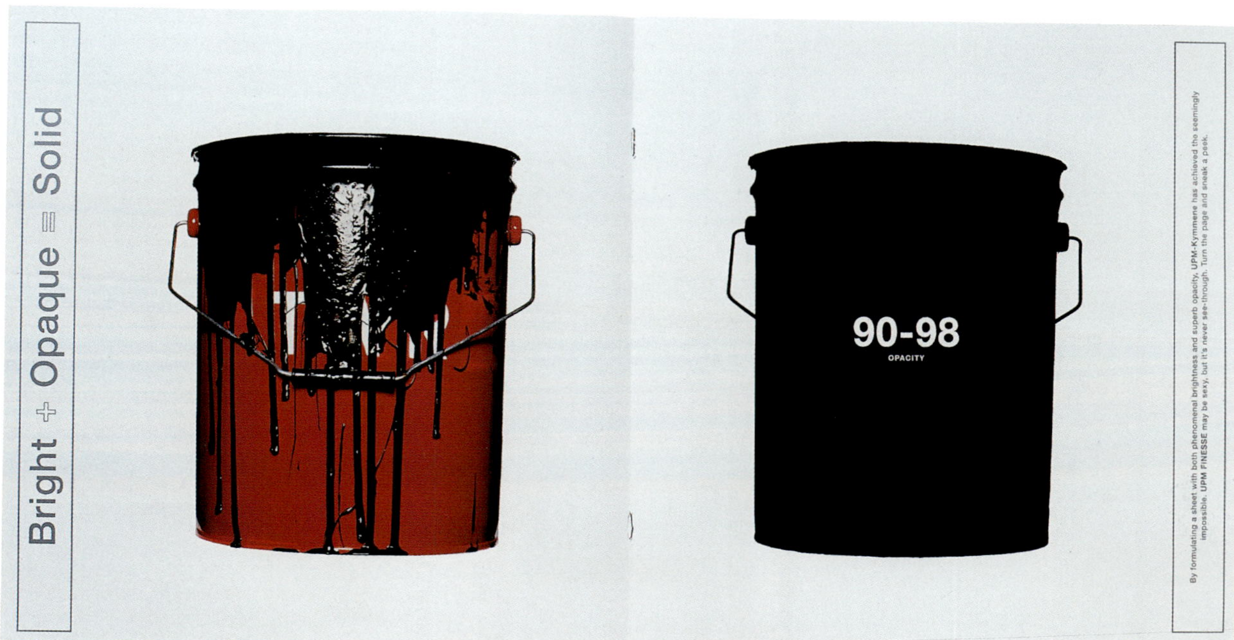

'Family Piece' Design Firm: Gage Creative Director: David Whitman Designer: Bob Goebel Copywriter: David Whitman Client: UPM

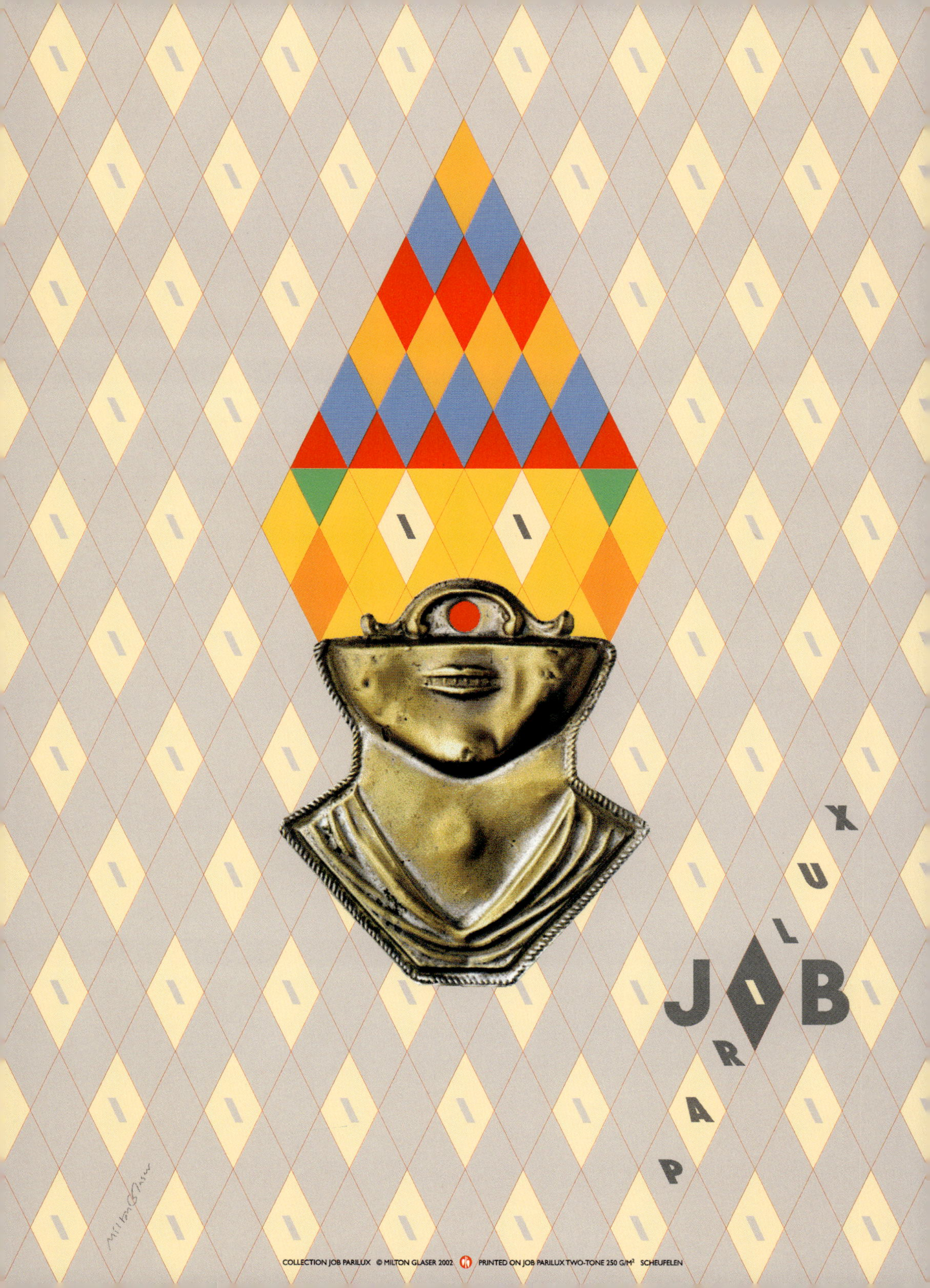
JOB
PARILUX
COLLECTION JOB PARILUX © MILTON GLASER 2002 PRINTED ON JOB PARILUX TWO-TONE 250 G/M² SCHEUFELEN

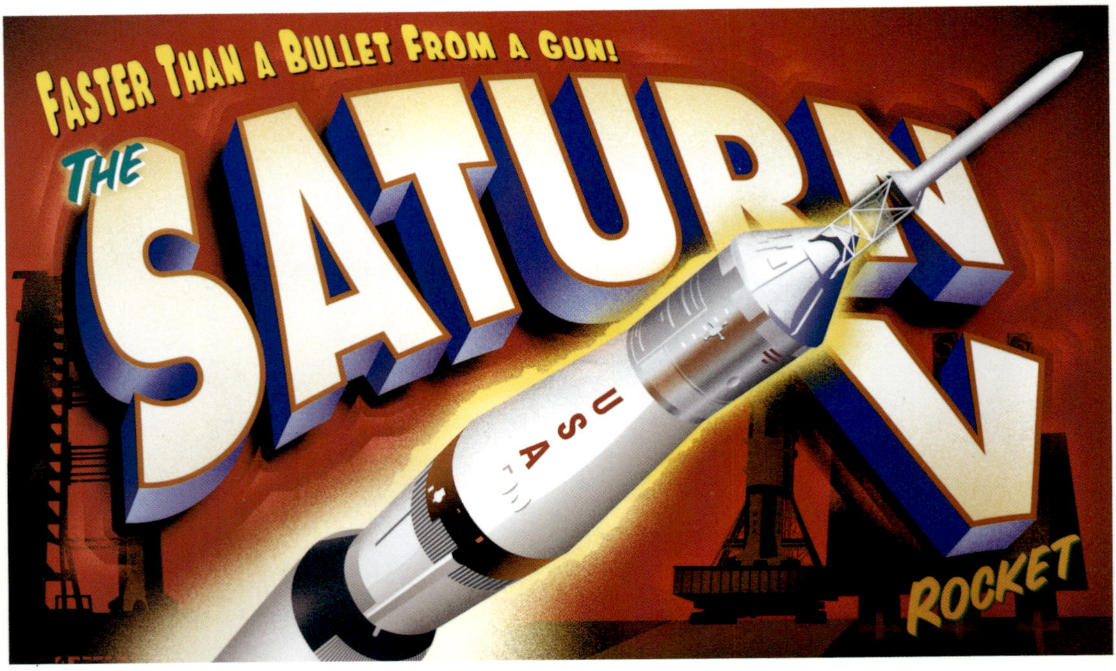
FASTER THAN A BULLET FROM A GUN!
THE
SATURN V
USA
ROCKET

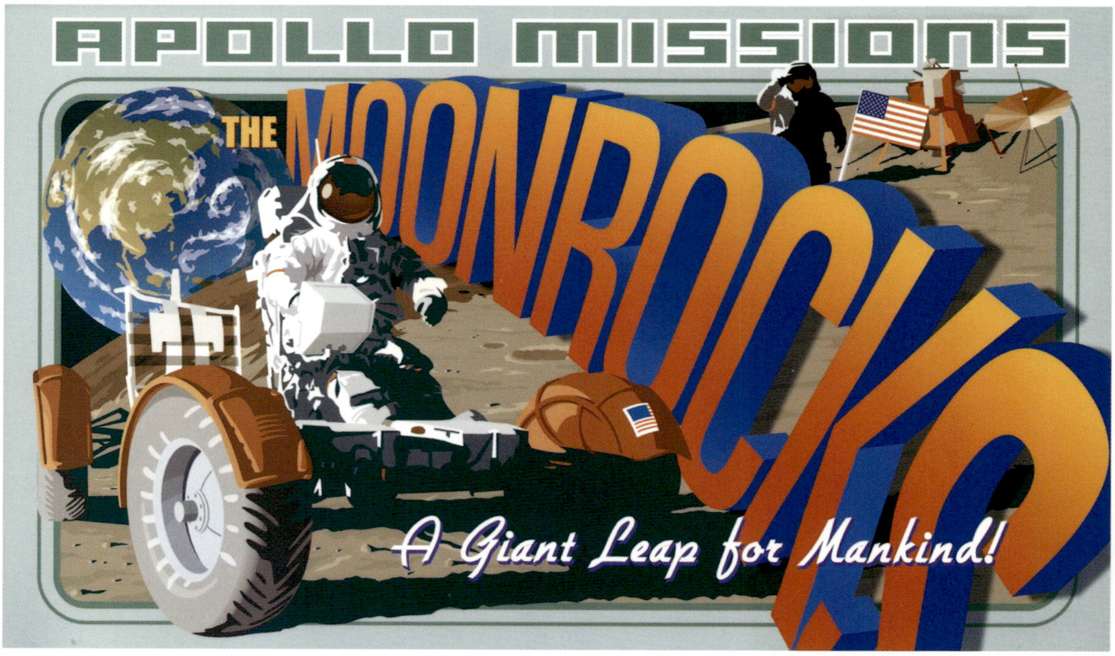
APOLLO MISSIONS
THE MOONROCKS
A Giant Leap for Mankind!

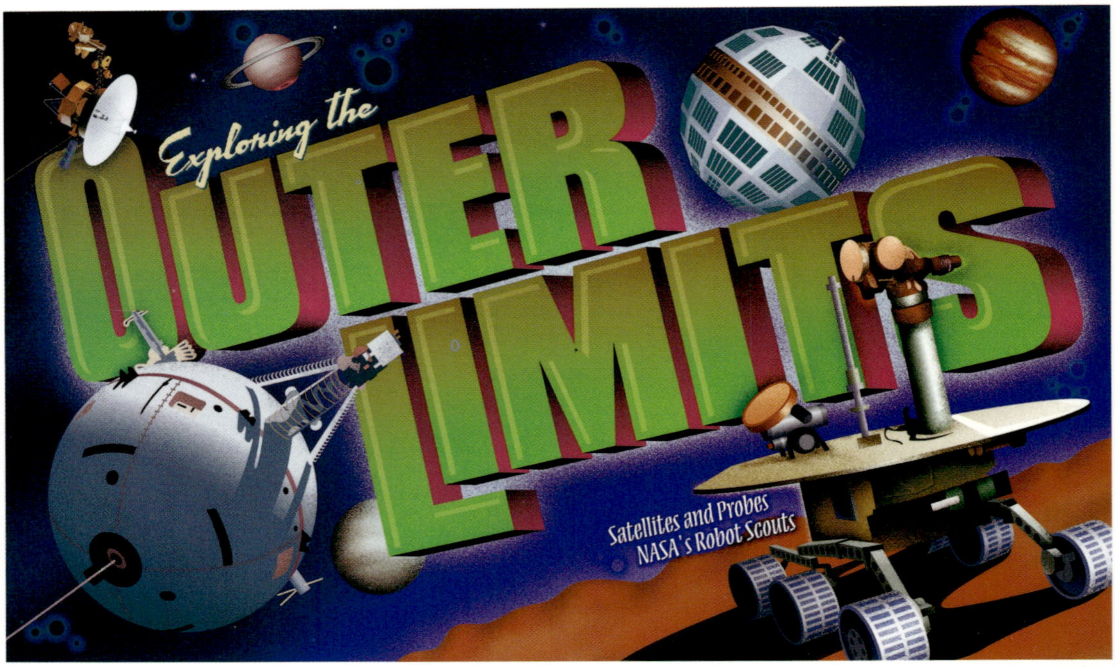
Exploring the
OUTER LIMITS
Satellites and Probes
NASA's Robot Scouts

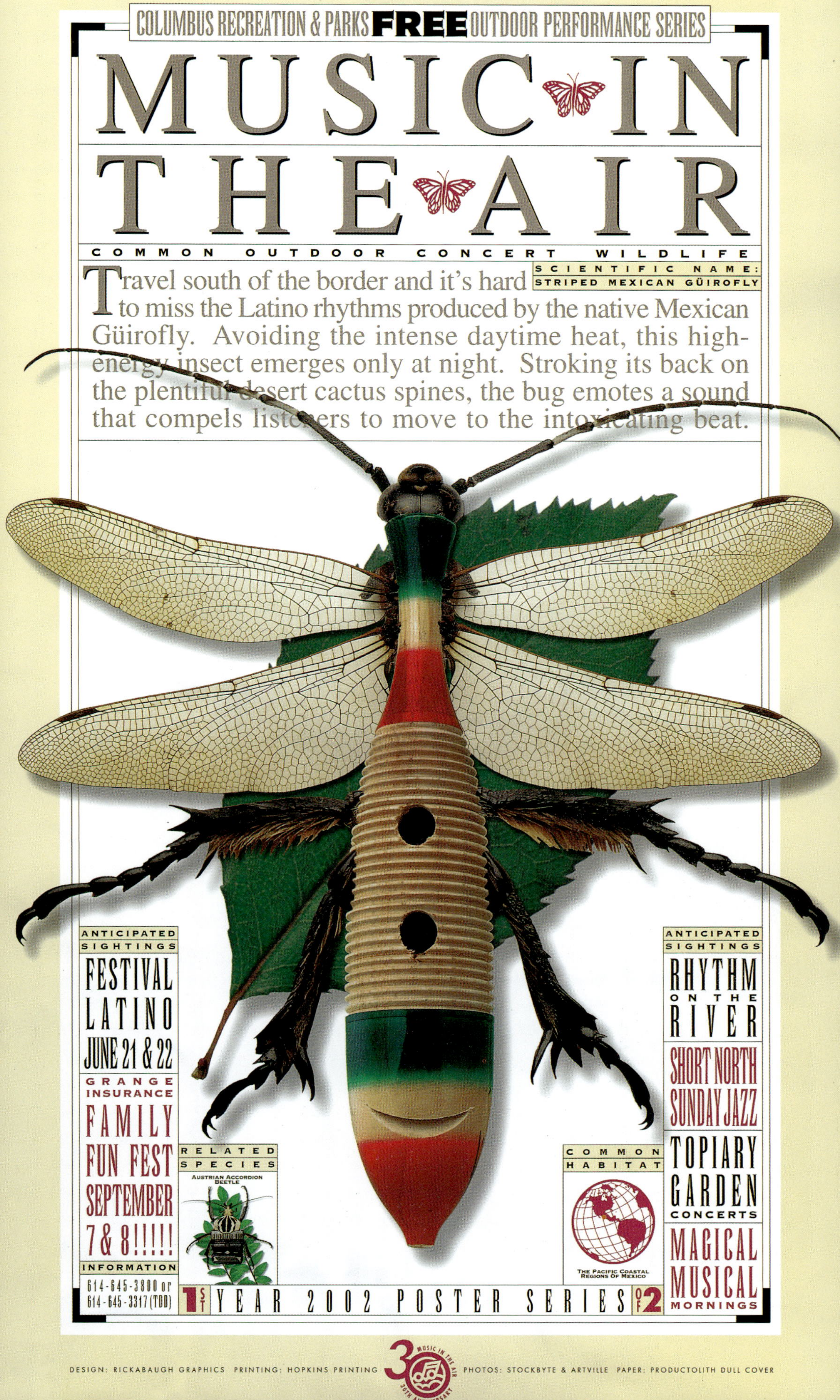
COLUMBUS RECREATION & PARKS FREE OUTDOOR PERFORMANCE SERIES
MUSIC IN THE AIR
COMMON OUTDOOR CONCERT WILDLIFE
SCIENTIFIC NAME: STRIPED MEXICAN GÜIROFLY
Travel south of the border and it's hard to miss the Latino rhythms produced by the native Mexican Güirofly. Avoiding the intense daytime heat, this high-energy insect emerges only at night. Stroking its back on the plentiful desert cactus spines, the bug emotes a sound that compels listeners to move to the intoxicating beat.
ANTICIPATED SIGHTINGS
FESTIVAL LATINO JUNE 21 & 22
GRANGE INSURANCE FAMILY FUN FEST SEPTEMBER 7 & 8!!!!!
INFORMATION
614-645-3800 or 614-645-3317 (TDD)
RELATED SPECIES
AUSTRIAN ACCORDION BEETLE
COMMON HABITAT
THE PACIFIC COASTAL REGIONS OF MEXICO
ANTICIPATED SIGHTINGS
RHYTHM ON THE RIVER
SHORT NORTH SUNDAY JAZZ
TOPIARY GARDEN CONCERTS
MAGICAL MUSICAL MORNINGS
1ST YEAR 2002 POSTER SERIES OF 2
DESIGN: RICKABAUGH GRAPHICS PRINTING: HOPKINS PRINTING PHOTOS: STOCKBYTE & ARTVILLE PAPER: PRODUCTOLITH DULL COVER
MUSIC IN THE AIR 30TH ANNIVERSARY

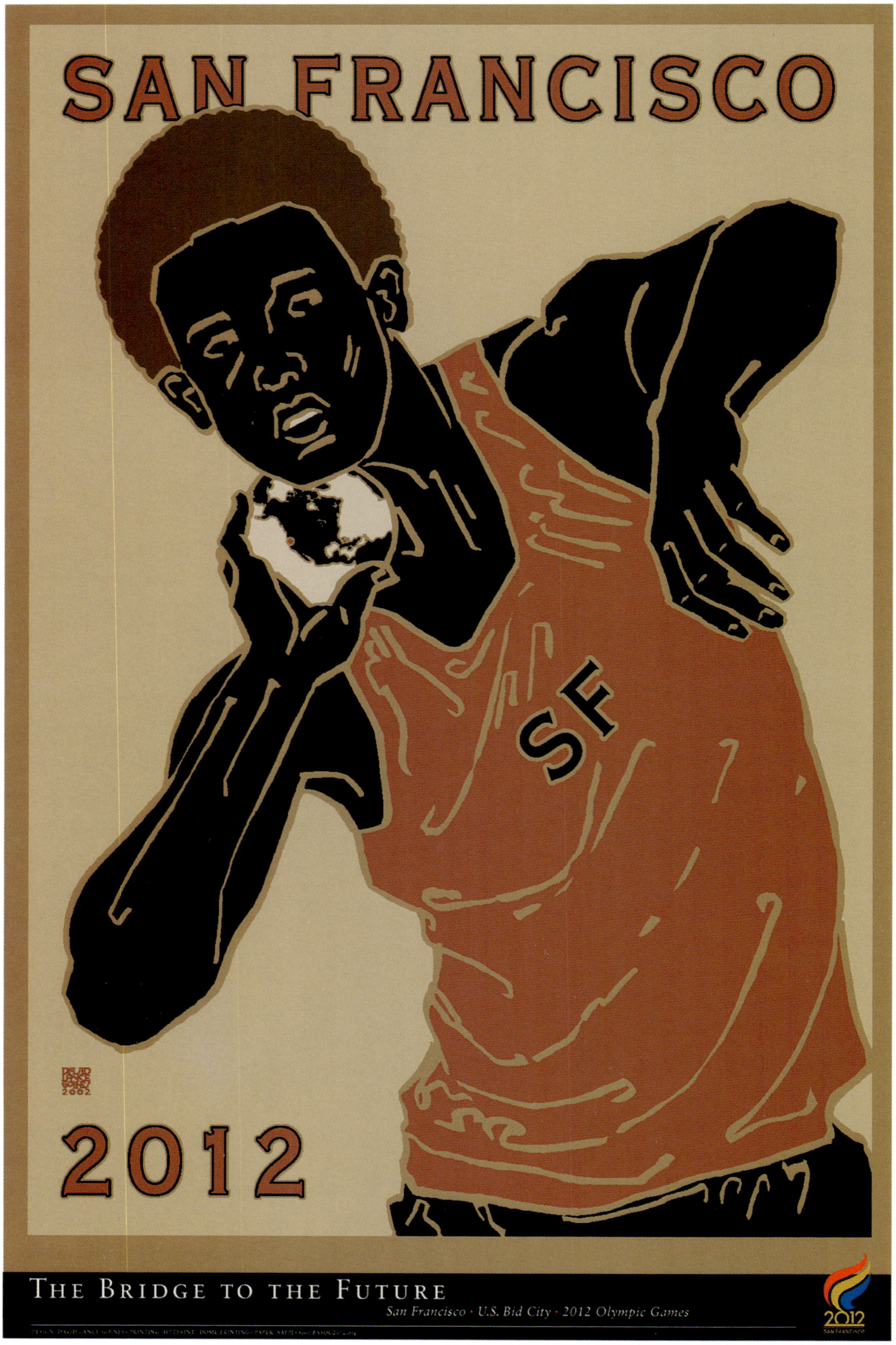

Design Firm: Saint Hieronymus Press Creative Director: David Lance Goines Art Director: David Lance Goines Designer: David Lance Goines Illustrator: David Lance Goines Client: Bay Area Sports Organizing Committee

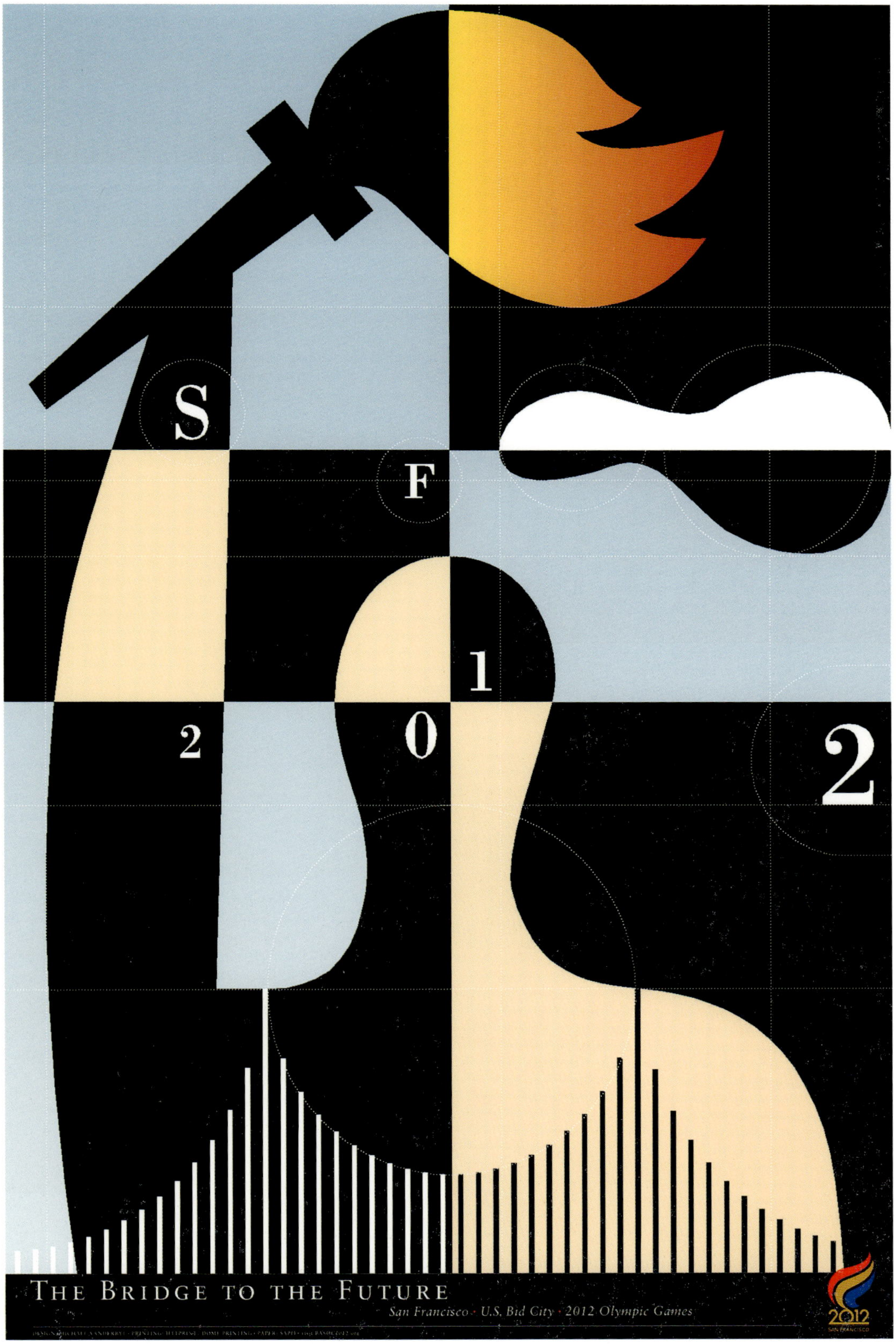

Design Firm: Vanderbyl Design Creative Director: Michael Vanderbyl Art Director: Michael Vanderbyl Designer: Michael Vanderbyl Illustrator: Michael Vanderbyl Client: Bay Area Sports Organizing Committee

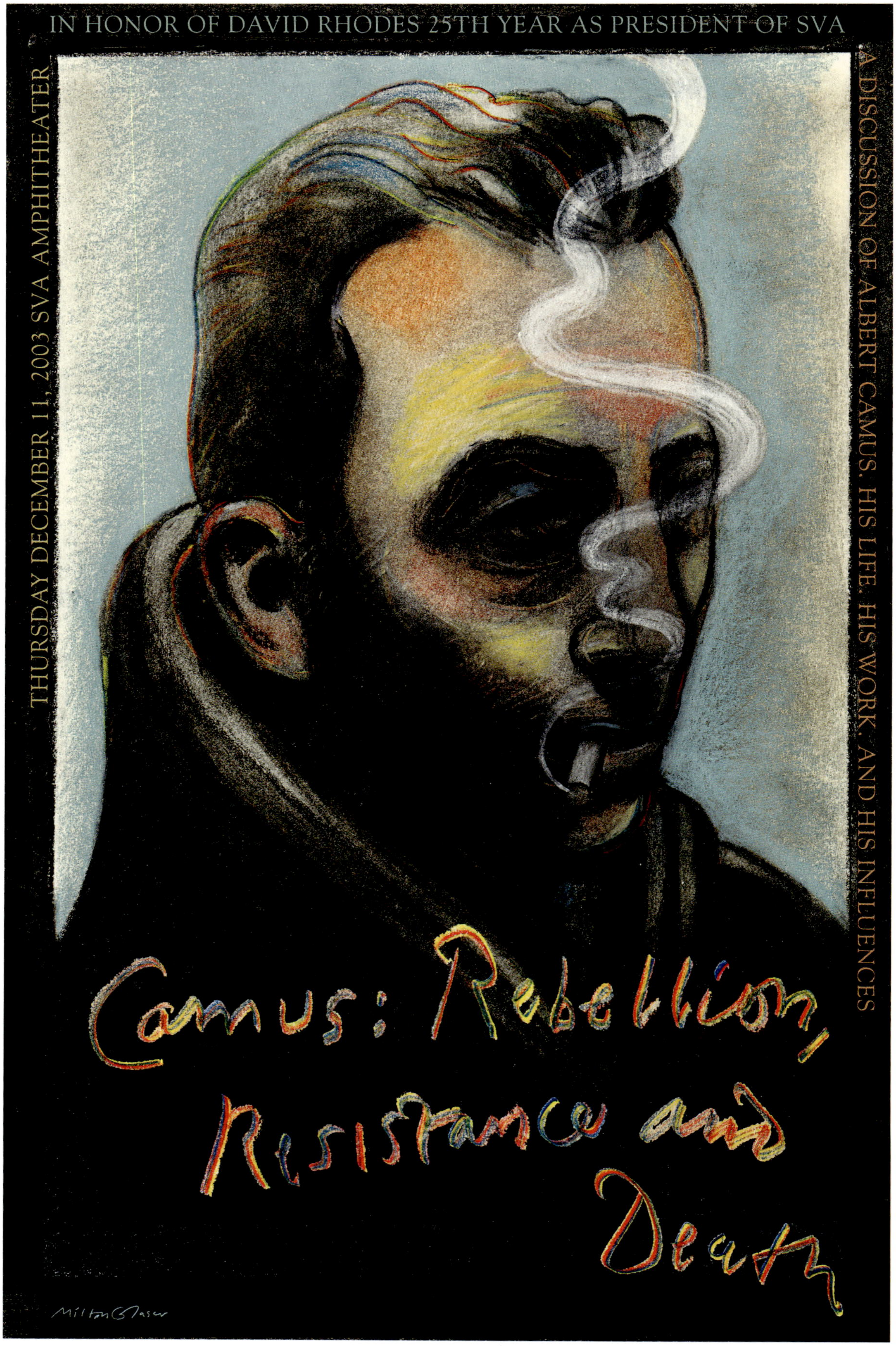

'Camus Poster' Design Firm: Milton Glaser Inc. Designer: Milton Glaser Illustrator: Milton Glaser Client: School of Visual Arts

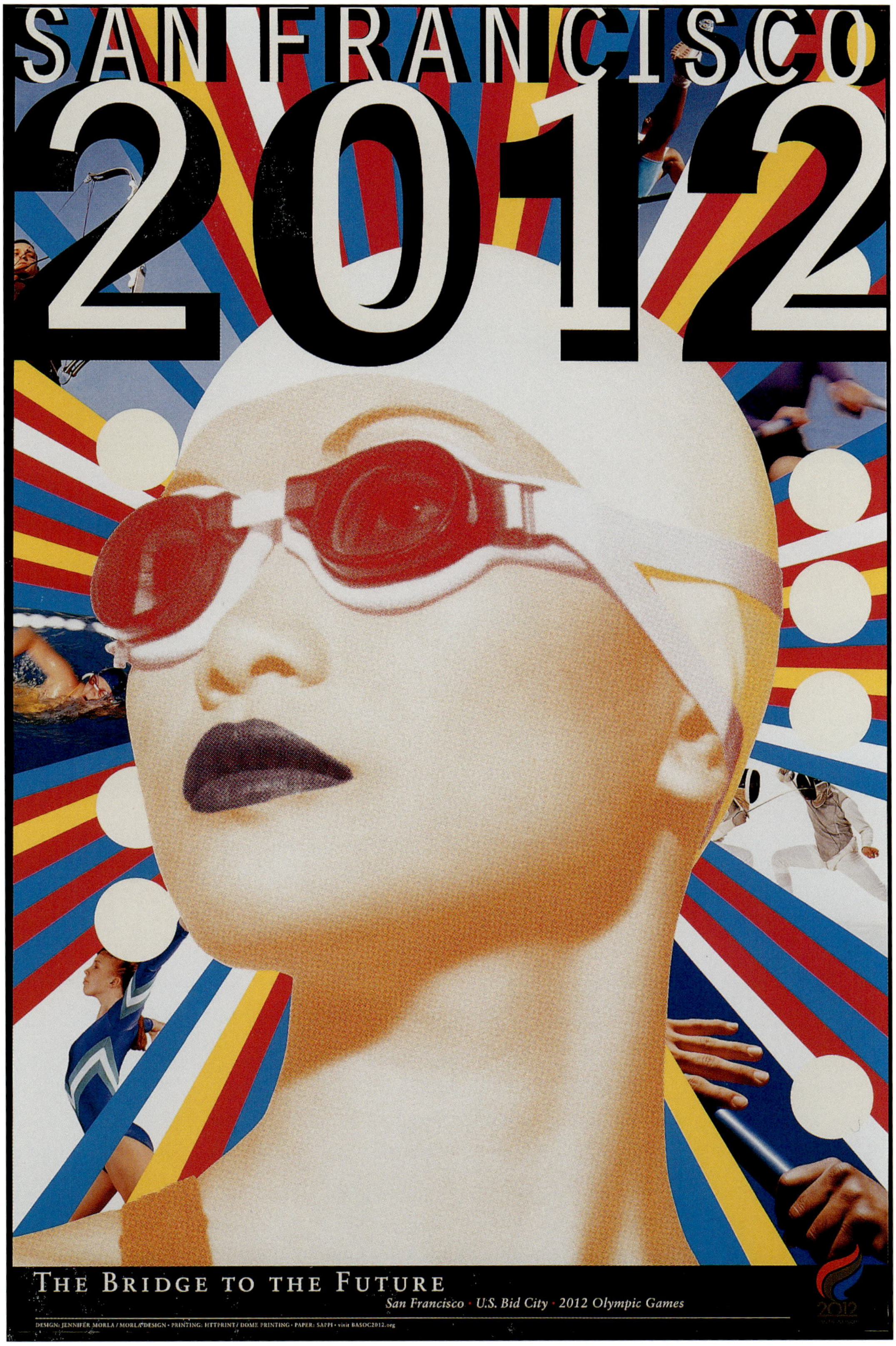

Design Firm: Morla Design Creative Director: Jennifer Morla Art Director: Jennifer Morla Designers: Jennifer Morla and Hizam Haron Photographer: Jock McDonald Client: San Francisco Bay Area Sports Organizing Committee

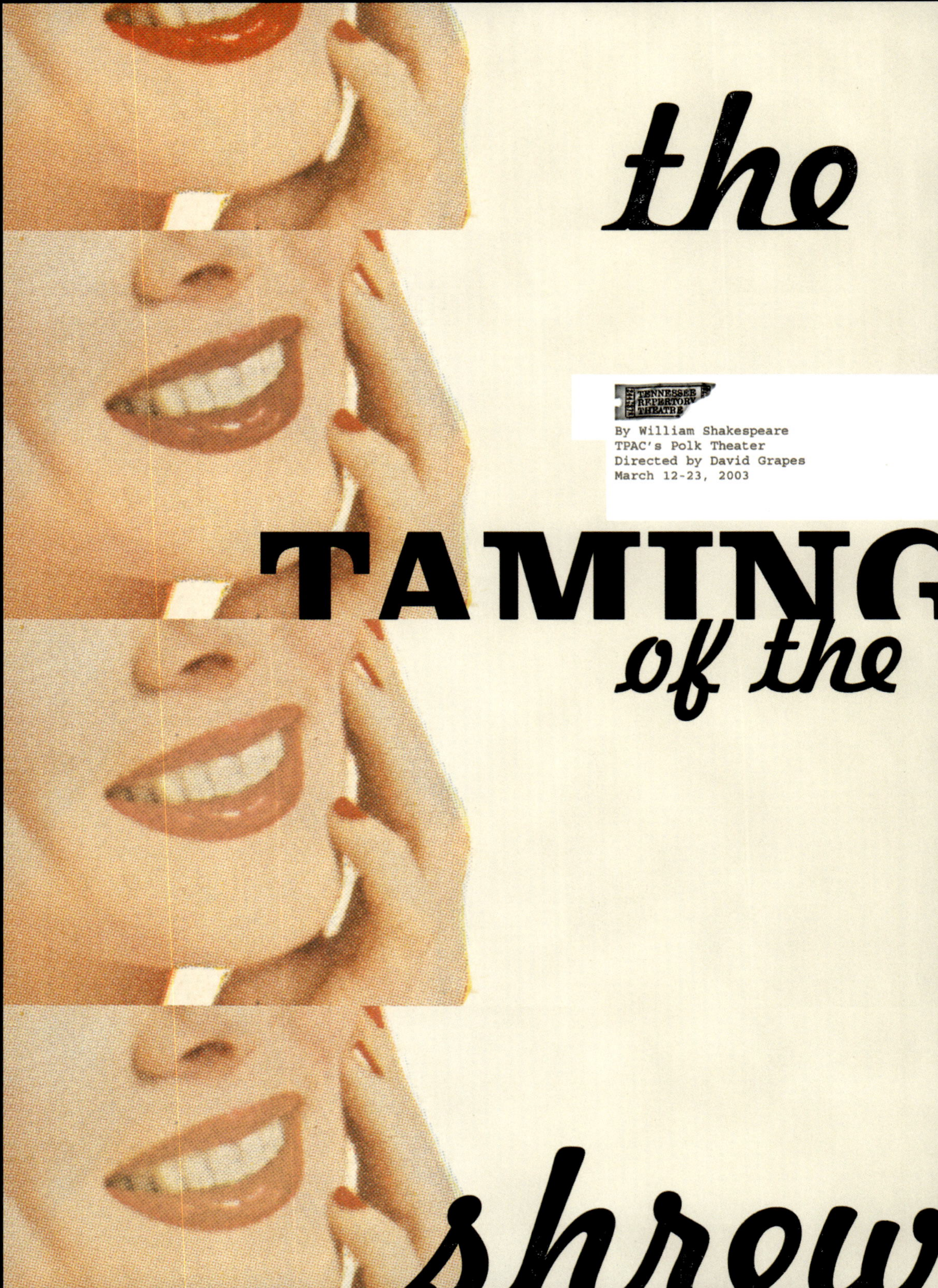

Taming of the Shrew' Design Firm: Th Designers: Blake Tannery and Clark Hook Client: Tennessee Repertory Theatre

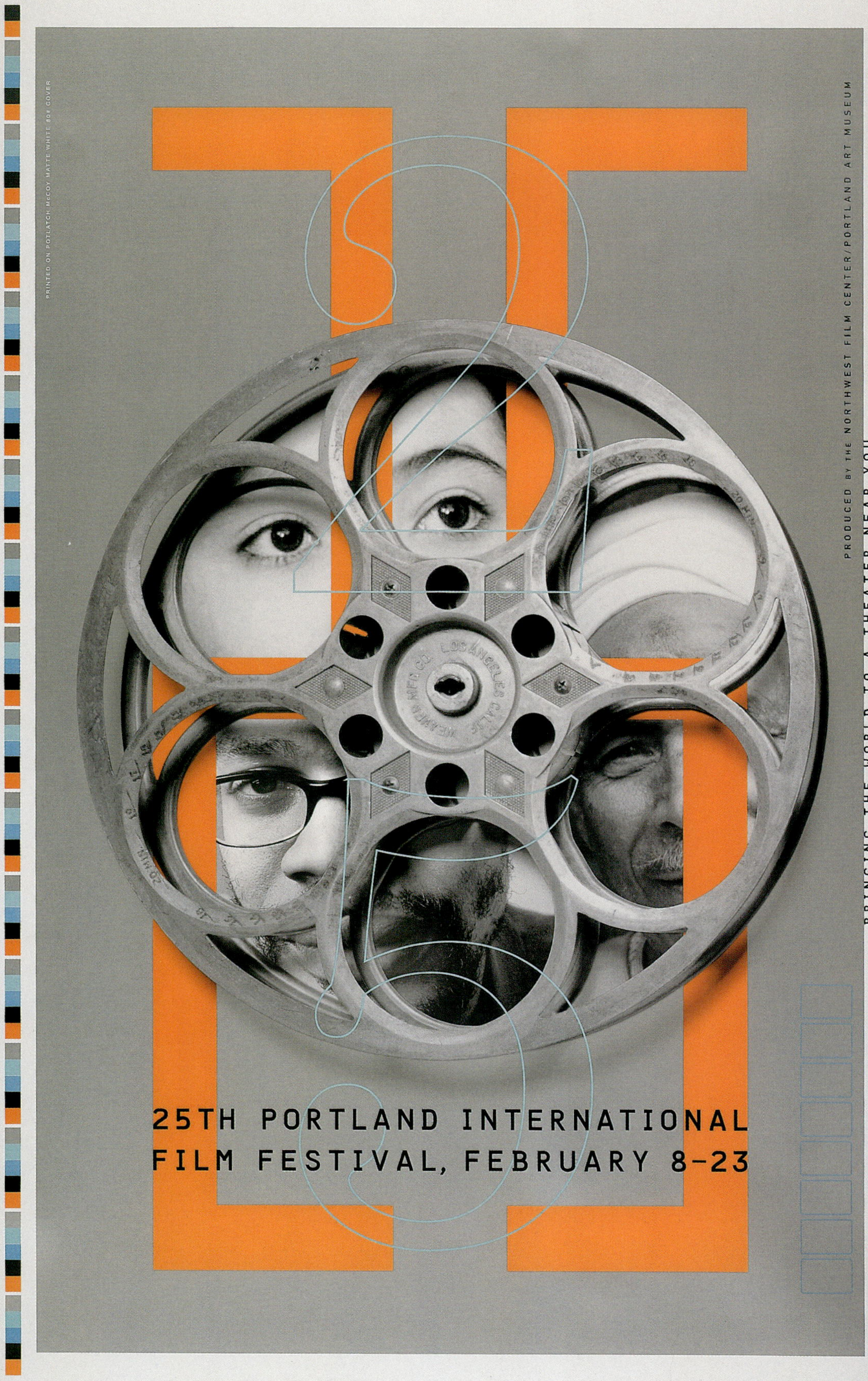
25TH PORTLAND INTERNATIONAL
FILM FESTIVAL, FEBRUARY 8–23
PRODUCED BY THE NORTHWEST FILM CENTER/PORTLAND ART MUSEUM
BRINGING THE WORLD TO A THEATER NEAR YOU
PRINTED ON POTLATCH MCCOY MATTE WHITE 80# COVER

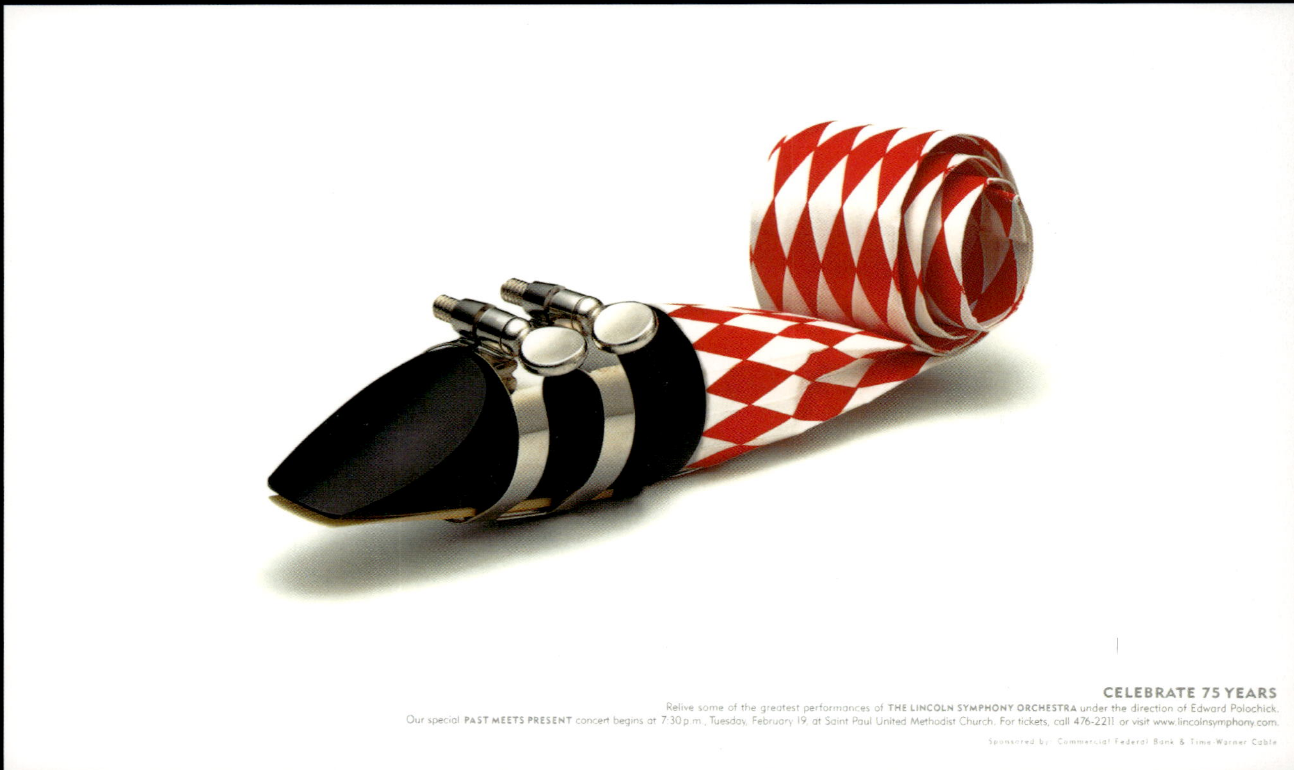

Bailey Lauerman Creative Director: Marty Amsler Art Director: Marty Amsler Designer: Thomas Irvin Photographer: Rick Neibel Account Coordinator: Becky Fujan Client: Lincoln Symphony

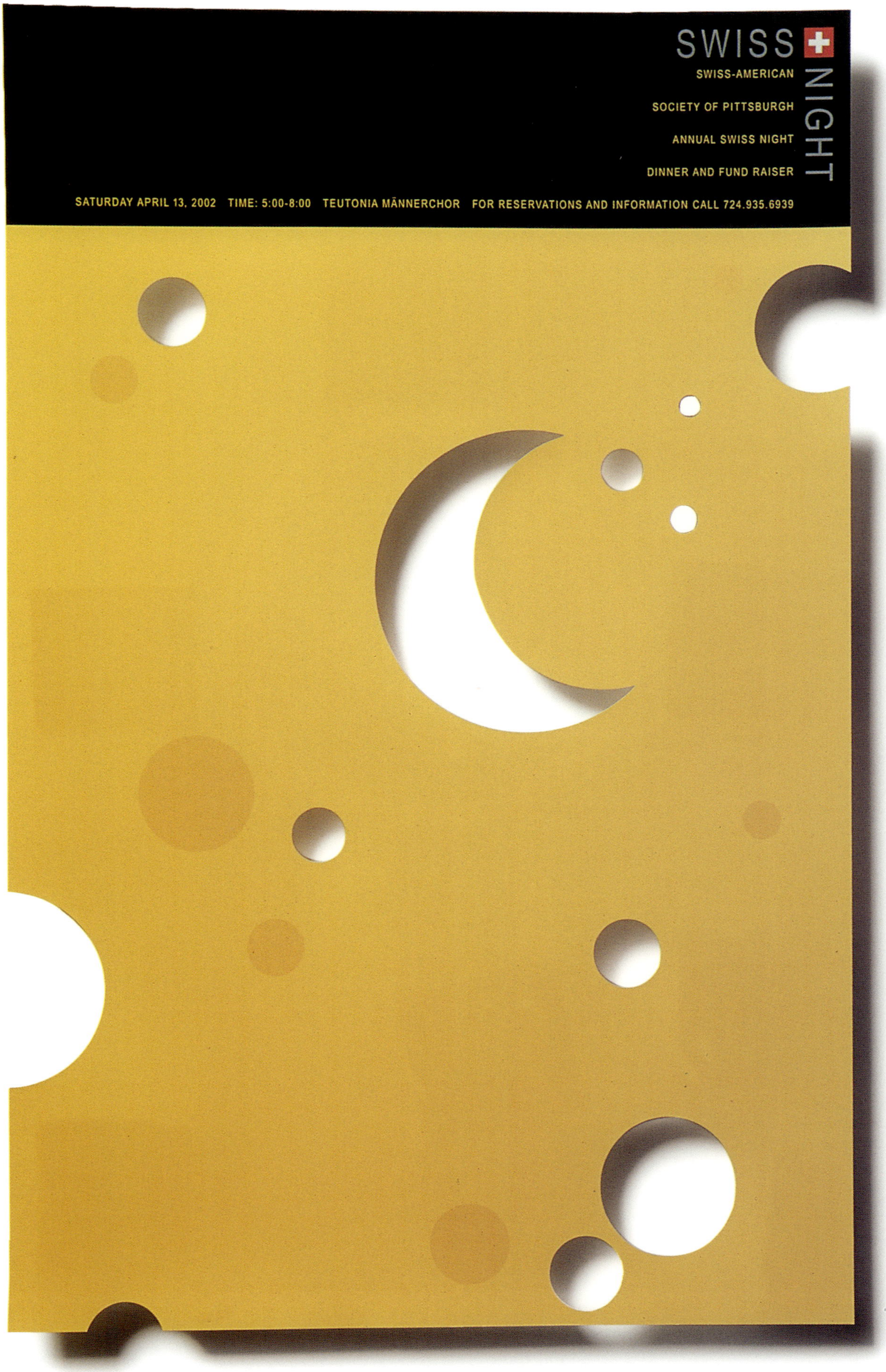

'Swiss Night' Design Firm: Blattner Brunner Creative Director: David Vissat Designer: David Vissat Production Supervisor: Ray Schmitt Client: Swiss American Society of Pittsburgh

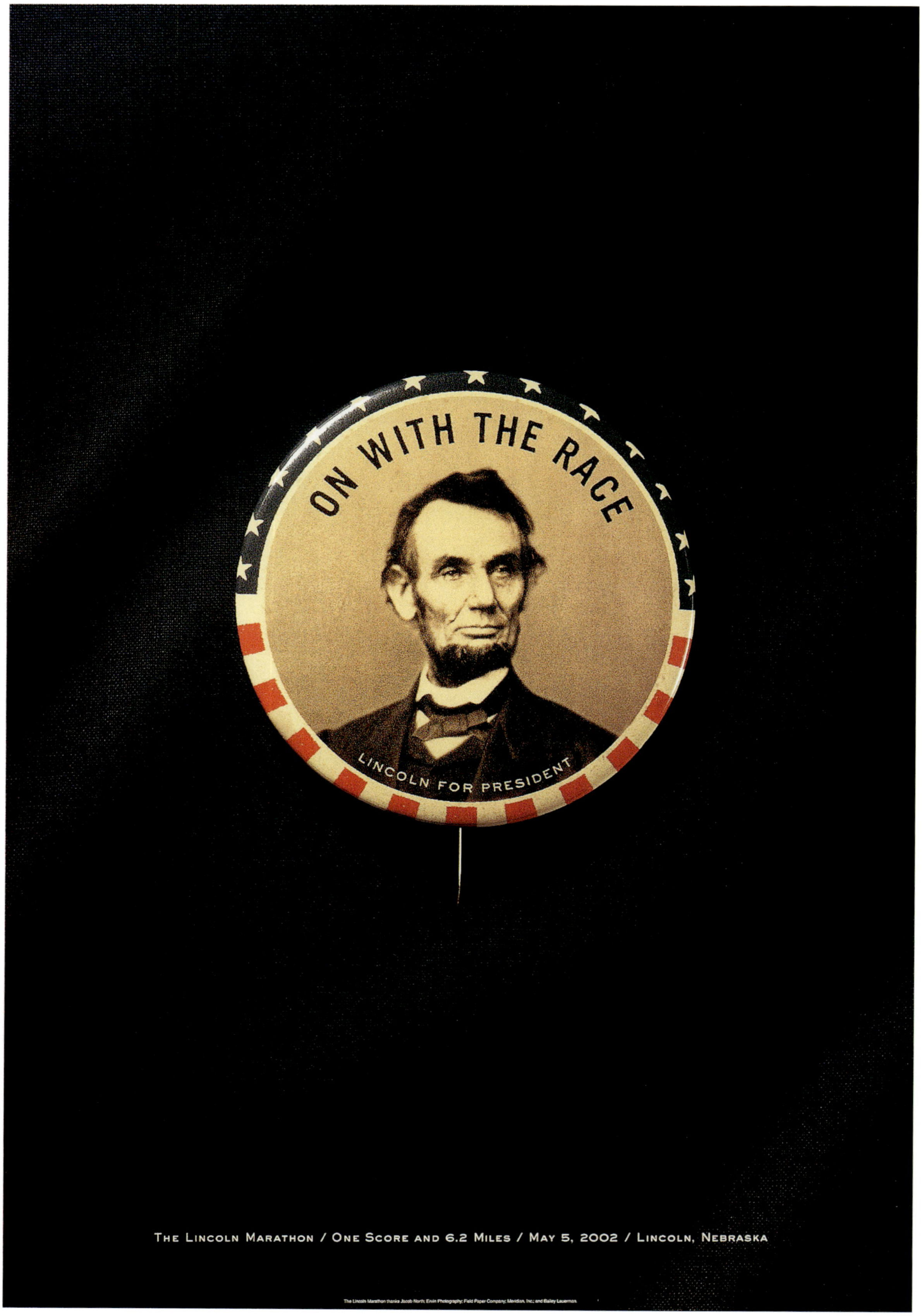

'On with the Race' Design Firm: Bailey Lauerman Creative Director: Carter Weitz Art Director: Ron Sack Designer: Ron Sack Photographers: Bob Ervin and Betteman Archive Illustrator: Joe McDermott Copywriter: John Vogel Client: Lincoln Marathon

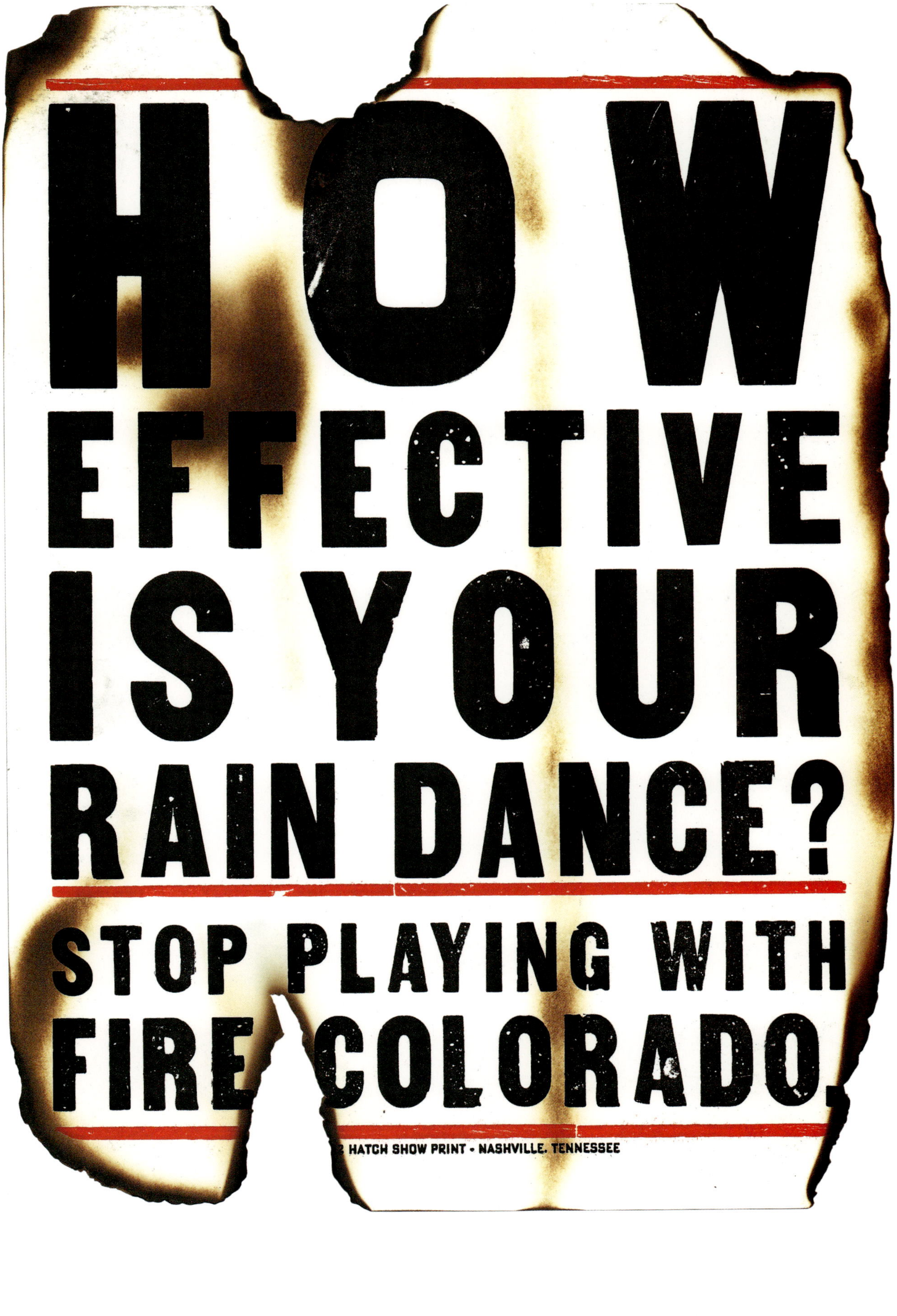

'Fire Poster' Design Firm: Cultivator Advertising & Design Creative Directors: Tim Abare and Chris Beatty Designers: Chris Beatty and August Sandberg Copywriter: Tim Abare Client: Colorado Wildlands

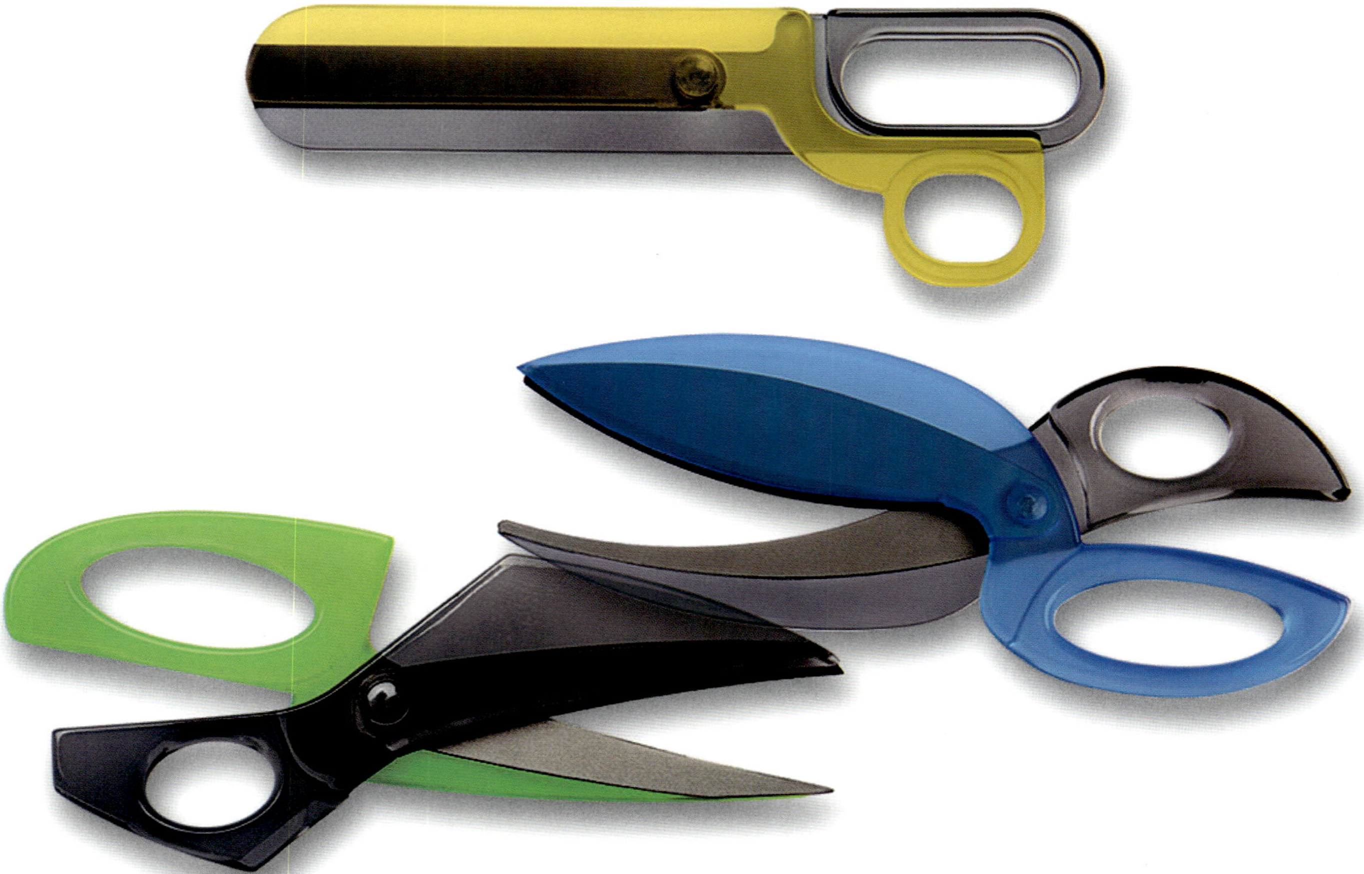

'X-Rays Scissor Product Design' Design Firm: Macey Noyes Associates Client: Acme UnitedDesign Firm Taku Satoh Design Office Inc. Art Director and Designer Taku Satoh Client Japan Graphic Designers Association Inc.

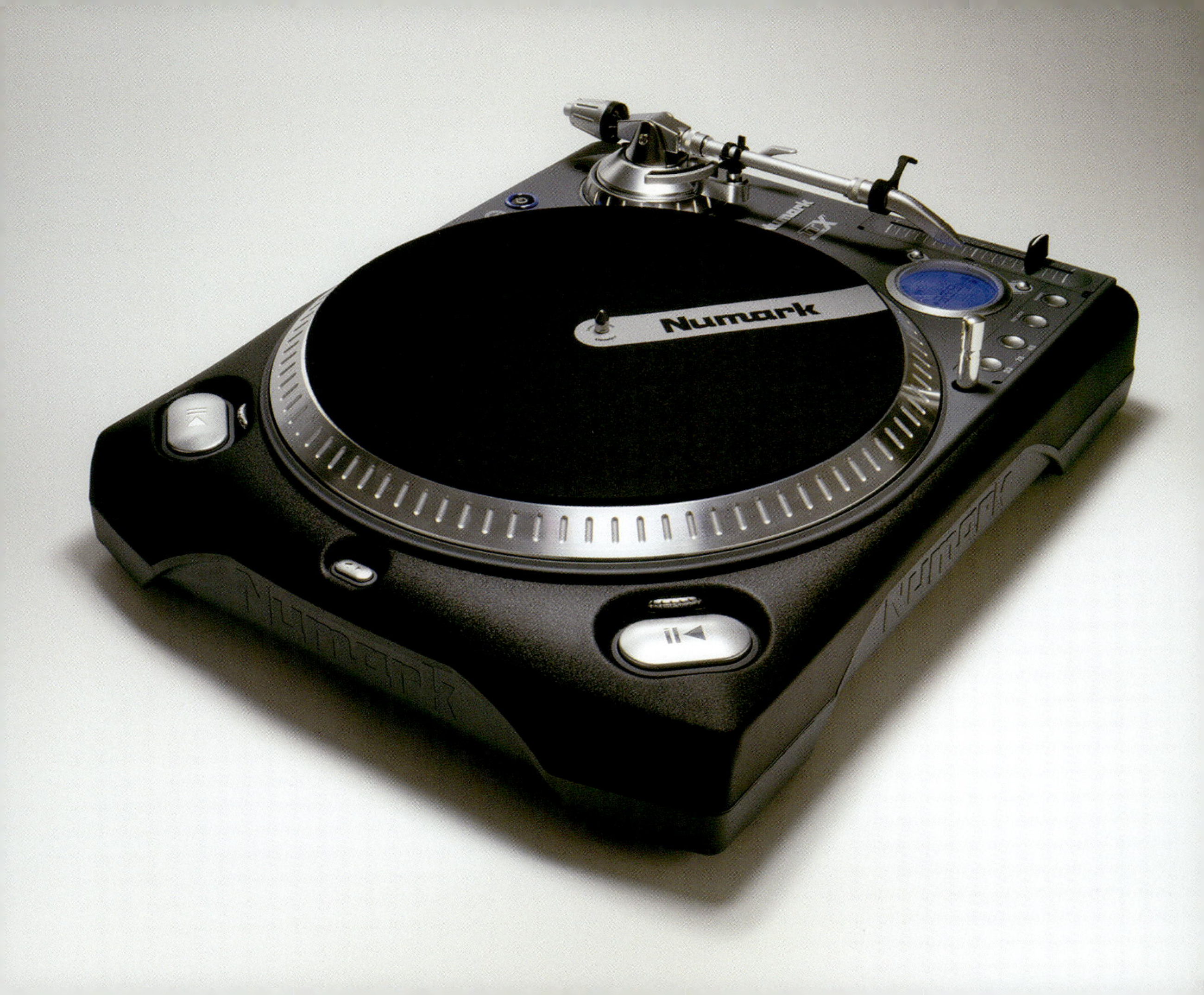
Numark

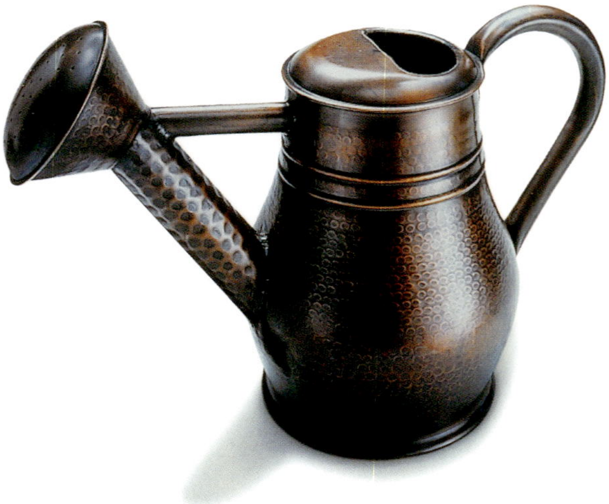

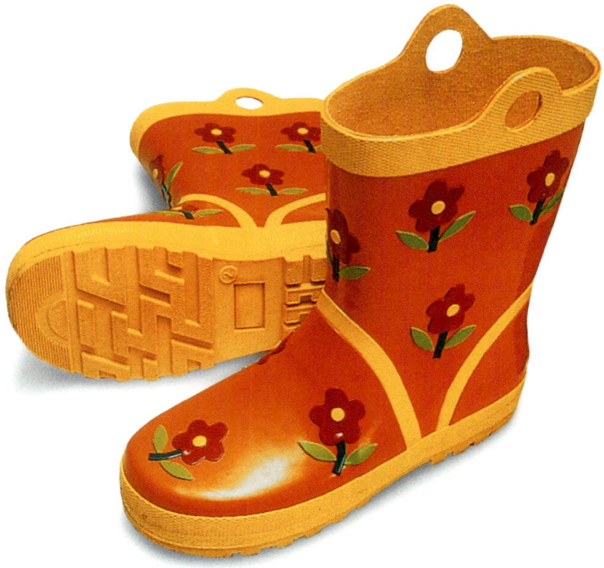

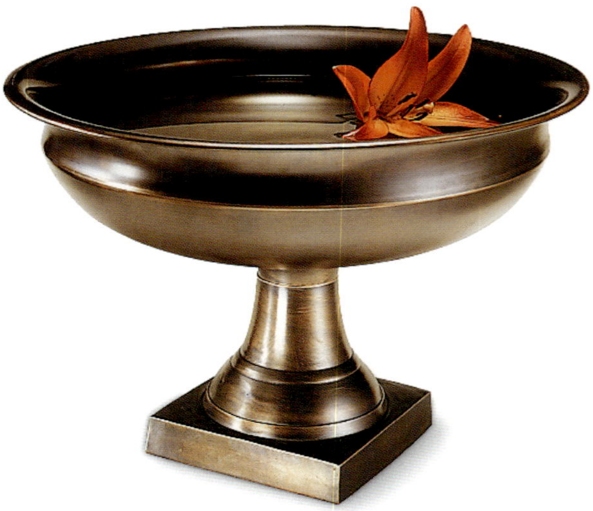

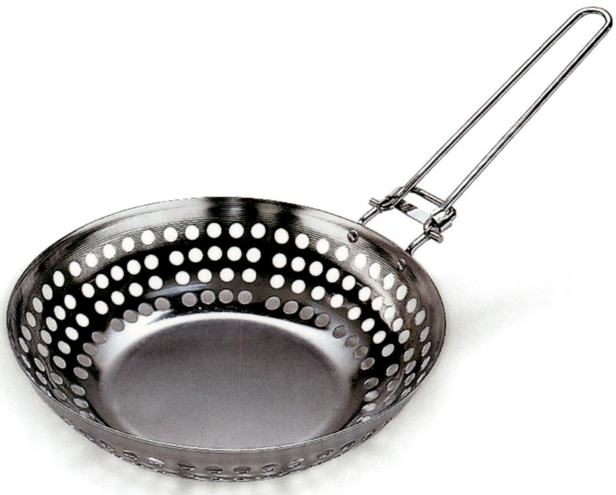

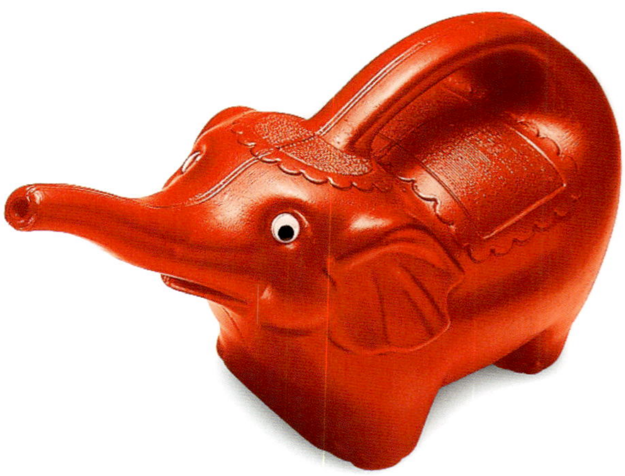

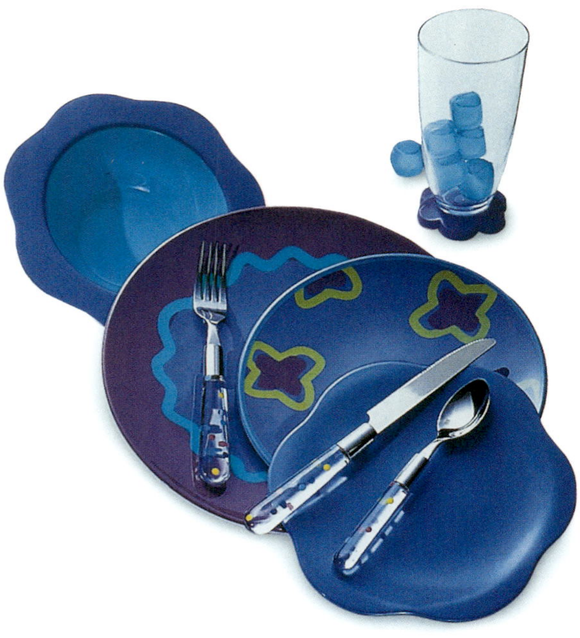

(this spread) 'Summer Entaining Press Kit' Design Firm: Graphic Culture Creative Director: Eric Erickson Art Directors: Cheryl Watson and John Mayhew Designer: Sharon McKendry Photographer: Patrick Fox Copywriter: Susan Bonne Client: Target Corporation

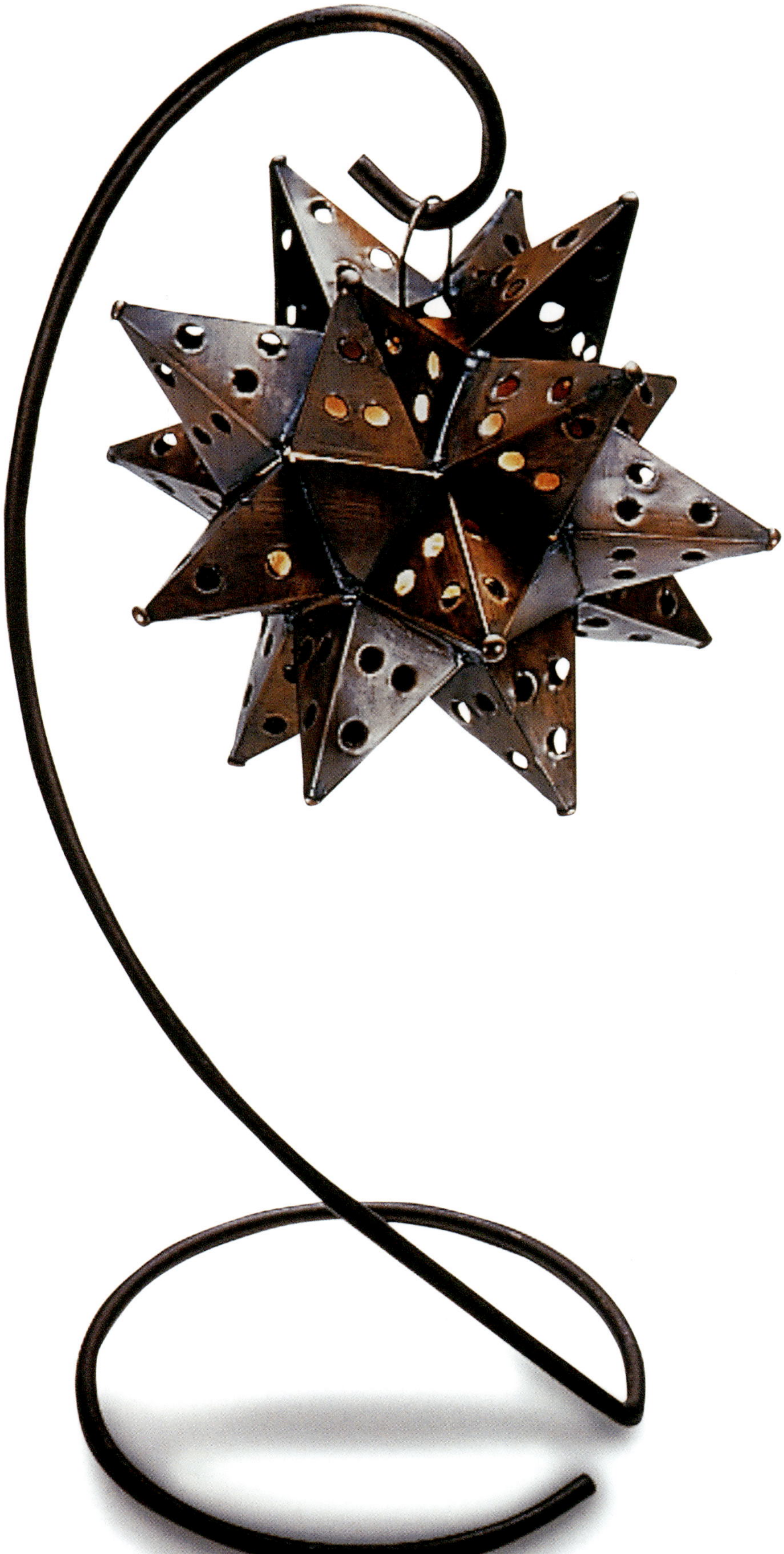

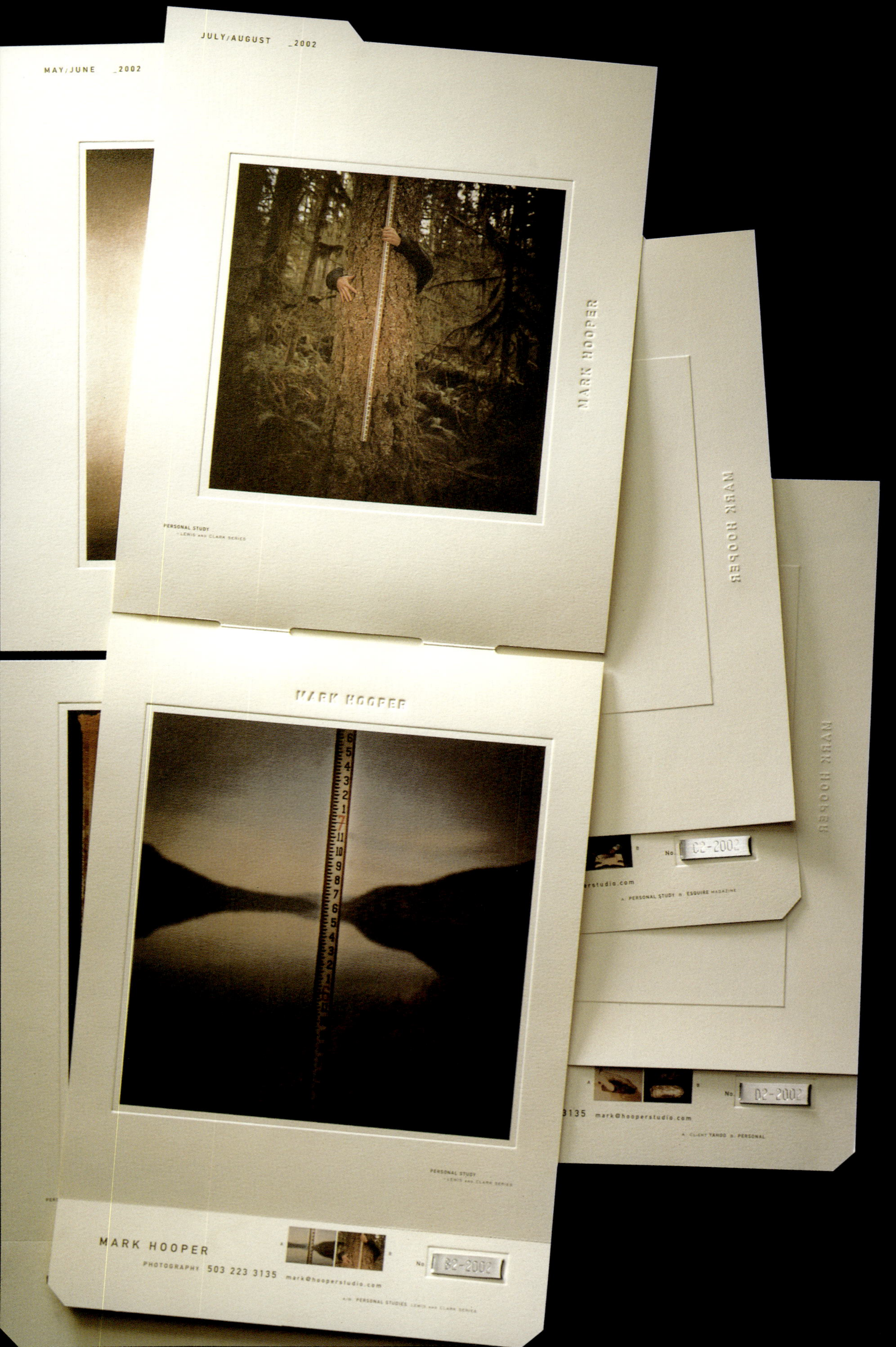
MAY/JUNE _2002
JULY/AUGUST _2002
MARK HOOPER
PERSONAL STUDY
LEWIS AND CLARK SERIES
MARK HOOPER
PHOTOGRAPHY 503 223 3135
mark@hooperstudio.com
No. 02-2002
A. PERSONAL STUDY B. ESQUIRE MAGAZINE

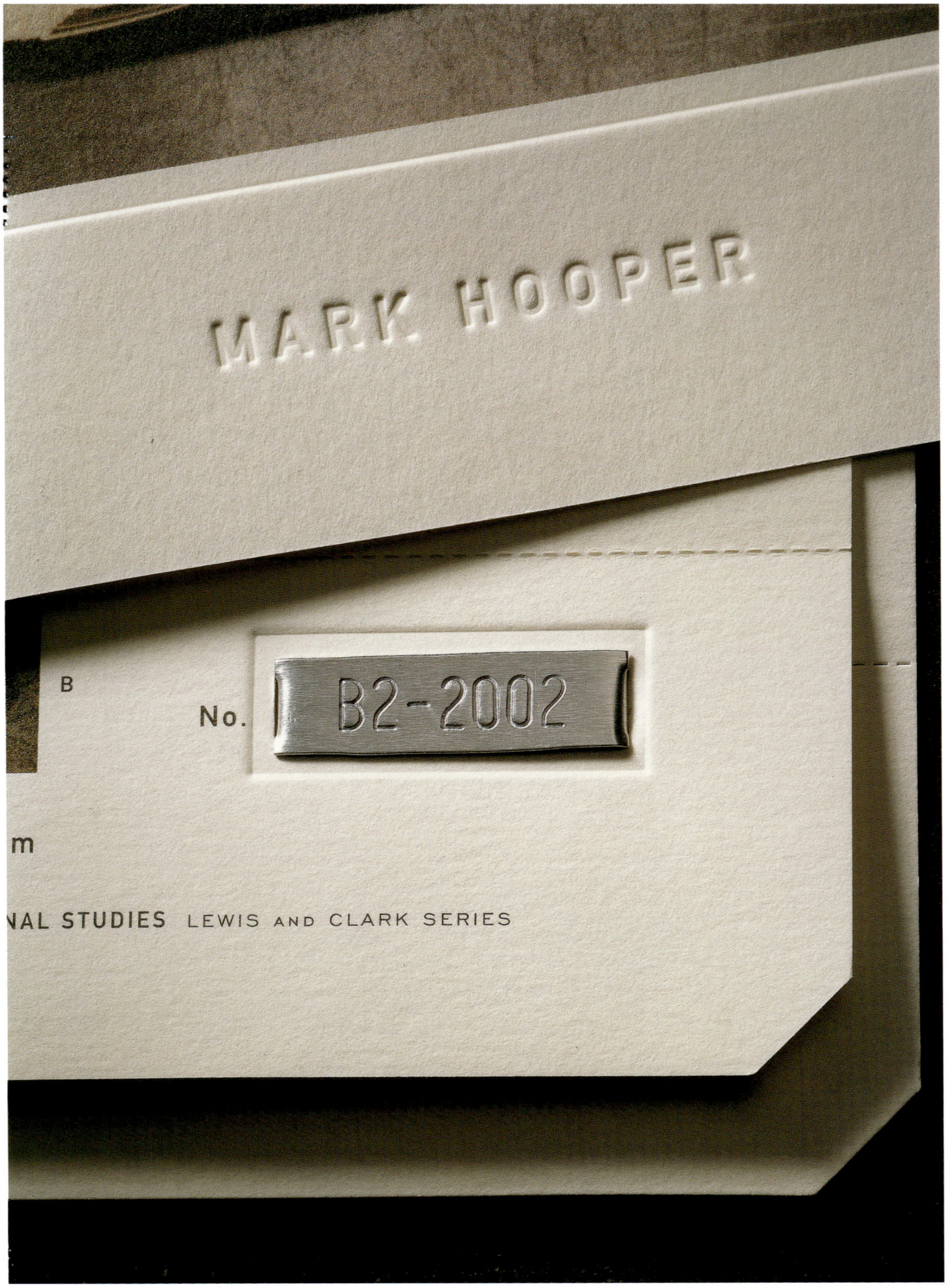

Design Firm: Sandstrom Design Creative Director: Steve Sandstrom Designer: Steve Sandstrom Photographer: Mark Hooper Production Designer: Starlee Matz Client: Mark Hooper

Creative Director: Stefan Sagmeister Art Director: Stefan Sagmeister Designer: Matthias Ernstberger Photographer: Tom Schierlitz Illustrator: Sabine Hug Copywriter: Stefan Sagmeister Client: Mak Vienna

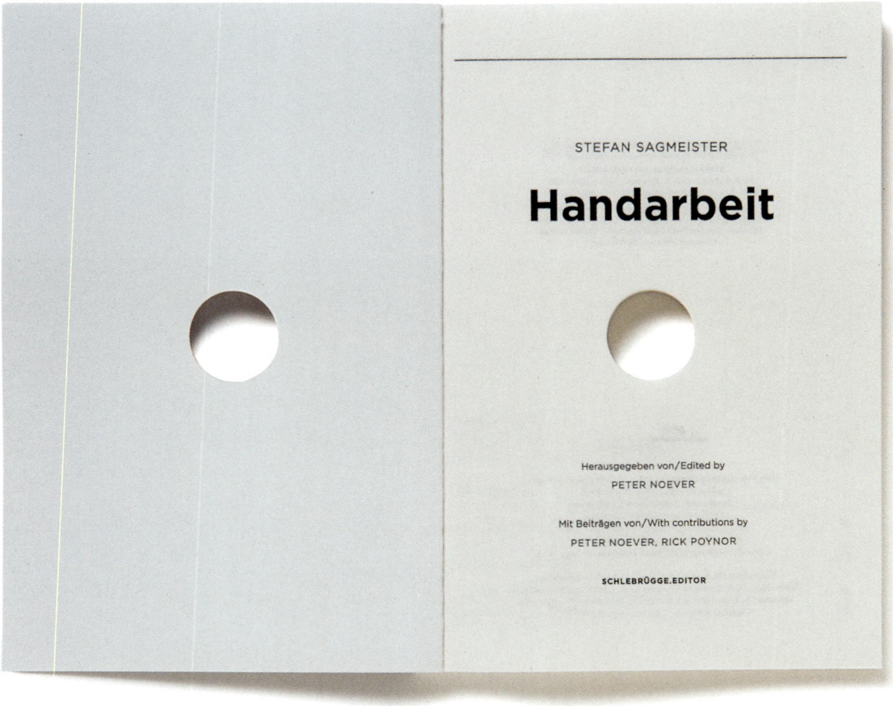

STEFAN SAGMEISTER

Handarbeit

Herausgegeben von/Edited by
PETER NOEVER

Mit Beiträgen von/With contributions by
PETER NOEVER, RICK POYNOR

SCHLEBRÜGGE.EDITOR

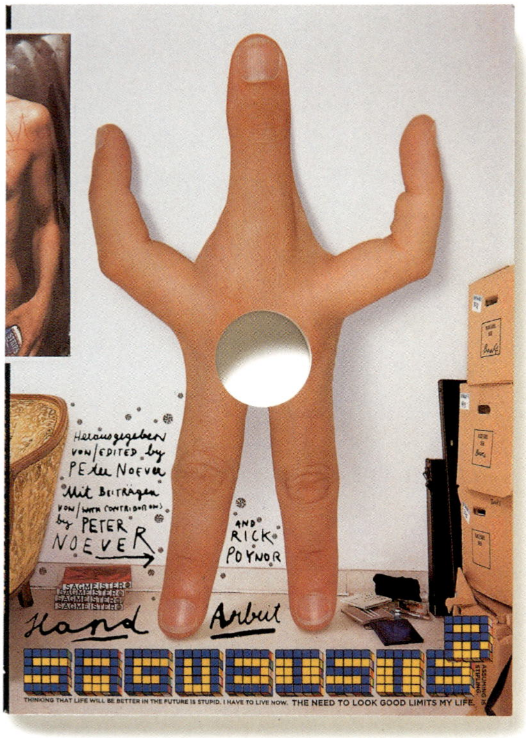

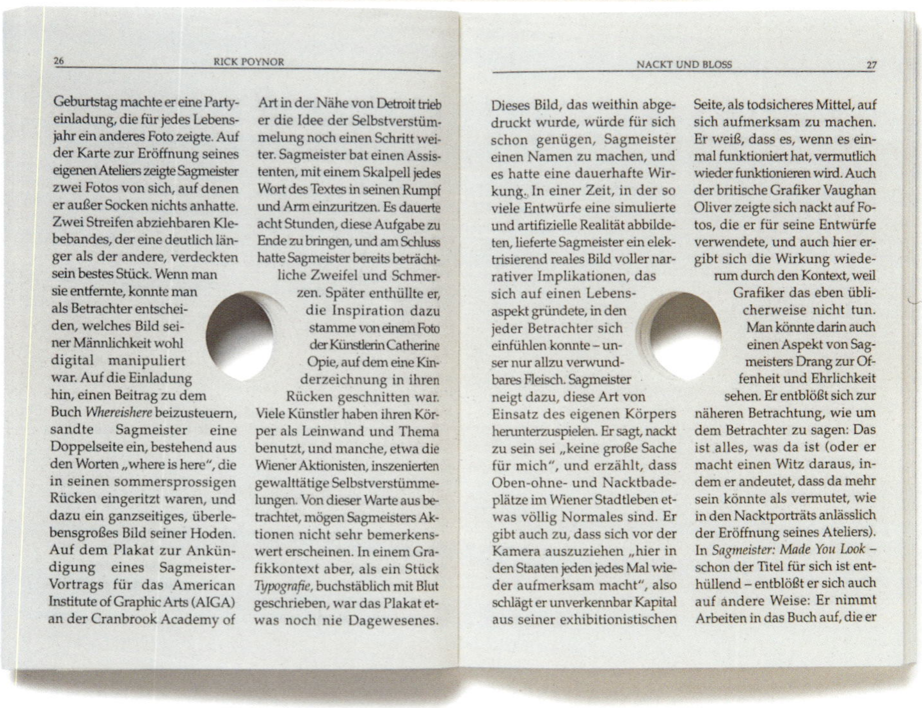

26 RICK POYNOR

Geburtstag machte er eine Partyeinladung, die für jedes Lebensjahr ein anderes Foto zeigte. Auf der Karte zur Eröffnung seines eigenen Ateliers zeigte Sagmeister zwei Fotos von sich, auf denen er außer Socken nichts anhatte. Zwei Streifen abziehbaren Klebebandes, der eine deutlich länger als der andere, verdeckten sein bestes Stück. Wenn man sie entfernte, konnte man als Betrachter entscheiden, welches Bild seiner Männlichkeit wohl digital manipuliert war. Auf die Einladung hin, einen Beitrag zu dem Buch *Whereishere* beizusteuern, sandte Sagmeister eine Doppelseite ein, bestehend aus den Worten „where is here", die in seinen sommersprossigen Rücken eingeritzt waren, und dazu ein ganzseitiges, überlebensgroßes Bild seiner Hoden. Auf dem Plakat zur Ankündigung eines Sagmeister-Vortrags für das American Institute of Graphic Arts (AIGA) an der Cranbrook Academy of Art in der Nähe von Detroit trieb er die Idee der Selbstverstümmelung noch einen Schritt weiter. Sagmeister bat einen Assistenten, mit einem Skalpell jedes Wort des Textes in seinen Rumpf und Arm einzuritzen. Es dauerte acht Stunden, diese Aufgabe zu Ende zu bringen, und am Schluss hatte Sagmeister bereits beträchtliche Zweifel und Schmerzen. Später enthüllte er, die Inspiration dazu stamme von einem Foto der Künstlerin Catherine Opie, auf dem eine Kinderzeichnung in ihren Rücken geschnitten war. Viele Künstler haben ihren Körper als Leinwand und Thema benutzt, und manche, etwa die Wiener Aktionisten, inszenierten gewalttätige Selbstverstümmelungen. Von dieser Warte aus betrachtet, mögen Sagmeisters Aktionen nicht sehr bemerkenswert erscheinen. In einem Grafikkontext aber, als ein Stück *Typografie*, buchstäblich mit Blut geschrieben, war das Plakat etwas noch nie Dagewesenes.

NACKT UND BLOSS 27

Dieses Bild, das weithin abgedruckt wurde, würde für sich schon genügen, Sagmeister einen Namen zu machen, und es hatte eine dauerhafte Wirkung. In einer Zeit, in der so viele Entwürfe eine simulierte und artifizielle Realität abbildeten, lieferte Sagmeister ein elektrisierend reales Bild voller narrativer Implikationen, das sich auf einen Lebensaspekt gründete, in den jeder Betrachter sich einfühlen konnte – unser nur allzu verwundbares Fleisch. Sagmeister neigt dazu, diese Art von Einsatz des eigenen Körpers herunterzuspielen. Er sagt, nackt zu sein sei „keine große Sache für mich", und erzählt, dass Oben-ohne- und Nacktbadeplätze im Wiener Stadtleben etwas völlig Normales sind. Er gibt auch zu, dass sich vor der Kamera auszuziehen „hier in den Staaten jeden jedes Mal wieder aufmerksam macht", also schlägt er unverkennbar Kapital aus seiner exhibitionistischen Seite, als todsicheres Mittel, auf sich aufmerksam zu machen. Er weiß, dass es, wenn es einmal funktioniert hat, vermutlich wieder funktionieren wird. Auch der britische Grafiker Vaughan Oliver zeigte sich nackt auf Fotos, die er für seine Entwürfe verwendete, und auch hier ergibt sich die Wirkung wiederum durch den Kontext, weil Grafiker das eben üblicherweise nicht tun. Man könnte darin auch einen Aspekt von Sagmeisters Drang zur Offenheit und Ehrlichkeit sehen. Er entblößt sich zur näheren Betrachtung, wie um dem Betrachter zu sagen: Das ist alles, was da ist (oder er macht einen Witz daraus, indem er andeutet, dass da mehr sein könnte als vermutet, wie in den Nacktporträts anlässlich der Eröffnung seines Ateliers). In *Sagmeister: Made You Look* – schon der Titel für sich ist enthüllend – entblößt er sich auch auf andere Weise: Er nimmt Arbeiten in das Buch auf, die er

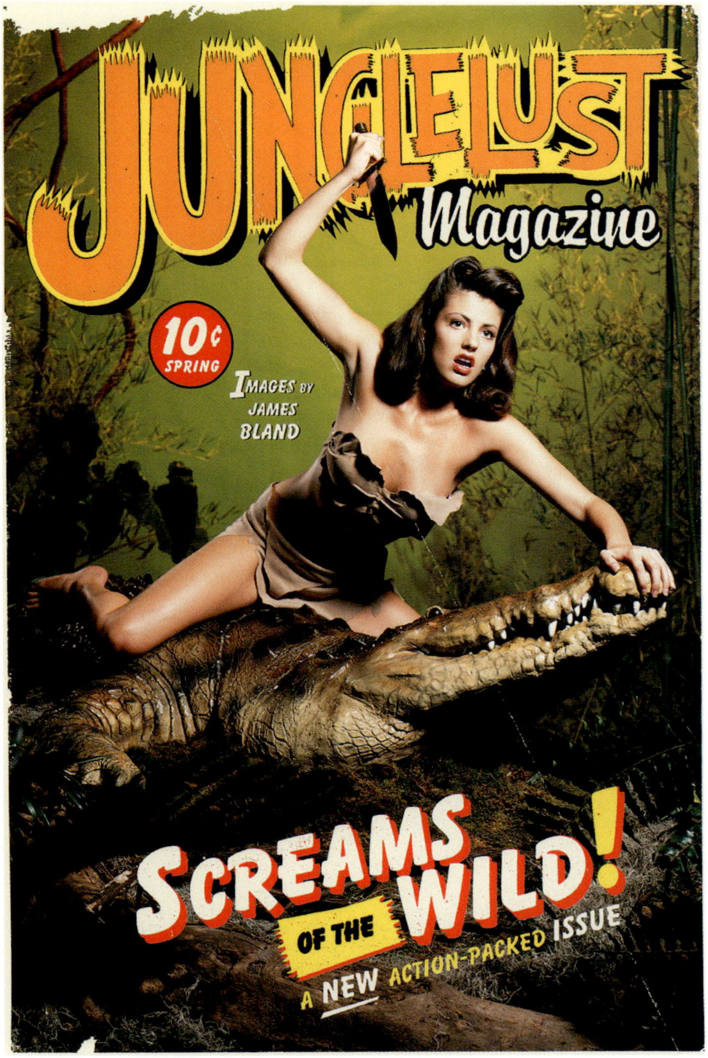

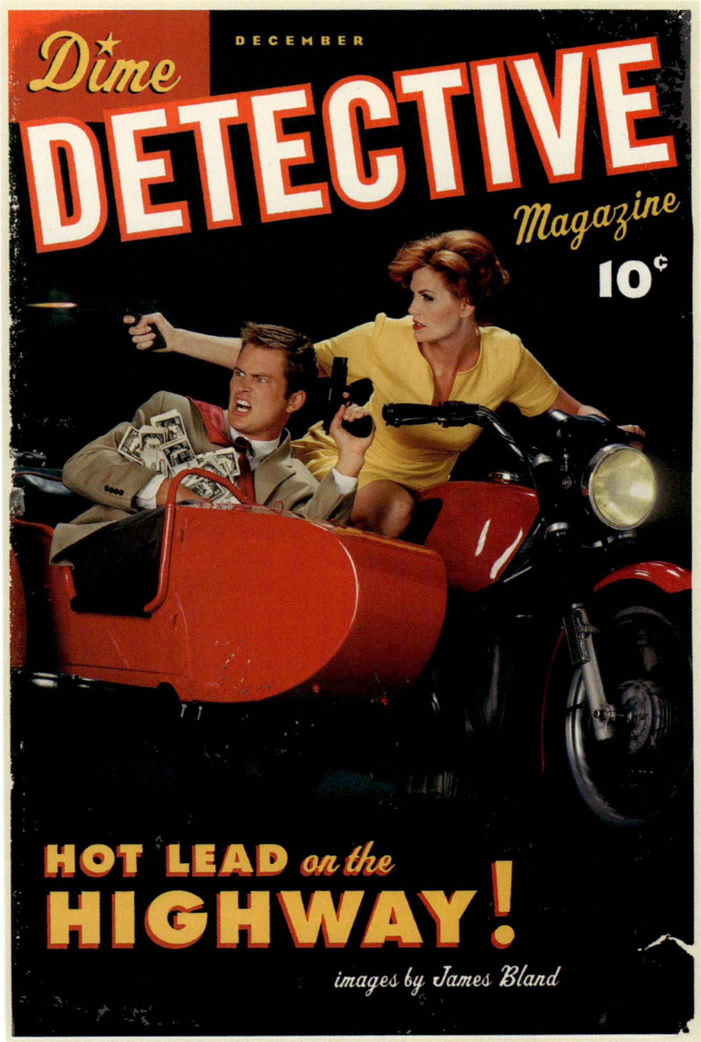

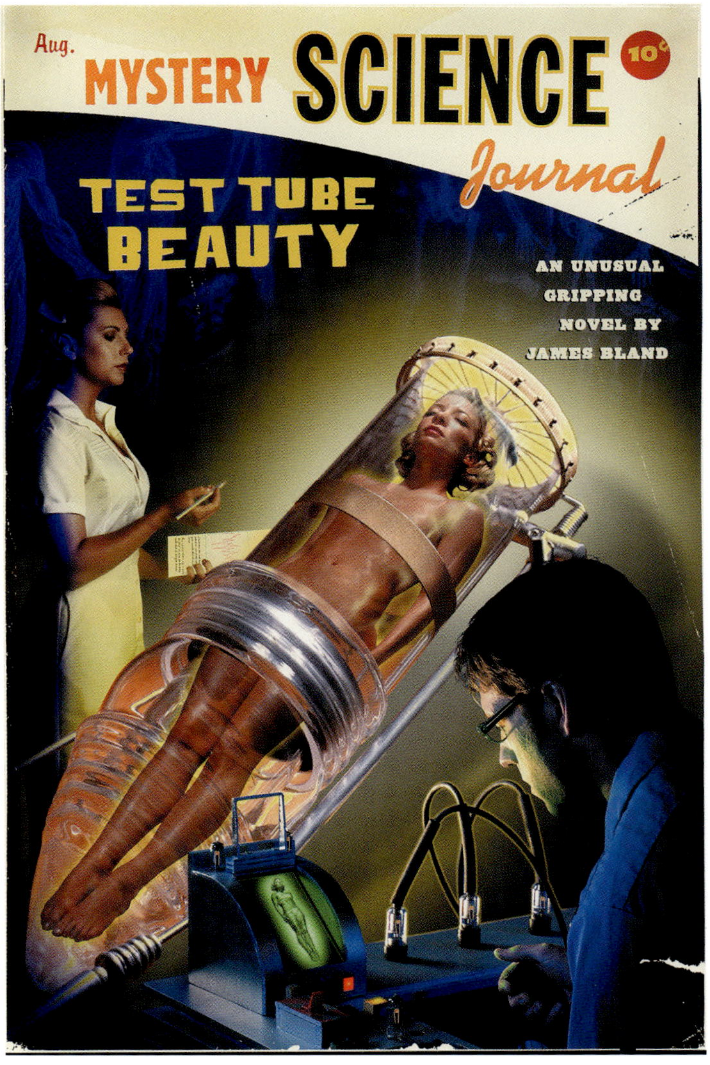

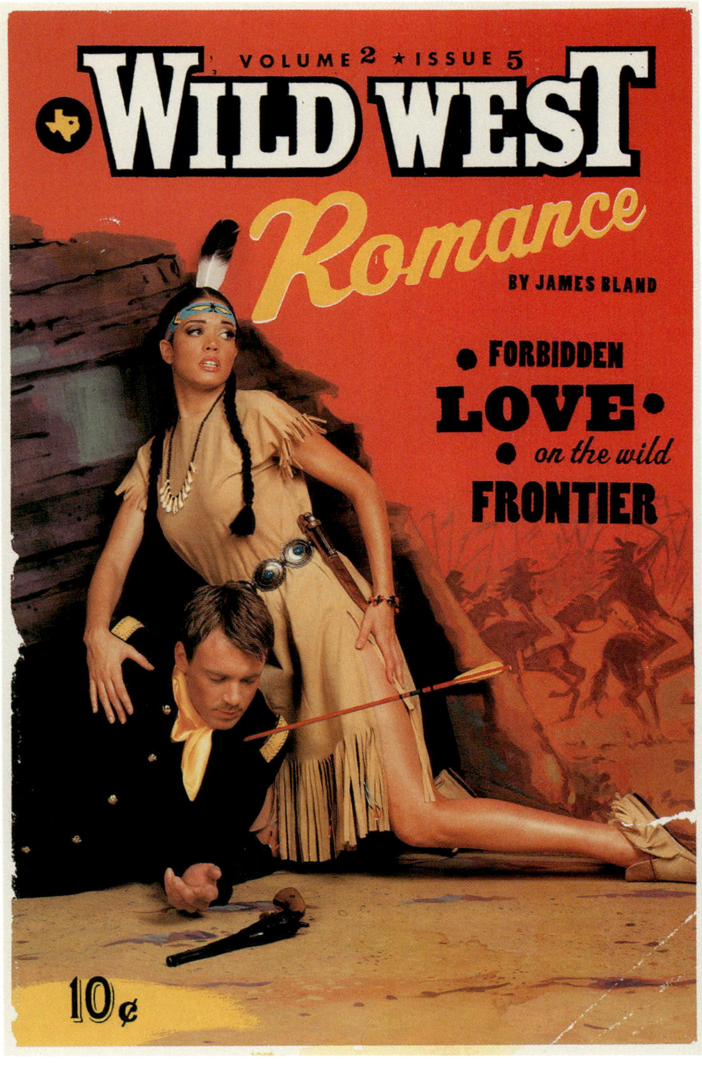

Design Firm: Squires and Company Creative Director: Brandon Murphy Art Director: James Bland Designers: Adam Hallmark, Bret Sano, Amy Folkins and Brandon Murphy Photographer: Max Wright Photo Retouching: Les Hall Copywriter: James Bland Client: James Bland

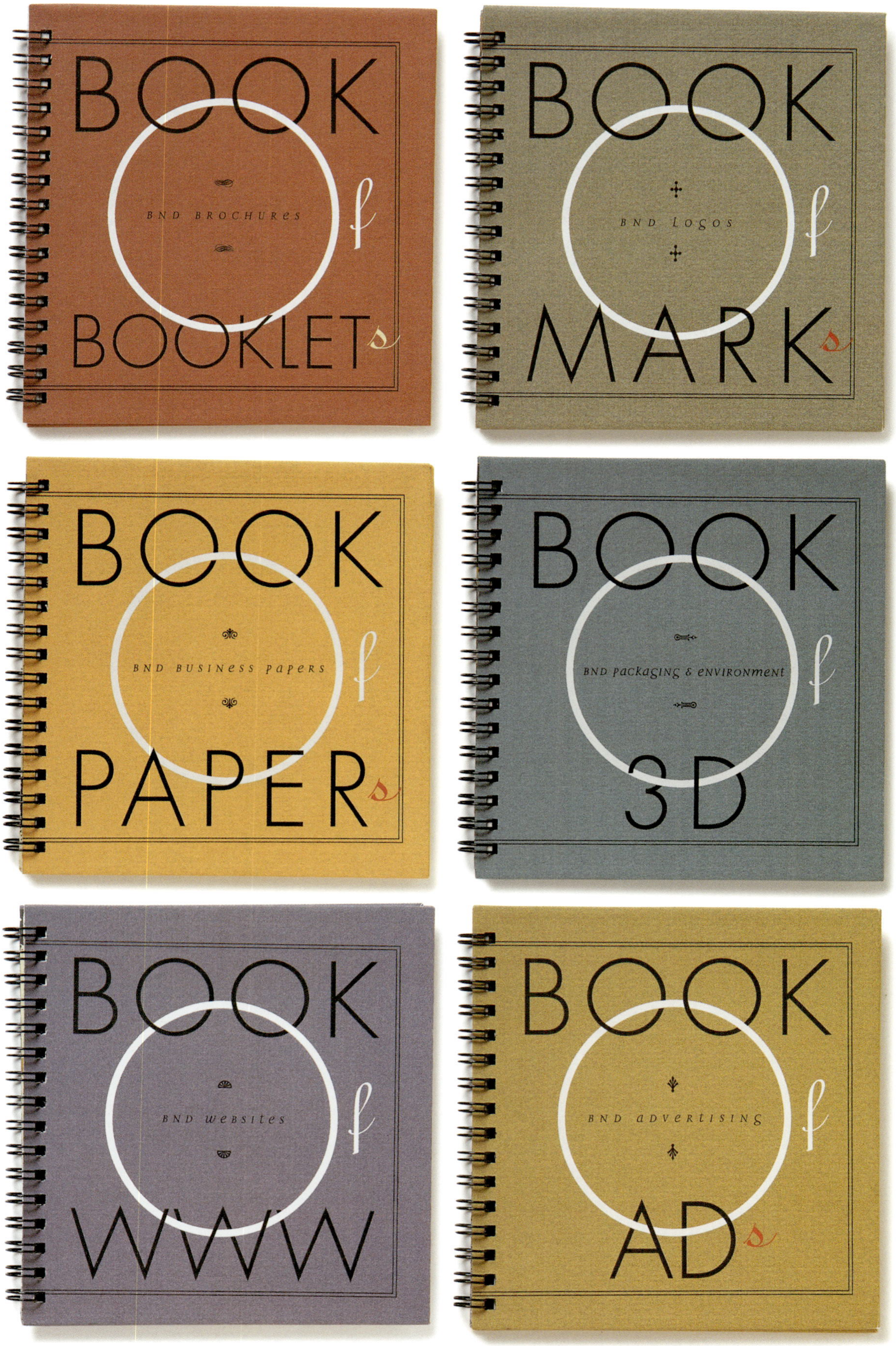

'BND Design Library' Design Firm: Brad Norr Design (BND) Art Director: Brad D. Norr Designers: Brad D. Norr, Daniel Landerson, Andrew Bessler and Michael White Illustrators: Darrell Gager and Steve Kemmerung Client: BND

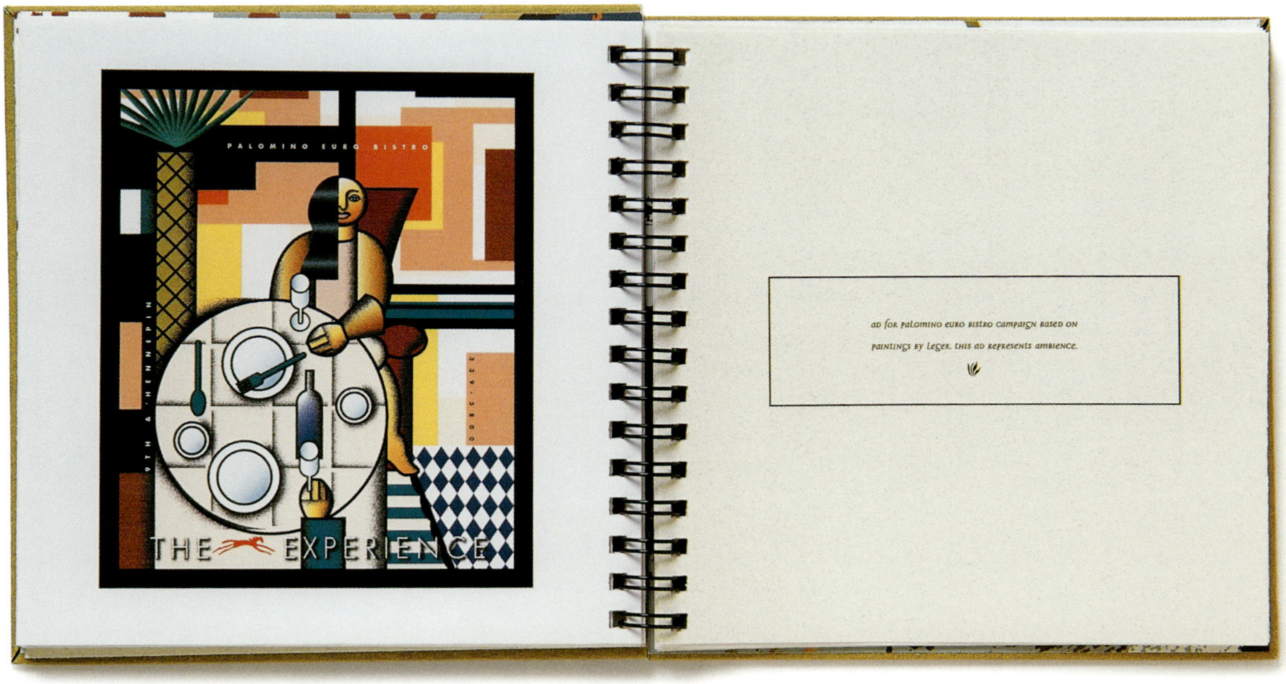

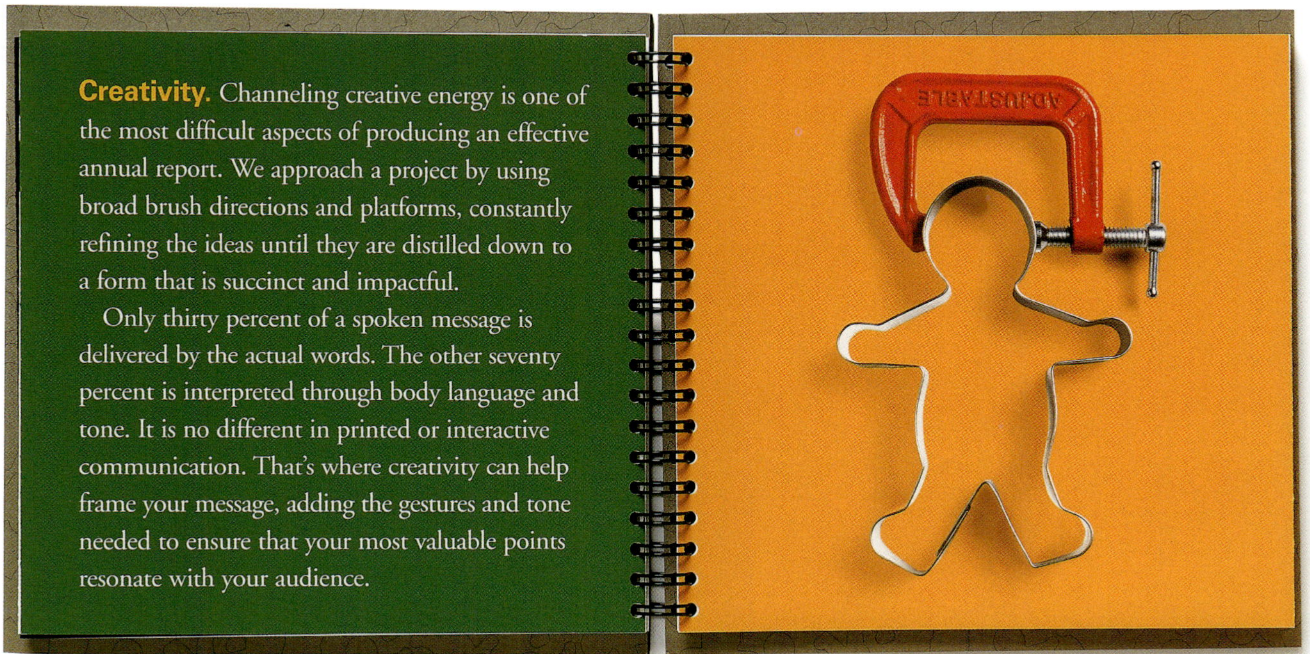

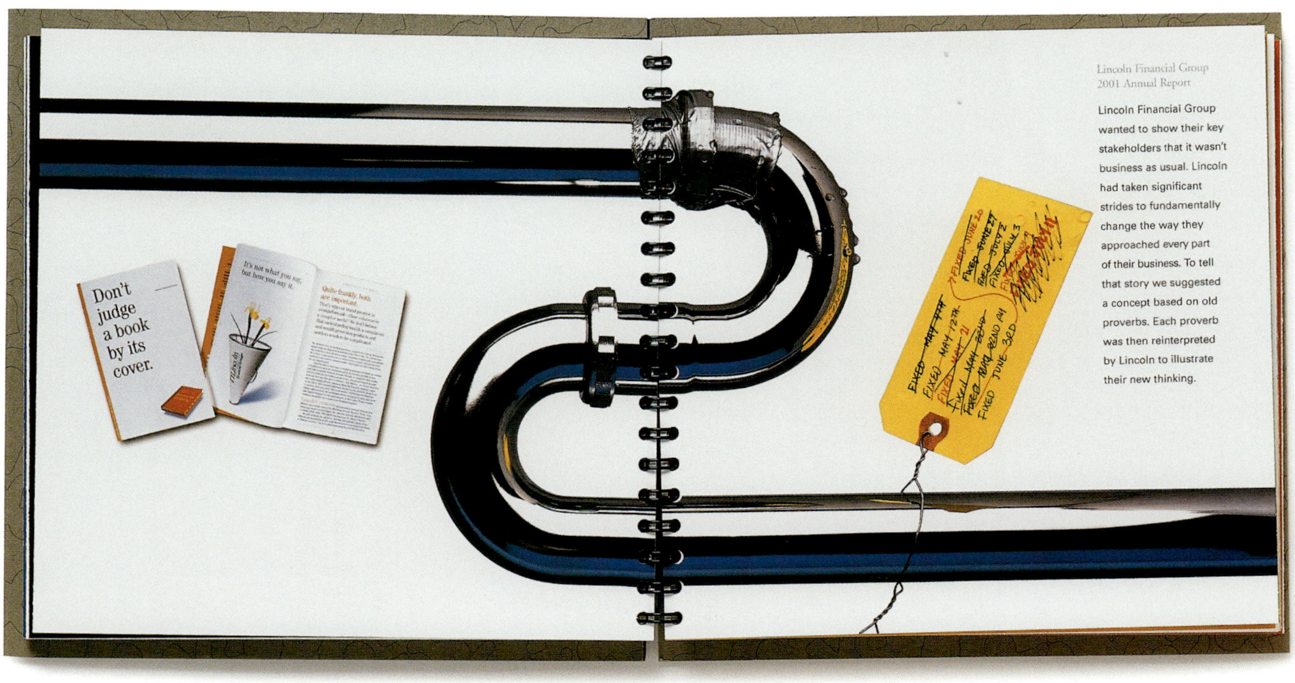

'Break The Mold' Design Firm: Bertz Design Group Art Director: Ted Bertz Designers: Chris Hyde and Andrew Wessels Copywriter: Chris Hyde Client: Bertz Design Group

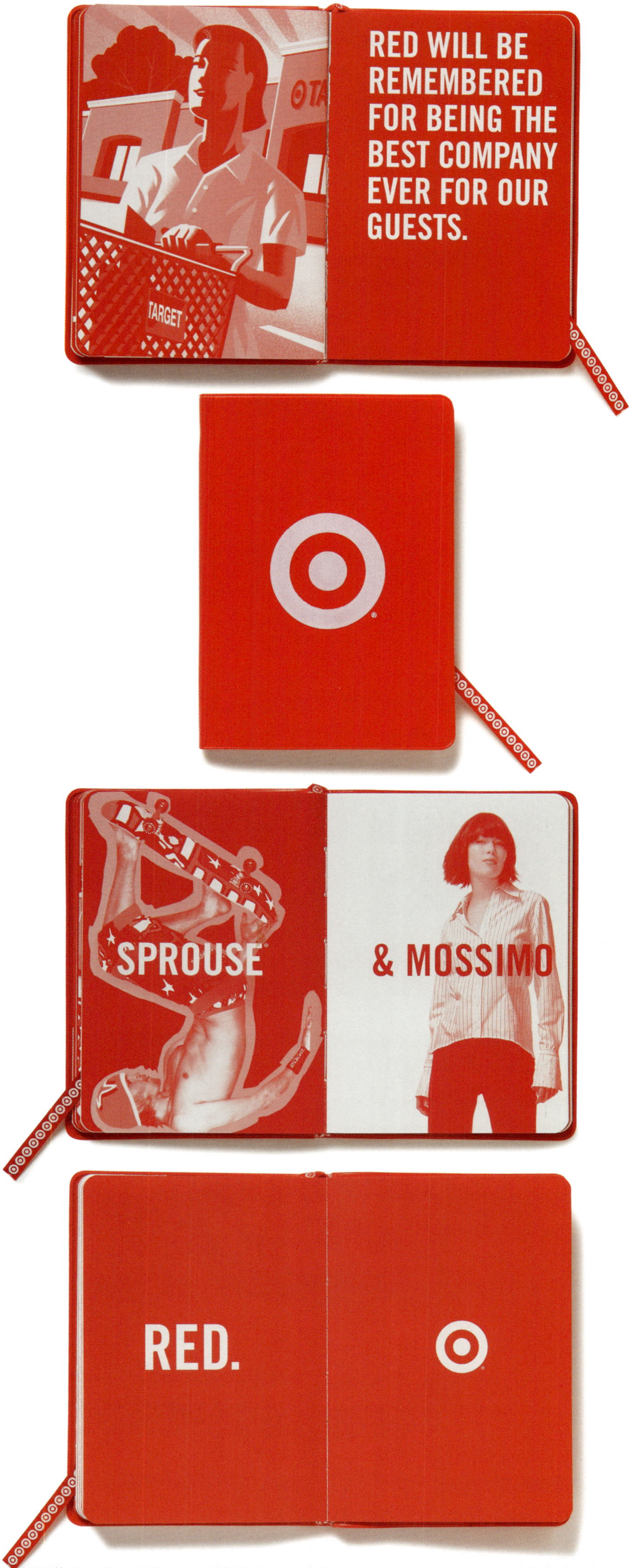

'The Ulrich Book' Design Firm: Little & Company Creative Director: Michael Schacherer Art Director: Michael Schacherer Designer: Monica Little Designer: Michael Schacherer Client: Target Corporation

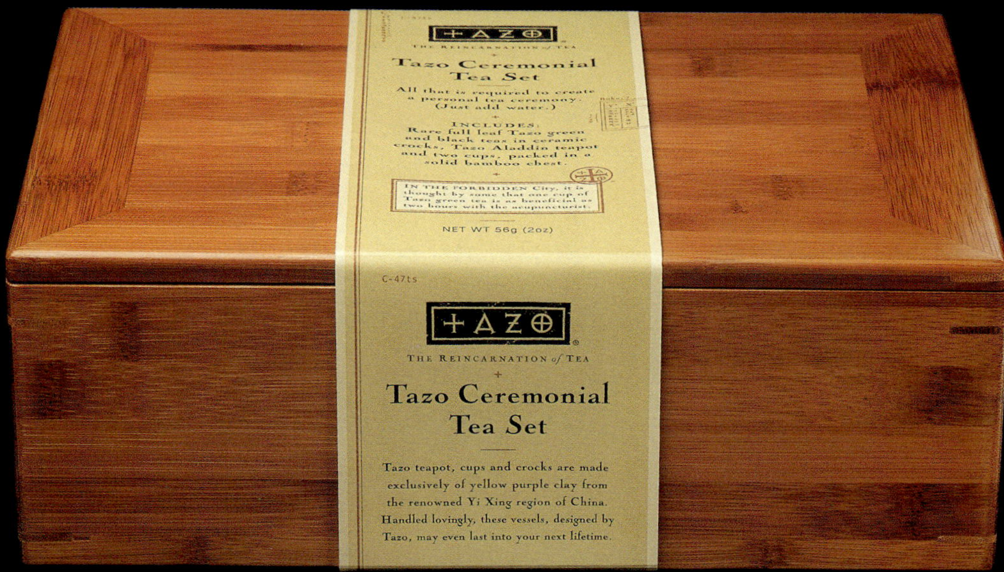

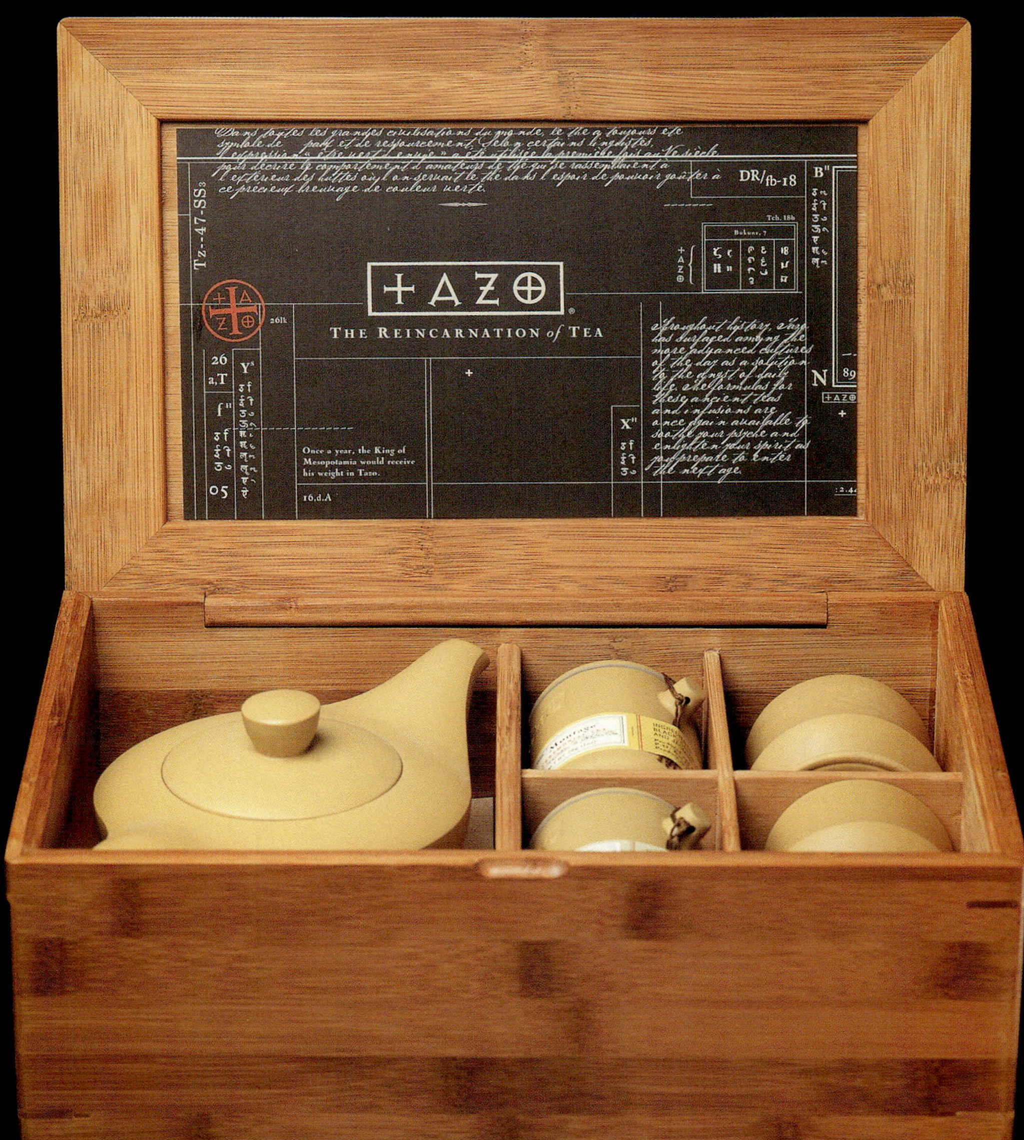

'Ceremonial Tea Set' Design Firm: Sandstrom Design Creative Director: Steve Sandstrom Art Directors: Steve Sandstrom and Steve Smith Designer: Steve Sandstrom Copywriter: Palmer Pettersen Client: Tazo

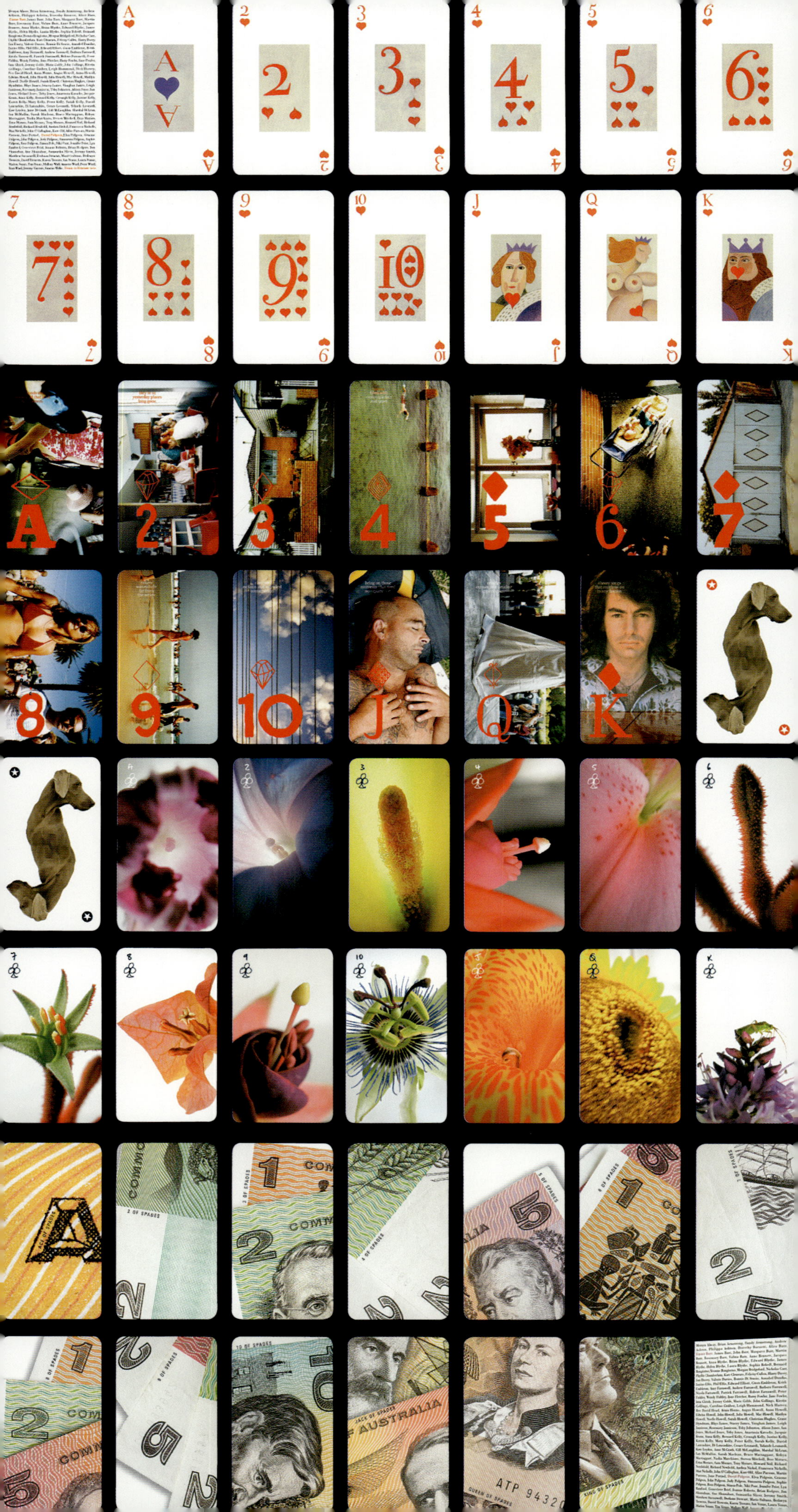

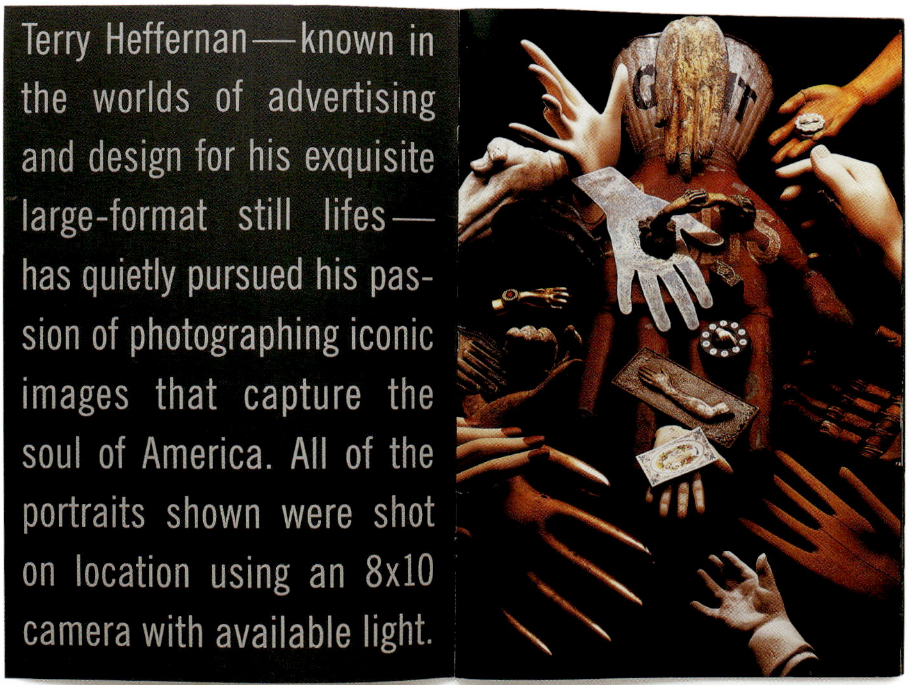

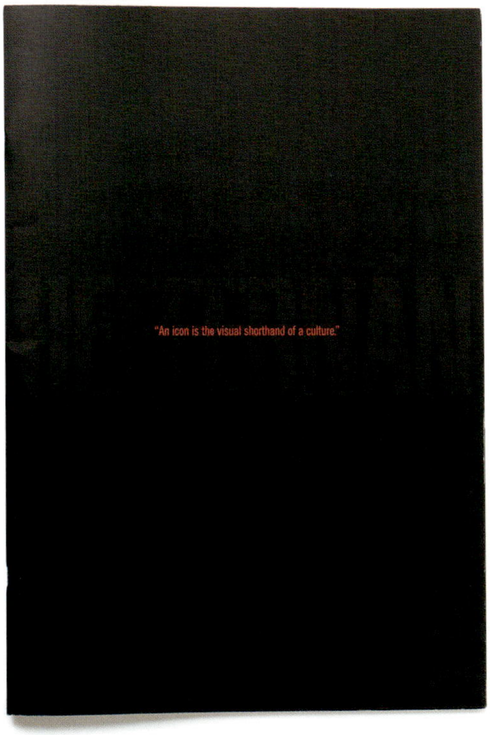

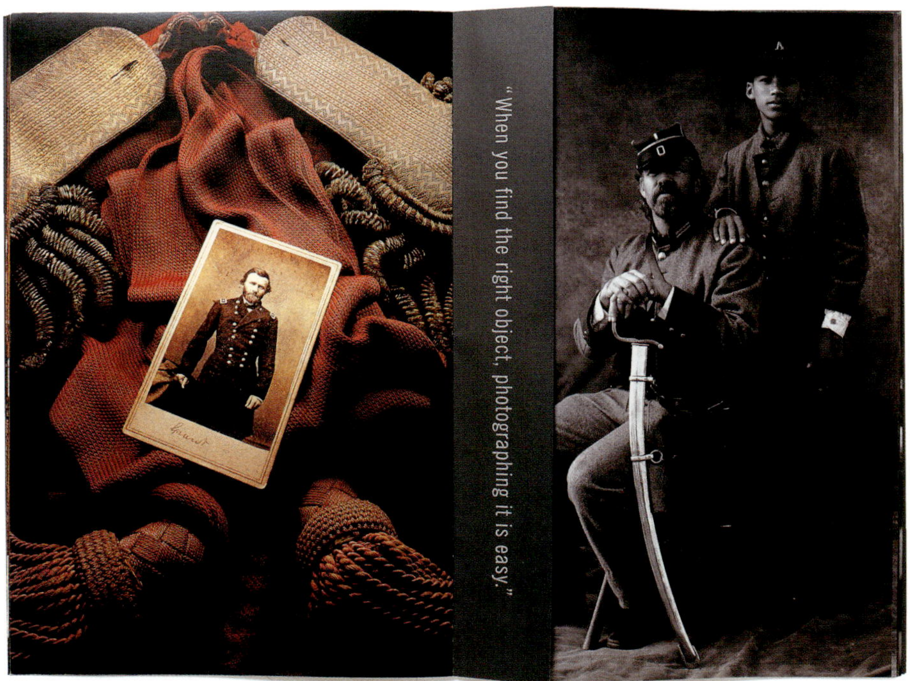

'Heffernan Icons' Design Firm: Pentagram SF Creative Director: Kit Hinrichs Art Director: David Asari Designer: David Asari Photographer: Terry Heffernan Copywriter: Delphine Hirasuna Client: Terry Heffernan

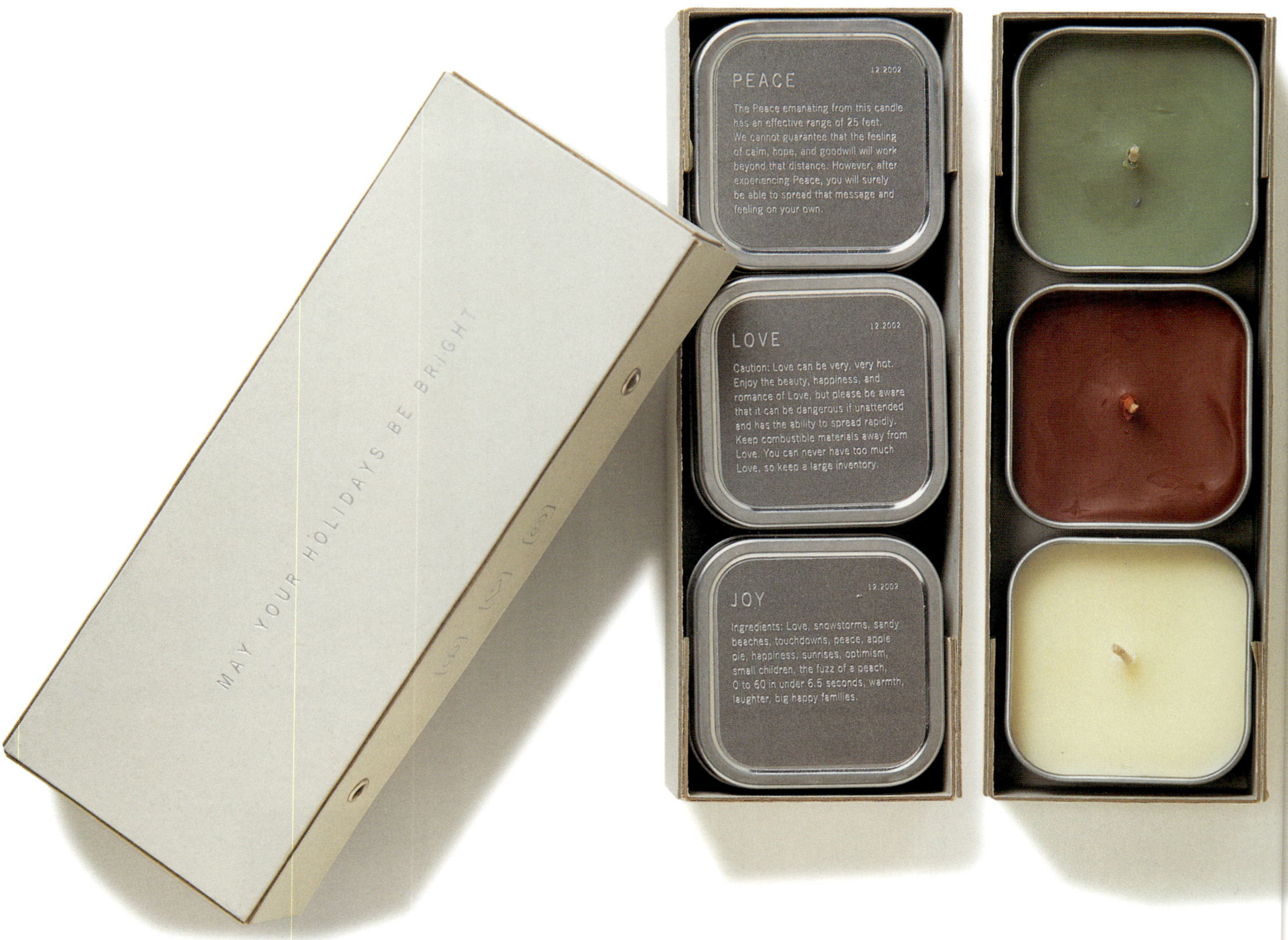

'2002 Holiday Gift' Design Firm: Sandstrom Design Creative Director: Steve Sandstrom Art Director: Steve Sandstrom Designer: Steve Sandstrom Copywriter: Jim Haven Client: Sandstrom Design

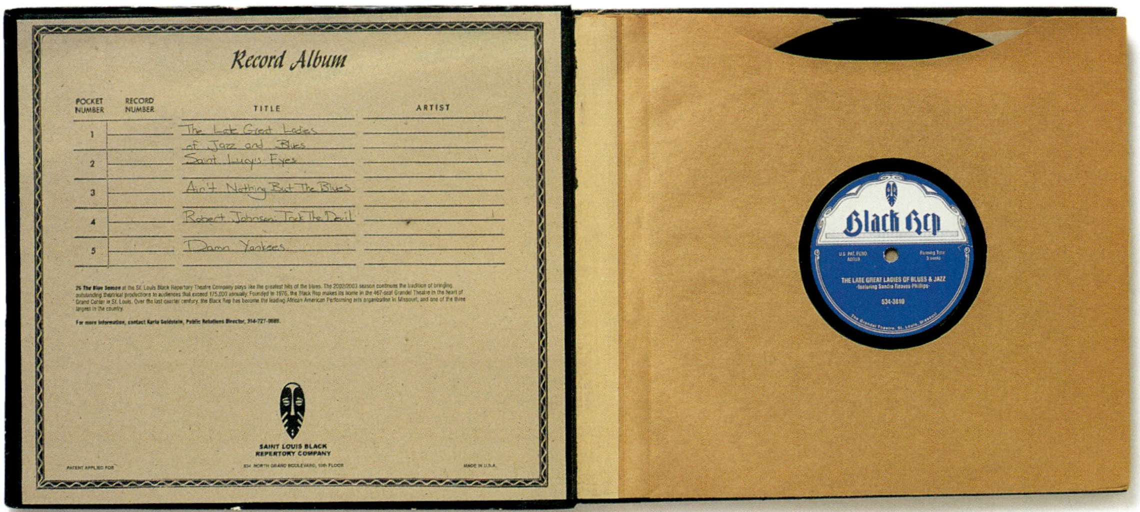

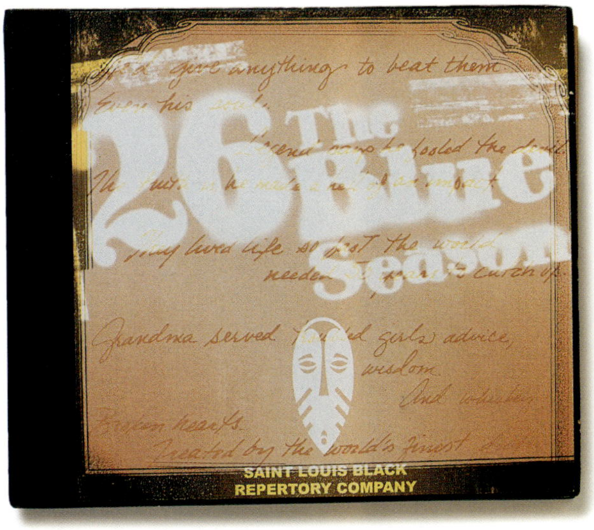

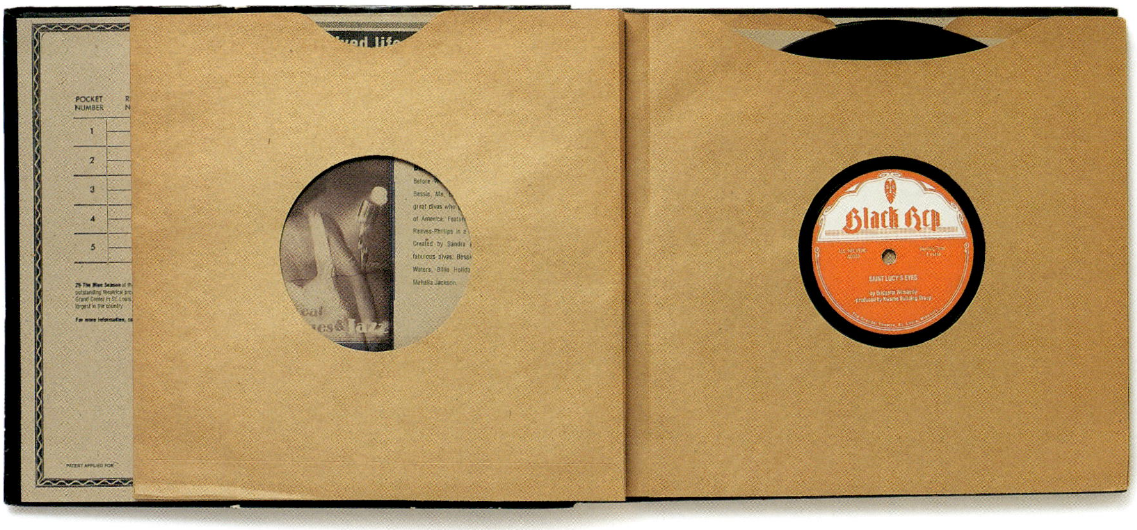

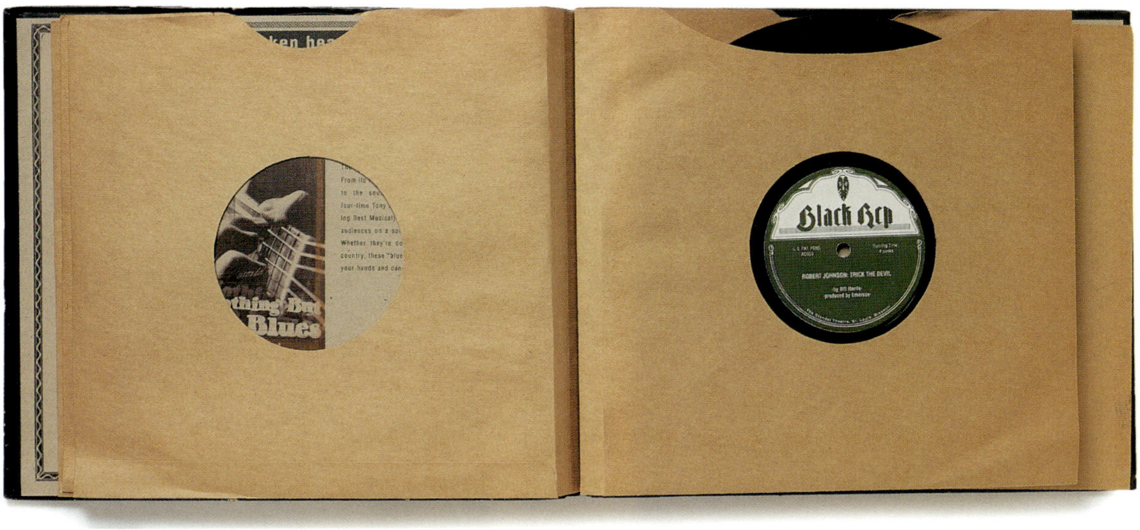

'Media Kit' Design Firm: Rodgers Townsend Creative Directors: Erik Mathre and Tom Hudder Art Director: Michelle Vesth Designer: Kris Wright Copywriter: Erik Mathre Client: Saint Louis Black Repertory Company

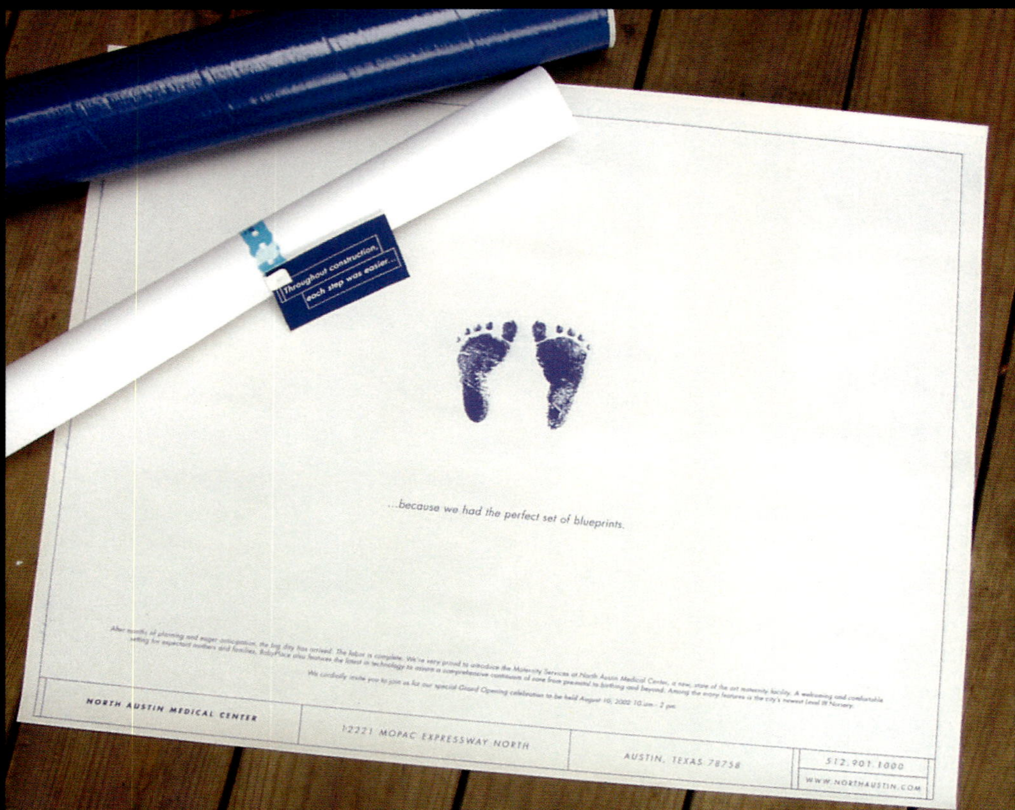

Design Firm: The Bradford Lawton Design Group Creative Director: Bradford Lawton Art Director: Bradford Lawton Designer: Jennifer Zinsmeyer Copywriter: Terry Roskin Client: St. Davids Medical Center

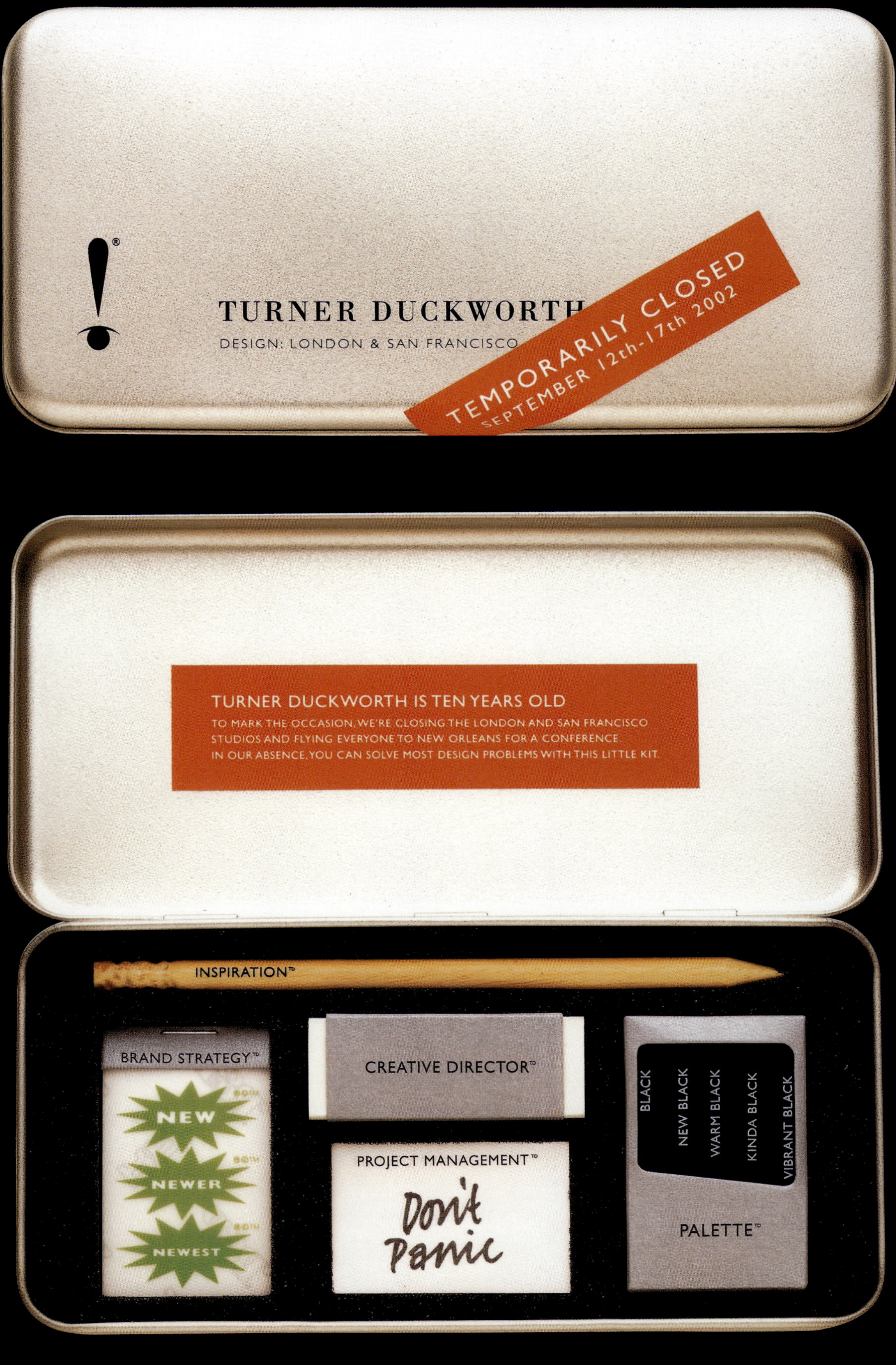

Temporarily Closed' Design Firm: Turner Duckworth Creative Directors: Bruce Duckworth and David Turner Designer: Mark Waters Account Manager: Moira Riddell Client: Turner Duckworth

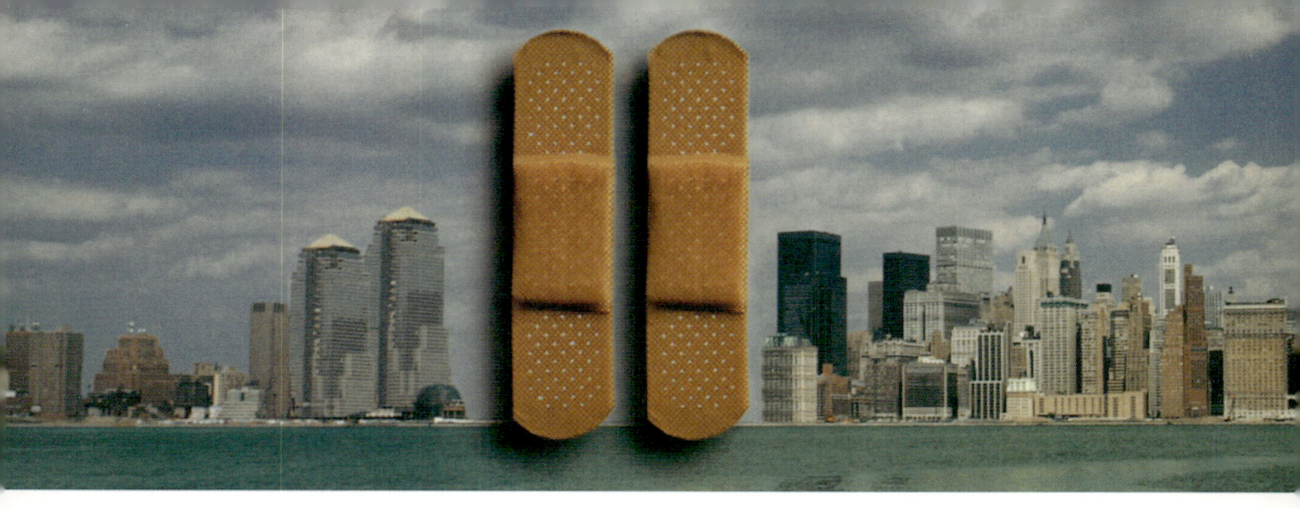

Merry Christmas and Peace on Earth. Marilyn & Carl Fischer

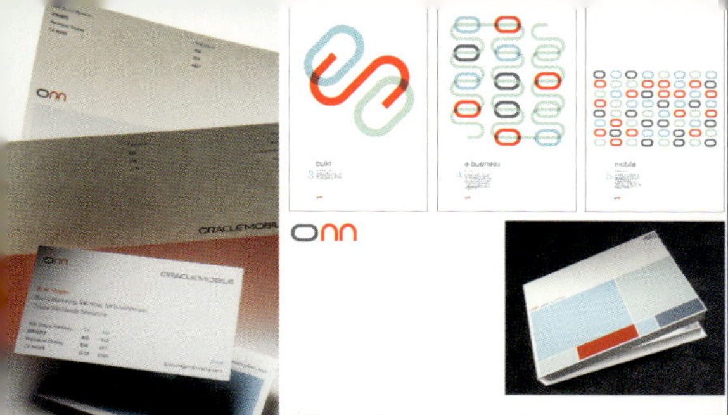

OracleMobile

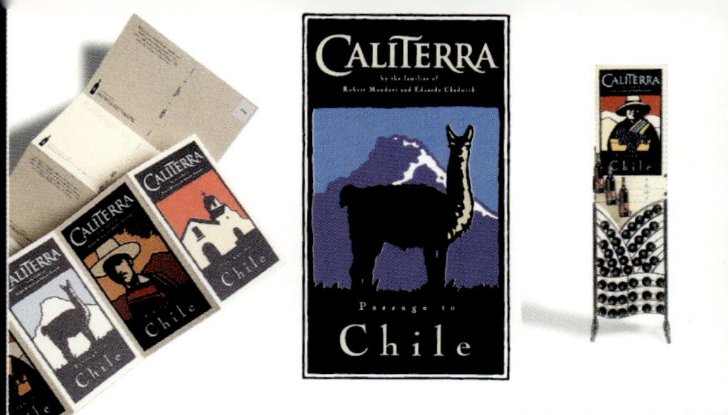

Robert Mondavi

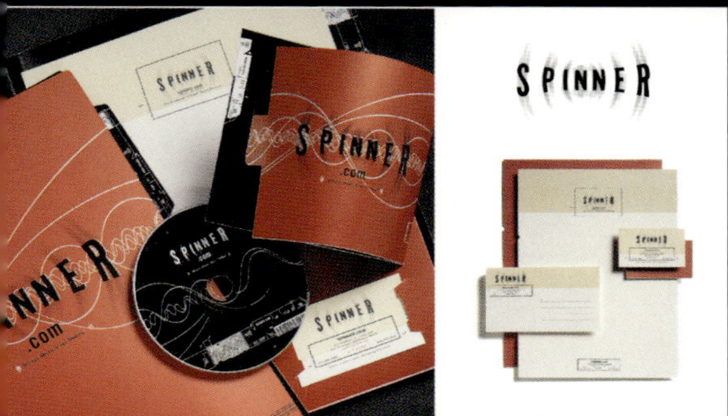

Spinner

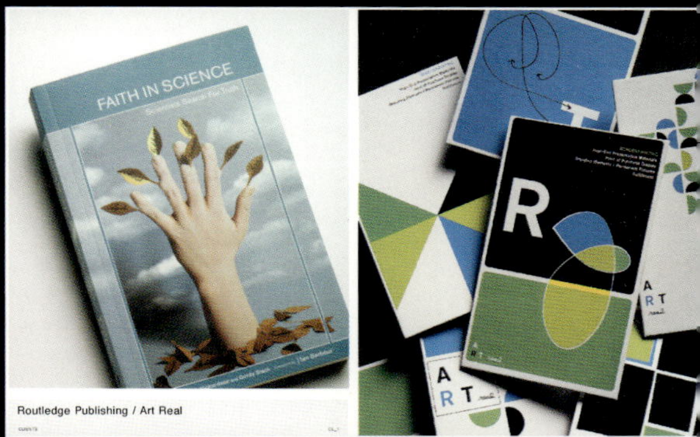

Routledge Publishing / Art Real

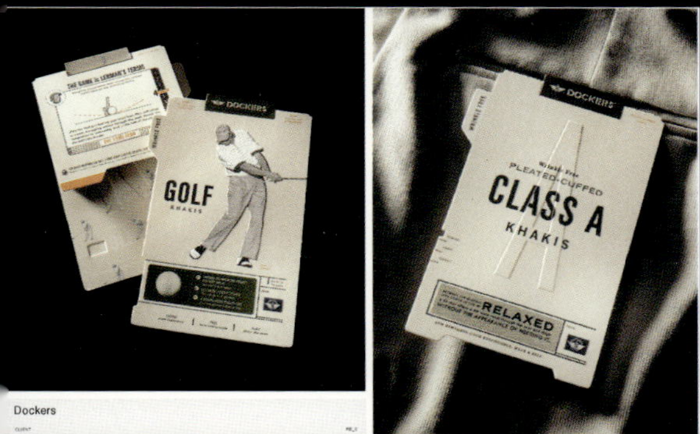

Dockers

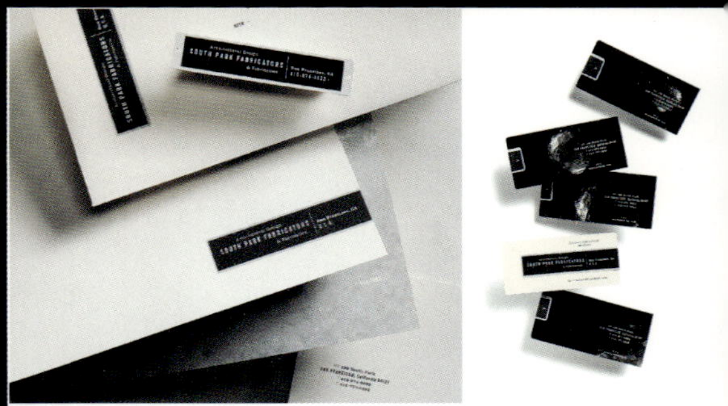

South Park Fabricators

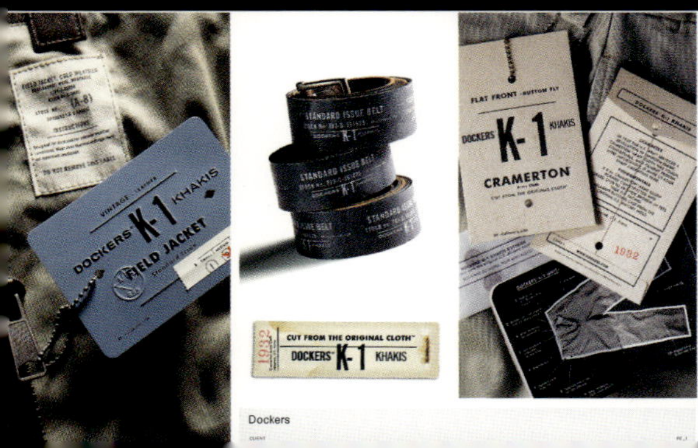

Dockers

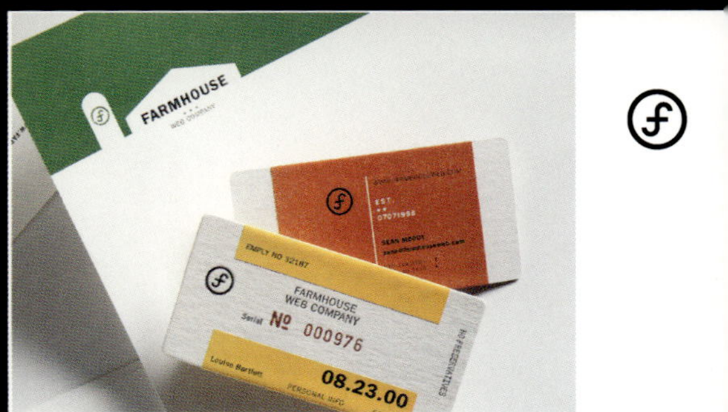

Farmhouse Web Co.

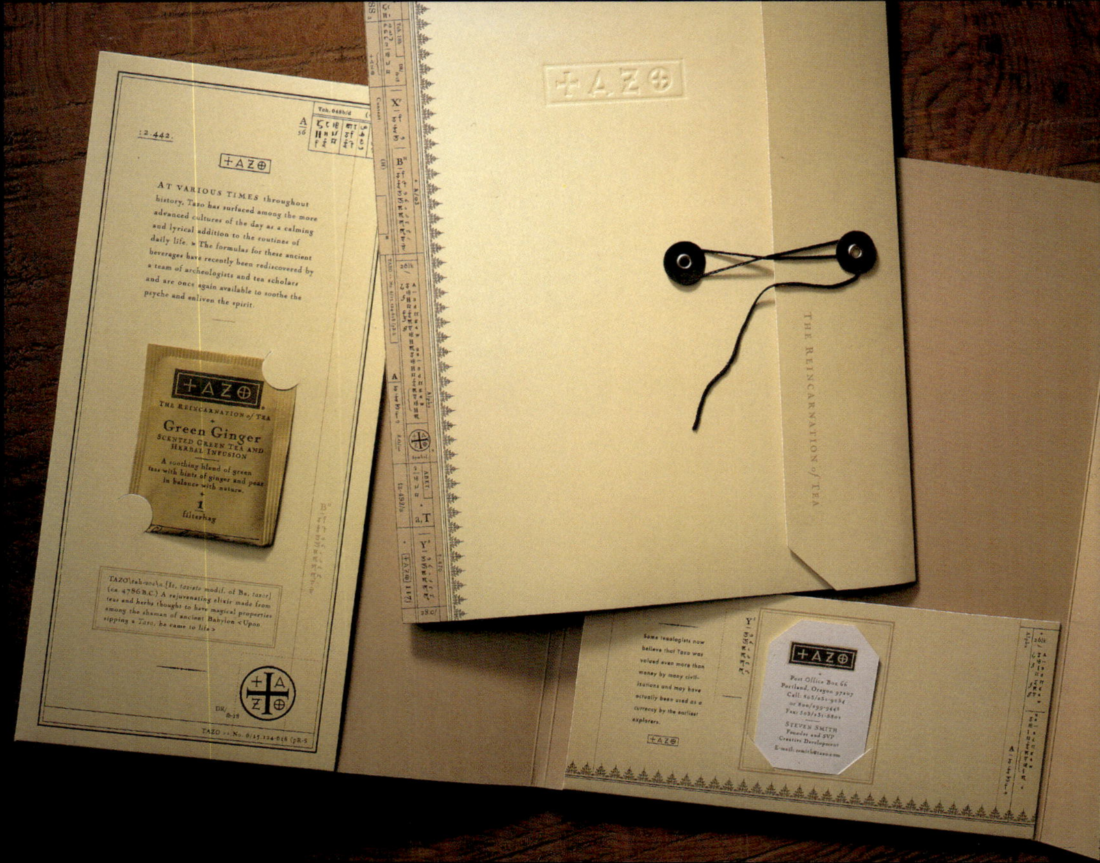

"The World According to Tazo" Design Firm: Sandstrom Design Creative Directors: Steve Sandstrom and Steve Sandoz Art Director: Steve Sandstrom
Designers: Steve Sandstrom and Steve Sandoz Photographers: Mark Hooper and Hiroshi Iwaya Production Designer: Andrew Randall Client: Tazo

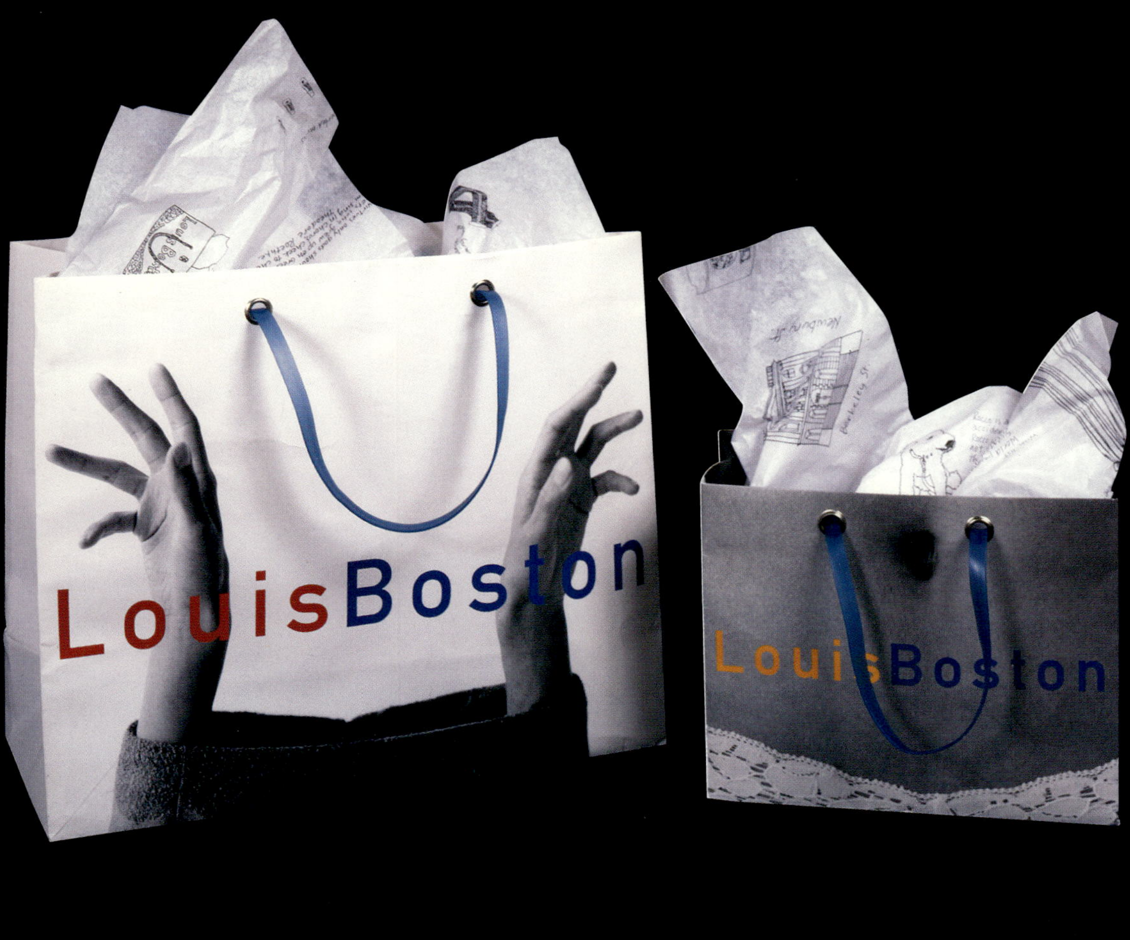

Design Firm: Heller Communications Creative Director: Cheryl Heller Designer: Cheryl Heller Photographer: Cheryl Heller Client: Louis Boston

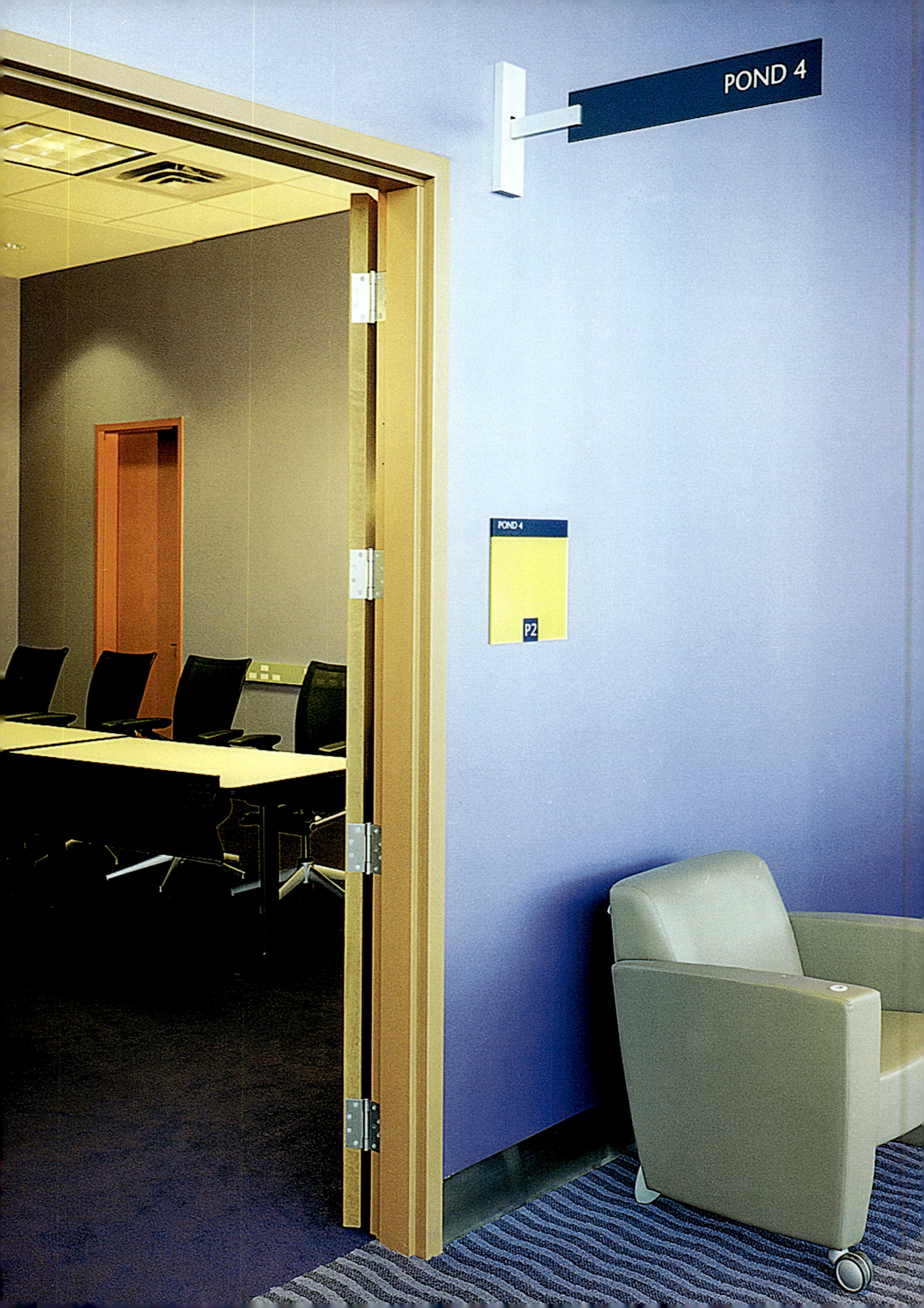
POND 4
POND 4
P2

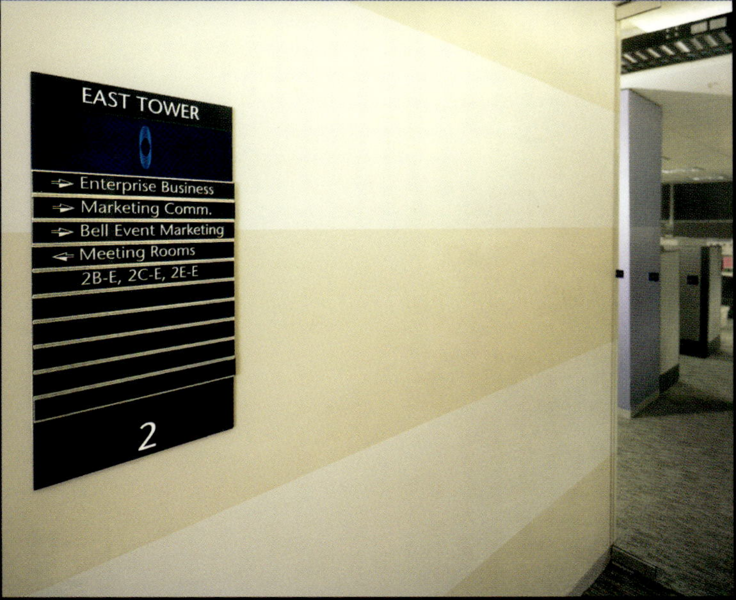

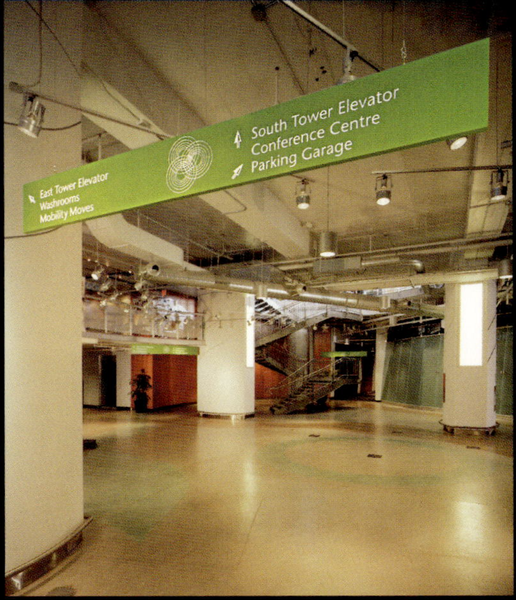

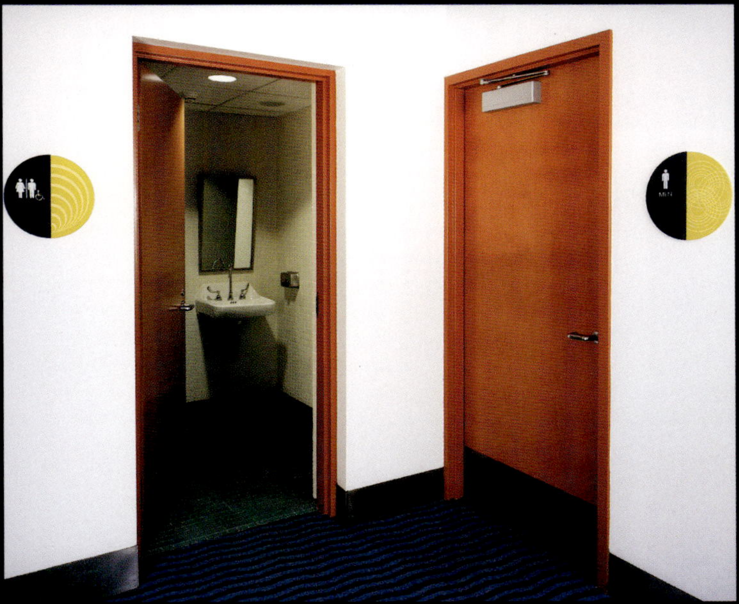

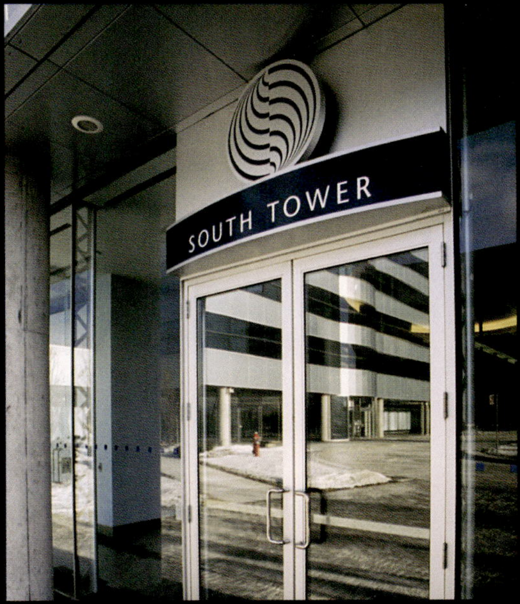

(this spread) Design Firm: Gottschalk & Ash International Art Director: Stuart Ash Designers: Jeff Inouye, Andrew McTavish and Udo Schliemann Client: Bell Mobility

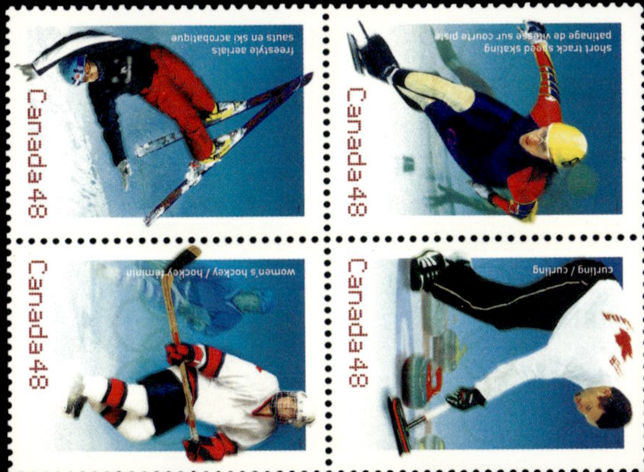

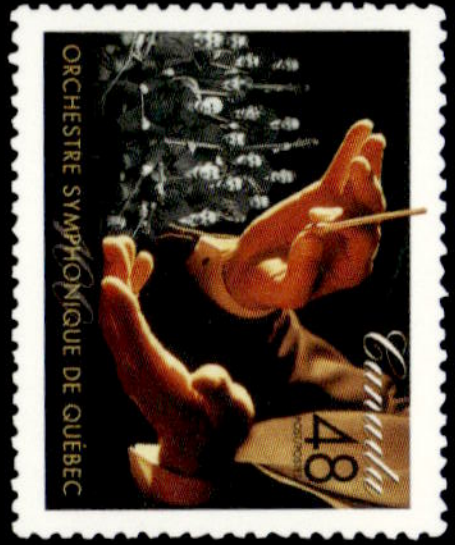

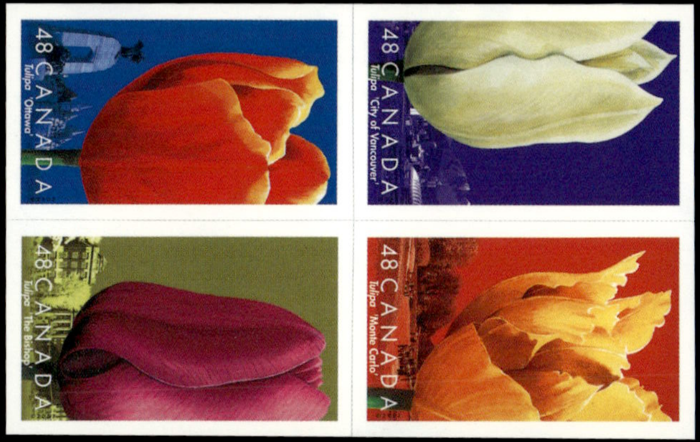

(from top) (1) 'Olympic Winter Games' Design Firm: Bhandari & Planter Inc. Designers: Sunil Bhandari and Watthew Wearn Photographers: Michael Burns, Patrick McCoy, Robert McNeill, Matthew Plaxman and Mike Ridgewood Client: Canada Post (2) 'Orchestra symphonique de Quebec' Designers: Monique Defour and Sofie Lafortune Photographers: ANQQ and Digital Vision Client: Canada Post (3) 'Tulips' Designers: Monique Defour and Sofie Lafortune Photographers: Malak Karsh, Peter Timmermans and The Ottawa Hospital Illustrator: Ghislain Lefebvre Client: Canada Post

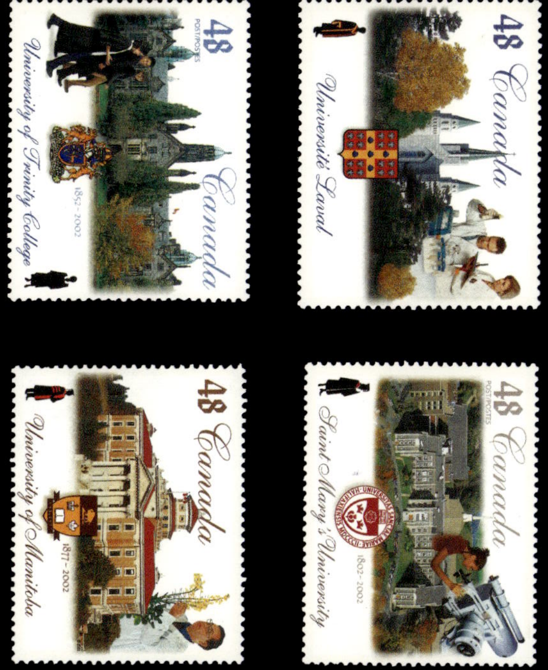

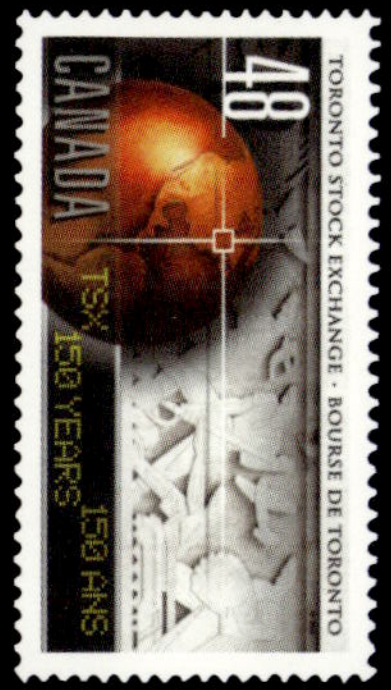

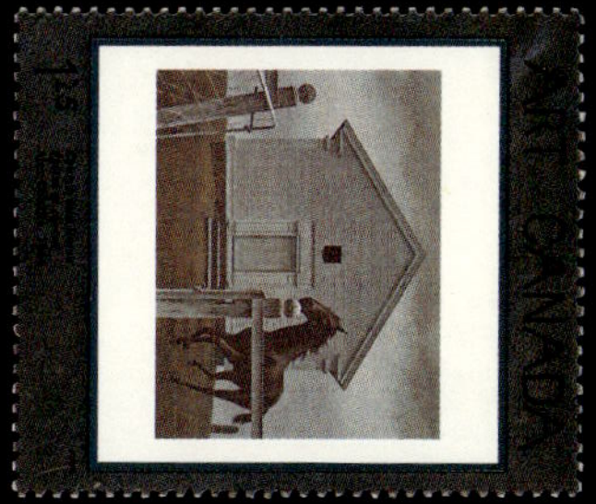

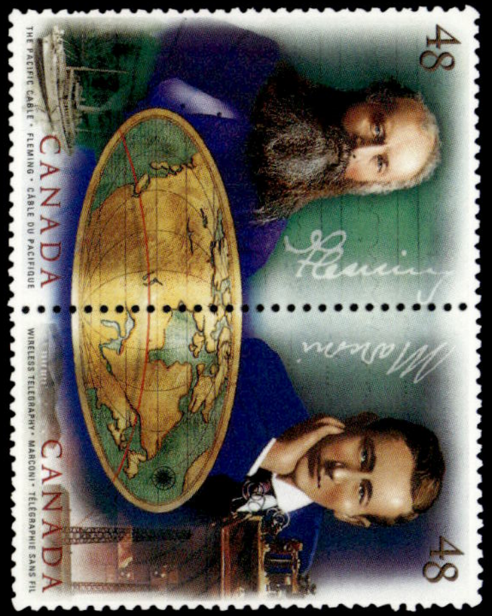

(from top) (1) 'Universities' Design Firm: Semaphor Design Co. Designer: Steven Slipp Illustrator: Bonnie Ross Client: Canada Post (2) 'Toronto Stock Exchange' Design Firm: Taylor/Sprules Corporation Designers: Ivan Novotny, John Taylor and Patrick Sayers Photographer: Tracy Clare Client: Canada Post (3) 'Masterpieces of Canadian Art' Designer: Pierre-Yves Pelletier Client: Canada Post (4) 'Communications Technology' Designer: Susan Warr Illustrator: Bonnie Ross Client: Canada Post

Masters of American Photography' Creative Director: Terrence McCaffrey Art Director: Derry Noyes Designer: Derry Noyes Typographer: Derry Noyes Client: United States Postal Service

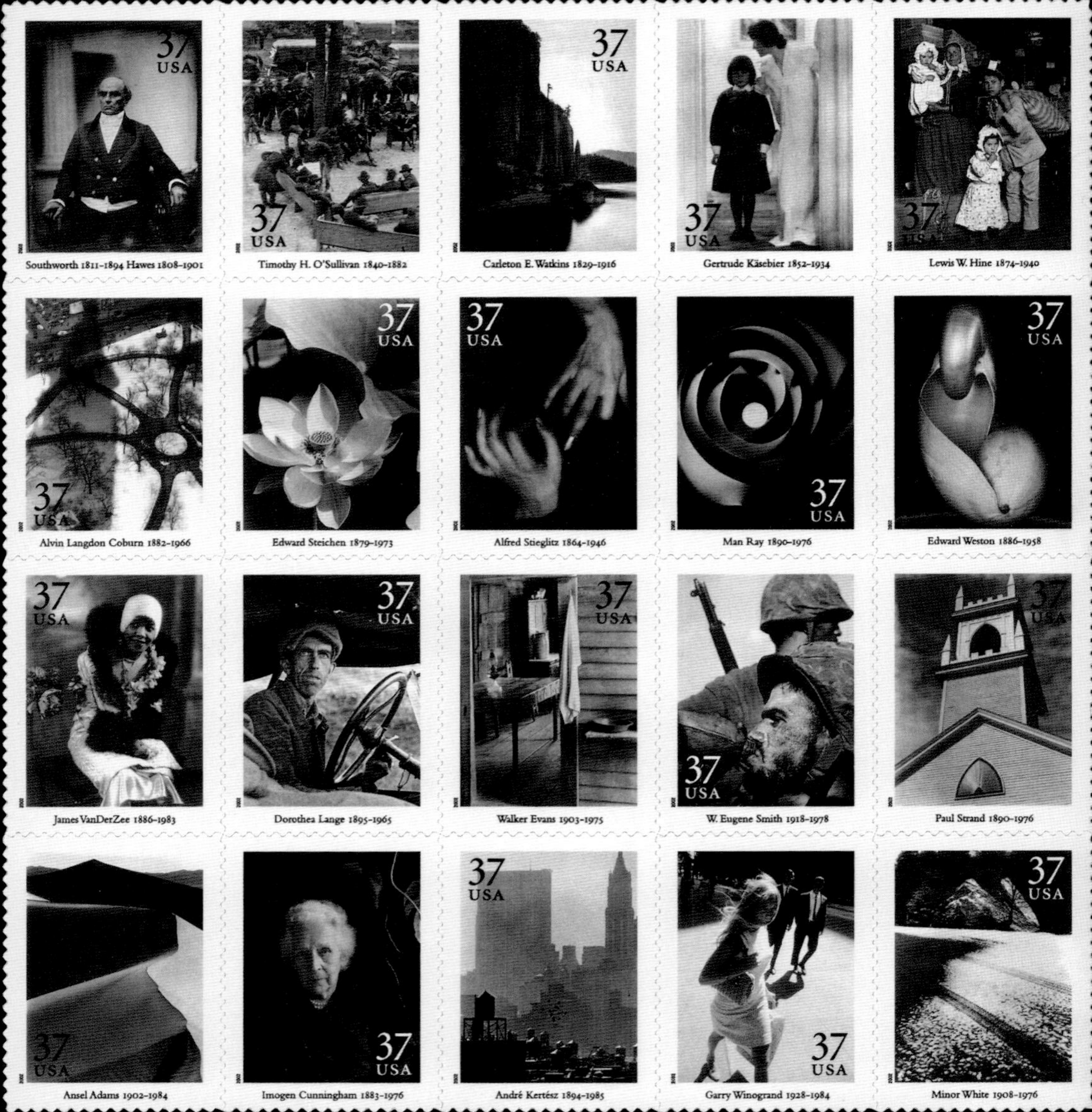

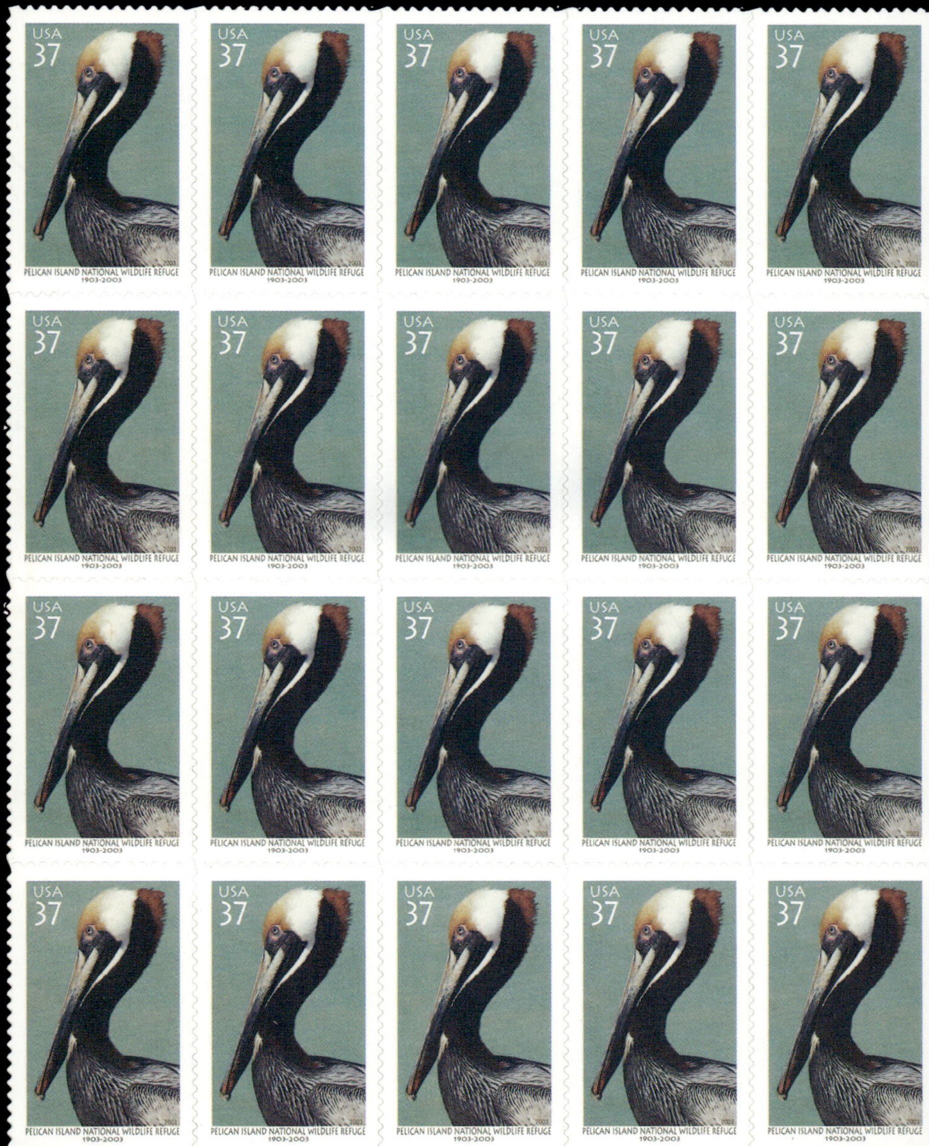

'Pelican Island National Wildlife Refuge' Creative Director: Terrence McCaffrey Art Director: Carl T. Herrman Designer: Carl T. Herrman Photographer: James D. Brandt, M.D. Typographer: Carl T. Herrman Client: United States

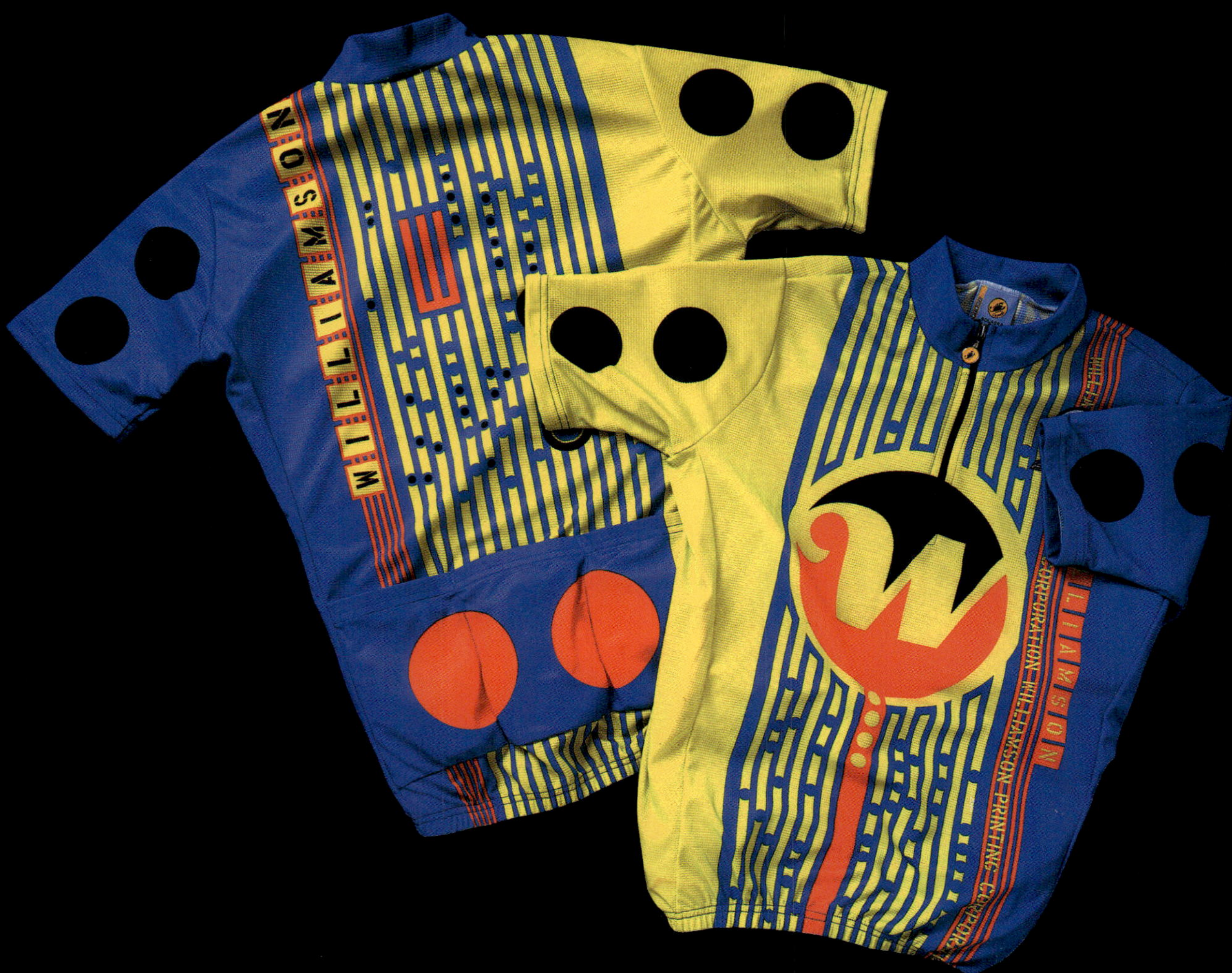

'Williamson Bike Jersey' Design Firm: Duffy Creative Director: Alan Colvin Designer: Charlie Ross Illustrator: Charlie Ross Client: Williamson Printing Corp.Inc.

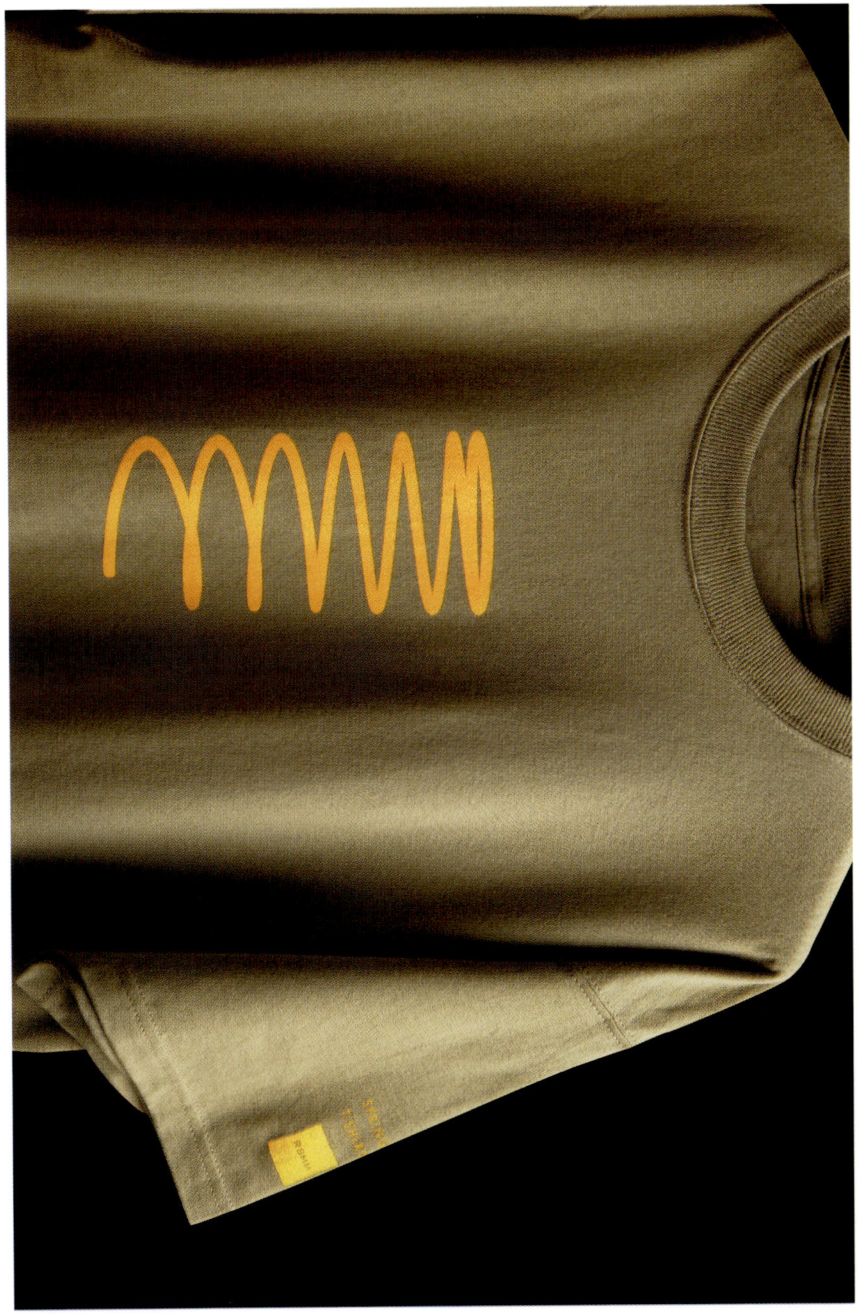

'Spring T-Shirt' Design Firm: RBMM Art Director: Dick Mitchell Designer: Jacob Ristau Illustrator: Jacob Ristau Client: RBMM (next page, left) '10 Year T-Shirt' Design Firm: Turner Duckworth Creative Directors: Bruce Duckworth and David Turner Designer: Anthony Biles Client: Turner Duckworth (next page, right) 'Midnite Oil' Design Firm: Webster Design Associates Creative Director: Dave Webster Art Director: Sean Heisler Client: Webster Design Associates

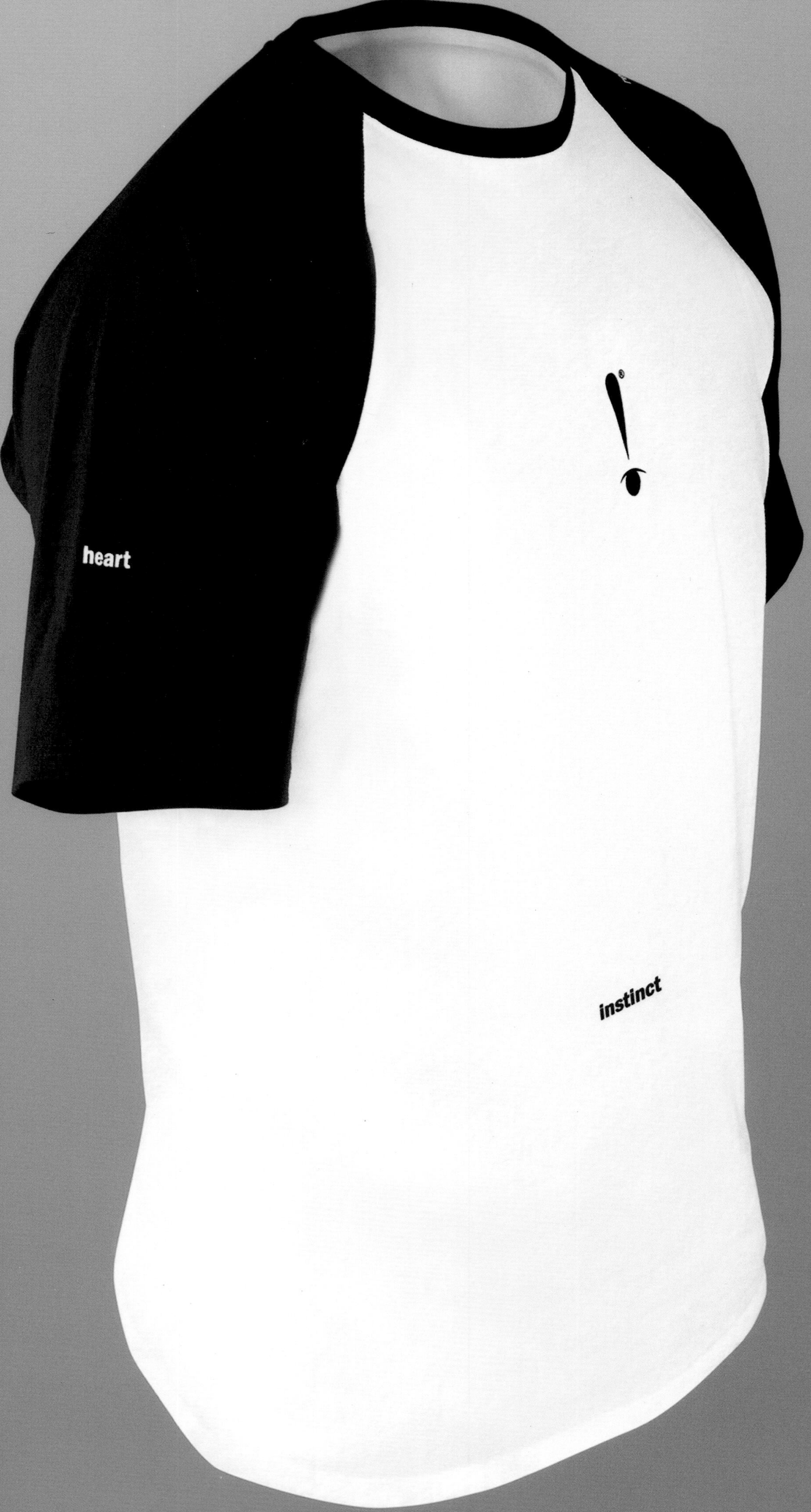
heart
instinct

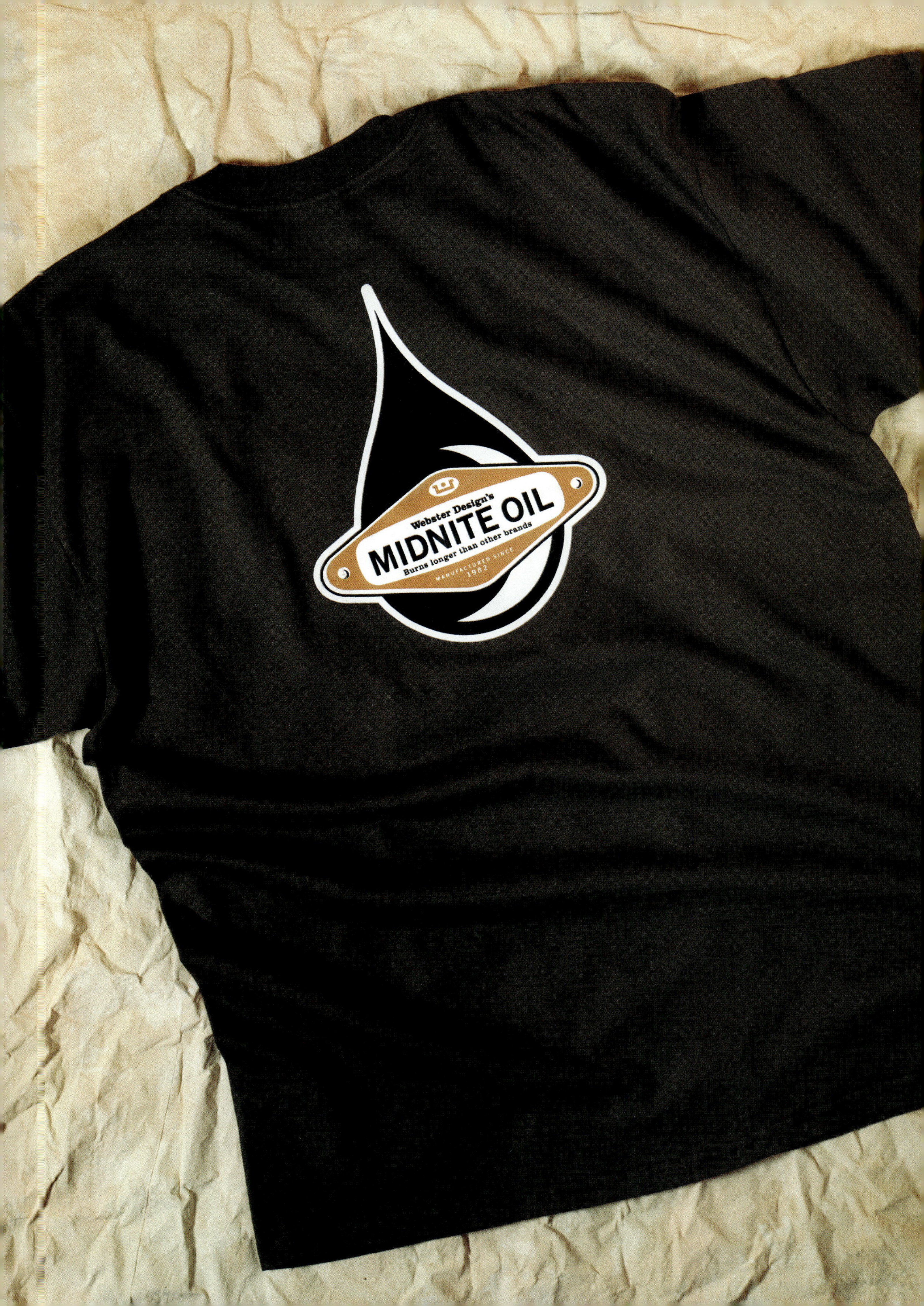
Webster Design's
MIDNITE OIL
Burns longer than other brands
MANUFACTURED SINCE
1982

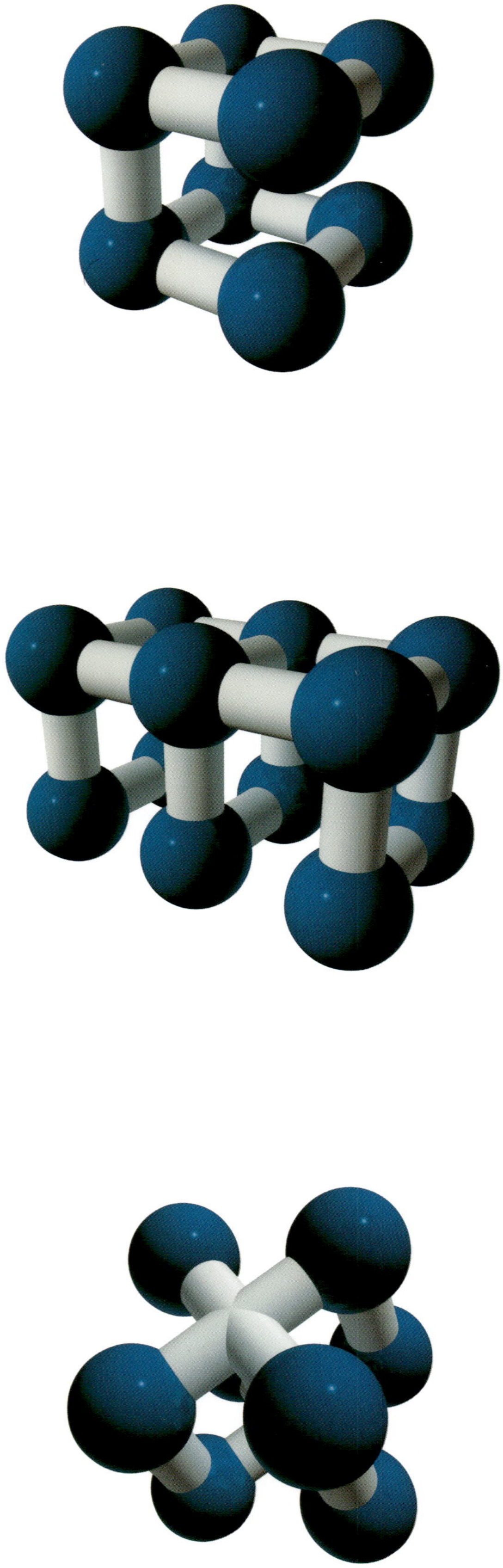

'MOLECULE 3D-cmx' Creative Director: Péter Vajda Art Director: Péter Vajda Designer: Péter Vajda Client: Alternativ Studio

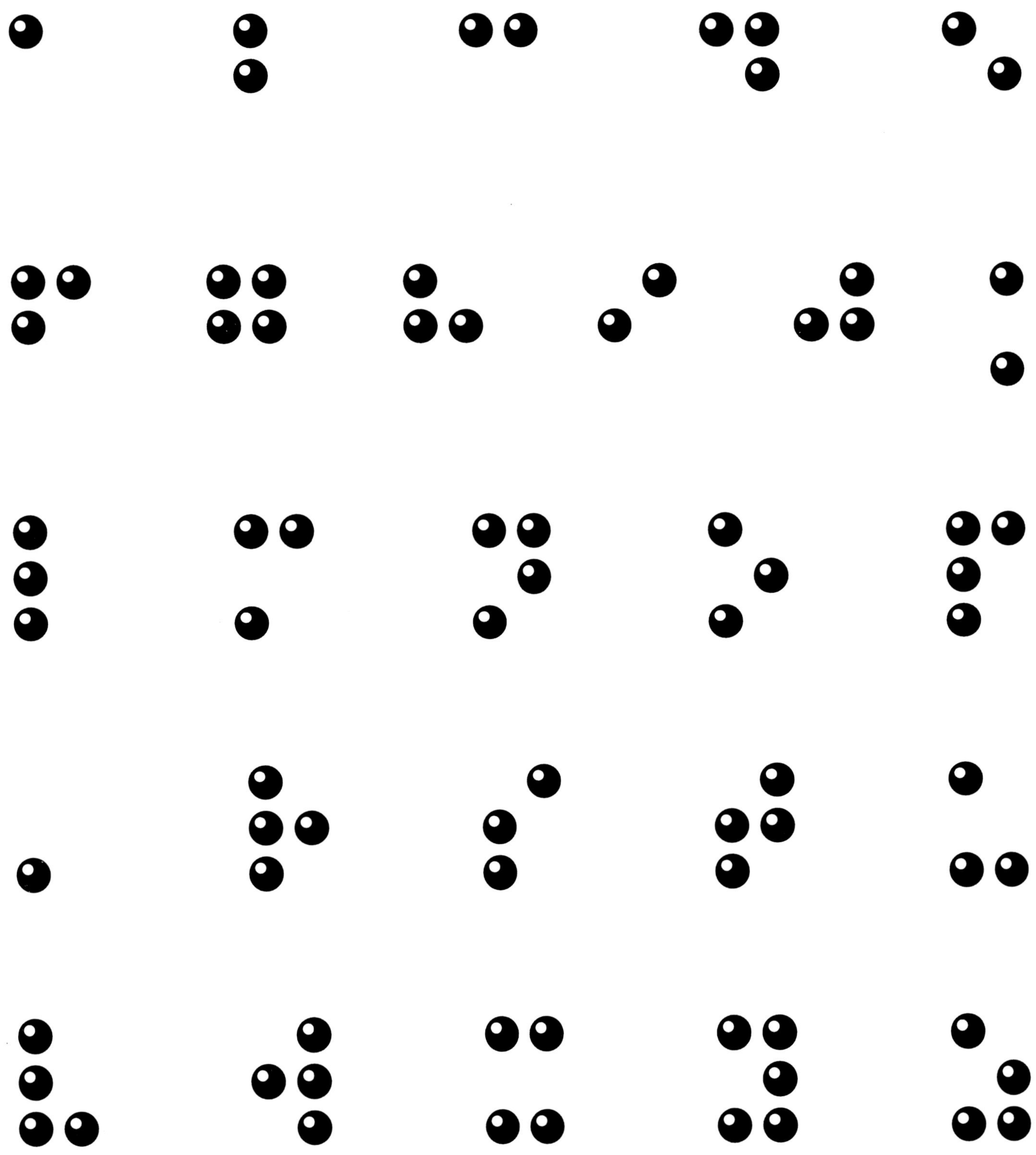

'MOLECULE-lowercase' Creative Director: Péter Vajda **Art Director:** Péter Vajda **Designer:** Péter Vajda **Client:** Alternativ Studio

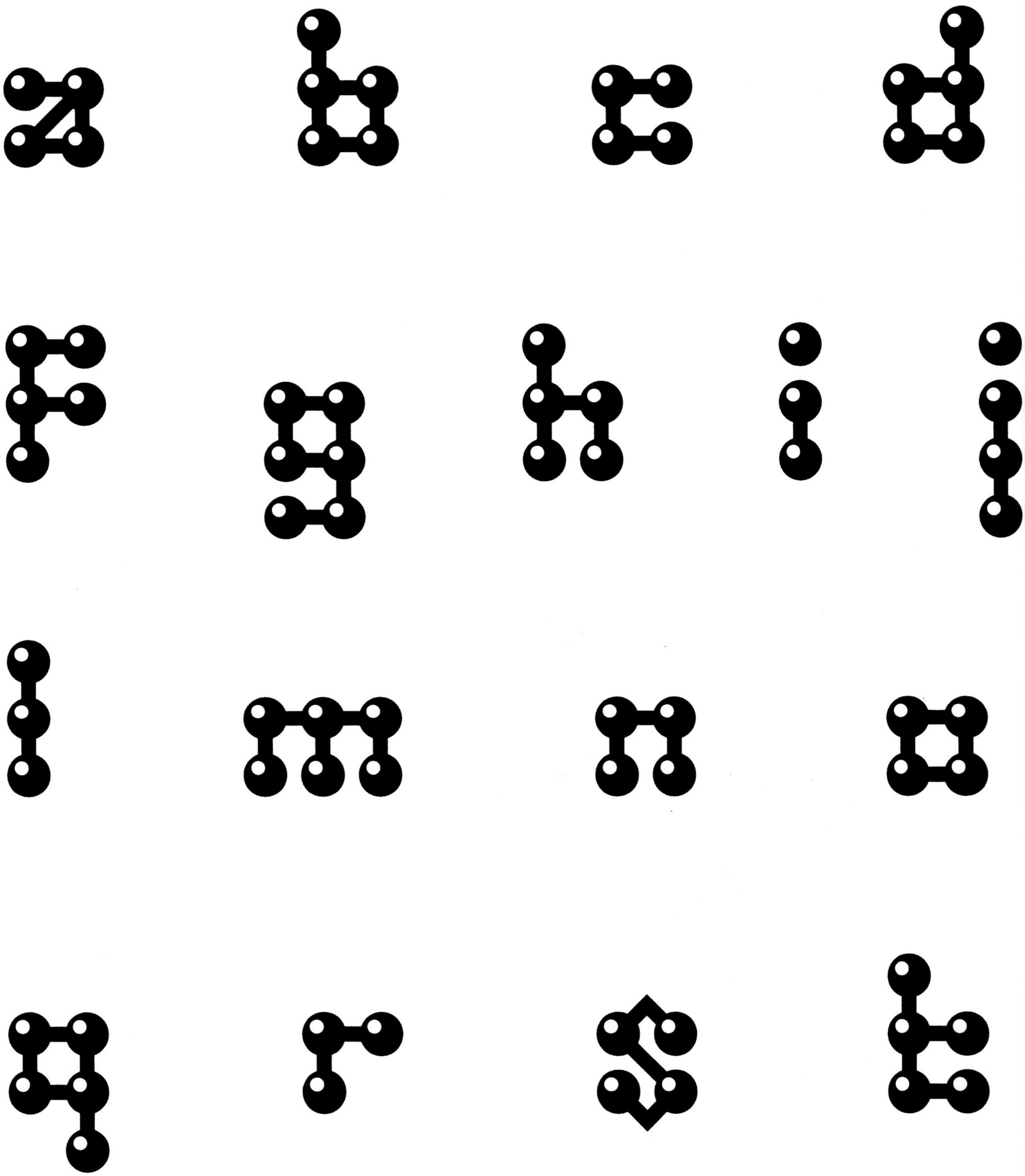

'MOLECULE-braille' Creative Director: Péter Vajda Art Director: Péter Vajda Designer: Péter Vajda Client: Alternativ Studio

Index

PhotographersIllustrators

Copywriters

DesignFirms

Clients

Directory of Design Firms

50,000 Feet Inc.
853 Broadway
Suite 1005
New York, NY 10003
Tel: 1 212 253 8222
Fax: 1 212 253 2798
www.50000feet.com

AIGA Boston
1 781 446 9082
www.boston.aiga.org

Apocalypse
199 Lafayette Street
New York, NY 10012
Tel: 1 212 334 0595
Fax: 1 212 334 6050
www.apocalypseworldwide.com

Apple Computers
1 Infinite Loop
Cupertino, CA 95014
www.apple.com

Art Center College of Design
1700 Lida Street
Pasadena, CA 91103
Tel: 1 626 396 2351
Fax: 1 626 795 0819
www.artcenter.edu

Artworks
H 1036 Budapest Csemete 10
Budapest, 1036
Tel: 36 14 37 1040
Fax: 36 14 37 1399

Axiom Design Group
210 West Clay, No. 9
Houston, TX 77019
Tel: 1 713 523 5711
Fax: 1 713 523 6083
www.axiomdg.com

Bailey Lauerman
900 Wells Fargo Center
Lincoln, NE 68508
Tel: 1 402 475 2800
Fax: 1 402 475 5115
www.baileylauerman.com

Barbarian Group
332 Newbury Street, 2nd Floor
Boston, MA 02115
Tel: 1 617 424 8887
Fax: 1 617 437 9499
www.barbariangroup.com

Benoit Design Inc
825 18th Street
Plano, TX 75074
Tel: 1 972 509 7588
Fax: 1 972 509 7589
www.benoitdesigninc.Com

Bertz Design Group
190 Washington Street
Middletown, CT 6457
Tel: 1 860 347 4332
Fax: 1 860 347 1008
www.bertzdesign.com

Bilbo
Ul Kotlarza 919
Katowice, Poland 40-139
Tel: 48 60 559 5747
Fax: 48 32 258 8497
www.bilbo.com.pl

Blattner Brunner
11 Stanwix Street, 5th Floor
Pittsburgh, PA 15222
Tel: 1 412 995 9500
www.blatbrun.com

BOWG Advertising
375 West 200th Street, Suite 300
Salt Lake City, UT 84101
Tel: 1 801 539 1818
Fax: 1 801 539 8484
www.bowg.com

Bozell
40 West 23rd Street
New York, NY 10010
Tel: 1 212 727 5982
Fax: 1 212 727 5298
www.bozell.com

Brad Norr Design (BND)
400 1st Avenue No. 312
Minneapolis, MN 55401
Tel: 1 612 339 2104
Fax: 1 612 339 9820
www.bradnorrdesign.com

Brandl & Scharer AG
Solothurnerstrasse 121
Olten, Switzerland 4601
Tel: 41 06 220 59040
Fax: 41 06 220 59045
www.brandl.ch

Business Architects Inc.
12 3 Gobancho
Chiyoda Ku Tokyo, Japan 102-0076
Tel: 81 33 51 22541
Fax: 81 33 51 22540
www.b-architects.com

Cahan & Associates
171 2nd Street, 5th Floor
San Francisco, CA 94105
Tel: 1 415 621 0915
Fax: 1 415 621 7642
www.cahanassociates.com

Carmichael Lynch Thornburn
800 Hennepin Avenue
Minneapolis, MN 55403
Tel: 1 612 334 6045
Fax: 1 612 334 6032
www.clynch.com

Catalyst Studios
126 North 3rd Street, Suite 100
Minneapolis, MN 55401
Tel: 1 612 339 0735
Fax: 1 612 339 0739
www.catalyststudios.com

Character
487 Bryant Street, 3rd Floor
San Francisco, CA 94107
Tel: 1 415 227 2100
Fax: 1 415 227 2191
www.charactersf.com

ComGroup
817 West Peachtree Street
Atlanta, GA 30308
Tel: 1 678 686 7913
Fax: 1 404 892 9176
www.comgroupmra.com

Cultivator Advertising & Design
1708 Walnut Street
Boulder, CO 80302
Tel: 1 303 444 4134
Fax: 1 800 783 4152
www.cultads.com

Dalton Advertising Inc.
111 Third Avenue South, Suite 130
Minneapolis, MN 55401
Tel: 1 612 341 2241
Fax: 1 612 341 2281
www.dalton-ideas.com

David Carter Design Associates
4112 Swiss Avenue
Dallas, TX 75204
Tel: 1 214 826 4631
Fax: 1 214 827 1938
www.dcadesign.com

DDB Worldwide
437 Madison Avenue
New York, NY 10022
Tel: 1 212 415 2811
Fax: 1 212 415 2811
www.ddb.com

DeAngelis Design
PO Box 5846
Santa Monica, CA 90409
Tel: 1 310 720 2931

Design Continuum
1220 Washington Street
West Newton, MA 2465
Tel: 1 617 928 9501
Fax: 1 617 969 2864
www.dcontinuum.com

Design Hoch Drei
Hallstrasse 25 A
Stuttgart, Germany 70376
Tel: 49 711 55037730
Fax: 49 711 55037755

design: mw
149 Wooster Street
New York, NY 10012
Tel: 1 212 982 7621
www.designmw.com

Deutsch Design Works
10 Arkansas Street
San Francisco, CA 94107
Tel: 1 415 487 8520
Fax: 1 415 587 8529
www.ddw.com

Direct Design Studio
PO Box 134
Moscow, Russia 127018
Tel: 70 95 961 8045
Fax: 70 95 792 0886
www.directdesign.ru

DNA Design
262-264 Thorndon Quay,
PO Box 3052
Wellington, New Zealand
Tel: 644 499 0828
Fax: 644 499 0888
www.dna.co.nz

Duffy
50 South 6th Street, Suite 2800
Minneapolis, MN 55402
Tel: 1 612 758 2333
Fax: 1 612 758 2334
www.duffy.com

Edward Walter Design
584 Broadway Suite 1108
New York, NY 10012
Tel: 1 212 966 7800
Fax: 1 212 966 7894

Elektra Records
75 Rockefeller Plaza, 13 Floor
New York, NY 10019
Tel: 1 212 275 4240
Fax: 1 212 974 7679
www.elektra.com

EPOS, Inc.
1639 16th Street
Santa Monica, CA 90404
Tel: 1 310 581 2418
Fax: 1 310 581 2422

Epoxy Communications
506 McGill Street, 5th Floor
Montreal, Quebec H2Y 2H6
Canada
Tel: 1 514 866 6900
Fax: 1 514 866 6300
www.epoxy.ca

Eric Chan Design Co. Ltd.
Unit 803 8F Park Comm
Hong Kong
Tel: 85 22 527 7773
Fax: 85 22 865 3929

Evolution Bureau
90 Tehama Street
San Francisco, CA 94108
Tel: 1 415 243 0859
Fax: 1 415 243 9255
www.evolutionbureau.com

Ford Weithman Design
431 NW Flanders, Suite 304
Portland, OR 97209
Tel: 1 503 222 0296
Fax: 1 503 222 0289

Fotografie Frank M. Orel
Baumreute 102/104
D-70199 Stuttgart
Germany
Tel: 49 711 640 80 04
Fax: 49 711 640 80 06

Françoise McAree
75 Elmgrove Avenue
Providence, RI 02906
Tel: 1 401 272 0832

Gage
10000 Highway 55
Minneapolis, MN 55441
Tel: 1 763 595 3800
Fax: 1 763 595 5812
www.gage.com

Gollings & Pidgeon
147 Chapel Street
St Kiloa 3182
Australia
Tel: 613 9537 0733
Fax: 613 9537 0187
www.gollings.com.au

good morning inc.
www.goodmorning.co.jp

Gottschalk & Ash International
11 Bishop Street
Toronto, Ontario M5r1n3
Canada
Tel: 1 416 963 9717
Fax: 1 416 963 9351
www.gottashzrh.com

Graf, Bertel, Buczek Werbeagentur
GmbH
Benratherstrasse 8
Dusseldorf 40231
Germany
Tel: 49 211 86 32400

Graham Hanson Design
222 Fifth Avenue, Floor 4
New York, NY 10001
Tel: 1 212 481 2858
Fax: 1 212 683 9304
www.grahamhanson.com

Graphème Branding & Design
2100 Drummond Street
Montréal, Québec H3G 1X1
Canada
Tel: 1 514 845 2727
Fax: 1 514 282 4742
www.cossette.com

Graphics & Designing Inc.
3-3-1 Shiroganedai Minato Ku
Tokyo 108-0071
Japan
Tel: 81 33 449 0651
Fax: 81 33 449 0653
www.quicheandtarte.com

Greteman Group
1425 E. Douglas, Suite 200
Wichita, KS 67211
Tel: 1 316 263 1004
Fax: 1 316 263 1060
www.gretemangroup.com

Hallmark Cards Inc.
2501 McGee
Kansas City, MO 64108
Tel: 1 816 274 7386
Fax: 1 816 274 5815
www.hallmark.com

Hambly & Woolley Inc.
130 Spadina Avenue, Suite 807
Toronto, Ontario M5V 2L4
Canada
Tel: 1 416 504 2742
Fax: 1 416 504 2745
www.hamblywoolley.com

Heller Communications
350 West 50th Street 15B
New York, NY 10019
Tel: 1 212 582 6429
www.hellercommunicationsinc.com

i.design
8653 San Leandro Drive
Dallas, TX 75218
Tel: 2143241405
Fax: 2143241405
www.ingramdesign.com

Iconologic
40 Inwood Circle
Atlanta, GA 30309
Tel: 1 404 260 4500
Fax: 1 404 260 4581
www.iconologic.com

Intellecta Branding & Design
PO Box 45045 Sueavagen 53
Stockholm, Sweden 10430
Tel: 46 87 299 600
Fax: 46 87 299 665

Jannuzzi Smith
10A Lane Street
London SE1 1QR
United Kingdom
Tel: 44 207 254 0557
Fax: 44 207 239 0558
www.jannuzzismith.com

Jon Cannell Design
43126 SE 175th Lane
North Bend, WA 98045
Tel: 1 425 831 5532
www.joncannelldesign.com

Kilmer & Kilmer
125 Truman NE, Suite 200
Albuquerque, NM 87108
Tel: 1 505 260 1175
Fax: 1 505 260 1155
www.kilmer2.com

Kosaka Identity & Design
115 West Micheltorena Street
Santa Barbara, CA 93101
Tel: 1 805 568 0350
Fax: 1 805 568 0360
www.kosakadesign.com

Kuhn, Kammann & Kuhn AG
Xantenerstrasse 105
Koln 50733
Germany
Tel: 49 221 9765 4122
Fax: 49 221 9765 4110
www.kkk-ag.de

Landesberg Design
1219 Bingham Street
Pittsburgh, PA 15203
Tel: 1 412 381 2220
Fax: 1 412 381 2413
www.landesbergdesign.com

Landor Associates
7525 Irvine Center Drive
Irvine, CA 92618
Tel: 1 949 754 2078
Fax: 1 949 754 2003
www.landor.com

Little & Company
1201 Marquette Avenue, Suite 200
Minneapolis, MN 55403
Tel: 1 612 375 0077
Fax: 1 612 375 0423
www.littleco.com

Lloyd & Co.
180 Varick Street, 10th Floor
New York, NY 10014
Tel: 1 212 414 3100
Fax: 1 212 414 3113
www.lloydandco.com

Lorenc+Yoo Design
109 Vickery Street
Roswell, GA 30075
Tel: 1 770 645 2828
Fax: 1 770 998 2452
www.lorencyoodesign.com

Louise Fili Ltd.
156 Fifth Avenue
New York, NY 10010
Tel: 1 212 989 9153
www.louisefili.com

Macey Noyes Associates
232 Panbury Road
Wilton, CT 6897
Tel: 1 203 762 9002
Fax: 1 203 762 2629
www.maceynoyes.com

Mark Oliver, Inc.
1984 Old Mission Drive, Suite A15
Solvang, CA 93463
Tel: 1 805 686 5166
Fax: 1 805 686 5224
www.markoliverinc.com

Matsumoto Incorporated
220 West 19th Street
New York, NY 10011
Tel: 1 212 807 0248
Fax: 1 212 807 1527

Michael Lee Advertising & Design
2615 Calder, Suite 150
Beaumont, TX 77702
Tel: 1 409 835 7564
Fax: 1 409 833 3822
www.michaelleeadv.com

Michael Schwab Studio
108 Tamalpais Avenue
San Anselmo, CA 94960
Tel: 1 415 257 5792
Fax: 1 415 257 5793
www.michaelschwab.com

Milton Glaser Inc.
207 East 32nd Street
New York, NY 10016
Tel: 1 212 889 3161
Fax: 1 212 213 4072
www.miltonglaser.com

Mirko Ilic Corp.
207 East 32nd Street
New York, NY 10016
Tel: 1 212 481 9737
Fax: 1 212 481 7088
www.mirkoilic.com

Morla Design
463 Bryant Street
San Francisco, CA 94107
Tel: 1 415 543 6548
Fax: 1 415 543 7214
www.morladesign.com

Moses Media
584 Broadway 607
New York, NY 10012
Tel: 1 212 625 0331
Fax: 1 212 625 0332
www.mosesmedia.com

Murillo Design
6933 Border Brook Drive, #312
San Antonio, TX 78238
Tel: 1 210 247 2717
Fax: 1 210 832 0007

Opto Design
214 Sullivan Street, 6C
New York, NY 10012
Tel: 1 212 254 4470
Fax: 1 212 254 5266
www.optodesign.com

Out of the Box
215 Hanford Drive
Fairfield, CT 06824
Tel: 1 203 254 1437
Fax: 1 203 256 8055
www.ootbdesign.com

Oxide Design Co.
4013 Farnam Street
Omaha, NE 68131
Tel: 1 402 344 0168
Fax: 1 402 344 0169
www.oxidedesignco.com

Paprika
400 Laurier West
Montreal, Quebec H2V 2K7
Canada
Tel: 1 514 276 6000
Fax: 1 514 276 6100

Pentagram SF
387 Tehama Street
San Francisco, CA 94103
Tel: 1 415 896 0499
Fax: 1 415 896 0555
www.pentagram.com

Peter Krämer
Lindemannstrasse 31
Dusseldorf 40237
Germany
Tel: 49 211 210 8087
Fax: 49 211 22 8541

Planet Propaganda
605 Williamson Street
Madison, WI 53703
Tel: 1 608 256 0000
www.planetpropaganda.com

Primo Angeli Fitch
101 15th Street
San Francisco, CA 94103
Tel: 1 415 551 1900
Fax: 1 415 551 1919
www.primo-fitch.com

Radical Media
435 Hudson Street
New York, NY 10014
Tel: 1 212 462 1500
Fax: 1 212 462 1600
www.radicalmedia.com

RBMM
7007 Twin Hills Suite 200
Dallas, TX 75231
Tel: 1 214 987 6500
Fax: 1 214 987 3662
www.rbmm.com

Rickabaugh Graphics
384 W. Johnstown Road
Gahanna, OH 43230
Tel: 1 614 337 2229
Fax: 1 614 337 2197

Rodgers Townsend
1310 Papin Streeet
Saint Louis, MO 63103
Tel: 1 314 436 9960
Fax: 1 314 436 9961
www.rodgerstownsend.com

Rutka Weadock Design
1627 East Baltimore Street
Baltimore, MA 21231
Tel: 1 410 563 2100
Fax: 1 410 563 0542

Ryan & Deslauriers
290 Place D'Youville
Montreal, Quebec H2Y 2B6
Canada
Tel: 1 514 287 1555
Fax: 1 514 287 1918

Sagmeister Inc.
222 West 14th Street
New York, NY 10011
Tel: 1 212 647 1789
Fax: 1 212 647 1788

Saint Hieronymus Press
1703 MLK Way
Berkeley, CA 94709
Tel: 1 510 549 1405
www.goines.net

Sandstrom Design
808 SW 3rd Avenue, Suite 610
Portland, OR 97204
Tel: 1 503 248 9466
Fax: 1 503 227 5035
www.sandstromdesign.com

Shapiro Walker Design
101 North Chestnut Street
Winston-Salem, NC 27101
Tel: 1 336 725 0110
Fax: 1 336 725 0120
www.shapirowalker.com

Shinnoske Inc.
602 Tsuriganecho 2-1-8 Chuoku
Osaka 540-0035
Japan
Tel: 81 66 943 9079
Fax: 81 66 943 9078
www.shinn.co.jp

SHR Perceptual Management
7702 E. Doubletree Ranch Road
Scottsdale, AZ 85203
Tel: 1 480 483 3700
Fax: 1 480 483 9675
www.shr.com

Sibley Peteet Design
3232 McKinney Avenue Suite 1200
Dallas, TX 75204
Tel: 1 214 969 1050
Fax: 1 214 969 7585
www.spddallas.com

Sony Music
550 Madison Avenue 29th Floor
New York, NY 10022
Tel: 1 212 833 4513
Fax: 1 212 833 4388
www.sonymusic.com

Squires & Company
2913 Canton
Dallas, TX 75226
Tel: 1 214 939 9194
Fax: 1 214 939 3464
www.squirescompany.com

Studio Ignition
116 South Hotel, Suite 203
Honolulu, HI 96813
Tel: 1 808 526 0500
Fax: 1 808 526 0212

TC Gruppe GmbH, Target Communications
Alt-Wuerttemberg-Allee 89
71638 Ludwigsburg
Germany
Tel: 49 7141 128 110
Fax: 49 7141 128 333
www.tc-gruppe.de

Templin Brink Design
720 Tehama Street
San Francisco, CA 94103
Tel: 1 415 255 9295
Fax: 1 415 255 9296
www.templinbrinkdesign.com

Tequila/Minneapolis
60 South 6th Street, Suite 2800
Minneapolis, MN 55408
Tel: 1 612 342 9844
Fax: 1 612 342 9700

Th
422 3 Main Street
Franklin, TN 37064
Tel: 1 615 790 2777
Fax: 1 615 790 2377
www.thwastaken.com

The Bradford Lawton Design Group
1020 Townsend Avenue
San Antonio, TX 78209
Tel: 1 210 832 0555
Fax: 1 210 832 0007
www.bradfordlawton.com

The Engine Room
610 22nd Street, Suite 307
San Francisco, CA 94107
Tel: 1 415 934 8180
Fax: 1 415 934 8190
www.theengineroom.cc

The Moderns, Ltd.
900 Broadway, Suite 903
New York, NY 10003
Tel: 1 212 387 8852
www.themoderns.com

Tom Fowler, Inc.
111 Westport Avenue
Norwalk, CT 6851
Tel: 1 203 845 0700
Fax: 1 203 846 6682
www.tomfowlerinc.com

Turner & Associates
487 Bryant Street, 2nd Floor
San Francisco, CA 94116
Tel: 1 415 344 0990
Fax: 1 415 344 0991
www.turnersf.com

Turner Duckworth
Voysey House
London W4 4PH
United Kingdom
Tel: 44 020 8994 7190
Fax: 44 020 8994 7192
www.turnerduckworth.com

Twist Inc.
9511 SW 264th Street
Vashon Island, WA 98070
Tel: 1 206 443 7661
www.twistdesign.biz

Vanderbyl Design
171 Second Street 2nd Floor
San Francisco, CA 94105
Tel: 1 415 543 8447
Fax: 1 415 543 9058
www.vanderbyldesign.com

VSA Partners
1347 South State Street
Chicago, IL 60605
Tel: 1 312 427 6413
Fax: 1 312 427 3246
www.vsapartners.com

Wages Design, Inc.
887 West Marietta Street, Suite S-111
Atlanta, GA 30318
Tel: 1 404 876 0874
Fax: 1 404 876 0578
www.wagesdesign.com

Wallace Church, Inc.
330 East 48th Street
New York, NY 10017
Tel: 1 212 755 2903
Fax: 1 212 355 6872
www.wallacechurch.com

Webster Design Associates
60 Dodge Street, Suite 2000
Omaha, NE 68132
Tel: 1 402 551 0503
Fax: 1 402 551 1410
www.websterdesign.com

Weymouth Design
332 Congress Street
Boston, MA 2210
Tel: 1 617 542 2647
Fax: 1 617 451 6233
www.weymouthdesign.com

Williams Murray Hamm
The Heals Building Alfred Mew
London, United Kingdom W1p 9lb
Tel: 44 207 255 3232
Fax: 44 207 637 8404
www.creatingdifference.com

Wink
417 First Avenue North #250
Minneapolis, MN 55401
Tel: 1 612 630 5139
Fax: 1 612 630 5157

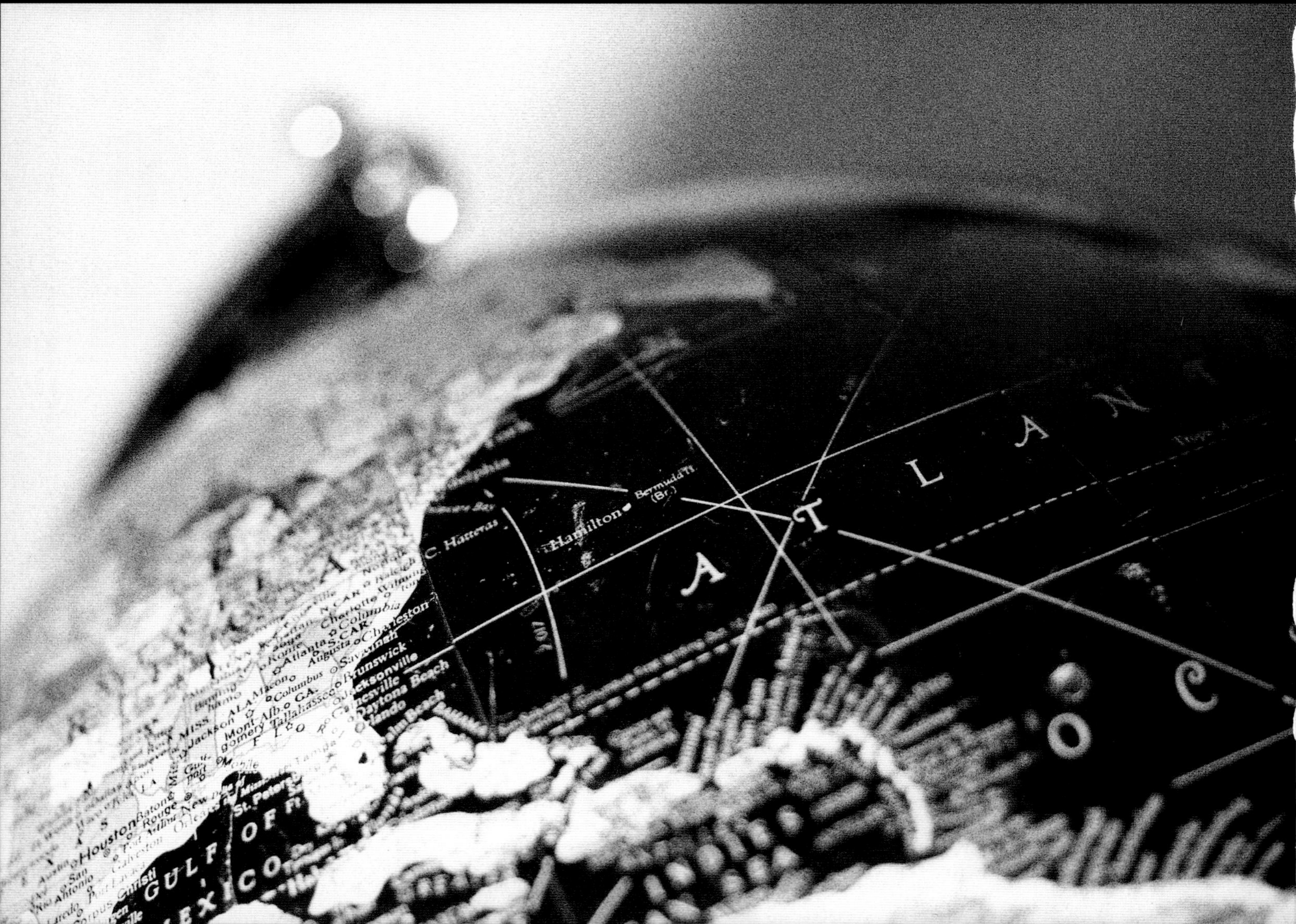
Hamilton
C. Hatteras
Charleston
Brunswick
Daytona Beach
Houston
GULF OF